# FORGOTTEN HEROES OF COMEDY

# ALSO BY ROBERT ROSS

*Marty Feldman: The Biography of a Comedy Legend* (Titan Books, 2011)
*Sid James: Cockney Rebel* (J.R. Books, 2009)
*The Goodies Rule OK* (Carlton Books, 2006)
*The Carry On Story* (Reynolds and Hearn Limited, 2005)
*The Complete Terry-Thomas* (Reynolds and Hearn Limited, 2002)
*Steptoe and Son* with Ray Galton
and Alan Simpson (BBC Worldwide Limited, 2002)
*The Complete Frankie Howerd* (Reynolds and Hearn Limited, 2001)
*Fawlty Towers: Fully Booked* (BBC Worldwide Limited, 2001)
*The Complete Goodies* (B.T. Batsford, 2000)
*The Complete Sid James* (Reynolds and Hearn Limited, 2000)
*Last of the Summer Wine: The Finest Vintage* with Morris Bright
(BBC Worldwide Limited, 2000)
*The Lost Carry Ons* with Morris Bright (Virgin Publishing, 2000)
*Mr Carry On: The Life and Work of Peter Rogers* with Morris Bright
(BBC Worldwide Limited, 2000)
*Benny Hill: Merry Master of Mirth* (B.T. Batsford, 1999)
*Carry On Uncensored* with Morris Bright (Boxtree, 1999)
*Monty Python Encyclopedia* (B.T. Batsford, 1998)
*The Carry On Companion* (B.T. Batsford, 1996)

★ **ROBERT ROSS** ★
PROUDLY PRESENTS

# FORGOTTEN HEROES OF COMEDY

AN ENCYCLOPEDIA OF THE
**COMEDY UNDERDOG**

unbound

First published in 2021

Unbound
Level 1, Devonshire House, One Mayfair Place, London W1J 8AJ
WWW.UNBOUND.COM

Text design by PDQ Digital Media Solutions Ltd

A CIP record for this book is available from the British Library

ISBN 978-1-78352-918-6 (hardback)
ISBN 978-1-78352-919-3 (ebook)

Printed in Great Britain by CPI Group (UK)

1 3 5 7 9 8 6 4 2

All that the comedian has to show for his years of work and aggravation is the echo of forgotten laughter.

*Fred Allen*

# Contents

# Foreword by Terry Jones

My advice to you is never share a meal and a bottle of wine with Robert Ross. There's a very certain chance that you will have such an enjoyable, relaxed, wildly amusing time that the conversation will invariably lead to one or both of you saying: 'Let's write a book!'

To be fair to Robert, the result of one such pleasant evening is in your hands now, and it was me, not him, who came up with the initial idea.

Allow me to set the scene. It was in my old house, in the old century. Robert had spent much of the day rummaging through my archive, collating information for the revised and up-dated edition of his excellent *Monty Python Encyclopedia*. It got to that certain time of day, so I ordered an Indian takeaway and set up a couple of bottles of Cabernet Sauvignon. Fatal!

Robert and I share a passion about a great many things: history, literature, politics – and comedy, of course. Always comedy. Our conversation turned to the 78rpm recordings I had collected as a child. They were old even when I was young, but I was obsessed with these music hall artistes – people like the grouchy Gus Elen, the rather naughty Ronald Frankau, the often-surreal Albert Whelan. Playing some of these dusty treasures, I was amazed that Robert had

The result of a fan letter from the author. Happily, it all started with a joke...

not only heard of the turns in question, but he knew most of the songs too. He was very well educated.

After an excited exchange of views on such delights as 'Let Me Carry Your Bag to Bagdad, Dad' and 'I'd Like to Have a Honeymoon with Her', I said: 'You should write a book about all these brilliant forgotten comedians. And if you do, I'll write the foreword!' And he has, and I have.

The fact that it's twenty years since that conversation is testimony to Robert's perspicacity and determination. It's also proof that most publishers don't know a great thing when they see it! Oh, we got close to a contract over the years. Some publishers had a problem with a perceived lack of focus to the choices – well, we both wanted to broaden the spectrum to celebrate our forgotten heroes not just from variety but also from the slapstick days of silent comedy, plus the shadowy figures who played their part in supporting the stars and those familiar character actors you can't quite remember the name of... They are all represented in *Forgotten Heroes of Comedy*.

Other publishers were even more dismissive just of the title – a title we always refused to budge on. '"Forgotten Heroes"?' they would bleat. 'Well, if they're forgotten, who cares? Who would want a book about them?'

It seems you would, so thank you.

Thank you, too, for supporting the amazing work of Unbound.

And thanks to Unbound, for having complete faith in this very worthwhile project. It's been quite the labour of love. I hope you treasure it as much as I will.

Terry Jones
Highgate, January 2016

# The Prologue

'The truth about variety is that it is unselfconsciously the poetry and song of the people.' So said John Betjeman. And so say all of us. And there are quite a lot of us, as is clear from the hefty weight of the tome you are holding – and it is by no means definitive. The pages aren't elastic, even at Unbound!

The selection process has had to be largely arbitrary; if Terry Jones or I were adamant to include them, then they were in, yet these sadly neglected clowns, drolls, wits and comedy actors are powerhouses who have inspired, informed and, yes, made me laugh out loud, over the years, whether through personal friendship or dim and distant memories of seeing them on television. This was back in the day when the major broadcasters would happily unleash classic comedy films on a Friday evening or Saturday morning. Now, alas, this happens less and less, and it is Talking Pictures TV that stands tall as the bastion of quality vintage broadcasting, merrily dishing out Old Mother Riley, Terry-Thomas and Laurel and Hardy.

And in this lies the mounting problem. Although more and more vintage film and television is being released on to DVD and Blu-ray, the punter has to literally search these out. One would only invest in a *Doctor in the House* box set if one knew what to expect from a *Doctor in the House* box set; thus, without regular terrestrial screenings, the marquee value of these gems of comedy is fast diminishing.

Some names included in this book could very well spin off into fully fledged biographies and reference works in their own right. Indeed, Marty Feldman is only missing from these pages because of my 2011 biography of that colossus of comedy. Peter Butterworth was only struck from the list of forgotten heroes because that's another book currently in my pipeline. Still, for every forgotten comedian who is eagerly pushed back into the spotlight, another one gets the last laugh.

Indeed, in the promotional film that helped to fund this book, Barry Cryer made a very important point. He remembered giving a presentation at Bristol's Slapstick Festival about his work and friendship with Kenny Everett. A group of under-forty-somethings were bowled over by the self-dubbed Cuddly Ken's comic genius. Of course they were. The worrying thing was that they had no idea who he was. For a comedian whose influence is equal to that of earlier pioneering surrealists Spike Milligan and Peter Cook, this is a sobering thought. While Milligan and Cook are still, quite rightly, celebrated in television retrospectives and documentaries, Everett rather frustratingly languishes in the vaults. My sister Fiona, who married a man called David Everett some twenty years ago, tells me that when she spelled out her new name to change bank accounts and other official documentation, she often heard: 'Oh, as in Kenny?' Now that never happens. It's much more likely to be: 'Oh, as in Rupert?'

Twenty years is a long time in comedy, particularly when your work is rarely given exposure. Even BBC Four's splendid 2012 biopic *Best Possible Taste: The Kenny Everett Story* couldn't kick-start a resurgence. The leather-clad raver Sid Snot, the bearded, big-busted movie starlet Cupid Stunt, the moronic punk Gizzard Puke... All were classroom favourites of my generation, but few younger than us can have any idea of his work.

It's hardly surprising, then, that a much earlier comedian, Sir George Robey, is equally underappreciated, despite being one of the few variety turns to receive a knighthood, not to mention playing Falstaff for Laurence Olivier in the 1944 film version of *Henry V*. These were achievements not to be sniffed at, following a career on the boards that saw his deadpan, throw-away style earn him the moniker The Prime Minister of Mirth. And this nearly a century before Boris Johnson!

Naturally, the variety theatres of yore are littered with casualties. Take the speciality act comedian Bob Nelson, who would try to ascend a huge pile of chairs or stagger about with a cannonball in his grasp, forever promising to toss it up and catch it on his back; his nonsensical, non sequitur question to the audience – 'Aren't plums cheap?' – still echoes today. Or Stainless Stephen, from Sheffield, who pimped his bowler hat with a stainless-steel rim. A true comedian, he delighted in the English language and in self-deprecation, introducing himself as 'Stainless Stephen comma comedian question mark'. A genius.

George Williams revolted against the impurities of the music halls and stuck to white-faced, white-book or family-friendly patter. So pale was he, in fact, that his endearing opening catchphrase, 'I'm not well! I'm not well at all. In fact, I'm properly poorly...' kept audiences in the palms of his hands for over sixty years. Marcel Marceau considered him 'Britain's most underrated comedian', but an arrest and conviction on charges of homosexuality in the early 1950s killed his career stone dead; in those horrendously intolerant times, the great man saw his contracts with the Moss Empires circuit and the BBC unceremoniously dropped.

Liverpudlian comedian Billy Danvers rode the punches of changing styles in comedy from Queen Victoria's time to the Swinging Sixties simply by sticking to his rustic one-liners. He was still working in variety at the Brixton Empress Theatre just a fortnight before his death. Charles Clapham and William Dwyer delighted variety audiences with their outrageous, occasionally near-the-knuckle cockney alphabet. Like many forgotten heroes, they smoulder on in the Will Hay anthology *Radio Parade of 1935*, with fresh-faced leading man Clifford Mollison the reluctant ringmaster to a big top of peerless but now neglected turns. Billy Russell enjoyed a seventy-two-year career as a character comedian and actor, memorably embracing the First World War cartoon figure 'Old Bill' and laudably using his early radio exposure to satirise the government 'on behalf of the working classes'. Bernard 'Bunny' Doyle was a pantomime favourite, delighting audiences across the country with his comic observation and silly songs. A survivor of the Great War, he even incorporated the

Compilation album *Listen to the Banned*, issued on the Living Era label in 1984.

words 'Late of 17th. Division Concert Party' in his playbill matter when he returned to variety and played his native Hull. A real forgotten hero.

Then there's Jack Beckitt, popular in Blackpool for the summer season, with his 'TV Talking Shoes' – seriously! He even went as far as to have his stage advertisements include the legend 'Not Solely Represented'. The man deserves respect for that, or at least a re-heel.

Music hall turns are by their very ephemerality like mayflies: captivating but short-lived. Even comparatively recent champions of the form, like impresario Alexander Bridge, can be forgotten because they determined to tread those sainted boards rather than take to television. As well as creating the *Palace of Varieties* show in 1963, Bridge presented solo performances by Jessie Matthews, was a much-sought-after pantomime dame and toured music halls around the provinces for nigh on thirty years. He was beloved within the business but today his legacy languishes in a dusty archive of old playbills. Even the legendary Jack Tripp, arguably the finest pantomime dame since Dan Leno – a pithy, withering, flirty imp of broad-brush greasepaint and multicoloured bloomers – is only really revered within the business itself.

The theatre is like the best summers – remembered through a haze of time. Still, this doesn't fully explain why some figures are forgotten and others not. Max Miller, George Formby and Will Hay were lucky to have their work preserved on film, and enjoy vibrant fan clubs to this day. Even admirers of those glorious eccentrics Jack Hulbert and Cicily Courtneidge foregather in celebration of their talents at the Concert Artistes' Association in London's Covent Garden. By contrast, the likes of Arthur Askey, Tommy Trinder and Leslie Fuller, who all had similarly prolific film careers, wallow half-forgotten in the mists of time. The irony for Trinder is that, with his brash cry of 'You lucky people!' and his aggressively popular patter, he stole great swathes of

Max Miller's material and, by so doing, stole great swathes of his audience; the rivalry was intense and well-documented, extending to Trinder actually buying a Brighton house right next door to Miller's – but there's no denying that Miller's place in the history books is far more secure, including a statue in Brighton and a face-in-hole board on the town's Palace Pier. Moreover, with a lineage of reverential front-cloth comedians from Ben Elton to Ross Noble consciously or unconsciously emulating him, the Cheeky Chappie is very much in the hive mind of the twenty-first century.

The inappropriate nature of a comedian's material sometimes explains why they are consigned to history. Olivier can still just about get away with being seen as Othello; comedy has a tougher deal – the BBC long ago dictated that there will never be repeats of *It Ain't Half Hot Mum*, for example. G. H. Elliott, the blackface variety turn in the whiter-than-white suit, was commonly known as 'The Chocolate Coloured Coon'; the very name will strike him from the footnotes of comedy history, despite working within the long minstrel tradition that continued to thrive on stage and television many years after his death. If the vast number of episodes of *The Black and White Minstrel Show* are never exhumed from the television archives, then the memory of old-timer Elliott will forever linger behind the 'last curtain' inscription on his Rottingdean grave. Other contemporaries share his fate: Eugene Stratton, 'The Dandy Coloured Coon', came direct from the minstrel tradition, scoring huge success in England with his sentimental ballads. His name may mean little today, even though many can still whistle his song 'The Lily of Laguna'. May Henderson was a child star and, later, a blackface artist performing in variety and pantomime as 'The Dusky Comedy Queen'. Playing a one-string fiddle, G. H. Chirgwin, 'The White-Eyed Kaffir', had an act as eccentric as his look and tirelessly worked as many as six music halls a night. It paid off, and he spent the last of his days on Devon's beautiful Burgh Island. Years after his death Spike Milligan saluted him, adopting his look in the 1974 film *The Great McGonagall*, appropriately enough on the stage of Wilton's Music Hall.

One fantastic performer, who, as a very young man, worked with G. H. Elliott and many other veterans of the music halls, was Jack Douglas. His 'Whey-hey!' twitching enriched everything from *Crackerjack!* ('Crackerjack!') to *The Arthur*

*Haynes Show*, while his lasting legacy resides in his tail-end contribution to the *Carry On* series. Yet, compared to the greats of those films, like Sid James and Kenneth Williams, Jack Douglas is rarely celebrated in the countless television documentaries that forever carry on. He is perilously close to being a forgotten hero.

My youth was far from misspent, wallowing in both Hollywood and Pinewood films until the familiar faces of the 1930s seemed like favourite relations irregularly popping round for tea. Can those glorious character actors of films by Preston Sturges or Mark Sandrich really be considered forgotten when their films are so celebrated? The bewildered gaze of Edward Everett Horton; the cheery best-friend roles so delightfully played by Una Merkel; those rotund, kindly gentlemen of Eugene Pallette; the prissy killjoys of Franklin Pangborn. The list goes on. Their names may always be on the tip of the tongue, but their legacy is a largely uncelebrated one.

Some readers may choke on their breakfast at the incongruity of Arthur Haynes, Harry Worth and Charlie Drake within these pages. These were massive stars who in their heyday commanded huge audience figures and huge fees. However, there's no denying that they too have fallen out of public consciousness. No afterlife on greetings cards or Christmas-fortnight repeat-screenings for them.

Tony Hancock, a contemporary of Haynes, remains an instantly recognisable icon of comedy. Both Hancock and Haynes were at their television peak in the early 1960s. Both also died tragically young, just over eighteen months apart, but it is Hancock and not Haynes who enjoys posthumous adoration. When film producer Betty Box gave Haynes a guest appearance in *Doctor in Clover* in 1966 it was just as intertextually knowing an embrace of small-screen stardom as when Box's film producer husband Peter Rogers gave Frankie Howerd a guest appearance in *Carry On Doctor* two years later. Both Haynes and Howerd were huge, recognisable stars channelling their television personas into a starry big-screen performance, but now, for those out of the know, Haynes's performance has completely lost its cachet, while Howerd's is every bit as imposing and playful.

There were some close-run heroes. Ted Ray, quite simply one of the best joke-tellers ever to have taken breath, a silver fox with a silver tongue, remains largely unheralded. His twilight years were spent retelling all the old favourites on *Jokers Wild*. Meat Processing King Al Read was more of a character comedian, reigning supreme over the great English Sunday lunchtime of the fifties and sixties with *The Al Read Show*. It was a showcase of hilarious everyday characters in, as he described them, 'pictures of life', with a string of unforgettable catchphrases. He was a 'right monkey!' that's for sure. Even Larry Grayson, who sprinkled my childhood with camp bon mots, skips between the raindrops of forgotten-hero status. With his gossipy monologues of Everard, Slack Alice and Apricot Lil, he was omnipresent in the 1970s, scoring his biggest personal triumph as the host of *The Generation Game*. It is a beloved perennial, but Bruce Forsyth's grip is hard to loosen. Larry Grayson did it with withering aplomb.

Even Max Wall, one of the greatest comic minds of his or any other age, isn't safe. Ahead of his appearances at the Edinburgh Festival Fringe in August 2017, Robin Ince tweeted: 'seems many comics haven't heard of Max Wall. I have just found a way of mentioning him in one or both shows' – one was Ince's show *Rorschach Test*, a wild wander through his inner thoughts; the other, *Pragmatic Insanity*, his reflection on idols in art and science. With his timeless funny bones, Max Wall inspired everything from soft-shoe shuffling to the interpretation of Beckett. Wall's recording of Ian Dury's 'England's Glory' on the Stiff Records label is surely Britain's alternative national anthem.

There are the veterans who found lasting fame late in life – like Jimmy Jewel who, whilst suffering a hilarious partnership with Hylda Baker in *Nearest and Dearest*, almost saw his near-legendary radio and stage partnership with Ben Warriss fall into obscurity. Peter Jones, universally loved as the melodic voice of the book in Douglas Adams's *Hitchhiker's Guide to the Galaxy*, utilised those dulcet tones on *Just a Minute* for years, as well as in his sitcom hits *The Rag Trade* and *Mr Digby Darling* – but what of his pioneering, early-1950s radio series *In All Directions*, with Peter Ustinov? Largely improvised, with the multi-talented duo playing most of the parts, just one edition currently resides in the BBC archives. Felix Bowness, who played Fred the downtrodden holiday-camp jockey in *Hi-de-Hi!*, was another whose real comedy legacy remains hidden under a bale of hay. For that beloved BBC sitcom, as well as for dozens of others, Felix was the top studio-audience warm-up man, whipping often hard-to-please, dispirited crowds into a comic frenzy before the main attraction. I saw Felix work a rabble many times, and his cheery way with people, coupled with an inexhaustible fund of good, punchy jokes, was a wonder to behold.

Arthur English was variety's 'Prince of the Wide Boys'. With his multicoloured kipper tie and his trilby hat at jaunty angles, he would sell his old grandmother for a profit and leave the stage yelling, 'Open the cage!' It was a towering variety turn, now completely overshadowed by his unforgettable role of Mr Harman in *Are You Being Served?* By rights, English should have landed the role of Private Walker in *Dad's Army*, but that was destined to be taken by James Beck, the first of the largely pensionable cast to fall out, ironically at the age of just forty-four.

Richard Beckinsale, who died at the even more ridiculously young age of thirty-one, could have fallen between the cracks but for the fact that he is still remembered with great fondness. His two greatest situation-comedy achievements, *Rising Damp* and *Porridge*, broadcast practically simultaneously on rival networks in the 1970s, have had a relentless repeat-programme ever since. For the interested researcher, these sitcom evergreens allow easier access to his more minor, although beautifully formed, hits *The Lovers* and *Going Straight*, as well as his fledgling film turn in *Rentadick*. The same applies to Yootha Joyce, whose monumental work with the Joan Littlewood Theatre Workshop is shamefully unheralded while her behemoth situation-comedy creation of Mildred Roper in endless ITV3 re-runs of *Man About the House* and *George and Mildred* keeps her name on the fabulous list.

An early death, even in the midst of a storming career, can condemn a legendary comedian to near anonymity. Take Ernie Kovacs, for example. His pioneering blend of surrealism and satire made him a staple of American television. He was a true eccentric (both on-set and off), once even wrestling a jaguar live on screen. As a comic performer and writer he was every bit as influential as Sid Caesar, but his death in a car crash at the horribly early age of forty-two came just as he might have reached superstardom, having been set to take a leading role in the epic feature film *It's A Mad, Mad, Mad, Mad World* for Stanley Kramer. His involvement in this box office hit and perennial television favourite would have kept him firmly in the public consciousness. Ironically, his role was filled by none other than Sid Caesar himself, forming a domestic double act with Kovacs's widow, the already-cast Edie Adams. What price fate?

Even ancient music hall turns aren't treated with parity. While little remains of their work save some faded sheet music and scratchy 78rpm recordings, even legendary masters like Gus Elen are very much forgotten men, while thanks to contemporary admirers who frequently reference him, and Peter Ackroyd's *Limehouse Golem* novel, the name of

Roy Hudd, a keen *Forgotten Heroes* supporter, points out his shared bill with Max Miller.

Dan Leno lingers on as part of the smog-filled Victorian and Edwardian London of Sherlock Holmes and Jack the Ripper. It is pure happenstance that allows the legacy of Dan Leno to have some resonance more than a century after his death, with his place at pantomime's top table keeping his name alive, while the 1960s satirist whizz-kid Lance Percival is somewhat underrated. A close friend of mine who works in television told me that a couple of her colleagues had each named their car Lance Percival. This tickled my young friend as, having lived in my world, she knew exactly who Lance Percival was. The girls in question had no idea, though. No idea about Lance's biting sketches on *That Was The Week That Was* or his knowing calypsos. Nor did they know him as the hapless chef, Haines, in *Carry On Cruising*, a perennial favourite for time-filling schedulers. Usually, even one *Carry On* appearance is the familiar public touchstone in the most crammed of CVs.

So, basically, there's no rhyme or reason why some are forgotten and some remain titans. It is undeniable, though, that for every Tommy Cooper there is a Dick Emery; for every Morecambe and Wise there is an Olsen and Johnson.

Instead, this book is a personal selection from those hundreds and hundreds of laughter-makers who, for one reason or another, have been left on the shelf.

Over this collection of one-hundred-odd essays, far, far more than one-hundred-odd heroes are profiled, but there are still always going to be plenty of names that you and I have forgotten and that someone else remembers with affection. These comedy heroes are lined up to form a possible second or third volume – or, with young Kenny Everett ever-fading from the collective memory, even *Forgotten Heroes of Comedy: The Next Generation.*

In the meantime, take your seats please in the Theatre Royal, Brighton, and have fun diving into and being entertained by this assembled A-Z collection of very funny folk. What a bill! From Avril Angers to Mario Zampi, these are my favourite forgotten heroes of comedy. Forgotten no longer.

Robert Ross
Buckinghamshire, December 2020

The author and Katy Brand look on in awe and affection as Terry Jones talks *Forgotten Heroes of Comedy*, in Highgate, November 2013.

# Avril Angers

## 1918–2005

A very funny lady, both on and offstage, and no mean actress.

*Brian Murphy*

Perhaps one of the most underrated of all British stand-ups, at the peak of her fame in the 1950s Avril Angers was described as a female Tony Hancock, a Betty Hutton with sophisticated subtlety, and England's answer to Lucille Ball. She could be all three of these things at once, for she had a quick wit and a versatility that sparked and fizzed like a freshly ignited Catherine wheel.

Despite the French name, she was born on 18 April 1918, in Liverpool to celebrated working-man's comic Harry Angers and original Fol-de-Rols girl Lillian Errol. Later joking that she was the only Liverpudlian who didn't play the guitar, by the age of fourteen she was in the chorus of a variety show on Brighton's Palace Pier and the following year took on the title role in *Cinderella* at the Alexandra Theatre, Birmingham, in which she starred opposite Wee Georgie Wood – well, he was opposite, but a lot lower down.

As dizzy, eccentric and beguiling as most of the characters she played, she seemed to breeze through life with an air of charming insanity. At five she went to Australia with her parents. 'I seem to have been on the move; ever since I can remember,' Avril remembered in 1957. 'I rarely stayed in one place for more than six months and I changed schools so frequently that the teachers hardly got to know me!' Her father alerted her to an audition and, from the age of fourteen, Avril danced with the celebrated Gordon Ray girls. The following year she joined her mother's old Pierrot troupe, the Fol-de-Rols. As with many of her comic generation, the Second World War proved something of a mixed blessing, and she went on to perform extensively with the Entertainments National Service Association, touring the Middle East and West Africa with the Out of the Blue concert party for two years. She was awarded the Africa Star and the 1939–45 Star for her services to morale: 'Just little awards that were made to me and which I admit I cherish more than any of the other possessions I have.' Crucially, while performing in Cairo she was spotted by BBC Radio producer Douglas Moodie, which landed her with her first broadcast with the corporation in May 1944, appearing on *Variety Bandbox*, *Merry-Go-Round* and *Navy Mixture*, and excelling as the scatty, easily distracted secretary of star-maker Carroll Levis in the presenter's eponymous 'discoveries' show. Avril's whirligig performance showcased her as one of the most sought-after foils in the business – every bit as versatile and valued as Dora Bryan, Joan Sims or June Whitfield. 'The Adventures of Avril Angers' even became a weekly comic strip in *Radio Fun*.

She was always ready with a steely gaze or a flirtatious smile, and an impressively eclectic roll call of comedy legends would benefit from the Angers touch over the decades: Arthur Askey (*Before Your Very Eyes*, Associated-Rediffusion, 1956), Les Dawson (*Dawson's Weekly*: 'All Pools Day', Yorkshire Television, 8 July 1975), Dick Emery (*The Dick Emery Show*, BBC1, 1967), Kenny Everett (*The Kenny Everett Show*, BBC1, 1985) and Roy Hudd (*Hudd*, BBC1, 1965).

None was more grateful than that pioneering maestro of television comedy, Terry-Thomas. Having been impressed by her versatility in the variety show *Stars in Your Eyes*, T-T wisely recruited Angers for his comedy sketch show *How Do You View?*. The relentless show put her flip chart of comic characterisations fully to the test though she was best loved as the resident BBC charlady Rosie Lee ('the girl with the tea'), forever choosing the most inconvenient point to interrupt the star comic's monologue simply to enquire on how he wanted his brew. At the end of every episode she would also play the object of his desire as they fell into a romantic, melodramatic fade-out embrace. The series ran with great success until Coronation year, leading

Dancing with Peter Sellers at the Astor Club, Mayfair, in 1955.

to the spin-off domestic situation comedy *Friends and Neighbours*, which ran for one series of six episodes from 27 January 1954 and recruited a barrel-load of beloved Terry-Thomas cohorts.

In the July of 1954 Angers landed her own series, *Dear Dotty*, which again saw the BBC recruit the *How Do You View?* scripting team of Talbot Rothwell and Sid Colin, as well as T-T's producer Bill Ward. In this forgotten gem, Angers was cast as Dotty Binns, a lowly writer on the staff of women's magazine *Lady Fare*.

Angers made her West End debut during the Second World War, performing with Cyril Fletcher in the frantically upbeat Palace Theatre revue *Keep Going*. In 1945 she appeared with Leslie Henson and Hermione Baddeley in *The Gaieties* at the Winter Gardens Theatre, Blackpool, and was back in the West End, opposite Max Wall, for the revue *Make It a Date* at the Duchess Theatre, in 1952.

A 1949 season at the Connaught Theatre in Worthing had offered her the challenge of more dramatic roles, and during her long stage career Angers ran the gamut from Miss Prue in William Congreve's *Love for Love* to Miss Marple in Agatha Christie's *A Murder is Announced*. Her favourite roles always allowed her maximum room for comedy, notably Billie Dawn in *Born Yesterday*, Eleanor Hunter in *No Sex Please, We're British* and Mrs Finney in Ray Cooney's production of *The Mating Game*, at the Apollo Theatre, London, from 14 June 1972.

Angers never lost her love of variety, and though she was annoyed that in 1959 the BBC dropped her topical musical spot 'Look Back with Angers' from the

How Do You Brew?: As the ever-cheerful canteen girl Rosie Lee, 'the girl with the tea', in the BBC Television sketch show *How Do You View?*

radio show *Roundabout*, she stormed through the early 1960s in a succession of theatrical hits. In 1962 she was in Australia for the intimate revue *Paris by Night* and spent much of 1964 touring in Jack Popplewell's *Busybody*. Immediately thereafter she took on the pivotal West End role of Belle Poitrine, 'that fabulous and fabled star of stage and screen', alongside Bruce Forsyth, in *Little Me*, at the Cambridge theatre.

One of her favourite writers was Noël Coward, and she often cited a regional tour as Madame Arcati in *Blithe Spirit* as her favourite role. Produced by Peter Saunders at the Vaudeville Theatre in spectacular tribute to theatrical manager C. B. Cochran, the 1973 revue *Cockie* afforded her Coward's heartbreaking showstopper 'If Love Were All', and she appeared in revivals of the master's obscure pieces *Post Mortem* and *Easy Virtue* at the King's Head pub theatre in Islington.

Angers had made her film debut as early as 1956 and was somewhat star-struck by the idea of a glamorous career on the silver screen. Despite her best efforts, that side of her career never fully materialised, the British film industry not really being equipped for a home-grown Lucille Ball. Still, she appeared alongside Richard Burton and Rex Harrison in *Staircase* (1969), as well as in Lance Comfort's unnerving British vampire film *Devils of Darkness* (1965). She could also embrace grim-up-North kitchen-sink drama, as she proved in Roy Boulting's *The Family Way* (1966), from which she gained a most incongruous connection with pop culture when a film still of her, in character as Liz Piper, was selected for the cover of the Smiths' single 'I Started Something I Couldn't Finish'. Morrissey, a self-proclaimed wallower in the cosy, no-nonsense waters of Britishness, had been something of a fan.

Angers was part of the furniture of British film and television. A reliable asset. There was always a warmth and familiarity about an Avril Angers performance, whether she was secretary or telephone operator, factory girl or fortune teller. Her appearances even spanned the nation's favourite soap, *Coronation Street*, from its inception in late 1960 to its thirtieth anniversary: two separate characters, Norah Dawson and Sylvia Crozier, in two separate stints.

The 1951 sheet music for one of the many songs Avril performed and made popular on radio.

Laudably, she was still happily in the pay of top comics towards the very end, being hand-picked by Victoria Wood to bring truth in small doses to a rambling rambler in *Victoria Wood*: 'Val de Ree (Ha Ha Ha Ha Ha)', in December 1989. If it was reassuring for Victoria Wood to have a shade from her viewing past in the company, it was equally irresistible for the rest of us. It was as fitting an autumn-years parade as could be wished for. Avril Angers was one of the best, keeping busy and keeping cheerful until her death, in London, on 9 November 2005, at the age of eighty-seven. Time to put the kettle on.

TREAT YOURSELF TO *The Green Man* on DVD (Studiocanal: B000HEZ7KC, 2006). George Cole is an unwitting vacuum-cleaner salesman on the trail of a methodical serial killer, played by Alastair Sim, with an eighth-reel burst of Terry-Thomas and lashings of Colin Gordon at his most supercilious. It was this film that first brought my undivided attention to Angers. Playing Marigold, the doe-eyed assistant, to Sim, her overly protective fussing and slowly dawning suspicions of her employer's shady deeds are a comic delight in this classic of frightfully British manners and frightfully British murders.

# Don Arrol

## 1929–67

A comedian of boundless energy and inventiveness.

*Sir Bruce Forsyth*

'You're going out a youngster but you've gotta come back a star!': so ebullient theatre director Julian Marsh (played by Warren Baxter) bellowed at chorus girl Peggy Sawyer (Ruby Keeler) in the 1933 film classic *42nd Street*. She did come back a star, of course – this was Hollywood and she was Ruby Keeler. Still, it was a phrase that influential television impresario Val Parnell could have used on the evening of Sunday, 16 September 1961, when a fresh-faced hopeful filled the enormous shoes of Bruce Forsyth. The show was the biggest thing on television, staged at the most prestigious theatre in the country: *Sunday Night at the London Palladium*. The callow youth who took his chance that evening was Don Arrol.

As all so-called overnight successes know, this was hardly the way it happened. Young Donald Angus Campbell was born on 11 August 1929, in Glasgow and, if not raised in a trunk, he came from a family that was certainly steeped in show business. His father was a comedian who tirelessly worked the clubs of the coal-mining community of Lanarkshire, and his down-to-earth, engaging style didn't fall far from the tree. While still in his teens, Arrol was working those same clubs, gaining a reputation as a turn who could alternate between surrealist flights of fancy and polished patter. He even cultivated a convincing transatlantic accent, making him an ideal compère. This was the early 1950s, after all, and everything American seemed to be bigger, brighter and just plain cooler than anything that ration-poleaxed Britain could muster. There was only one venue where Arrol would let his accent slip back into native Scots, and that was the Glasgow Empire, whose audience were notoriously unforgiving of any comedian from over the border.

It was during pantomime season in Glasgow that he met singer and fellow comedian Norman Meadows. The two young coves, both doing only reasonably well at the time, decided to team up as a double act. Meadows was the straight man to Arrol's fall guy, and almost immediately the team began making inroads on the Scottish variety circuit. Having been signed up by agent Cyril Berlin, Arrol and Meadows began playing the number-two and number-three music halls south of the border too, and a stint entertaining the troops in Germany saw them supporting such top-line acts as Ronnie Hilton and Vic Oliver.

The duo agreed from the outset that their partnership must be flexible, however. While pantomime season together was set in stone, and variety offers for their act were fair for the plucking if both agreed, the summer season was sacrosanct. That was precious time to work on their solo routines. Every year, Norman Meadows would head for Eastbourne Pier and support veteran turn Sandy Powell [qv] – an assignment Meadows would honour for twenty years. Arrol, meanwhile, would indulge in his laid-back and lucrative compèring duties.

In the early summer of 1960 he was attached to a rock 'n' roll show touring Britain with dream-team teen headliners Conway Twitty, Freddy Cannon and Johnny Preston. At the end of May, Arrol joined another such package, *Seeing Stars*, starring home-grown talent Adam Faith and the John Barry Seven, and played the Blackpool Hippodrome for the season. Fortuitously replacing Des O'Connor who, ironically, had been switched to the London Palladium, Don

Who's in charge? Bruce Forsyth hands over his compere duties on *Sunday Night at the London Palladium*, September 1960.

was as relaxed at the microphone as ever. When it was his turn to dish out the comedy Arrol could be just as explosive and astounding as any young rock 'n' roller; his playbill matter, 'Dial "M" for Madness', said it all. It was on one fateful June day of the tour that Arrol hit Newquay and Val Parnell happened to be in the audience.

Parnell had found himself in a quandary. *Val Parnell's Sunday Night at the London Palladium* – to give it its full on-screen title – was his baby and it was a heavyweight, also making a national sensation out of Bruce Forsyth. Indeed, even today it's hard to say 'Sunday Night at the London Palladium' without lapsing into a sing-song Brucie croon. In a show that went out live and involved both attention-sapping guest-stars and intricate games played by folk from the provinces, Forsyth had been a television revelation. His uncanny ability – combining all-round entertainer with quirky comic and delivering it all with a totally at-ease, down-to-earth way with the general public – was gold dust. The problem that faced Parnell that evening as he took his seat in Newquay was that Brucie's doctor had ordered him complete rest in light of a suspected duodenal ulcer that had forced him to bow out of the show's sixth series, scheduled to start that September. Then Parnell spotted Don Arrol.

Arrol seemed to have the same winning combination of style and silliness. He could work a crowd. He could sing. He could also take his comedy down completely unexpected avenues. Often he would appear onstage in a huge, oversized overcoat, squared at the shoulders. He would then saunter towards the microphone, leaving the coat literally behind him, sing a standard, standardly dressed, while his live-in coat (complete with hanging cutlery, and pots and pans), would await his return. Other times, Arrol would bound onto the stage dressed as a horse. He was that kind of comic. Parnell struck the deal and Arrol compèred the sixth series of *Sunday Night at the London Palladium* with seasoned aplomb, introducing such international stars and home-audience favourites as Tommy Steele, Shirley Bassey, Frankie Vaughan, Petula Clark, Eartha Kitt, and Morecambe and Wise. On 6 November 1960, the headliner was none other than 'The Mighty Atom' himself, Bruce Forsyth.

This was Brucie's terrain and he certainly didn't want to relinquish control completely, certainly not with Arrol holding the show together so expertly. Moreover, it was clear that Arrol didn't feel the pressure from his rigorous schedule, juggling his breakthrough television work with a regular comedian-and-compère spot with the Fol-de-Rols' summer season in Bournemouth, where he was hosting eight shows a week, two on Saturday, before bombing up to London for *Sunday Night at the London Palladium*.

Arrol owned every show of the sixth series, which ended on 18 June 1961, but the position was never anything more than temporary. Everyone accepted this, and Bruce was back at the helm at the start of the seventh series, in September 1961. As Arrol admitted at the time: 'every time I did it, it was like working with a ghost behind me. Let's face it – it's Bruce's show'.

It had certainly done Arrol's career the power of good, though. In January 1961, Decca Records released his single 'Ev'rybody Likes It' coupled with 'It's All Happening Here'. Immediately after his London Palladium exposure Don joined comedian Al Read's summer season troupe in *Fun and Fancy Free*, at the Queen's theatre, Blackpool. He also walked into a glut of compèring jobs, starting with *Thank Your Lucky Stars* at the end of 1961 and continuing with *Candid Camera*, from March, 1962.

Guest spots on *Comedy Bandbox* and *Big Night Out* and a third Blackpool summer season, this time with Albert Modley [qv] on the Central Pier, kept him frantically busy throughout 1962 and into 1963 – lucky breaks such as he'd landed don't come along that often so the game was on to utilise that precious exposure. But the pressure took its toll on his wife, Heather. Having suffered a nervous breakdown, she discharged herself from hospital in Scotland and began the long drive home to the Sussex coast with the couple's nine-year-old daughter, Donna. Just outside Darlington, the family car broke down and a replacement vehicle was provided. It was green, a colour his wife had always been superstitious of, and tragedy hit near Scotch Corner, Yorkshire, when she clipped a lorry, careered off the road and struck a tree. She was killed instantly. Donna suffered only minor injuries.

Arrol continued to work. He had to. He was contracted to host *Blackpool Night Out* for ABC Television and subsequently accepted radio work for the BBC, notably taking centre stage on *Light Up the Night*, for producers John Browell and Richard Wilcox. Arrol's professional appeal was noted as: 'an extension of his shy, modest self, abetted by an engaging warmth of manner'.

It was a skill that BBC producers of variety series *The Black and White Minstrel Show* were keen to embrace. By the mid 1960s, the show was a television phenomenon attracting viewers in more than 21 million homes. Arrol was its host for almost three of its most popular years, leading to the BBC's decision to choose the show as the light entertainment series to spearhead colour television in the summer of 1967. By then, however, Arrol was dead, having succumbed to a heart attack on 13 May. He was just thirty-eight.

Arrol certainly wasn't an overnight success, and the fact that his television glory days were restricted to just six years at the top seems beyond cruel. By all accounts a winning and likeable sort of bloke, Arrol's epitaph should be much, much more than the only host of *Sunday Night at the London Palladium* you have never heard of. So, ladies and gentlemen, *now* you know. (That's your cue to applaud.)

TREAT YOURSELF TO Arrol's single ('Ev'rybody Likes It'/'It's All Happening Here', Decca: F11318, 1961), which was orchestrated by *Sunday Night at the London Palladium*'s composer Eric Rogers. It is light and jaunty stuff typical of both Decca and Rogers, although the A-side, 'Ev'rybody Likes It', does indulge Arrol's skill for madcap comedy, with a Jerry Lewis-like rant metamorphosing into a rumbling baritone. Treasure it.

JOE BAKER

# Joe Baker

## 1928–2001

I loved Joe like a brother. He was the perfect stage partner. We fitted like a dovetail joint. He was hilarious, mad and totally frustrating! He knew I was bloody furious when he broke up the act, but I also knew he had to do what he did. By the grace of God, he ended his days as my dear friend across the ocean. I will miss him until I exit stage left.

*Jack Douglas*

Joe Baker was a roly-poly, dough-faced clown and a born mimic. He was also the man born to be Lou Costello, so akin was Joe's comedic awkwardness to the great vaudevillian; Lou's daughter, Chris Costello, once told Baker: 'You do my dad better than anyone!' In fact, Joe spent the majority of his working life in England fantasising about making the transition to Hollywood. As his long-time comedy partner Jack Douglas remembered: 'Joe was obsessed with the States ever since I met him – and that was way, way back in the forties! He dressed like an American, he wisecracked like an American. He even drank Jack Daniel's whisky to complete the image.'

Baker was born to music-hall-performer parents, Joe and Olga Baker, in London, on 14 December 1928. Saturated with greasepaint and variety throughout his formative years, he made his mark just after the Second World War. While serving as a sergeant, his erstwhile superior officer, Jack Douglas, met him in Germany, was struck by his winning stage craft, and offered him an early demob if he could make himself available for pantomime; he was directing *Dick Whittington* at the Kingston Empire and was desperate for a Captain's Mate. Baker readily agreed. When the actor cast as the Captain was unavoidably detained at the eleventh hour, Douglas, as the only other member of the company who knew the part, was forced to draft himself in as replacement.

In the audience on that very first night was influential agent Hyman Zahl. Approaching Douglas and Baker once the curtain had fallen, he waxed lyrical and wondered aloud how long the two had been a team. Douglas looked at his watch and gave the flippant-sounding but gospel-truth answer: 'Two hours, twenty minutes!' Thus was born a comedy double act. Instantly. From that first performance together would grow an act that wowed audiences ranging from American army bases to the Astor Club in Mayfair.

As part of the Moss Empire circuit, Douglas and Baker toured the country and cut their teeth on the fading British music hall scene. They were gainfully employed in pantomime and summer season work, performing in venues everywhere, from the Chiswick Empire to Butlin's Clacton. There never were such times! The pair's television break came in 1955, with the fledgling children's favourite *Crackerjack!* ('Crackerjack!') which brought silly slapstick and playful puns to a delighted junior audience. Joe's father, Joe Baker Snr., as the sour-faced Mr Grumble, was often the butt of the joke. Another influential television opportunity came along in 1957, when producer Brian Tesler included the act in his variety series *New Look*. As the title suggested, the show was geared towards showcasing fresh talent, and its liberating, ramshackle, anything-goes attitude to song, dance and sketch-comedy suited the team down to the ground. *New Look* and *Crackerjack!* ('Crackerjack!') formed their training ground, providing a paid apprenticeship in comedy acting and expert tomfoolery.

Everyone was shocked, none more so than Jack Douglas, when Joe Baker announced he was breaking up the act. It seemed complete madness, for the two had just appeared in their first feature film with an admittedly brief, albeit beautifully self-contained, bit of plate-smashing opposite Kenneth Connor in the Royal Air Force comedy *Nearly a Nasty Accident* (1961). A sort of 'Carry On Flying', it certainly pointed the way forward for Douglas, but to

Aye aye, that's yer lot! Jack Douglas, Jimmy Wheeler and Joe in *Robin Hood*, at the Alhambra, Bradford, 1960–61 season.

Baker it simply pointed out that his career was stagnating. Together they had clocked up fourteen years touring the music halls, taking slosh in the face and judging knobbly-knee competitions. After completing their run as the comic merry men in *Robin Hood* at the Alhambra Theatre in Bradford, time was up. Douglas was devastated and not a little miffed, with one particular grievance: 'Laurel and Hardy were my absolute comedy heroes. Their legendary producer Hal Roach had seen our act and offered us the opportunity to remake all their old films. It would have been wonderful. Joe's decision put paid to that.' Notwithstanding the fact that Roach seemed to make that offer to pretty much everyone, from Dick Van Dyke to Kenneth Williams, one can see Douglas's point of view. Still, one can also see Baker's. Both Douglas and Baker needed a new comedy direction. In the immediate aftermath of the break-up, Douglas would team up with other comedians. Baker would go it alone. A rotund comedian in search of a stooge. There would be other shoes to fill however, and after the death of his inspiration Lou Costello, in March 1959, the biggest clown shoes of all. But not quite yet.

Having flicked off the dust and custard pie of regional theatre from his baggy trousers and cultivated a more sophisticated, transatlantic style of delivery, Baker first worked the London cabaret and club circuit. His reputation was initially boosted by West End exposure in *Joey, Joey*, which opened at the Saville on 11 October 1966. It was a pet project of Ron Moody, who played nineteenth-century clown Joe Grimaldi. Alas, this life story of The Great Grimaldi charmed neither audiences nor critics and the show closed after just twenty-three performances. Baker went back to television, a medium that persistently saw him as: 'a short, fat comedian' – yes, that phrase was actually used in the press handout for his first solo television success, suitably enough entitled *The Joe Baker Show*, for ATV in 1965.

He had already made his mark in situation comedy, landing a supporting role in the 1964 series *Fire Crackers*, starring droll comedian Alfred Marks. This wacky tale of bumbling firefighting didn't help Baker's typecasting – he was given the part of the bumbling man-child Jumbo, very much like the Graham Moffatt [qv] role in the 1940 film *Where's That Fire?* on which the series was unofficially based – but it did lead to his first sitcom lead, in *My Man Joe*, in February 1967. Joe's master, Lord Peregrine Hansford, was played with fine faded élan by Francis Matthews, while Baker happily mugged and pratfell as the clumsy, ever-enthused manservant, forever coming up with unsuccessful schemes to re-stock the Lord's empty coffers. The show lasted just one series of six, but still ATV had enough faith in Baker to offer him *Baker's Half-Dozen*, in 1967. A platform for various comedy characters and situations, it was a veritable Joe Baker comedy playhouse. The sixth and final instalment of the series 'The Guy Fawkes Night Massacre' – which saw Joe as a hapless baker dealing with a problematic wedding cake on Bonfire Night – didn't air in the London area until the September of 1976 due to its incendiary title. By then, Baker had finally made the move to America – but it seems he may have left it a little too late. Lou Costello was long dead; Bud Abbott had gone too. So any wild dreams of resurrecting that celebrated teamwork with Lou's estranged partner had gone with the wind, despite Bud providing his own voice for the Abbott and Costello cartoons, opposite Stan Irwin, and being very much in work mode until the end thanks to dogged taxation.

Baker found steady, if plodding, work in America and, ironically, enjoyed his greatest successes following in the footsteps of his heroes. Costello had been a semi-regular godsend for Steve Allen back in the late 1950s, and there was a sugar-sweet delight in Baker finding a regular slot on *The Steve Allen Comedy*

*Hour* (NBC, 1980–81). There was a minor role as Merlini in 'Murder Is A Parlor Game', a March 1979 episode of the NBC crime series *Mrs Columbo* and a bit part as a peasant in Mel Brooks's *Robin Hood: Men in Tights* (1993), but there was no escaping the fact that it was just like playing the Alhambra in Bradford, only with better weather.

Baker featured in the films *Waxwork* (1988) and *Waxwork II: Lost in Time* (1992) opposite horror-franchise favourite Zach Galligan, and, as Barnard, brought his many years of comic expertise to Peter Farrelly's *Dumb and Dumber* (1994). Back in England, Baker had chalked up one-off appearances in such drama series as *No Hiding Place* (in the episode 'Cover Story', Associated-Rediffusion, 5 June 1962) and the last ever *Strange Report* ('Report 4977: Swindle – Square Root of Evil', ITC, 28 October 1969). While in Hollywood there were welcome turns in the likes of *Fantasy Island* ('Rogues to Riches'/'Stark Terror', ABC, 19 January 1980) and *Highway to Heaven*, in the 'Man's Best Friend' two-parter transmitted on NBC on 16 and 23 September 1987. There were nods and winks as Jewish tailors and refined butlers, but for juicier, fat-idiot parts Hollywood already had Buddy Hackett; it would always prefer to use one of its own, but that was particularly the case now that Baker, who had been the ultimate pseudo-American in Britain, seemed determined to heighten his Englishness to Wodehouse absurdity for the American audience.

His saving grace was his lifetime's skill at mimicry and funny voices. Indeed, he once claimed to have taught Sir Laurence Olivier how to 'do' Donald Duck. Animated cartoons were churned out of Hollywood like kosher sausages and Baker found a lucrative position as one of the city's busiest voice artistes. Occasionally he would hit pay dirt, as with his memorable characterisation of Lon in Walt Disney's 1995 classic *Pocahontas*, but usually it was the factory treadmill of Hanna-Barbera that paid his grocery bills.

Fittingly enough, his stand-out vocal performance was as another hero from Hollywood's 'golden age' of comedy, Larry Fine. The trio of Larry, Moe, and Curly had appeared in cartoon form before, but in 1977, with all the original Stooges dead, Baker landed the role of Larry in *The Robonic Stooges*. The bizarre premise – the Stooges are now robots with superhero powers – first appeared as five-minute, throwaway inserts in the 1977 CBS children's show *The Skatebirds*.

Joe's 1965 album of comic prank calls.

It was sort of like *The Banana Splits* but with chaps in furry bird outfits – on skates. The Three Stooges segments were easily the most popular element, and a series of half-hour adventures was hastily commissioned. Joe Baker had finally made it as a Hollywood star-comedian but he had to wear a dead man's shoes to do it. And the wrong dead man's shoes at that.

Commercials and telly bit parts kept Baker active until his death, in Los Angeles, on 16 May 2001. His old sparring partner, Jack Douglas, was deeply affected by Baker's loss: 'We had never really fallen out,' he remembered, 'but equally things had never quite been the same since the act broke up. He knew how I felt about it, but life goes on. And we both did pretty well on our own, didn't we?'

TREAT YOURSELF TO Joe Baker's long-playing record *Dial Joe Baker* (Parlophone: PMC 1251, 1965). Clearly inspired by the American trend for funny crank calls, and utilising his dazzling array of regional accents and impromptu wit, this LP predates Jon Culshaw and Dom Joly by decades, with Baker chatting to everyone, from the manager of a London Turkish bath to a bewildered receptionist of an American servicemen's club. And I guarantee you'll be singing 'There's a rose between my toes...' for days afterwards!

# Eric Barker and Pearl Hackney

## 1912–90 and 1916–2009

I used Eric Barker often in my films. Pearl Hackney not at all. Both were fantastic artists. Regrets, I've had a few...

*Peter Rogers*

It seems strange for a comedian significant enough to appear in both the first and last of the original, twenty-one-year run of *Carry On* films to be considered forgotten, but Eric Barker is one such talent. Indeed, the Indian summer of character-acting in films saw him pick up a British Academy award for his performance as a frantic Labour Party agent in the satirical *Left, Right and Centre* (1959). He played the officious Man from the Ministry of Education in several of the *St Trinian's* comedies and proved an energetic comic buffer for Bob Monkhouse and Kenneth Connor in the *Dentist* films. Despite this glut of familiar and popular British cinema romps, Barker was already established as something of a comic renaissance man. A man of many voices and a writer with a proven ability to amuse, his long and winding career perfectly played out in three distinct acts.

Despite enjoying an acting career that stretched back to childhood – he appears in the 1918 film *Nelson* – first and foremost, he was obsessed with the written word. To say he started at the very bottom is to put it mildly. After an education at Whitgift School in Croydon, the young Barker was put to work in his father's wholesale paper business – he'd been surrounded by paper for so long that he eventually started writing stuff down on it! By the time he was twenty-one, in 1933, he had written lyrics and sketches for André Charlot's revues, written and produced two plays, seen his novels *Day Gone By: The Tragedy of a Fool* (Ward, Lock & Co., 1932) and *The Watch Hunt* (Ward, Lock & Co., 1933) become best-sellers. Eric would even have a short story included in P. G. Wodehouse's landmark anthology *A Century of Humour* (Hutchinson & Co. Ltd., 1938), Wodehouse noting that Barker had 'a real talent for humorous writing'. Just before the outbreak of war in 1939, he had turned his attention to radio, penning both the words and music for the ambitious operetta *His Majesty's Pleasure*.

Barker had long combined his love of the written word with an ease for performance: by his late teens he was playing juvenile Shakespearian roles at the Q Theatre in West London, and in 1934 he played opposite Joan Hickson as Dick Whittington with the Oxford Repertory Company. Twenty-five years later, the two would be reunited on the set of *Carry On, Constable*; what a business – for Barker, an awful lot of carrying-on had preceded it. His other repertory theatre experience had included assignments at Birmingham and Croydon, and he had enjoyed lots of lowbrow fun with George Royle and Greatrex Newman's Fol-de-Rols seaside troupe, a long-established variety show that would also boast Arthur Askey and Norman Wisdom amongst its number.

The ultimate showcase came when Barker was taking his self-penned impressionist routines to the Windmill Theatre (which triumphantly 'never closed' during the Blitz). It was during one such attachment that he met Pearl Hackney, who, having been employed for the chorus at the age of fifteen, had already graduated to principal dancer. Originally hailing from Burton upon Trent, and spending her formative years in Liverpool, she had not only trained as a ballet dancer, under the tutelage of Anna Pavlova, but also ingested a local wit that would inform her comedy. Pearl and Eric married in 1936 and remained together until the end, skilfully projecting to the public the joy of their very domesticity. It was never gentle, but real; never saccharine, but enchanting.

The year after their marriage, Barker made further inroads into feature films, giving his stagebound antics a wider audience in *Concert Party* and *Carry On London* (both, 1937). It

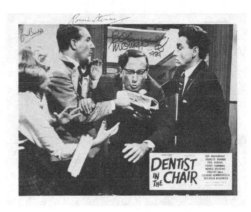

Orthodontic hilarity with Peggy Cummins, Ronnie Stevens, Eric Barker and Bob Monkhouse in *Dentist in the Chair* (1960).

was another twenty years before his role as the bombastic Captain Potts in the first, official, Peter Rogers created, *Carry On* film, *Carry On Sergeant* (1958), came along.

In the meantime, it was radio that made him a star. From 1940 to 1945 Barker served as a lieutenant in the Royal Naval Volunteer Reserves, but his heart was really in his weekly radio broadcast, *Merry-Go-Round*. Such was the morale-boosting clout of this show that Barker was often allowed time off specifically to write, record and promote it, which in turn enabled him to spend plenty of time away at the family home, Hillside cottage, in Stalisfield Green, Kent. After victory, Barker continued to make some of the best-loved and most happily subversive comedy ever broadcast by the BBC. Shows such as *Waterlogged Spa*, from September 1948, *Barker's Folly*, from March 1959, and, perhaps most treasured of all, *Just Fancy*. Running from 1951, the sterling supporting cast included Deryck Guyler [qv] and Kenneth Connor, whose wholesome and often pithy interactions added to the blurred comic edges. The playful shorthand that Barker and Hackney brought to the wireless made them beloved family friends and, via their shows, eagerly welcomed into millions of homes across the country. The series kept them at the top of the tree with a seemingly never-ending supply of catchphrases. Lines like 'Oh, I say! I rather care for that!' and 'Steady, Barker!' would follow them around like lost puppies for the rest of their lives – with *Steady, Barker!* also the title of Eric's 1956 autobiography.

Playing Paper Theatre with daughter, and future actress, Petronella, at their Kent cottage in 1948.

Unsurprisingly, television was quick to capitalise on their popularity, with Eric's own shows *Look At It This Way* (BBC, 1955), a satirical revue in brash strokes, and *The Eric Barker Half-Hour* (BBC, 1951–53), which had required no introduction at all. This show, in particular, allowed a more structured, character-centric shade in order to ease out the more base material of Eric's earlier comedy. Producer Richard Afton had already capitalised on this in *The Newcomer*, a fifteen minute slice of televised domestic disarray from 1950. Pearl, again, was instrumental in this more grounded, groundbreaking style. She was very much more sitcom in her nuanced performance. It was a quality that, decades later, she would bestow on established hits: the role of Mrs Grainger in *Are You Being Served?*: 'The Clock', for example. As a direct result of her advice, Barker even found time for straight supporting turns, notably the recurring role of Inspector Mole in the BBC crime serial *Cluff*. In 1957 Barker had become an indispensable part of the backbone of British film character actors, thanks entirely to British film polymaths the Boulting Brothers. As a mild-mannered master of slightly off-kilter comedy, Barker was cast as the ever-efficient clerk of the law firm at the centre of *Brothers in Law* (1957), and while the likes of Richard Attenborough, Terry-Thomas, Peter Sellers and Ian Carmichael would carry this and other Boulting films, it was Barker's detailed character studies that gave full richness to *Happy is the Bride* (1958) and *Heavens Above!* (1963).

In 1959 Barker was handed a bunch of scripts originating from Sid Caesar over on NBC. The result was *Something in the City*, a sitcom concerning three commuters, played by Eric, Deryck Guyler, and Peter Hammond. It was a doomed Associated-Rediffusion series, not least because Pearl was cast as the wife of Guyler rather than the wife of Barker!

The *Carry On*, *St Trinian's* and *Dentist* romps would deploy comedy of a broader nature but allow him the greatest comic opportunities of his career. The irresistible combination of a bemused scowl and suppressed laughter informed all of these, notably, *Dentist in the Chair* (1960) and *Dentist on the Job* (1961), which gave him dual roles to sink his teeth into: with a reprise of the Dean of the Dental School from the first film, as well as playing his cousin, the rather unscrupulous Colonel Proudfoot of Proudfoot Industries. It is the nearest Barker got to being Alastair Sim or Alec Guinness. *Carry On Spying* (1964) cast him as the determined but awkwardly cowardly Chief, scoring maximum subtle innuendo-points in high-octane sparring with both Richard Wattis and Kenneth Williams. It was flared nostrils at dawn. Indeed, Eric had written a treatment for a *Carry On Cruising*, giving Dickie Wattis and Miles Malleson plum parts; as well as himself, of course. Still, apart from the undeniable fact that both had a ship in them, there was very little of Barker's script in the finished film, released in 1962. At times anarchic but mostly archaic, Eric's plot was much more Portsmouth procedure than P and O pleasure. He still received a 'based on an original story' credit though.

However, by the time he had completed the 1965 Ken Annakin epic *Those Magnificent Men in Their Flying Machines* (a film which employed almost every comic working in Britain at the time) and the last of three consecutive *St Trinian's* films, *The Great St Trinian's Train Robbery* (1966), Barker was not a well man. Illness forced his early retirement.

Pearl happily soldiered on, joining the cast of ATV series *The Best Things in Life*, in June 1970, opposite Bob Todd as June Whitfield's interfering parents. Dream casting! She appeared in 'The Importance of Being Hairy', a Kingsley Amis scripted *Comedy Playhouse*, in May 1971, 'Another Fine Mess', the *Seven of One* episode that indulged Roy Castle and Ronnie Barker as Laurel and Hardy impersonators, and *The Life of Riley*, a Bill Maynard vehicle for Granada, in early 1975. Pearl was Mrs Pringle, a typically fussy portrait of maternity that she keenly essayed at the drop of a hat in everything from playing Gillian Taylforth's mother (this time round, Pearl was married to Derek Benfield) in the February 1981 *Hi-de-Hi!* episode 'Desire in the Mickey Mouse Grotto', to *The Hound of the Baskervilles*. The Peter Cook one! She certainly deployed stern discipline for her Maggie Clarkson in Vince Powell's Liverpudlian comedy *The Wackers* (Thames Television, 1975). Moreover, she was a natural as Mrs Pike in the BBC Radio 4 run of *Dad's Army*, from 1974 until 1976.

While immobility didn't deter Eric from regular contributions on Radio Kent, Pearl was an active member of the Stalisfield Parish Council. The couple were also in-laws to Anthony Hopkins, to whom their actress daughter Petronella was married from 1966 to 1972.

He was a devout Anglican who supported many worthy causes. Notably he became a strong campaigner for the disabled. This often led to the misconception that he was confined to a wheelchair himself: that and a fondness for watching the television detective series *Ironside*. In written correspondence he maintained that 'unlike Raymond Burr, I have never sat in one in my life', though by the 1970s he could only muster enough energy for the smallest of guest-turns on film and television. Among the last of these was as the aged Admiral in *Carry On Emmannuelle* (1978), in a wordless but poignant vignette of wistfully remembered sexual agility. Old comic soldier Eric Leslie Barker did carry on, though, fading away on 1 June 1990, at the age of seventy-eight.

With several careers packed into one life, Barker's legacy deserves full recognition.

It was a flame that Pearl tendered for nigh on twenty years, slipping away on 18 September 2009, at the grand old age of ninety-two. They were reunited, and interred together in the churchyard of St. Mary's. It's a beautiful corner of Kent which is forever them. What a marriage. What a partnership. What larks they had, and shared.

TREAT YOURSELF TO a few days in *Darling Buds of May* country, for the essence of Kent seeped into the collective work of Barker and Hackney. Robust and good-natured, it does the soul a power of good.

# Alfie Bass and Bill Fraser

## 1916–87 and 1908–87

As a child, I lived in Africa for a bit over three years, coming back in 1962. The great sensation for me as I settled back into the rather small, greyish country I had longed for and dreamed of for those seemingly interminable years was television, which I had never seen in my life; there was certainly none in Northern Rhodesia. I fell in love with the little box in the corner of the room dispensing non-stop entertainment. And the zenith of my viewing was *Bootsie and Snudge*. My next-door neighbour Billy Brown and I used to live for Fridays, when his mum would cook us bangers and mash and we would lock ourselves in front of what we weren't allowed to call the 'telly'. We adored the unending battle between bossy Snudge and cheeky Bootsie: Alfie Bass with his ever-mobile features, a street urchin in uniform; and Bill Fraser, a towering presence, his face a mask of scorn and hauteur, his vowels tortured into some semblance of poshness, always chasing Bootsie and always failing to catch him. It was a servant-and-master relationship, except that – and this was the glorious sting in the tail – they were actually both servants. The pecking order, so beloved of the Britain in which I grew up, had them in its vice-like grip.

I had never seen *The Army Game*, the show from which they had demobbed themselves into the world of London's rather grand clubland, and by 1962 they were onto the third series of *Bootsie and Snudge*, so I knew nothing of their military history, hovering in the background, or of the 1950s world out of which they had sprung. For me, they were perfectly real, though now of course I see that they were essentially stock characters whose origins go back to the commedia dell'arte, and before that to the Roman comedy of Plautus and Terence. Perhaps because of these deep roots, their playing had a richness and a depth to it. These were actors in their own right, not mere puppets of sitcom. Of course, in the 1960s a sitcom series wasn't a matter of half a dozen episodes; series one *Bootsie and Snudge* had forty weekly episodes. Series three, where I came in, twenty-nine. So they and their writers, who included Marty Feldman, Barry Took, John Antrobus, Stanley Myers and Jack Rosenthal – the crème de la crème of comedy writers – had a chance to develop and enrich them. Both Bass and Fraser were seasoned actors and seized their opportunities. So much of the great comedy of the 1960s was created not by comedians but by actors who instinctively fleshed out the comic archetypes – Arthur Lowe, Warren Mitchell, Harry H. Corbett, Wilfrid Brambell. (And, of course, there were comedians who became actors, notably Frankie Howerd and Tony Hancock.)

Alfie Bass, né Basalinsky, from Bethnal Green, had a background in the famous, left-wing Unity Theatre in Camden, for whom he acted (with Paul Robeson, no less, in the 1930s) and directed. In 1956, at the Arts Theatre in the West End, he had played the leading part in an adaptation by Wolf Mankowitz of Gogol's story 'The Overcoat'; it was turned into a short film, *The Bespoke Overcoat*, which won an Oscar the following year. Bill Fraser, a Scot from Perth, started life as a bank clerk but ran away to London to become an actor. At first he failed, spending many a night sleeping rough on the Embankment, but before the Second World War he rose to be the manager and leading actor of the Connaught Theatre in Worthing.

These men had real heft as actors, as they demonstrated rather astonishingly, to me, who knew nothing then of their backgrounds, by appearing in the grandest of venues and revealing themselves to be major actors. Alfie Bass took over from Topol in *Fiddler on the Roof* at Her Majesty's Theatre: he was superb – I saw them both, and believe me, Bass was better. Topol was absurdly good looking and healthy; Bass knew about starvation, he knew about being henpecked, he knew about being frightened of Russian soldiers – his relationship to God and to his fellow human beings was rooted in reality, not a musical comedy version of all those things. He knew about clinging to your community for survival, and his humour was a survivor's. Bootsie was in there somewhere; an older, wiser, sadder Bootsie.

In 1967 I was working at the National Theatre, at the Old Vic, in the box office – so of course I knew everything that was going on before anyone else did – when I saw on some memo that Bill Fraser was joining Laurence Olivier's company. I could scarcely believe my eyes – or my luck. He'd never stopped working all that time, of course, always popping up in this or that, but here he was in an early play of Shaw's, *Mrs Warren's Profession*, with the great Coral Browne and Sarah Badel. Whatever I expected of him – to do it just like Snudge, perhaps – I was astonished by his elegance and subtlety, and the air of corruption he brought with him onto the stage. Then, of course, I saw everything he did – at the National, in the West End, at the Mermaid. Often it was Shaw, a writer who requires extraordinary brilliance in phrasing and inhabiting the language. This Bill Fraser did supremely well, as he had with Claude Snudge. I never met him at the National – he kept himself to himself – but I saw his performances again and again (the advantage of being in the box office) and stored them in my mind. I often think of him now when I'm approaching a part.

And I'm still kicking myself over something that happened, or didn't happen, over fifty years ago. I went to school in Chelsea – to the

London Oratory, in those days at the tip of Sydney Street. At the other end of the street was the King's Road, and on the corner was the old Chelsea Palace of Varieties, bought up by Granada in 1951 and from 1957 a television studio from which, among other things, *The Army Game* and, later, *Bootsie and Snudge*, were transmitted. You could just nip in and get a ticket for the transmission; I walked past it every day, but I never went and got a ticket. Why? Perhaps I didn't want to think of them as performers, but as people. Idiot. It riles me still.

*Simon Callow CBE*

Alfie Bass and Bill Fraser were not Laurel and Hardy. They weren't even Abbott and Costello. They weren't a double act at all, not in the strictest sense of the word. Still, like Tony Hancock and Sid James, or Walter Matthau and Jack Lemmon, they were two brilliant comedic actors who became cemented together in the minds and hearts of their audience.

As the diminutive, work-shy, ever-cheerful and deeply philosophical Bootsie, Alfie Bass was the beleaguered Everyman, a benighted and beloved microcosm of the working-class fall guy. As the squinting, scheming and bombastically self-important Snudge, Bill Fraser was a pressure cooker of suppressed rage, a jumped-up, pompous jobsworth who wore his delusions of grandeur and aspirations of cultural betterment like military medals. Together, Bass and Fraser made the tail end of the 1950s and the pre-Beatles 1960s laugh out loud, well up and reflect upon a Britain that had dragged itself through the Blitz and national service and upon the promise of never having had it so good. If sitcom characters can come to represent the nation that loves them – and they can – then none other sums up the complex period between the fall of Herr Hitler and the rise of Merseybeat better than Bootise and Snudge.

Both Bass and Fraser were well into their respective careers by the time *The Army Game* came along and introduced a 'beans on toast' mentality to the British sitcom, in which millions of working-class families would sit down to an evening in front of the telly invariably with their tea on their lap. *The Army Game* was that flagship ITV show that made them stars. They were being beamed into millions of homes on a week-by-week basis, thirty-nine weeks of the year. It was a sitcom soap opera, and that level of fame could never have been imagined for jobbing character actors from the realms of regional repertory and film bit parts. Suddenly, they were pop stars, mobbed by devoted, frenzied fans in the street. There was a 1959 summer season at the Hippodrome, Blackpool. There was even a board game in which

He's in the money!: The return of *Bootsie and Snudge*, after a decade, on 15 October 1974.

you could join in with the antics of the boys from Hut 29. *The Army Game* was big, and its effect on the actors was life-changing and long-lasting.

Suitably enough, Bass's and Fraser's humble rises and rises have many parallels. Bass, almost inevitably, had been born to Russian Jewish immigrant parents and, again almost inevitably, had eked out a living in the environs of North London as a messenger boy, a shop-window dresser, even a tailor's apprentice. Fraser was born a decade earlier into refined austerity. A practical young chap, he made a meagre living as a bank clerk before throwing up the security for a life on the stage. Years and years of struggle resulted. He was the very nemesis of an overnight success. His determined and positive attitude to the over-populated world of theatre gave him a hard edge and a loyal group of friends. Friends in the same unemployed position, but friends all the same. Success came to Fraser at the Connaught Theatre in Worthing; for Bass, it was the Unity Theatre in Camden.

When war broke out in 1939, both Bass and Fraser dutifully enlisted to fight for king and country. Bass served with the Middlesex Regiment, indulging his passion in various army concert parties and even making his debut on film with the Army Film and Photographic Unit. Fraser had joined the Royal Air Force and, by the end of the war, had reached the rank of flight lieutenant. More importantly, in terms of his burgeoning career in comedy, he met and befriended a young writer by the name of Eric Sykes. Upon demobilisation, Fraser would employ Sykes; over the subsequent years, Sykes would return the favour tenfold.

Throughout the late 1940s and early 1950s, Bass and Fraser became familiar faces on British film and television. They were efficient, effective and efflorescent. Flitting from stiff-upper-lipped war flick to slop-drenched television show, Bass and Fraser would have a line of dialogue or a pie in the face, then immediately prepare for the next job.

Busy and popular but very much not a star, Bass left his biggest mark as part of *The Lavender Hill Mob* (1951) at Ealing Studios. Like his fellow tea leaf, Sid James, Bass is in only a third of the film, but in his proud, working-class criminal is a lifetime of experience; it's his pre-Bootsie career in a nutshell. Cult stardom was to follow in September 1955 when Bass was cast to replace David Kossoff as Lemmy Barnet in the BBC Light Programme sci-fi favourite *Journey into Space*: it was Bootsie as the cosmic hobo.

Fraser, however, had no such top press cuttings to pull out at parties. He was busy, certainly, but busy in shows that were very much other people's successes. Perhaps the most important success story to which he was a footnote was that of Tony Hancock. Meeting the great comedian via Eric Sykes, in 1957 Fraser was awarded a regular role in the *Hancock's Half-Hour* BBC Television repertory company. Lovely bits and pieces featuring clerks and coppers always saw Hancock come a cropper, while Fraser's razor-sharp timing and mischievous delight ensured each vignette was fresh, funny and truthful. One episode in particular, 'The Lawyer: The Crown v James S.', broadcast live on 2 December 1957, in which Fraser's deadpan, precise police desk-sergeant castigates bumbling solicitor Hancock over myriad broken laws, was very much the blueprint for things to come. Fraser is so at ease with the comedy business he even whistles the show's theme tune. It's a moment of intertextuality to relish.

Things were to come for Bass before Fraser, however. The very first series of *The Army Game* saw the pontificating William Hartnell as the key source of dread. Bass was cast as the milksop Private Bisley, nicknamed 'Excused Boots', and later simply 'Bootsie', because his delicate plates gained him permission to wear soft plimsolls instead of army-issue, clodhopping footwear. With his throwaway catchphrase – 'Still, ne'er mind, eh?' – here was a lovely soul and an endearingly etched character. Alongside actor Michael Medwin's smart alec, the lumbering Bernard Bresslaw, the supercilious Charles Hawtrey and the down-to-earth Norman Rossington, Bass became part of the merriest and most popular band of funsters on British television.

Bill Fraser was recruited from December 1957, adding to and then usurping the barking authority of William Hartnell. Fraser's Sergeant Major Claude Snudge was a snobbish man who took on the hopeless troop of Nether Hopping Surplus Ordnance Depot as his own personal mission, whipping them into shape, glowering at failure and singling out 'Bootsie' as his target for mental and physical torture. He was, naturally, still in awe of a higher authority than himself, and would cower and toad to officers with the grinning, handwringing subservience of Uriah Heap. ''Ave no fear, Snudge is here!' would serve as the catalyst for literally hundreds of military mishaps over the years.

By the end of the fourth series, in the summer of 1960, Granada had convinced itself that Bootsie and Snudge could and should have an afterlife. With the return of William Hartnell, *The Army Game* marched on for one more year while Bass and Fraser found themselves on Civvy Street. Meanwhile, writers Barry Took and Marty Feldman, who had cut their teeth on scripts for the show, were signed up to pen the further adventures of Bootsie and Snudge. The schedule was equally punishing, with a forty-week first series, but the effect was immediate. Not only did the audience figures soar but the skilful, challenging scripts, and tried-and-tested interplay between Bass and Fraser, took the comedy into brave, new, weird directions.

The stars would break the fourth wall, reveal their innermost thoughts via voice-over, chat with furry friends or inanimate objects, and even subliminally plug the *TV Times* (when Snudge warbled the latest advertising jingle whilst taking a bath). On one occasion they would even meet the devil. All this within the so-called cosy confines of a three-set ITV situation comedy.

The basic premise was perfect. Both got jobs with an exclusive London club. Snudge, naturally, was slightly higher in authority; Bootsie was the dogsbody who would always take the moral high ground. The two shared a bedroom, shared flights of fancy, shared day trips out. The other corners of the square were provided by Clive Dunn, as the aged bootboy, and Robert Dorning, as the club's befuddled, perpetually sweating secretary. As often as not, the four leads would be the only actors used. They would be trapped in a room together or stranded on a roof or in a broken-down car in the English countryside. The comedy became more about

Michael Medwin, Norman Rossington and Alfie Bass in Hammer Films' *I Only Arsked!*, directed by Montgomery Tully, for release in November 1958.

relationships and aspirations rather than bickering and innuendo. It became a thing of beauty.

After three long, long series of *Bootsie and Snudge*, everyone involved with the show was exhausted and spent, but Bass and Fraser were so intertwined in the consciousness of the public that at the start of 1964 Barry Took and Granada reunited them for *Foreign Affairs*, putting Bootsie and Snudge back in harness after just over six months off-screen. This time they were employed by the British Embassy in pseudo-European country Bosnik. Snudge naturally had his eye on the ambassador position played by the clipped and witheringly inefficient Nicholas Phipps, while Bootsie was the underling once more, misfiring and misunderstanding at every turn. This time only eight episodes were made and thereafter it seemed the characters were to be mothballed for ever more.

But on April Fool's Day 1967 Bass and Fraser were back together again in the ABC series *Vacant Lot*. Milo Lewis was the director, a safe pair of hands who had steered *The Army Game* and *Bootsie and Snudge* through many episodes.

Although playing to type, this time Bass and Fraser were family. Fraser was cast as the belligerent William Bendlove, the managing director of a building firm. Bass was his slovenly and shifty works foreman – and brother-in-law – Alf Grimble. The Bootsie-and-Snudge iconography and small-minded battles were always just a petulant grimace away.

Finally, in 1974, Granada gave in to pressure and officially brought back *Bootsie and Snudge*. It was something of a renaissance for 1960s revivals, with *Steptoe and Son* and *Whatever Happened to the Likely Lads?* riding high over at the BBC. For just six episodes and now in full colour, the power had shifted, with Bootsie as a £1 million pools-winner employing Snudge as his financial adviser.

The last time the two appeared on screen together was back in khaki for a special *This Is Your Life* celebrating the twenty-first birthday of ITV, in September 1976. Alfie Bass is there from the start, alongside a hardly altered Harry Fowler (*The Army Game*'s 'Flogger' Hoskins) and a clearly bamboozled Charles Hawtrey. Bill Fraser looks set to miss the party completely until his joyous, bellowing, last-minute appearance from the back of the auditorium. As swansongs go, it's flawless.

The 1970s were fruitful times indeed for both Bass and Fraser. Both cropped up in typical form in *The Goodies,* although, alas, not in the same episode; Fraser being an ex-sergeant major in the March 1973 episode 'Way Outward Bound', and Bass an unscrupulous man from the ministry in the December 1973 episode 'Camelot'. Later that month Bass was back on the show, to play the tiniest giant in pantomime in the Christmas Eve special 'The Goodies and the Beanstalk'; Fraser had chalked up appearances in Frankie Howerd's trilogy of *Up...* film comedies (1971–72); Bass represented the working classes in the big-screen presentation of writers Galton and Simpson's 'Impasse' in *The Magnificent Seven Deadly Sins* (1971); Fraser was the sour-faced studio commissionaire in Reg Varney's behind-the-scenes, film-making romp *Go for a Take* (1972).

They continued to enjoy regular work even during their twilight years, with Bass enlivening the ensemble fun of *Are You Being Served?* (BBC1, 1979) and *Dick Turpin* (London Weekend Television, 1979–81). Fraser soldiered on until the end too: as late as 1986 his West End run in J. B. Priestley's *When We Are Married* at the Whitehall theatre won him the Laurence Olivier Award for Best Comedy Performance.

And with perfect comedy timing, the end for Bass and Fraser was connected, too. On 15 July 1987, Alfie Bass suffered a heart attack and died; less than two months later, on 9 September, Bill Fraser succumbed to emphysema. ('I'll be leaving you now, sir...')

TREAT YOURSELF TO *Bootsie and Snudge: The Complete First Series* (Network: 7953178, 2009) and enjoy one of the finest of all sitcoms – a funny, often surreal and unfairly neglected masterwork.

# Michael Bates

## 1920–78

Michael Bates was a tremendous comedy technician. He was a very well-known theatre comedian, which suited the early episodes of *Last of the Summer Wine*. He spent a great deal of time showing me how to hit someone over the head with a tin tray. He would say: 'Wait, Jane. Pause... think... Now!' He was wonderful.

*Jane Freeman*

After twenty years as a jobbing actor, in the mid 1970s Michael Bates found himself at the epicentre of two very different, very popular BBC situation comedies. He had been with the cast of both shows from the very beginning, and both would continue long after his death, at the age of 57, on 11 January 1978. One show would go on for a handful of years; the other would last for decades: *Last of the Summer Wine* – or, as the original *Comedy Playhouse* episode was entitled 'The Last of the Summer Wine'. That opening tale of three over-the-age-limit but never over-the-hill man-children was dubbed 'Of Funerals and

Fish'. The action is typically sedate, with scenes moving from chapel to library to café, but the conversation is brittle and barmy; the casting impeccable. Peter Sallis and Bill Owen would wander through the Yorkshire Dales for the rest of the century; Michael Bates, the first incarnation of what became known as 'the third man', lasted just two series.

'I had known Michael since 1953,' Peter Sallis once told me. 'We'd done some plays together, including *Rhinoceros* with Laurence Olivier, which was directed by Orson Welles. Michael was meticulous. He was basically a theatre actor; he played television as though it was theatre. Everything had to be exactly right for Michael. Even if he bought a round of drinks, he liked to have the exact money on him.'

That's practically the character Bates was given: Cyril Blamire, the officious, ex-military gentleman with a sense of pride and style, delightfully allowed the actor's fastidious characteristics to rise to the surface. Michael Aldridge, Frank Thornton and, most successfully of all, Brian Wilde would fill the post-Bates void in the coming years, but it was Bates who pioneered the supposedly calm, upright pillar of authority who could instantly lose his head, and his posh accent, when the latest hare-brained scheme escaped his grip.

Born in Jhansi, British India, to a military family on 4 December 1920, the young Bates could speak English. It was the world of Rudyard Kipling, a world Bates relished, even recording Kipling's verse in 1971 for inclusion in *The English Poets* range from Argo Records. Being an actor, he may well have been most at home on the stage, but it was radio that first made him a star of comedy: *The Navy Lark*, on the Light Programme from March 1959, allowed Bates to stretch his skills for playing eccentric, befuddled types, his character usually caught up in the hilarious naval disasters that hit every week for nigh on twenty years. He also had a string of minor roles in British films, including *I'm All Right, Jack* (1959), *No Sex, Please – We're British* (1973) and *The Rise and Rise of Michael Rimmer* (1970), in which he personified the Everyman sick to the back teeth of having a referendum on absolutely everything.

Before *Last of the Summer Wine* Bates had carved out a lucrative career playing bombastic figures of officialdom, earlier proving a valuable asset in the Peter Cook film *Bedazzled* (1967) as the dogged detective relentlessly on the trail

*To Robert with all good
wishes from Michael Bates
1977.*

Forever *Last of the Summer Wine*'s
Cyril Blamire.

of Dudley Moore. The Bates CV certainly took intriguing U-turns: Alfred Hitchcock cast him, again as the policeman, in *Frenzy* (1972), while Stanley Kubrick had forced his jobsworth swagger to crumble to dust, as the prison guard who viciously strip-searches our wayward hero in *A Clockwork Orange* (1971). Undoubtedly his finest and most prestigious film performance was as Field Marshal Montgomery in the Oscar-winning *Patton*. Of course, as Patton, George C. Scott got all the awards for the film; he may not have accepted them all but he got them. Bates, though, was never destined to be a big film star. He just wasn't the type.

However, as one of the busiest of character actors, he was seldom out of work – particularly in television. One of his earliest small-screen successes was something of meat and drink to him: playing Bardolph in the December 1957 presentation of *The Life of Henry V*. He also notched up one-off appearances in popular fare of the day including *Dixon of Dock Green* (as Jimmy in the episode 'A Little Bit of Luck', BBC, 22 November 1958) and *The Four Just Men* (as Corporal Bates in 'The Deserter', ITC, 29 October 1959). In 1965 Bates secured the regular role of Inspector Mole in the BBC1 detective series *Cluff* and relished the offbeat humour of author R. S. Surtees's *Mr John Jorrocks*. A classy, eight-part production broadcast on BBC2 from July 1966, it starred Jimmy Edwards [qv] as the cockney chancer who becomes the squire of Handley Cross. Bates played the dotty Duke of Donkeyton. Enough said, really.

Bates joined Peter Jones and Sheila Hancock's ever-bickering characters in the Yorkshire Television sitcom *Mr Digby, Darling*, for the third series from December 1970, and guest-starred in the *Six Dates with Barker* episode 'Come in and Lie Down' (London Weekend Television, 5 February 1971). For this script, by John Cleese, Bates gives a sinister performance of facial tics and uneasy subterfuge. It's a thing of the disturbing, and of the dark.

Bates had also appeared opposite Richard Vernon and Bernard Bresslaw in the May 1968 *Comedy Playhouse* episode 'Stiff Upper Lip'. No series resulted, but the idea was adapted by one Barry Took, the very man who oversaw *Last of the Summer Wine* a few short years later. It's a small, square world in comedy.

In 1972, Bates landed the lead role in *Turnbull's Finest Half-Hour*. Directed by Bill Hitchcock at Yorkshire Television, it concerned the ups and downs of Pentagon Television, a very minor hub of broadcasting. Itself something of a

Rangi Ram in *It Ain't Half Hot Mum*: Michael's favourite role.

forgotten gem, the show lasted just one series of six episodes but clearly pointed the way towards Bates's snobbish, overbearing *Last of the Summer Wine* persona.

However, the role closest to Bates's heart was to come in 1973, when David Croft cast him as the Indian character Rangi Ram in *It Ain't Half Hot Mum*. For Bates, the role was a love letter to his youth. Caked in brown slap (and thus controversial ever since) and decorating his turban with the same snake belt he'd worn as a lad, he gave a beautifully judged performance, enthusiastically clearing his throat for near-the-knuckle moments, and working within the storyline and around it in order to address the audience. It was the lead role of his life. Co-star Christopher Mitchell [qv] remembered: 'On the first episode Michael had to take me aside to talk to me. On the recording it was the first time that he did that bit of business of clearing his throat but not spitting. Michael got a huge laugh, as did I because I couldn't help reacting to it. I had never seen it before! He was clever. He knew to save it for the actual take. I almost wanted to turn to the audience and say: "He didn't do that in rehearsal!" He was a wonderful actor. A wonderful man.'

Sadly, when he started to suffer from the cancer that would kill him, Bates was forced to choose between Rangi and Balmire. The location shoots in Yorkshire

'Bridge Over the River Hipong', broadcast on 1 November 1977, from Michael's fifth and final series of *It Ain't Half Hot Mum,* with Melvyn Hayes, Mike Kinsey, Barbar Bhatti, Kenneth MacDonald, Don Estelle, Stuart McGugan, John Clegg, Christopher Mitchell, Dino Shafeek, Donald Hewlett and Windsor Davies blocking Michael Knowles!

were too long and arduous, and since he preferred playing Rangi anyway, he gave his all to the Indian part, right to the end of his allotted thirty-six episodes, despite being in pain. David Croft would allow him to remain seated during rehearsals, though Bates insisted on standing for takes and would feign severe displeasure if he felt seated interludes were being written in deliberately to ease his situation. 'The Eternal Quadrangle', his last episode of *It Ain't Half Hot Mum,* was broadcast at the end of November 1977. Less than two months later he was dead.

Even if only for his Rangi Ram, Michael Bates deserves to be remembered as one of the truly great sitcom actors. A performance of such joy and warmth, it is Bates's real moment in the sun.

TREAT YOURSELF TO the DVD set *It Ain't Half Hot Mum: Complete Fifth Series* (BBC: CCTV30328, 2006) and watch Bates's last hurrah with the added love and respect it deserves.

# David Battley

## 1935–2003

A brother in laughter.

*Eric Idle*

The chances are that on the very rare occasion you hear the name David Battley he will be described as 'lugubrious' and his abiding comedy credit will be a guest appearance in *The Good Life* Christmas special. He was indeed lugubrious – very lugubrious. And he was in 'Silly, But It's Fun...', that wonderfully Christmassy special episode of *The Good Life* broadcast on Boxing Day 1977. It's probably safe to say that this particular episode has been screened every Christmas since. Somewhere, anyway. It certainly has been by me. You can bet the old homestead on the fact that the Beeb will blow the dust off that crudely animated bird-and-bee title sequence and screen it again next Christmas too. And why not? It's joyous. And one of the great joys in it is David Battley, giving a masterclass in perfect pauses and his stock-in-trade placid expression. As the department store delivery man who delivers a Christmas tree a full quarter-of-an-inch

37

shorter than the one ordered, Battley's browbeaten tradesman goes head-to-head with Margo Leadbetter (one of telly's greatest comic creations, as played by Penelope Keith) as Richard Briers's Tom mutters: 'You've picked the wrong house here, mate...' Battley is on-screen for less than three minutes but in that time he warbles a snatch of 'White Christmas', shares Royal Air Force memories with Tom and observes everything from Margo's wallpaper to her shoes. He is a minion who knows his place and accepts the inevitable – that he'll have to take back the Yuletide paraphernalia. Within those few minutes, Battley creates a full and rich personality for the man; he has no name but he has a soul. His monotone cheerfulness hangs over the scene like a clown's shroud. The writers, Bob Larbey and John Esmonde, also provide him with a killer exit line. After all the attention he has paid to Margo, Barbara – that lust-object of self-sufficiency, as played by Felicity Kendal – asks whether he has observed anything about her. 'Yes', he replies in that disinterested drone, 'your eyes. They're the kind of eyes a man could kill for, the sort of eyes that hint at a deeply sexual nature. Merry Christmas!' And with that, he is gone.

Still, David Battley didn't vanish as quickly. During the 1970s, in particular, he seemed to be everywhere. Certainly, television comedy would have been much the poorer without him. He chalked up a *Hark at Barker* (the 'Rustless in Pigtails' episode, London Weekend Television, 25 April 1969) there, a *Father, Dear Father* ('A Book for the Bishop', Thames Television, 11 October 1971) here. He found an irregular niche in the worlds of Eric Sykes, being particularly notable as a – yes, you guessed it – lugubrious floor manager in *The Likes of Sykes* (Thames, New Year's Day 1980). Battley also proved memorable as a sparring partner for Sid James in *Bless This House*: 'Watch the Birdie!' (Thames, 12 March 1973). All Battley's Mr Jones wants is for Sid to take a photographic portrait of his dead parrot!

Producers loved him. He was a quick-witted, polished and totally professional actor. There were no tantrums, no problems. Just bloody good work and split-second timing. Hence the repeat invitation from William G. Stewart to *Bless This House*, making an appearance as a different character in the 2 December 1974, episode 'Freedom Is...'. Battley's tramp, Wally, is so well-rounded a character, and so poignantly played, that the star of the show, Sid James, seems strangely detached and muted in comparison.

On film, Battley was equally busy and equally lugubrious. He enjoyed a rare starring role in the short-lived situation comedy *That's Your Funeral* (1972) but Hammer Films were so hungry for sitcom spin-offs that the seven telly episodes lead to a big-screen version, complete with Dennis Price as guest star and a slapstick finale. Meanwhile, Battley's grasp on the pratfall was seen at its definitive best in the 1969 film short *The Waiters*, where he and Benny Hill were the serving-disaster-areas in question.

Battley was the desk sergeant in *Rentadick* and the army cook in *Up The Front* (both, 1972). He turned in a knowing cameo as a country yokel in the Leslie Phillips farce *Don't Just Lie There, Say Something!* (1974) and, most memorably of all, played the cynical schoolteacher Mr Turkentine in *Willy Wonka and the Chocolate Factory* (1971). As per usual, it was the tiniest of roles, but in his one scene Battley sums up the very essence of Roald Dahl's distrust of grown-ups.

Bizarrely, it's the film he should have made, but didn't, that would have assured him a major place in comedy history. Having been involved in the 1960s satire movement onstage and on television (notably the 1966 BBC1 series *BBC-3*), Battley was a natural choice to join Eric Idle's *Rutland Weekend Television* team (BBC2, 1975–76). Battley's quick, instinctive style suited the sketch show perfectly and such was its happily spontaneous nature that when his hitherto unknown skill for juggling was discovered it was incorporated into the series. In the episode transmitted on 19 May 1975, to be precise. Battley's dry, laconic delivery was particularly suited to Stig O'Hara, the George Harrison character within the band The Rutles. Also including Idle, John Halsey and Neil Innes, the prefab four remain the most vibrant legacy of *Rutland*'s two-series run, performing 'I Must Be in Love' in the opening episode of the second series, on 12 November 1976. The team even performed on *Saturday Night Live*, from Studio 8H at NBC, New York City. Lovingly recreating snapshots from The Beatles' days on *The Ed Sullivan Show* or filming *Help!*, The Rutles were a pinpoint-accurate, laughter-tinged kiss to the group. Yet when *All You Need Is Cash* was made in 1978, Battley's role was played by the more musically savvy Ricky Fataar.

Perhaps Battley pinned his hopes on the epic disaster-movie-to-end-all-disaster-movies: *S.O.S. Titanic* (1979). In a star-studded cast featuring David Janssen and

*Truly, Madly, Bletchley*, BBC Radio 4, 1997–99, with Toby Longworth, Julian Dutton, Simon Godley and Liz Fraser.

Cloris Leachman, Battley landed a decent supporting role as chief crewman Stebbing. Disappointingly, but appropriately enough, the film sank without trace.

Nonetheless, Battley remained much in demand throughout the 1980s and 1990s. He was particularly effective as Ergo the Magnificent in *Krull* (1983). Battley played the part as per usual, his Eeyore-like countenance anything but magnificent – that's why it worked so well, of course. On television he continued to accept tiny roles and make something brilliant out of them all. He was a police sergeant ('Super Gran and the Day at the Sea', Tyne Tees Television, 24 March 1985), a barman (*The Beiderbecke Tapes*, Yorkshire Television, December 1987), a cab driver (*Grange Hill*, BBC1, 13 March 1997), a golf attendant (*Tee Off, Mr Bean*, Central Independent Television, 20 September 1995) and even a carpet-fitter (*One Foot in the Grave*: 'The Eternal Quadrangle', BBC1, 1 February 1990).

Unbeknownst to all but family and friends, David John Battley (the son of Clapham's first labour member of parliament, John Battley), had been born, on 5 November 1935, with a hole in the heart. As a result, he had been educated largely at home and later failed to complete a course at the Camberwell School of Arts and Crafts. Battley would eagerly explain that acting was his escape route; he could be somebody else, even if that person was always, reassuringly, the same somebody else, and a life in front of the camera was certainly more appealing than a career with the family printing firm, Battley Brothers, which he had stuck at for a matter of months. Even a life on the stage was tough, although once he had graduated from the Royal Academy of Dramatic Arts he quickly joined the Liverpool Repertory Company and clocked up West End credits including Henry England's *There'll Be Some Changes Made*, with Gemma Jones and Alan Lake, at the Fortune Theatre, in 1969.

However, his forte remained television and film, and despite ill health he soldiered on with both into the new century. Radio was a more sedate luxury, that he truly loved, and in 1997 he gratefully joined the regular cast of Radio 4 comedy series *Truly, Madly, Bletchley* – a surreal but effective mix of small-town politics and intimate cabaret, written by and starring Julian Dutton.

As Percy, with Bill Fraser and Raymond Huntley, in Hammer Films' *That's Your Funeral*, directed by John Robins, for a Christmas 1972 release.

The Battley heart gave out in the end, though, on 20 January 2003, leaving behind a rich legacy of comedy. For me, at least, the David Battley hound-dog gaze is as much part of Christmas as mistletoe and wine.

TREAT YOURSELF TO the dead funny Hammer Films comedy *That's Your Funeral* (Strawberry Media: B06XTXYHBQ, 2017). Not only is it the thirty-third and final appearance for that wide-eyed mascot for the studio, Michael Ripper, it also showcases a lovely Battley performance; it's also the only time you'll ever own anything on which he gets top billing on the cover!

# Michael Bentine

## 1922–96

In the early sixties I was on the crew recording *It's a Square World* – operating camera four, I think. Michael Bentine wanted his famous 'flea circus' (usually just a tray of sand being flicked up and down, with Bentine's great commentary) to land on the surface of the moon. Michael and the production crew had the effrontery and bravery to go into the next studio and ask Ray Barrett – Australian actor, known later for *The Troubleshooters* – who was recording a Second World War play about Singapore called *White Rabbit*, to help them out in our studio. He amazingly agreed, and I was given the task of taking a very big close-up of Ray's pockmarked cheek (which in black-and-white days looked exactly like the surface of the moon), and then, as Michael commentated that his flea circus had landed somewhere quite special, I tracked out (on a very tight lens, which was pretty tricky) to reveal the smiling face of Ray. Michael Bentine was one of my heroes. He was very special.

*Clive Doig*

Michael Bentine was more than likely correct that he was 'the only Peruvian born in Watford' in his day, as he so often claimed – and he is most certainly the forgotten Goon. Although he was a founding father of the group, almost the full extent of Bentine's contribution to the genre-bending comedy movement has been wiped from the archives. In the wake of Spike Milligan's place as chief Goon – and, even regardless of its alleged roots in Popeye cartoons – Bentine would often assert that the term was directly aimed at him, in a 1948 *Picture Post* review of his off-kilter variety act. Here was a true Goon.

As such, he found a natural habitat in Jimmy Grafton's family-owned Bloomsbury watering hole, the Grafton Arms, and together with that fellow inn-frequenter and Windmill Theatre veteran Harry Secombe, he starred in the New Year's Day 1949 broadcast *Rooftop Rendezvous*. Mere weeks later, the show's producer Pat Dixon cast him in the programme *Third Division* 'Some Vulgar Fractions' alongside Patricia Hayes and Benny Hill. The comedic clout of Bentine and Secombe fully connected with another likely lad, Peter Sellers.

Jimmy Grafton added Spike to the mix to form a four-pronged radio team proper in 1951. These were unique and Crazy People indeed, although, dubbed the Junior Crazy Gang, they were forced to bask in reflected glory for that first series. They weren't basking in other people's glory for long, mind you: by the second series, the programme was officially branded The Goon Show and the rest is comedy history.

It wasn't long before Bentine was history, too. At the end of the second series, after forty-two episodes, he departed the group, but in terms of Goon mythology he's still a titan. His Captain or Professor (depending on the plot) Osric Pureheart was at the very heart of the madness in those fledgling days. During Bentine's run in the show, Pureheart had a hand in building the Suez Canal, Croydon airport and a time machine. He also first introduced his aunt, Minnie Bannister, who appeared in the shape of a gurgling Spike Milligan. She was destined to be a Goon mainstay.

Rumours of why Bentine left when he did have flown around ever since. Bentine himself claimed to find the radio environment too restrictive for his surreal flights of fancy, while the BBC has been quoted as finding him just too silly and actively jettisoning him, along with producer Dennis Main Wilson.

Still, Sellers and Secombe remained close to their fallen comrade. Bentine had a habit of calling everyone he met a 'genius' and, given that Bentine was the most educated of the quartet, both Sellers and Secombe happily believed him. Milligan was less taken in. He considered Bentine's comedy forced, fake, and far too crazy. And if Milligan thought you were crazy, you were in serious trouble.

Bentine was certainly nobody's fool. Born Michael James Bentine, on 26 January 1922, and, yes, in Watford, and, yes, to a Peruvian scientist father and an English mother, he was educated at Eton College and served with the Royal Air Force during the Second World War. He was transferred to intelligence after a medical mishap ruined his eyesight, and helped to lay out the blueprint for the counterterrorist wing within the 22nd SAS Regiment, ultimately helping to liberate Belsen concentration camp. Quite understandably, the experience had the most profound effect on him. As a result, he needed to find the soothing balm of comedy in anything and everything – and the most bizarre, surreal comedy at that. He had tried his hand at amateur dramatics before the war and was working with Robert Atkin's Shakespeare company in Regent's Park when his call-up papers finally caught up with him.

After the war, he honed his comedy skills with old Etonian pal Tony Sherwood, forming a double act called Sherwood and Forrest. Michael Bentine was Forrest, of course, and the act appeared at the renowned Windmill Theatre in 1946, and on television in 1947, but he hastily reverted to Bentine with the chance to go solo at the Windmill. His offbeat delivery, chesty laugh and inventive use of props made him one of the most distinctive of the returning-hero comedians of the late 1940s. He galloped over the boards for years afterwards, always barely contained within the space, particularly when the occasion was as grand as storming the London Palladium in April 1968 as comedy support for the headliner Tom Jones, or through that August and September performing similar duties for Frank Ifield at the Winter Gardens, Bournemouth.

Cheeky Goon acolyte Graham Stark would dismiss Bentine's comedy as a gimmick. 'It's all he could do!' maintained Stark. 'He would have the broken chair-back and mime a comb or a machine gun or whatever – he did it forever.' Still, it was funny. So funny, in fact, that the young Bentine was chosen to perform this routine for the 1949 Royal Variety Performance at the London

Coliseum. Funny, too, was his gobbledegook language of Slobodian and his wild-haired professor character whose protruding teeth and insane stare were the things of nightmarish laughter. It was in this guise that Bentine contributed to the ramshackle but historically vital feature film *Down Among the Z-Men* (1952) – the only film to feature all four Goons.

In the aftermath of leaving the Goons, Bentine made working trips to Australia and the United States, including appearances on three editions of *The Ed Sullivan Show*. At home, Bentine was perfect as Teddy Brewster in the *ITV Play of the Week* presentation of *Arsenic and Old Lace* on 20 August 1958. Bentine played him as 'a slightly barmy professor'. He interacted with live actors and cartoon characters for *After Hours* (BBC Television, 1958–59) which Bentine not only hosted but also co-wrote, with film-maker Richard Lester. However, Bentine scored his biggest personal triumph with *It's a Square World* (BBC, 1960–64). A pioneering comedy classic, the show, its less-remembered sequel *All Square* (ATV, 1966–67) and its less-still remembered BBC1 revival, *Michael Bentine's Square World*, in April 1977, all laudably indulged Bentine's Olympian insanity. It also won Bentine the 1962 BAFTA for Best Comedy Performance, and a special edition, screened by the BBC in April 1963, won that year's Golden Rose of Montreux.

*It's a Square World* sits comfortably somewhere between Terry-Thomas's *How Do You View?* and *Monty Python's Flying Circus*. While nearly every sketch show pre-*Python* has been dubbed a major influence on it, *It's A Square World* really was a radical attack on the codes and conventions of broadcasting: from newsreaders replaced midway through a bulletin (because Bentine suddenly fits a police identikit and is dragged away, much to the delight of fresh presenter Frank Thornton) to an elaborate animated history of aviation. *It's A Square World* was certainly the first comedy show to poke fun at *Doctor Who*, with Clive Dunn as a white-wigged time-traveller in 'The Doctor's New Invention' sketch, broadcast 31 December 1963, just over two months since *Doctor Who* itself had started! *It's A Square World* was just as quick to mercilessly rib the newly opened BBC Television Centre.

A sense of destruction runs through Bentine's work like the word 'anarchy' through a particularly explosive stick of dynamite. A passion for science saw him hold his own alongside Arthur C. Clarke and Patrick Moore on *The Sky At Night*, although his contributions to the BBC1 show in the late seventies were always naturally tinged with intellectually silly humour. Bentine also had a deep interest in the paranormal. His published works on the subject – *The Door Marked Summer* (Granada Publishing, 1981) and *Doors of the Mind* (Granada Publishing, 1984) – both reflect a need for something, anything, beyond our confined perception of reality. The mass canvas of destroyed youth that he had witnessed during the war, and the personal trauma of the early deaths of two of his five children, gave him an unbreakable inner-peace; an air of childlike kindness that seemed to mask the heartache he had suffered.

Suitably, it is as an architect of children's television that Bentine was at his happiest – it would be a kind of therapy. As early as February 1954, he was writing and presenting the science fiction puppet series *The Bumblies*. He seemed perfectly at ease in the company of characters fashioned from latex and felt, and *Michael Bentine's Potty Time* (Thames Television, 1973–80) brought him to a whole new audience of adoring, enchanted admirers. The Potties themselves were heavily hirsute, myopic-looking bundles of material who – in the thousand-and-one voices of Bentine – would constantly whine, chortle and jabber.

Hair neatly coiffured, and dressed in tie, shirt and club blazer, the self-styled Potty narrator was brilliant. He would present ten-minute vignettes on everything from Christopher Columbus to Dick Turpin, with a relentless supply of corny wordplay and subversive education. Thanks to Bentine's galaxy of vocal impersonations, old radio chums like Peter Sellers, Spike Milligan and Dick Bentley would be magically channelled through the Potties. And this was a man who didn't talk down to children but confided in them. Not an ounce of condescension crept into the show's eight-year history, for within the maelstrom of silly voices and uncontrolled giggles, the actual historical facts were pinpoint accurate, and always conveyed within the sugar-coated pill of humour.

Bentine was also canny enough to get four credits on the show: one in the title itself, one as writer and devisor, another for the voices and a fourth for actually designing the puppets. He was the arts and crafts Charlie Chaplin. Throughout, Bentine's cheery, winning, ageing-uncle figure was the cement to the madness, our sane, head-shaking representative in the potty world around him.

Bentine himself did not go gentle into that good night. While his Goon pals enjoyed diverse popularity, Bentine experimented with an all-star, silent slapstick homage for his one and only starring film vehicle, *The Sandwich Man*, in 1966. The reaction of his old cohorts, none of whom took part,

September birthday boys Harry Secombe and Peter Sellers celebrating with their old Goon chum. Forever united in nuttiness.

are left unrecorded. Thankfully, it would appear those wounds of separation were not that deep after all. Bentine had reunited with Sellers as early as 1952 for the doomed *Trial Gallop*, a BBC sketch show of silliness scuppered by the death of King George VI, and with the olive branch accepted, Bentine was soon invited back for a guest appearance in *The Goon Show*'s fourth-series episode 'The Giant Bombardon', broadcast on Boxing Day 1953. From February 1957 he bolstered the relationship with script and performance contributions to *Yes, It's the Cathode-Ray Tube Show!*, again with Peter Sellers.

Bentine had also been involved in the inventive *Goonreel*, a spoof television newsreel broadcast 2 July 1952, with Graham Stark, Sam Kydd, Eunice Gayson and Leslie Crowther. Written by Bentine, Jimmy Grafton and Spike Milligan, the show also featured a pre-recorded appearance from Harry Secombe. The ever-affable Secombe invited Bentine to be a guest on his ATV variety series *Secombe and Friends* in November 1967, working with old chum Tony Hancock on a script by Jimmy Grafton, no less, and the paths of the old drinking pals would inevitably cross at premieres and charity parties. Bentine even shared some marquee space once more with Spike Milligan, although the film in question, *Rentadick* (1972), kept them firmly apart. Bentine's out-of-control and out-of-context turn, as a foreign diplomat, pretty much steals the film by stopping the plot in its tracks entirely. It was the only sensible course of action.

In later years he tirelessly toured his autobiographical one-man show, bringing it to the Haymarket, Basingstoke, where, as a young Goonite, I

The wild-haired craziness of Professor Osric Pureheart. Mike would never lose his zeal for the zany.

wallowed in Bentine's open-hearted affability. In the nick of time he was, quite rightly, awarded a CBE, and even had one final 'ridiculous, funny conversation' with friend, admirer, and crowned head of the Seagoons, Prince Charles, just hours before his death, in the Royal Marsden Hospital, on 26 November 1996. Even as Bentine fought the dreaded lurgy that would claim him, he fought the BBC's policy of using four-man *Goon Show* publicity photographs for their double-cassette *Goon Show Classics* releases – publicity photographs that would shamelessly crop his face from the image. He may not have been there at the last but he was there at the beginning, and once a Goon, always a Goon.

TREAT YOURSELF TO *Michael Bentine's Potty Time: The Complete First Series* (Network: 7952194, 2003). You just can't beat Bentine when he's surrounded by his beloved balls of fabric and fun, and the series captures his humane and inclusive ethos. 'People are within, not without,' he explained. 'A Potty is a character who can change his nature with the help of the costume or design department. He is neither black nor white, Jew nor Christian, hippy nor bureaucrat, but can be transformed into anything at the whim of the programme.' This opening collection of bite-sized episodes is your perfect portal, if only for the Sheriff of Nottingham's canter through Sherwood Forest. A lovely call-back to Bentine's ancient double-act days, his line 'I'm only here for the deer!' will reduce you to a puddle of mirth.

# Harold Berens

## 1903–95

Our man of many dialects and the best-dressed artist in the profession.

*Bert Weedon OBE*

Over his lengthy and prolific life and career – which the man himself attributed to a daily breakfast of muesli and mashed bananas – Harold Berens ('no relation to ball bearings') became the archetypal Jewish raconteur, with a winning sense of chutzpah that made him a radio natural. A love for show business and the good it can do saw Berens embrace a distinguished association with the Grand Order of Water Rats, while his sheer gusto secured him a productive tenure with both the P&O and Cunard cruise lines, providing joyous, good old-fashioned cabaret for a gleefully captive, floating audience.

Despite relishing the air of a long-established East End tailor, Berens was actually the son of an art dealer and a native of Glasgow. While still a young man he moved with the family down to Brighton. The taste of cockles and sea air were nothing to Berens compared with the multiple delights of the Brighton

Hippodrome on a Monday night, and the young Berens practically became a season-ticket-holder. He learned his craft from the best in the business and, over the many years to come, would happily regale students of music hall with tall tales of the turns he had known and loved.

Indeed, his parents were so immersed in a love of the arts and theatricals that out of town variety comedians would often visit the family home, with Robb Wilton [qv], in particular, being greatly impressed by Harold's relentless comic patter. Music hall shtick was in his very bones. However, the boy was no starstruck fool and appreciated the need for a proper trade to fall back on. With his father's know-how, Harold's tailoring instinct was nurtured. It made him a good living, and ultimately, with a lot of skill and a touch of flimflam, gave him a reputation in the business. As the self-proclaimed 'shirtmaker to the stars' he counted among his clientele the fabulously influential Canadian talent scout Carroll Levis. Purely by chance, Berens became one of his famous 'discoveries': 'He lifted up a manhole cover and there I was!' Berens would joke. A formal introduction to BBC producer Ernest Longstaffe led to invaluable advice on his twelve-minute comedy act as well as irregular exposure on the radio.

By 1939 Berens had risen to such heights that when he returned to his beloved Hippodrome he was the one onstage, as a support act to jazz pianist extraordinaire Fats Waller. Berens also enjoyed cabaret assignments at the Café Anglais sharing the bill with Terry-Thomas, the highest-paid comedian in the country at the time. Berens was singled out as the year's most exciting newcomer, with one reviewer proclaiming: 'He slips in and out of character with the ease of a bus driver changing gear.'

He was a godsend to radio, compèring outside broadcasts for Maurice Winnick and his Band from the Dorchester Hotel, hosting the Beeb's faux West End nightspot the *Golden Slipper Club* and finally signing for his own, lucrative show on Radio Luxembourg. So effortless were his vocal shifts that even the peerless Peter Sellers came to him for tips on how to perfect his Pakistani accent. Indeed, Sellers was a lifelong admirer of Berens and happily advocated him as 'the man with a thousand voices'. Decades later, Sellers gratefully invited him to play the hotel clerk in *The Pink Panther Strikes Again*, in 1976, although

Berens's scenes were edited out of the finished film, only finally appearing in *Trail of the Pink Panther*, released in December 1982, over two years since the death of Sellers.

As Luigi, with Eric Phillips and Jewell & Warriss, recording comedy-thriller *Jimmy and Ben*, in 1950.

Berens's *Panther* part was just one of many chopped and changed roles in a career that would encompass some 200 cameos, from the wartime thriller *Candlelight in Algeria* (1944) to *The Pure Hell of St Trinian's* (1960) via Carol Reed's *A Kid for Two Farthings* (1955). Frankly, if I had been Harold Berens and I hadn't got a job on that film of East End stall-holders and petty crooks I'd have had palpitations!

Michael Bentine, too, would embrace the multitalented Berens as part of his select band of brothers in his sixties television series *It's A Square World*, while other small-screen appearances included such cult classics as *Randall and Hopkirk (Deceased)* – (in the episode 'That's How Murder Snowballs', ITC, 19 October 1969) and as Number 113, the Tally Ho journalist in *The Prisoner* ('Free for All', ITC, 22 October 1967), who the show's creative force, Patrick McGoohan, said he signed up to 'bring some laughs on the set'.

Still, this late-1960s resurgence of cool came only after a hard-fought return to the spotlight. As for many of his generation, Harold's fledgling career had been completely derailed by war service, and Berens had every right to be more bitter than most, with the Second World War being declared just two days after signing his contract with Radio Luxembourg. Still, the conflict proved a fruitful training ground for his ever-improving delivery, with him clocking up hundreds of military concerts and benefits during its course.

Even before the war came to an end, he was back keeping the home fires burning from November 1944 in the radio series *Hoop-La!*, starring his old champion Robb Wilton. Providing the listener with 'all the fun of the fair on the air', Berens played the frightfully smooth Guy who, like everyone tuning

Well-groomed and in great demand as a character actor throughout the 1950s and 60s.

in, was obsessed with the shortage of butter during these darks days of rationing. The nation could engage with Berens, and loved his female characterisations, too, notably cheery cook Mrs Twiddleswitch: 'spelled T with a W, I double diddle, S double which!', while from October 1954 he delighted audiences as Ted Ray's cleaner Mrs Mosseltoff in *Ted Ray Time*.

With his radio success complemented by a relentless commitment to touring variety theatres, Berens quickly became a bigger star than he had been before the war. Week-in, week-out, he earned the hugest laughs on the panel game *Ignorance is Bliss*. The show ran from 1946 to 1950 and made Berens something of a national sensation – no mean feat in a cast of wits, storytellers and mannered maniacs including Gladys Hay, Sid Millward and His Nitwits, and Dr Crock and His Crackpots. Be honest! Host Stewart MacPherson (who, after a lengthy radio career, died just weeks before Berens) presided over the insane goings-on as panellists gamely tried to discuss a staggeringly vast range of topics. Berens could cut through all the nonsense with a beautifully timed 'What a geezer!' and bring the house down – no contest.

*Beat the Band* followed quickly after, with Berens now elevated to star status, interviewing various members of the general public, Gawd bless 'em, and challenging them to identify obscure musical numbers performed by the house band. The joke was that these tunes got so obscure that few if anybody could identify them, and Berens absolutely loved the ridiculous inconsequence of it all.

There followed years of old-time music hall, including a notable period with fellow old-timer Max Wall. Berens delighted in being the oldest working comedian in the country; he chalked up two final film appearances just shy of his ninetieth birthday – a poignant bit part as an aged bandleader in *Hear My Song* (1991), the story of singer Josef Locke, and a laugh-out-loud cameo, as leather-clad Cecil the Torturer, cheerfully stretching Jack Douglas on the rack, in *Carry On Columbus* (1992). As Berens wrote, in answer to a fan letter at the time: 'I'm still working after all the years in the profession. I just couldn't give it up!!' And he didn't. Berens happily waited for the telephone to ring right up until his death, on 10 May 1995. He was ninety-two. Wot a geezer indeed!

Always one of the best-dressed chaps in the business, Harold was still dapper in his dotage and eager to work.

TREAT YOURSELF TO *Harold Berens: Wot a Geezer* (Windyridge: VAR87, 2017) on which Windyridge CDs has painstakingly collated live recordings of a selection of Berens's radio performances on *Variety Bandbox*, *Midday Music Hall* and *All Change*, transcribed from privately owned acetate discs. As a bonus there's his memorable parody of that suave 'tec Dick Barton: Dick Berens (Special Agent).

# Willie Best

## 1916–62

The best actor I know.

*Bob Hope KBE*

During the cool, cool days of the early 1960s, a black all-round entertainer named Sammy Davis Jr joined the in-crowd. As part of the Rat Pack he swung and sung his way through an effortless utopia of booze, birds and barbiturates. In a climate of social unrest, he was game for a laugh. Frank Sinatra and Dean Martin sent him up; Davis sent himself up. During his solo Las Vegas sets he would impersonate old movie stars and cast himself as the terrified coloured manservant. He would conjure up the image of a monochrome haunted house, with dusty cobwebs and secret panels and, for all his street cred and hipness, he'd confess that if indeed he ever did find himself in such a situation, he would blanche and mutter: 'Feet, do your thang!' If an owl hooted or a door creaked he admitted he would revert to type and say: 'Who dat?' Although he never name-checked him, what Sammy was doing was saluting the comic persona of Willie Best.

The best-loved and career-defining film appearance of Willie Best is undoubtedly in the 1940 spoof spook film *The Ghost Breakers*, Paramount Pictures' hasty re-teaming of Bob Hope and Paulette Goddard following their scare-fest duty in *The Cat and the Canary* the year before. Like the earlier film, *The Ghost Breakers* tends to take its shivers quite seriously. Despite the wisecracking, teeth-flashing New York modernity of the sleek-haired Bob Hope (who is pretty much in tip-top form throughout), the actual backwater-haunted-mansion and the hunt for buried treasure offer up thrills that are genuinely frightening, making the jokes and japes all the more powerful as refreshing relief from the horror. Although Best was playing the manservant, as was typical for black actors in Hollywood at the time, he was at least credited with a name, Alex, for his character. Many black performers were shamefully identified as simply 'shoe shine boy' or 'elevator attendant' – Willie had suffered such indignity in the past and would continue to do so (if producers bothered to credit him at all). But in *The Ghost Breakers* he was Bob Hope's comedic equal, very much the Laurel to his Hardy, the Abbott to his Costello. Unsurprisingly, Best was recruited to play Samuel, Hope's slack-jawed, slow-witted manservant in the third, and least known, film in the trio with Goddard, *Nothing But the Truth* (1941). Ghosts were out and a knowing satire on big business was in, with Best giving admirable support once again; all bewildered looks and weary gripes at his hapless boss.

He was less lucky in other films. He had a bit part as a waiter on a train in the Laurel and Hardy frightmare *A-Haunting We Will Go* (1942), played another waiter in the Red Skelton comedy *Maisie Gets Her Man* (1942), and had supported the three Marx Brothers in *At the Circus* (1939) before the ultimate indignity, an uncredited performance as a lavatory attendant in the George Murphy musical *The Powers Girl* (1943).

Like his fellow black pioneer Stepin Fetchit, Willie Best first found fame by embracing a stage name that highlighted the racist attitude of the country in which he was born. While his friend played dogsbodies who would, indeed, just step and fetch something when his white masters demanded it, Willie Best found fame as Sleep 'n' Eat. The stereotype of the lazy, work-shy negro, all he seemed to do on camera was sleep and eat. His first film, the Harold Lloyd comedy

As Sleepy in the Wheeler & Woolsey comedy mystery *The Nitwits*, 1935.

*Feet First*, released in November 1930, actually credited him as Sleep 'n' Eat, and while this lasted only for four more films – including the superior 1932 haunted-house romp *The Monster Walks* – the name and the stigma stuck throughout his life.

He was born on 27 May 1913, in Sunflower, Mississippi, and eventually set foot in Hollywood through a stereotypical, subservient bit part: as a chauffeur. (He would play many on-screen throughout his twenty-year career.) But it was with a touring minstrel show that he first found show business popularity, excelling at slow-talking comedy banter and energetic physical pratfalls. Although few film-makers took full advantage of his clowning skills, comedy producer supreme Hal Roach considered him one of the greatest talents he had ever worked with. Indeed, during the 1950s when the black community turned against him and other black actors who had embraced the stereotype and taken the white man's coin, Roach gave him near-constant employment on his television shows *The Stu Erwin Show* (ABC, 1950–55) and *My Little Margie* (CBS, 1952–53/NBC, 1953–55). The roles were still slow-thinking elevator boys and handymen, but he was usually giving a character name and that character name was invariably and charmingly Willie. And it was work, at a time that Willie really needed work.

For the the race-campaigners, Best had played to the terrified negro stereotype enough. Films like *The Smiling Ghost* (1941), *The Body Disappears* (1941), and *The Hidden Hand* (1942) hadn't stretched him as an actor but had paid his bills. Nonetheless, he was only ever employed to drive the white hero around and to jump at his own shadow; Hollywood press-blurb even blurred the edges of reality between actor and slave, comically claiming that

Best would work just for three square meals a day and a corner to sleep in.

Still, this was the system Willie found himself in, so he took the roles and played them with all the gusto he could muster. While a champion like *The Ghost Breakers* director George Marshall would subvert this manservant image and

As Drowsy, with Arthur Treacher as the erudite manservant, in *Thank You, Jeeves!*, 1936.

allow him more scope, albeit whilst still casting him as a manservant, other Poverty Row productions like the *Charlie Chan* and *Scattergood Baines* film series gave him regular, albeit more inconsequential, work. In his *Charlie Chan* films – *The Red Dragon* (1945) and *Dangerous Money* (1946) – Best lifted the character of Chattanooga Brown into orbit. He was Drowsy – both by name and by deed – in *Thank You, Jeeves!* (1936). His pivotal turn as Simon Templer's butler, Algernon, opposite George Sanders in *The Saint Strikes Back* (1939), went uncredited – frankly unbelievable, but as a black actor in Hollywood, Willie could hope for no better.

However, when he died of cancer on 27 February 1962, at the age of just 45, his funeral was paid for by the Motion Picture Relief Fund. He hadn't worked in nearly ten years. They were foot soldiers caught in the crossfire, these fine black actors who had to take what they were offered. The greats like Noble Johnson and Mantan Moreland – and, yes, Willie Best – kept their heads above the waves in a city of dreams that would never dream of acknowledging equality.

Willie Best may have lived just long enough to hear Sammy Davis Jr affectionately send up the very essence of the actor's career. He would have been in on the joke from the hollow position of suppression. But that natural, likeable comedy manservant in *The Ghost Breakers* isn't funny because he is black and scared. He's just funny. We warm to him, we laugh and shiver with him. It was not a racist role; it was a part of American society. A society

'I'm befuddled!': A trade press advertisement for *The Ghost Breakers*, the summer 1940 spooked comedy classic from Paramount Pictures.

whose film and music industries would be in the hands of African Americans a generation after Willie Best's death. I can see his wide eyes getting even wider at that pleasing revelation.

TREAT YOURSELF TO *The Ghost Breakers* (Kino Lorber: B08BWFVZXS, 2020), and rediscover Willie Best's comic genius in one of the most pleasing performances in all film comedy.

# Alec Bregonzi and Michael Ward

## 1930–2006 and 1909–97

'What with tweed?': a Talbot Rothwell one-liner from *Carry On Cabby* delivered in Michael Ward's effeminate style first brought him to my attention, although I had undoubtedly seen him in many a post-war British film prior to that. He was one of that troupe of great character actors which the British film industry seemed awash with and whose performances I've more often than not found more interesting than the stars'. Whilst the Sam Kydds and Sydney Taflers are rightly lauded, many of their compatriots are now sadly forgotten and Ward is certainly one of these. His distinctive air of upper-class nervousness remained a constant whether he was playing a petulant photographer with Norman Wisdom in *Man of the Moment* or Archimedes in *Carry On Cleo*. Next time you're watching a Boulting Brothers film, keep an eye out for him – a master of the cameo.

I've often thought that Alec Bregonzi was the television character actor equivalent of Michael Ward. They shared the same aquiline features and aristocratic air, although Bregonzi was perhaps more kitchen-sink, in keeping with the times.

He was one of the Hancock-crew oarsmen, along with Mario Fabrizi, Johnny Vyvyan and Arthur Mullard, and worked with all the greats, including Dick Emery, Benny Hill and, latterly, Kenny Everett. Although he had the occasional lead he was more than happy with the bit parts and in his later years was happy to recount tales of the numerous stars he had worked with. I met him only once (at the British Film Institute's fortieth-anniversary-celebration of the *Carry On* films at the Museum of the Moving Image in 1998), and he delighted in telling me about his appearance in *Carry On At Your Convenience*, which ended up on the cutting room floor.

I'm glad that both actors are being recognised in this book, and I'm sure they would be thrilled to take their rightful place in this salute to forgotten comedy stars.

*Alan Coles*

Two delightfully fey men of character who were undoubtedly cut from the same cloth (a particularly fine piece of tweed), Alec Bregonzi and Michael Ward flounced through dozens of film and television supporting turns, as often as not leaving a cloud of talcum powder in their wake.

Despite their similarities in comedic style, they would often occupy the same professional space, playing interchangeable roles. Both were touched by the innuendo-encrusted screen successes of Peter Rogers and Gerald Thomas. Alec Bregonzi was in with the *Carry On* films from the get-go, kitting out the hapless squaddies in *Carry On Sergeant* (1958). Michael Ward wafted through a gallery of effete cameos, starting with an unforgettable photographic session with Kenneth Williams in *Carry On Regardless* (1961). Both Bregonzi and Ward would spar with Tony Hancock during his BBC glory days, with Ward particularly effective in the classic television *Hancock's Half Hour* episode 'The Economy Drive', broadcast 25 September 1959, where the lad himself's disgusting concoction of bread roll and free sauces puts our man Ward right off his tuck. It's a winning performance of haughty superiority and childlike weakness.

One of Hancock's favoured repertory-company actors, Alec Bregonzi was rarely out of East Cheam in the late 1950s and early 1960s, and his newly-married, frantic young juror in 'Twelve Angry Men', broadcast 16 October 1959, lingers long in the memory. He was a near-permanent feature of life on London's South Bank in the 1990s. I would often bump into him on the way to our respective trains at Waterloo Station or, even more frequently, in the bar at the National Film Theatre before seeing the same –

Always dignity! Alec happily embracing the madness of *The Kenny Everett Television Show*, in February 1985.

or a different – film; regardless, we would hook up afterwards to discuss the either joyous experience or whether we had selected the wrong film to savour.

Very much the comedian's friend, in 1961 Bregonzi graduated from Tony Hancock to Sid James, occupying very much the same comic universe when he cropped up regularly in *Citizen James*. There was also memorable 1961 BBC Television work opposite Michael Bentine in *It's A Square World*, as well as later in *Benny Hill* (as a fop – of course! – in 'Portrait of a Bridegroom', BBC Television, 23 December 1962) and Eric Sykes (*Sykes*: 'Marriage', BBC1, 30 November 1972) situation-comedy. Later, Bregonzi would play everything from a vicar to Queen Victoria for *The Two Ronnies* (BBC1, 1975–1987), and knowingly lent his comedic respectability to small-screen anarchists Kenny Everett (*The Kenny Everett Television Show*, BBC1, 1982–85), *Cannon and Ball* (as Roger the Barman, London Weekend Television, 1985), and Little and Large (*The Little and Large Show*, BBC1, 1987–91). He was an eternally happy, grateful actor, seemingly always working on one commercial or another, or just about to start on yet another busy schedule of television bits and pieces.

Born rather wonderfully (and rather unsurprisingly) George William Everard Yeo, on 9 April 1909, Michael Ward had been a man of the theatre, first

Mike gets the giggles with director Ralph Thomas, Liz Fraser, Joan Sims and Irene Handl during the filming of *Doctor in Love* (1960).

and foremost, dressing the legendary Donald Wolfit in his barnstorming days and making an early mark in British cinema with refreshingly concise performances in *Sleeping Car to Trieste* (1948) and *Helter Skelter* (1949). Always aware of the precarious nature of the acting profession, Ward was a qualified accountant as well as a realist. Gleefully typecast as the effete fusspot from an early age, he provided withering looks and bird-like elegance in support of Norman Wisdom in a long run of his box-office-hit comedies for the Rank Organisation. The battle of the window-dressers in *Trouble in Store* (1953), encouraged by a calmly malign presiding Ian Wilson, remains a classic of slapstick. The Wisdom association reaches heights of delirium in *Up in the World* (1956) where Ward is not only a sympathetic character for once but also throws himself merrily into a musical interlude that happily ends in chaos: Ward on piano and Wisdom on drums! Wisdom would remain a firm friend, checking in on Ward well into the 90s.

At the end of the 1950s, Ward popped up as an effeminate journalist in the chintzy home of Peter Sellers's Fred Kite in *I'm All Right Jack* (1959). The die had been cast, and even the most straightforward of his roles would forever have the camp twist of the Michael Ward treatment, be it a Labour MP in the *Rising Damp* episode 'Stand Up and Be Counted' (Yorkshire Television, 17 January 1975) or a surreal mental-institution inmate in Hammer Films' *Frankenstein and the Monster from Hell* (1974).

In the big-screen version of *Man About the House* (another 1974 Hammer release), Ward's casting completely threw caution to the wind and cheerfully had him parade around the pub with his toy boy, played by Melvyn Hayes. It is a blistering essay in gay pride. The man himself, even when, at the end of his days, alone and lonely in a London nursing room, would forever deny speculations about his sexuality. He was an actor; he played the parts he was offered.

However, Ward was proud of his association with the great and the good of British film. The last time we spoke on the phone, I had just been to a screening of *Carry On Cleo* (1964) at the Barbican. As usual with the *Carry On* films, Ward's part was small but beautifully formed. In answer to Kenneth Williams's arrogant announcement: 'I represent the Roman Empire!', Ward mutters: 'No thank you. Not today!'

'Did I get a laugh?' he asked me nervously. He did. A belter. And I told him so.

'Really? Did I, really? Oh, how lovely!' The excitement and joy in his voice will stay with me forever.

A codicil: following Alec Bregonzi's funeral, Ray Galton and I repaired to the nearest pub. Naturally. Bregonzi had been very loyal to Tony Hancock, and Galton always appreciated the supporting actors. Our bar room conversation inevitably turned to both Bregonzi and Ward: 'Alec and Mike were terrific,' said Ray, 'reassuringly good actors. Lovely people. We should raise a pink gin to them both.' So we did.

TREAT YOURSELF TO *Revenge of the Pink Panther* (Twentieth Century Fox: B001JK6P8G, 2009), that cheerful, scattergun showcase for Peter Sellers at his most self-indulgent. The film is a glorious salute to excess, with fart gags, cross-dressing, high-speed car chases – and the only occasion our two heroes, Bregonzi and Ward, appear in the same film. Alas, these gracious wisps of serenity are kept apart so as not to cancel each other out, and, even more outrageously, Alec Bregonzi's performance – largely restricted to the pre-credit sequence – is dubbed. Still, his flamboyantly, steely attitude radiates off of the screen. Michael Ward, meanwhile, in this – his last – film appearance, is an energetic, distressed and wildly camp estate agent besieged by the ongoing battle between Clouseau and Cato. It's ridiculous, of course, but enriched by a supporting cast hand-picked from the top drawer. Bregonzi and Ward are the plums!

# Billy Burden

## 1914–94

The best country bumpkin in the business!

*David Croft OBE*

David Croft was right. And he should know. At the very end of Billy Burden's fifty-year career, Croft gifted him two plum parts that encapsulated all the rustic charm of this comic original.

Beloved as the bumbling, cider-quaffing, ooh-aching yokel from the West Country, Burden strolled through stage and screen assignments without ever changing his act. Why should he? It served him beautifully. Moreover it proved inspiration for Bernard Miles' farmer characterisation, Jon Pertwee's Worzel Gummidge, and almost the entire act of The Wurzels.

William George Burden was born on 15 June 1914, in Wimborne Minster, Dorset. A natural affection for saucy innuendo bled into his personality and took him into show business. He enjoyed experience in local amateur dramatics before turning professional for local summer seasons and pantomime, in which he became a regular favourite for producer Frank Maddox, at the Theatre Royal, Bath. Burden's stage attire was of muddy boots and battered hat. He would appear, invariably, with a jug of scrumpy in one hand and a chicken in the other. Then he would giggle and gurgle his way through outrageously funny monologues, full of fruity observations about his gardening chords. The likes of 'I'm holding a big pear in m'hands!' and 'I've been laying 'em all out on the bed!' would be coupled with a leery wink. Ribald laughter from his audience would be guaranteed.

Simply give Billy a hammer and it would be instant, self-inflicted, slapstick gold.

By the sixties he was headlining his own variety shows on the Moss Empire theatre circuit and had a ten-year run guest-starring with *The Rick Jango Road Show*. Burden also joined the legendary Clarkson Rose in her long-running revue *Twinkle*, at the Pavilion Eastbourne Theatre. The showstopper was the Rose and Burden duet on 'There's a Hole in My Bucket'.

Burden's gravel-voiced, suggestive, rib-poking character would also pop up all over television comedy, memorably as Dickie Henderson's pal William, in the situation comedy *A Present for Dickie* (Thames Television, 1969–70).

Burden swiftly proved himself a popular support to such top comedians as Harry Secombe (in *The Harry Secombe Show*, BBC1, 1969), Brian Murphy (in the 1978 *George & Mildred* episode 'Nappy Days', Thames), and Tommy Cannon and Bobby Ball, in their only film, *The Boys in Blue* (1982). Typically, Burden was cast as a crafty herdsman!

By which point, David Croft had entered his story. *Oh Happy Band!* (BBC1, 1980) was a rare misfire from Croft and co-writer Jimmy Perry. Harry Worth starred as the conductor of a brass band, but Burden was a revelation as Mr Sowerby. It was his stage persona, lock, stock and barrel, and it was perfection. Croft cast him as the minor character of camper Mr Thompson in 'It's Murder',

Top-billed at the sadly long-gone Cosy Nook, Newquay for the summer season, 1984.

a January 1986 episode of hit BBC1 situation comedy *Hi-de-Hi!*

When the eighth series kicked off with 'Pigs Might Fly', in November 1986, Burden was brought back. At the time cast changes were rife, and Ben Aris had been signed up as ballroom dancer Julian Dalrymple-Sykes. The character's life was centred around his pig farm and it required just a few utterances from Burden to give the plot line total credibility. Burden was back for 'September Song', in December 1986, clearly revelling in the muck as he carried prim and proper Yvonne Stuart-Hargreaves (as played by Diane Holland). Burden was also there for *Hi-de-Hi!*'s emotional wrap-up, 'The Wind of Change', in January 1988. Billy was no stranger to porcine practices, for he had made a thoroughly selfish, slow, silly but ultimately resourceful Pig in the 1970 Philips record release of *The Owl and the Pussycat Went to See...*

And it was all grunts and smells when David Croft resurrected his *Are You Being Served?* team for *Grace & Favour* (BBC1, 1992–93), Burden got the call again. Quite naturally, for the simple premise dropped the Grace Brothers department store favourites into a country manor house setting. This time Burden was playing a saucy farmer called Maurice Moulterd and, with the expected hilarious play on his name (he, of course, pronounced it mole turd), it was comic business as usual. Breathing in the scent of manure with the gusto of a bracing stroll on Boscombe Pier, it was the part Burden was born to play.

A seasoned scene-stealer, this twilight television stardom added further marquee value to his pantomime appearances – usually with a glamorous chorus girl on his arm – and even gave him a following in America, where the *Are You Being Served?* cast were cult figures: 'I keep getting fan mail from American women,' he said. 'I didn't think they would understand the dialect over there but they think I'm the funniest character they have ever seen.'

Burden also used his enhanced fame to cap some thirty years' charity work for the Variety Club of Great Britain, and active membership of The Grand Order of Water Rats. Everybody loved Billy, especially kids. Simon Wright remembers: 'I saw him in panto in *Little Bo-Peep and Her Sheep*, in 1972 at the Theatre Royal in Bath. I got taken onto the stage and Mr Burden, as the dame, put a basket on my head. I was only six but thrilled with having held the great man's hand (and even more thrilled with the goodie bag he gave me). I've dined out on the story ever since!' This was Burden's rustic charm. Reeking with kindness.

With fellow Forgotten Hero Norman Vaughan, for the pantomime season at the Playhouse, Bournemouth, from 20 December 1975 to 24 January 1976.

Still living in Wimborne Minster, he died on 3 June 1994, just two weeks shy of his eightieth birthday celebrations, but that whiff of comic genius kind of lingers. As he would sign off on comedy monologue broadcasts: 'Oh, well, it's bin lovely havin' a chat. I'd better be goin' now. 'Tis a long way back to Dorset. Cheerio!'

TREAT YOURSELF TO *Grace & Favour: The Complete Series* (Eureka Entertainment: B01BFFTX18, 2016). David Croft and Jeremy Lloyd's hilarious revival, more blatantly called *Are You Being Served? Again!* in international screenings, gives Billy Burden the television part of a lifetime. Each of the twelve episodes reeks with his unique charm.

# Douglas Byng

## 1893–1987

The meeting place for the leaders of the profession in those days was The Ivy, a restaurant built on a triangular site appropriately opposite two theatres, the St Martin's and the Ambassadors, off Charing Cross Road. Here sat Douglas Byng entertaining lavishly and always complaining about the bill: his famous twitch jerked his head from left to right, taking his jaw nearly round to his shoulder (caused, it was said, by sitting too often with his back to The Ivy's door). 'This is quite exorbitant – there must be a mistake. Bring me the head waiter.' The head waiter checked the bill and could find no fault. 'But this is disgraceful – nobody can be expected to pay a bill of this size. It's outrageous! Send for Mario!' Mario appeared. 'What are you doing to me? For a very simple lunch I am presented with this enormous bill. I may never come here again!' Mario tried to mollify him and explained that, after all, he had entertained five guests; they had consumed six bottles of wine, plus brandy and liqueurs, and the asparagus was out of season. Byng's twitch became more violent and he trumpeted: 'In which case, I demand to see Ivy herself!'

*Sir Donald Sinden CBE*

In the early 1980s, my family holiday destination of choice was Brighton. We flirted with other British seaside favourites, but after a first single, rain-sodden day trip, we were hooked. Admittedly, my parents had already booked a week's holiday and, despite the wails of protest from his children that this place was horrible and it rained all the time, my dad was belligerent: he had booked a week's bleeding holiday for that summer, and we were going to take a week's bleeding holiday in the summer. Whether we liked it or not. And oh, how we liked it. We returned for every halcyon summer of my youth: a joyous time of miniature golf and miniature trains, candy floss and rock climbing, and endless, endless strolls round the antique-festooned Lanes.

Brighton also fuelled my blossoming obsession with comedy. One of the first things we did each visit was take a jaunt to Max Miller's house, reverently pausing outside for a moment, my dad usually attired in something bright and flashy – naturally: Brighton dripped with comedy credentials. We even spotted Arthur Lowe mucking about on his boat in the Brighton marina. We may also have strolled past a certain silver-haired gentleman, dapperly attired, with a pink-champagne smile and an air of decadence, on the promenade. Back then, I wouldn't have given him a second glance; I certainly wouldn't have recognised him. But it was perfectly fitting that Brighton was the proud manor of one Douglas Byng.

In an era where homosexuality was not only against the law but pretty much punishable with a good horsewhipping, Douglas Byng blazed the trail for Danny La Rue, Paul O'Grady, Julian Clary and so many others. But Douglas Byng was not camp. He was far too outrageous for such a damp squib of a word. He was gay – in the strictest, most profound sense. Life was a joyous thing, and Duggie Byng was going to live it to the full.

He was born Douglas Coy Byng on 17 March 1893, in Basford, Nottingham, to staid bank manager father Joseph T. Byng and prim schoolmistress mother Mary Coy, who both actively discouraged his ambitions to follow his grandfather onto the boards. Byng recalled his 'first cabaret appearance, apparently in the drawing room at about two years of age, standing on a hassock (stage sense now developing) reciting the story of Mr Punch or Mrs Bunch (memory now failing), but I can vividly recall giving a rendering (still on a hassock) of "Twinkle, Twinkle, Little Star" as it would be recited by a lady.'

Indeed, having been bewitched by myriad variety turns, the young Byng was desperate to embrace every stage himself, and always with an attitude of no-holds-barred fun. Once, his mortally embarrassed mother whisked him away from a social gathering because little Douglas couldn't stop laughing at a large lady giving a spirited rendition of 'Every Morn I Bring Thee Violets'. The sight of this grand woman with prominent teeth would inspire 'Spring', the first of a great many comic songs Byng would write: 'Come out, come out, don't flop about, for spring is in the air!'

His mother refused to condone a life of professional buffoonery. Instead, the young Byng was shipped off to Germany, where his elder brother owned a lace factory. Here he studied German (the best place for it) and music (ditto) while latching onto the world of fashion as an outlet for his flamboyant energies. He returned home, to London, to work for costume designer Charles Alias.

But his ability to amuse burnt bright, and in 1914 he responded to an advertisement for a light comedian to join a seaside concert party decamped at the Pelham Palacette theatre, Hastings. The gang had an exhausting schedule, often performing seven shows a day, delivering fun and frolics in every available space, from town halls to tiny local cinemas. Byng later toured as Professor Charcot in the musical comedy *The Girl in the Taxi*, which transferred to the Gaiety Theatre, London: Byng's spiritual home.

Byng was one of the greatest exponents and champions of pantomime, making his debut as the Grand Vizier in *Aladdin* in 1920 at the London Palladium. He taught the mirror routine – in which one comic mirrors another to mask an absent mirror – to the soon-to-be legendary Jack Tripp who in turn taught it to the patron saint of music hall, Roy Hudd. Wheels within wheels, my friends. Wheels within wheels.

Byng performed the first of his many pantomime dames, Eliza in *Dick Whittington and His Cat*, at the New Theatre in Oxford for the 1924–25 season. The following year he was back at the Palladium, appearing in the Noël Coward revue *On with the Dance*, for producer C. B. Cochran. He was pressed into service by Cochran for the next five years, during which time Byng opened his own nightclub in Central London – again, shades of Danny La Rue (a generation later).

Noël Coward later said of Byng that he was: 'the most refined vulgarity in London', and his burlesque routines were undoubtedly that. With self-penned songs such as 'Mexican Minnie', 'Sex-appeal Sarah', 'The Lass Who Leaned Against the Tower of Pisa', 'Doris, the Goddess of Wind', and even 'I'm Milly, A Messy Old Mermaid', his act was outrageousness personified. He would heighten the flamboyance of his performance by taking to the stage by walking down a gangplank, preceded by a clutch of sailors

One of the Great Old Queens of England.

and a diminutive hotel bellhop. Byng would be clad in a top hat and tails, before donning a flamboyant wig, a feather boa and the frontage piece of a lavish ballgown to launch into a number such as 'Ceres, the Goddess of Plenty': '...and plenty I've had in my time!'

By 1931 Duggie had taken the New York club scene by storm, headlining at the Lido Chonette and the Blue Angel. Cole Porter became a huge admirer and wrote 'Miss Otis Regrets' specifically for Byng, in the character of a refined British butler making apologises for his mistress. Indeed, the very first recording of the classic song was by Byng for Decca Records, in 1934.

Paris also fell for his bejewelled charms, but it was London that Byng loved most of all. He was the first cabaret star to have his name in neon lights in the West End, and the first female impersonator to broadcast on television. By 17 March 1938 he had been given a regular BBC Television slot, with the gloriously entitled *Byng-Ho!*. His appearances were a revelation, typically twenty or thirty minute bursts of live variety performed at 3 p.m. and then again at 9 p.m.

Other BBC Television outings for his saucy songs included *Variety* (7 July 1947), *Stars in Your Eyes* (3 October 1948) and *Rooftop Rendezvous*

'An intimate revue' which ran at the
St. Martin's Theatre, London, 1952.
On the pull is Hattie Jacques!

(2 July 1949). He was still outrageously at it nearly two decades later when he happily dusted off a frock or two for Alan Melville's *Before the Fringe* (BBC2, 1967), which he undoubtedly was! Straighter West End credits included his role as Prince Zorpan in *Maritza*, although even this production couldn't resist putting him in drag for one sequence, as a viola-player who claimed to be 'the pest of Budapest that turned the Danube so blue!' He played Monsieur Martin opposite Alec Guinness in *Hotel Paradiso* at the Winter Garden Theatre, Drury Lane, from 2 May 1956, and later at Henry Miller's Theatre in New York, running from April to July 1957. Later still, Byng reprised his role in the 1966 film version, making his big-screen debut, at the age of 72, opposite Gina Lolobrigida. It's so Duggie Byng!

However, it was his cabaret act that made his fame and fortune, though he was happy to go unpaid for concerts put on by the Entertainments National Service Association for the troops in India and Burma during the Second World War, his kindness and skill bringing much-needed, down-to-earth fun to those beleaguered heroes. It was not for nothing that his stage billing was 'Bawdy ... but British'. He was a plump peahen with something extra as he cheekily explained: 'My songs are said to be a trifle risqué and made the nicest dowagers so frisky. Sedate black bosoms heaved with laughter; their daughter pointed jokes out to them after!' As critic James Agate once noted, Byng's act wasn't so much near the knuckle, 'it was the knuckle itself'.

Byng never actually retired, but fan Patrick Newley picked him up in 1967 for something of a comeback tour nonetheless. In 1970 Byng published his memoirs, *As You Were*, and in 1977 made a showstopping appearance, alongside Broadway star Carol Channing, on the *Parkinson* chat show. Having renewed public interest in Byng's lengthy career, Newley teamed him with fellow veteran performer Billy Milton for a regional tour entitled *Those Thirties Memories*.

Douglas Byng worked almost to the end, taking his final bow, in 1987, in a one-man show at the National Theatre. Sadly, during his last few months he had to leave his beloved Brighton and take up residency in Denville Hall, the care home for the entertainment industry. As his health increasingly failed, he would lament, 'You know all this is down to the devil, dearie?'

In his last days, he provided his own heartbreaking epitaph: 'So here you are, old Douglas, a derelict at last. Before your eyes what visions rise of your vermilion past. Mad revelry beneath the stars, hot clasping by the lake. You need not sigh, you can't deny, you've had your bit of cake.'

He died on 24 August 1987 at the age of 94. His ashes were scattered outside his former home in Arundel Terrace, Brighton. I never did meet him, which is a pity, but I did write him a fan letter (and, delightfully, got a reply). I don't know where I stumbled across him to prompt my letter of admiration – possibly on a *Wogan* television interview or maybe one of his old 78rpm recordings collected on a long-player of my dad's called *Listen to the Banned* – for he was banned by the BBC (of course he was). Duggie would fill with heavenly satisfaction to know that he would be celebrated on BBC Radio 4 when, in November 2010, his spiritual descendant Julian Clary played his ghost, giving one final return performance, in *The Byng Ballads*.

And you can still take a ride on Douglas Byng in Brighton. The number 903 bus is named after him. One can imagine his beaming smile and twinkling eyes as he chortled, 'Room for one more inside, dearie...' One of the greatest queens of England.

TREAT YOURSELF TO *Douglas Byng Looks Back* (Decca Ace of Clubs: ACL 1155, 1963), Byng's essential rerecording of some of his greatest cabaret numbers. From 'Nanna of the Manor' to 'Flora MacDonald', all his bewigged and bejewelled ladies are here, resurrected in a sort of autobiographical gallop. Byng is in mischievous, reflective mood, and he never sounded better or more vital than on this precious platter. Moreover, the recording was overseen by fledging *Carry On* maestro Eric Rogers – a match made in blue heaven if ever there was one.

# Marti Caine

## 1945–95

I was a kid in the seventies, growing up with great light-entertainment shows every Saturday night. *New Faces*, the talent show that paved the way for *The X Factor*, was the first time professionals as well as the public could pass sentence on emerging talent. I remember seeing a glamorous, red-headed chanteuse in a slinky dress launching into a sultry torch song. As she moved to reach the obligatory stool to perch on, she made an ungainly trip in her high heels and beautiful dress. She then broke into patter and we realised that the sexy lady singing a song of seduction was more Gracie Fields than Shirley Bassey. The judges and the audience fell in love with the zany, self-deprecating funny-girl. Her name was Marti Caine.

When I grew up, my childhood fantasies of becoming a Saturday-night telly star came true – at least for the last, golden days of TV variety. I was an impressionist, and was one of London Weekend Television's

*Copy Cats* team as well as Bobby Davro's partner on *Bobby Davro's TV Weekly*. One of our parodies was sending up *New Faces*, now hosted by the by-now big star Marti Caine. I would mimic her low-voiced Yorkshire tones and utter her catchphrase: 'Press your buttons now!'

The circle was complete when I was invited to be a showbiz judge on the real *New Faces* and met the great lady herself. Her thin physique was part of her Olive Oyl appeal but she was sharp as a pin, a total professional who took her role as hostess as seriously as she would her own act – checking that the gags worked, the wording edited to create the full effect. She was utterly lovely and encouraging to me, the new girl in the biz. Only in retrospect do I realise that she was probably ill at that time. Maybe she wasn't aware of it herself. But I certainly admired her: a British female performer who'd held her own, been to Vegas and back, and could offer us home-grown comedy with glamour and style. I'm glad she has not been forgotten here.

*Jessica Martin*

Cast very much from the mould of the sassy, beautiful and self-confident American comedienne Lucille Ball, the sassy, beautiful and self-confident Marti Caine was all ours: a glowing, multitalented invention of Sheffield-born Lynne Denise Shepherd, who, having married at seventeen to the local butcher's lad, fell into a working-class dream of escape via fame and fortune. Yes, Marti Caine was an invention. She could wear luxurious gowns and say outrageous things – gowns and things that the shy and retiring Lynne Shepherd could have only dared to consider before shrinking back to rejoin the other shrinking violets in her area.

From an early age she had been dispirited by her appearance: a nose she thought was just a little too big, a figure that was just a little too lean, and a voice that was just a little too masculine to complement the romantic ballads with which she wanted to wow the world's most discerning audiences. It was only through necessity that she ventured onto the stage in the first place, the result of a notoriously tough childhood culminating in the death of her mother when fledgling Marti was just nineteen years old. Unable to raise the £150 funeral fee,

The 'Midnight at the Oasis' dance number for *The Marti Caine Show*, BBC2, 1 March 1982.

she chose two songs – 'Puppet on a String' and 'Summertime' – and auditioned for Ernest 'Honest' Johns at the Chapeltown Working Men's Club.

She arrived with her married name, Lynne Stringer, and left with a job and a brand-new handle, Sunny Smith. This ephemeral stage name lasted all of one week, as did the equally insipid Zoe Bond. It was her husband, Mal, who suddenly hit inspiration in a gardening catalogue when he spotted a bargain price for a 'tomato cane'. Wait, bear with me – this was rather clever and exactly how it really happened. His wife did resemble a bean pole, after all; it was one of her torturous bugbears. Tomato Cane might not look great in lights, but how about Marta Cane? Sold! (Well, nearly.)

With her next booking, that very evening, fresh-faced Zoe Bond phoned the club's manager to inform him that she wouldn't be performing after all. It would be Marta Cane in her stead. With divine showbiz intervention, the name was misheard and misspelled, and Marti Caine was born – and the name stuck. But you knew that would happen.

The bright lights of London seemed an impossible dream, as the young Marti blossomed as a performer in the clubs and bars of the North of England. Ostensibly a singer, her nervousness and keenness to be liked led her to add amusing banter to the act. As the laughs came, so the songs were sidelined. The songs would always be there, of course, but comedy became the focal point. Ronnie Hazlehurst, the musical director for her last album of songs, released posthumously in 1996, lamented: 'I was working with arguably the best female singer around, but who was, unfortunately, always thought of, first and foremost, as a comedienne.' And she really was that good a singer. Four previous albums of songs featured pitch-perfect tributes to Gladys Knight, while her phrasing of Broadway numbers proved she was indeed a loss to musical theatre. When she did eventually indulge this passion, notably starring as Fanny Brice in a regional tour of *Funny Girl*, audiences and critics were enraptured.

In the early 1970s she was still serving her apprenticeship in-between rounds of beer and the meat raffle – a section of her career preserved forever in her single appearance on Granada Television's *The Wheeltappers and Shunters Social Club*, broadcast 29 March 1975. Caine, with her elegant glamour and earthy humour, was perfect for the show. At this point her comedy was still of the rather ignoble Sheffield housewife, but her image was already more Broadway than Barnsley. Bernard Manning's introduction is perfectly in tune with Caine's presence as a vision of loveliness in a male-dominated world. Still, she was nobody's fool. Lynne Shepherd may have been living on her nerves, but Marti Caine was poised to embrace the big time.

Her newly acquired agent, Johnnie Peller, knew this too. Having seen her hone her craft in the bear pit of the club circuit, he pressed her to have a stab at *New Faces*. Caine was typically reluctant, still believing she needed more time beyond the decade she had already spent in the belch-and-fag-smoke environs of her home county, but she steeled herself and applied.

In 1975, in a season that also included Lenny Henry and Victoria Wood, Marti Caine won. Her success was instant. Crowned victorious in July, by August she was reprising much of her popular heats' material, in tandem with Henry and Wood, for the five-week ATV run of *The Summer Show*. By the following year she was starring in her very own television series, *Nobody Does It Like Marti*, for producer-director Colin Clews. And that same year the title would also be adopted for her debut album, for Pye Records.

By 1977 she was certainly famous enough to justify ATV giving her a television show simply called *Marti*. Long obsessed by her supposedly huge nose, she'd had cosmetic surgery so that it would no longer keep 'knocking people off bicycles'. Throughout the series she appeared in a succession of flowing, revealing and drop-dead gorgeous frocks, the theory being that a beautiful woman of poise slipping on a banana skin would be all the funnier. She was right.

But ATV was about to lose its prized asset. The BBC had spotted a diamond on the floor and picked it up. They built a tantalising variety series around her, with an impressive writers' room of Spike Mullins, Neil Shand, Laurence Marks and Maurice Gran. A BBC2 special of *The Marti Caine Show* on 3 October 1977 was followed by a full series of four, broadcast in January 1979. *The Marti Caine Show* ran for five series until 1984, making Caine both financially secure and professionally respected.

She appeared on the bill of the Royal Variety Performances for both 1978 and 1979, and in March 1978 had been surprised by Eamonn Andrews in Sheffield for her *This Is Your Life*; she was also cast away by Roy Plomley on *Desert Island Discs*. (She requested a solar-heated bath, with bubble bath, as her luxury item.)

By the end of the decade, Caine was more than used to the luxury life. She had invested in five health clubs in the North of England and bought her husband a butchery business. The couple divorced soon after and she subsequently married ex-actor and television producer Kenneth Ives. The year was 1984, the year of her *Funny Girl* tour, which kicked off at her local venue, the Crucible Theatre in Sheffield. The year also saw the start of her sitcom *Hilary* (BBC2, 1984–86). Domestic sketches had featured in her variety shows, so Peter Robinson and Peter Vincent penned this especially for her. Cast as the endearingly scatty Hilary Myers, a single mum and researcher for Eagle Television, she was blessed with distinguished and experienced actors Philip Madoc and Jack Smethurst in supporting roles. A second series followed in 1986, and although her television work made her a comedy hero to millions, she decided to go full circle and once more unleash her all-round entertainer stage personality in a solo show at the Donmar Warehouse. A musical autobiography, it coincided with her happily signing up to the challenge of hosting the revival of the show that had made her name, *New Faces*.

Very much a performer for the people, Caine took to the task immediately, relishing her rather bland catchphrase – 'Press your buttons now!' – and making the show pure variety gold. The resurrection lasted until 1989, by which time Caine had received the news that would dominate the rest of her life.

In October 1988, doctors informed Marti Caine that she was suffering from lymphatic cancer. At the age of just forty-three, she was given a year to live. It was no laughing matter but, typically, Marti laughed about it, asking: 'Does this mean I'm a lymphomaniac?' In the end, she got seven years – seven years dominated by a cancer she refused to tolerate. She accepted every press interview or chat show invitation, including another stint on *Desert Island Discs*, in March 1991, this time with Sue Lawley in the chair. Again, Caine gleefully bent the luxury-item rules by taking a full set of power tools in order to build herself a private hotel.

In November 1994 she was, once again, a victim of *This Is Your Life*, this time under the auspices of Michael Aspel, who caught her out at Woburn Golf Club. Each appearance was a celebration of her talents, inevitably tempered by the latest progress report on her cancer. It became part of her act

Promoting the third series of *The Marti Caine Show*, in March 1981.

– it had to. It was the only way to kick it in the teeth, as it so richly deserved.

Her memoir, *A Coward's Chronicles* (Century, 1990), was refreshingly candid, the title mocking the bravery that was apparent to all and that she could never seriously acknowledge. Still, she was very serious about using her fame as a way of empowering and supporting other people. To that end she founded the Marti Caine Children with Leukaemia Trust.

And she kept on working. A Christmas special for Central Television with guest Joan Rivers on 18 December 1989 was followed, in May 1992, by twelve weeks hosting BBC1's *Joker in the Pack*, in which Caine travelled the country in search of real people with a gag to tell. It was the perfect vehicle for her, delightfully building up the show at the time by saying: 'comic coppers, witty city slickers and humorous hairdressers prove that Britain is a cut above the rest when it comes to cracking jokes. We uncover comedians in every corner – proving that talent will out wherever it lies'. Her final television appearance was in *Call Up the Stars* (BBC1, 8 May 1995), a celebration of past variety performers resurrected by the biggest stars of the day, in which she paid tribute to one of her comedy heroes, Gracie Fields, singing 'The Biggest Aspidistra in the World'.

Delighting as Miss Marie Lloyd for a music hall medley on *The Marti Caine Show*, 16 January 1982.

Other stars on call included Ronnie Corbett as Arthur Askey and Mike Yarwood as Max Miller.

Caine was resolute about living life to the full. She gratefully accepted an honorary doctorate from Sheffield University which saluted her life achievements and contribution to entertainment. Sculptor Mick Farrell designed his work *Sheen* for installation outside Sheffield Hallam University. Caine died two weeks before she was due to unveil the piece and, as a result, it is now affectionately dubbed 'Marti'.

Working to the end, she was due to star as the Red Queen in *Snow White* opposite comedian Ted Rogers at the Basingstoke Anvil for the 1995–96 pantomime season. Sadly, she was forced to pull out of rehearsals, and died on 4 November 1995. She was fifty. *Keeping Up Appearances* star Mary Millar replaced Caine and the show went on. Of course it did – it's what Caine would have wanted.

Marti once said: 'I'd rather have thirty-five years of my own life than seventy years of anybody else's,' and she spent the best part of that life making us smile. You should smile every time you think of her – and you should think of her a lot.

TREAT YOURSELF TO her final album, *Marti* (Carlton Home Entertainment: B000024MV8, 1996), on which she sings standards with the Ronnie Hazlehurst Orchestra. It's a real tonic to hear that unique voice deliver 'Send in the Clowns' and 'I've Loved These Days' with such passion. Besides, a quid of your money went towards the Marti Caine Fund for the Children with Leukaemia Trust. She was still bringing a little sunshine, ya see.

# Esma Cannon

## 1905–72

In my early years of movie-watching she seemed to be everywhere, but it was a long time before I discovered her name. Esma Cannon. Four feet tall and built like a chaffinch, there she'd be in film after film, teapot or duster in hand, lighting up front parlour scenes in the likes of *I'm All Right Jack*, or *Sailor Beware!*. Regularly cast as wing woman to the likes of Peggy Mount and Irene Handl, Esma Cannon was all angles and giggles, dancing tiny attendance on a roll call of British stars who could do nothing but watch as this Tinker Bell in a housecoat stole scene after scene after scene.

When her characters ventured outside, they usually did so in sensible coats and startling hats, and always with an umbrella sturdy enough to administer instant justice should officialdom or ne'er-do-wells be foolish enough to come in range (in *Carry On, Constable*, this weapon of choice is a baguette). And she could be flirty: it might be stretching a point to compare the ping-pong match between Esma and Kenneth Williams in *Carry On Cruising* to the McQueen–Dunaway chess game in *The Thomas Crown Affair*, but there's a spark there – and it's not coming from Kenneth Williams.

It wasn't until I got to drama school that I discovered people who felt the same way I did about Esma Cannon. They also felt that way about Franklin Pangborn. And S. Z. Sakall, and Edward Everett Horton. And (later, and on this side of the Atlantic) Sam Kydd and Michael Ripper. Consummate actors all, actors who added lustre to any film in which they appeared, but actors whose names never appeared above – or even close to – the title.

Esma Cannon was immensely talented; what she was known for was not all she could do. As well as her long list of film and television credits, she had a varied and distinguished stage career. When she wasn't working she would withdraw from show business into her family life, and so complete was that withdrawal that her death in 1972 went entirely unnoticed. But when she was working, she was absolutely unmissable. I loved her as a boy, and as a drama student I came to understand the skill and craft that underpinned those extraordinary creations of hers. No film featuring Esma Cannon can be entirely bad, and no afternoon spent watching an Esma Cannon movie is ever wasted.

*Neil Pearson*

From the late 1930s to her retirement in the early 1960s, whenever British film-makers needed a fussy, bewildered or dithering little old maid, the call would invariably go out to Esma Cannon. She specialised in female companions, telephone-exchange operators, shop assistants and landladies, usually cockney, who could pop in for a scene or two, lift the spirit of the audiences, and hastily vanish again. She was one of the smallest funny-bones practitioners in the business and her CV is packed to the rafters with notable film and television assignments, though it's thanks almost solely – and inevitably – to the *Carry On* films that her work is now enjoyed by a whole new generation, even though most would struggle to put a name to her face. Described as 'that mad little pixie' by Captain Sid James in *Carry On Cruising* (1962), Cannon flapped her way through four of the early

*Carry On* films before turning her back on the business entirely.

Like Sid James, she was in fact born many miles from the sound of Bow Bells. Esma Ellen Charlotte Cannon hailed from Randwick, New South Wales. Records of her Australian theatrical career are scratchy. Indeed, records of almost everything she did in life are pretty unreliable. Still, it seems she trod the boards for the first time at the age of four: she is credited with an appearance in *Madam Butterfly* as early as 1910 and she successfully carved out a career in her home country before

A demure publicity session as the naive and ill-fated Elsie Dawson in *Holiday Camp*, 1947.

eventually upping sticks with her mother in 1931. They headed for England and settled in Paddington, the young Esma securing gainful employment as assistant stage manager at the Arts Theatre, though with very small parts – as she often explained, her tiny stature meant she could play little else.

She chalked up her first important maid role in *All Rights Reserved*, in which she made her West End debut, at the Criterion Theatre in 1935. The following year she was cast as Ethel, another maid, in Frank Vosper's adaptation of the Agatha Christie story *Love from a Stranger*. After the play transferred to the Queen's Theatre in the May of 1936, Cannon stayed for all 149 performances. She repeated the role for the live television presentation on the 23 November 1938.

Two years previously, she had made her feature film debut – typically as the waitress, Emily – in director Michael Powell's *The Man Behind the Mask*, released in August 1936. She may only have been a waitress, but she was a waitress at the top of the film business, and she quickly became a familiar little face on the big screen. She was perfectly in tune with star comedians and, most notably, chalked up appearances in four George Formby films. All but the last of these – *Trouble Brewing*, in 1939 – were uncredited performances, and even in this she was only another maid (listening intently to Formby's singing of 'Fanlight

Fanny'), but the films gave her brief, eye-catching moments of comedy gold. *I See Ice* (1938), for example, sees her as the shy bride in a fit of the giggles as photographer George captures the happiest day of her life. Her performance as Blanche in *Feather Your Nest* (1937) is much the same, while *It's in the Air* (1938) cast her as an employee of the stuffy Sir Philip, played by C. Denier Warren – you've guessed it: Esma is the maid.

Cannon was yet another maid, Ada, opposite Max Miller in *Asking for Trouble* (1942), and a decade or so later popped up alongside the bright young things Frankie Howerd – in *A Touch of the Sun* (1956) and Hammer Films' *Further Up the Creek* (1958) – and Norman Wisdom – during his sentimental rendition of 'Don't Laugh at Me 'Cause I'm a Fool', in *Trouble in Store* (1953). Here, still uncredited, Cannon absent-mindedly drops myriad sugar cubes into her tea. The sentimentalist within me sees this as a nostalgic kiss to her George Formby days, but the actor herself probably felt more that she was treading water.

Still, she was working – and working a lot. Her film career ranged from the prestigious – she was cast once more by Michael Powell, in *The Spy in Black*, in 1939 – to the frivolous – *It's in the Bag*, with Elsie and Doris Waters [qv], in 1944 – but the roles rarely got her beyond a scene or two. She was trapped in the maze in the 1956 film version of *Three Men in a Boat*, and her film career seemed to be as frustratingly restrictive. Even as late as 1959 she was popping out only to film roles as ill-fated crones in *Jack the Ripper* and *The Flesh and the Fiends* or as increasingly older maids, notably Spencer in the employ of Margaret Rutherford in *I'm All Right Jack*. She even swept the floors – uncredited – in *Expresso Bongo*.

In terms of clout, her finest performance must be as Agnes in Powell and Pressburger's *A Canterbury Tale* (1944). Cannon's cheery familiarity adds an air of grounded focus to the fantastic, disturbing folklore in arguably the most beautiful and lyrical film ever made in Britain.

It was maids in lowbrow comedies that gave her the greatest pleasure at the time, though. Her encounters – again uncredited – with a ghostly Richard Bird in *Don't Take it to Heart* (1944) include some of her finest moments on-screen. Indeed, with a snappier title it could have been a minor classic. As it is, few have heard of it; even fewer have actually seen it.

Cannon's most celebrated pre-*Carry On* film role was perhaps in the 1956 film version of *Sailors, Beware!*, in which she played Edie Hornett, the archetypal meek and mild punchbag into which bossy Peggy Mount punches. Cannon later worked with Mount, a larger-than-life force of humour, in the 1960 stage sequel *Watch it Sailor!*, at the Aldwych Theatre. Surprisingly, she wasn't picked up for the Hammer Films production.

Esma Cannon's landmark year had come in 1947. She was again playing the serving girl, Lindy Wicks in *Jassy*, but this was also a rare chance to flex her considerable acting muscles within a lavishly shot melodrama. Lindy was a mute character, poignantly played, with Margaret Lockwood and Dennis Price looking haughty in the foreground. That same year, Esma was cast in the far-less-glamorous, but altogether more grounded, *Holiday Camp*. As the plain, ageing maid Elsie Dawson, she etches a touching and desperate character-study again opposite Dennis Price, still playing a swine, whose intentions are anything but honourable (in fact, he's downright murderous). The film would be important for Cannon for two reasons. Firstly, it would lead to a series of spin-off films for down-to-earth fun-seekers the Huggetts, as played by Jack Warner and Kathleen Harrison. Esma Cannon would notch up appearances in three of these films, playing various roles usually associated with the Girl Guides. *Holiday Camp* would also be the big break for a young scriptwriter by the name of Peter Rogers, who, when he turned producer, would employ Cannon on a regular basis, starting with one of his earliest credits, *Marry Me!*, in 1949.

Cannon's roles started out small: the deaf old landlady in *Raising the Wind* (1961), the equally deaf old lady who gives Kenneth Williams a bashing in *Carry On, Constable* (1960). Gradually, they developed; she was Sid's helping hand in *Carry On Regardless* (1961) and the prissy Mrs Jones in *Nurse on Wheels* (1963) – she even got her name on the poster for that one. Esma Cannon, with her name on the poster – boy, was she famous.

The *Carry On* films and, even more powerfully, her role as the gutsy Lily in *The Rag Trade* on BBC Television from October 1961, made her something of a star, albeit for just a year or two. This gave her the opportunity to take on meatier roles, most touchingly of which was the lonely Mrs Raikes, faced with

*The Rag Trade* album, with Sheila Hancock, Peter Jones, Esma Cannon, Reg Varney and Miriam Karlin.

the death of her pet, in Leslie Phillips's veterinary comedy *In the Doghouse*, released in May 1962, slap bang in the middle of her final series of *The Rag Trade*. That such fast and loose bits of comic flotsam and jetsam as *In the Doghouse* could pause to embrace such emotive moments gives Cannon's performances within them all the heart in the world.

Cannon's own personal favourite was the BBC Television *Maigret* episode 'A Crime For Christmas', for Boxing Day 1961, which not only afforded her a jaunt to Paris but also gave her another touching vignette, this time as an isolated French spinster.

By the time she was shooting her final *Carry On* film, *Carry On Cabby*, in the spring of 1963, she had set her heart on retirement. 'Until now,' she said at the time, 'I've always played fluttery parts. My height made it difficult to play anything else. But as Flo, I really do get a chance to show that little women can be a character to reckon with.' After *Carry On Cabby* there was just one more film appearance, as a tea lady in the thriller *Hide and Seek,* before retirement. Always an intensely private person, she lived the last ten years of her life with her family in Camden. She was so private, in fact, that the industry at large only became aware of her death when *Films and Filming* magazine ran a 'Where Are They Now?' feature on her several years later. The truth of the matter was that Esma had retired to live in Saint-Benoît-la-Forêt, Indre-et-Loire, France, with her husband Ernst Littman, whom she had married in 1945. Esma died there, on 18 October 1972. She was sixty-six, which seems unbelievably young for the eternal comedic maiden aunt. Her exit was appropriately quiet and refined for a little lady who gave the nation such gentle pleasure. That heartwarming smile can brighten the gloomiest day. Instantly.

TREAT YOURSELF TO *What a Carve Up!* (Platform Entertainment: B00198QRJ0, 2008), not only an exceedingly good haunted-house comedy with Sid James, Kenneth Connor and Dennis Price, even here, after all those years, the smoothest of swines, having the time of their lives, but a

'I'm Glad.' 'So am I!' All aboard the Happy Wanderer, with Liz Fraser and Jimmy Thompson, in *Carry On Cruising*, 1962.

pretty-near definitive encapsulation of Esma Cannon's dotty-old-maid performances. Here, as Connor's Aunt Emily, she lives in a bygone world of suffragettes and George Bernard Shaw. Humoured, loved and, in the end, not such a silly old bird at all, her character makes this the perfect Esma Cannon film, and perfect for a winter's day in front of a roaring fire. Another cup, dear? Esma will pour. After all, the film was released for that cold autumn of 1961 and, hot on its heels, from 19 December 1961, Esma was capitalising on small-screen popularity in *The Rag Trade* stage show, at the Prince of Wales Theatre. *What a Carve Up!* delights in the glow of Esma's Indian summer, and she's loving it.

# Patrick Cargill

## 1918–96

Having worked with Patrick – playing Anna, his elder daughter, in the Thames Television series *Father, Dear Father* – I enjoyed his company, relished his wit and appreciated his generosity generally – and especially as an actor – at close quarters over a number of very happy years. As the series came to an end, I met and married actor Paul Copley. There was a feature film made of *Father, Dear Father* – Paul was involved in that briefly and so I was able to introduce him to my televisual family.

Sometime later, when Paul and I were finally deciding that we might be able to afford to stop renting in NW8 and actually buy somewhere to live, Paul was rehearsing at the old BBC Acton rehearsal rooms. This was a place like no other in London; much of the BBC's output was rehearsed there before it moved into Television Centre. In the canteen on the top floor it was possible, and probable, to queue up for lunch with actors, comedians and turns of every description, at all levels of fame and accomplishment, from ingénues to huge stars. So it was that Paul bumped into Patrick whilst collecting his plate of grub, they exchanged pleasantries, and it came out that we were looking to buy a flat. Patrick had quite recently turned his beautiful Edwardian family home in SW14 into a maisonette for himself plus two leasehold flats; the attic flat was about to go on the market. Patrick was overjoyed that us buying and moving in to his house might be a possibility. Having spent happy times in that very house during the series – the house where Patrick had entertained The Beatles during filming *Help!* – I too was overjoyed and keen to see how the house had been developed.

We bought the flat, with its alcoves and skylights and dormer windows, and I was as happy there as at any time before or since. Patrick could make me giggle or roar with laughter at the drop of a hat ('Chuckle, wheeze, fall about' was one of my ad libs for the show, that Patrick made me keep in and often reminded me about). We lived there for three happy years. We moved on – still in SW14, which we had grown to know and appreciate. Patrick moved on too. He was a firm friend, gave me good advice and gave the most lavish and enjoyable parties it's been my pleasure to attend. He was proud to know me as his screen daughter and I was proud and privileged to know, work with and learn from him.

*Natasha Pyne*

Patrick was part of a long line of 'debonair actors' which included Leslie Phillips, Terry-Thomas and, of course, David Niven. They all represented a part of English society that is sadly no longer with us – a cartoon version of the ever so slightly camp English gentleman, but at the same time, fiercely heterosexual! Very few actors could get away with wearing a silk dressing gown and cravat on-screen as often as Patrick. We all know how ridiculous it would look, but he made it seem the most natural thing in the world.

He created a rather glamorous bubble around himself, and the humour is when the bubble bursts and we see the wonderful expressions of bewilderment, fake horror and delicious impotent rage. It was always lovely to be there, to take part in the bursting of that bubble.

He never minded us teasing him, which we did all the time, especially about his toupée – of course, there would be a raised eyebrow if we ever went too far. (And we did!)

One of the last times I saw him was when he was playing the dame at Richmond Theatre. From Sandhurst to Widow Twankey – quite a journey, Patrick.

*Annie Holloway*

If the fictional tome *Illustrated Dictionary of Definition* demanded representation of 'lounge lizard', you could do a lot worse than a picture of Patrick Cargill. For that was the image he cultivated so skilfully through his glut of stage and screen performances: the wispy, grey hair; the elegant, colourful cravat; the cigarette perched playfully between the forefinger and the middle; the oh-so-seventies wardrobe of a florid, man-about-town cad; the witty, at-ease way with women. This was the persona Cargill perfected. Whether it was the much-married playboy of *The Many Wives of Patrick* (London Weekend Television, 1976–78) or the domestically addled novelist-father of two teenage daughters in *Father, Dear Father* (Thames Television, 1968–73), there was always that air of sophistication about him. Even after farcical and slapstick nonsense bemused and angered the characters he played, the Bentley-loving, champagne-sipping dilettante that was at the heart of Cargill remained reassuringly intact.

Born on 3 June 1918, in Bexhill-on-Sea, East Sussex, Edward Sydney Patrick Cargill was educated the military way at Haileybury and Imperial Service College, and the Royal Military Academy Sandhurst, before getting his commission in the Indian Army. It was, he reflected years later, 'good disciplinary training'. Still, the army life was not for him, and the stage soon became his lifelong love. He started out with Bexhill Amateur Theatrical Society before joining the Buxton Repertory Theatre, under company actor-manager Anthony Hawtrey. It was during this association that he wowed a young master of farce, Tim Brooke-Taylor. 'Patrick Cargill was our local hero,' Brooke-Taylor remembered. 'He used to come round to our house and listen to gramophone records. He wrote the pantomimes and was so innovative onstage – he would play Buttons on roller skates – I was left in a state of sheer delight.' Cargill would still be doing

the pantomime roller skates
into the 1980s! After Buxton
there followed a seven-year
stint with John Counsell's
repertory company at the
Theatre Royal in Windsor.
The crowning glory – quite
literally – of this period was
the attendance of the Queen
and a party of her guests at a
performance of the revue *The
World's the Limit*.

Giving Frankie Howerd his BBC medical for the
first episode of Frank's eponymous TV series,
directed by Duncan Wood, for 11 December 1964.

Cargill made his West End debut in 1953, playing opposite Ian Carmichael
and Joan Sims, in another revue, *High Spirits*, at the London Hippodrome. He
spent much of the decade on the West End stage and co-wrote a number of plays
with dramatist Jack Beale. The most famous of them now is a medical comedy
drama called *Ring for Catty*, which was staged at the Lyric Theatre in 1956.
Producer Peter Rogers bought the film rights and screen credited the source
when he made *Carry On Nurse* in 1958, although scant traces of the original
play remained, apart from the hospital-ward setting. Four years later Rogers
made *Twice Round the Daffodils*, which was more in tune with the bittersweet
dynamic of the Cargill and Beale play and incorporated elements of his earlier,
sanatorium-based effort *Time on Their Hands*. Still, although the tragicomedy
was there, it was again told in broader strokes; scriptwriter Norman Hudis said
'they should have called it *Carry On Coughing*'.

Cargill's landmark West End run was typical. Cast as Bernard, the Lothario
besieged by numerous air hostesses, in the original West End production of
*Boeing-Boeing* at the Apollo in 1962, this insouciant man of wit and slapstick
flitted through the complex settings like an elusive hawk-moth. By this stage
in his career, Cargill had mastered the art of film and television scene-stealing.
He had played the languid and refined Scottish doctor in the classic *Hancock*
episode 'The Blood Donor' (BBC Television, 23 June 1961), where, faced by
the star's outrageous Scottish gibberish, Cargill brought the house down with

Hand-picked by the star to play store manager Mr Stone in the first *Hancock* for ATV, 1963.

his limp: 'We're not all Rob Roys!' In the March of 1961 he had been on the big screen in *Carry On Regardless*, as a lip-smacking scoundrel who finds a scantily clad Liz Fraser in the Popsy Cupboard.

Cargill returned to the *Carry On* series and proved his restraint in front of the camera by playing the foppish, arch-Spanish governor in the historical seafaring romp *Carry On Jack* (1964). Later still, he relished the opportunity of being directed by Charlie Chaplin in *A Countess from Hong Kong* (1967). However, none of his film roles are as gleeful or satisfying as his glorified cameo as the police superintendent in the roller-coaster Beatles comedy *Help!* (1965). Convincing the lads that he can impersonate them to save their lives, he smugly waxes lyrical on his skills as an impressionist: 'Jimmy Cagney...' he boasts, with a nonchalant wave of the hand, as he adopts broad Scouse down the blower and George Harrison mutters: 'Not a bit like Cagney...' It's a free-wheelin', madcap bubble of 1960s cool and, despite being the figure of authority, Cargill was right there at the swinging heart of the matter.

But it was the stage that really bewitched him. In 1966 he starred in Keith Waterhouse and Willis Hall's *Say Who You Are* at Her Majesty's Theatre and, in 1968, directed the Ray Cooney and John Chapman farce *Not Now, Darling* at the Strand Theatre. He starred opposite Dorothy Tutin in *Play on Love* at the St. Martin's Theatre in 1970, and later that year relished the ultimate lightness of touch leading man challenge, of Charles Condomine in Noël Coward's *Blithe Spirit*, at the Globe Theatre (now the Gielgud). I've seen many a fine Condomine but, oh, what I would give to have seen Cargill's. What spine-tingling casting. Not to mention, Madame Arcati was played by Beryl Reid.

Cargill notched up supporting roles opposite almost every top comedian, including Peter Sellers (in *Up the Creek*, 1958), Norman Wisdom (*A Stitch in Time*, 1963), Marty Feldman (*Every Home Should Have One*, 1970), Tommy Cooper (*It's Tommy Cooper*, LWT, 14 March 1970) and, on many occasions, Frankie Howerd; Cargill's cynical and calculated Nero in the 1971 film of *Up Pompeii* was the perfect antidote to Howerd's audience-pleasing mugging. When, in 1986, Howerd returned to togas and serving maidens, in the Chichester and Piccadilly theatres' revival of *A Funny Thing Happened on the Way to the Forum*, it was a natural progression that Cargill would do so too, in the role of Senex. Although Cargill was less than amused when Howerd would veer off piste of the script, turn to the audience and dish out a few of his trusty old catchphrases!

In between his stage roles, Cargill had honed and perfected his farce skills on television. His biggest personal success, *Father, Dear Father*, ran for seven series, even making a guest spot, in character as Patrick Glover, on *The Edward Woodward Hour* in August 1971. He revisited the show as part of a Thames Television special *Patrick, Dear Patrick*, in January 1972, and returned for a new series for the 7 Network in Australia from June 1978. Predictably entitled *Father, Dear Father in Australia*, the show, which also recruited Noel Dyson as 'Nanny' from the original, ran down under until June 1980, with, always three or four months behind, a concurrent screening back in Britain. Cargill had proved himself the master of comic business on the Australian stage, too. Displaying relentless vitality as George in the 1975 Comedy Theatre Melbourne production of *Two and Two Make Sex*, juggling wife, girlfriend, false teeth and a chest-expander with a life of its own, he had played the Cambridge Theatre in the West End, for over a year from 30 August 1973, before enjoying hugely successful tours of Australia and Canada. They were homes from home that always loved to make a truly British comic icon feel very welcome.

Forever keen and agile, it was rather apt that Cargill would deliver his television swan song as Neville Chamberlain in 1990's *Heil Honey I'm Home!*, a one-off comic pot-shot at 1950s Americana. Guaranteed and designed to offend just about everybody, it was a brilliantly inventive misfire for the satellite channel, Galaxy. That same year Cargill took on his last major stage assignment, as Captain Beaky at the West End's Playhouse Theatre, and continued to appear

With champion chums Annie Holloway and Natasha Pyne in the *Father Dear Father* film, directed by William G. Stewart, for a May 1973 release.

with the frightfully proper and legendary Hilton Playhouse and British Airways tours, under the auspices of his good friend Derek Nimmo.

At home, Cargill surrounded himself with pets, from ever-faithful dogs to a monkey and a parrot. He lived for the life of the actor; when illness struck, at the end of 1995, he was determined to soldier on – and he did. Anything else just wouldn't be cricket, old boy. This most urbane of actors slipped away peacefully in his sleep, in a hospice in Richmond, on 23 May 1996. He was seventy-seven. One hopes, in his pleasant dreams, Patrick Cargill was speeding through the lush English countryside in his beloved black and dark green Bentley Drop-Head. How very civilised.

TREAT YOURSELF TO *Father, Dear Father* (Madman Entertainment: MMA5045, 2010), the feature film spin-off of Patrick Cargill's biggest television success – a distillation of all the raised eyebrows, parental worry and effortless charm of the series, plus an enlightening commentary (moderated by me) with his charming screen daughters Natasha Pyne and Ann Holloway. But this is where you came in...

# Jimmy Clitheroe
# and Danny Ross

## 1921–73 and 1930–76

As a child of the sixties, Sunday lunchtime comedy on Radio 2 (or the Light Programme, in old money) was just as important an ingredient, for me, as the lamb chops and mint sauce I was busy scoffing before being allowed out to play football again. My own personal favourite? *The Clitheroe Kid*, starring squeaky-voiced, vertically challenged Jimmy Clitheroe – the archetypal cheeky and eternally youthful Northern chappie who made Peter Pan seem world-weary by comparison – ably supported by Danny Ross as his friend Alfie Hall, the hapless sidekicks' hapless sidekick. In short – and, indeed, in shorts: peerless, end-of-the-pier comedy. I was even lucky enough to see Jimmy in panto one year, at the Theatre Royal, Nottingham. Aye. And I still had change for the bus home.

*Johnny Immaterial, ex-stand-up comedian; Johnny Meres, actor*
*of character; Jonathan Meres, author of the World of Norm books*

When I first started in this glorious game, I met a lovely chap who would happily tell all and sundry that he used to be the stunt double and stand-in for Jimmy Clitheroe. Naturally, I was rather more impressed and in awe of this fact than most. Let's be fair: I was the *only* one impressed and in awe of this fact. If anybody else actually bothered to pursue this line of enquiry and expressed their ignorance of who in actual fact this Jimmy Clitheroe chap was, this affable stand-in would say: 'You know Jimmy Krankie off of the Krankies, right? Jimmy was like him... umm, her... only before you were born...' That's quite a desperate attempt to link to fame.

Still, without doubt, little Jimmy Krankie is the modern-day touchstone of who exactly Jimmy Clitheroe was. For eighteen years, *The Clitheroe Kid* was one of BBC Radio's flagship successes, and the delightfully cheeky schoolboy trapped within an adult's body was avidly listened to by millions of people across the country. Even into the twenty-first century, his legacy kind of lingers. The Fall's release of their *Live in Clitheroe* concert, from 2013, featured a variety-style poster of the lad on its cover, with the 'Jimmy' in 'The Fall Live in Jimmy Clitheroe' scrawled out. Now there's a fun back-handed compliment if ever I saw one.

Jimmy Clitheroe, who was born on Christmas Eve, 1921, in Clitheroe, Lancashire, and actually called Clitheroe, was the only child of a couple of Lancastrian cotton weavers. Bitten by the performing bug at an early age, he was the life and soul of parties and the playground, but it soon became clear that this funny little boy was going to always be little. Suffering from a rare genetic condition, he reached four foot three and stayed there. The voice of a ten-year-old-boy refused to mature, too. It was the blessing and the curse that would make his fame and fortune. By the time he was fourteen, the family had moved to the town of Nelson and young Jimmy was proving something of a success in regional variety. Not only did he prove himself an accomplished accordion player, but that childlike voice lent itself spectacularly to female impersonation. Having been spotted by a local talent scout, Jimmy toured his act through variety theatres across the country and in 1940 was picked up by Butcher's Film Service to support Arthur Lucan and Kitty McShane in *Old Mother Riley in Business*, released in cinemas early in 1941. Later, Jimmy proved a likeable screen foil to George Formby in *Much Too Shy* (1942), a sweet, endearing friend to the toothy awkwardness of the star turn.

But it was onstage, and in particular in variety in the north, that Clitheroe was a star. Now in his early twenties, young Jimmy's knowing bill matter – 'Don't Some Mothers 'Ave 'Em' – caught the eye of James Casey, son of the great music hall comedian Jimmy James, who was casting for the part of a mischievous schoolboy. The role demanded an actor with the maturity of a seasoned professional. Stand up, please, Jimmy Clitheroe.

Alf Hall's kindly, submissive catchphrase 'I'm not bothered' became the title of Danny's 1956 ATV series.

The production was the *Northern Variety Parade* show, which Casey had written for his legendary father, and its popularity led directly to Clitheroe's first chance at radio stardom. In October 1948 Jimmy was cast as yet another naughty schoolboy, opposite yet another music hall great, in Norman Evans's radio series *Over the Garden Wall*. Meanwhile, James Casey was busy writing a radio show of his own. *Call Boy*, first heard on 18 October 1955, would feature Clitheroe in a monthly and, from 1956, weekly domestic skit. He was the schoolboy tearaway again, and audiences adored him – so much so that Casey saw the clear potential for a series built completely around this Clitheroe kid.

Initially broadcast only in the North of England, public demand dictated that, after two very successful years, *The Clitheroe Kid* went nationwide. Some at the BBC questioned whether a small man in his late twenties playing a thirteen-year-old schoolboy was quite the thing the Corporation should be peddling. These concerns fuelled Clitheroe's own demons of self-doubt and inadequacy. But whenever he was onstage Doctor Theatre dispelled any such angst and Clitheroe's perfectly timed misadventures made him one of the country's most popular and best-loved comedians.

With no London-based Command Performance in 1959, Manchester's Palace Theatre welcomed the royals on 23 June and Jimmy Clitheroe was on the bill. The changing times were reflected by the inclusion of rock 'n' roll impresario Jack Good's package featuring Cliff Richard, Marty Wilde, and Lord Rockingham's XI, but the kid held his own. He also played the London Casino, the Victoria Palace theatre and most of producer Emile Littler's premiere venues across the country.

The support cast of the radio series was enriched by Peter Sinclair as Jimmy's grandfather, and Renée Houston as the young lad's long-suffering mother. That wonderfully dour character actor Tony Melody played the wonderfully dour next-door neighbour Mr Higginbottom, while Diana Day was cast as Jimmy's extremely snobbish older sister, Susan.

In 1961, with the fourth series now attracting millions of listeners across the country, Susan secured herself a gormless boyfriend by the name of Alfie Hall. Enter Danny Ross, an Oldham lad, born Ronald Crabtree on 30 April 1930, who had trained as a serious actor and trodden the boards with various repertory companies. Ross's major show business break came when he met Glenn Melvyn [qv]. Melvyn, writer and co-star of the successful stage play and subsequent film *The Love Match*, spotted the comedic quality at the heart of Ross's work. The actor brought bumbling charm and balletic slapstick to his lovesick role of Alfie Hall and, taking the part from stage to screen, Alf gave Ross a public identity that refused to budge. Danny and Alfie instantly and forever became welded together as one entity: actor and character as one. Chuffed to secure regular employment, Danny sacrificed his varied career to embrace this multilayered performance of an ineffectual buffoon. The wildly energetic and mischievous schoolboy of Jimmy and the slow-witted, eager-to-please simpleton of Danny made the perfect team. For years, Clitheroe and Ross reeled out free-wheeling, carefree and just plain daft comedy recorded in the auditorium of the Hulme Hippodrome in Manchester, and broadcast to loyal families gathered round the dim, yellow lights of their wireless sets; Jimmy, the leader of the gang, forever thinking up naughty wheezes and playful criminal activities, and Danny chatting away in gloriously scrambled non-sequiturs, always one step and one thought behind the latest cunning plan.

With Jimmy in full school uniform in front of the radio microphone and Danny effortlessly incorporating silent pratfalls within and around his scripted dialogue, the invited audience had double the show that the listening millions heard. Indeed, more laughs per minute were undoubtedly generated away from the page as from it, with much of the process being completely unintelligible to the home audience.

It wasn't effortless, of course, and for Jimmy in particular it wasn't jolly. Although revelling in the stardom that the role in *The Clitheroe Kid* afforded him, as a man he was shy, frustrated and sick to the back teeth of well-meaning members of the general public still treating him like a child.

In the 1960s, now in his forties, Jimmy was still living with his beloved mother in Blackpool. It was a complex double life, for even when a role out of school uniform was offered it was, of course, still a role of diminished height; he grabbed the chance to play Tom Thumb in the feature film adventure *Jules Verne's Rocket to the Moon* (1967), though it led to nothing.

At the BBC, *The Clitheroe Kid* was still one of the cornerstone radio successes, and Clitheroe could command huge fees and expect huge audiences for his headlining appearances throughout the summer season and in pantomime. In order to both cultivate a loyal audience and make geographical sense, Jimmy usually opted to perform in Blackpool for the summer season. Danny Ross was happy to tag along to wherever the need of the gormless Alfie would take him.

One step too far, however, was ATV's attempt to transfer the team to television. Despite the ever-reliable Mollie Sugden putting in sterling work as Jimmy's third theatrical mother (Patricia Burke having now taken over from Renee Houston on radio, in 1958), *That's My Boy* proved something of a curate's egg. The loveable and silly antics of the Clitheroe Kid were as loveable and silly as ever, and Danny Ross, though now rather incongruously cast as Cousin Danny but just as gullible, was as perfect a foil as he ever had been, too. In actual fact, for Danny, television was rather a revelation: always a very visual, physical actor onstage, his natural ability for slapstick had, quite naturally, proved redundant on radio. In *That's My Boy* he is like a free spirit. He had an array of facial expressions using muscles as fluid as quicksand, while his expressive and excessive hair almost had a life of its own.

The major problem was Jimmy Clitheroe himself. A man in his forties playing a teenage boy could fool all of the people all of the time on radio. Even

James Robinson Clitheroe promoting the last of his ABC TV series *Just Jimmy*, 1968.

on the stage, thanks to the distance between the footlights and the front row, the magic of greasepaint and Clitheroe's assured performance could conjure up a jolly smokescreen. In a small television studio, with hot lights, constricted sets and huge cameras literally in your face for reaction sets, it was patently clear that Clitheroe was a small, middle-aged man in a school uniform. Rather disconcerting, it certainly distracted from the rather desperate, old-fashioned, *Just William-*styled charades on display.

Still, on radio *The Clitheroe Kid* continued throughout the sixties, but it had been around so long it was practically collecting its pension, and both Jimmy and Danny knew in their heart of hearts that the innocent fun and games could only last so much longer. When the final curtain did fall, on the 13 August 1972, it marked the end of an incredible run of 280 half-hours. Never twee, never gentle, the real force of the comedy was in the Clitheroe-and-Ross conspiracy – there was real anarchy at work. A very British, very silly coup, it was a series that the nation had taken deep to its collective heart.

Clitheroe's own heart was already in pieces, when within days of the cancellation of *The Clitheroe Kid*, his long-time female companion, Sally, died in a motor accident. Less than a year later, Jimmy's mother died too. With the two people closest to him gone, and the show he loved no more, it was all too much for Jimmy Clitheroe. On 6 June 1973, the day of his mother's funeral, Jimmy was found dead in the Blackpool bungalow the two had shared for so many years. A coroner's verdict recorded accidental death due to the effects of barbiturates and alcohol.

As for Danny Ross, he continued to play variety theatres with his tried-and-tested befuddled comedy act. Though only in his early forties, he was not a well man himself and would gratefully accept any assignment he was offered. One such opportunity arose on 2 February 1976, when a fellow comedian fell ill suddenly and the spot on the playbill urgently needed filling. As the theatre was close to his Lancashire home, Ross happily stepped into the breach. Alas, it was one job too many. Whilst en route to the venue he suffered a massive heart attack. He was dead at just forty-five years old.

It was an unfairly cruel farewell for a delightfully knockabout coupling that gave such joy for so many years, but on distant airwaves they are eternally stuck in aspic – the cheeky scamp and his bewildered friend, together getting into scrapes and happily muddling through for all time.

Jimmy with Hylda Baker, during the dress rehearsal for *Jack and the Beanstalk* at the Liverpool Empire, ahead of an opening on 23 December 1959.

TREAT YOURSELF TO the only official BBC release of *The Clitheroe Kid* currently available (BBC Radio Collection: ZBBC1104, 1990): four gloriously funny episodes, with Clitheroe and Ross at their mischievous best. All the beloved characters are here, including Diana Day as Alf's girlfriend and the Kid's teenage sister 'Scraggy Neck' Susan and Tony Melody as Mr Higginbottom who is forever threatening to give Jimmy a good hiding. No wonder the show regularly attracted over 10 million loyal listeners. Even the episode titles start me smiling: 'Clitheroe and the Hound Dog', 'A Load of Chinese Junk', 'The Evils of Tomato Juice' and 'Beware of the Neighbour'. Joyous fun.

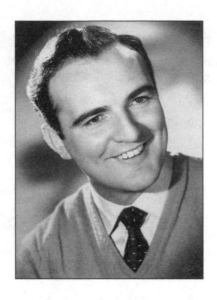

# Billy Dainty

## 1927–86

You must forgive me waxing eloquent in my summing up of Bill. He was one of my best friends. He was, quite simply, stunning. He could switch from comedy to pathos (never bathos) in the blink of an eye. I get very angry indeed when I think of just what we have all missed by his early death. I miss him every day.

*Roy Hudd OBE*

When you are a child, the death of someone famous is an odd and almost compelling moment in time. I have distinct memories of the national gut-wrench when Eric Morecambe departed stage left. I have dim recollections of the hysteria when John Lennon was shot in New York City. However, the show business death that affected me most profoundly of all was Billy Dainty. I was a little older, perhaps a little wiser, but I suppose you can say the day that Billy finally succumbed to cancer on 19 November 1986 was the final nail in the coffin of my childhood; a slow death that started with the departure of Tom

Baker from *Doctor Who* and the end of *The Goodies*, but that is the date on the certificate. That was the day – the day that Billy went out, eccentric-dancing-feet first, from his aptly named home, 'Cobblers', in Godalming, Surrey.

He had been around throughout my childhood. He seemed to be in every Royal Variety Performance, though of course he wasn't. In fact, he appeared in just three – the first, in 1974, in front of his biggest royal admirer, the Queen Mother. I'm sure I would have seen Dainty perform only in the 1982 presentation, but what a performance it was: legs flying akimbo, that cheesy grin of pure music hall beaming out at me from the television screen via the hallowed boards of the Theatre Royal, Drury Lane.

Billy was a staple of the Children's Royal Variety Performance, and of that other favourite in the Ross household, the *3–2–1* Christmas special – he brought his gentle charm and brain-stuffed-with-shtick to the table in both the 1983 and 1984 shows. Then there was *Emu's Broadcasting Company*. *EBC* was probably the most subversively silly show on children's television and it certainly engendered within me a lifelong obsession with the workings of a broadcasting unit. My sister and I were such fans that we would bombard the BBC with correspondence on a regular basis – as far as we were concerned, the BBC was simply the home of *EBC*. Barbara New was the tea lady, Rod Hull and that bloody bird held the entire show together – but, for us, it was Billy who made the programme. Billy played Billy, the ever-reliable, ever-jovial cameraman. It was a masterclass in physical and verbal comedy, and we adored him.

The show had a fairly lengthy run, from 1975 to 1980, but despite the career of Rod Hull and Emu encompassing everything from pantomime to a pink windmill, they are forever cemented in my mind as those *EBC* characters, with Billy Dainty in tow.

Born William Hooper Frank John Dainty, on 22 February 1927, in Dudley, Worcestershire, Dainty was star-struck at an early age. His father owned and ran a florist's shop, Hoopers, from the front of the family home, while his mother nursed bitterness at missing the opportunity to be a dancer. Her children would not suffer as she had done, and as soon as the young Billy could stand she enrolled him in ballet lessons at Madame Whistin's Music School. He was the Billy Elliot of the Black Country, flaunting his skills in taut limb-dancing in a class full of girls, one of whom was his sister, Betty. By the time Billy was twelve he had joined a local dance troupe, the Dancing Babes, and added to his already considerable hoofing talents thanks to tap-dancing tutelage from vaudeville hero Buddy Bradley.

Billy won a scholarship to the Royal Academy of Dramatic Art and made his professional stage debut in 1942, opposite Norman Evans in *Mother Goose* at the London Coliseum. It was the most inauspicious, clichéd start to any career, for Billy was the back end of a dancing donkey by the name of Asbestos. That's starting at the bottom, for sure. His chum John Shackelle was luckier and got the carrot-munching half. Still, never one to be downhearted, at the end of the run in 1943 Billy secured work as a chorus boy in the influential Sid Field revue *Strike a New Note* at the Prince of Wales theatre.

Called up for national service on his eighteenth birthday, Billy toured the Far East with the Stars in Battledress for just under two years, honing that teeth-and-twinkle expression. So nimble of foot was he that his right leg would not touch the ground as he careered across the length of the stage on his left. It was quite extraordinary. No less extraordinary were the impersonations with which he was continually fleshing out his act – by the mid-1950s he was incorporating singing starlet Shirley Bassey alongside his dance-based impressions of Fred Astaire and Rudolf Nureyev, whom he gleefully reinterpreted as 'Rudolf Near-Enough'. It was a joke that good friends Eric 'n' Ernie would utilise in the 1970s.

Billy had become a mainstay of British television variety, with peerless support from his long-term comic feed Len Lowe. He had wowed them on a *Sunday Night at the London Palladium*, having made the first of several guest clown appearances on 24 March 1957. Dainty and Lowe were particularly suited to *Kindly Leave the Stage* (BBC1, 1968), a variety showcase that positively revelled in the most awful jokes in music hall's armoury. Even better were Dainty's regular appearances on *The Good Old Days* (BBC1, 1966–83). Blessed with funny bones and often cited as the only contemporary performer with the true essence of music hall coursing through his veins, Dainty could be both of the now and very much of the then. With a song, a dance and a cheeky wink, he had one foot in the pie 'n' mash and one foot in the caviar.

It was no surprise that Thames Television gave him his very own show, *Billy Dainty, Esq.*, which, although producing just a September 1975 pilot and one series, in the spring of 1976, showcased him at his very best. Perhaps he just wasn't cut out to carry an entire project on his wobbly, scattergun legs. An attempt to star him in his own ABC situation comedy in 1967 had also been unsuccessful, despite the perfect premise of Dainty as winsome cabaret star Billy Cook, and including fine support from June Whitfield and Kenneth Connor, with

*Just a Verse & Chorus* transferred to the Greenwich Theatre in April 1981.

scripts by Vince Powell and Harry Driver. The title, of the show alas, summed up its failure: *That's Show Business.*

One of Billy's happiest collaborations was with his great chum, Roy Hudd. *Just a Verse & Chorus* was a musical celebration of songwriting monologuists R. P. Weston and Bert Lee, whose songs had been interpreted by the likes of Gracie Fields and Stanley Holloway. The show was first produced at the Haymarket Theatre in Leicester: a poignant and hilarious salute to variety from two proper old pros. It was as part of a brilliant ensemble that Billy worked best, be it *BBC* on television or a glut of pantomimes across the country, and across the decades. Having proved a likeable Simple Simon and Aladdin, in 1964 he was persuaded to play the dame for the very first time. It was in *Merry King Cole*, opposite the merry old soul of Harry Worth at the Bristol Hippodrome, that Billy was hailed almost instantly as one of the great panto dames. He was invited to wax lyrical on the subject in the 1982 documentary *The Pantomime Dame*. Alas, he had only a handful of seasons left in him.

'Going Mad – Coming!' as his variety bill matter had it: those dainty Dainty limbs launched a thousand laughs.

In 1985 he was in Nottingham for *Aladdin* when he was forced to make an early withdrawal from the production. It was the final curtain. He was a laudably modest man throughout his career. 'I don't really look upon myself as a success,' he said in the 1960s. 'A success in this business is a man who can fill the theatre fifty-two weeks a year, and I'm not one.' However, he did have the seemingly effortless ability to fill a theatre with laughter each and every time he appeared. It was a gift.

THERE'S SO LITTLE of Billy Dainty commercially available, and that's not just a digital-age thing; he was a man of the music halls. Although it's a shame to keep this whirling genius restricted to sound alone, do treat yourself to his single for Decca Records, 'Cry Upon My Shoulder', with 'If I'd Known You' on the other side, (Decca: F11499, 1962). It's a delight. (Well, Decca had to make up for turning down The Beatles somehow.)

# Janet Davies

## 1927–86

It was lovely to get the part of Pike's mother in the *Dad's Army* film, even though I still think I was far too young for the role! It must have been upsetting for Janet Davies. She was so good on television, but that sometimes happens. I played the matron in *Whack-O* and didn't get the film. I didn't try to imitate Janet's performance, but I hope I did her justice. She was wonderful.

*Liz Fraser*

*Dad's Army* is still one of the nation's favourite situation comedies. Saturday-night repeats pull in an incredible 2 million viewers. Not bad for a fifty-year-old series. The magnificent seven and their motley supporting troupe have become the stuff of British folklore, almost an indelible image of the Second World War rather than just an affectionate mockery of the dogged Home Guard.

Janet Davies, however, remains unheralded. She was rather unheralded at the time, and she was certainly forgotten by Columbia Pictures when they were casting the 1971 feature film version. Yet her television and stage performance as Private Pike's overly protective mother was perfectly judged – a performance of loneliness, unconditional love, over-compensating compassion, wartime morale and, yes, patriotic pride. From the very first episode, 'The Man and the Hour' on 31 July 1968, to the very last, 'Never Too Old' on 13 November 1977, Janet Davies was there, fussing about the cleanliness and manners of her beloved son and embarrassingly insisting on his wearing his woolly scarf; coyly rebuffing the charms of smooth-talking Sergeant Wilson in public while clearly finding solace in his arms behind blacked-out windows.

Janet Kathleen Davies was born on 14 September 1927, in Wakefield, Yorkshire, and followed in the footsteps of her late father by training as a solicitor. She decided against a career in law, however, and learned shorthand and typing instead, securing a secretarial role at the BBC shortly before the Second World War.

She had long nursed ambitions to go on the stage and, from 1948, she appeared with repertory companies in Bedford, Leatherhead, Northampton, Shrewsbury and Watford. She had a bit part as a motorist in the 1955 film version of Glenn Melvyn's *The Love Match* (having been in the original stage production), and played a cockney wife in the 1966 film *The Ghost Goes Gear*. There had been a handful of stage and television roles in-between but nothing particularly eye-catching and certainly nothing regular. Still, she had signed up as a client of theatrical agent Ann Callender and when work was tight, as it often was, Davies would be employed as Callender's secretary instead.

It just so happened that Callender was married to the director–producer David Croft, and Janet Davies was working in the office when that very first script of *Dad's Army* landed on the desk. She knew a great script when she read one, and this was a great script. Using her initiative and grabbing the prime opportunity in front of her, Davies eagerly threw her hat into the ring. As Croft later recalled, 'She hastened to suggest herself for the part. After all, being in the office where the script first saw the light of day, she knew the requirements well.' Ann Callender was obviously keen for her to secure the role too.

With the popularity and exposure of *Dad's Army* came other featured roles in situation comedy. Davies played a Grace Brothers' customer in the *Are You*

*Being Served?* episode 'Diamonds Are a Man's Best Friend' (BBC1, 18 April 1973), she appeared opposite Brian Marshall in *Hey Brian!* (Yorkshire Television, 19 June 1973) and with Leslie Phillips in *Casanova '73* (BBC1, 15 October 1973). She also chalked up two appearances as the nervy librarian Miss Jones in the early *Last of the Summer Wine* episodes 'Who's That Dancing with Nora Batty Then?', broadcast 12 March 1975, and 'Some Enchanted Evening', a fortnight later. All were lovely variations on her Mrs Pike theme, her own personal comfort zone. She was the housewife, not the show business legend, Ethel Merman in *The Fall and Rise of Reginald Perrin* episode 'Communal Social Evenings' (BBC1, 27 December 1978), and appeared in *The Dick Emery Show* (BBC1, 7 February 1981) and in the *Open All Hours* episode 'The Man From Down Under' (BBC1, 18 April 1982). She was Florrie in a couple of episodes of *Don't Wait Up* (BBC1, 8 November 1983/27 January 1986) and Mrs Lacy, twice, in *That's My Boy*: 'Hello Young Mothers' and 'The Bypass' (Yorkshire Television, 15 February 1985/21 March 1986). There was a rather splendid Mrs Hill in the 1980 BBC2 adaptation of *Pride and Prejudice*, a receptionist in *Sadie, It's Cold Outside* (Thames Television, 5 May 1975) and a saleswoman in *Angels* episode 'The Visitor' (BBC1, 19 June 1978).

Her very last role, now being credited as Jan Davies, was as a lowly DHSS claimant in the first episode of the BBC1 sitcom *Bread* on 1 May 1986, but even that indignity paled next to her disappointment at not getting the 1971 film of *Dad's Army*. Though known as 'Generous Jan' due to her charitable contributions, she couldn't find it in her charitable heart to forgive Columbia Pictures for embracing the marquee value of Liz Fraser over her own original and long-time performance as Mrs Pike. It was a disappointment she took to her early grave, but it is her thirty episodes of the television show, not the seventies' film – nor indeed the radio series nor the stage revival nor the 2016 big-screen resurrection – that gets that regular audience of 2 million, week in and week out. There's a kind of justice in that.

Treat yourself to *Dad's Army – The Complete Collection* (2entertain: B000VA3JK, 2007). Quite frankly, no self-respecting comedy aficionado should be without it, but the gently subversive, kindly manipulative performance of Janet Davies is her lasting legacy – and quite a legacy it is.

# Florence Desmond

## 1905–93

A relative newcomer to the joy that is Florence Desmond, my first chuckle at her hands came from the very title of her wartime song 'The Deepest Shelter in Town'. And the chuckles continued, as the song itself doesn't disappoint. Chock-full of delightful double entendres, she perfectly walks a charming tightrope between Blitz-spirit bonhomie and saucy sexuality that's still funny almost eighty years later. But to me she appeals not just because she's a great comedian and singer, but also a perfect mimic and natural actor: *A Hollywood Party* is a masterclass in elegant aping. A true talent that deserves to be remembered.

*Rebecca Vaughan*

As a London-born comic who specialised in mimicry, it is perhaps fitting that Florence Desmond's most widely seen performance is a film which convinced me as a lad that she was actually a Scot. It is the Max Miller vehicle *Hoots Mon!* (1940), and not only is it the cheeky chappie's best and most important film work, it also preserves forever the amazing dexterity of Florence Desmond's act of quick-change famous impersonations. Writing about her in 1934, the critic James Agate observed: 'she has not only a white-hot sense of the ridiculous but can present it in a dozen different disguises'.

I was first introduced to the multi-talented Desmond in a mid-1980s Channel 4 television screening of *Hoots Mon!* that I recorded on VHS. I watched it over and over again. (In fact, I still have the original, well-worn tape!) There was a vivaciousness about her that appealed, so much so that I wrote her a gushing fan letter. She was well into her eighties at the time and long retired but, charmingly, she not only replied but also preserved my besotted illusion by sending me a huge sepia signed photograph, circa 1939.

In the film she plays Jenny McTavish, a bright and breezy Scottish music hall star who has the vim and vigour to include an impression of flashy cockney comedian Harry Hawkins in her act. Hawkins is, of course, Max Miller – in every sense; the onstage routines – clad in floral suit and squeezing risqué jokes past the stage management – form the most vibrant record of Miller, the stage colossus, in the archives. Hal Walters, Miller's ill-fated film stooge, is also quite brilliant here, giving just the right balance of subservience and superiority. The joke of *Hoots Mon!* is that Miller is an arrogant swine who insists that the impression of him – an extremely good one – is dropped. Refusal leads to him pulling every nasty trick in the book to scupper the rival turn. Finally, it's the challenge: with Desmond's character having proved her popularity in London, Miller's character must play to an audience north of the border – an English comic's nightmare, at a time when mention of the Glasgow Empire would make the blood run cold for even the most successful turn. The outcome is endearing if implausible – but, hey, who cares? It was a match made in heaven, so much so that Desmond subsequently supported Miller in his 1941 London Palladium spectacular *Apple Sauce!*.

She was born Florence Dawson, on 31 May 1905, and took to the stage at the age of ten, although her education certainly wasn't put to the sword, studying at the highly respected Dame Alice Owen's School in Islington. At the age of eleven she was performing ballet in pantomime, and after leaving school at fifteen, she returned to variety theatres along with her brother, Fred, forming the comedy acrobatics team of Desmond and Marks.

She had taken London by storm in the revue *Still Dancing*, which ran at the London Pavilion from 1925. From November 1928, co-starring with Noël Coward, no less, Desmond wowed Broadway audiences with the 'Dance, Little Lady' number in *This Year of Grace*, at the Selwyn Theatre.

Florence could have become a massive star in America if she had chosen to stay. Her forte was impersonations of great film stars and, as always, the greatest and most instantly recognisable were American. In fact, her British variety act could have been performed in America with very little tweaking. Still, it was in the West End revue *Charlot's Masquerade*, at the Cambridge theatre in 1931, that her gift was first fully recognised. Her very first recording, *A Hollywood Party*, followed quickly on its heels in August 1932, and provides definitive evidence of her transatlantic appeal. On it she plays Gracie Fields visiting a swanky bash hosted by Janet Gaynor. At the party, Gracie meets Greta Garbo, Marie Dressler, Marlene Dietrich, Tallulah Bankhead and other great stars of the day – even Jimmy Durante. Each impersonation is uncannily accurate, and pleasantly backed by the band of Ray Noble. Then Gracie Fields starts to sing. Desmond had had the opportunity of studying Gracie at close quarters while co-starring with her in the 1931 film *Sally in Our Alley*. The impersonation is absolutely perfect – but of course it is. They all are.

It wasn't only the monumental release of *A Hollywood Party*, that made 1932 a landmark year for Desmond. Having now featured in several feature films, she was picked by producer Irving Asher to star in the five-reel comedy *High Society*, and later that year also made *The River House Ghost* at Warner Brothers First National Studios, Teddington. She also shot a snatch of her act for *Radio Parade* (1933).

It is more than likely that Desmond proved the inspiration for dexterous impersonator Carlotta Adams in the fiendish 1933 Agatha Christie novel *Lord Edgware Dies*. In 1933, Desmond was back in the West End, at the Palace Theatre, to star in *Why Not Tonight?*, a musical revue written by Herbert Farjeon. In the mid 1930s she fleetingly tasted the thrill of Hollywood when – in a string of films – Hollywood came to her. She starred with Douglas Fairbanks Jr in *Accused* at Worton Hall Studios, Isleworth, and there had been encounters with Will Rogers (in *Mr Skitch*, 1933) and Sophie Tucker (in *Gay Love*, 1934).

But there was always George Formby to keep her feet on the ground. Indeed, as Florrie, she breezed through two of George's very best films: *No Limit* (1935) and *Keep Your Seats Please!* (1936).

While the Second World War was raging in Europe in 1940, Desmond appeared with Stanley Lupino in *Funny Side Up*, at His Majesty's Theatre. As the bombs fell over the West End, Florence starred opposite Arthur Askey in *Jack and Jill*, at the Palace Theatre, in 1942 (Florence was Jack, Kathleen Moody was Jill); and Bud Flanagan and Chesney Allen in *Hi-de-Hi*, at the Stoll Theatre, in 1943. She happily kept the funny side up throughout

In the centre of the curtain call and, oh, what a civilised showtime.

the war. It's a cliché but laughter really did help keep the home fires burning during Britain's darkest hour, and the irrepressible impressions of Florence Desmond became a firm favourite on the radio. She could perform an all-star variety bill all on her own and her sheer good-natured joy came through each and every broadcast. She was quite simply a tonic.

Even more rousing were her clutch of wartime recordings for His Master's Voice, including 1941's tongue-poking attack on Italian fascist Benito Mussolini, 'Oh! What a Surprise for the Du-ce!' and, best of all, the extremely racy flip-side 'The Deepest Shelter in Town' – beautifully sung but with outrageous lyrics; within the introduction Florence eagerly admits to not being a lady of the highest virtue before asking any patriotic man who happens along to come back to her flat and sample the deepest shelter in town. Well, quite!

After the war, she returned to America, perhaps in an attempt to do what she thought she should have done back in the late 1920s. She certainly proved her mettle as Guest Impressionist on Jackie Gleason's *Cavalcade of Stars* (DuMont Television Network, 9 February 1951) and five-times guest on *The Milton Berle Show* (NBC, 1948–53). Seemingly satisfied, she came back home

Sassy and saucy and supremely talented, Florence teased out many a depression-era giggle and morale-boosting wartime titter.

to play a supporting role in the Max Bygraves film *Charley Moon* (1956), and was happy to grab the role of a bitter and manipulative stage revue diva. Nothing like herself at all.

Having appeared on the bill of the 1937 Royal Variety Performance, she got the call for the second time in 1951. The following year she gave her most ambitious and celebrated stage appearance when she starred in the thriller *The Apples of Eve*, at the Comedy Theatre. Set in an institution for the insane, the head of the outfit is found dead and the suspect list is narrowed down to five patients, including a discombobulated acrobat, a member of the gentry who likes a tipple, and a cockney charlady. Florence Desmond played them all! It was an audacious theatrical trick and one she pulled off with style.

Deciding to leave the business on a high, she announced her retirement in 1953 and duly published her memoirs with Harrap & Co., amusingly entitled *Florence Desmond By Herself*. She couldn't keep out of the spotlight for long, however, and triumphantly returned to star opposite Beatrice Lillie in *Auntie Mame*, at the Adelphi Theatre in 1958. Only then did Florence really retire, and happily spent the rest of her days doings bits of show business for famous fans like Derek Nimmo (in *Just a Nimmo*, BBC2, 25 March 1974), going through the old routine for charity events, and recounting the good old days with Denis Norden, and still with a contented smile, on *Looks Familiar* (Thames Television, 20 September 1984). Her last film role had been as the charming Lady Manderley in the psychedelic Bulldog Drummond classic *Some Girls Do* (1969), with Richard Johnson.

It was a role that suited her down to the ground – she had pluck, adventure, romance and fortitude in her spirit. Florence was bewitched by a daredevil.

She was something of a spitfire herself, after all, and she fell in love with aviator Tom Campbell Black. She may have been besotted but wouldn't accept his proposal of marriage until he had piloted the *Grosvenor House* to victory in the London to Melbourne air-race, in October 1934. Speaking at the time, Florence confirmed: 'I wanted to say, "Yes," but I thought it would help him more if I delayed my answer until he won this race.' The couple married in March 1935 but, tragically, Campbell Black died in a ground collision at Speke Airport, Liverpool, in September 1936. The following

The cool way to listen to your 78rpms. Bandleader Henry Hall joins Florence in sampling the brand new gramophone refrigerator from HMV, in March 1934.

year Florence married his friend and fellow aviator Charles Hughesdon, and settled in to life at Dunsborough Park in Ripley, Surrey.

A rare beauty, even in her dotage, on 16 January 1993, Florence Desmond died at the age of eighty-seven, in St Luke's Hospital, Guildford. She was on a ward subsequently renamed after her. Her husband passed away in the summer of 2014, at the age of one hundred and four. Glamorous, romantic and thoroughly bewitching, there is something eternally vivacious and vital about Florence and the era she illuminated. Forever brilliant. Forever in the spotlight. A personality that just seems to make everything seem better, somehow.

TREAT YOURSELF TO *Florence Desmond – Hollywood Party* (Windyridge: VAR66, 2013), which not only showcases Desmond's finest impersonations on such recordings as 'A Hollywood Bridge Game' and 'In Love Again' but that glorious platter of wartime sauce, 'The Deepest Shelter in Town'. Fall in love, with gas mask in hand.

# Jerry Desmonde
# and Eddie Leslie

## 1908–67 and 1903–75

Jerry Desmonde always struck me as an immensely charismatic actor. He was the perfect foil for Norman Wisdom, beautifully playing a high-class gentleman whilst attempting to maintain dignity as Pitkin clung to his trousers with his trademark hysterical laugh. He would often react with an exhale or growl of sheer disdain for Norman's antics before bellowing, 'Get out!' The pair got on famously. When I asked Norman about Jerry, he replied, 'Jerry Desmonde was a smashing bloke and a gentleman. It was marvellous working with him.' *Follow a Star* is one of Jerry's best, playing the ageing crooner Vernon Carew. It allows him ample screen time to play off Norman's shy and inexperienced character, and vice versa. Much like Edward Chapman, he played authority figures brilliantly, clearly pulling on his music hall background when the situation demanded.

As for Eddie Leslie, I found it heartwarming to learn that he had known and worked with Norman since the 1940s. The pair were thick as thieves by the time Rank came knocking on Norman's door. So close was their friendship that Eddie was made godfather to Norman's daughter, Jacqui. Both Nick and Jacqui Wisdom remember Eddie for being a kind-hearted man and a lot of fun, enjoying pool parties at Norman's family home in West Chiltington, Sussex, where Eddie also lived.

I'm glad to see him being remembered.

*Jack Lane, actor and writer of* Wisdom of a Fool

Like any great clown, Norman Wisdom worked tirelessly at his routines and timed every pratfall trip and knowing gurn to perfection. He was also blessed with a fine repertory company of performers who happily took a custard pie in the face, all in the name of quality slapstick. None took the pie with such aplomb as Jerry Desmonde: the finest straight man in the business. Always immaculately dressed, with elegant, greased, wavy hair and the look of an ageing giraffe that can smell rotting foliage, the steely-eyed and unflappable Jerry Desmonde was the perfect foil to the most popular British film comedian of the post-war era.

Born James Robert Sadler, on 20 July 1908, in Linthorpe, Middlesbrough, he had toured Scotland and the North of England with his performing family for many years before joining the family act as Jimmy Sadler, at the age of eleven, to form The Four Sadlers. His forte was song and dance, and indeed, even when plastered in slosh in a Norman Wisdom comedy, there is always the poised air of debonair musical star Jack Buchanan about him – Jack Buchanan with a particularly big chip on his shoulder, but Jack Buchanan nevertheless. This image is further cemented when one considers his 1928–29 tour of America, when he appeared in the popular revue *This Year of Grace*, starring Noël Coward and Beatrice Lillie, no less. Style personified.

In 1934, Desmonde met and married Peggy Duncan and the two formed a dance and comedy double act known, appropriately enough, as Peg and Jerry. They proved popular, particularly north of the border, but Peggy soon retired to start a family (the couple had a son and a daughter), leaving Jerry at something of a loose end. Salvation arrived in early 1940, when he teamed up with knockabout comedian Dave Willis, with Jerry proving the strait-laced, snooty, sophisticated and perpetually petulant straight man stooge.

In 1942 he worked for the first time with Sid Field. It was, and continues to be, one of the most accomplished and influential double acts in comedy history. And it really was a double act: Jerry wasn't simply a foil. Sid Field and the audience knew that Jerry's dry commentary on the madcap antics of his bumbling chum were instrumental to the laughs. He was the wry, knowing, slightly contemptuous representative of the audience, and the scarce and sacred remnants of filmed material of the team together are comic artefacts of the highest importance, the Dead Sea Scrolls of variety.

Jerry's high-profile moonlighting with Frankie Howerd in *Out of This World* at the London Palladium in 1948 notwithstanding, the team of Field and Desmonde were together pretty much continually from 1942 until Sid's untimely death in 1950. The smash-hit revue *Strike a New Note*, at the Prince of Wales Theatre in 1943, was the one that made Sid Field an 'overnight' star after years on the regional variety circuit, and Jerry Desmonde continued to lend the buffoon his unique touch of class.

A further stage revue, *Strike It Again,* back at the Prince of Wales, in 1944, was another huge success, and the duo's popularity reached such a height that they were invited to perform their golfing sketch for the Royal Command Performance held at the London Coliseum on Bonfire Night 1945, the first since the start of the Second World War. In 1946, Field and Desmonde starred in another West End hit revue at the Prince of Wales, *Piccadilly Hayride*, performing its 'Snooker' sketch at the London Palladium for the Royal Command Performance on 4 November. As on the golf course, Field was the novice and Desmonde was the old hand.

The same year saw the release of *London Town*, the much-maligned, commercially disastrous film that is, regardless, a historically crucial film record of their partnership. Thanks to all the Hollywood glamour, Technicolor and backstage panache that Hollywood director Wesley Ruggles could muster on a Pinewood Studios sound stage, the film conjures up a charming glimpse of what life might have been like at the Prince of Wales Theatre. It certainly preserves three landmark sketches that would have gone the way of all flesh without it.

The list of comedians these sketches inspired is practically limitless. Most immediately, they included Tony Hancock, Dick Emery, Tommy Cooper, Benny Hill and Eric Morecambe. Be it the golfer or the spiv, the effeminate photographer or the embodiment of the nerve-racked comedian within Field's autobiographic performance, this is the stuff that variety dreams are made of. Throughout, Jerry Desmonde is the consummate professional. His barked annoyance and withering glances are always on the money,

Jerry as Augustus Freeman, with Norman Wisdom in *Trouble in Store*, 1953.

nowhere more so than when aimed at Field's dunderhead golfer. Ridiculous exchanges like 'Address the ball...': 'Dear ball!' have passed into legend. And quite rightly too. They are beyond funny. They are the Bayeux Tapestry of comedy.

The regret for the partnership was the way it ended. It was all rather sad. With the failure of glossy *London Town* swept under the carpet, Pinewood Studios threw Field into a historical costume romp with Margaret Lockwood. *Cardboard Cavalier,* released in March 1949, is a kind of 'Carry On Gainsborough', a decade before there could have been such a thing, with Jerry Desmonde as Colonel Lovelace, once more dogged and dignified as the authoritative counterpoint to the clownish Field.

In 1950, Field and Desmonde were reunited on the stage of the Prince of Wales Theatre, this time not in a revue but in the subtle comedy of alcoholic manifestations, *Harvey*. Field, by now a hopeless alcoholic himself, was a shoo-in for the dipsomaniac dreamer Elwood P. Dowd. Desmonde's role was the ineffectual voice of reason. Reassuring, really.

In the fifteen or so years that followed, Desmonde flirted and fooled with some of the best comics in the business, memorably teaming up for a short time with rubber-limbed Nat Jackley [qv]. As early as 1951, Desmonde was also providing straight man support for Arthur Askey, in BBC Television's *Starlight: Arthur Askey*, broadcast live from the Radio Show at Earls Court, followed by a closing-night spectacular for the annual trade show, *Holiday Camp*. From 1956, Desmonde became a regular part of Arthur Askey's team for the Associated-Rediffusion sketch comedy *Before Your Very Eyes*. In the early 1950s Jerry even proved an endearing foil to Bob Hope on radio (*The Bob Hope Show*, NBC, 1951–53), and in 1963 he appeared alongside Bud Flanagan and the occasional Crazy Gang guest-star in the ATV series *Bud*. Jerry's film roles ranged from the effortless: as sex-starved actor Martin Paul, opposite Helping Hand Joan Sims, in *Carry On Regardless* (1961), to the downright bizarre: as the Great Galaxian in the Kenneth Connor sci-fi comedy musical *Gonks Go Beat* (1964). Jerry even took on blackface, to play the Grand Vizier in the *Coronation Street* universe, Arthur Lowe sitcom *Pardon the Expression* episode 'A Sheik in the Night' (Granada Television, 18 April 1966).

However, it was Norman Wisdom with whom Desmonde secured his most long-lasting and most productive comedy partnership. Although Edward Chapman's five appearances with Wisdom overshadow Desmonde in memorability (after all, no one could forget the recipient of that screamed 'Mr Grimsdale!'), unlike Chapman, Jerry Desmonde was there from the start of Wisdom's film stardom. In the very first scene of *Trouble in Store*, Norman's first starring vehicle for the Rank Organisation in 1953, Desmonde, typically snooty and sophisticated, is stuck in his chauffeur-driven Rolls-Royce behind a traffic light hanging on red. Norman, the lowly employee of Desmonde's grand department store, appears to be sitting next to him; in fact, he's on his bicycle, stationed alongside. Desmonde is not amused; Norman's hand is clutching the side of his vehicle. He swipes at it with his glove. Norman instinctively moves it. Swipe. Move. Swipe. Move. It is a thing of slapstick beauty, timed to the split second. It was an old gag even then, but it proved an irresistible introduction of Norman the 'Gump'; the cap-wearing, eager-to-please simpleton. The star's comic value had been a gamble on the part of the Rank Organisation, and many within it were sceptical it would be a success. Wisdom respected his stooge's work with Sid Field, and valued his presence in the film. Jerry Desmonde would be a lucky talisman, for there would follow another six feature film collaborations, as well as two stage ventures at the London Palladium in the 1950s – *The 1954 Gay Palladium Show* and *Painting the Town*. He also played Sir Francis Chesney in Wisdom's variation on *Charley's Aunt*, called *Where's Charley?*, at the Palace Theatre, from February 1958.

Desmonde's contribution to the Wisdom films could last a matter of moments and be uncredited, as in *Just My Luck* (1957). Still, it is pleasing that his last Wisdom role, and indeed his last feature film of any kind, was *The Early Bird*, released in November 1965, in which Desmonde is given due respect and a glorious exit as the typically pompous Mr Hunter, whose house, car and little bit of forever-England is mercilessly put to the sword by the hapless antics of Norman's Pitkin. It's a bright and breezy satire of the little man taking on the mighty conglomerate, and it is a delight to see Desmonde – older and more world-weary now, but still in prime comic condition – giving those dismayed and dishevelled looks for one last time.

It was also the last on-screen contribution to the Wisdom legacy by long-time cohort and master of the sight-gag Eddie Leslie. If Norman Wisdom was the single most popular screen comedian in post-war Britain, then Eddie Leslie was his shadow. Though he bearly receives a footnote in the history of the Wisdom comedies and is rarely mentioned in documentaries, it's fair to say that the Wisdom persona recognisable throughout great chunks of the civilised world would never have developed in the way it did without Eddie Leslie.

Born Frederick Edward Leslie Whittaker on 11 October 1903, in Camberwell, South London, Leslie met Wisdom early on when the two appeared on the same variety bill. Theirs was an immediate friendship, from the instant comedy chemistry of opposites attract: Wisdom the eager-to-please, overly enthused little man; Leslie the scowling, wearisome cynic. Leslie had the look that spoke of years of graft and maybe, just maybe, a little time at His Majesty's pleasure. He was the tired, frustrated and just plain angry underbelly of the working-class chirpiness embodied in Wisdom's persona, and Wisdom was all the funnier because of it.

When The Rank Organisation set its sights on making Wisdom a star, Eddie Leslie was very much part of the package. He secured a writing credit on *Trouble*

Wisdom, practising his golf during the filming of *The Early Bird*, 1965. The caddy, a step or two behind, is Leslie.

*in Store* (1953) and, crucially, he is the reliable stooge in Wisdom's most natural and naturally funny scene in the film. It's a tense scene, heightened by Leslie's performance. He looks like a heavy from a gangster picture. The perfect foil, as our hapless hero is force-fed knockout drops. Norman protests that he can't swallow pills; Leslie doesn't believe him. A glass of water, even a ham sandwich, nothing can ease that pill down the Wisdom gullet. It is rehearsed to perfection. They must have been subconsciously rehearsing it for years, just for this occasion. It's a stage routine that's beautifully resurrected lock, stock and barrel for the big screen, and Leslie's ever-growing disbelief gives Wisdom the comic confidence to soar with the idea and milk every last laugh out of the routine. It's quite simply breathtaking teamwork.

Unsurprisingly, Leslie found himself on the writing staff (both credited and uncredited) of the Wisdom comedies up to and including his departure from the Rank Organisation, with *Press for Time*, in 1966. On television, too, Leslie crafted routines and sketches for his partner, starting with *The Norman Wisdom Show,* a 60 minute comedy spectacular in February 1952, also aiding and abetting on the small-screen pantomime *Robinson Crusoe*, in 1964.

Eddie Leslie excelled in several other on-screen supporting roles in the Wisdom comedies, notably as the petulant medical officer in surely the funniest and most polished of the lot, *The Square Peg* (1959). Those halcyon days of the late 1950s also saw him play bully boy Max in *Up in the World* (1956), the gas man in *Just My Luck* (1957), and Harold Franklin in *Follow a Star* (1959). So loyal was Leslie that he even stuck around for an uncredited cough as the piccolo-player in *A Stitch in Time* (1963) – Wisdom's biggest box-office success – and another uncredited spit as Slater in *The Early Bird* (1965).

Leslie did work with other comedians, of course, but not that often. There was the matey role of Bert in the Freddie Frinton–Thora Hird sitcom *Meet the Wife* ('Coming Home', BBC1, 28 April 1964). He was the mayor in the 1959 small-screen panto *Mother Goose*, supporting Frankie Howerd, and in 1961 he was back for more television panto, as the baron opposite broker's men Jimmy

Norman and Eddie are here to tell you that *The Norman Wisdom Collection* is a knock-out!

Jewel and Ben Warriss, in *Cinderella*. He played the stage manager in five episodes of the Jimmy Clitheroe series *Call Boy* in 1957, and flexed his more serious acting muscles as the regular character of Wally Farnes in the first series of *Taxi!* (BBC Television, 1963), starring Sid James.

But it was Norman Wisdom who defined him. It was a partnership of completely unequal standing, but if Leslie ever minded it didn't get mentioned, and it certainly didn't show. He was the perfect comic's foil: unassuming, focused, and absolutely on the money at all times. He was the yin to Wisdom's yang; the countermelody; the cement that kept the whole wonky wall standing.

Hugh Stewart, Wisdom's long-time and very indulgent producer, remembered actively adding bits and pieces to certain films just to have the excuse to employ Jerry Desmonde and to keep the lead comedian focused and entertained during breaks in filming on set. Eddie Leslie needed no such favour. He had the ear of the star, and the star knew he was essential. Here's a thoroughly deserved pat on the back to Jerry Desmonde and Eddie Leslie: the very lucky mascots of British cinema's most commercially successful star comedian.

TREAT YOURSELF TO *The Norman Wisdom Collection* (ITV Studios Home Entertainment: 3711529483, 2008), a complete collection of the box-office smashing comedy films from the Rank Organisation. The inspiration and influence of Jerry Desmonde and Eddie Leslie is all over it like a benign Banquo's ghost.

# Maidie Dickson

## 1922–2010

Chic was the best, and he couldn't have done it without his doll.

*Sir Billy Connolly CBE*

It is as the power behind the throne of one of the greatest of all comedians, Chic Murray, that Maidie Dickson has her footnote in history. But she was so much more than just 'the small doll' to his 'tall droll'.

Maidie Dickson made her stage debut at the age of four. She recalled years later that 'I went onstage for a show at Leith Hospital and wouldn't stop singing – they had to carry me off. It felt great to hear the applause and I knew I had to be a performer.' As a child she became an accomplished buck dancer (naturally in blackface as it originated from African slaves in North Carolina) but, with her pronounced lisp, her singing was even more endearing, particularly in audience favourite 'Walkin' My Baby Back Home'.

By the age of six she had added accordion-playing to her list of stage skills, learning her craft by performing alongside the finest names in Scottish entertainment, and none finer than celebrated comedian Will Fyffe. The two performed on the same bill in Burntisland, Fife, in 1933, and Fyffe was so impressed that he presented her with a ten-bob note signed 'To a very clever wee lassie. Yours aye, Will Fyffe.' It is testament to how important this gift was to the Scots lass that she treasured it for the rest of her life.

But even more life-changing was Maidie's booking on the variety bill at the Greenock Empire in 1944. Her digs for the night were at the home of Isabella Murray and her gangly son, Charles – it was Charles the musician in those days, not yet Chic the comedian, playing with amateur group The Whinhillbillies and, latterly, Chic and His Chicks.

Maidie was clearly taken with Chic from that first meeting – she often said it was 'love at first night'. It clearly was, for the couple married in St Giles's Cathedral just a year later and, although she was firmly established as a solo attraction, she gladly began giving Chic small parts within her popular stage act.

She supported her husband's local gigs, but increasingly noted that it was his relaxed, laid-back comedy patter in-between the songs that seemed to most delight the audiences. Insisting that he leave his 'proper' employment – in the Greenock shipyards – and concentrate on show business full-time, Maidie formed a comedy double act with Chic.

A year after their marriage, the couple had a son, Douglas, and later a daughter, Annabelle, and Maidie juggled stage and home commitments. She studied and moulded Chic's comedic delivery, encouraging him to talk more precisely and pause between words to maximise opportunities for laughter; she even wrote down his material and inserted the occasional 'Ha ha' of encouragement where she knew he could wait for an extra laugh. To her horror, Chic actually vocalised the 'Ha ha' – and got a huge laugh for it. The gimmick remained in the act. By such accident, genius is born.

Maidie was very much the initiator of ideas and bookings, honing the couple's cross-talk music hall turn to perfection. Not only was it verbally dexterous; visually it was comedy gold, with Chic towering over his four-foot-eleven-inch partner. The team topped variety bills and became regular guests on television. Under the auspices of agent Billy Marsh and the Bernard Delfont

Organisation, they toured the whole of the United Kingdom, incorporating a major West End success at the Prince of Wales Theatre.

By 1956 Chic and Maidie, as they were known, were popular enough to be invited to appear in the Royal Variety Performance at the London Palladium. Frustratingly, the Suez Crisis reared its ugly head at the most inopportune moment and led to the cancellation of the show. Maidie, for one, long nursed bitterness at missing their chance to hit the very top. Still, the team were not disheartened. They were already variety and pantomime legends in Scotland. Dickson knew 'we were part of something unique in theatre history'.

But their success was not to last. Under the pressures of both touring and raising a family, the act broke up and, in the sixties, Chic flourished as a solo stand-up comic. He would become one of the greatest comics of all time, adored by his audiences and respected by his peers: being named The Comedian's Comedian in 2005. Chic, alas, did not live to see the accolade. He remained friends with Maidie after their professional and domestic break-up, but Maidie retired completely from show business and turned the Edinburgh family home they had once shared into a hotel. At the end of January 1985, Chic made the journey to see his ex-wife and valued friend. Arriving in Edinburgh much later than planned, in the wee, small hours of the morning, he opted to stay with friends next door rather than disturb Maidie's sleep. He never woke from his own sleep that night. Maidie later reflected that: 'I felt very sad. It was worse knowing he was just next door.'

In the years after Chic's death, Maidie kept the hotel and his memory thriving, often reminiscing about the couple's shared success in the limelight over a dram or two with guests in the bar, whose walls were festooned with playbills. With her children, Maidie founded Chic Murray Enterprises Limited to preserve the genius of her late husband in releases of script books, and CDs of his routines.

At the time of Maidie's death, Chic's daughter, Annabelle Meredith, touchingly reflected: 'The Small Doll has joined the Tall Droll. Maidie was one of the greatest gals, with the biggest heart, variety theatre has ever seen. She paved the way for so many other artists.'

Indeed, as a pioneering female comic and music hall entrepreneur, Maidie Dickson more than held her own in a male-dominated industry. More importantly, she nurtured the fledgling talent of one of the true giants of comedy. So, always remember: there would categorically not have been a Chic Murray without his Maidie Dickson. For that, she deserves all our thanks and respect. Here's tae ye, Maidie!

TREAT YOURSELF TO *Chic Murray – A World of His Own* (Universal: B00004R74Z, 1999). You'll have to dust off your old VHS player for this long out-of-print gem, but it's a comedy essential: a brief but concise collection of the great Scot featuring both archive footage and interview soundbites from the ever-loyal Maidie, still keeping a canny custodian's eye on the old flame.

Chic and Maidie: The Tall Droll with his Small Doll, off-stage and happy in each other's company, 1968.

# Charlie Drake

## 1925–2006

It was quite amazing for me because it was well known in the business that Charlie Drake was not an easy person to work with, but we instantly clicked. From the moment Jim Davidson brought him over and introduced me as 'Prince Charming'; Charlie Drake just smiled and said, 'Hello Pwrince!' and that was it. Maybe it was because I was from that tradition of repertory theatre and respecting your peers. I was certainly in awe of him. When I was younger he was a big, big star.

All through rehearsals of *Sinderella* we got on really well, so Jim asked me if I could look after Charlie on tour. He did get a bit confused, but everything was provided for him. Jim made sure there was a television in his dressing room so he could watch the show and wait for his cue. While he did that, he chain-smoked and drank a lot, so it was also down to me to make sure he was there for his first entrance. As soon as he was on he would be fine, but different theatres could confuse him. I remember one matinee in Cambridge: I walked him onto the stage and said, 'Have a great show,' and he replied, 'Will do, Pwrince!' and promptly walked out of the fire door and into the flower market outside! He was wandering round the market dressed as Baron Hardon and all the stall-owners were shouting: 'Oi, Charlie! You're in the wrong place here, mate!' Meanwhile Jim was frantically ad-libbing. Eventually Charlie found the front of the theatre and, typical of him, asked the prettiest usherette how the hell he could get to the stage. He walked up the aisle with this beautiful girl on his arm and Jim made great comedy out of it all until Charlie got back to the script! Anyway, he did the scene, came off, and got confused again. He got lost in the scenery and was making false entrances for the whole matinee. It was hilarious.

We were all in awe of his stage presence and Jim never, ever tried to top him. Charlie stole the show anyway, but we all had tremendous affection for him. All his suggestions were listened to because he had so much experience.

He finished up in Brinsworth House, with 'Fluff' Freeman on one side and Richard O'Sullivan on the other (I would visit them) because they were all great mates. Charles was wired up to all sorts of medical paraphernalia but still telling jokes. Bless him: he would forget the tag – he would even forget he had started telling the joke – but he had had a tremendous life. We would reminisce about *Sinderella*. It was so special for me, and it was very clever to cast him. He bought in to it, like we all did. In the end, you're just telling the story. It didn't enter your head that it was smut until you stopped to think what you were saying, but we were all laughing too much to do that!

Charlie Drake was a small man with gigantic charisma, and he was absolutely brilliant at what he did. Looking back, that was a lovely last job for him. He would laugh more than any of us, and he was spoiled rotten. I've done some pantomimes where the old pro was not so good any more and was given a few bits as the king, and treated very shabbily by the management. Not Charlie Drake. He finished in a production with the total respect of everybody involved and everybody out front in the audience. I'm very proud to have been a part of that, and I'm very proud to be Charlie's champion for this book.

*Jess Conrad OBE*

Sid James was a consummate professional. He loved acting but always saw it as a means to an end. He would learn the lines, gets the laughs, and get home to his family. Ideally, with the minimum of fuss. However, in the late sixties, during rehearsals for a recording of his popular ATV sitcom *George and the Dragon*, a certain vital prop was missing. It was missing on the next run-through too. Enough was enough – Sid pulled himself up to his full height and screamed at the crew: 'Do I have to behave like Charlie Drake in order to get anything done around here?' It spoke volumes. In the business in the 1960s, the name of the diminutive and very successful Charlie Drake was easy shorthand for how *not* to behave.

Outside of the business, it was a totally different matter, of course. During the 1950s and 1960s, Charlie Drake was arguably the nation's best-loved comedian. By 1968 Drake's big-screen comedies were already notorious as some of the most expensive in British film history, while his television work was securing him an international reputation.

Not too bad for a hustler from The Elephant and Castle, for that's what young Charles Edward Springall was. His father was a newspaper-seller with a profitable sideline in placing illegal bets, and for Charlie the ducking-and-diving existence of a street trader came as second nature. Always something of a pipsqueak, Drake explained, 'I was raised on condensed milk!' He also had a pugnacious attitude, determined to get to the top. At just eight years old he queued for hours for the opportunity to audition for the great music hall comedian Harry Champion. Rather cheekily, the young 'un sang 'Boiled Beef and Carrots', which Champion had made famous, and wangled himself a place in the chorus for the star turn's closing number, 'Any Old Iron'. It was a week-long engagement advertised by the South London Press. Charlie pocketed 7/6d.

It was an inauspicious start but a start none the less, and he soon negotiated a deal with the manager of the local picture palace. If Charlie won the top, ten-shilling prize for every amateur talent show, Charlie would in turn give the manager half. During the Second World War he had been a messenger boy for Air Raid Precautions and a baker in a NAAFI. His small stature had seen him rejected by the navy but the Royal Air Force took him on and trained him up as a rear gunner. Typically, Drake saw the war as a potential leg up on the show business ladder, but even the infamous, influential RAF Gang Shows eluded him.

After the war, he formed a double act with his friend Sidney Cant. They performed their act, featuring a spirited rendition of 'A Bird in a Gilded Cage', at their local pub, the King's Arms. They were given the bird, and not asked back. Drake's audition for the BBC *Workers' Playtime* proved equally dispiriting. Hoping for a comedy spot on the popular variety showcase, Drake performed thirty minutes of his best material. In a premise that would later inspire his befuddled 'little man' persona, Drake was in the wrong studio. The radio producer never saw the

Charlie starred as wannabe playwright Percy Pointer in his fourth and final feature film for the Associated British Picture Corporation.

audition, and Drake failed. A change of style, from just jokes to observational comedy, and a change of name, to Charlie Smart, saw Drake finally get a foot on the ladder of variety bills, as well as radio broadcasts. But alas, he was pointedly informed that there was an organist by the name of Charlie Smart already on the airwaves, so it was back to square one.

The 'Drake' moniker, then, was a keeper, but the clown himself was still at rock bottom. He failed an audition with the Windmill Theatre, and after becoming a Butlin's Redcoat in 1953, he was dismissed after just one season – by the great Billy Butlin himself; Drake had been accused of light-fingered shenanigans with the bingo money. It was this cavalier attitude to pretty much everything that would shade his entire life. Interestingly, though nothing was formally discussed, Drake was writer David Croft's first choice to play the holiday-camp big cheese Joe Maplin in *Hi-de-Hi!*, if that character had ever appeared. He never did, but what perfect casting that would have been.

Disappointment and hardship formed the bedrock of Drake's comedy. He had left both school and home at fourteen, and gone through a quick-fire rotation of jobs starting with a position as an electrician's mate. This scattergun employment would provide invaluable anecdotal reference for his greatest comedy triumphs. They all seized on the simple but effective format of the square peg in a round hole. Most notable was, of course, *The Worker*, his long-running ATV sitcom that, from the first broadcast on 27 February 1965 cast him opposite, originally, the long-suffering Percy Herbert as beleaguered employment agent and fall guy Mr Whittaker and then, from 2 October 1965 and on into the seventies, opposite the long-suffering Henry McGee as beleaguered employment agent and fall guy Mr Pugh. Every week a different job; every week relentless, hilarious, meticulously rehearsed slapstick that, with a pleading glance and a winning grin, effortlessly endeared the audience to Drake's day-to-day foibles.

The premise itself had been used for Charlie's first major television success. Theatrical agent Phyllis Rounce had teamed him with an old Royal Air Force chum, lofty Northern Irish stooge Jack Edwardes, and the new double act proved a hit on children's television – so much so that when BBC department boss Michael Westmore decamped to Associated-Rediffusion, he took Drake and Edwardes with him. With a change of name to Mick and Montmorency, the popular double act headlined *Jobstoppers*. It proved a staple of commercial television practically from its inception in September 1955, which heralded the eternal Drake catchphrase: 'Hello, my darlings!' The success of the series even resulted in their own *TV Fun* comic strip.

Moreover, Ronnie Waldman at the BBC determined to tempt them back. *Laughter in Store* was broadcast on 3 January 1957, with *Drake's Progress* coming that May, much to Drake's smug satisfaction. By this stage, Jack Edwardes had been unceremoniously elbowed out of the equation as Drake determined to become a star. A year or so later, the experienced scriptwriters Sid Green and Dick Hills were similarly dismissed when Drake himself insisted on writing the show.

The 1960s was undoubtedly Drake's decade, when he became something of a multimedia icon. He made the first of nine Royal Variety Performance appearances, and his comedy singles were chart-busters. 'My Boomerang Won't Come Back', produced by comedy-record guru George Martin, no less, reached no. 14 in the charts in October 1961 and became a top favourite with children. Moreover, 'Splish Splash', having made the Top Ten in 1958, was still a genuinely funny rock 'n' roll reworking of the original. (Indeed, years later, on Drake's second *This Is Your Life*, in 1995, theatrical impresario Bill Kenwright maintained it was better than the Bobby Darin version!)

Typically, the British film industry now sat up and took notice, with experienced comedy director and Norman Wisdom's original collaborator John Paddy Carstairs handling Drake's first starring vehicle, *Sands of the Desert* (1960). For a few glorious years, Drake's cinematic outings were the most lavish, elephantine and just plain expensive-looking films for any British comedian. Ever. Peppered with big-name guest-stars and in Cinemascope and full Technicolor when even the all-conquering Norman Wisdom was retained in black and white, films like *Petticoat Pirates* (1961) and *The Cracksman* (1963) were relentless and exhausting to watch. But, boy, were they funny. Very, very funny.

Drake's film popularity coincided with his huge success on BBC Television. *The Charlie Drake Show* ran for three series from November 1960 and cast our hapless hero in a series of self-contained parodies, often putting him slap bang in the middle of a murder-mystery or espionage plot. The title, if not the format, was deployed again at the end of 1967 when the star comic returned to the corporation for a series of 45-minute sketch-based spectaculars. Super-stooge Henry McGee was recruited as his chief cohort, and these BBC2 programmes in full colour remain arguably Drake's most ambitious and evocative television work, showcasing just what a fine comedy performer he could be with a producer as skilled as Ernest Maxin at the wheel. Drake indulged in pathos, of course, but these sketches also showed him as a brilliant mime artiste, physical clown and refreshing exponent of slapstick. There is one extraordinary sequence which has Drake play the conductor and every member of a concert orchestra in a performance of the 1812 Overture. It is exquisite. Little wonder then that it was included in the thirty-five minute compilation, *The World of Charlie Drake* (BBC2, 14 April 1968), that won the Golden Rose of Montreux that year.

However, an attempt at a more pathos-driven television series, and accompanying plaintive single release, 'Who is Sylvia?', on the Pye Records label in 1967, saw the rot set in. Charlie had made a mark the previous year as Joey in an *Armchair Theatre* play 'The Battersea Miracle' (ABC Television, 26 March 1966), but audiences didn't want Charlie to be serious. They wanted him stepping into

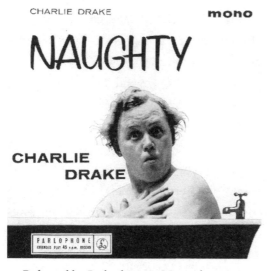

Released by Parlophone in November 1960, this EP also includes 'Starkie Starkie', 'Old Mr Shadow' and 'Google Eye Ghee'.

cement and falling off ladders. To that end, his greatest success of the 1970s was a revival of *The Worker*. The show's old home, ATV, had brought *The Worker* back for a year, from 29 December 1969, with Henry McGee still in tow. The cherry on the top was a sketch within the *All-Star Comedy Carnival*, on Christmas Day 1970. Then, from 7 October 1978, Drake and McGee were back. Within the Saturday evening spectacular of *Bruce Forsyth's Big Night*, London Weekend Television presented tasty fifteen-minute chunks of *The Worker*, the last as part of that year's *Bruce Forsyth's Christmas Eve*.

Still, despite this renewed interest, by the mid 1970s Drake's film appearances had dwindled to the self-scripted Children's Film Foundation serial *Professor Popper's Problems* (1974).

Onstage he was facing personal problems too. A regular star of television pantomime in the late 1950s, he had made his stage panto debut in 1958, in *Sleeping Beauty* at the London Palladium. The cast had included television headliners Bruce Forsyth and Bernard Bresslaw, but Drake demanded, and got, the number-one dressing room nonetheless. His obstinance would remain for nearly twenty years. Working his way through the country, and through myriad chorus girls – who would be callously dismissed and replaced if not wholly accepting of Drake's advances – things came to a head at the Alhambra Theatre in Bradford, in 1974. Drake had insisted that a certain local girl should have a featured role. She wasn't a performer, just a friend of the star comic – and the star comic was used to getting his own way. Not this time, though. Equity stepped in and not only quashed the idea but fined and banned Drake from regional theatre for twelve months. He never got over his anger.

Although he determinedly returned to the venue, to play Buttons in *Cinderella* for the 1977–78 season, pantomime ultimately became a dirty word for him – and that word was *Sinderella* (with the emphasis on 'sin'), in 1995. Eagerly joining Jim Davidson's adults-only touring panto company, Drake returned to the pun-cracking, girl-chasing role of Baron Hardon as late as 2004, for the even dirtier *Sinderella Comes Again*.

Drake had continued to display his slapstick expertise, notably for Eric Sykes's majestic, almost-mute comedies for Thames Television *The Plank* (17 December 1979), *Rhubarb Rhubarb!* (15 December 1980) and *Mr H is Late* (15 February 1988). Even more impressive was Charlie's belated re-dabble in more dramatic fare. His performance as Davies in Harold Pinter's *The Caretaker*, at the Royal Exchange, Manchester, in 1983, won him plaudits and respect. On television he played Smallweed in the 1985 BBC adaptation of Charles Dickens's *Bleak House*, and made for an unforgettable Nagg in Tony Coe's 1989 presentation of Samuel Beckett's *Endgame*.

In September 1991 Drake starred as a rather seedy old man on the lookout for a young wife in the *Screen One* single drama 'Filipina Dreamgirls'. (In reality, his two marriages, both to chorus girls, had ended in divorce.) One of his final television appearances was in 1992 when Michael Aspel hosted LWT's *The Trouble with the Fifties*, which was ironic for several reasons, not least because the anecdote discussed with Drake was from 1961. It involved a clip that was the stuff of television legend at the time. In 'Bingo Madness', an episode from *The Charlie Drake Show* that prematurely curtailed the series mid-run, one live television stunt called for Drake to be thrown through a bookcase, then through a window and, ultimately, through a door. Needless to say, something went horribly wrong and Drake was in a coma and hospitalised as a result.

*The Trouble with the Fifties* interview saw Drake at his most relaxed and likeable; it was a petulant, arrogant and self-satisfied likability, but he was likeable none the less. Urged by Aspel to relate the story, Drake insists that he can't: 'I was unconscious at the time!' he explains, with perfectly straight face.

He suffered health issues for the last decade of his life and found final solace in the variety-performers' home Brinsworth House, in Twickenham. I remember

Hello, my darlings! The Little Man comic persona that saw him at his peak in the early sixties.

seeing him several times, always sitting at the bar scowling. It was Mr Drake to strangers; Charles to those lucky enough to be in his inner sanctum; and never, ever Charlie. Those who did address him that way got a stare to make Paddington Bear grovel. He died two days shy of Christmas 2006.

Like the cliché, this man who could make us cry with laughter cut a rather sad figure, never quite at peace with himself or the world. It's heartbreaking, really, for during those halcyon moments in the 1960s he was truly one of the greatest there has ever been. His legacy should be celebrated.

TREAT YOURSELF TO *The Worker – The Complete Series* (Network: BoooNDETTC, 2007). A veritable slapstick smorgasbord, the five-DVD set also laudably features what's left of Drake's vignettes on *Bruce Forsyth's Big Night*. Essential remnants.

# Jimmy Edwards

## 1920–88

Television didn't arrive at Baker Towers until 1953 (we had to see the coronation, like everybody else), so the radio played a huge part in my childhood, and Sundays were by far the best day. The Home Service provided us with the most wonderful Sunday afternoons, with *Life with the Lyons* (and if you had told me that Ben Lyon would be my first agent I would have thought you were mad), *Educating Archie*, *Ray's A Laugh* and, at teatime, *Take It from Here* – with Dick Bentley, Joy Nichols and the wonderful, larger-than-life, hyper-moustachioed Jimmy Edwards. Part of the programme included a regular item featuring The Glums, when Pa Glum, played by Edwards, invariably interrupted his courting daughter and her boyfriend with what became one of his booming catchphrases: ''Allo, 'allo, 'allo!'

The man himself was larger than life, and so were his characters. Well worth a play on Radio 4 Extra – please! Playing Professor James Edwards in *Whack-O!* on television, he was the antithesis of all that should be considered headmasterly. Fond of a tipple, bombastic and charmingly corrupt, he schemed and bamboozled his staff, including the wonderfully put-upon Pettigrew, played by Arthur Howard.

The moustache was a huge part of who he was. When he applied for his first job at the infamous Windmill theatre, he was told to keep it, as it was 'the only funny thing about his act'. I loved the fact that he was such a huge, irrepressible character, always. Lurking beneath the surface was mischief and mayhem – very attractive to the schoolboy-me (and his glory days of *Take It from Here* precisely occupied my school years). His booming tones provided a glimpse of another, funnier world, of naughtiness, when I was living in a world where that was frowned upon.

The success of *Big Bad Mouse* – as a result of his and Eric Sykes's decision to 'have a bit of fun' with the play when it received bad reviews and was failing – is a testament to his innate ability as a performer and comedian. It then ran for years.

An early product of Cambridge Footlights, he was an accomplished musician, using the trombone to great comic effect many times, and he even stood for Parliament – sadly unsuccessfully, or perhaps it was just as well. Gerald Nabarro MP had a bigger moustache.

*Colin Baker*

One particular drunken weekend with my Sussex-based pal, Rick Blackman, in the 1990s, turned into something of a comedy pilgrimage for us two relatively young chaps with a healthy devotion to variety comedians. Rick had told me that when Jimmy Edwards found his fame slipping, he went into semi-retirement and moved to his brother's farm down in Fletching in the beautiful South Downs. Rick also told me how the larger-than-life Edwards had loved a pint or three in the village's Rose and Crown pub, with its rustic charm. Indeed, Jim loved a pint so much that by the end of his life he had become nuisance enough for the landlord to bar him from the premises.

Both Rick and I felt affronted by this and needed to pay our tribute to the great man in the best way possible – by having a pint in the very pub Edwards had been barred from. Then we had a silly wheeze. When the barman called time, we ordered three pints of ale.

Now, it's hardly unusual for drinkers to get an extra one or two in just under the bell. Still, one of these pints was not meant for us. Once we'd drunk our own respective pints, I smuggled the full, foaming third out

Tony Hancock and Joan Turner clowning with the 'Professor' in his dressing room for *The Talk of the Town*, 1954.

under my coat. The Fletching graveyard is just across the road from the pub, and there we found our man: 'In Memory of James Keith O'Neill Edwards, D.F.C., M.A., M.E.H., "Professor Jimmy", 1920–88, of Atheralls Farm.' Respectfully I poured the pint over Edwards's final resting place and stood the empty glass up by his grave. It was one in the eye for that barman of years past, and one final pint for the 'Professor' to enjoy.

Although the 'Professor' may have been a stage affectation, the Distinguished Flying Cross was not. A war hero of the highest order, Edwards joined the Royal Air Force hotfoot from graduating from St John's College, Cambridge (during which time he wrote a witty serial of *Adventures for Professor Thronkinspoop* in the university newspaper). While flying a Dakota over Arnhem in 1944, he was shot down by enemy fire. He suffered substantial facial wounds and was subjected to experimental plastic surgery at Queen Victoria Hospital, East Grinstead. As a result, he became a member of the Guinea Pig Club, along with other such heroes, the institution having been founded as a drinking club to help the patients regain their confidence. The club's anthem contained the line: 'we'd rather drink than fight...' Amen to that.

The most life-changing effect of this plastic surgery, however, was the impressive handlebar moustache Edwards grew to conceal his unsightly scars. The moustache would become his trademark, bristling with each off-colour quip and flaring with each sip of brown ale. The opening line of his memoir,

*Six of the Best* (Robson Books, 1984), states: 'I embarked on this story a couple of years ago and had spent the advance royalties before I had written many chapters...'

Pretty much exactly the same offstage as he was on, he was a devoted supporter of fox hunting and would don hunting pink whenever out in the hills and downs of Sussex. He was also a lifelong true blue, and even stood – unsuccessfully – to be the member of parliament for Paddington North in the 1964 general election. The personal detail that perhaps most surprised his admirers was that his decade-long marriage to Valerie Seymour was in effect a smokescreen to conceal his homosexuality. (When the marriage ended, in 1969, he was attached to singer Joan Savage, but the union led to nothing.) Although the revelation, in the early 1970s, angered Edwards, it had little effect on his career or standing in the profession. Illegal no longer, it was simply the truth.

There is a pleasing, full-circle quality to the forty-year comedy career of Jimmy Edwards. Immediately after the Second World War he took to variety and became one of the greatest names in the history of the Windmill Theatre. A tubby, distinguished and rather fruity comic presence, he retained the air of an RAF officer throughout his life, and was rarely onstage without his trusted trombone. While Harry Secombe had his shaving brush and Michael Bentine had his chair-back, Edwards effortlessly brought his instrument to life in a routine that displayed both his musical and juggling skills. It was his comedy stooge. Playing it, dismantling it, and abusing it, were turned into comedy gold. His final television appearance, on 28 December 1987, when Jimmy performed his trusted old routine on *Wogan's Radio Fun*, was a masterly, chest-puffing last stand.

His connection with the Windmill Theatre had led to his first brush with cinema, an admittedly ramshackle, but historically important, little comedy thriller called *Murder at the Windmill* (1949). In my youthful innocence I had always imagined this might deal with a killer who bashed people over the head with a bag of flour, but it was even more exciting than that: a post-war glimpse into the legendary theatre that 'never closed' during the Blitz, and a snippet of the fledgling variety turn of Jimmy Edwards. It is gold dust. Val Guest's script and direction has the quality of someone knowing it's all fairly lacklustre but is laudably bestowing a preservation order at the same time.

Edwards would never become a major force in British film but he chalked up some very good ones, including the 1952 romp *Treasure Hunt*, a trombone-blowing cameo in the wacky creature feature *An Alligator Named Daisy* (1955), and a frightfully British interlude in the multi-story *Innocents in Paris* (1953) in which he plays experienced continental traveller Captain George Stilton, who, having boasted of his Parisian knowledge to gormless airport chum Frank Muir, spends the entire weekend drinking pale ale and playing darts in a perfectly reconstructed English village pub right in the heart of 'Gay Paree'.

His hale-and-hearty, never-trust-Johnny-Foreigner persona was resurrected lock, stock and barrel for by far his finest film, Ken Annakin's *Three Men in a Boat* (1956) a beautifully coloured, elegantly written adaptation of the immortal comic tale by Jerome K. Jerome. Edwards stars alongside Laurence Harvey and David Tomlinson, and it's all soggy flannels and cricket whites, boozy lunches and wide-eyed debutantes, the perfect encapsulation of the fun, foibles and follies of Edwardian life, Jimmy style. In fact, it's a crime still unsolved why it failed so miserably at the box office and has been pretty much universally panned ever since.

Edwards certainly didn't worry. By the late 1950s he was one of the country's best-loved and busiest comedians, thanks in the main to his sterling work with writers Frank Muir and Denis Norden. Their radio comedy *Take It from Here* was a long-running and influential collection of songs, sketches and outrageous puns. Broadcast from 12 March 1948 and quickly shortened to *TIFH* (pronounced 'Tife' by radio announcer David Dunhill), it ran to an unlucky thirteen series, ending at the very dawn of the sixties. A love for words and history informed the programme and some of the best-known and oft-quoted jokes of all time have their parentage within its scripts, not least the 'Infamy! Infamy!' line from *Carry On Cleo* (1964). In terms of the career of Jimmy Edwards, the most lasting element of *Take It from Here* was The Glums. A sort of Giles cartoon made flesh, the series of radio vignettes cast him opposite Dick Bentley, as his slow-witted son Ron, and June Whitfield, who had joined the team when Joy Nichols had left just as Colin Baker got his first television role in June 1953, as Ron's pert, high-pitched fiancée, Eth. So popular and culturally embedded were these characters that in the late 1970s they were added to the

A slapstick kiss to his RAF past as Group Captain Kingsley in *Nearly a Nasty Accident*, directed by Don Chaffey, for a May 1961 release.

nostalgic mix of *Bruce Forsyth's Big Night* (London Weekend Television, 1978), just as Charlie Drake had been. The little insights into the life of The Glums, still reassuringly rooted in the 1950s, led to a full-blown series for London Weekend Television in 1979. Edwards, and writers Muir and Norden were the established bedrock, while Ian Lavender and Patricia Brake were brought in as the not-so-bright young things. It was nostalgic, hilarious, and utterly, utterly charming.

Muir and Norden had also created Edwards's other long-lasting persona, that of the deliciously cynical, hip-flask-concealing, cane-wielding portly headmaster of public school Chiselbury. The vehicle for this character, *Whack-O!*, was a monumentally popular and pioneering television situation comedy which ran from 4 October 1956 to 27 December 1960. The vaults of the BBC alas have very little left as a record, but the character lingered on, appearing in a feature-film version, *Bottoms Up* , released in March 1960, just ahead of the sixth series on television. A thirteen week colour resurrection on BBC1 and now styled *Whacko!* (without the hypen!), began on 27 November 1971. The essence of the character – a self-centred, carefree bounder in a position of authority – suited Edwards down to the ground. His relish can be detected in every curl of his moustache and every whack of willow on schoolboy shorts. 'Bend over, Wendover!' became a familiar cry in every playground across the country. There was even not one but two board games based on the show: Chiselbury Capers and Whack-O!.

Edwards's BBC television career went from strength to strength with *The Seven Faces of Jim* (1961), *Six More Faces of Jim* (1962) and *More Faces of Jim* (1963), which indulged him in self-contained adventures from the boundless imagination of *TIFH*'s Muir and Norden, and blessed him with peerless support from June Whitfield and Ronnie Barker. At the start of 1969 Edwards moved over to London Weekend Television and away from this anthology format to play James Fossett, a devious writer of 'penny dreadfuls', in *The Fossett Saga*. Scripted by Dave Freeman, and featuring omnipresent actor Sam Kydd as Herbert Quince, this Victorian romp proved popular, not least because the BBC's epic drama, *The Forsyte Saga*, was enjoying a repeat season at the time!

Edwards had also devised and took a seat on the panel of the radio game *Does the Team Think?*, which started a twenty-year run on 20 October 1957. An all-comedian affair initially hosted by Peter Haigh and, subsequently, McDonald Hobley, the premise was simple: questions were posed by members of the studio audience, and Edwards and his comic chums, including Arthur Askey, Ted Ray, and Tommy Trinder, had to answer. In the funniest way, of course. It subsequently transferred to Thames Television in 1982, where Tim Brooke-Taylor was in the chair, valiantly keeping order over regular players Frankie Howerd, Beryl Reid, Willie Rushton and, of course, Jimmy Edwards.

But it was his long-running and breathtaking collaboration with Eric Sykes that gave Jimmy Edwards probably the most fun of his professional career. He took major roles in *The Plank* (both the 1967 cinema version and the 1979 remake for television) and *Rhubarb* (1969) as well as one of his last assignments, *Mr H Is Late*, broadcast in February 1988, about a troublesome corpse that refuses to stay nailed down and in one place.

Sykes had written and starred in a breakneck, television version of *Charley's Aunt* (Yorkshire Television, 29 December 1977) in which he donned the drag, and Edwards was completely taken in as Stephen Spettigue.

And then there is *Big Bad Mouse*. The 1972 Thames Television screening from the Prince of Wales Theatre can only hint at a smidgen of the chaos of the line fluffs, prop malfunctions and sheer free-falling insanity of the stage production. Nationwide tours, West End success and major excursions throughout the Middle East and Australia (with either Eric Sykes or Roy Castle): all would generally break down into slapstick and shtick. It became the stuff of legend.

Edwards's other stage work could be equally uproarious, including *London Laughs*, a 1951–52 revue with Tony Hancock and Vera Lynn, at the Adelphi

Theatre; *Cinderella*, with Tommy Steele, at the London Coliseum for the 1958–59 season; Mr Bumble in *Oliver!*, with Roy Hudd, at the Theatre Royal, Newcastle, in 1983; and a self-penned farce, *Oh! Sir James!*, with Kenneth Connor, at the Theatre Royal, Brighton, in 1979. The programme notes for the latter explained that it 'was inspired by Jimmy's reluctance to go on paying Author's Royalties to other people, and by the prospect of unlimited champagne to be drunk during the performance. It was written in Perth, Adelaide, Sydney, Honolulu and Solihull.'

Raising the wind throughout his comedy career, from his days at the Windmill Theatre in the late forties.

By the 1980s the round belly had become a solid barrel, the hair had gone save for snow-white side clumps, and the moustache had got bigger and bushier so that it could now comfortably serve as refuge for two owls and a hen, four larks and a wren. Edwards was an old-time character, with a voice echoing with cadged booze, woodbines and those vibrating whiskers; a gentleman, scholar, hero and wit who enriched the culture with the unique sense of a true bon vivant. Here's to the final round.

TREAT YOURSELF TO *The Glums – The Complete Series* (Network: B004W2FZHK, 2011), the bombastic 1970s television comeback for Pa and the family. And yes, the scraps from *Bruce Forsyth's Big Night* are included as an extra tidbit.

# Gus Elen

## 1862–1940

One of the great Edwardian comedians.

*Kenneth Williams*

With a face like patent leather and a voice reminiscent of hobnailed boots tramping through Borough Market, Gus Elen was the 'Famous Coster Comedian', adopting the uniform of striped jersey and skew-whiff peaked cap of the cockney traders, or costermongers, who would peddle fruit and vegetables from their barrows. This earthy comic reality informed his performance, and with a clay pipe as oft as not protruding from his down-turned mouth, Elen was almost a true cockney, being born just out of earshot of the bells of St. Mary-le-Bow, in Pimlico. His background was poor and rough, and his most popular songs reflected this; he had lived the life he sang about.

Elen was no character actor. As a youngster he had busked the streets of London, graduating to his local pubs with impersonations of the stars of the day. Looking back from cosy semi-retirement in the 1930s, he remembered his tough, formative days: 'Years before I entered the ranks of music hall performers proper, I used to contribute to the programmes of the weekly sing-songs held at such places as Poppy Lords in Lisson Grove, the Magpie and Stump, Battersea, or the George Street Recital Hall. At the last-named hall, the salaries ranged from a shilling to three-and-sixpence a night with a cup of coffee and a bun thrown in by way of refreshment. In those days I often filled in a season on the "waxeys" – waxworks exhibitions – at Margate and Ramsgate in a Negro minstrel troupe.'

He eventually found his natural footing at the Old Mo, the Middlesex Music Hall, on Drury Lane, Holborn. Although only in his late twenties, he brought sincerity, with genuine bitterness, to such memorable end of the century numbers as 'If it Wasn't for the 'Ouses in Between' and 'Never Introduce Your Donah to a Pal'. The songs told of the cramped living conditions of the East End and the perils of parading your girlfriend in front of your chums, but although they were steeped in melancholy, Elen's delivery was also one of resigned acceptance. He didn't wallow in the despair of his almost fellow cockney; he simply sang about it from the heart. He could unite a huge crowd with just a few bars of "Arf a Pint of Ale' – a glorious salute to the joys of alcohol at every meal: 'Now for breakfast I never thinks of having tea, I likes me 'arf a pint of ale. For dinner I likes a little bit of meat and 'arf a pint of ale. For tea I likes a little bit of fish and 'arf a pint of ale. And for supper I likes a crust of bread and cheese and a barrel and an 'arf of ale!' Sheer poetry.

One proud Londoner whose family heritage was fermented in the songs of Gus Elen was Kenneth Williams. During the 1983 recording of his memoirs on the BBC Television series *Comic Roots*, Williams recalled: 'My parents spent many happy hours at The Boot [pub] with their friends Alf and Edie Palmer. The Palmers ... would trundle their piano across for an evening in the pub. A song that was a great favourite of my father's was sung by Gus Elen. It was a song that was ... totally on the side of the bloke, and anti-feminine.' And so it was. All of Elen's songs were, none more so than the one Williams gave as an example. The 1895 ditty 'It's A Great Big Shame!' tells the woeful tale of Elen's bruiser of a mate being tamed and domesticated by his diminutive wife: 'He's a brewer's drayman with a leg-of-mutton fist, and as strong as a bullock or a horse. Yet in her hands, he's like a little kid, oh I wish as I could get him a divorce.' Elen's performance would be so impassioned that lyrics such as 'If she belonged to me, I'd let her know who's who!' would be accompanied with raised fists and thrown punches. This was domestic violence as music hall entertainment. Disturbing, though fascinating in context.

His anger would be further emphasised by a swinging of an implement in time to the drumbeats during the number. Indeed, Elen tirelessly made notes on his stage moves and the delivery of certain lines. Each performance would be practically identical to every other and, as a result, he became one of the nation's favourite

"E dunno where E are."

Edwardian postcard featuring Gus in typical Coster Comedian pose.

music hall performers. Audiences would flock to see him perform these most cherished songs, safe in the knowledge that they could not only sing along but pretty much set their watches to Elen's muscle-memory stage business.

Elen topped the bill in theatres for nearly thirty years. He even took his act on tour throughout America and his idiosyncratic cockney was a surprise hit. Vaudeville manager and agent William Morris had spotted Elen on the London stage, and thought him ideal for the American audience. Celebrated turn and chief coster comic rival Albert Chevalier had already paved the way. And Elen was the genuine article. He was so financially successful that when he returned to England he was able to retire from the business, and lived in great comfort in his home in Clapham. As early as 1896 Clapham had been noted as a 'music hall colony' and Elen's property singled out as 'a comfortable little villa backed by a pleasant stretch of greensward, around which one can see evident signs of the owner's taste for animals, gardening, and those healthy pursuits which form an indispensable part of country life'. His great passion was fishing, and 'everything about him suggested the "homely" man; there was neither the suggestion of the "halls" in his manner nor his dress, and the only things likely to strike the observer on a first meeting were his bright, shrewd-looking dark eyes and

YOU HAVE MADE A NICE OLD MESS OF IT

Sung by GUS ELEN

OGDEN'S CIGARETTES

CLASSIC RECORDINGS BY THE GREAT MUSIC HALL ARTIST

A definitive and vibrant celebration of Gus's music hall legacy, Tropic Records, 1979.

a certain resolute expression which indicated that Mr Elen in private life, as on the stage, has a pronounced individuality.'

The stage was in Elen's blood. It could still quicken his pulse. A 1932 Pathé newsreel had reported that 'a striking feature of entertainment today has been the popular revival of old-time songs and melodies' and shown Elen as a force unleashed, the camera capturing him performing some of his best-loved numbers. He returned to wow stage audiences all over again, regularly performing on the London variety circuit throughout the 1930s and being honoured as a special guest in the 1935 Royal Command Performance.

Beloved by children, every Christmas Elen would distribute toys to the poor of Balham, Battersea, Clapham and Wandsworth. (Incidentally, the popular so-called Coster Doll – a jointed, wooden figure that could be made to dance in the hand – was named in tribute to his beloved music hall persona.) When Gus died, on 17 February 1940, there was something akin to national mourning. He was buried in Streatham Park Cemetery. In 1979 a commemorative blue plaque was erected by the Greater London Council on his home at 3 Thurleigh Avenue, Clapham, with the simple inscription 'Gus Elen, Music Hall Comedian, lived here'. He lived on too in the hearts and minds of the people, as one of their own who had made good and enjoyed all he had made. I like to think that, as much as London is built up and knocked down and rebuilt again, you will always be able to see a little bit of Gus Elen in the streets of the capital. If it wasn't for the 'ouses in between...

TREAT YOURSELF TO *You Have Made a Nice Old Mess of It* (Topic Records: 12T396, 1979), a vintage vinyl compilation of fifteen great Gus Elen numbers. The cover is an evocative joy and, believe me, the old boy has never sounded better.

# Ray Ellington

## 1916–85

Our brilliant colour sergeant.

*Spike Milligan KBE*

With a hazy, lazy, beautifully soporific 'That's nice...!', pioneering bandleader and musician of repute Ray Ellington effortlessly left his mark on the history of popular music. He also stamped his name into the fabric of the most surreal wireless success Britain has ever known, *The Goon Show* – a show of its time, and for all time. Outrageous characters and catchphrases had been a staple of BBC Radio's *It's That Man Again* back in the 1940s, but now comedy was tempered by the threat of death and destruction that all the Goon generation had faced a few short years earlier; the stench of conflict still filled the nostrils of the purveyors of this very silly universe of barrack-room badinage and jet-black humour.

But this wildest of airwave parties still required musical breaks to punctuate the comedy. That had been an essential in variety before and during the Second

World War, of course, but, like *The Young Ones* a comedy generation later, *The Goon Show* used music as a vital part of the madness, not as a counterbalance to it.

Ray Ellington's gang of hard-drinking, hard-working musicians fitted the show's style to perfection; they were the house band for the Goons simply because they were hand-picked by the Goons. In terms of his musical experiments, Ray Ellington was as erudite and off-the-wall as Milligan was mentally muddled, which was as often as not.

Ellington was born Henry Pitts Brown in Kennington, London, on 17 March 1916. His mother, Eva Stenkell Rosenthal, was a Russian Jew. His father, Harry Pitts Brown, a successful African-American vaudeville comedian who had travelled to England to make his name. Sadly, the raucous patter of Mr Brown senior was silenced before his son's fifth birthday. Brought up an Orthodox Jew, Ray enjoyed his first taste of acting at the age of twelve. However, he left full-time education at fourteen to become an apprentice cabinet-maker at his uncle's business. But that life was not for him; jazz riffs and roll-ups were the thing, and in 1937 he got his first break into music, replacing drummer Joe Daniels in the Harry Roy Orchestra. Ellington's talent on the skins was indisputable, while his cool and hot jazzy way with a lyric put Roy in mind of Nat King Cole. Indeed, on that very first session with the band, Ellington was given free vocal rein on 'Swing for Sale'. Not bad for the new boy.

Ellington's fledgling success was rudely interrupted by his call-up for duty with the Royal Air Force, in May 1940. Ostensibly employed as a physical training instructor, he inevitably got involved in putting together various RAF bands. Upon demob after the five-year hiatus, Ellington threw himself back into the London jazz scene, his musical melting pot now containing all sorts of styles. For one thing, the war years had certainly opened up his ears to the sounds emanating from America. The pioneering rock 'n' roll 'jump music' of Louis Jordan was a key influence but, equally, folk songs and nursery rhymes became delightful Ellington ear-hauntings and resisted all attempts at exorcism.

Ellington happily shared his talent between several popular British dance bands, including that of Tito Burns, the group's number sadly having been diminished by the recent conflict. Ellington even rejoined Harry Roy for a few months, but his aim was to push forward with his own, unique blend of musical tastes. He teamed up with an established group, the Caribbean Trio, and their outfit became Ray Ellington's loyal band, the established trio being Dick Katz on piano, Coleridge Goode on bass guitar and Lauderic Caton on rhythm guitar. Under Ellington's influence, Caton would revolutionise British jazz and introduce an amplified electric guitar early on in their success.

In *Walking on Air* (1936), the British film jazz showcase directed by Aveling Ginever, at Marylebone Studios.

Debuting together on Sunday, 7 December 1947, the Ray Ellington Quartet were booked to play during bandleader Ted Heath's residency at the London Palladium. A recording contract with Parlophone followed, with stints for Decca and Columbia after that. The choicest cuts from these were collected in the Castle Pulse anthology *Let the Good Times Roll*, and for a definitive taster of Ellington at his purest it is very hard to beat. The Ray Ellington Quartet appeared in films, notably doing his thing in the musical spectacular *Walking on Air* (1946), and Roy Ward Baker's thriller *Paper Orchid* (1949). Riding high in the public eye, Ellington joined forces with Latin American bandleader Edmundo Ros for the March 1954 Light Programme radio show *Mr Ros and Mr Ray*, the script written by Jimmy Grafton.

Cue three ex-servicemen, each already steeped in music, gravitating towards Ellington and his sound: Harry Secombe, a bel canto singer who could belt them from as far back as the Rhondda Valley, was slightly outside Ellington's musical territory, but drummer Peter Sellers and trumpeter Spike Milligan inhabited it for years. Michael Bentine, too, though gone from the Goons team before Ellington's initiation, was on the shared wavelength of belly-laughs and foot-taps.

As leader of the Goon house band, it was also inevitable that Ray Ellington would step away from the rostrum and closer to the BBC microphone. Just as radio announcer Wallace Greenslade became an integral part of the show, so

Newly recorded *Goon Show Hits* issued on the
BBC Records label in 1974.

too did Ray Ellington, right back in 1951 when it was still billed as *Crazy People*. Most often, and predictably, cast as a deep-voiced, stereotypical African native, Ellington could also turn his hand to Arab chieftains, American Indians, furious Scotsmen – and, once, even a sexy female secretary. Brilliantly, all of these were played with the exact same baritone earthiness of Ellington's natural delivery.

I make no apologies for comedy of over half a century ago; Ray Ellington's *Goon Show* performances are beyond racism and beyond sexism. Indeed, they are beyond criticism. They perfectly nailed the Goonish ethos and should be relished for the pure joy they continue to illicit. He cheerfully adopted the Goon mythology that he was originally from Ghana, so this Ghanaian from London Town added unquestionably to the freewheeling fun of the show.

In November 1962, after his *Goon* success, Ellington took musical charge at The Madison, and played the White Elephant Club in Chelsea. He later took a long-term residency at the London Hilton's rooftop restaurant, on Park Lane. What a glorious way to spend some time that must have been. He also added style to such television hits as *The Eric Barker Half-Hour* (BBC Television, 1951–52), *Alfred Marks Time* (Associated-Rediffusion, 1959–60), Tommy Cooper's *Cooperama* (ABC, 18 June 1966) and, of course, *Milligan in...Autumn* on 1 October 1972. Four days on saw the broadcast of the *Last Goon Show Of All* reunion show. Ellington had even cropped up in the 1969 film *The Undertakers*, with Bernard Cribbins as Mr Rigor and Wilfrid Brambell as Mr Mortis. Spike had been in that too. Of course he had!

The groovy Ellington genes were still finger-clicking in his son Lance Ellington who had competed in and won *New Faces* in 1977. He became the voice of the *Strictly Come Dancing* house band, and played Ray himself in *The Life and Death of Peter Sellers* (2004). He's a real chip off of the old block, and no mistake, and in this most touching tribute he injects the perfect note of humour to the Britt Ekland wedding night scene.

It's 1952 and those crazy people Milligan, Secombe, Sellers and Bentine are on the fiddle, with Ray's quartet member, guitarist Lauderic Caton, and unidentified double bassist.

TREAT YOURSELF TO *The Goon Show Compendium Volume Four* (BBC Physical Audio: 9781408410462, 2010), featuring some choice cuts of Ray Ellington, both in song and in character, including a sparkling rendition of 'Who's Got the Money?' and an unforgettable turn as native bearer O'Brien in the episode 'The House of Teeth'. So kick off your shoes, pour yourself a drink, and listen to the unbridled glee of Ray Ellington. You'll cherish the day when you first hear him as Bloodnok's bilious batman, Ellinga, the Major's arch enemy, the Red Bladder, or the gravel-voiced Gladys. It's a sin to tell a lie...

# Dick Emery

## 1915–83

Dick Emery's drag really intrigued me as a young girl. All his characters were so specifically individual but his women were always naughty, barely controlled. And he clearly loved them. They were middle-aged housewives with nylon scarves and unspoken demands. Even his floozies seemed to be the ones mocking the man wielding the microphone. I saw a male fascination with the mystery of femaleness being played out as some kind of art installation. Like those seventies feminist artists who went around in a wig and an entirely constructed persona. His is the only catchphrase I still want to use every day.

*Samira Ahmed*

At first glance, to find Dick Emery residing within these pages seems incongruous indeed. At the peak of his success, his eponymous television series generated a gallery of hilarious characters, while every playground resounded to cries of 'Ooh, you are awful... But I like you.' The tales of many celebrated

comedians in this book stand
testimony to the passage of time
dulling a great career and, even
more so, a lasting legacy. Dick
Emery, however, has had the
occasional documentary and
book in salute. His name still
chimes. But he has fallen foul of
the curse of his era: the seventies
– the decade that taste forgot
and decorum shunned. We are

Lance Percival, Sid James, Sylvia Syms and
Dick, on location at Wormwood Scrubs, for
*The Big Job*, 1965.

told that Emery's comedy is now watched almost from behind one's fingers, if it
is watched at all. A camp, risqué, politically incorrect barrage of sketchy sketches
and one-note characterisations; a stream of comic consciousness that could only
ever exist in the era of flared trousers and glam rock. This is nonsense, of course,
but such labels stick, and they have unfairly stuck to Dick Emery.

I was the perfect laughter fodder for Emery's relentless kaleidoscope of
outrageous humour. I am a child of the seventies and *The Dick Emery Show* was
never short of essential in our house; his death within a year after the conclusion
of *Emery Presents...Legacy of Murder*, and less than a fortnight before the
second batch, *Jack of Diamonds*, was originally due to start transmission on
13 January, was keenly felt by all of us. That dawn of the 1980s that saw great
swathes of comedy heroes cut down way before their time – Marty Feldman,
Tommy Cooper, Eric Morecambe: Dick Emery was very much in their rank. He
was part of the family.

He was also part of that family of comedians, including Hancock and the
Goons, that burst from the blood, sweat and tears of the Second World War into
a brave new Britain of the National Health Service and a healthy disregard for
authority. This was an age where anything could go. The essence of the Ralph
Reader RAF Gang Shows concert party, on which Emery cut his comedic teeth,
was suitably cast off like an ill-fitting demob suit. But he was always more at
ease onstage – when in drag, in any case. It was during the conflict that the
'forces' sweetheart' Vera Thin – a less than subtle nod to Vera Lynn – was born,

Presenting his best-loved TV characters at the ABC Theatre, Blackpool, for the 1976 summer season.

and the glitz and glamour of sequins and high heels fired Emery's comic imagination for the rest of his days.

It was gleefully ironic, therefore, that it was a return to military uniform, for *The Army Game*, that first made Emery a star of television. He had honed his gift for impersonation and near-the-knuckle tomfoolery at the usual places: onstage at the Windmill Theatre, and on radio's *Workers' Playtime*. But as far as television viewers were concerned, *The Army Game*, was the tops. By the time Dick Emery joined the gang from September 1960, original star William Hartnell had headlined, left in a huff, and returned once more to the khaki chaos.

Emery's slightly effete Private 'Chubby' Catchpole – aided and abetted by blistering scripts from Marty Feldman and Barry Took – gave birth to the cry of 'Hello, Honky Tonks!' that would become legendary. If it hadn't had been for all that earlier wallowing with the likes of Sellers and Milligan, it could be argued that *The Army Game* shaped his whole comic personality.

Dick Emery, like Kenneth Connor, was something of an also-Goon in the late 1950s. His comedy style perfectly slotted in to the established disestablishment of the radio series, not to mention the most delicious slice of Goonery ever filmed, *The Case of the Mukkinesse Battle-Horn* (1956). My absolute passion for this film is widely known. One of the truly great short comedies, as a twenty-year-old curio of joy it was picked up by the Pythons as the supporting film for *Monty Python and the Holy Grail* (1975), and its irregular television exposure in the 1980s bewitched my comedy senses. I devoured it. The scene that Emery's museum curator shares with detectives Sellers and Milligan is sheer perfection. Moreover, Emery's beleaguered, doggedly cheerful, fourth-wall-breaking cameo as Maurice Ponk was a sequence that could reduce me to near-hysteria. It still has the power to leave me quite literally breathless with laughter. Comedy that can nearly kill you is to be celebrated indeed.

Finally getting his own BBC Television series, *The Dick Emery Show*, first broadcast from 13 July 1963, the star found his happy place in a gloriously silly world of sketch comedy. Emery's chief writers David Cumming, Eric Davidson, Peter Robinson, John Singer, and John Warren wrote superbly to his strengths as a character comedian. Week in, week out, over an incredible eighteen years, Emery's show was a children's comic come to life for all the family. We always expected, wanted, and got those beloved characters: Clarence the effeminate sauce-pot; College the educated tramp; Hetty the bespectacled spinster; Lampwick the befuddled pensioner; Mandy the peroxide tease... *Ooh... You Are Awful* (1972) was a feature film outing for this gallery of characters and, as conman Charlie Tully, it allowed Emery to expose the method behind the make-up. Despite a release in America, as *Get Charlie Tully*, the film's disappointing box office receipts curtailed Emery's advanced plans for his production company to remake *Kind Hearts and Coronets*. Emery was to star in the Alec Guinness roles. Intriguing! Although many may know of Dick Emery, most don't really know him at all. He was a carnivalesque character. A larger-than-life performer who lived life large. The gadgets, gimmicks, fast cars and fast ladies superficially cast him as an ersatz Peter Sellers. Indeed, when Steve Coogan was compared to Sellers, he modestly refused such an accolade and declared himself more like a modern-day Dick Emery. A backhanded compliment, maybe, but a compliment none the less, for – putting the questionable depiction of race, sexuality and gender to one side (as one has to for much 1970s comedy) – the bare-bones comedic skill of Emery is extraordinary. He deserves to swim free of the rock pool of misunderstanding and reluctant tolerance. He is much, much more than a questionable footnote in comedy history. He is one of the titans.

TREAT YOURSELF TO some vintage vinyl with *Dick Emery Sings* (Pye Records: NSPL 18411, 1973), a collection of original numbers providing a stage for Emery's community of perfect comic creations. Gems include his toothy man-of-the-cloth singing 'The Vicar of Belching-by-the-Sea' and a poignant, straight performance on 'I've Got to Make Them Laugh'. (And he did.) The last track on the album, the desire within its title serving both as Dick Emery's mantra and epitaph.

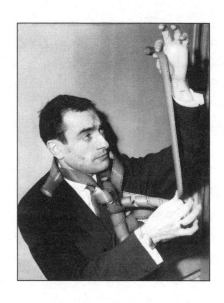

# Pierre Étaix

## 1928–2016

In 2010 I spent a glorious week in Bologna at Il Cinema Ritrovato experiencing the delights of their screenings of newly restored classic films, and it was at that festival that I first discovered the genius clowning of Pierre Étaix.

Completely unknown to me previously, it was a screening of his 1962 masterpiece short film *Heureux Anniversaire/Happy Birthday* in the large, outdoor piazza that first delighted and charmed me. I mean: 'Who is this extraordinary performer? And why haven't I heard of him?' The film was full of surprises and absurdist humour, masterful clowning at the level of – yes, I will say it – Buster Keaton and Jacques Tati.

Following this we watched every film we could that had Étaix's name on it: *Le Soupirant/The Suitor*, *Yoyo* and the extraordinary and beautifully observed, much underrated, *Le Grand Amour/The Great Love*.

Determined to champion this unsung hero of visual comedy and master of clowning, we were delighted when he accepted our invitation to receive the Aardman Slapstick award for excellence in visual comedy, in 2012. At the Slapstick Festival in Bristol he appeared onstage at Colston Hall following a screening of *Heureux Anniversaire* to rousing applause from a 1,500-strong audience, and seemed as delighted and charmed by this audience that was only just now discovering him as he was by the award, presented the next day.

It was a privilege to have the opportunity to meet and to work with him in this way. He was truly modest, gentle and wonderfully mischievous – exactly as you would hope he would be. A true genius of the screen.

*Chris Daniels, Director, Slapstick Festival*

Pierre Étaix is as near as you can get to a true forgotten genius of comedy, with his tale perhaps the most frustrating of them all.

Born in Roanne, France, on 23 November 1928, Étaix graduated from magazine illustrator to cabaret and music hall performer, taking the stage in such high-class Parisian venues as Le Théâtre des Deux Anes and Le Crazy Horse. Under the tutelage of circus performer extraordinaire Nino, the young Étaix tuned his athletic feats to the comedic act. In 1954 he met a genius. A genius of comedy and of film-making. That genius was Jacques Tati. Eventually Étaix worked as his assistant on the masterwork *Mon Oncle/My Uncle* (1958), writing sight gags, designing sets and even creating the poster for the film. The influence of the great Tati was to leave a clear and lasting impression on Étaix's own oeuvre. As he told the *Los Angeles Times*: 'Not having any idea of cinematic language before then, I learned everything from Tati.' Moreover, the slapstick style of the great silent clowns Chaplin, Keaton, Lloyd and Langdon merged with his own unsentimental physicality to make him arguably the last of the great film slapstick artists.

Throughout the 1960s, Étaix directed a string of hugely successful short subject and feature films – including *Heureux Anniversaire/Happy Anniversary* (1962), which won the Oscar for Best Short Subject, and his own personal favourite, *Yoyo* (1965). The film cast him as both a billionaire father and his independently wealthy idler son who loses everything on the

Forcing a happy moment, *The Suitor*, 1962.

stock market and finds true happiness by running away with the circus. It was definitive Étaix: beautifully shot and elegantly funny with a key awareness of its cinematic roots. As was often the case, the script benefited hugely from a collaboration with Jean-Claude Carrière, while Claudine Auger provided perfect support as the lowly love of his life. The film was a contender at that year's Cannes Film Festival.

Étaix's directorial career came to a rather abrupt end with the documentary *Pays de Cocagne/Land of Milk and Honey* (1971), which examined the state of French society and the thoughts of its people through candid, *vox populi* interviews. Never downhearted, he embraced his passion for circus by founding the National Circus School with his wife Annie Fratellini and subsequently spent much of the 1970s touring.

That other master comedy film-maker Jerry Lewis had once remarked that he grasped the meaning of the word genius only twice in his life: the first when he looked it up in the dictionary, the second when he met Pierre Étaix, casting him in his notoriously unreleased *The Day the Clown Cried*, in 1972. Étaix would crop up in other people's films for the rest of his days, notably Philip Kaufman's *Henry & June* (1990) and Otar Iosseliani's *Chant d'Hiver/Winter Song* (2015).

Tragically, his own films had been forgotten in a vault for a lifetime due to a petty dispute over legal ownership with his distribution company. It wasn't until 2009 that the situation was resolved and work commenced on a definitive release of his greatest films both as director and star. Joyously, he lived long enough to see the project released to wild enthusiasm, and to receive several plaudits and honours for his truly unique contribution to slapstick comedy. His work was celebrated with a *Vive Pierre Étaix!* season at the Festival Lumière in Lyons, and the Film Forum in New York showcased a retrospective. He even made the trip to Bristol to accept his Aardman Slapstick Visual Comedy Award for lifetime achievement. A master of his art who languished far too long in the shadows, Pierre Étaix is now, quite rightly, discussed alongside the true greats of film comedy.

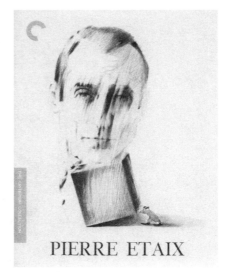

PIERRE ÉTAIX

TREAT YOURSELF TO that long-awaited, beautifully packaged presentation of Pierre Étaix's finest film work (Criterion Collection: B00B2BYYiM, 2013), even if only for the beautifully imaginative

The stunning inner sleeve of the Pierre Étaix Criterion Collection release, overseen and fully approved by the comic genius film-maker.

travelling-bed dream sequence in his first colour film, *Le Grand Amour/ The Great Love*. It is a vital record of an unfairly neglected comedy film-maker, now rightly re-evaluated. Vive Pierre Étaix, indeed!

Honoured with the suitably attired Morph in a Glass Dome: the Aardman Slapstick Visual Comedy Award recipient, in January 2012.

# Barry Evans

## 1943–97

Barry was a complicated man but his life was his own and he lived it the way he wanted to. Working with Barry was a dream as he was a 'giving' actor. He was a perfectionist in his work. The one thing that Barry wanted was to be taken seriously in his work; that is why theatre work was so important to him. He hated being admired for his looks but loved being admired for his work. So he should have!

I loved Barry because he was a truly good, honest friend who would tell you the truth whether you liked it or not. I appreciated his candour, and I salute his comedic timing.

*Françoise Pascal*

From his inauspicious beginnings, as a foundling on the streets of Guildford, Surrey, to his tragic death after an evening's shift as a minicab driver around the streets of Claybrooke Magna, Leicestershire, the life of Barry Evans has an air of intriguing mystery about it.

A Barnardo's boy, an early desire to become an actor was encouraged by the organisation, which helpfully arranged a drama school audition that ultimately led to two years with the National Theatre. A painfully beautiful young man and an actor of deep intensity, Evans first came to prominence as Jamie McGregor in Clive Donner's pivotal, controversial, groundbreaking and very Sixties film *Here We Go Round the Mulberry Bush* (1968). It was an exciting and career-defining role, subsequently elevated to 'Cool Britannia' status by its convention-twisting approach to sex and the potent soundtrack from the Spencer Davis Group and the band Traffic. A close friendship with the director saw Evans give a performance that is both naive and knowing.

Donner and Evans, cast as Ingild, would quickly reunite for the historical epic *Alfred the Great* (1969). However, a fledgling film career was soon curtailed when a lucrative and irresistible offer came from London Weekend Television. It was turning Richard Gordon's extraordinarily funny *Doctor* books into a television series and saw its perfect lead actor in the gauche, uneasy but always likeable Barry Evans. Although actually far too old for medical school, Evans's eternally youthful features easily masked that anachronism and, from its first episode, 'Why Do You Want to be a Doctor?', on 12 July 1969, *Doctor in the House* proved an instant success for Frank Muir's beans-on-toast sitcom initiative. The popular *Doctor* film series may have been on the wane, but television could capitalise on the student-doctor boozing, rugby-playing and nurse-chasing for the home audience instead. The antics of Dirk Bogarde and Donald Sinden had been raucous, of course, but they very much reeked of the austerity and politeness of 1950s Britain. Following the Sixties' revolution, it was not only acceptable to discuss sex and debauchery – it was practically compulsory! Barry Evans is the clear benefactor of Bogarde's mild-mannered and nervy leading role, for while the other cast members energetically drool over scantily clad nurses, throw themselves into student shenanigans and drink for England, Barry was usually sitting, quiet and studious, cramming for forthcoming exams. It was a perfect sitcom vehicle for him.

The success was almost too much for him, though. Having starred in all twenty-six episodes of *Doctor in the House* he was reluctant to do more. Eventually he relented and took on a further run as Mike Upton, in *Doctor at*

In the *Doctor in the House* writers' room in 1969, with Graham Chapman, Richard Gordon, John Cleese, Graeme Garden, Barry Cryer and Bill Oddie.

*Large*, from February 1971, but it was a stethoscope too far and after a brief sketch in *Mike and Bernie Winters' All-Star Christmas Comedy Carnival* that year Evans determined to mothball his white coat. The various *Doctor* series would run and run, however, with stars Geoffrey Davies, George Layton and Robin Nedwell returning to their medical roles. Indeed, even as late as 1977 they showed no signs of slowing down, and in a poignant *TV Times* interview Evans admitted that he had been 'incredibly stupid' not to stay with the show, that spring having realised a second series of *Doctor On the Go*. He would return to the franchise in the seventies, however, touring *Doctor in Love* across Canada with his old telly colleagues Geoffrey Davies and Ernest Clark, and wearily agreeing to take on the old Dirk Bogarde film role of Dr Simon Sparrow, for a bottom-of-the-bill special-guest role with his fading *Doctor* marquee value, opposite Jimmy Edwards as Sir Lancelot Spratt, in a 1977 UK tour of *Doctor in the House*. Evans was even persuaded to star in the rather hilarious but still, for him, rather desperate sex comedy *Under the Doctor* (1976), which naturally exploited his association with the *Doctor* comedies.

He had clearly signed up for the plastic-mac brigade, having starred as Joe North in *Adventures of a Taxi Driver* (1976), the first of a trio of film rivals to the *Confessions* series from producer Stanley Long. Barry Evans wouldn't return for the other two. He didn't need to.

The aforementioned *TV Times* interview had him grudgingly admit that he had been forced to join the dole queue. The ordeal had been too much and, swallowing his pride, he had gone cap in hand to London Weekend Television and begged for a job. The job offered came from that masterful scriptwriter Vince Powell [qv], who saw in Evans the perfect, loveable authority figure for his new series set in a school that taught English as a foreign language. Premiering at the end of December 1977, *Mind Your Language* was the hit series that Evans desperately needed, and his subtle, gentle, understanding delivery made his character, Jeremy Brown, the perfect foil for the flamboyant misunderstandings that surrounded him.

As with much of Vince Powell's television work, the show is often dismissed as xenophobic or even racist, but it was the ludicrous nature of the English language that was the real

Having a ball with Françoise Pascal at a London Weekend Television press junket for *Mind Your Language*, 1977.

joke, and nations across the globe – notably those represented by the students struggling with verbs and pronouns on screen – lapped up the series. Twenty-nine episodes were chalked up by the end of the 1970s, and an eager Evans returned to the series, under the production of Powell and cast member Albert Moses, for thirteen more episodes, in 1986. These did not prove a success, with its old home of LWT even refusing to broadcast the series, but Barry was desperate to work again. The roles had dried up to a trickle, and only an enjoyable comic detective partnership with Dick Emery on *Emery Presents...Legacy of Murder* (BBC1, 1982) had briefly brought him back into the limelight.

A victim of his youthful looks, he was by now too old to be comfortable in juvenile leads but far too fresh-faced for casting directors to assign him more mature roles. The decline and fall was a lingering and painful one, with ambitions to secure a regular role in *EastEnders* or indeed anything, repeatedly thwarted. The bitterest pill to swallow was that the phone remained silent when the BBC chose to pick up the *Doctor* franchise for the spring 1991 season. Davies, Layton and Nedwell were back in harness, and even an ailing Ernest Clarke returned as Sir Geoffrey Loftus. Apart from a flippant mention in the opening episode of *Doctor at the Top*, alleging that Dr Mike Upton had

A high-profile guest spot, as Simon Sparrow, in the autumn 1977 regional tour of *Doctor in the House*, along with fellow Forgotten Heroes Jimmy Edwards and Hugh Lloyd.

had an affair with the wife of Nedwell's Dr Waring character, there wasn't a sniff for Evans.

His final acting role came as Bazzard in the April 1993 A&E presentation of Charles Dickens's *The Mystery of Edwin Drood*. An adaptation of a famously unfinished novel was rather apt, for even now there is something not quite resolved about the life and work of Barry Evans. He fluttered through the insanity of this business with a fragile grace. What he left behind is something to cherish.

Treat yourself to *Doctor at Large – The Complete Series* (Network: B000NDETT2, 2007), with Barry's Mike Upton freshly graduated and taking centre stage. Actively told not to play it funny, his performance is even more joyous for his ongoing mild panic and frustration in response to a catalogue of misadventures. As one of the scriptwriters, John Cleese was actually castigated for writing deliberately funny dialogue for the actor; he simply didn't need it. This collection includes both series across four DVDs, including the black and white episodes resourcefully recorded during the ITV technical strike; 'No Ill Feeling!', from May 1971, Cleese's embryonic *Fawlty Towers* with a frantic and poignant turn from Roy Kinnear; and some lovely material from Graham Chapman and Graeme Garden – quite literally script doctors – revolving around father and daughter Arthur Lowe and Madeline Smith. It'll do you the world of good. Doctor's orders!

# Mario Fabrizi

## 1924–63

Dear old Mario. He tried and tried but he never quite became the star he should have become. Top bloke!

*Harry Fowler MBE*

Born in Holborn, on 25 June 1924, and of proud and obvious Italian descent, Mario Edgio Pantaleone Fabrizi has one of the shortest yet most vibrant British film-and-television-comedy CVs to be found within these pages. With his distinctive waxed moustache and slicked-back hair, he cut an impressive figure, and even in the smallest of supporting roles always stole the scene.

His screen persona was of the East End barrow boy or cunning spiv. His eyes always seemed to be on the lookout for the next sucker or the nearest policeman, his suits were as sharp as his tongue, and he could fleece or flaunt opposite the greatest comedy actors in the business.

Peter Sellers was besotted with Fabrizi and yearned to utilise his comic charms at every opportunity, including the fledgling attempts to transfer Goon humour

With Tony Hancock and Kevin Brennan in
*The Punch and Judy Man*, 1963.

to television, such as *Son of Fred* (Associated-Rediffusion, 1956) and *The April 8th Show (Seven Days Early)*, transmitted on BBC Television, April Fools Day 1958. And it was opposite Sellers that Fabrizi made his first feature film appearance (uncredited), as a wildly enthused fan of Sonny MacGregor in Mario Zampi's jet-black comedy *The Naked Truth* (1957). Fabrizi was even better, though still uncredited, as Deputy Minister of Gaillardia in *Carlton-Browne of the F.O.* (1959). It was almost inevitable that he would join other Sellers satellites Graham Stark and David Lodge to throw himself energetically into Richard Lester's sublimely surreal, Oscar-nominated short *The Running Jumping & Standing Still Film* (1959), and he was awarded an actual character name, Jones the van driver, although still uncredited, in the prison comedy *Two-Way Stretch* (1960)

Indeed he became such a vital member of the Goon repertory company, and an instant signifier for the hip and happening comedy of surrealism, that it was only natural that others would snap up the bizarre, other-worldly figure of Mario Fabrizi. He supported Benny Hill in the 1958 run of *The Benny Hill Show* for BBC Television, as well as Eric Sykes and Hattie Jacques in *Sykes and a Movie Camera* (BBC Television, 11 August 1960). He would rejoin Sykes in the big-budget British MGM comedy romance *Village of Daughters* (1962), filmed in Sicily and displaying a gentle calm lacking in much of Fabrizi's other work. He was perfectly cast as Antonio Durigo and frolicked with almost every other professional foreigner in British film at the time – from Harold Kasket and Roger Delgado to Eric Pohlmann and Grégoire Aslan.

But it was the Granada situation comedy *The Army Game* that levitated Fabrizi to near-stardom. Cast in the second phase of the series – after the initial, square-bashing days of William Hartnell, Michael Medwin, Bernard Bresslaw and Charles Hawtrey – Fabrizi was recruited to play Corporal

'Moosh' Merryweather in the fourth series, from October 1959. The wheeler-dealer, ne'er-do-well, crafty fixer of Hut 29, he struck up a firm friendship – both on- and off-screen – with Harry Fowler, who had replaced the faux cockney Medwin with some real clout. The chemistry of Fowler and Fabrizi gave the series the desired kick up the khaki it required and allowed it to march on way beyond the

Mario Fabrizi and Harry Fowler display the catalogue number for their HMV single release of 'Buddies', 1961.

abolition of national service in Britain. The Fowler and Fabrizi partnership also delivered a His Master's Voice single release of 'Buddies', in July 1961.

Professionally secure and enjoying the money that the regular television employment offered him, Mario had married beauty expert Katherine Boyne on 28 May 1960. The following June the couple welcomed a son, Franciso Anthony.

If *The Army Game* had improved Fabrizi's bank balance, then it was *Hancock's Half Hour* that had heightened his prestige. From August 1956 to November 1959 he appeared in twenty-two episodes of the BBC Television series, playing everything from a Viking to a tree-hugger for hire; he was the dogged tray-snatcher in 'The Economy Drive' (25 September 1959), the juror who goes bonkers in the 'Twelve Angry Men' episode (16 October 1959), and, perhaps most memorable of all, washed the very shirt off of his back in 'The Big Night' (6 November 1959). During those happy *Hancock* repeats of the 1980s, Nick Kamen in the Levi's 501 adverts certainly had nothing to worry about. In fact, in a cheeky reference to bodybuilder Mickey Hargitay, Hancock spies Fabrizi's near-skeletal frame, nudges Sid James and mutters: 'Jayne Mansfield's old man!' Always the same – emaciated, moustachioed and rather world-weary – Fabrizi could pop up for just a few moments and lift the whole show.

More importantly, Fabrizi was an actor who could lift the spirits of Hancock, and thus lift Hancock's performance. Having people of the calibre of Mario Fabrizi was key to Hancock's comedic ease, and he proved something of a pit prop when he made just one appearance in Hancock's ill-fated but really rather good series for ATV. 'The Assistant', broadcast in Janaury 1963, was the very first episode of *Hancock* and saw the star incredulous, as always, as a shop assistant challenged to work for one week without arguing with a customer. This was made all the harder for being forced into the Uncle Bunny rabbit suit. Fabrizi has great fun as the cheery predecessor of the furry costume.

Fabrizi was also cast in Hancock's major big-screen outings, memorably as the not-so-continental attendant of a Soho coffee bar in *The Rebel* (1961) and as the anxious beach photographer Nevil Shanks in *The Punch and Judy Man* (1963). The film was still on general release when Fabrizi collapsed and died at his London home on 6 April 1963. He was just thirty-eight. A week before his death he had officially announced his retirement from acting; disgruntled at not having worked for four weeks, he'd intended to join a firm selling television advertisement slots. His actors' agent later said: 'He was a man loved by everybody, and the sad thing about his death is that his last part – and his best part – was in Tony Hancock's latest film, *The Punch and Judy Man*. In that, he had virtually a star part and he was absolutely marvellous.'

He had also recently wrapped on several other important films, including one of his finest, *The Mouse on the Moon* (1963), in which he performs the wordless, prat-falling and gentle pantomime of Mario, valet to Ron Moody's scheming prime minister. And he had, once again, proved himself something of a talisman to Peter Sellers when he was cast (uncredited) as the hotel manager in *The Pink Panther* – the last role he played. The film was finally released in January 1964, almost a full year after his death. It is practically a given that Sellers would have persuaded director Blake Edwards to find a place for Mario in the sequel, *A Shot in the Dark* (1964), thus rejoining Graham Stark and David Lodge on the friendly Sellers gravy train.

There could have been even more regular employment in another comedy franchise where Fabrizi had only recently left his mark. As one of the ship's cooks, alongside Anthony Sagar, in *Carry On Cruising* (1962), he turned the stomach and repelled the taste buds of chef Lance Percival. The next film, *Carry On Cabby* (1963), had just started production at the time of Mario's death, but as a reliable and recognisable comedy character actor he was undoubtedly in director Gerald Thomas's keepnet.

Having hung onto the hems of comedy greatness in Hancock, Sellers, Milligan, Sykes et al, Mario

He has his father's moustache! Mario, at home with his five-month-old son, Franciso Anthony, in November 1961.

had proved himself more than just a stooge. His performances, while ostensibly the same, were layered with bitterness, cunning and pathos. With a stroke of that trademark moustache or a roll of those hound-dog eyes, he could turn the comic tension of a scene up to eleven. That was the gift that he gave in his all-too-short life. And he keeps on giving.

TREAT YOURSELF TO *The Army Game Collection* (Network: B001B8CBNY, 2008). With 1,250 minutes of classic comedy from the earliest days of commercial television, this essential release showcases a glut of our forgotten heroes, including great swathes of the unsung and sainted Mario – peerless stuff from this prince of the bit part.

# Doug Fisher

## 1941–2000

Doug was fabulous. He had a wicked sense of humour. He was also very well read; he spoke about four languages.

We especially had fun when we were soaked for the *Man About the House* movie. Richard O'Sullivan personally asked if he could soak us and I think he enjoyed it... Cheeky! Doug was very chivalrous and hugged me to keep warm – obviously it didn't work as he was as wet as me!

I miss him and think he would have gone to the top in his career.

*Sally Thomsett*

Every classic situation comedy had the archetypal bloke. Either as a leading character or a supporting 'King Leer', there was always some randy, smirking, tousle-haired, tight-trousered lad, a beer in one hand and a bird in the other. Undoubtedly the most unsung and joyous of these was Doug Fisher. As Larry Simmonds in *Man About the House* (Thames Television, 1973–76), he longed for the great good fortune of his best mate, Robin Tripp, played by Richard

O'Sullivan (in an even tighter pair of trousers), who was rooming with two lovely ladies. This was the situation from which the majority of the comedy derived. Doug, never without a quip, a cheeky grin and a knowing wink, could only wistfully look on while the star of the show juggled life, love and limited funds alongside the ample charms of Paula Wilcox's Chrissy and Sally Thomsett's Jo.

Richard O'Sullivan inventing the Ice Bucket Challenge forty years early, drenching Doug Fisher and Sally Thomsett during the making of the *Man About the House* film, Elstree Studios, 1974.

Still, although he notched up only brief appearances in only half the episodes, Doug Fisher's character was an effortlessly winning one, played with the care and devotion of an actor who could have, and perhaps, should have, been doing silly things with Monty Python at the time. But he wasn't. He was dishing out lounge-lizard corn on ITV. And doing it brilliantly.

Fisher read French and Russian at Oxford, where his contemporaries included Terry Jones and Michael Palin. Indeed, the three wrote and performed *The Oxford Revue* of 1964. Fisher, who also directed the production, took it to the Edinburgh Festival, where its air of surrealism – notably the sketches 'Song About a Toad' and 'I've Invented a Long-Range Telescope' – won it great acclaim.

Terry Jones remembered Doug as 'a very good friend of mine at Oxford. He was also a very good person to be onstage with, and we were onstage a lot at university. He was so funny – far, far funnier than I could ever be. He would often leave me crying with laughter. If life had been kinder, he would have done lots more than he did.'

*The Oxford Revue* proved popular enough for a London transfer to The Establishment nightclub in Greek Street. Like many of his Oxbridge contemporaries his studies didn't signpost his career path. 'They didn't offer me a job spying in Europe,' Fisher quipped, 'so I went into television instead.' Through the 1960s he chalked up appearances on *Not So Much a Programme, More a Way of Life* (BBC1, 1964–65), *The Illustrated Weekly Hudd* (BBC1, 1966–67) and *According to Dora* (BBC1, 1969). He also sparred with the fledgling Two Ronnies in sketches for *Frost on Sunday* (London Weekend Television, 1968–70), having worked extensively with Ronnie Corbett during the early days at Danny La Rue's nightclub. 'The audiences there were raw and unsophisticated, in the best sense,' Fisher remembered. 'If they didn't like you, they threw ice cubes!'

His career was subsequently steered towards the cosy sitcom world that would form his favourite environs, with appearances in *That's Your Funeral* (as Alf in 'Unholy Deadlock', BBC1, 19 February 1971), *His and Hers* (as a pub landlord in 'Morals', Yorkshire Television, 28 July 1970), and *Father, Dear Father* – as Leslie in an episode called, would you believe it, 'A Man About the House' on 16 June 1970 – oh, yes! Fisher's big break came with another ITV sitcom, *All Our Saturdays* (Yorkshire Television, 1973), in which platinum-blonde bombshell Diana Dors starred as Northern lass Di Dorkins, the ball-crushing manager of an amateur rugby league team. Fisher played the smooth Jack the Lad, Ronnie Rendell – Larry Simmonds in embryo.

It was nothing more than a toning down of the accent that led to *Man About the House* and Fisher's finest hour – a ragbag of delightfully coy and cute comedy situations with an endearing, perfectly selected cast giggling, groaning and gurning their way through a never-never land of bright colours, outrageous fashions and affectionate political incorrectness; in other words, the 1970s. In terms of television comedy in Britain, it was a decade of booze, fags, flares and dolly birds. Doug Fisher was an expert in all of them. It was certainly no surprise when Hammer Films brought the whole gang to the big screen and gave Fisher a sizeable slab of the action. The cinema could have found its new Sid James in Fisher, for he followed the *Man About the House* film with more of the same but cranked right up. The character Sammy in Jackie Collins's blockbusters *The Stud* (1978) and *The Bitch* (1979), both starring Joan Collins, was basically Fisher's sitcom persona in a cartoon world of drugs, nightclubs and infidelity.

However, once the excess of the seventies had segued into the gloom of the 1980s, Fisher's career seemed to stagnate. He was rather splendid, however, in the *Yes Minister* episode 'The Challenge' (BBC2, 18 November 1982) and fitted nicely into the domestic angst of *Home to Roost*, with John Thaw and Reece Dinsdale, in the episode 'Paper Chase' (Yorkshire Television, 5 December 1987).

Penelope Nice, Sally Thomsett, Richard O'Sullivan, Doug Fisher, Yootha Joyce and Judy Matheson celebrate the record-breaking autumn 1975 tour of *Boeing-Boeing*.

Still, by the early 1990s Fisher was reduced to playing a cameo as a chirpy cabbie in *The Detectives*: 'Studs' (BBC1, 24 February 1993). He had proved himself skilled at more dramatic fare, notably as Edward Harvey in the first *Prime Suspect* (Granada Television, 1991), and Kevin Medhurst's father, Jim, in *London's Burning* (London Weekend Television, 1988–93) – but there was certainly no going back after the character was unceremoniously killed off.

There were suitably comic featured roles in the first episode of *Jonathan Creek*: 'The Wrestler's Tomb' (BBC1, 10 May 1997), *Heartbeat*: 'In on the Act' (Yorkshire Television, 7 December 1997) and, most touchingly of all, the *Goodnight Sweetheart* episode 'How Long Has This Been Going On?' (BBC1, 15 April 1997), where his bit part as Stanley can genuinely bring a lump to the throat of an old comedy softie like me. The part was a beautifully written, self-aware morsel of cockney charm for Fisher, by now a half-familiar actor whose face got viewers clicking their fingers, pointing and pondering... 'Wasn't he in... umm... oh, you know!'

Onstage, Fisher had appeared in everything from Shakespeare to Beckett. Reflecting on the years since his early work at Danny La Rue's venue, he said: 'There is a certain comfort knowing, years later, that if an audience doesn't like you in *Volpone*, the members will not throw ice cubes!' He had also been more than happy to embrace the cache of *Man About the House* stardom when he co-starred opposite Richard O'Sullivan, Yootha Joyce, and Sally Thomsett in a 1975 tour of the jet-age farce *Boeing-Boeing*. Perfectly cast as the suave and sophisticated, crumpet-mad Bernard, Fisher also directed the production and, due to necessary cast changes, oversaw a fresh staging of the piece when he and Richard O'Sullivan took it to Sydney, Australia, in July 1977.

He had also appeared with repertory companies in Glasgow, Leicester, Watford, and Worcester, acted opposite David Hemmings at the Hampstead Theatre Club, and starred in John Heilpern's solo show *The Man Who Almost Knew Eamonn Andrews*, at the Edinburgh Fringe. He later took it to Glasgow, Manchester, Richmond in West London, and Amsterdam, filming it as a *BBC2 Playhouse* episode in 1981.

A founder member of Frank Dunlop's Young Vic company, Fisher became a pioneer of the controversial and the challenging in British theatre. All he lacked was ambition, as he admitted when the Australian run of *Boeing-Boeing* came to an end in October 1977. His co-star, Richard O'Sullivan, was hotfooting it back to England to do yet another television series. Doug was keen to get back to England too, but to toil in his garden in Chelsea: 'There is lots of pruning to do at that time of year,' he said at the time.

His final appearance, uncredited, was as a clergyman in ITV's highly prestigious 1999 production of *Oliver Twist*, starring Robert Lindsay as Fagin, my dear. Fisher always had a Dickensian heartbeat about him. What laughs and thrills his early death denied us.

TREAT YOURSELF TO what else but *Man About the House – The Complete Series* (Network: B001B1G4XY, 2008), which collects, complete and uncut, every knowingly raised eyebrow and indecent suggestion in the Doug Fisher armoury. A comedic masterclass.

# Ronald Frankau

## 1894–1951

The unlikely poster boy for this entire project, for without an unceremonious spinning of a Ronald Frankau 78 rpm we would never have come up with the idea. So thank you, you wonderfully naughty gentleman, you.

*Terry Jones*

Ronald Frankau's predominant reputation is as the naughtiest comedian of the 1930s. Yes, even naughtier than Max Miller. In a way, Max – with his flamboyant, floral suit and relentless pushing of his blue book of dirty jokes – was a twinkling-and-winking given. He was an obvious saucepot from the moment he took to the stage. Frankau, on the other hand, with his dinner jacket, bow tie, public-school demeanour and frightfully clipped vowels, was officer class; good gracious, he could even have been working on the Board of Governors of the BBC. As it was, he was a no-frills smut-monger who delighted in the most risqué of material. Indeed, some of his Parlophone song recordings were banned outright by the Beeb. The deceptively childlike 'Winnie the Worm', recorded in

July 1931, was anything but; the innuendo all too obvious, even now. 'I'd Like to Have a Honeymoon with Her' didn't bother with any second meaning. It was about sex, impure and simple. It's unlikely that 'Everyone's Got Sex Appeal For Someone', from October 1933, was even offered to the BBC Radio playlist, given the sheer outrage and, more than likely, bafflement of broadcasting bigwigs towards Frankau's material, as beautifully preserved in the film *Radio Parade of 1935* (1934), in which Will Hay personifies humourless respectability. In the film, Frankau's breathy and buoyant rendition of 'Let's Go Wild' engenders a barrage of scornful expressions and what can only be described as worried concern for Frankau's sanity. Of course, the best way to shift anything is to ban it. Ronald Frankau's records sold over 100,000 copies in 1932 alone.

As his demeanour attests Frankau was born into an affluent family, his grandfather having established a thriving cigar business. Frankau's mother was the satirical novelist Julia Davis. Young Ronald's upbringing was clearly steeped in literature: his older brother, Gilbert, was a Great War poet and novelist; sadly, his younger brother, Jack, was killed in Gaza in 1917 before his writings could fully find voice. His sister, Joan, was a literary scholar and Cambridge don.

Ronald himself married Renee Roberts, now best remembered as the flustered Miss Gatsby in every episode of *Fawlty Towers*. Their daughter Rosemary became an actor too, with her top comedy credit as Terry and June's long-suffering next-door neighbour Beattie; their son John was a distinguished TV director. Adding to the dynasty, Rosemary's son Sam Bain is the creator of the television comedies *Peep Show* and *Fresh Meat*. What a comedy-rooted family tree.

A ripe fruit falling from such an illustrious orchard, Ronald Frankau gladly became the daring bad apple of British comedy. He had worked as a chorus boy at Daly's Theatre in London in 1911 before joining the army in 1914 and supervising military concerts both in Africa and back home in Blighty. He then worked as a straight actor before forming his own concert party in 1921. It was during a stint in London's nightclubs that he met the extraordinarily talented pianist Monte Crick. It was Crick who scored musical accompaniment to Frankau's 1929 book of children's verse, *Oh, Dear, Dear*. This was, in actual fact, good clean fun. After all, it was published by Frederick Warne and Co., the publisher who had taken a chance and found everlasting stability with the work of Beatrix Potter, and the Parlophone recording was a big seller. But one can see the look of disappointment of listeners latterly stumbling upon it and expecting the near-the-knuckle gleefulness of Frankau's 1930s output. Crick would play the piano on the majority of Frankau's earthier, best-selling releases, too, his musical talents and sense of sheer fun a perfect sounding board for Frankau's wry and cheeky bonbons of bawdiness.

by RONALD FRANKAU
pictured by Laurie Tayler

Published in the early months of the conflict in Europe, in the spring of 1940.

In terms of a vocal sounding board, Frankau found his perfect match in 1934 when he teamed up with the fast-talking Liverpudlian comedian Tommy Handley to form Mr Murgatroyd and Mr Winterbottom. Long before his greatest success *It's That Man Again*, Handley had himself been no stranger to comedic controversy, and the two happily now made merry hell with the BBC's strict broadcasting code; as with most things, these rules and regulations were slackened slightly during the Second World War.

For Frankau, the conflict was a very personal one. Not only had he fought, and lost a brother in Europe's first innings, but his paternal grandfather, a German Jew, had long since left the benighted country for the safety of England. It is unsurprising, therefore, that Frankau threw himself into satirical propaganda during the rise of Fascism in the early thirties and throughout the war years – be it home-fire-burning, goodwill favourites like 'The Navy, the Army and the Police', from 1935, or finger-wagging, tongue-poking attacks like 'Heil Hitler! Ja! Ja! Ja!', from the height of the Blitz. He also wrote humorous verse aimed squarely at cheering up battle-bashed Britain. Both *DiVersions* and *He's a Perfect Little Gentleman, the Swine* were books published by Raphael Tuck & Sons and energetically illustrated by Laurie Taylor. The latter, in particular, hit home with a firm clout in 1940, depicting the Führer as nothing more than a pig with power.

Although cinema never fully knew what to do with Frankau – other than the bits of variety as himself – he contributed to the script for the wartime George Formby hit *Much Too Shy* (1942). The supporting cast included a youthful-looking Charles Hawtrey, who subsequently cast Frankau in his own directorial debut, the musical mystery *What Do We Do Now?*, in 1945. Even at the time, the reviews considered it old-fashioned variety; indeed, it seems Hawtrey simply threw together a few swing bands and a handful of comedians some time past their sell-by date. The film is now missing, believed lost.

Frankau fared somewhat better in *The Ghosts of Berkeley Square* (1947) directed by the ever-underappreciated Vernon Sewell. He was cast in the kind of role he could really enjoy, as the babbling, blustering buffoon Tex Farnum, a pompous oaf unable to outfox the supernatural in the form of comical players Felix Aylmer and Robert Morley. Later the same year, Frankau also appeared in the crime drama *Dual Alibi*, starring Herbert Lom, but sadly this fledgling career as a character actor was cut short by ill health.

Pretty much retired for the last few years of his life, Frankau found sanctuary by the Sussex coast, in Eastbourne. One hopes he whistled the odd dirty ditty as the refined gentlewomen strolled by.

His fruity collection of always filthy, often gently cheeky, often bitingly satirical, often gloriously and wildly inappropriate songs have lost none of their vigour, and the impish sense of dangerous fun in Frankau's very best recordings is as fresh and wicked as ever. Every time I listen to one, I can see his twinkling eyes, polished, bald head and brandy-bowl cheeks as he defies his strait-laced generation and regimented class to laugh. They always did. Who could help it?

TREAT YOURSELF TO *Ronald Frankau – Upper Class Love* (Windyridge: VAR4, 2004), another extraordinary collection of digital remasters from this record label, performed by the great man between 1929 and 1940. The selection includes 'Nothing Ever Happens to Some Girls', 'They Have a Much Better Time When They're Naughty', and 'I'd Rather Be A Savage'.

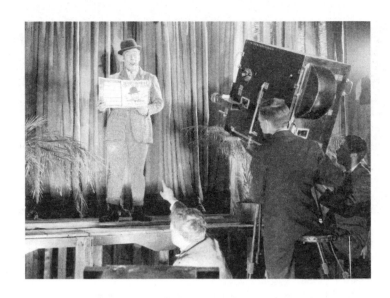

# Leslie Fuller

## 1888–1948

The top comic of his day.

*Sir John Mills CBE*

Leslie Fuller was indeed the top comic of his day, that day being the depression years of the early 1930s. Working class and as often as not in a tweed suit several sizes too small for him, he was rubber-faced and quick to lost his temper. Nevertheless, he was a salt of the earth kind of bloke, as synonymous with the seaside town of Margate as Max Miller was with Brighton.

Born on 9 October 1888, in London's Bethnal Green, as a lad Fuller worked for his father's printing firm while longing to play the music halls. Although he always considered himself a 'bad baritone', his desire was enough to propel him to learn three songs off by heart and join a minstrel troupe in Brighton. More than willing to travel far afield to hone his talents, between 1909 and 1912 he and his brother Dave performed with the Silloth Pierrots at Silloth in Cumbria.

As down-on-his-luck comedian Bill Potter saddled with a stray greyhound, *The Outcast*, 1934.

When the First World War broke out in 1914, young Albert Leslie Fuller became a second lieutenant of the Huntingdonshire Cyclist Battalion; he was a keen cyclist and had been something of a champion on Civvy Street. When he was invited to form a Battalion concert party, he leapt at the chance and, in reference to all that peddling, rather cheekily dubbed the troupe 'The Ped'lers'! The group, in various incarnations, would be part of his life for more than thirty years.

The initial performances, at The Coliseum Theatre, Whitby, proved hugely popular, and when Fuller was demobbed in 1919 he cannily retained the rights to the troupe's name and material. Having settled in Margate, Kent, with his wife Beatrice Witham – a dancer and male impersonator whom he'd married just before the war – he presented The Ped'lars at the town's Clifton Concert Hall, only a handful of his original cast having survived combat. By the end of the 1920s, Fuller had become Margate's comedy darling, headlining both summer seasons and pantomimes. He had also toured the theatres owned by Sir Oswald Stoll (later co-founder of the Stoll Moss Group) and broken onto the London scene with appearances at the Coliseum and the Alhambra Theatre.

His droll, world-weary tones gave a fillip to several radio variety slots, but it was a meeting with film producer Joe Rock that elevated Fuller to star-comedian status. Rock had previously worked with Stan Laurel and saw potential in Fuller's rogue Everyman personality. In 1930 he starred Fuller in his first feature film, *Why Sailors Leave Home*. In it Fuller played a cheery British sailor, Bill Biggles, who is mistaken for a powerful Arabian sheikh. The director was Monty Banks. Things would stay pretty much the same for the next eight years: Banks, an assured comedian and director with a fiery temperament, would direct many of the early Fuller comedies and, invariably, Fuller would play Bill, the downtrodden but good natured bloke. His second film, *Kiss Me Sergeant* (1932), saw his return as Bill Biggles but this time serving in the British Indian Army. Over the twenty-plus films Fuller starred in, he would as often as not play Bill Smith, Bill Smithers or Bill someone or other. It was reassuringly familiar for his audience.

He would also find himself working with the cream of British cinema. Future scriptwriter and director Val Guest cut his teeth as a bit-part actor in the Fuller comedies; Frank Launder directed one of the most assured of them, *The Last Coupon*, in 1932, while, in 1934, a sprightly John Mills teamed up with Fuller for

'His famous Ped'lers' concert party long tickled Margate's funny bone.

the films *A Political Party* and *Doctor's Orders*. Still, it was another character comedian, Syd Courtenay, who had been writing stage routines for him since 1919, who really shaped his screen persona. Fuller was a brusque and burly performer, skilled at physical comedy. In one film, *Hawleys of High Street* (1933), this battling business was taken to unique heights with a fight with a rival local council electee, played by Moore Marriott, deploying weapons of joints of meat!

In *The Pride of the Force* (1933) Fuller played two roles, that of identical twins: one the popular policeman of the title who yearns to run away and join the circus; the other a clownish farm-hand who yearns to join the force! Norman Lee, the director of this and several of Fuller's most popular films, explained his appeal: 'It need be neither scintillating nor witty – it is enough if it be funny. Broadly funny. A Fuller joke is often a familiar one, because Leslie believes that people laugh most heartily at the jokes they know best.' This familiarity was essential to his appeal. In one film, *What a Night!* (1931), Fuller would investigate a reputed haunting. In another, *The Outcast* (1934), he returned to his roots to play a producer for a theatre troupe. His bluff, likeable style of comedy proved so successful that for *Strictly Illegal* (1935) he and long-time producer Joe

A welcome addition to Network DVD's essential British Film range, in 2014.

Rock set up independent production companies, and distributed through Gaumont British. Sticking to the tried and tested formula of keeping writer, supporting player and pal Syd Courtenay close, and playing a character called Bill, Fuller enjoyed continued success with films *The Stoker* (1935), and race-horsing comedy *One Good Turn* (1936). By 1935 Joe Rock had taken over the Neptune studios at Elstree. Such assured box office attractions were the Leslie Fuller films that the studios dubbed him the Clark Gable of Borehamwood. At the time Gable had been given the title of the King of Hollywood. Leslie Fuller was indeed the King of Borehamwood.

However, *Boys Will Be Girls* (1937) broke this run of popularity. Fuller was cast as the hard-drinking Bill Jenkins, who must stay sober in order to inherit a fortune. The film proved to be his last starring role.

After three years in the wilderness, he finally returned for *The Middle Watch* (1940), a naval comedy starring Jack Buchanan. Fuller's was a relatively minor, supporting role as a cheeky mariner, cementing his fate as a familiar face who popped up as an old lag or a policeman. He would never again headline a film, his robust earthiness seemingly at odds with what the public now really wanted. His last film saw him playing a bit part as a taxi-driver opposite star comedian George Moon in *What Do We Do Now?* (1945), for director Charles Hawtrey. (Yes, *that* Charles Hawtrey!)

Fuller settled in Teddington with his second wife, ex-bareback-elephant-rider and concert-party dancer Nancy Bates, who had been his leading lady in *The Pride of the Force*. The couple then upped sticks and moved back to Fuller's beloved Margate. There he got heavily involved in local charities and even got himself elected as an independent councillor for the town's Cliftonville ward.

In 1946 he successfully revived The Ped'lars for one last hurrah at Cliftonville's Lido Theatre. He died two years later from a massive brain haemorrhage, on 24 April 1948, and was buried in Margate Cemetery.

Without doubt one of the biggest and best-loved stars of British film comedy of the 1930s, Leslie Fuller was once up there with the likes of Will Hay and George Formby. Fame at its most fickle, after the morale-boosting war years, robbed him of his popularity and, in the years after his death, has robbed him of his immortality. Still, his work remains fit for reappraisal in light of his place as a First World War Tommy who returned to the brave new world he helped to create and could happily laugh along with. He was a vital example of the returning comic hero. In Margate, though, he was always a comic hero; still a King. Even in shows after the war Fuller was being billed as 'Margate's Favourite Comedian and Film Star', and he remained a local personality until his final days. Uncouth, uncompromising and unapologetically vulgar, Leslie Fuller deserves to be celebrated. His comic persona has the essence of the loveable sitcom slob about it. His cynical, selfish demeanour feels very contemporary, and his vivacious lust for life is happily and brutally honest. So, do invest some time in getting to know him. He's good company. A good man. And a very good comedian.

IT IS THE peerless Network that really fills the gaps other DVD companies leave, and which allows you to treat yourself to some rare Leslie Fuller from its 'The British Film' collection. I'm even recommending you double-dip and pick up both *Captain Bill* (Network: B00OU0JQII, 2015), which sees our hero at his most popular, as a Bill (this time a Bill who happens to be a Thames river bargee), and the aforementioned *A Political Party* (Network: B00O489701, 2014), which stars our man as a lowly chimney sweep who stands for Parliament. Go on: vote for Leslie Fuller!

# Dustin Gee

## 1942–86

A great trouper and entertainer.

*Russ Abbot*

You could barely turn on your television in the early 1980s without being confronted by the widely talented, towering comic impressionist that was Dustin Gee. With his gaudy jackets and radioactive-blond hair, he was like the computer-animated Max Headroom made flesh. A winning-war baby, he was born Gerald Harrison in York on 24 June 1942, and after studying art in Manchester returned home to work on York Minster's famed stained glass windows. By night, however, he unleashed his wilder side by playing in the rock band Gerry B and the Hornets. Even when the group changed their name to Gerry B and the Rockafellas, fame and fortune were hardly knocking the door down so, disenchanted and disgruntled, they broke up. Few people noticed.

Still, Gee was not going to give up his dreams of show business success so easily. Having a relaxed friendliness in front of an audience, he tried his hand as a compère and, subsequently, comedian. He had discovered a talent for mimicry that amused his friends, and it was this forte for impressions that would make his name. He was no mere shade of the famous, however – in fact, to call them impressions is to do him a disservice. Gee 'became' the people he impersonated. He was a master. His collection of familiar personalities was wide-ranging but it was the stars of popular television for which he became best known. Gee could morph into John Cleese in full-blown Basil Fawlty rant – Cleese said at the time that it was 'the best

Dustin Gee and Les Dennis with the Ray Cornell Dancers, promoting *The All Laughter Show*, 1985.

he had ever seen'. Another target of Gee's friendly fire was Larry Grayson, who was so impressed by Gee's encapsulation of his delivery and stage persona that he went on to become a close personal friend and would even join him onstage in mid flow. Gee, like Larry Grayson, was instantly liked by the public. A beloved comic friend.

He came to national attention in 1982, on the ITV talent show *Success* though he had already carved out a career in cabaret and he had joined the ensemble fun of *Russ Abbot's Madhouse* (LWT, 1980–85). There he teamed up with his life-long double-act partner, Les Dennis, the two working particularly well together on a parody of Mavis and Vera from *Coronation Street*. Gee remembered how the inspiration to lovingly send up *Corrie* came through sheer desperation. Russ Abbot had been the lead in a sketch about a peddler selling comedy sketches from a barrow. 'We had to pop up from behind the barrow doing particular impressions, but we got the sequence a bit wrong,' Gee recalled. 'Russ had already got Mavis Riley [Les Dennis] beside him and he said, "And what am I bid for a Bet Lynch?" I said, "You can't have a Bet Lynch, but here's a Vera Duckworth," because I was halfway dressed as Vera. I appeared and

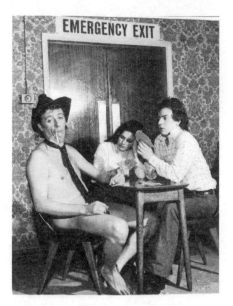

Dustin doing his celebrated Robert
Mitchum impression, here in a losing
game of strip poker!

began talking to "Mavis" in character. After that, we began to appear more regularly, eventually on *Live From Her Majesty's* as well as the Royal Variety show.'

Although the sketches themselves may be distant memories, Les Dennis's 'I don't really know!' has become part of the Mavis Riley legend. Actor Thelma Barlow insists that she never actually said it in the show but it still resonated, and was put to teeth-achingly good effect in Les Dennis's episode of *Extras,* in October 2005. Similarly, at the peak of Dennis and Gee's success, Dustin had seized upon Vera Duckworth's habit of calling everybody 'cock' and making it far saucier than Elizabeth Dawn had ever intended. Gee would shrill: 'You know what you need...' and leave the slightest of pauses before adding 'cock!' It was a riotous double act – seasoned pros at the very top of their game.

On 15 April 1984, when Tommy Cooper collapsed and died onstage during the broadcast of *Live From Her Majesty's,* Dennis and Gee were the act scheduled to follow him on the bill. The compère that night was Jimmy Tarbuck, who later recounted how Tommy 'was a big bloke and very heavy; we just couldn't move him. And this show was live, don't forget, so I told Les Dennis and Dustin Gee, who were up next, that they'd have to work in front of the curtain. Dustin said that they needed more room and I replied, "Well, you ain't gonna get it. You're professionals: just get on with it." And they did.' At the time Dustin told his comedy partner that that was the way he would like to die. On stage.

Just over a year later, in May 1985, Gee himself had a massive heart attack. It was the opening night of a sell-out six-month engagement starring in *The All Laughter Show,* on Blackpool's North Pier. It wasn't such a surprise to Gee, however, having been born with an enlarged heart. Against doctor's orders, he gamely returned to the Blackpool assignment just a month later to mark his forty-third birthday, and went on to complete the run.

From 20 December 1985, Dustin was back onstage with Les Dennis. The duo were playing the Ugly Sisters, Mavis and Vera, in *Cinderella*, at the Southport Theatre. But on New Year's Eve Gee suffered a second heart attack. The show's company manager, Basil Soper, revived him

Dustin's bizarre but brilliant album, from 1976.

and, along with Gee's personal assistant Roger Edwards, accompanied him to the Southport General Infirmary. He died there three days later. For Les Dennis, Gee was 'my best friend ... the most charismatic and talented man I ever knew'. Gee's tragically early death was keenly felt by the rest of us too, and his simple, good-natured humour is still much missed. Missed by lots of us. At its peak, *The Laughter Show* was regularly attracting television viewing figures of over 12 million. Dustin Gee gave us all a renewed love of variety. He was very much part of my own formative television viewing, and is, to me, now the essence of a lost summer. Perhaps our collective lost summer – of bumper editions of favourite comics, sand in your shoes and the affordable thrills of variety on the pier. Dustin Gee is almost next to John Betjeman in his ability to transport me back to my youth.

TREAT YOURSELF TO Gee's quite extraordinary vintage long-playing record *Plastered with the Pink Elephant* (Indigo Studios: IDS 51601, 1976), an unbelievably eccentric and eclectic collection of covers including David Bowie's 'Space Oddity' and George Harrison's 'Piggies', and rounded off with a rousing rendition of Bing Crosby's 'I'll Take You Home Again, Kathleen'. This is Dustin's intimate, personal odyssey. Indulge.

# Peter Glaze

## 1917–83

Laugh your grey, knee-length school socks off at his slapstick, or sit bemused by it; you couldn't ignore Peter Glaze in the 1970s. His loud, physically involved and at times belligerent routines were as much a part of any British teatime as Mr Kipling, Spam and dehydrated mashed potato. Five to five was *Crackerjack!* ('Crackerjack!') time, and *Crackerjack!* could not have been *Crackerjack!* without his bumbling, bespectacled figure constantly chastising his sidekick, Don Maclean, for things that were clearly his own fault... Doh!

*Simon Donald, him off the* Viz

Television may have sounded the death knell to variety theatres but it was that selfsame small screen in the corner of your living room that kept the custard pies flying well in to the twenty-first century. It was children's television, to boot, that nourished the tangible link with the old vaudeville tradition. And this wasn't nostalgia or homage, kids. This was the real thing!

The essences of the pratfall and the slow burn were encapsulated in the diminutive frame of just one man: Peter Glaze. Short, tubby, bespectacled and the master of the baited authority figure, Glaze was the comedy bedrock of *Crackerjack!* ('Crackerjack!'). For nearly a quarter of a century, starting in 1960, Glaze's traditional slapstick was the very foundation of the show. It was intrinsically, eternally funny. Not only that, but only Glaze could irk even the usually unflappable Eamonn Andrews. In an October 1962 edition Andrews whacks a caveman-styled Glaze with a club and mutters: 'I've been waiting months to do that...'

Glaze took it on the chin – and in the stomach, and on the arse: a human punchbag for punchlines, a real-life cartoon character for whom no demeaning bit of stage business was too demeaning. Whether faced with effrontery, innuendo or indeed anything that was attempting to send up his self-importance and sophistication, Glaze would never retaliate. He would roll all his angst up in to one tiny word: 'Doh!' It expressed his dissatisfaction with his lot, his pain, his anxiety, his frustration – even with us, his audience. A simple 'Doh!' spoke volumes.

Long before Homer Simpson picked 'Doh!' for his own branded usage, Glaze had digested the phrase from James Finlayson. If it was good enough for the balding Scot to bellow while Laurel and Hardy haplessly tried to flog him a Christmas tree in *Big Business* (1929), then it was certainly good enough for Glaze to unleash in the face of an idiotic comment from *Crackerjack!*'s resident comedian Leslie Crowther.

Glaze was at the peak of his 1970s fame and comic genius when he was teamed with *Crackerjack!*'s then resident comedian Don Maclean. The Don-and-Pete segment was a five-minute celebration of slapstick and saw Glaze in his absolute element, working every sight gag in the book. These perfect micro-keystone comedies proved hugely popular within and without *Crackerjack!*, and Glaze's passion for the ways of the slosh was increasingly indulged. When Maclean left the show in 1978, Glaze decided to soldier on, diminished but not dulled.

Glaze was the perfect, dependable comedy conduit, having learned his craft through working the music halls. Comedy was in his very bones. His family

*Those Crackerjack Silents*, with Don and Pete.

had been steeped in the business. His father had been a successful actor and manager, so it was little surprise that the young Pete had the taste for greasepaint. Having got his first break into comedy at the legendary Windmill Theatre, Glaze discovered his natural, slop-filled home as an understudy for most of that madcap stage and screen comic collective the Crazy Gang. He always had an essence of the Gang members Jimmy Nervo and Teddy Knox about him as he had so often fallen down, tripped up and slid across the stage of the Victoria Palace Theatre alongside them – as often as not when Glaze was doubling for one of the other Crazy Gang boys and the majority of the audience thought they were actually laughing at Charlie Naughton or Jimmy Gold. Almost a constant in the Crazy Gang troop, Glaze even landed the role – albeit a minor, supporting one – of a scene-shifter in their final film, *Life Is a Circus*, in 1958.

Glaze would chalk up some notable guest-spots on television, though certainly not as many as he should have done. There was a memorable, twilight turn as Joe Spratt in *The Sweeney* (the 'Big Spender' episode, Euston Films, 13 March 1975) and appearances in *Citizen James* ('The Football Team', BBC Television, 30 October 1961) and *Billy Bunter of Greyfriars School* ('Hunter-Bunter', BBC Television, 10 June 1961). He had been schoolteacher R P Trench MA in the third series of *Whack-O!* (BBC Television, 1958), and Ralph, a cockney busker, in the *Comedy Playhouse* episode 'Thank You Sir, Thank You Madam' (BBC1, 31 May 1968). He played Cyril Wedgewood, the earnest Romeo to Frankie Abbott's hypochondriacal mother in *The Fenn Street Gang* ('Ménagerie à Trois', London Weekend Television, 5 November 1972), snogging, singing and strutting his stuff on the living room floor, and was the head juror who sent Anthony Newley's fantasy dreamer down for having no sense of humour in *The Strange World of Gurney Slade* (ATV, 12 November 1960) . He truly shone as the animal impersonator of 'The Bowmans' in that unforgettable 2 June 1961 episode of *Hancock*, the star of the show skipping through the accents, from Welsh hill farmer to Robert Newton, allowing his disgruntled, written-out character Joshua Merriweather 'a last wish: that my dear old dog be buried alongside of me!' Without a word of dialogue, without even a bark, Glaze's double-take reaction and shocked, open-mouthed outrage is the very definition of scene-stealing.

For science fiction fans, Glaze's finest moment was probably as the line-fluffing, slightly portly Third Sensorite in the William Hartnell *Doctor Who* serial *The Sensorites* (BBC1, 27 June-1 August 1964). Behind the narrow eyes, tufted jowels and the zip up the back, that voice was instantly recognisable, and it was still funny. One hopes that some television back-room boy got the joke when, years later, Glaze was cast as a cherubic Brigadier, and even had a little dance with Doreen the Dalek, opposite Maclean's Dr Why in a 21 March 1975 *Crackerjack!* spoof. For *Crackerjack!* was where Glaze's comedy muscles were fully flexed. He did everything the producers requested of him, even if that meant donning a bald pate and a leather jacket emblazoned with a swastika, or badly singing badly arranged renditions of the pop hits of the day. There are few more beguiling and intriguing sights than Glaze, dressed as an Edwardian gentleman, struggling through the latest platter from Sparks or David Bowie. It is the very image of the generation gap, but somehow we bought in to it.

Unsurprisingly, basking in his television success, Glaze found himself in great demand for summer seasons and pantomimes. His natural ease onstage and his years of standing in the business were a boon for any space staging a tatty end-of-pier romp or a trip to never-never land. For Glaze, the falling-down business was always booming.

Glaze tried his hand at legitimate theatre as well. Actor Simon Treves had, as a child, appeared in the Christmas 1967 episode of *Crackerjack!*. In 1981 he bumped into Glaze again: 'He was playing Chasuble in *The Importance of Being Earnest*. He played it exactly like *Crackerjack!*. (I was rehearsing *Chips with Everything*.) All I remember is he had a blue nose – from drink, I think.' Oh, for Glaze's Mr Micawber... In 1949 Glaze had understudied for Arthur Askey in *The Kid from*

It's Friday, it's five to five, and it's *Crackerjack!* ('Crackerjack!'). Leslie Crowther and Pete, back for the eleventh series, from 1 October 1965.

*Stratford*, at the Winter Garden Theatre, Drury Lane; in 1976 he had played the Comedy Theatre, supporting Kenneth Williams and Peggy Mount in *Signed & Sealed*, and there was one final West End hurrah: a celebration of music hall for the 1982 Royal Command Performance, for which Glaze collaborated with Roy Hudd in a tribute to The Crazy Gang – talk about full circle.

Glaze was not to go gentle into that good night. He had just reached retirement age but retirement was a dirty word to this bastion of slapstick. After sixty-five years of falling over, Pete took his final bow after the Saturday evening performance of *Underneath the Arches*, that Crazy Gang musical, on 19 February 1983. The following day Pete died of a heart attack, at his home in Dartford, Kent. A roly-poly, energetic, slosh-splattered personification of childlike anarchy, he died with the scent of custard pie in his nostrils. Quite right too.

TREAT YOURSELF TO the one and only official *Crackerjack!* album (BBC Records: REC185, 1974), in which Peter Glaze takes top billing and is joined by Jacqueline Clarke and Don Maclean in a handful of tasty cuts from the series. Colour me nostalgic.

# Ken Goodwin

## 1933–2012

I worked with Ken Goodwin in panto and a few variety shows which I compèred, and it was always a treat to 'settle down' and listen to the wit of this very underrated and charming performer.

*Linda Regan*

The 1970s was a different planet – for all sorts of reasons, some good and some bad. It was not so much the dying days of variety as the second coming. An air of faded grandeur had descended. While some shone brightly (and, of them, many continue so to do), other turns had their moment in the limelight then vanished. Ken Goodwin was one such case and, for him at least, the step back into the shadows was for the most poignant of reasons.

Ken Goodwin was a funny man – funny in that beautiful way that children are funny. His comedy was rehearsed to the nth degree, of course, but he had a gentle, innocent, giggling way with the Christmas-cracker-style gag that won millions of us over. His self-effacing humour was also rooted in Northern poverty and that made him something of a working-class hero.

He was born William Kenneth Unwin in Manchester, on 7 April 1933, and by the time he could legally light up a cigarette he was effectively alone. His mother had left the family home while Ken was still a toddler, and by the time he reached the age of sixteen his father was dead. That's growing up fast. If you haven't got a sense of humour by then, you develop one pretty sharpish, or go under trying.

As a boy, Goodwin was obsessed with the toothy grin of Lancashire's own George Formby and would entertain his school friends with his pretty good impersonation. With his serviceable banjo skills, Goodwin performed in school concerts, and by his late teens was playing local social clubs – the smoke-filled, beer-stained bear pits full of wannabes and no-hopers desperately trying to break through the rowdy melee and the embittered MC. Goodwin supplemented his meagre club earnings with hard graft, working as everything from coal man to travelling salesman, millworker to market gardener. Anything that put bread and dripping on the table.

It was his ever-loyal wife, Pat Earith, whom he had married in 1956, who helped hone his stage craft. The jokes had to be funny – silly, but funny. His winning style of almost begging his audience to laugh was key. Ken Goodwin was someone you liked. You laughed because you liked him. Pat was the one who gave him the tongue-in-cheek, audience-calming line 'Settle down, now. Settle down.' It was a catchphrase that would linger among his quips for the rest of his career.

Like a cheeky kid, Goodwin would laugh at his own jokes. His own daftness would amuse him. A twinkle would light up those soulful eyes, there'd be a grin, a shrug of the shoulder and a nervous giggle, and we'd be in the palm of his hand. 'I don't know how I've got the nerve to tell terrible jokes like I do,' he reflected, 'but it works. It's all in the character. The way I tell the jokes: I'm just Simple Simon. I come over all nervous and shy, and most of the audience is laughing at me before I've said a word.' Actually, the key was that they were laughing *with* him.

As critic Eric Braun wrote in his review of *Babes in the Wood* for the 1985–86 season at the Richmond Theatre: 'the warmth of Ken Goodwin always seems ideal for pantomime: his Freddie the Jester, with a harking back to George Formby and his ukulele, is yet another comedy style that blends neatly in with the rest of the Sherwood Forest'. The show was written by Jimmy Perry, and starred Spike Milligan and Bill Pertwee as the robbers, with Peter Wyngarde's high-kicking Sheriff of Nottingham stopping the show with a spirited rendition of 'If They Could See Me Now'. Even Evelyn Laye flew in as the Fairy Godmother. Boy, what a cast!

A sold-out London Palladium season for *The Comedians*: Charlie Williams, Ken, Mike Reid, Dave Butler, Bernard Manning and Jos White, February 1972.

It was in fact his wife Pat he had to thank for his very beginnings, for it was she who had persuaded him to enter a talent contest in Leek, Staffordshire. The first prize was a hundred quid; at the end of the night, that wodge was in Goodwin's pocket.

But it was something of a rollercoaster ride from there on. In 1964 he was sharing the bill at Salford's working men's club with singer Gerry Dorsey (who later changed his name to Engelbert Humperdinck), and within months Goodwin had won his segment of *Opportunity Knocks*. Although an accident kept him out of the series final, his confidence was boosted and his profile heightened enough to bring him the all-important showcase of *The Comedians*, first transmitted in June 1971. The inspired brainchild of Granada Television producer Johnnie Hamp, the show's aim was to hand-pick the cream of the crop of club comedians and unleash them onto television. No satire, no sketches; just joke, upon joke, upon joke. Hamp had seen Goodwin in a club in Chester and thought him perfect. *The Comedians* made stars of Frank Carson, Bernard Manning, Mike Reid, Charlie Williams and so many others – and none more so than Ken Goodwin, whose streak of naive charm slotted ideally alongside the more robust and earthy style of some acts.

By the November the same year, Goodwin was on the bill of the Royal Command Performance. He returned in 1972, too, and was even invited to give

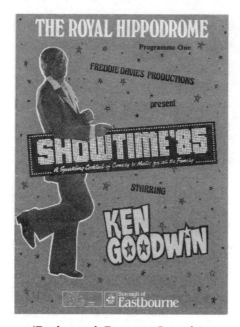

'Eastbourne's Favourite Comic', in residence at the Royal Hippodrome in 1985, featuring singer Susan Maughan and Ken's 'Nostalgic Look Back to 1945'.

a private show at Buckingham Palace. He won the Supreme Bernard Delfont Award and was voted Comedian of the Year. He topped the bill at the London Palladium in the April of 1972, and thrice embraced retro variety through the early seventies for BBC Television's very own old time music hall, *The Good Old Days*. He even got his own comic strip, 'It's Ken Goodwin', in *Look-In* magazine. Boy, was he famous! *Ken Goodwin's Year*, a Baz Taylor documentary film for television, followed Goodwin back to see family and friends in Manchester. The year was 1972. And what a year it had been!

*The Comedians* brought him fame, fortune and a villa in Alicante, but when Pat was taken seriously ill, in 1973, he left the show and abandoned his career to care for her. After Pat's death, in 1977, Goodwin returned to playing London cabaret spots and summer seasons. He was dubbed Eastbourne's Favourite Comedian, with his regular *Holiday Showtime* at the Hippodrome theatre providing guaranteed family fun, and his *Aladdin* for the 1979–80 season cementing the love and respect the East Sussex town felt for him. Goodwin continued to work throughout the 1980s, with a cabaret tour of Australia in 1980, reprising his role of Aladdin, for the 1981–82 season, at the Alfred Beck Centre, Hayes, and starring in *Dick Whittington*, at the Theatre Royal, Newcastle, for 1982–83. Still, Ken preferred preferred to spend more and more time in Spain with his second wife, dancer and singer Vicki Lane.

His last great hurrah came in 1993 when Granada Television staged *The Comedians Christmas Cracker*. Despite a decade's fight against stomach cancer, Ken was determined to take part, his eager enthusiasm undimmed by the twenty-year hiatus. If anything, that enthusiasm was heightened, masking a lack of confidence that he would conquer by pacing his dressing room and singing snatches of familiar songs to himself. He was a clown in serious preparation.

Latterly, resident in a nursing home in Rhos-on-Sea, eventually Alzheimer's clouded his lifetime's memories of laughter. When he died, on 18 February 2012, the media barely flickered in response. Still, his sweet and silly legacy will not fade. At his most vibrant onstage he would quip: 'I'm too good for this place.' You know what? I really think he was.

TREAT YOURSELF TO *Settle Down With Ken Goodwin* (Granada Television Records Ltd.: SGTV 1003, 1972), a cosy armchair collection vinyl collectable of his favourite standards, including 'All I Do Is Dream of You', 'Harbour Lights' and 'Wrap Your Troubles in Dreams'. The album happily embraces his comic catchphrase, while allowing Goodwin to indulge his pleasant singing voice. Like every great club comedian he could carry a tune, and this is a delightful keepsake of a beloved talent. There's no better company.

# Bernard Gorcey

## 1886–1955

His films had a lot of appeal to real kids of that era and even enjoyed some popularity when they were released to TV.

*Jim Willard*

Show business is full of the children of famous stars following in their parents' footsteps and making a success of it. Occasionally, the career of the youngster outstrips that of the elder but, almost uniquely, in the case of Bernard Gorcey his biggest moment of fame didn't come until after his famous son was already one of the busiest character actors in Hollywood.

The son was very busy indeed – very busy in cheap potboilers, but that's beside the point. They had a winning charm all of their own, and through reverse nepotism Bernard Gorcey became an invaluable asset to them. The son was pint-sized Leo Gorcey, and the films the seemingly never-ending run of *Bowery Boys* adventures that would be churned out at the rate of up to five fun-packed pictures a year for more than a decade. Gorcey senior was himself rather pint-sized; in fact, compared to his diminutive father Leo Gorcey looked eight feet tall and bulletproof – even though he couldn't even look legendary box-standing leading man Alan Ladd in the eye without himself standing on a box.

What I'm trying to say here is that Bernard Gorcey was short. He was born on 9 January 1886, in Russia of Swiss–Jewish descent and he grew no higher than four feet, ten inches in his stocking feet. At the outbreak of the First World War he married Irish Catholic Josephine Condon, over twenty years his junior, and together they emigrated to America to find work in vaudeville. Leo, their middle child, was born when Josephine was barely sixteen – he was scarcely born in a trunk, rather on a kitchen table. They were very poor, and Leo later recalled 'we moved so many times that we could have made a hummingbird seem like a statue'. Still, Bernard Gorcey had work. While his wife looked after the home, he was appearing on Broadway in productions like Oscar Hammerstein's musical *Song of the Flame* , which opened at the 44th Street Theatre on 30 December 1925.

It had been in 1922 that Gorcey had hit real pay dirt, when he landed the role of Isaac Cohen in *Abie's Irish Rose*. The play opened at the Fulton Theatre on 23 May 1922 and, suitably enough, it told of the comedic ups and downs of a Jewish man and his Irish wife. It ran for nearly six years. Gorcey was with it for almost the entire run. In 1929 he recreated the role in a film version. Other film bits came along, as did continued success on Broadway, notably playing Moses in *Joy of Living* (Theatre Masque – now John Golden Theatre, 1931), and Kent J. Goldstein in *Keeping Expenses Down* (National Theatre – now Nederlander Theatre, 1932). From January 1935 he was at the Vanderbilt Theatre, playing Mr Goodman in *Creeping Fire*. He also accepted regular work on the *Popeye the Sailor* radio show, broadcast on the NBC Red Network from September 1935. Gorcey landed the role of Max Goldblatz in the farce *Satellite*, at the Bijou Theatre. It opened and closed on the evening of 20th November 1935, and it certainly didn't help to salvage his failing marriage. His wife cantered through a number of affairs and Gorcey left, deserting his three young sons.

It was many years later that he reconciled with Leo and youngest son, David. The boys hadn't had the peachiest of times with their old man and Gorcey senior was keen to make amends. He was encouraging of their ambition to follow in his footsteps, and in 1937 suggested they both audition for a new Broadway play. The play was *Dead End*, and they both got a positive callback – for Leo it was for a prominent role. Moreover, both father and son were signed up for the Warner Brothers film adaptation, which proved the touchstone for Leo's career; he played a variation on the wisecracking, streetwise wheeler-dealer for the rest of his days. Bernard Gorcey, meanwhile, had found renewed fame with an old favourite. From May 1937, *Abie's Irish Rose* was revived on Broadway, at the Little Theatre (now the Hayes Theater), and once more he was cast as Isaac Cohen.

Hollywood also came a-knocking on Bernard's door, with a handful of extremely small bit parts in some great and good films immediately before America joined the war. Charlie Chaplin rallied the nation with *The Great Dictator* (1940) and Gorcey cropped up as Mr Mann opposite the warm, flip side of Chaplin's dual role. Gorcey also delighted audiences with his role as a very small man carrying a load of tyres in the *Ellery Queen* detective films, with two different Ellery Queens: Ralph Bellamy in *Ellery Queen and the Perfect Crime* (1941), and William Gargan in *A Desperate Chance for Ellery Queen* (1942). (You couldn't make this stuff up.) He also played a cabbie and a shop-keeper, respectively, in the 1942 Bela Lugosi crime thrillers *Black Dragons*, and *Bowery at Midnight*; a prophesy of his biggest film success, for he would spend the rest of his career as the elder statesman of the *Bowery Boys* films, wallowing in Hollywood's version of New York's slum.

Leo Gorcey and his chums had developed from the hard-boiled *Dead End* ragamuffins to the rather more endearing *East Side Kids* for a series of Monogram Pictures, from 1940. Now they were foiling crooks and battling ghouls – a certain Bela Lugosi amongst them – and it was in these environs that young Leo got his father gainfully employed. In 1943 he was a liquor-store owner in *Clancy Street Boys*, and, soon after, director William Beaudine cast him as Mr Johnson in *Bowery Champs* (1944).

Beaudine would direct a vast quantity of the *Bowery Boys* series and Leo Gorcey had a lot of clout with Monogram Pictures. It may have been the poorest studio in town but Leo's failure to get a 100 per cent pay rise on the *East Side Kids* pictures resulted in his leaving the series, which ended immediately. Fellow East Side Kid

Bobby Jordan suggested Leo meet with his agent, Jan Grippo, and Leo not only secured a 40 per cent share in Jan Grippo Productions but also a say in scripting and casting. The series had been billed as starring Leo Gorcey and the Bowery Boys, don't forget, so his marquee value was high.

Bernard, Leo and the Boys focus on Huntz Hall in *Private Eyes*, December 1953.

As early as the second film in the *Bowery Boys* series, *In Fast Company* (1946), Leo had found roles both for his younger brother and his dear old dad: Bernard was cast as the loveable and naive malt-store owner Louis Dumbrowski. Louie's Sweet Shop on 3rd and Canal Street would be the focal point of the early part of each film, the boys hanging out and chewing the cud before the real adventure began.

Over the years Bernard Gorcey became more and more embroiled in the plot. In *High Society* (1955 – released a full eight months before the celebrated Cole Porter musical!) he joined the boys in tuxedos, smoking huge cigars. In *Let's Go Navy!* (1951) he ended up aboard, his chronic seasickness a source of much humour. Yes, he even gets the goosebumps when *The Bowery Boys Meet the Monsters* (1954). It was low-rent Abbott and Costello, but for a decade he was making up to five films a year playing the aged P of the *Bowery Boys* and would have continued for a few years more if fate hadn't intervened. On 31 August 1955 Bernard's car collided with a bus at 4th and La Brea, Los Angeles. He died of his injuries two weeks later. *Dig That Uranium* was released on Christmas Day the same year and Bernard had yet another *Bowery Boys* film in the can for release in 1956 – the rather unfortunately titled *Crashing Las Vegas*.

But already that was that for Leo Gorcey. Bernard had been drinking heavily during production of the last few films and once *Crashing Las Vegas* had wrapped he had gone berserk at Monogram and trashed the set. It all proved too much for Leo. When the studio refused to increase his percentage share he left

Dropping off Bela Lugosi in *Black Dragons* (1942): a companion piece to the East Side Kids film *Let's Get Tough!* (1942).

the *Bowery Boys* film series too, leaving the leading role in the films to his highly-skilled dumb-cluck stooge and cohort Huntz Hall. The wisecracking element was picked up by another young tearaway actor, Stanley Clements, but it was never the same again. How could it be? Leo Gorcey had been the beating heart of the series. Even the deadpan clowning of Huntz Hall and the family tie to David Gorcey, both of whom stayed with the series until the end, couldn't prevent the steam running out of the *Bowery Boys* series, in 1958, after an incredible forty-eight films.

Bernard Gorcey's lasting legacy – the crumple-faced, endearing, frantic, petulant, forever-hen-pecked, forever-fooled butt of scattergun humour – cheered up America during some of her darkest days and created some of her brightest. Like father, like son. The Gorceys are the very soul of New York City; down in the gutter, perhaps, but never completely out.

TREAT YOURSELF TO *The Bowery Boys – Volume Three* (Warner Brothers Archive Collection: B00FJYXQCG, 2018), and a multi-region player, for a definitive fix of Bernard Gorcey, including such highlights as *Feudin' Fools* (1952), *Paris Playboys* (1954), as well as his last hurrah, *Crashing Las Vegas* (1956).

# Bert Gordon

## 1895–1974

One of the comedy heroes from my youth. And that's a very long time ago!

*Carl Reiner*

I urge you not to Google 'The Mad Russian'. If you do, you'll get lurid tales of unscrupulous therapist Yefim Shubentsov or brutal serial killer Sergey Golovkin, and nobody wants that! No, the only Mad Russian that matters to the popular culture which fuels my personal happiness is our man Bert Gordon.

Born Barney Gorodetsky in Manhattan, New York, on 8 April 1895, his first professional japery was in a series of *School Days* sketches with Gus Edwards' Newsboys Sextette. Subsequent work alongside Joe Wood's Nine Crazy Kids led to Gordon becoming a popular turn on the vaudeville circuit, but it wasn't until 1930 that fate stepped in and made him a star. The George and Ira Gershwin musical *Girl Crazy*, at the Alvin Theatre, featured Russian actor Gregory Ratoff as Gieber Goldfarb; much lower down the cast was a certain Bert Gordon. When canny Ratoff bought the rights to the show he happily opted out of all that shouting in the evening and allowed Gordon to take over his role: all wild hair, ever-popping eyes and a constant stream of cod Russian.

Many other Broadway shows and cabaret assignments followed while the full effect of Ratoff's bequest lay dormant, biding its time, until the day in 1935 when Eddie Cantor came a-calling. *The Eddie Cantor Show* on NBC needed a man of character comedy, and, with his profile high thanks to *Girl Crazy*, the man approached for the task was Bert Gordon. By 1937, when the show had morphed into *Texaco Town*, all the traits and ticks of the Mad Russian were mined remorselessly.

By the end of the 1930s Eddie Cantor was hosting *Camel Caravan* and Bert Gordon was naturally called upon to bring guaranteed laughs. Gordon's every appearance was heralded by his elongated and exaggerated 'How doooo you do?' It was a belter of a catchphrase that worked each and every time, and effortlessly slipped into the national consciousness. Gordon was now rolling in work. It was always in support of a star comedian – be it Milton Berle, Mel Blanc, or Abbott and Costello – but he was a reassuringly fixed point in the comedy landscape.

Gordon remained fiercely loyal to Eddie Cantor until the very end of the 1940s, when Bert's Russian schtick was irretrievably scuppered by international events. In 1942 Cantor had started referring to him as 'our Russian friend' in order to avoid potential offence to Russia's turncoat support of the allied forces under the influence of Joseph Stalin. By the end of the conflict and the chilly frost of the Cold War, any kind of Russian – mad, friendly or otherwise – was anathema to the United States.

The character was unceremoniously dropped, although the cheap and cheerful Producers Releasing Corporation had given him one last, albeit horrendously badly timed, home run: in December 1945 Gordon starred in the film *How DOoo You Do*. No question mark, just the catchphrase and the film poster screaming: 'I Got Comedians. I Got Babes. I Got Detectives.' It also got 'radio's top announcer' Harry Von Zell, Charlie Chan's number one son, Keye Luke, and Ella Mae Morse, 'The Cow-Cow Boogie Girl'. Gordon, who played himself, was clearly one of the promised comedians in the gloriously ragbag plot line which saw him desperately trying to escape female wiles and finding himself up to his neck in a bizarre murder mystery.

Gordon's film appearances were surprisingly few and far between. He cropped up in *New Faces of 1937* as Count Mischa Moody, in the July of that year, performing for Milton Berle's corrupt theatrical producer who is looking for a flop having over-sold shares in a show to investors. This was thirty years before Mel Brooks' *The*

Eddie Cantor's Wednesday evening show kept National Broadcasting Company listeners in stitches from 1940–46.

*Producers*. Gordon also featured in the musical comedy film *Outside of Paradise* (1938); and happily appeared for a gag in his pal Eddie Cantor's wonderfully self-deprecating *Thank Your Lucky Stars* (1943). In 1941 he had officially brought the Mad Russian to the screen in *Sing For Your Supper*, while his interchangeable Boris Rascalnikoff character carried the comic weight of *Laugh Your Blues Away* (1942) and *Let's Have Fun* (1943), to limited box office socko. No, if the Mad Russian is known at all today it is thanks to the oft-repeated *Merrie Melodies* cartoons of the Warner Brothers stable. For a full decade, from *Porky's Movie Mystery* in 1939 to *Paying the Piper* in 1949, Bert Gordon's mannerisms and catchphrases were wedged in to elicit audiences' guaranteed laughs of instant recognition and affection. Perhaps the most delightful example is the 1944 Bugs Bunny classic *Hare-Ribbin'* in which a dog, voiced by Sam Glaser, appears in full Cossack regalia, complete with furry hat, and the full Mad Russian persona. 'How doooo you do?' guffaws the affable canine. On the scene's countless television outings, it's doubtful whether any kid, baby boomer or beyond, had any idea of the reference. I know I didn't.

Thankfully, for Bert Gordon there was one final, beautiful sunset. During the third season of CBS's *The Dick Van Dyke Show*, in 'The Return of Edwin Carp', the episode broadcast, suitably enough, on April Fool's Day 1964, our hapless television-writer hero Rob Petrie, as played by Dick Van Dyke, hits upon the idea of putting radio on television. It guest-starred London-born surrealist and nasal-heavy character actor Richard Haydn as the eponymous and

Bert joins Richard Haydn and *The Dick Van Dyke Show* regulars Morey Amsterdam, Richard Deacon and Rose Marie, in harkening to Arlene Harris, 1964.

fictitious fish impersonator and monologist. To give the show some authenticity and charm, broadcasting veteran Arlene Harris was lovingly showcased with a sparkling performance of her classic one-way telephone conversation shtick, while the affectionate attempt to contact the Mad Russian easily locates Bert Gordon. Answering the phone with, inevitably, 'How doooo you do?' the intervening years disappear in an instant. It's a television moment to bring a wistful tear of joy to the eye. Performed with perfect dignity some thirty years after *Girl Crazy* had launched him, it was also Gordon's last professional assignment. He took his final bow, in sunny California, on 30 November 1974. He was seventy-nine.

A true comic original, indelibly set in aspic, Bert Gordon is a unique, timelessly enchanting giver of joy.

TREAT YOURSELF TO *A Golden Hour of Comedy* (On The Air: 101901, 1994), an invaluable CD compilation from Portugal, of all places, which kicks off with a tasty morsel of radio revelry from Eddie Cantor and Bert Gordon, as the Mad Russian neighbour Boris Tsoris (that's Yiddish for trouble, folks!). Further treats for your ears come from cover stars Laurel and Hardy, Burns and Allen and Groucho Marx, as well as Fred Allen, Jack Benny, Ernie Kovacs, Milton Berle, Red Skelton and Abbott and Costello's 'Who's on First' routine.

# 'Monsewer' Eddie Gray

## 1898–1969

I'm delighted to say I have worked with many people in this book, but I will never forget being in the same digs as 'Monsewer' Eddie Gray. Mealtimes with him were so funny: he said everything in his mangled French accent and caused such laughter at the table, it was almost impossible to eat.

*Dame June Whitfield*

'Well, you can't have big stuff all the time, you know. You've got to have some little stuff in-between!' So saying, the outrageously faux-French 'Monsewer', beneath the big top, introduces his tried and tested juggling act, which comes in the wake of Genie Lionel Jeffries and some particularly miraculous doings in the very last Crazy Gang film, *Life Is a Circus* (1960). The film is itself a threadbare reworking of a Crazy Gang hit from twenty years earlier – when Alastair Sim had played the genie in *Alf's Button Afloat* (1938). Still, *Life Is a Circus* is awash with treats, not least of which is the glorious preservation of the mighty Monsewer's

NO ONE ALLOWED IN THIS SECTION

Eddie joined Flanagan, Knox, Naughton, Nervo and Gold, for *These Foolish Kings*.

stage patter. If it doesn't give you a tantalising thrill, you may as well close this book now.

Comedically, it is the grumpy, bespectacled Monsewer, with cod French, cod moustache, cod everything, who steals the whole picture. With that fake 'tache aquiver and the almost tangible beery breath beneath the throbbing, claret conk, the Monsewer relentlessly sends up everything: the plot, the other actors and, both within and without of the narrative, the very flea-bitten circus and flea-bitten film production in which the character and the man find themselves. It is a very modern performance; almost postmodern in its concept. It's Walt Disney's Grumpy dwarf made flesh – an arrogant, beguiling, almost malevolent spirit of dissent in a world of song, sniggers, and sentiment. It was a triumphant return to the gang, for other than rejoining them for the 1948 Royal Command Performance at the London Palladium, Gray had been *en absence irrégulière* since *la guerre*. Absent without leave since the war, peasants!

Born to Rebecca and Edward Earl Gray in Pimlico, London, on 10 June 1898, Eddie grew up just a stone's throw from the sainted Victoria Palace Theatre that would be the Crazy Gang's playground for so many years. One of nine children, his skill as a comedy juggler-deluxe developed from an early passion. Like the booze-addled genius that was W. C. Fields, before him, he had to be proficient at the art before he could make mock, but by the age of nine Eddie and his brother Danny were good enough to join a juggling troupe that would tour America, Europe and the Far East. To relieve the boredom of his easy skills while he wowed his audience, Eddie added casual comic asides. It was the start of a self-deprecation and disrespect for everything within the act that would make him a star.

By the late 1910s he was sharing a variety bill with comedian Jimmy Nervo, and when, in 1919, Nervo teamed up with fellow eccentric dancer and knockabout comic Teddy Knox, it seemed a natural progression to recruit Gray too. However, Gray doggedly kept his individuality within the act. He was a more sophisticated madman looking into the jaws of the asylum; a more urbane and cultured counterbalance (albeit with tongue firmly in cheek) to the slapstick antics and slow-motion comedy wrestling of his gloriously insane cohorts. Touring with them throughout the 1920s, Gray determined to schedule solo spots too, memorably joining the company of Scots entertainer Harry Launder to tour Australia and South Africa.

Now wallowing in international plaudits, in 1931 the trio had a watershed year. Eddie married Patti Loftus, of the famous variety act the Loftus Sisters, and joined Nervo and Knox for the London Palladium revue *Crazy Week* – an appropriate and indeed prophetic title, for the bill also included the energetic double act of those other soon-to-be Crazy Gangers Charlie Naughton and Jimmy Gold. These inspired clowns were already experts in spontaneous mayhem when other *Crazy Week*, and *Crazy Month*, revues followed. By 1932 Bud Flanagan and Chesney Allen had joined in the fun, and the following year all seven played the Royal Variety Performance at the London Palladium. Though Gray gave a memorable film appearance as a goose trainer in the Jessie Matthews cross-dressing comedy of manners *First a Girl* (1935), after the obligatory turn in Nervo and Knox's romp *Skylarks* (1936) the following year all three were swallowed up within the larger team, now officially dubbed The Crazy Gang. Their annual London Palladium shows *London Rhapsody* (1937), *These Foolish Things* (1938) and *The Little Dog Laughed* (1939) kept West End audiences in stitches in the years immediately before the Second World War.

However, when the 1936 stage romp *O-Kay For Sound* became a film the following year Gray had been absent. Indeed, he would also be absent from all the Crazy Gang films produced during the war years. Apart from a cough and a spit in the George Formby comedy *Keep Smiling* (1938), during this period Gray concentrated his efforts on the stage, perfecting his 'cockney French' juggling act and bringing the house down with a wry look to the stalls, a cynical adjustment of

Ooh la la! As the proprietor of a Riviera cafe, with Sonya Cordeau, *These Foolish Kings*, 1956.

his top hat and a burst of continental lunacy. He even added the odd word of German for seasoning. But then came the 1948 Royal Command Performance and a re-call to arms for the Crazy Gang. Laurel and Hardy were the top-line comedy act that night – and which comic trooper could possibly turn that down? Certainly not the 'Monsewer'.

With *Life Is a Circus* and the television reunion *Together Again* (Associated-Rediffusion, 1957) being as far as Chesney Allen was willing to take his return to show business at the time, it was a five-strong Crazy Gang that soldiered on through the remaining Victoria Palace Theatre shows. Although Gray didn't join in the fun of *Jokers Wild* in 1954, Vera Day, who bravely suffered the itching-powder pranks of the old boys, remembers that: 'the "Monsewer" would come and see the show all the time. He was just pals of them all; he was always there. He was there more times than the Queen Mother, and she was there a lot. We had to acknowledge her in the royal box!'

By the time they reconvened for their silver anniversary show, *These Foolish Kings*, in 1956, the Gang was already a national treasure and Eddie Gray was firmly back in the cast. Robert Tee, in his review for the *Daily Mirror*, proclaimed the show had 'more laughs than a chemist has aspirins'. Unsurprisingly, the Gang, with the 'Monsewer' on board, were back for more Victoria Palace insanity with *Clown Jewels* in 1959 and, finally, *Young in Heart*, which ran for nigh on eighteen months from the Christmas of 1960. Poignantly titled and tinged with emotion, it was always designed to be the gang's swansong. So historically important was its last night, of 19 May 1962, it was recorded for television, broadcast by ATV from 8.25pm. the following evening.

Eddie Gray didn't have retirement on his mind, though – it was the dirtiest word he knew, and he knew a lot of dirty words! The following year he took to the West End stage again, as Senex, at the Strand Theatre, opposite Frankie Howerd, Jon Pertwee, Kenneth Connor and seasoned old-timer Robertson Hare, in the original London production of Stephen Sondheim's *A Funny Thing Happened on the Way to the Forum*. Reviewing the production for the *Observer*, Bamber Gascoigne noted 'the highest laurels must go to Eddie Gray and Frankie Howerd for a wonderful quality of detachment. They both make a comic routine ten times funnier by plodding through it as though it occupies only one-fifth of their attention.' Even when clad in a toga and singing 'Everybody Ought to Have a Maid', this was the Eddie Gray of the fluorescent nose and joke-shop moustache. A veteran variety turn in ancient Rome: exactly what Stephen Sondheim had had in mind.

Throughout the 1960s, Gray continued to mangle language, as well as most of his limbs, in the pursuit of laughter. He even resurrected Crazy Gang ties, when Bud Flanagan took on his first television situation comedy, *Bud*. ATV, who had showcased their final stage appearance, ran the six episode series from July 1963. The premise was deliciously meta, featuring Bud – with old pal Charlie Naughton in tow – now out of work after the gang has disbanded, and in need of another job. Gray happily popped in and out for old times' sake, as did Chesney Allen, in his positively last reunion with his old comic partner.

In September 1969 Gray made an unscheduled and uproarious appearance in comedy double act Elsie and Doris Waters' show at the Royal Hippodrome Theatre in Eastbourne. Those lucky enough to be there noted his clear emotion at the wave of love from the audience that greeted his spontaneous interjection. The 'Monsewer' died just three days later at his home in Shoreham-by-Sea, West Sussex, but what a way to go. Always leave 'em laughing.

TREAT YOURSELF TO *Life Is a Circus* (Network The British Film Collection: 7953966, 2013). If 'Monsewer' Eddie Gray's bombastic, ageless sense of world-weariness doesn't floor you, check your funny bone.

# Raymond Griffith

## 1895–1957

Dapper and debonair, Raymond Griffith was a slapstick sophisticate. Not only was he a true comedy auteur but he was an excellent character comic too, which means his films, and even his brief appearances elsewhere, spill over with brilliantly played gags and an avalanche of charm.

*Pamela Hutchinson, Silent London*

January 1926 saw the release of one of the greatest silent comedy films. The film is also universally acknowledged to be not just one of the great silent films but also one of the great films, period. An epic, comedic look at the American Civil War, it tells of a spy for the Confederate States of America, on the trail of a shipment of gold, who comes face to face with Abraham Lincoln, Sitting Bull and a bunch of irate American Indians.

Now if that sounds a little bit like – and yet an awful lot not like – Buster Keaton's *The General*, that's because that masterpiece didn't start shooting until June 1926, with a release the following February – a full year after Clarence G. Badger's constantly hilarious, awe-inspiringly inventive *Hands Up!* – the ultimate unsung classic of silent comedy. And its star was Raymond Griffith.

*Hands Up!* – 'an historical incident, with variations', as the credits explain, allows our smooth hero to leap from one beautifully staged set piece to another. Along the way, Griffith distracts a firing squad, gatecrashes an American Indian war dance and skilfully juggles the affections of two women.

As with all his successful contemporaries, Griffith had an instantly recognisable look. He was the off-centre toff, complete with top hat, white tie and tails, and as often as not doing full-on sophistication with a flowing cape and a natty, steel-tipped cane. He was Fred Astaire with a Max Linder moustache.

Having made his first inroads into film comedy in 1915 with the L-KO Kompany (which at the time boasted Hank Mann, and comedy innovator Fred Karno stalwart Billie Ritchie on its roll call), Griffith joined Keystone Pictures Studio in 1916. Perhaps his finest film of that initial year was *A Scoundrel's Toll*, which cast him as a lowly tram conductor nursing ambitions to be a crazy inventor.

Griffith became part of director Tod Browning's repertory company (which often credited him as Ray Griffith) and actor and director worked together on the 1923 film dramas *The Day of Faith* and *White Tiger*. Griffith had already proved useful as screenwriter and director, under the guidance of film-making 'King of Comedy' Mack Sennett, before adapting the 1904 musical comedy *The Yankee Consul* for the screen with director Lewis Milestone.

On-screen, Griffith's acting range was impressive, but it was as Igor in *Open All Night* (1924), a winning comedy of social manners and one-upmanship, that he shone brightest. In January 1925, he played the Honorable Bertie Bird in the Bebe Daniels farce *Miss Bluebeard*. In it he is the personification of dandy and fop. Thankfully, the film still survives, making one ache for more discoveries.

Some audacious bedroom scenes in *Forty Winks* (1925) – in which he starred as a dogged detective aided and abetted by his dog – made this film a hit, while *The Night Club* (also, 1925) was the blackest of romps, with Griffith's lovesick

As crime-busting coroner Mr Green, with Dorothy Sebastian, solving the Friday the 13th mystery in *You'd Be Surprised*, 1926.

Romero preferring to hire assassin Wallace Beery rather than live without Vera Reynolds. Shades of Bernard McKenna's *The Odd Job* which appeared forty odd years later. It proved a smash hit, and it fully made Griffith a star comedy attraction.

Immediately before collaborating on *Hands Up!*, Griffith and director Clarence Badger presented the breakneck-chase comedy *Paths to Paradise*, released in June 1925. Based on the 1914 Paul Armstrong play *The Heart of a Thief*, it was produced by Adolph Zukor for his fledging Paramount Pictures.

*You'd Be Surprised* (1926) sees our star playing coroner Mr Green in a wry comedy mystery with romantic interest provided by Dorothy Sebastian. The 1925 film *He's a Prince!* (also know as *A Regular Fellow)*, with director Edward Sutherland at the helm, was a success in America but fell foul of distribution in Britain due its satire of the Prince of Wales.

Shortly after, Griffith fell victim to the arrival of sound in the cinema. Due to a childhood accident, he could barely speak above a whisper. His last starring vehicle, *Trent's Last Case* (1929), was released by Fox in both silent and sound versions, with the latter saddled with a clunky explanation of his subdued vocal delivery. Touchingly, he was at his best at what he used to do, with a performance of emotive mime as an ill-fated French soldier in *All Quiet on the Western Front* (1930), the directorial masterpiece of his old chum Lewis Milestone. The film also featured Griffith's wife, Bertha Mann, uncredited as Sister Libertine. The couple had two children.

As sound cinema vanquished the silents, Griffith made a fair living as writer and co-producer in Hollywood's fast and furious era before the Hays Code. But disillusioned by the sanctified restrictions the Motion Picture Producers and Distributors of America put on Hollywood from the mid-1930s, he retired to a comfortable life of tall tales and telltales. He died on 25 November 1957, following a choking fit in the Masquers Club, Los Angeles.

For one perfect year, in 1926, Raymond Griffith had made the world laugh uproariously. It was a champagne-bubble of a career, and one of the finest vintage.

TREAT YOURSELF TO *Hands Up!* (Grapevine Video: B002YP8Y98, 2007), a gem that deserves constant admiration. Laudably, America's

The extant films of this unfairly forgotten screen star handsomely reward the viewer a century since his roaring twenties fame.

National Film Registry placed a copy in its archives in 2005, considering it culturally, historically and aesthetically significant. No self-respecting comedy collection is complete without it.

# Deryck Guyler

## 1914–99

A top-class comic actor. Superb.

*John Cleese*

There is an actor who has been performing in a hit West End play for over sixty years. He is still in the cast and he has never missed a performance. Eight shows a week since 1952, his dulcet tones have set up the murderous premise of the world's most famous mystery. It's a record that remains all the more remarkable seeing as the actor in question has been dead since the turn of the century.

The play is, of course, Agatha Christie's *The Mousetrap*, and the actor is, of course, Deryck Guyler. Those refined, cultured, BBC tones are unmistakable and unmissable as his steady voice radiates from the wireless in Monkswell Manor. Guyler's slight Liverpudlian accent gives those rounded vowels a deep authority as he reveals the description of a fiendish killer who has struck in London and vanished into the night. We then meet our gallery of suspects and Guyler is heard no more, but it's a very reassuring talisman of continued success. (Comedy actor

Henry McGee, it should be equally noted, was very proud to hold the opposite distinction. Fulfilling a two-week contract as a hasty replacement for an indisposed cast member, he enjoyed the shortest stint in the world's longest run.)

The association between Guyler and radio is apt for, in his long and prolific career, he became something of a broadcasting expert. He reckoned to have chalked up an incredible 6,000 broadcasts since his debut in 1935 and, crucially for this most sophisticated of Scousers, he was proud to be the first broadcaster to use that distinctive Liverpudlian accent. He utilised its broadest form to great comic effect when, just after the war, in September 1946 he was hand-picked by star comic Tommy Handley for his radio comedy team in *It's That Man Again*. As the series writer, Ted Kavanagh, noted in his 1949 biography of Handley, 'Deryck Guyler, who hailed from Wallasey, Cheshire, and knew Liverpool as well as Tommy himself ... had already had some useful work to his credit as Sir Percy Palaver in the previous Tomtopia series, apart from an immense variety of serious parts in radio drama, and was in this [tenth] series to create the delightful characters of Dan Dungeon the Castle Guide, Sir Short Supply and the immortal Frisby Dyke'. This slow-witted loon quickly became an audience favourite and over the years Guyler would happily turn on the Scouse at the drop of a chequebook, even enjoying a supporting role as – what else – a police inspector opposite The Beatles in *A Hard Day's Night* (1964). It is ironic that in the early 1930s he had taken elocution lessons to flatten his regional accent for delivering the essential King's English of theatre and radio.

In 1935 he joined Liverpool's prestigious repertory company and found his forte in the plays of William Shakespeare. This experience stood him in good stead for, after being invalided out of the Royal Air Force Police during the Second World War, he was accepted into the BBC Repertory Company, memorably portraying Macduff opposite John Gielgud's Macbeth. It remained one of his proudest achievements. That and being a virtuoso on the washboard!

But for the rest of his career it was his flawless ability to be second banana to star comedians that made him a near-permanent fixture of the light entertainment scene. Radio was his natural habitat and after *It's That Man Again* came to an end in 1949, he went on to join the comedy troupe of fellow Forgotten Hero Eric Barker's *Just Fancy*. A gentle comedy of eccentric characters,

Guyler and Barker created the two most endearing characters, a couple of elderly gentlemen, long-time residents of the Cranbourne Towers Hotel, maintaining that it is only by listening to the other fellow, that you get the other fellow's point of view. Guyler reached his comedy broadcasting pinnacle opposite the equally clipped Richard Murdoch [qv] in *The Men from the Ministry*. The programme had started in 1962 with Wilfrid Hyde-White in the lead role, but on his departure in 1966 Guyler took up the baton and the show became even more successful. It lasted until August 1977, falling by the wayside in the Silver Jubilee year, which also saw the demise of the even longer-running *The Navy Lark*. *The Men from the Ministry* was cut from similar cloth: a very British kind of leg-pulling. *The Men from the Ministry* scripts, in the main written and produced by Edward Taylor, saw Guyler and Murdoch poke gentle fun at the politics of the nation. By the time the series came to an end, in a Britain of gobbing punks and the rise of Margaret Thatcher, it was gloriously old-fashioned. It always had been. Not so much satire as mild-mannered lampooning, it was scarcely *Spitting Image*; it wasn't even *Yes, Minister* but the affectionate ribbing of these bumbling buffoons in *The Men from the Ministry* left a pleasant aftertaste. It also made Guyler something of an omnipresence player on the wireless. Indeed, a March 1977 edition of radio comedy show *The Burkiss Way* featured a sketch concerning the impossibility of having a radio comedy show without Deryck Guyler. Although he never appeared in *The Burkiss Way*!

Guyler himself was well aware that he was, at best, an ensemble player. He wasn't star material but he preferred it that way: 'It's the old thing,' he reflected. 'It's nicer to sit back and play first violin, and let the conductor carry the can.' It was John Alderton and a load of unruly kids, far too old and cool for school, who carried the can in Guyler's first television sitcom success. Launching in November 1968, *Please Sir!* was a pioneering part of the new London Weekend Television and comedy writer Frank Muir's attempt to attract a common-denominator, Friday-night audience. Guyler had first swum into the ken of *Please Sir!* writers Bob Larbey and John Esmonde when he had starred in their radio comedy series *You're Only Young Once* the previous year. The emphasis, like that of other successes such as *On the Buses*, was on loud, broad and brash comedy strokes; the subtlety was sprinkled by the prestige performers.

Co-star Joan Sanderson would also leave her harridan handprints all over *Please Sir!*, but it was Guyler, as the irascible and pompous school caretaker, Potter, who secured the majority of laughs. He was a bombastic figure of fun – much akin to Stephen Lewis's Cyril Blakey in *On the Buses* – with his proud, elaborate accounts of Desert Rats duty and his officious running of the school as if it were a military outpost, merging with his jobsworth's attitude to his work. Deryck even released a Columbia single, in character, in 1971. '(You Can't Kill An Old) Desert Rat' failed to chart!

Caretaker Norman Potter, a beloved sitcom orgy, tried and failed to gain respect in all 55 episodes of *Please Sir!*

Interestingly, Guyler's aptitude for the more mild-mannered style of comedy had originally seen him cast as the show's ineffectual headmaster – a role subsequently played, rather brilliantly, by Noel Howlett. The shifting authority between the Head and his helper was invested with charm and gall by the two actors, giving real heart to the show. It certainly heightened the pathos within the slapstick comedy moments and in the sarcastic, undermining comments to which the horrors of form 5C subjected poor old Potter.

As was typical of the time, a full-length feature film sprang from the loins of *Please Sir!* in 1971, as did a spin-off, *The Fenn Street Gang* (London Weekend Television, 1971–73). For a period this ran concurrently with the final series of *Please Sir!*, which saw a fresh crop of youngsters recruited to take Potter's patience to breaking point.

Members of the Fenn Street Secondary Modern staff popped in for the odd guest role in *The Fenn Street Gang*, but not Guyler. Still, the actor had no employment worries, for in 1972 he was cherry-picked by one of the country's finest comedy brains, Eric Sykes, for his eponymous BBC series. It had proved a hit in the 1960s and – again, as with many such successes – it was revived, in colour, in the 1970s. Guyler was once more the authority figure – the local police constable, Turnbull – but was an altogether warmer, more jolly, even

Eric, Hat and Del took *The Eric Sykes Show* on stage, at the Winter Gardens, Blackpool, in 1977.

naive creation than Potter. Known affectionately as Corky, this bobby on the beat was more *Dixon of Dock Green* than *The Sweeney*, and would get involved in the mad misadventures of Eric and on-screen sister Hattie Jacques with always a weary shake of the head. For nigh on a decade this rather soppy, simple, sweet and innocent upholder of the law happily put an additional, cheery spanner in the works at 28 Sebastopol Terrace. Every perfectly timed twitch, sniff and kindly chuckle was just plain lovely, and he became one of the nation's favourite sitcom characters.

Corky was such an endearing and recognisable character that much of that comic persona merged effortlessly into Guyler's rare excursions into film, most notably shining in a glittering gallery of British character actors in Walt Disney's 1975 romp *One of Our Dinosaurs Is Missing*. As the bemused security guard of the Natural History Museum, Guyler's astonished reaction to a seemingly re-animated brontosaurus skeleton is a masterclass.

Guyler remained a familiar face on television for years after *Sykes* came to an end, in 1979, but eventually emigrated to Australia, in the early 1990s, a happy man and a contented man, enjoying his lifelong hobby of painting model soldiers and creating meticulously detailed, historically accurate settings for them, with his little corner of a foreign field. His legacy, particularly in television sitcom, is a rich one indeed. And there's always *The Mousetrap*. This charming play will forever feature Guyler's scene-setting performance, and its run will simply go on and on. So, if you've seen it, please keep the secret of *The Mousetrap*, if only for the sake of keeping Deryck Guyler in the West End.

TREAT YOURSELF TO *Sykes – The Complete Series* (Network: 7954602, 2017), twelve discs of glorious comedy featuring every single moment of Deryck Guyler's PC Corky Turnbull. Arrestingly amusing. H'oh, yes!

# Brian Hall

## 1937–97

Comedy is teamwork: even a solo stand-up needs an audience to use as an energy conduit or target for banter. In double acts there's always a straight man, in slapstick there's always someone to lay down the banana skin. And in a sitcom the funniest characters can only be so if their surroundings showcase them at their best. *Fawlty Towers* is one of the greatest sitcoms of all, but its brilliantly memorable lead characters didn't exist in a vacuum. Basil's awfulness would be nothing if we didn't see him patronising the guests, getting furious with builders or trying to suck up to the gentry. And Basil – and Manuel and Sybil for that matter – would not be as effective without something, or someone, normal to act as a contrast to the glorious largesse of their characterisations.

I was always taken with Brian Hall's performance as Terry in the second series – not because he was a consistent source of belly laughs, but actually because he wasn't. With everyone around him giving career-best performances and creating icons in the process, Hall provided a solid backdrop for the craziness to bounce off. It needn't have been that way, for Terry is no dull straight man – he is dishonest with Basil when trying to get a few quid extra out of him, and his kitchen hygiene is open to question – but Hall never tries to steal the laughs. In an age when cockney characters often reminded you how cockney they were by jutting out their jaws, cor-blimeying their way out of trouble or adopting the high-pitched whine favoured by work-shy privates languishing at the bottom of the cast list of any number of British war films, Hall lets the character speak for himself. Lesser actors might have gurned their way into prominence but Hall plays Terry as a real person, not a walking embodiment of 'cockney chef', and is more quietly impressive for that.

He's a convincing part of the set-up too; he has an especially believable dynamic with John Cleese's Basil and Connie Booth's Polly. As writers they must have been grateful that someone was happy to serve their script rather than mug their way into the centre of proceedings, and Terry becomes a vital part of the *Fawlty Towers* team. Cleese was very kind about Hall in later life and was clearly happy with his work. While they were lucky with Ballard Berkeley as Major Gowen and strong turns in virtuoso guest-roles from the likes of Bernard Cribbins, Joan Sanderson and Bruce Boa, those parts were, frankly, hard to mess up. Yes, they benefitted from the input of the skilled actors mentioned, but Hall had a harder job with a role less vividly rendered on the page. It is to his credit that Terry remains memorable for all the right reasons and not for any unnecessary attempts at scene-stealing in a character who wasn't there for that purpose. What he did was unfussy, competent and faultless, allowing the story and the characters around him to prosper.

It was always fun seeing him turn up in other things – he lends credibility to *The Long Good Friday*, memorably endures the ire of Colin Firth in *Tumbledown* and, having missed out on the TV version for some inexplicable reason, crops up in *Doctor Who* in one of its rare sabbaticals on radio, appearing opposite Jon Pertwee in *The Paradise of Death*, during its thirtieth anniversary year in 1993.

He was a face you recognised and were happy to do so – he was reliable and welcome, and a distinguishing feature of the television landscape of the 1970s and 1980s. Not every actor can be a star, but really good supporting actors help those stars to shine.

*Toby Hadoke*

It's still almost impossible to believe that *Fawlty Towers* ran only to twelve half-hour episodes. So densely plotted and fast-paced were the John Cleese and Connie Booth scripts that at least three episodes' worth of plot are at play at one single time. It's even harder to believe that Brian Hall, as the cheerful cockney hotel chef Terry, appeared in only six episodes. He was brought in for the second series, in 1979, and displayed such a lightness of comic touch and such deep understanding of the character that you can see his backstory and swinging social life in every chilled-out meal preparation.

He certainly bonded – both on screen and off – with the four principals: John Cleese and Prunella Scales as hotel-owning married couple Basil and Sybil Fawlty, Connie Booth as the flirty wannabe-artist-cum-waitress Polly, and Andrew Sachs as Manuel, the clumsy waiter from Barcelona. Into this perfect cube of situation comedy greatness came Brian Hall.

From that very first episode of the second series, the classic 'Communication Problems', on 19 February 1979, with Joan Sanderson as a hard-of-hearing guest, Hall hits the floor running. His presence as part of the hotel staff isn't explained; it doesn't need to be. Unflappable in the kitchen and with a cheeky-chappie grin, the role of Terry helped sustain and widen the situation.

For John Cleese, the very best episode ever was the very last episode ever, 'Basil the Rat', which owing to a strike at the BBC was broadcast half a year after the rest of the series, on 25 October 1979. In the plot a spiralling series of catastrophic events emanate directly from Terry's manor, the Fawlty Towers kitchen. It is faced with closure due to its sloppy conditions, so the impending, crucial visit of the health inspector is potentially damning. And Manuel's pet rat is on the loose. A poisoned slice of veal is put down for the rat but, naturally, veal is what the health inspector has ordered for lunch. Moreover, the hotel cat has had a nibble. It's the comedy of confusion but, typically, Terry the chef is calm and matter of fact: 'Right. How's the cat?' he asks. 'How's the cat?' Basil explodes, but Terry is no fool. If the cat is all right, the bit of veal he has tasted is all right; it can be trimmed and served up. Problem solved. As a feed to Basil, Terry's cool attitude is less flamboyant than Manuel's but all the funnier for it.

With his close-cropped hair, lightweight-boxer physique and cockney swagger, Brian Hall brought a knowing quality to the role of Terry; you certainly believed his character could look after himself, and it was hardly surprising when the series revealed that Terry's hobby was karate.

For Hall, it was something of a blessing to be cast in a sitcom, for he had spent much of his career pigeonholed as the hard man. Adding a lighter touch allowed Hall to flex his acting muscles. Happily, *Fawlty Towers* wouldn't undermine his gangster image completely. His television CV would include all the usual '70s and '80s suspects: *The Sweeney* (in the 'Trap' episode, Euston Films, 6 October 1975), *The Professionals* ('Not a Very Civil Civil Servant', London Weekend Television, 18 November 1978), *Minder* ('You Gotta Have Friends', Euston Films, 21 January 1980), *C.A.T.S. Eyes* ('Cross My Palm with Silver', TVS, 17 May 1985), *Big Deal* ('Deals on Wheels', BBC1, 16 September 1986) and *Boon* ('Do Not Forsake Me', Central Television, 20 November 1989). Perhaps most effective of all was his performance as a knowing taxi driver in 'It Must Be the Suit', the opening episode of Trevor Preston's *Out* (Thames Television, 24 July 1978). Dropping off the recently released convict (played by Tom Bell) he refuses payment – he's been inside himself and knows the angst-sweats of returning to normality. Again, in just one brief scene Hall conjures a whole backstory.

On film, Hall played a bloke on the 'phone in the Amicus horror portmanteau *From Beyond the Grave* and a Nazi confronted by dinosaurs in *The Land that Time Forgot* (both, 1974); his on-screen geezer pedigree also made him a shoo-in for the lyrical violence of both *Sweeney 2* (1978) and *McVicar* (1980) – it's tantalising to think that the latter's Terry Stokes is our Terry from *Fawlty Towers* back on the cloudy side of the street.

Although a Brighton boy, Hall always brought the confidence of a Covent Garden chancer to a role. He also brought a sense of mischief, often leaving cast and crew in fits of laughter at his relentless, straight-faced streams of made-up cockney rhyming slang. He was fun even when making an advert for tea, as co-conspirator and actor David Barry remembers: 'The setting was a wedding, and Brian and I were making speeches as a groom and his best man at the wedding breakfast. We were saying the most outrageous things, which went way beyond innuendo, because the speeches were not recorded for sound. Instead there would be a jingle playing over the pictures. But as someone later pointed out, lots of lip-reading deaf people would either be shocked or have a great laugh!'

Hall had started his career with local amateur dramatics while in his teens; even then, his pugilistic attitude saw him cast as hard men. While working as a taxi driver he was spotted by theatrical agent Richard Ireson who encouraged him to give acting another go. Hall swiftly became a favourite at the Royal Court Theatre in John Antrobus's *Crete and Sergeant Pepper*, opening on 24 May 1972. He appeared in Ron Daniels's 1974 production of *Afore Night Come* at the Other Place, Stratford-upon-Avon, for the Royal Shakespeare Company, and proved he could turn his heels to a good old knees-up, too, playing the roguish Harry Adair in the musical *Liza of Lambeth*, at the Shaftesbury Theatre, from 8 June 1976.

As a playwright Hall collaborated on *Made It Ma* with farce specialist John Chapman, at the Royal Court in 1976, and in 1984 worked with Tunde Ikoli on *Bit a' Business* for the National Theatre. His first break on television came with *Softly, Softly: Task Force* (BBC1, 1969–76), in which he landed the regular role of copper Ted Drake. Even when on the right side of the law, Hall seemed to be from the wrong side of the tracks. It would happen in comedy, too, when he was another Terry, in the George Baker gangland sitcom *Bowler* – it was just one episode, 'The Ides of March', (LWT, 29 July 1973), but it sets out Hall's stall as a right hard nut. He was a particular bastard of a British serviceman in *Adolf Hitler: My Part in His Downfall* (1973), and even his removal man in *Confessions of A Window Cleaner* (1974) is a bit dodgy.

The *Fawlty Towers* effect certainly lightened the tone of his comedy, and it increased his output too. In comedy fare of the '80s and '90s he cropped up in *Cannon and Ball* (LWT, 10 May 1986), *The Little and Large Show* (BBC1, 13 February 1988), *Terry and June* ('The Artistic Touch', BBC1. 5 December 1983), *2point4 Children* ('Leader of the Pack', BBC1, 3 September 1991), *The Upper*

As Harry Adair in *Liza of Lambeth*, a musical adaptation of W. Somerset Maugham's first novel, at the Shaftesbury Theatre in 1976. Brian's songs included 'Gawd Bless Yer'. How very apt.

*Hand* ('Sex, Lies and Exercise Tape' and 'To Let or Not to Let', Central, 3 November/28 December 1992) and *Birds of a Feather* ('Non Starter', BBC1, 19 September 1993). He enjoyed playing Brian the barman in the Jim Davidson sitcom *Up the Elephant and Round the Castle* (Thames Television, 1983–85) and relished his best comedy role of the 1980s, as Pat the milkman in the Diane Keen and Tim Brooke-Taylor domestic sitcom *You Must Be the Husband* (BBC1, 1987–88), with Hall gleefully pinpointing the ever-increasing impotence and irrelevance of the paranoid, frustrated house husband. As the imp on Tim's shoulder, Hall was a great catalyst for laughs.

Even serious illness couldn't dampen his pluck. Talking about his cancer diagnosis to the *Mirror* in 1996, Hall showed typical determination and sheer bloody-mindedness: 'Cancer is a bully and I hate bullies. This old boy cancer will get about as much change out of me as all the other bullies I've met – nothing.' Brian succumbed, in Worthing, Sussex, on 17 September 1997, at the age of just fifty-nine, but there was zero respect right up to the final curtain. One thing is for sure: Brian Hall went out punching.

IN THE UNLIKELY scenario that you don't already own it, you must treat yourself to *Fawlty Towers – Series 2* (2 Entertain Video: B00005NGUQ, 2001). It's the master chef's masterwork.

# Lloyd Hamilton

## 1891–1935

Lloyd 'Ham' Hamilton is today mostly forgotten despite his reputation as a 'comedian's comedian'. Charlie Chaplin, Harold Lloyd, Buster Keaton, Mack Sennett and Charley Chase all professed their admiration for him – indeed, Chaplin is said to have described him as 'the one actor I am jealous of'.

Sadly the bulk of his movies are lost, and only a few examples of his work can be seen today. A big, pug-faced man with a mincing walk and often with a flat cap perched precariously like a pancake on his head, his performance is appealing and his gags inventive, but without access to the movies of his golden period, with Educational Pictures in the 1920s, it's hard to see why the comedy greats put him on such a high pedestal. Film historian Kevin Brownlow has a theory that Chaplin, Keaton and Co. became so tired of being asked which comedian they most admired they got together and agreed to nominate the unlikely figure of Hamilton as a joke. It's an unkind theory, as Hamilton's surviving work shows a subtly and inventiveness that suggest the possibility that his lost movies were indeed great.

Lloyd Hamilton died aged forty-three, beset by personal and alcohol problems. Perhaps one day enough of his work will surface to allow us to make a proper judgement. For the time being, I'm happy to take the word of Chaplin, Keaton, Lloyd, Sennett and Chase.

*Graeme Garden OBE*

I've long admired and supported the Bristol Slapstick Festival. Although it primarily celebrates the custard pies and arse-kicking of Charlie Chaplin, Buster Keaton and Harold Lloyd, its remit is wide enough to embrace everything from Mary Pickford to *The Young Ones*. During the 2012 convention, a running joke erupted involving the genius or otherwise of a forgotten hero of silent comedy: Lloyd Hamilton. He was hugely respected by his peers, with Keaton reflecting he was 'one of the funniest men in pictures'. So was this an industry send-up floating within a time bubble from nearly a century before, or was it genuine praise?

Many delegates were sceptical. It smacked of mockery and insincerity: like Stewart Lee lavishing praise upon James Corden. The proof of this particular comic pudding was in the eating, and when we were actually shown some Hamilton material, I, for one, was very impressed indeed. For the uneducated, Hamilton's style resembles Oliver Hardy and Harry Langdon in a blender. Chubby and walking as if he has just sat up from a damp patch, he glows with a boyish neediness lightly touched by surrealism. That baby face as malleable as Play-Doh.

Hamilton was certainly challenging the boundaries of film-making, with one of his finest surviving films, *The Movies* (1925), featuring our hapless hero as a country boy bidding farewell to the farm, yet the shining city of dreams in which he hopes to make his fortune is located directly next door. It is this imaginative streak, encouraged by his director Roscoe Arbuckle, that established him as a great film comedian. It was a flourish that would have undoubtedly impressed Keaton and Hamilton's other peers.

Lloyd Vernon Hamilton, or 'Ham' as he became known both professionally and personally, first trod the boards in 1909 working for theatrical and operatic troupes in Northern California. He entered films as an extra just before the outbreak of the First World War, making his mark in a double act with diminutive dimwit Bud Duncan. The 'Ham and Bud' comedies ran for just over three years and, in a makeshift fashion, served as the blueprint for every physically contrasting comedy double act ever since. The fat man plus the small man equalled funny. That was until the winter of 1917, when Hamilton tired of the relationship, dropped Duncan like a hot peanut and signed up with Fox.

*The Educator*, a comedy two-reeler, directed by Lloyd Bacon, 1922, Educational Pictures.

In 1920 Hamilton and directors Charley Chase and Jack White started Mermaid Comedies, a special film unit tailor-made to churn out two-reeler comedies with Hamilton, looking typically bewildered, in the lead. *Moonshine* and *The Simp* were released that same year and each proved popular.

The following year, Hamilton starred in *The Vagrant* and in *Robinson Crusoe, Ltd.*, which prompted praise from critic James W. Dean: 'Lloyd Hamilton is hereby nominated for a place in the hall of comic immortals. Chaplin, Lloyd and Keaton must crowd up a bit to give him room.' And that was no joke.

In the safe, workmanlike hands of director Norman Taurog, Hamilton starred in a string of comic shorts before, almost inevitably, ego and demons led to his downfall. *His Darker Self* (1924), Hamilton's first attempt at a feature-length comedy, was a financial disaster. Hamilton played a wannabe detective infiltrating a black community to solve a murder case. The film was almost solely reliant on blackface confusion and racial stereotyping for laughs, and now survives only as a cut-down two-reeler. His second feature, rather unfortunately called *A Self-Made Failure* (1924), also bombed at the box office and, with

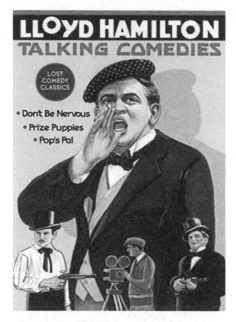

A 2016 Alpha Video release for three 'Lost Comedy Classics' released between 1929 and 1933.

his tail between his legs, Hamilton returned to comedy shorts.

While Keaton, Lloyd and Chaplin continued to flourish in features, Hamilton became something of a forgotten man. His increasing dependence on alcohol and his wilderness years are the textbook case of the downfall of a silent clown. Both of his short-lived marriages ended in divorce. The first, to actress Ethel Lloyd in May 1913, ended in a bitter two-year court battle; the second, in June 1927, to Irene Dalton, who had appeared in many of his films, lasted just one year and ended in her unsubstantiated claims that he beat her while drunk. In 1929 Hamilton's reputation was further tarnished by his suspected involvement in the street-brawl death of boxer Eddie Diggens. As in the case of his friend and colleague Roscoe Arbuckle, Hollywood mud didn't brush off.

Educational Pictures laudably signed Hamilton for a series of *Lloyd Hamilton Talking Comedies*. The best of these – *Toot Sweet!* (1929), *Polished Ivory* (1930), and *False Impressions* (1932) – deliver much of his reputation, and although those once-frantically-mobile boyish looks show signs of weariness, the comic energy remains high. He later joined Mack Sennett at Universal, but when his contract came up for renewal and producer Hal Roach's interest in his career started to wane, Hamilton hungrily accepted a few bit parts back at Educational Pictures.

In October 1933 Hamilton was twice arrested and jailed for drunken behaviour. After a year without work, on 18 January 1935, he was tracked down by friends to a rented room in downtown Hollywood. Rushed into hospital suffering stomach ulcers, he died the following day. He was just forty-three.

This personal tragedy was compounded two years after his death, when a laboratory fire destroyed the only surviving prints of dozens of his finest films.

Only a handful of classics and jagged remnants remain, though fortunately more than enough to confirm once and for all that the great and the good of slapstick were not sending him up all those years ago. 'Ham' is indeed one of the greats of silent comedy, and forgotten no more.

TREAT YOURSELF TO *Lloyd Hamilton – Talking Comedies 1929–1933* (Alpha Video: B01BMH1NGO, 2016), a collection of three 'lost comedy classics': *Don't Be Nervous* (1929), *Prize Puppies* (1930) and *Pop's Pal* (1933). As Mack Sennett said: 'Lloyd Hamilton had

As Breezy in *A Self-Made Failure*, with Ben Alexander as Sonny. The feature film was directed by William Beaudine, for a June 1924 release from Associated First National Pictures. Alas, no print is known to survive.

it. Comic motion. He would just walk across the room and apparently do nothing, but just make you laugh.' Amen to that.

# Arthur Haynes

## 1914–66

The greatest of forgotten comedians.

*Paul Merton*

My ultimate ambition for all the forgotten heroes celebrated within these pages would be for them to wriggle out of obscurity and be heralded once more. Over the time I've spent researching and writing this book, the only one of them who has got near to achieving this is Arthur Haynes. Though he was one of the top television comedy stars of the 1960s, for years and years his vast catalogue of recorded work languished in the archives. Only his supporting turn as a sarcastic hospital patient in the 1966 film *Doctor in Clover* has served as a reminder of his comic genius whenever it is occasionally televised – for contemporary audiences a clear indicator of Haynes's television clout, now something of a disconnected remnant, a sole echo of a glittering career. A role filmed, ironically, just before his untimely death, the bedridden moaner Tarquin Wendover fully captures Haynes's multilayered comedy persona. He was the world-weary loser; the cynic;

the hard-done-by Everyman who wasn't prepared to take it any more. It could sum up Haynes's legacy.

Thankfully, in recent years comedian Paul Merton has been a vocal champion, fully celebrating him in a clip-stuffed BBC4 retrospective in 2011, and by 2013 those lovely chaps at Network established a complete release programme of *The Arthur Haynes Show* resulting in seven volumes and amounting to a whopping forty-five hours. They form an essential investment for the serious comedy devotee.

It is not unfair to say that as soon as Tony Hancock left his greatest writers and the BBC behind, in 1961, Arthur Haynes easily filled the gap. He was the common man within a comedy sketch. We were in on the joke. We were *in* the joke. He would bait and beat authority. Indeed, he was often in the criminal class, but only ever as an endearing rogue.

For the champagne socialist extraordinaire, East End boy and Arthur Haynes's chief television writer Johnny Speight, the idea of a tramp with careful disregard for money or status came to him when his Rolls-Royce was waiting at a set of traffic lights. An opinionated vagrant promptly got into the vehicle and sat down – and bingo: the fully formed comedy character of the belligerent down-and-out who was never downhearted when encountering figures of authority was born. He was always referred to in production paperwork as 'Hobo Haynes', and Speight used that very first encounter to inform a battle over a taxi cab with a top-hatted toff, played by Nicholas Parsons, in a sketch featured in *The Arthur Haynes Show*, broadcast 8 December 1960.

Like Hancock, Haynes was more of a comedy actor than a comedian, and just as Hancock was at his best within the confines of the imaginations of writers Ray Galton and Alan Simpson, Arthur Haynes had his own distinct comedy Jiminy Cricket in Speight. Before he created the immortal sitcom figure of Alf Garnett, Johnny Speight had Haynes to voice his views on politics, religion and every other contentious topic that Garnett would grouch on about for the next thirty years – indeed, Haynes's anti-establishment rants are often peppered with instances of Garnettesque 'Innit marvellous!' and 'Cor blimey'. In one sketch, in *The Arthur Haynes Show* transmitted on 30 March 1961, Haynes eyeballs the doctor, played by Nicholas Parsons, and rambles on about the unfairness of his sick pay being stopped, and his requirement of new boots and a hospital bed on the NHS – it's very much the Alf prototype.

Again like Hancock, Haynes was an intuitive performer. In those days of live or 'as live' recordings, he could work a failed prop or lapsed line of dialogue to his advantage. Absolutely nothing phased him. He would chew for ever on a stubborn bit of food before he would take the scripted mouthful of booze or deliver the scripted line. As often as not, the more audience laughter these departures from the script produced, the more Haynes did it, and the more he did it the louder and more raucous the laughter became, whether he was bleating on about his experience of the Second World War, when he was 'up to my neck in muck and bullets', delighting in the company of Irish sparring partner Dermot Kelly, or delivering bewitching, mischievous mime as odd 'everyman' Oscar Pennyfeather. There was even a heated debate between cheerful cat-burglars, in which Haynes was partnered by a promising newcomer called Michael Caine. Comic sparks fly in this classic sketch, featured in *The Arthur Haynes Show* of 8 December 1962. Whatever the occasion, Haynes could work the ATV studio audience like the conductor of an orchestra.

Also like Hancock, he was adept at the monologue. A great example is the classic scene in the 23 May 1962 edition of *The Arthur Haynes Show* where, in his celebrated tramp guise, he tries to use all his wiles to secure a police-cell bed for the night. Apart from the odd interjection from the desk sergeant, the scene is minutes of pure Haynes pondering. The desk sergeant, played by Haynes's long-standing – actually sitting down here – straight man Tony Fayne, does nothing but glance up from his work with a look of disdain. The comedy is in the throwaway reaction shots, and in the twist of the knife that Haynes did so well.

Haynes was a rascal of the old school; not unpleasant, just persistent. He could try the patience of a saint and, opposite Tony Fayne's inexhaustible galley of vicars, clergymen, and priests, often did. With a few well-chosen words of praise and humility, Haynes could have his feet up in front of your fire, carving your turkey and guzzling your brandy as soon as look at you. He was a master of deception and of human nature. The combination of Johnny Speight as the intelligent scribe and Haynes as the brilliant marionette remains one of the most dazzling of comedy collaborations.

As for so many of his generation, it was the outbreak of the Second World War that set the seal on Haynes's life as a comedian. The only child of a London baker, Haynes racked up a string of jobs including plumber, joiner and painter. During the war he served with the Royal Engineers, and it was here that he met comic 'Cheerful' Charlie Chester and a firm friendship was established. Chester was already part of the army concert party Stars in Battledress and encouraged his friend to continue performing once the war was over. After the two had been

As the taxi driver in *Strange Bedfellows*, directed by Melvin Frank, 1965, Universal Pictures.

demobbed, they unexpectedly worked together again on the BBC Radio series *Stand Easy*, broadcast from 11 February 1946. Although originally intended as a starring vehicle for Chester, Haynes were featured more and more as part of Cheerful Charlie's gang, and by the time the series had come to its natural end, in 1949, the two were very much a double act in the eyes and ears of the nation. So much so that, thanks to popular demand of the listeners, the BBC brought them and the variety sketch show format back, as *Keep Smiling*, in 1951.

Thanks to his popularity following a string of summer season, pantomime and variety theatre engagements, Haynes was given his first television spot, with ATV, on 21 February 1956. The show, *Strike a New Note*, was written by Dick Barry, Johnny Speight and John Antrobus, and featured Nicholas Parsons as the ever-unflappable straight man. Haynes and his writing team provided similar sketch-based fun for *Get Happy* (ATV, 1957), and it wasn't long before the Haynes, Parsons and Speight team were spearheading *The Arthur Haynes Show*, which was first broadcast on 2 January 1957. The blend of star comic Haynes and urbane stooge Parsons was perfect; intuitive. The partnership was poetic. One sketch sees them as two dogged club members fighting over the one available chair. It is a ballet of one-upmanship and tactics, and quite, quite

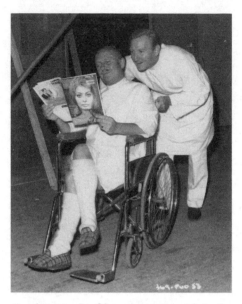

Catching up on film star gossip with Leslie Phillips during the making of *Doctor in Clover*, shot in late 1965.

beautiful. There's even a gloriously bizarre scene, suitably enough in the Hallowe'en night 1964 edition, where both Haynes and Parsons are almost unrecognisable behind dog masks. It's surreal, silly, and hilariously funny. The pair just had the right chemistry.

The format of the show hardly changed at all during its run – there was no need. With tongue-in-cheek musical interludes from Aileen Cochrane and from Pearl Carr and Teddy Johnson, Haynes himself preferred to keep his singing voice (though not unpleasant) largely under wraps on television, though he did record a number of serious, heart-warming numbers for commercial release and happily sent up any delusions of hit-parade grandeur when, for *The Arthur Haynes Show* of 23 February 1963, he teamed up with Dickie Valentine to form the hilarious Haynes Brothers with each singing alternate words! Respect for the pop world was demonstrated by guest appearances from The Springfields, the Dave Clark Five, Joe Brown and the Bruvvers, and even The Rolling Stones.

*The Arthur Haynes Show* would keep Haynes extremely busy for the rest of his life. Indeed, over 150 episodes were aired over one decade, with a sixteenth series due to go before the cameras just before his death on 19 November 1966. The success of the series saw Haynes on the bill of the Royal Variety Performance at the Prince of Wales Theatre on 6 November 1961, and Speight also scripted the show for radio from 1962 to 1965, with support from regular second banana Nicholas Parsons. Speight also wrote another radio outing for Parsons and Haynes, *Arthur Again*, in 1962. Even America sat up and took notice: Haynes's guest appearance as a London cab driver in the Rock Hudson and Gina Lollobrigida romantic comedy *Strange Bedfellows* (1965) was hardly going to set the world alight but his casting within the Swinging Sixties London scene – along with Terry-Thomas, who played an assistant mortician in the film – spoke volumes of his place as a comic signifer. Every British act was cool in 1966 and Haynes was pretty much the coolest comedian around. A trip from Hollywood to New York to appear on *The Ed Sullivan Show* (CBS, 6 November 1966) was the icing on the cake. Less than a fortnight later Arthur Haynes was dead. He was on the cusp of superstardom.

All this while retaining the calm and relaxed persona of a working-class boy made good. There was to be no compromise: Arthur Haynes was British through and through. After all, if his old mucker Michael Caine could wow the Americans, why not Haynes?

Alas, we would never know. His tragically early death at the age of just fifty-two curtailed a star comedy career just before it peaked. Internationally, potentially. Without Arthur Haynes, the world may not have seen the creation of Alf Garnett, and thus, in turn, no Archie Bunker. ITV may not have plugged the gap in their schedules by courting and eventually headhunting Benny Hill. Who knows? What is clear, however, is that following his death Haynes's shows seem bizarrely to have been promptly filed away and forgotten about. There were no 1980s repeat-seasons (unlike Tony Hancock) even though there was no excuse (unlike Sid Field), leaving almost the full collection of Haynes's television work languishing in the archives, gathering dust. Thankfully, this oversight has since been rectified; it may be thirty years too late, but it is rectified. Unquestionably the most popular comedian of commercial television's fledgling years, Haynes has left a rich legacy of laughter that rewards countless revisits.

TREAT YOURSELF TO *The Collected Arthur Haynes Show* (Network: 7954774, 2017): the whole surviving kit and caboodle – 101 episodes spread over seventeen discs – which 'returns him to his rightful place among the comedy greats'. What are you waiting for?

# Richard Hearne

## 1908–79

Richard Hearne, or Mr Pastry as we all knew and loved him, is a very underrated clown. His dancing is remarkable. My only real memory is of him wrestling with a deckchair, but what a fantastically fit actor he was. I would have loved to see him getting into the T.A.R.D.I.S. – it could do with some slapstick! Robert, you are just the man to introduce him to a new generation. I'm so glad he's in the book.

*Mike Grady*

Such is the all-consuming power of playing Doctor Who that it can practically obliterate the rest of your life and work. Doctor Who number three, Jon Pertwee, is hardly a forgotten man – but a forgotten hero of comedy? Quite possibly. A versatile man of a thousand voices, Pertwee was a gift to radio, whether as the conniving Chief Petty Officer Pertwee in *The Navy Lark* or the bumbling Puffney Post Office Postman ('Tear 'em up!') Pertwee in *Waterlogged Spa*. Utilising Pertwee for characters certainly helped make that name, but still the Time Lord legacy is universal – quite literally. The effect could take hold even if you didn't end up playing the part. Take Geoffrey Bayldon, for example. Despite delighting a generation as both that wacky wizard Catweazle and the rather disturbing crow man in *Worzel Gummidge*, he is remembered almost as much for turning down the opportunity to star in *Doctor Who* from the very start, in 1963. Even those fabulous entertainers Ron Moody and Jim Dale, Fagins in *Oliver!* both, have rather too many paragraphs on *not* being Doctor Who cluttering up write-ups on their vast and varied careers.

As for Richard Hearne, he is merely a footnote in television history, rather better remembered for not being Doctor Who IV, eventually played by Tom Baker, than for anything he had achieved up to that point. In 1974 *Doctor Who* producer Barry Letts offered Hearne the role and, with a gleeful blurring of the edges between actor and character, his reaction was that '"Pastry" wasn't quite right for the part.' As with Jon Pertwee before him (who had, incidentally, worked alongside Mr Pastry in many an edition of his television series), it wasn't this reassuring screen persona that the producer required but the actor himself. But just who was Mr Pastry, and why couldn't he have been Doctor Who?

Well, as any well-informed fool knows, Mr Pastry was the accident-prone, kind-hearted, slapstick-proof comic-genius creation of Richard Lewis Hearne. Hearne's father, Richard senior, had been an acrobat, and this seemingly genetic ability to fall over without hurting oneself informed Hearne's entire comic persona. Mr Pastry was a loner, a gentle outcast, clad in tattered jacket and battered bowler hat. The whole hilarious sorry state was topped off with a huge walrus moustache, and for thirty years, looking out from within this bundle of shabby stage wear, Hearne spun his own unique brand of small-screen magic.

The Pastry character evolved slightly over the years since Hearne first unleashed him onstage at the Saville Theatre, supporting portly comic turn Fred Emney in the 1936 musical *Big Boy*. Still, most of the familiar elements were in place from the outset: an old but agile man, clumsy, but endearingly sentimental. In 1937, with Hearne on sousaphone and Emney on the piano, the two teamed up with comic droll Leslie Henson, playing the cello, for a televised act *The Worse Than Narkington Quartette*. Mr Pastry further invaded Hearne's West End stage success at the old Gaiety Theatre, in the comedy revue

In Mr Pastry Richard created a unique comic character, here about to pedal off on another misadventure!

*Running Riot*, selected scenes of which were performed for the 1938 Royal Command Performance at the London Coliseum. In was in this show that Hearne premiered his celebrated 'Lancers' act, an hilarious eccentric dance routine, which he had adopted from the late comedian Tom D. Newall. By the time Hearne made his television debut on 19 August 1946 in the one-off ten-minute sketch 'The Village Store' for the BBC *Variety* series, Pastry was pretty much fully formed. In those pioneering days at Alexandra Palace, the John Logie Baird system allowed for a ninety-second delay between performance and transmission, affording Hearne the opportunity to complete his slapstick routine, canter down a corridor, and actually watch his turn go out to the nation. During the 1950s, Hearne would relentlessly go through his slapstick paces for an enthralled generation, with an early series *Mr Pastry's Progress* (BBC Television, 1951) being produced by none other than Ian Carmichael, who was a BBC staffer before becoming an actor. Another claim to fame, Hearne was the first television comedian afforded his own signature tune – the Folk Dance Band recording of *Pop Goes the Weasel*.

These programmes were usually very compact – fifteen minutes was the average – and extremely messy; perfect for easily distracted children, in fact, and a staple that made bank holidays more special for many. In *For the Children*, April Fool's Day 1951, all Hearne had at his disposal was a mound of pastry. So Pastry made pastry. It was more than enough – of course it was! This bumbling handyman character with no odd job too odd, and with a thousand-and-one ways of making a fool of himself, quickly became part of the British psyche.

And it didn't happen just in Britain. In France, where Mr Pastry was rather endearingly known as Papa Gâteau, he was considered a comedy god in the same breath as Chaplin. In Germany he was a hit under the name Sugar Tart. In America he made a record-breaking number of thirteen appearances on

*The Ed Sullivan Show* (CBS, 1954–68) and proved so popular that even Buster Keaton counted himself a fan. There is no higher accolade in all of comedy. In fact, Keaton was such a champion that in the summer of 1958 he travelled to England to star alongside Hearne in *The Adventures of Mr Pastry* for ATV. Suitably enough, Hearne played the pupil to Keaton's professor, albeit an unwitting, gullible one falling for a con trick. In a perfect piece of casting, Peggy Mount played their bossy landlady. Sadly, this fascinating prospect was curtailed after just one episode, transmitted on 21 June 1958, owing to Keaton's illness forcing him

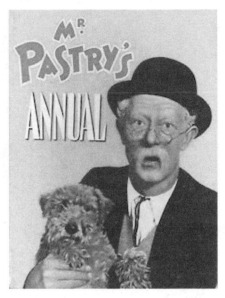

For children of all ages, this was found under many a Christmas tree in 1956, published by Morrison and Gibb Limited.

to return home. Pastry ploughed on though, with a return to the BBC in a run of self-contained twenty-five minute programmes throughout the early 1960s, as well as full series of *Leave It to Pastry* (BBC Television, 1960), *Ask Mr Pastry* (BBC Television, 1961) and *Mr Pastry's Pet Shop* (BBC Television, 1962). Give that comedy powerhouse a few buckets of slosh, a vat of flour and an endless supply of objects to fall into and over, and he could have slapsticked you into eternity. He certainly relished his seemingly never-ending regional tour of *Mr Pastry Comes to Town*, when kids of all ages could meet and greet the man himself.

Still, when real old age started to catch up with Hearne, and Mr Pastry needed less and less sprinkled flour in his hair to create the desired decrepit effect, he began to scream into the wind of light entertainment. He would decry the ever-increasing reliance on lewd humour in television comedy. Although Hearne often complained bitterly that Mr Pastry was an alter ego that had unfairly overshadowed his other acting roles – he had been Gregory Peck's orderly in the 1951 film *Captain Horatio Hornblower R.N.*, for heaven's sake – the character was a spectre of fun that made an awful lot of people very happy

The beautiful quad poster for *Miss Robin Hood* (1952).

indeed. It didn't take much persuasion for Hearne to don the well-worn Pastry attire once more. One of Mr Pastry's last outings was in the nostalgia-wallowing setting of *The Good Old Days*, which welcomed Hearne in the March of 1976. He came out of semi-retirement one more time, when he replaced an indisposed Deryck Guyler [qv] as the Baron in *Cinderella* for the London Palladium Panto season of 1977–78. Fresh posters were printed to bill Richard (Mr Pastry) Hearne, and he played it as Baron Pastry, of course!

For an often charitable lifetime delighting the young and the young at heart, Hearne certainly deserved his OBE, though it should also have been for keeping in work dry cleaners, glazers, decorators... for there's no denying he was one of the finest practitioners of the art of relentless slapstick.

TREAT YOURSELF TO one of the rare feature-film outings that allowed Hearne to escape the mantle of Mr Pastry. *Miss Robin Hood* (Showbox Home Entertainment: B000OMCIMC, 2007) is a delightful Group 3 comedy fantasy from 1952, starring Hearne as comic-strip writer Henry Wrigley and Margaret Rutherford as the deliciously dotty Miss Honey. She is so obsessed with his fictional teenage safe-cracker that she takes on her mantle in order to fundraise for an orphanage faced with closure. It's all lovely stuff and exposes Hearne's real heart, not to mention the much more youthful features that all the Pastry paraphernalia had obscured for so long. What's more, in a cast as rich as any British comedy's of the day, you can wallow in the company of Sid James, as Rutherford's chauffeur, as well as Hearne's one-time producer Ian Carmichael, lowly and callow in the newspaper office from which our hero is dismissed!

# Dickie Henderson

## 1922–85

Following my six wins on television's *Opportunity Knocks*, my first professional stage engagement was supporting Jack Jones and Dickie Henderson at the London Palladium for two weeks, in October to November 1972. Whilst Jack was, shall we say, less than welcoming, Dickie rallied round this nervous newcomer and took me under his wing.

I'd long been a fan of Dickie's, remembering him from his television series when I was growing up in the 1960s and his exploits with Tanya the Elephant. His classic routine as a Frank Sinatra wannabe was a lesson in style and perfect comic timing. Dickie was a great all-rounder and a very underrated performer. His casual style was more like that of an American performer and it's my belief that American audiences would have loved him and made him an international star, had he not been so loyal to the UK.

Following the Palladium season, Dickie insisted that I was brought in as 'special guest-star' on his summer season show at the Congress Theatre, Eastbourne, the following year. There I got to know him well, along with his lovely wife Gwynneth and his daughter Linda, who, being a similar age, became a special pal.

I'm privileged to have known Dickie and worked with him – a true gentleman and a real class act.

*Bobby Crush*

A copper-bottomed Mr Showbiz, whose long and winding road of a career had a strong whiff of Hollywood razzmatazz, Richard Matthew Michael Henderson was born in Stepney, London, on 30 October 1922, steeped in the traditions of greasepaint and the red nose and the big boots. His father, the rotund, bowler-hatted droll Dick Henderson, was a huge star of variety and the first British artist to record the song 'Tiptoe Through the Tulips', to his own ukulele accompaniment, which he would use as his opening stage number. Meanwhile, Dickie's two sisters toured the music halls as close-harmony singers the Henderson Twins.

Having performed to great acclaim across America from 1924, Henderson Sr. took California by storm in a handful of Vitaphone short comedies and feature films at Warner Brothers. Dick Henderson packed up his troubles and his family, and returned to settle in Hollywood in 1933. Young Dickie's Californian education would undoubtedly shape his destiny. He would pick up an easy, laid-back, transatlantic style that made him an attractive prospect in British variety, and he had his first taste of stardom when British director Frank Lloyd cast him in Noël Coward's *Cavalcade* (1933), playing Master Edward, the son of Brits in Hollywood Clive Brook and Diana Wynyard. Ironically, Dickie had fully embraced Americanisms: 'They gave me an English tutor and made me read English comics,' he later explained. 'While I was struggling to say "carn't" and "darnse" I was itching to be out there pitching with a baseball team!' In March 1934, *Cavalcade* won the Best Picture Oscar and director George Cukor offered Dickie the lead in Charles Dickens's *David Copperfield* at MGM.

However, Dickie's father was reluctant for his son to become entangled in the Hollywood rat race, so it was back home to Blighty for the pair of them. Years later, Dickie was philosophical about missing out on such a career-defining role: 'It was a daunting experience at the time and I had no aspirations to become a movie star – it was just a giggle. The stage was the big attraction. I watched my father working and he gave me encouragement and advice. I'll never forget him saying: "Show Business is 90 per cent luck and 10 per cent talent. But don't bother trying if you haven't got that 10 per cent talent.'"

Max Miller with Dick and Dickie Henderson, in *Things Are Looking Up* (1935).

Bandleader and theatre impresario Jack Hylton spotted Dickie's 10 per cent and offered him a job as a props boy for one pound a week – it wasn't much, but the young lad gratefully accepted it. This wannabe song-and-dance man would take any excuse to be in a theatre, although his father warned him: 'If you want to be Fred Astaire, you practise ten hours a day. But if you want to be a comedian you don't have to practise at all!'

Dickie quickly proved his natural talent for comedy, touring the variety circuit with his father and even teaming up for a film together, sparring with Max Miller and Cicely Courtneidge in *Things Are Looking Up* (1935), Dickie a confident, stylish and pugnacious version of his old man.

Dickie sang, danced and joked his way through variety until the Second World War broke out, when he joined up with the Royal Army Service Corps. As soon as he was demobbed it was back to revues, pantomimes and summer seasons. Dickie recalled he 'clowned my way up', making his debut at the London Palladium in 1950.

In 1953 he broke into television with his particular brand of good-natured wisecracks and polished banter in *Face the Music*, introduced by genial host and bandleader Henry Hall. Dickie's confident and casual manner was perfect for the intimate warmth of television, and, from that February, he became a regular, with Diana Decker, on Arthur Askey's BBC variety show *Before Your Very Eyes*. The distinctive glint in Henderson's eye effortlessly connected with West End audiences, too, when he starred at the London Casino in the 1953 musical cabaret *Wish You Were Here*. This success was immediately followed by his own personal favourite, a twenty-month run from 17 January 1955, as Sakini the Okinawan interpreter in *The Teahouse of the August Moon* at Her Majesty's Theatre.

Producer Brian Tesler had used Henderson in many a variety show, and when he left the BBC for ATV in 1956 he lured Henderson with an offer to temporarily take over from Tommy Trinder as the guest host of *Val Parnell's Sunday Night at the London Palladium*. Henderson would be associated with the show, on and off, until 1960.

Now basking in celebrity, Henderson played a comedian in the film drama *Time Without Pity* (1957), and he and Arthur Askey reunited for the advertising satire film *Make Mine a Million* (1959).

It was with Askey's daughter, Anthea, that Dickie had become a sitcom star, with *The Dickie Henderson Half-Hour*, presented by his former boss Jack Hylton. The show ran on Associated-Rediffusion for two series, from July 1958 to June 1959, and the pairing of Henderson and Askey proved so popular that there followed a stage version and even a cartoon strip *The Dickie Henderson Family*, in *TV Comic*. The series was a mash-up of the modern domestic mishaps and misunderstandings of American shows *I Love Lucy* and Sid Caesar's *Your Show of Shows*. Indeed, the writing of Neil Simon, Mel Brooks and other sharp scribes for the America series was bought lock, stock, and barrel, in a canny cost-sharing deal that Hylton had struck with NBC, and funnelled through the transatlantic Babel Fish translator of Jimmy Grafton, a very safe pair of comedy hands, who was recruited as script associate. Experienced variety television director Bill Hitchcock coaxed winning performances from his stars.

In 1959 Dickie Henderson and June Laverick were cast as married couple Andy and Nicky Persichetti, in Jack Hylton's musical production *When in Rome* at the Adelphi Theatre. In this show Dickie was the mild-mannered husband, as well as the raucous hero Tiger Joe, his alter ego within his wife's sensational novel *Rock-a-Bye Baby*. The pairing of Henderson and Laverick worked so well that, in 1960, during the run of the stage show, Hylton and Associated-Rediffusion cast them as husband and wife, Dickie and June, in *The Dickie Henderson Show*. Dickie was his cool and confident self. June was rather wacky and disorganised, causing domestic mayhem at every turn. Lionel Murton brought cigar-chewing clout to the role of his friend and agent, Jack. Albeit with various cast changes (his only son was played by John Parsons and later Danny Grover, and following Laverick's retirement from the business Isla Blair was cast as Henderson's wife for the ninth and final series), *The Dickie Henderson Show* chalked up one hundred and sixteen episodes between 14 November 1960 and 20 March 1968. But it was practically beer-and-skittles money for Dickie, ostensibly playing himself, with stage and screen work often referenced within the plots. Still, it was an effortless charm that was polished to perfection, and Henderson embraced the 'show must go on' mentality even when his wife, Dixie Ross, of the American singing contortionist act the Ross Sisters, died, at just thirty-three, while he was making the fifth series in July 1963. Concurrently to television work, Henderson was starring in theatrical hits including *Show Time*, for the 1968 summer season at the Pavilion Theatre, Bournemouth, and *Stand By Your Bedouin*, for the 1969 summer season at the Pavilion Theatre, Torquay. Throughout the 1960s and 1970s, Dickie also wowed audiences at the London Palladium and toured America, Canada, South Africa and Australia. His patter was effortless; his physical comedy a poetic contrast to the cool, Sinatra style he cultivated. Indeed, despite a chilled-as-vintage-champagne delivery of a gem from the American songbook, it was the nadir of this Sinatra cliché that made him such a popular stage turn. He would pretend to battle an anonymous stagehand for the microphone, much to his embarrassment and desperation. He would emulate the saloon-style singing of the 'chairman of the board' then disrupt the suave performance by clumsily burning his lips, getting drunk and slipping off the bar stool.

His easy way with the standards of Cole Porter and the Gershwins certainly had a sincere side too and, from the late fifties to the early seventies, he proved it with guest spots on such television staples as *The Ed Sullivan Show* (CBS, 1958–71), and *Jack Paar Tonite* (ABC, 16 October 1973). Still, it was those pitch perfect comic routines that most delighted audiences.

The legendary 'One For My Baby' routine – a deconstruction and celebration of the legendary American singers he always wanted to be a part of – was a masterclass in milking every last possible guffaw out of a simple but

As Buttons, reunited with Arthur Askey for Charles King's *Cinderella*, Birmingham Hippodrome, 1972–73 season.

precise comedy situation. It was subtle and hilarious. It was enough to bewitch impresario Bernie Delfont and secure Henderson no less than eight Royal Variety Performances. A 1967 routine with Tanya the baby elephant has passed into variety legend, with the delightful pachyderm bonding with the star and winning the hearts of the Queen, the Duke of Edinburgh and the entire London Palladium audience – the very definition of showstopper as her trunk lifted a banner that read 'I work for peanuts'. The elephant escapade was such nationwide news that a whole television series was built around it. *A Present For Dickie* (Thames Television, 1969–70) featured Dickie returning home from a tour of the Far East, with Mini, an Indian elephant, in tow! His much-discussed wife – travelling home on a slow boat from Australia – only appeared in the last episode. A lovely touch, she was played by an out-of-retirement-for-one-night-only June Laverick: his erstwhile wife from *The Dickie Henderson Show*.

Henderson's subsequent by-royal-appointment appearances ranged from a Monte Carlo cabaret for Prince Rainier and Princess Grace of Monaco to a special private concert for the Queen and the Royal Family at Windsor Castle.

He always found time to lend his talents in support of the Stars Organisation for Spastics, a tireless charity commitment that earned him an OBE in 1977. That same year he teamed up with the only comic who could match his transatlantic charm for *I'm Bob, He's Dickie*, and when the Monkhouse partnership ended amicably in 1978, he sang, danced and joked on, in May and October, with two hour-long ATV variety spectaculars *I'm Dickie – That's Showbusiness*. It certainly was.

His last great achievement was the staging of *An Evening with Dickie Henderson* at the Bob Hope Theatre in Eltham on 17 September 1982. Both Henderson and Hope were golf-crazy; indeed, Henderson would try to play every single day, getting his handicap down to eight. His obsession was no secret, and when he featured on *Desert Island Discs* in the summer of 1960, his luxury item comprised his golf bag and balls, and his choice of book the mythical *How to Play Your Best Golf All the Time*. As for his final choice of disc for the island, that was Ethel Merman belting out 'There's No Business Like Show Business'. There's his own personal anthem, right there.

At his happiest, on the golf course, with Mini the Elephant, promoting Thames Television's *A Present For Dickie*, 1969.

For Dickie Henderson, it was show business until the end. He left a lot of joy – joy that has frustratingly been forgotten over the years.

Dickie Henderson was an entertainer who made you happy with his very presence onstage, that problematic microphone in one hand and a cigarette in the other, that winning grin firmly in place, and those eyes that sparkled with glee. Here was a chap you would warm to instantly and who guaranteed a fun, swinging, feel-good time. His charisma was Las Vegas with a very British streak, and oh, how we loved him for it.

TREAT YOURSELF TO the sensational vinyl album *Sincerely, Dickie* (Beacon Records: SBEAB10, 1969), a glorious collection of standards, produced by Phil Carson, allowing Henderson to ditch the slapstick shtick and breath-taking hoofing so pivotal to his stage appearances, and sing 'em from the heart. As the sleeve note puts it: 'we can't put those falls on to record, nor his scintillating dancing but here is the voice... It strikes us he would have made the top as a singer alone if he'd not been so energetic and multi-talented but that's the kind of man Dickie is – a true entertainer.' Truth.

# Gerard Hoffnung

## 1925–59

When I was about eleven, a friend of mine played me a cassette tape she had found of an old man having a conversation with an American guy, about his life and work. It was hands down one of the funniest things I'd ever heard. We lay in her room in the dark, listening and snorting with laughter until we were told once and for all to 'keep the noise down'. The cassette was a home-made recording that my friend had found in a box of mixed junk at a jumble sale, and was not marked in any way. We had absolutely no idea who this man was, or why the recording had been made (we didn't even know if it was real or played by actors), but it was so brilliant and odd that I made my own copy of her tape and played it over and over again at home, rocking with glee.

It was several months before I discovered that the old man was in fact the famous cartoonist, broadcaster, musician and writer Gerard Hoffnung, and the recording was from a series of comic interviews with Charles Richardson called *The Importance of Being Hoffnung*. The mystery had lingered in that charming but frustrating pre-internet age, but once I knew who this comedy god was, I was in for a treat – because what followed was a minor obsession with his many other broadcasts and musical endeavours, and particularly his astonishing, magical cartoons (many of which I heavily plagiarised for home-made birthday cards and so on).

His drawings captivated me – whole worlds in black ink, the detail, the visual gags. I would stare at them for hours. He died tragically young, at thirty-four, but if he had lived he would no doubt be far better known and given the public approbation he deserves. Gerard Hoffnung was a playful genius with a great and hilarious comic mind.

*Katy Brand*

Some people are just born brilliant. Brilliantly brilliant. None more so than Gerard Hoffnung, who I am convinced was born a middle-aged intellectual. By the time of his early death, he sounded as though he had survived the Crimean War to spend half his life in a deep, leather chair with a cigar in one hand and an eternally topped-up brandy balloon in the other. He would often state: 'I was born at the age of two.' More like seventy-two!

Hoffnung was a humanitarian, a scholar, a cartoonist, a wit, a raconteur, a musician, a wordsmith, a linguist, a gentleman. In other words, the 'Profession' strip of his passport was never going to be big enough. He was quite simply the most poly of polymaths.

He was raised in Hampstead Garden Suburb and educated at Highgate School. With the distilled air of the flask hanging to his leather-patched smoking jacket, he was a sophisticated chap who would prop up the bar while chewing the cud about everything from world politics to the latest cricket scores. And he would always keep the most important things until last.

He was a wildly precocious talent. Heavily involved with *Lilliput*, the monthly humorous magazine, his first cartoon was published under the editorship of Tom Hopkinson, while Hoffnung was still studying at Highgate. He graduated to Hornsey College of Art and, like most of its best students, it seems, was promptly expelled. The Harrow School of Art followed, and then life as a schoolteacher. His first gainful employment came at Stamford School,

Lincolnshire, while also submitting illustrations published in the *Stamford Mercury*. He then returned to Harrow to teach art, but life could never be that simple for Hoffnung.

Born Gerhard Hoffnung in Berlin, on 22 March 1925, he was taken from Germany to London while still a boy to escape the upsurge of the Nazi Party. A sense of justice, of anarchy and an indefatigable sense of mischief informed his talent for both art and music. As early as 1949 Hoffnung had staged a successful one-man exhibition at the Little Gallery in Piccadilly. His published cartoons had often seen the funny side of classical music. Hoffnung could see the funny side of almost anything. Indeed, it was his beloved tuba that propelled him to fame, playing with the Morley College Orchestra in the fifties, always with an eccentric flourish.

In 1950 this satirical gene had been given voice, when Hoffnung made his wireless debut on the BBC. He was a broadcasting natural, and his flair for language and fruity rhetoric would enliven scores of panel games and interview broadcasts. His intelligence was the size of Africa, his sense of the absurd completely without boundaries. He was born for the radio, with his intimate, almost conspiratorial style with the microphone, his self-awareness, his delicious mockery of 'the Corporation' and, above all, a way of making every single thing he talked about endlessly fascinating. Here was the very embodiment of the post-war wit. Even that ever-poised tinge of pompous grumpiness was dissipated by his sense of sheer, irrepressible joy.

That joy was most memorably showcased in the Roy Plomley-hosted radio panel game *One Minute Please*, from the summer of 1951. Devised and produced by Ian Messiter, and very much a blueprint for *Just a Minute*, it required players to talk on a given subject for sixty seconds, without pause, repeats, or deviation. Hoffnung continually stole the show with his acrid sense of humour and seemingly endless supply of hilarious anecdotes. He also reigned supreme with the highest ever score of 17 points, four times the average!

Also in 1951 he took to the Royal Festival Hall with the first in a series of hilarious and stimulating classical concerts. The sheer charm and cheek of these concerts was captured in his publication *The Hoffnung Symphony Orchestra* (Dobson, 1954), an absolutely typical slice of gentle and affectionate mockery.

By 1956 the Royal Festival Hall played host to the first pioneering and influential Hoffnung Music Festival. A further hilarious assault on the senses, the Hoffnung Interplanetary Music Festival, which was staged there in 1958, put him at the cutting edge of raucous ridicule of British culture. Being a real renaissance man, it was of course his beloved classical music that formed the arrowhead of his best work. Hoffnung loved the music, and it showed, in the remorseless and wicked deconstruct. It was done with

A Hoffnung self-portrait, with 'myself (I think!)' at the bottom of the sketch.

affection, and panache. So much so that fellow satirist, pianist Donald Swann, along with the celebrated conductor Malcolm Arnold, gleefully joined in with the liberating insanity of Hoffnung's musical soirées. The Hoffnung Music Festival events were ambitious, irreverent and deliciously unpretentious. Indeed, the inaugural one delighted in a grand overture for symphony orchestra, organ, rifles, three vacuum cleaners, and an electric floor polisher. It was pure Hoffnung.

The all-too-few recordings of Hoffnung show him as an Everyman; a man of conscious and of compassionate wit; truly a man for all eras. He would have stormed *Have I Got News For You* and beaten all comers on *Mock the Week*. He would have dominated *QI* with just a tenth of his brainpower and run rings round those who profess to govern us on *Question Time*. In short, Hoffnung was a born orator. The fact that he only had a few short years in which to do so is a tragedy for all of us. His subversive silliness ploughed on without him and within others. The Royal Festival Hall staged the Hoffnung Astronautical Music Festival in 1961, while the 1969 concert was in aid of the Notting Hill Housing Trust and featured guest conductor Dudley Moore, very much Hoffnung's spiritual son. The concert made allocation for community coughing, requesting patrons reserve any coughs for this designated two-minute period. In February

'Tired Man Playing the Horn Tuba': a typically playful Hoffnung musical cartoon.

1988, the Royal Festival Hall presented two days of concert, resurrecting pieces from previous shows, and touchingly featuring guest appearances from Hoffnung's widow, Annetta, and their timpanist daughter, Emily.

Hoffnung's last public appearance had been at his beloved Royal Festival Hall, but this time for a campaign for nuclear disarmament, not a slice of musical whimsy. A devoted Quaker, Hoffnung was not only a very funny man but a very humane one. He would debate for the good of the nation on discussion programmes and in correspondence. He too would frequently visit disadvantaged prison inmates, a campaigner for better living conditions for all.

All the genius, all the good work, all the magnificent thoughts were curtailed on 28 September 1959, when he suddenly collapsed and died from a cerebral haemorrhage. It was so bloody cruel.

Undoubtedly his most famous recording had taken place less than a year earlier: on 4 December 1958 he delivered his Oxford Union address. The entire speech is a joy, but the best-loved section details a letter published by the Federation of Civil Engineering Contractors. The letter is read as an explanation of an unfortunate accident that had befallen a poor chap who had been trying, rather unsuccessfully, to collect some loose bricks from atop a building site. Filling an empty barrel with said bricks, the hapless individual explains that: 'unfortunately, the barrel of bricks was heavier than I was and before I knew what was happening, the barrel started down, jerking me off the ground. I decided to hang on!' The relentless tale of woe is quite simply one of the funniest things you will ever, ever hear. The beauty is not in the story itself (it's a fairly obvious string of slapstick vignettes). The pure delight is in Hoffnung's gurgling, playful and beautifully mischievous glee in the telling. It is a towering performance. For that alone, Hoffnung must never ever be allowed to be forgotten. In fact, I vote for a lovingly crafted bronze statue of the great man to be prominently placed outside the Royal Festival Hall – where else?

THE SOUND OF HOFFNUNG mono

COLUMBIA

*The Sound of Hoffnung* EP, a 1958 release from Columbia which features 'Punkt Contrapunkt' and 'A Dissertation on the Tuba'.

TREAT YOURSELF TO *Hoffnung – A Last Encore* (BBC Radio Collection: 0563226161, 2002) which features not only the Oxford Union bricklayer speech but all the Hoffnung recordings preserved within the BBC archive, including a hilarious interview with radio presenter Charles Richardson. Essential. Just ask Katy Brand...

# Shemp Howard

## 1895–1955

The humour was the most undistilled form of low comedy.

*Ted Okuda and Edward Watz*

The Three Stooges are one of the greatest of all film comedy teams. They churned out literally hundreds of two-reelers for Columbia Pictures throughout the 1930s, 1940s and 1950s. Their images have been recreated on T-shirts, collectible figurines, wall clocks and every other bit of authorised home-cluttering tat imaginable. Indeed, at the time of writing, offspring of the team are crowdfunding a junior film comeback with *The Three Little Stooges*.

The iconic line-up is as omnipresent in American culture as the three-man team of *Last of the Summer Wine* is to a British audience. Like the Yorkshire Dales romp, the line-up of The Three Stooges was wont to change in personnel, but the type was constant. There was the wild-haired lunatic – always Larry Fine; there was the pudding-basin hair-cutted leader – always Moe Howard; and there was the childlike slaphead – originally Moe's brother, Jerry 'Curly'

Howard, but not always, though Jerry's bald-pated Stooge figure became the best loved and most instantly recognisable of the trio. When the filmmaking brothers Bobby and Peter Farrelly resurrected the franchise with *The Three Stooges*, in 2012, it was the Larry, Moe and Curly line-up they embraced. Of course it was – it was those

Larry, Moe and Shemp welcome back Curly – in a gag role, with hair! – for the 100th Stooges short, *Hold That Lion!*, 1947.

original shorts that had been repeated on television (relentlessly in America and in England very rarely) over the years. Actor Will Sasso was cast as the 'Curly' for the twenty-first century.

There were others before Sasso. Joe Besser – well loved as the man-child who continually bettered Lou in television's *The Abbott and Costello Show* – was suitably hairless for the job. Then came Joe DeRita, who reluctantly took on the mantle of Curly-Joe DeRita to complete the illusion. It is DeRita who is probably the most aired third Stooge on British television, as it was he who joined Larry and Moe for their 1963 *It's A Mad, Mad, Mad, Mad World* cameo. Subsequently, a run of cartoons – even one series that depicted robotic Stooges! – also had a bald third Stooge. But there is a forgotten Stooge – one with hair! And his name is Shemp Howard.

Yet another Howard brother, he was born Shmuel Horwitz, in Manhattan, New York City, on 11 March 1895; Shmuel was hastily Anglicised to Samuel and forever Shemp, due to his Lithuanian mother's struggle to pronounce Sam. Shemp was there from the very beginning, teaming up with his older brother Moe in the 1920s as a vaudeville blackface double act called 'Howard and Howard: A Study in Black'. The duo never made the big time and instead Moe joined forces with an old school friend, Ted Healy. Spotting Shemp in the audience one day, Moe ad-libbed him a line – Shemp threw a one-liner right back and was invited onstage. Ted Healy and His Racketeers – they weren't

As Dizzy, with Lou Costello and Bud Abbott, in the peacetime draft comedy *In the Navy*, 1941, Universal Pictures.

dubbed The Stooges until the days of Curly – finally made it to Hollywood in 1930 with *Soup to Nuts*, for Fox. The studio wanted more, but it didn't want Healy. Various shenanigans, back-stabbing activity and even a threat to bomb theatres they were playing finally led to Shemp's decision to leave the team – with Healy nestling back in as the headliner – in 1932.

Almost immediately, Shemp was signed up by the Vitaphone film studio in Brooklyn, New York, initially supporting Roscoe Arbuckle before working his way through the ranks and starring in his own short films in the mid 1930s. In 1935 Vitaphone secured the rights to the *Joe Palooka* comic strip, the misadventures of a heavyweight boxer, created by Ham Fisher, and cast Shemp as fast-talking manager Knobby Walsh – a character who quickly became the focal point of the series. Shemp's energetic comic timing and surprise deviations from the script were a budget-film-makers' dream. He could improvise enough material to power three short films in a day.

By 1937 Shemp was settled in Hollywood. Eye-catching, albeit uncredited, bit parts, as Wacky in *Another Thin Man* (1939) and as Pickpocket Joe in *The Lone Wolf Meets a Lady* (1940), brought him to the attention of producers who needed a fast-working, fast-talking actor to lift a picture. In 1941 alone Shemp appeared in fourteen feature films, among them the film that made Abbott and Costello the darlings of Universal, *Buck Privates*, and the film that remains a monument to Olsen and Johnson [qv] and one of the funniest ever committed to celluloid, *Hellzapoppin'*. As Louie, the cinema projectionist – who is more interested in the gargantuan blonde usherette, played by Jody Gilbert – Shemp skilfully flits in and out of the action on-screen in a surreal performance of dizzying bewilderment for both him and the audience watching.

Shemp continued to steal scenes in some of the best Abbott and Costello comedies – much to the chagrin of the stars themselves. His cameo as a frustrated soda jerk in *Hold That Ghost* (1941) injects pure vaudevillian madness and helps make the film the slickest of all the Abbott and Costello comedies.

Naturally, Shemp was a shoo-in for comic relief in many other films too. He was in the John Wayne industrial drama *Pittsburgh* (1942) and the Virginia Bruce fantasy *The Invisible Woman* (the lightness of touch of this 1940 film, and John Barrymore's deliciously hammy performance make it an impossible sell as a full-blown horror). Shemp even played Sinbad opposite exotic-adventure-essentials Jon Hall, Maria Montez and Sabu in the 1942 three-strip Technicolor epic *Arabian Nights*.

Moreover, Shemp had established himself as a popular comedy star with Columbia's short-subject department. He sparred with comic galoots including Tom Kennedy and Charley Rogers, and sparked off regular Stooges glamour puss Christine McIntyre, even resurrecting some vintage Stooge plot lines for his own starring vehicles. By 1946 he was churning out two-reel masterpieces such as *Mr Noisy*, in which his loud-mouthed bore ruins several sporting events. He was so famous by now that he often simply played Shemp Howard in these twenty-minute wonders.

Meanwhile, in a parallel studio at Columbia, The Three Stooges were in a state of turmoil. Throughout 1946 Curly was often below par, slurring his lines, mistiming slapstick business and generally being propped up by Moe and Larry. In the May of that year, Curly suffered a stroke on set. Although everyone hoped for a full recovery at some point, Moe desperately turned to brother Shemp to fill in for the good of the act. Shemp was, unsurprisingly, reluctant – he was already doing very nicely at Columbia, thank you very much – but the brand and, more importantly, family loyalty won through. Shemp agreed to rejoin the troupe, but only with the proviso that it was a temporary situation until Curly recovered. Alas, Curly never did recover, and by the time Curly died, in 1952, Shemp was well and truly back in the fold, even though his wages were practically half those of his ultra-busy days as a character actor. He would eventually make nearly eighty films for Columbia as part of the Three Stooges team, all of them shorts except for a comedy Western *Gold Raiders* (1951), and even that clocks in at under an hour.

In 1949 Moe, Larry and Shemp filmed a television pilot for the ABC network for a series provisionally called *Jerks of All Trades*, and on the following New Year's Day the trio guest-starred on CBS's *The Frank Sinatra Show*. And still the Columbia short films kept rolling out at an electrifying rate – until, in 1952, the studio announced it was downsizing its short-subject unit. The usual four-days-per-film schedule was reduced to a two-day shoot. The use of footage from vintage Stooges shorts helped ease the pressure but Shemp, in particular, was disgusted by the sloppy way producer and director Jules White was treating the team's material.

Shemp had moonlighted with other comedians: most notably, he had reunited with Abbott and Costello for the film *Africa Screams* released in May 1949, but brotherly love was a hard bond to break. Shemp made his last television appearance, with Moe and Larry, on the syndicated anthology series *The Eddie Cantor Comedy Theatre* ('What Do You Want in a Show', Ziv Television Programs, 18 July 1955), and though he must have been distraught and disinterested, he stuck with the reduced Three Stooges shorts at Columbia Pictures. *Blunder Boys* – historically fascinating as Hollywood's first spoof of a television series, in this case *Dragnet* – was released on 3 November 1955. It was the typical, joyous mixture of pratfalls, pokes in the eye, hits to the body and shovelfuls of dirt in the face that had kept audiences laughing for years. It was also the last Stooges film Shemp completed. He died in Hollywood at the age of sixty, less than three weeks after the film's release. It seems his heart just couldn't take any more.

Still, with ghoulish disrespect, Shemp starred in four further Stooges films in 1956. With wholesale scenes from earlier films, random Shemp vocals from other sources, new footage with just Larry and Moe and, to the utter disgust of Moe, a stand-in Shemp, Jules White kept the Stooges going until the end of the year. The fake Shemp, bit player Joe Palma, was often and obviously seen from behind, sometimes in a huddle with the real Stooges and sometimes even half-heartedly recreating Shemp's trademark warble of 'Bee, bee, bee...' It was comedy grave-robbing.

When a full-time third man was at last recruited, bald was beautiful again – for ever – but Shemp's vital contribution must not be overlooked. The term 'Fake Shemp' is still used in the film industry when an actor is replaced by somebody else. Most don't know the origin and this should certainly never be Shemp's only lasting achievement of fame. Some of the funniest Stooges shorts are from Shemp's post-war period, and despite – or perhaps because of – the fact that his failing heart wasn't always in it, he remains a personal favourite. An endearing, reluctant hero, giving his all and giving his last for a timeless comedy team.

Detectives Shemp, Moe and Larry were '3 times as hilarious in 3-D!', taking on a kidnapping case and a gorilla in *Spooks*, directed by Jules White, for a June 1953 release.

TREAT YOURSELF TO *The Three Stooges Collection, Volume 6, 1949–1951* (Sony Pictures: B0024396EM, 2009), a beautifully remastered collection of twenty-four Stooges shorts. With Shemp at the peak of his comedy powers and Columbia still investing time and money into the films, this treasure trove is definitive. Standouts are *The Ghost Talks* from February 1949, *Malice in the Palace*, from that September, and *Three Arabian Nuts*, released in January 1951.

# Nat Jackley

## 1909—88

A unique performer. Every serious student of comedy should study
those very funny bones.

*Ronnie Corbett CBE*

*Magical Mystery Tour*, the avant-garde home movie from The Beatles that
greeted a bemused and bewildered BBC Television audience on Boxing Day
1967, was stuffed to the rafters with wild and wonderful things. It was a delayed
postcard from the Summer of Love, conjuring everything from the Fab Four
themselves, as effeminate wizards, to the proverbial fat lady, Jessie Robins singing
'You Made Me Love You'. It was also populated by the weirdest of gentlemen.
Considering that one of the sanest moments was when the Bonzo Dog Doo-
Dah Band sang 'Death Cab for Cutie', everyone from dour poet Ivor Cutler
to midget drunk George Claydon in a World Cup Willie mask contributed to
a nightmare scenario that could have come from the fevered imagination of the
Marquis de Sade.

Only someone very weird indeed would stand out from that crowd of beautiful people, but that's exactly what eccentric dancer and elastic man of slapstick Nat Jackley did. Sadly he isn't called upon to do very much in the film. He certainly doesn't dance like an Indian rubber plant on steroids, which was his tour de force. He simply sits in the coach, sings along with the singalongs and generally exudes an air of slightly creepy happiness. Credited as Happy Nat the Rubber Man, his playbill matter for the music halls – his domain for many years – had been the Indian Rubber Man. Much of his *Magical Mystery Tour* material was directed by variety devotee John Lennon, including a legendary missing sequence where Nat lustily chased scantily clad young ladies around the swimming pool of the Atlantic Hotel in Newquay.

When the film was exhumed for Blu-ray release at the end of 2012, Ringo Starr recalled that Nat Jackley had been 'seen by someone on a television show...' Well, quite. Nat had indeed been a familiar fixture on the box since the early 1950s, but he had been seen by many, many people onstage from as early as the 1920s.

Born Nathaniel Tristram Jackley-Hirsch in Sunderland, on 16 July 1909, he had a very good six-degrees-of-separation rating – from Charlie Chaplin. Nat joined the well-loved clog-dancing act The Eight Lancashire Lads. The troupe of junior performers was founded by Bill Cawley and J. W. Jackson at the end of the nineteenth century, and it was during these early days that the pair gave the ten-year-old Chaplin his break into show business (a seal of approval they delighted in exploiting during Chaplin's monumental fame in the 1920s). Touring with the act for almost five years, Nat then started a double act with his sister Joy. It was with Joy that Nat made his London debut, at the Alhambra in 1928. This was straight song and dance, with piano accompaniment. The madness was just around the corner.

As a variety turn Nat started out as the straight man to comedian Jack Clifford, but his crazy moves quickly became the funny heart of the act. Having been trained in ballet during his time with The Eight Lancashire Lads, Jackley was more than just an eccentric dancer. He was a classically trained eccentric dancer. Every discordant jerk had class. He simply was funny. A rake-thin frame that he could contort into bizarre shapes; a giraffe-like neck and rubber features that could equal the peculiar speech patterns that he accentuated for laughter. In short, a unique, hilarious grotesque.

As with many a comedy invention, the secret of Jackley's success lay in an accident. Having to hastily cover for an overweight turn, Jackley donned the fat man trousers and coat, sans shirt. The incongruous image got a laugh. Jackley's impromptu neck waggling and leg shaking got an even bigger laugh. Bingo. Those staring eyes, elastic limbs, elongated neck muscles and sheer showbiz breeding shone through every disjointed movement.

Show business certainly was in those funny, bendy bones of his. His father, George, was the leading comic for theatre impresarios the Melville Brothers headlining fourteen consecutive pantomimes at the Lyceum Theatre, while his grandfather, Nathan, had toured America with his own comedy troupe, The Jackley Wonders. By the time he went solo in 1931, Nat himself had become a major draw on the British variety circuit. He had married scriptwriter and performer Marianne Lincoln and she joined Nat onstage as his comedy stooge, the split to his banana. Yet with his unique vocal dexterity and unsettlingly vibrant dancing, it became obvious that Nat was a solo comedic force. In any case, the relationship between him and Marianne was, by all accounts, a very stormy one, so it seemed best for all concerned for Marianne to leave the limelight to Nat, while she wrote material for him and managed his affairs. Show business proved very lucrative indeed for them. Summer seasons merged into pantomime time, which merged into the next summer season.

Jackley was an odd brick; a complete one-off. He was so off-the-wall that his speciality performance seemed at home in any context, purely because it never felt a cohesive part of the show – any show. It was gloriously abstract, both within and without any structured entertainment.

He was fundamentally a mime but, as Jackley himself always implied, that could get a bit boring for an audience. While abstract movement was key to his sketch characters – be it a soldier or a job-seeker – Jackley's special language of mutters, and elongated vowels was a childlike delight. It made him perfect for pantomime and he found a niche as the dame. It was a fantasy environment that was made just that little bit more fantastical by his presence, and he was still treading the boards in pantomime, notably in *Snow White* at the Theatre

Royal Newcastle for the 1983–84 season. By then he was one of the oldest handbag-swingers in town, though he still managed to shoehorn his celebrated Girl-Guide-on-parade business into every performance.

Back in the first flush of stardom, it was no surprise when the doyen of low-budget, working-class, variety-act film-makers Mancunian Films soon came a-knocking. The company teamed Nat opposite variety droll Norman Evans in two hugely popular

Lennon directs Nat on *Magical Mystery Tour*, in Newquay, September 1967.

comedies, *Demobbed* and *Under New Management* (both 1946), and both for film-maker John E. Blakeley and his makeshift ways. Clearly the Blakeley way of simply hiring great music hall turns, plonking them in front of a film camera, and telling them to be funny was the only way to showcase Nat's act, for he didn't make another film for a decade. That would be *Stars in Your Eyes* (1957), a colourful, backstage comedy romance co-starring Pat Kirkwood.

Not that Nat minded the spasmodic film work. By 1946 he had reached the topper-most, with a long-running revue at the London Palladium, no less. *High Time* was exactly what the public wanted, as it shook the rubble of war from its feet and looked optimistically past the immediate future of bomb craters and rationing. It was only natural, then, that when, in November that year, the Royal Variety Performance was staged at the Palladium, Nat was on the bill.

In 1948 Nat was back at the Palladium for another knockout revue, *Out of This World*. It gave an early break to Frankie Howerd, and one can only imagine the interaction between Frankie's 'Ooohs' and Nat's glorious gurning. The show proved so popular that it later transferred to the candyfloss-and-dodgem-car audience of Blackpool for a lengthy run at the Opera House, in 1950. Rather bizarrely, in the 1950 Royal Variety Performance at the London Palladium Nat appeared alongside Binnie Hale, Max Wall and The Crazy Gang in a 'Do You Remember' nostalgia section. Nat was certainly no variety dinosaur, for as a direct result of a snippet from *Out of This World* being broadcast within a 1950 programme called *The Symbol of Entertainment Supreme*, celebrating shows on Blackpool's Golden Mile, Nat became a television sensation.

He had been a regular performer on both radio and television, simply dropping his distinct comic traits in as a high-profile guest-turn. A canny business brain saw him continually refresh and reimagine routines for his stage appearances, thus keeping at the top of the variety tree with the 1950 revue *Off the Record* at the Victoria Palace Theatre and, in 1952, the punningly entitled *Singing in the Reign*, at – where else – the Queen's Theatre, Blackpool (Reign, get it!?). This 1952 spectacular caught the zeitgeist of Coronation fever and Nat remained a long-standing favourite of the Royal Family. And then, in 1956, BBC Television tried to make him a star. Two episodes of *Nat's in the Belfry*, produced by Richard Afton in April and May, were a winning combination of songs, sketches and silly behaviour, and captured his music hall vitality to perfection. But something must have been amiss, for no more were forthcoming, and it was back to the abundant stage work and special guest appearances. Notably a touring version of *Nats in the Belfrey*, 'the laugh-time of a lifetime', that producer Duggie Chapman assembled as a platform for Nat and his Happy Gang.

Forever faithful to variety theatre, Nat Jackley and Company toured a knockabout comedy sketch *Why Should England Tremble?*, and teamed up with other seasoned old-timers like Bob & Alf Pearson, and Leslie Sarony, for *The Golden Years of Music Hall*. Pantomime too kept him agile. Hardly still for a moment, this man in a frock galloped through season after season. He was there when *Babes in the Wood* saw the Empire Palace Theatre, Leeds, go dark forever in 1961, and he became a favourite with the crowds at the Liverpool Empire.

As dwindling audiences saw the variety theatres starting to close and his bendy limbs starting to hurt, Nat drifted into character acting. He made a fair stab at it too. He basked in The Beatles' reflected glory as a pub singer in the band Herman's Hermits' film *Mrs Brown, You've Got a Lovely Daughter* (1968), there were a couple of appearances as shipyard veteran Joe Prestwick in the third series of the BBC1 drama *When the Boat Comes In* (in the episodes 'Letters from Afar' and 'The Father of Lies', 10/17 November 1977), a *Tales of the Unexpected* ('Bosom Friends', Anglia Television, 5 July 1981) and an episode of *Minder* ('Give Us This Day Arthur Daley's Bread', Euston Films, 4 September 1985). Jackley even performed Shakespeare, appearing as Snout in director Elijah Moshinsky's 1981 BBC film production of *A Midsummer Night's Dream*, opposite Brian Glover's Bottom. In 1983 Nat was cast as the father of a

Carol Leroy joins Nat on the Newcastle City Walls, 1983, to launch the Theatre Royal panto *Snow White*.

gutter journalist in *The Ploughman's Lunch*, Richard Eyre's deconstruction of Margaret Thatcher's Britain for *Film on Four*.

On 10 April 1980 Nat had been the subject of *This is Your Life* and he eagerly wallowed in nostalgia when interviewed for his episode of *The Old Boy Network* (BBC2, 30 September 1981), a loving salute to variety's veterans. Donald Sayer's documentary profile showed a very happy Nat indeed, relating his theatrical follies and fortunes in an intimate chat filmed at his beloved Southport Theatre. Nat had the spirit of variety in his very bones, and it was a fitting tribute to his sixty glorious years in the business. He was a balletic, extraordinary, and often absolutely breathtaking performer. Truly unique.

TREAT YOURSELF TO the scrumptious Network Blu-ray of *Stars in Your Eyes* (The British Film: 5027626834548, 2020), the crowning glory of Aldephi Films Ltd., and, playing enthusiastic but ramshackle comedian Jimmy Knowles, an invaluable record of Nat Jackley's eccentric stage routines. Shot in Eastman Color and CameraScope, it's a lavish celebration of fifties variety. Nat is having a ball throughout. Not surprisingly, within five minutes he gets an onstage snog from luscious and vivacious Vera Day!

# Rex Jameson

## 1924–83

Growing up in the fifties, it seemed to me that Mrs Shufflewick was always on the wireless. I don't remember any of her material but it was obviously more genteel than the stream of double entendres and swearing she regaled us with in later life. For me, one of Jameson's major comedy achievements was getting away with the name 'Shufflewick', a slang term for masturbation, but in those more innocent times I don't think many people would have made the connection. I don't think Mrs Hand-Shandy would have got away with it though.

In 1980, while working for the BBC, I attended a record reception at a London hotel. For some reason Jameson had been hired to perform to a room full of people only interested in chatting and necking as much free booze as possible in the allotted time. He'd obviously had a few but gamely struggled on, despite being mostly ignored, until finally announcing: 'Right, that's it, I'm off. And if I never see any of you again it'll be too fucking soon.' (Exit. No applause.)

*Paul Cole*

'Your favourite laughter appetiser poured straight from a Guinness bottle: Mrs Shufflewick!' And so it was that for the best part of a quarter of a century Rex Jameson's cockney alter ego of a slightly sozzled, earthy woman took to the stage and delivered steadily bluer and bluer observations on East End life, the characters of the snug bar and her rather outrageous experiences with the men of her acquaintance. But this was the tail-end Shufflewick, the more bawdry end of the spectrum, when this spirited music hall turn and radio star had become dispirited and cynical, when the fine line between characterisation and catty despair had gone for good.

It is fitting that Jameson's best recordings were actually in front of an audience of excessive drinkers; more than just another female impersonator, his Mrs Shufflewick was the embodiment of the four-ale taproom. His flights of surreal fancy and lewd wit had all been fuelled by his beloved, mythical spiritual home, the Cock & Comfort, where the cheap gin and tonic could hit the spot and revelations of her fur coat made of 'genuine untouched pussy' could be revealed. Oh, yes – Mrs Slocombe owes more than a debt to the hilarious ramblings of Mrs Shufflewick.

Rex Jameson, a foundling, had been abandoned on the steps of Trinity Hospital, in Greenwich. Adopted by George and Mabel Costar, there followed a lonely childhood in Southend-on-Sea, bullied and ridiculed by his peers. As a young man Rex drifted towards the delights of the Southend Hippodrome and the Finsbury Park Empire, learning from the best in the business. Variety was an irresistible itch that war-time recruitment into the Royal Air Force allowed him to scratch. There he was introduced to Ralph Reader and his legendary RAF Gang Shows concert party. Ralph Reader and Ten Blokes from the Gang Show toured Cyprus, Italy and North Africa, where the lure of brothels was eschewed in favour of down-at-heel bars. Rex and Tony Hancock, his flight sergeant superior, would get paralytic on whiskey; his stage name of Jameson was a nod to his favourite brand.

After being demobbed, Jameson spent the late 1940s touring with *The Bryan Michie Happy Hour*. Like fellow Ralph Reader graduate Dick Emery [qv], Jameson had a galaxy of grotesque comic characters that would serve both as his recurring act and as his audition piece for BBC Light Entertainment producer Bryan Sears. Also like Emery, Jameson had a comical vicar in his repertoire. However, even at this early stage of his career Jameson could go too far for what was considered acceptable for broadcast. Outraged at the behaviour of much of his congregation, this less-than-puritanical man of the cloth was wont to tell them all to 'Flock off!' Unsurprisingly, this was not for Auntie Beeb and it was suggested that his slightly more subtle cockney charlady character should be utilised instead. So in May 1950 Jameson's Mrs Shufflewick made her broadcasting debut, enjoying near instantaneous success. Agent Joe Collins took Jameson on, and he provided camp-as-Christmas support for singing sensation Dorothy Squires. Then he would hotfoot it to the more relaxed cabaret atmosphere of the Talk of the Town or the Astor. Jameson's character comedy soon attracted the attention of Vivian Van Damm, whose Windmill Theatre, on Great Windmill Street in racy Soho 'never closed' and, as often as not, never clothed its female artistes. Having rubbed shoulders with fledgling greats in the Gang Shows, Jameson was now offered work at a venue that was already a haven for the cream of the comic crop, who would ply their trade in-between the nude tableaux.

Jameson's drag act of gossipy bitching was a stinging contrast to the naked glamour around him, with an initial six-week trial at the Windmill eventually extending to three years. With financial and professional security came a healthy embrace of smut onstage, and a flagrant disregard for concealing his sexuality, and impressive alcohol intake, off.

The relentless slog of six shows a day for the duration of a working week coupled with the frequent disinterest of the clientele – who were there for the real girls – took its toll, however, and with a quick change to civvies pretty much pointless, Jameson took to grabbing quick liquid respite in the welcoming womb of the Bear & Staff in full Shufflewick garb. Rex Jameson was fast vanishing within the female persona in any case. By November 1954 he was a regular guest star alongside Terry Scott in *It's a Great Life* (BBC Television, 1954–55),

By the late sixties Rex Jameson was rather lost without his Mrs Shufflewick alter ego.

and by April 1955 the character was at her zenith, chalking up regular radio work opposite Jon Pertwee in *Pertwee's Progress*. For the 1956 summer season Rex's Mrs Shufflewick was comic support for *The Dave King Show*, at the Winter Garden Pavilion Blackpool.

As a direct result of all this exposure and just before signing the Blackpool deal, BBC Television producer Richard Afton signed up Jameson – well, Shufflewick – to support that great Northern drag comedian from *The Norman Evans Show* in a new programme, *The Saturday Comedy Hour*, of which four episodes were broadcast, from 21 April to 13 October 1956. Talking about his experience with Norman Evans, Jameson recalled: 'you would have thought that the two of us clashed but he was unique. We got on very well together. It was Northern and Southern comedy. It just merged.'

Endless tours of variety theatres kept Jameson busy for the rest of the fifties, and regular television exposure even saw Mrs Shufflewick named the *TV Times* Personality of the Year for 1962. It was something of a watershed. Such was the popularity of the character that Jameson was invited to join the bill of old pros that gathered to say a fond and final farewell to the Metropolitan Theatre on the Edgware Road. They had all played the 'Met'; even the greatest of them all, Max Miller, had made a near-legendary recording at the fading home of variety. Variety itself was now fading, and Jameson was now fading right alongside it. He was declared bankrupt just weeks after the 'Met' closed for good.

By the 1960s Jameson's own identity had all but disappeared, and both man and character were together known simply as 'Shuff'. He often performed under the influence and enjoyed it, finding a natural habitat in the Northern working men's clubs of Batley and Barnsley. But Jameson was most at home

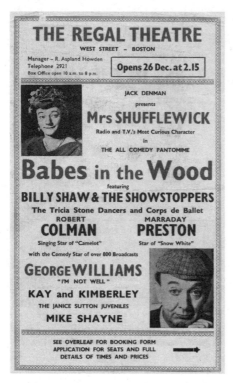

## THE REGAL THEATRE
WEST STREET – BOSTON

Manager – R. Aspland Howden
Telephone 2921
Box Office open 10 a.m. to 8 p.m.

**Opens 26 Dec. at 2.15**

JACK DENMAN
presents

## Mrs SHUFFLEWICK
Radio and T.V.'s Most Curious Character
in
THE ALL COMEDY PANTOMIME

# Babes in the Wood
featuring

## BILLY SHAW & THE SHOWSTOPPERS
The Tricia Stone Dancers and Corps de Ballet

ROBERT
**COLMAN**
Singing Star of "Camelot"

MARRADAY
**PRESTON**
Star of "Snow White"

with the Comedy Star of over 800 Broadcasts

### GEORGE WILLIAMS
"I'M NOT WELL"

**KAY and KIMBERLEY**
THE JANICE SUTTON JUVENILES

**MIKE SHAYNE**

SEE OVERLEAF FOR BOOKING FORM
APPLICATION FOR SEATS AND FULL
DETAILS OF TIMES AND PRICES

Rex's Mrs Shufflewick, billed as 'Radio and TV's Most Curious Character'.

on the closeted London gay circuit: the Royal Vauxhall Tavern, the Skinners Arms in Kennington, the Theatre Royal, Stratford. In these venues a progressively more lewd and refreshed Shuff would perform to huge acclaim every Sunday night.

On 5 March 1983, Jameson died from a heart attack after a performance at one of his most celebrated revues, at the Black Cap in Camden Town. He was just fifty-eight. His final curtain was at Golders Green Crematorium in front of a packed house who laughed and lingered and stirred up a loud sing-song for his closing number, music-hall legend Marie Lloyd's hit 'My Old Man (Said Follow the Van)'.

Yet the spirit of Shuff is forever with us. As long as the freewheeling workers can release their inner carnivalesque spirit, as long as we can booze and belch and bunk up on a breezy day out, then the nose-tapping innuendo and the port-and-lemon-fuelled ramblings of this once all-conquering comic creation will never be silenced.

I URGE YOU to hunt through the racks of old vinyl at your local charity shops and treat yourself to *The Amazing Mrs Shufflewick – Live! At the New Black Cap* (London Records: SW99545, 1972), Shuff's definitive recording, still wowing 'em in Camden Town after all those years. If variety was dead in 1972, then this is the joyous order of service.

# Roy Jay

## 1949–2008

A comedian with a style all his own.

*Bob Monkhouse OBE*

The 1980s was a wild and crazy time for television comedy. While Frankie Howerd and Benny Hill, the near-extinct dinosaurs of post-war titters, were hanging on for dear life, Ben Elton and the so-called 'alternative' brigade were dishing out right-on comedy against the right wing. Smack bang in the middle of this unofficial battle of jaded experience and cocky youth was a batch of turns who, while young, harked back to the pre-war days of variety. There was Roy Walker, the silver-fox joke-teller with gentle Irish whimsy. There was Duncan Norvelle, mincing about in polyester and begging everyone to 'Chase me!' And then there was Roy Jay.

For a very short spell in the mid 1980s, Roy Jay seemed to be everywhere. I'm convinced he was on every panel game I watched as a child, and in every Royal Variety Performance of my pre-pubescent years. He certainly appeared on shows with Bob Monkhouse and Mike Yarwood and Little & Large, as well as with Larry Grayson, on *The Main Attraction* (BBC1, 30 July 1983). And it seems as though he guest-starred in every single episode of Les Dennis and Dustin Gee's *The Laughter Show* on BBC1. In actual fact he was in only five episodes in 1984 and '85, but his act left a mark on everyone of my generation. To me and my sister, this strange bloke in the cartoon-like convict outfit (he donned white gloves, moved slowly and had a grey suit covered in arrows) was the funniest person in the world. His act consisted of nothing more than hesitantly walking around a television studio, stopping suddenly, looking menacingly into camera and muttering a single word: 'Slither!' That was pretty much it, and that's certainly the impression I would do at family parties and weddings. For years and years I did it. My sister Fiona would always cry with laughter. I'm certain if I do it the next time I see her she'll cry with laughter again. He had something, did Roy Jay.

What he didn't have was good jokes – he would labour over Christmas-cracker-type puns and other dreadful wordplay – but what he had was this unnerving and just plain weird persona that made him unique. He would crack a joke about his girlfriend, which would never be that funny, then he would stop short, jump backwards and say: 'Spook!' 'Spook!' was the endgame to almost all his funny stories. Like 'Slither!', it worked on the Spike Milligan principle that if you say something enough times it becomes hilarious. 'Spook!' became hilarious. His snake-like preamble, monotone delivery and drugged-to-the-eyeballs expression was duplicated in school playgrounds across the country.

Despite the odd, transatlantic drawl in which Jay delivered his bonbons of half-amusements, he was actually born in the village of Uffculme in Devon. He had honed his madcap comedy talents as a Bluecoat for Pontins. Having been stationed at its Morecambe branch during the late 1970s, he soon made a name for himself on variety bills, albeit rather low down. He would perform in working men's clubs in the North of England and in other entertainment venues, too, like the Circus Tavern in Purfleet. He was obviously doing something right, for by 1983 Roy Jay was the special guest supporting the UK tour of American singing star Johnny Mathis. That same year Jay made his first mark on television in the Chas 'n' Dave variety showcase *Knees-Up*, on LWT.

The decade of greed and nuttiness was perfect for Roy Jay. Something akin to the Emperor's new clothes, if you didn't get his humour you were probably over the age of eighteen and had aspirations of sophistication. Still, the youth of the country took him into their hearts – and, eventually, so did everybody else. 'You'll all be doing it tomorrow,' he would chatter at the cameras.

He became so famous he even made a comedy record in 1984. A

Spooky! With Dustin Gee on BBC1's *The Laughter Show*, in April 1984.

romantic ballad performed in his usual style, what else could it be called but 'Spooky Love'. Jay also signed up for an advertising campaign on behalf of Schweppes. He was certainly no William Franklyn, the actor who memorably fronted the adverts from 1965, but in his usual stage attire Roy Jay methodically wandered onto the floor of a disco, drank his tonic water and slowed down the entire world. It was, well, weird.

His last appearance on British television seems to have been an edition of *Pebble Mill at One* in February 1986, when he was desperately plugging another single that would never chart. This one was called 'Spooky Down the Street'. Enough said, I think.

Of all the forgotten heroes in this book, the fate of Roy Jay is one of the most bizarre and tragic, with a very sudden fall from grace. Both close friends and enemies seem to agree that even before he made it big in show business, Jay loved a drink a little too often. A bit of fame and some extra cash in the back pocket simply fuelled this addiction. His love of gambling didn't help keep him solvent for long either. Coupled with his excessive spinning of the wheel and repeated swigging of the bottle was his love of the ladies. Ex-squeezes testify that Jay was extremely well blessed in the trouser-snake department. Allegedly, during one post-booze-up appearance Jay was so out of it that he dragged out his huge throbber onstage, in front of the audience. The universal cry of 'You'll never work again' rang out across the industry and, to all intents and purposes, he didn't.

Jump-cut nearly twenty years to 2005 and poor Roy Jay was eking out a living in the bars and clubs of Benidorm. Now a hopeless alcoholic and pretty much penniless, he was appearing as Roy 'Slither' Jay for tourists as inelegantly wasted as himself. Brits on the razz would half remember him from their youth, heckle him with the confidence of fifteen lagers inside them and see a once-beloved comedian crumble into desperate pleas for their laughs. During these thankless days he regularly appeared as support for a very special speciality act who called herself Sticky Vicky. Now, this young lady became something of a legend thanks to her ability to squeeze out ping-pong balls and pull flags of all nations from her love tunnel.

It was a particularly ignoble end for Roy Jay: though the exact date of his death is unknown, his body was found towards the end of 2008, several weeks after booze had taken its ultimate revenge. A local businessman and friend of Jay's paid the burial costs. Man, I wish I had met him, just once, and shaken him by the hand. He was a true comedy hero. Oh, and one more thing: 'Slither!'

TREAT YOURSELF TO the truly incredible *Roy Jay* album (Clubland Records: SJP 837, 1982), featuring the most bizarre versions of 'Love on the Rocks', 'Dimples' and 'A Whiter Shade of Pale' you'll ever own. Spook!

# Spike Jones

## 1911–65

The Mozart of Mayhem.

*Billy Crystal*

When I was a young lad, the family holiday was always in Brighton. It was always on a budget, with self-catering in Lower Rock Gardens, miles from the Pavilion, and every meal in the Wimpy carefully totted up. Still, we were happy. My parents always indulged our collecting frenzies, with a reasonably priced old doll for my sister and a *Wonder Book* or two for me. My parents would always put themselves last, of course. As long as we could go back to the accommodation in the evening to change – my dad's favourite bit – and had enough money for four seats in the cheap seats at the Theatre Royal, everything was fine. One sacrifice has never left me though. I was never able to resist a second-hand book shop, and on one last day of a holiday we found a veritable treasure trove of temptation. The bottom line was that there was money enough for one last purchase and my dad gave in to my pleas for *The Films of Boris Karloff*, putting his own favourite back on the shelves. My choice is still treasured to this day, but the book that got away became something of an obsession for my dad. From the very moment we got on the train to go home, he wistfully regretted not buying it. Naturally it was gone when we returned the following year, and another copy could never be found. He even mentioned it on his deathbed without a trace of malice, and while it was hardly his Rosebud, it still played on the mind of this completist who'd never actually owned it. The book in question was a complete discography of every musical permutation of abused instruments that the genius, crazed bandleader of the anvil and the revolver interlude, Spike Jones, ever recorded. A zoot-suited native of Long Beach, California, who put the phony in cacophony!

Young Lindley Armstrong Jones was born on 14 December 1911, and earned his lifelong nickname at an early age owing to his ultra-thin physique, which was said to give him the appearance of a railroad spike. Having got his first drum kit at the ripe old age of eleven, the ambitious bandleader grudgingly learned his trade with other outfits before forming Spike Jones and his Five Tracks, who adopted the cheap and very cheerful habit of utilising the banging of kitchen implements borrowed from a friendly railroad-restaurant chef. This incorporation of household objects and manufacturing equipment into his orchestra would become his unique gimmick.

By the 1930s Jones was already getting radio exposure with the Victor Young Orchestra, but such a scattergun creative force couldn't be content with playing the same old notes over and over again, night after night. Gathering a tight-knit group of like-minded frustrated anarchists, Jones took to recording their impromptu musical efforts simply for their own amusement, and also to play to family and friends back home. One such recording found its way to the ears of an RCA Victor executive, who signed up Jones along with his brilliant rabble of musical misfits. The first session, on 8 August 1941, resulted in four cuts: 'Barstool Cowboy from Old Barstow', 'Behind Those Swinging Doors', 'Red Wing' and 'The Covered Wagon Rolled Right Along', all featuring Del Porter on vocals. But it was the recording session held the following April that produced the first huge success of wild, baton-wielding Spike Jones and his motley but experienced gang of musicians, dubbed his City Slickers. 'Der Fuehrer's

Face' captured the zeitgeist of imminent world war, with America joining the conflict seemingly inevitable. With a healthy disregard for Adolf Hitler and every strangled 'Heil!' warranting a loud raspberry, the recording was a smash hit and even inspired Walt Disney to cast Donald Duck in his own Oscar-winning attack on the Nazis – complete

Doodles Weaver gives his all on CBS's *The Spike Jones Show*, June 1949.

with Jones's omnipresent song, of course. (In 1943, Tommy Trinder made a recording of it for the British market.)

As a direct result of 'Der Fuehrer's Face', Jones became a sensation overnight, arguably thanks to a strike by the American Federation of Musicians that meant until 1944 he could make records only for radio broadcast. Still, these 'standard transcription' recordings, and his subsequent return to the studio, engendered some of the most hilarious three-minute pop songs anyone, anywhere, has ever recorded. 'Cocktails for Two' ripped the sentimental ambiance of the original apart with a booze-induced hiccupping delivery, complemented by a cornucopia of car-horn honks. Jones had long nurtured drinking songs, and in January 1942 had enlisted comic voice maestro Mel Blanc for hiccup duty on 'Clink, Clink', a track whose relentlessly gleeful drinking spree should make it the anthem for every New Year's Eve. Trumpet player and singer George Rock could rustle up a mean Liberace impersonation, memorably deploying it for 'I'm in the Mood for Love' and lifting the seasonal favourite 'All I Want for Christmas is My Two Front Teeth' with his trademark childlike lead vocals. The incongruous sight of hulking gentle giant George Rock recreating this number on television made the song even funnier, if such a thing were possible.

In a February 1947 recording session, Rock would lend his adenoidal whine to '(I'm Forever) Blowing Bubble Gum' while, in an October session that year, that other City Slicker star, Doodles Weaver, had fun as a sports commentator

Soulmates and playmates Spike Jones and Helen Grayco were married in 1949. Here promoting CBS TV's *The Spike Jones Show*, 1960.

with a passion for puns and an energetic abuse of Rossini's 'William Tell Overture', where deadbeat horse Beetlebaum was an unlikely winner. On 'Dance of the Hours', with Weaver's commentator character again to the fore, there was an even more unlikely winner. It's not beyond the realms of possibility that Blur were Spike Jones fans when they included 'Beetlebum' as the opening track of their self-titled album in 1997. After all, Damon Albarn sampled vintage American radio comedian Lord Buckley on his 2014 solo release *Everyday Robots*.

The 1955 Spike Jones recording of 'The Man on the Flying Trapeze' indulged Weaver's skill for spoonerism, mangling the original George Leybourne lyrics into a collection of stutty numbles, I mean nutty stumbles, via his Professor Feitlebaum character. He was also the father of actress Sigourney Weaver and fell foul of the birds in Alfred Hitchcock's film, but 'Flying Trapeze' is undoubtedly the greatest contribution to popular culture that Doodles Weaver ever made. It's a masterpiece.

In 1947 'My Old Flame', a beautiful torch song, was just ripe for the wacky Spike Jones treatment. The recording begins with a straight rendition by crooner Paul Judson, with the singer subsequently revelleing in the unintentionally macabre lyrics. The illusion of romance is shattered with a fire engine siren breaking through the sentiment. Radio comedian Paul Frees adds to the fear factor with his Peter Lorre-style ghoul. The sinister screen star had appeared in *The Beast with Five Fingers*, the previous year. 'Chloe' (1945) undermined romantic bliss with yelled insults, while 'The Glow Worm' (1946) featured a serious-minded operatic duet between Red Ingle and Aileen Carlisle, frequently lapsing into white-trash bickering. 'Rhapsody from Hunger' (1951) cast Jones himself alongside his multitalented wife Helen Grayco as a pair of lovesick kids, with proper anvil-bashing action and a stunning Dick Gardner violin solo. The same line-up had performed 'None But the Lonely Heart (A Soaperatta)' (1949), with Grayco, in particular, languidly wafting through the intricate and complicated marital status of all concerned, finally breaking character with an incongruous and frustrated: 'I must go away somewhere and figure this thing out!' before returning to wistful, perfectly over-played melodrama. Jones, as her gauche cuckold, is, for once, left standing in comic awe.

A timeless running commentary on the action came with 'Popcorn Snack', in which The Boys in the Back Room warble about their distaste of cinema-goers more interested in filling their faces than watching the show. (Nothing has changed in sixty years.) That 'Man of a Thousand Voices' Paul Frees gave his uncanny impersonation of Edward G. Robinson on that one. On 'I'm in the Mood for Love', 'The Jones Laughing Record' and many broadcasts, Jones incorporated the peerless sneezing of City Slicker pianist Frank Leithner. Hey, it's a comic gift – you try doing it as well as Leithner did!

*The Spike Jones Show* radio series ran and ran until 1949, and from 1954 to 1961, Jones and his ever-changing roster of musicians enjoyed their own television shows on the NBC and CBS networks. These were seriously funny variety shows and, naturally, kept Jones a popular recording artiste right up until the end of the fifties. For despite his deadpan acknowledgement of his audience's often ironic applause, Jones was a true musician. He may have been playing the base of a bathtub but, boy, he played it in tune.

Moreover, he could get very serious, and brilliantly so, as Spike Jones and His Other Orchestra – which he formed in 1946 as an antidote to the musical madness of his City Slickers recordings – proved beyond doubt. Even so, the zenith of this musically exquisite venture is 'Laura', which starts deceptively pure and melodic before the impossible-to-contain insanity breaks through in the second half, with Jimmy Cassidy's vocals valiantly competing with the perfectly impertinent tuba-action from Joe 'Country' Washburne. The flip side of that recording, 'When Yuba Plays the Rumba on the Tuba', gave Washburne even more scope, and is arguably Jones's definitive recording.

Spike, with musical revolver in hand, posing for, arguably, the first 'Star with Packed Audience' photograph. How very twenty-first century!

TREAT YOURSELF TO *Spike Jones and his City Slickers – The Radio Years, Volume 1* (Rhino Records: R2 71156). Licensed from Jones's estate, this album collates not one but two episodes from the late 1940s, guest-starring horror-film icons Boris Karloff and, yes, the real Peter Lorre, who begs Spike: 'Stop the music! You're driving me sane!' Peerless, completely unclassifiable comic genius. The Peter Lorre broadcast is an edition of *The Spike Jones Show* from 10 December 1948, while the Boris Karloff guest appearance is on a *Spotlight Revue* first broadcast on 9 April 1949. But, hey, this is where you came in! The Karloff book is still safely gathered in. As for that Spike Jones discography... if you have a spare copy, do get in touch!

# John Junkin

## *1930–2006*

I met John when I appeared on *Bob Says Opportunity Knocks* in April 1989 along with my double-act partner Mandy Craig. John was Bob Monkhouse's writer, and we were quite star-struck when we met him as we were both Beatles fans and to us he would always be Shake, The Beatles' roadie in *A Hard Day's Night*. We didn't get to speak to him until the actual show. We'd endured the tortuous 'clapometer' bit, where we had to smile at the studio audience while the applause was judged on a sliding scale. It wasn't very high and as we came offstage we must have looked traumatised, as there was John with an arm around each of us whispering, 'It's just a bit of cardboard and a person backstage; it's not accurate.' Bless him: he made us feel tons better and, lo and behold, the following week we watched at home as Bob announced the results of the phone vote. We'd come second behind three-times show-winner Matt Mudd. Not bad going, and guess what? 'Shake' stopped us shaking. Thanks John, you lovely fella. x

*Jayne Tunnicliffe*

John, Baz and Timbo lean on Denis King. The *Hello Cheeky* gang: a BBC Radio 2 sensation from 1973 to 1979.

John Junkin was a self-confessed grumpy old man. He looked like a grumpy old man even as a grumpy young man. When his renaissance finally came, in the twilight of his years, with a regular place as suspicious pensioner Ernie Johnson in the cast of *EastEnders*, in 2001 and 2002, he used the renewed exposure to complain that he had been forgotten by the industry. And he had.

Junkin had worked with the great and the good of British comedy, both as performer and writer. He'd even starred opposite The Beatles, for Heaven's sake, so one could see his point. However, like beloved contemporaries Eric Sykes and Spike Milligan, by the 1990s Junkin could scarcely get arrested. He *was* gainfully, albeit desperately, employed as consultant on *Gagtags* (BBC1, 1994–96), the fun but untaxing battle of comic wits, but that was more than likely down to a good word from chum and regular panellist Bob Monkhouse.

But there was no more worthy consultant. From the 1950s to the 1990s, and with a particularly rich harvest of work in the 1960s and 1970s, Junkin was a comic cornerstone writer, actor, stooge, and trusted conduit. In the earliest days, there was work with Benny Hill (*The Benny Hill Show*, BBC Television, 16 December 1961), the biggest star on the small screen, and with Peter Sellers, the biggest star on the big, with Junkin popping up unannounced and uncredited in comic criminal capers *The Wrong Arm of the Law* and *Heavens Above!* (both, 1963). First seeing the light of day as late as 1990, on the EMI CD release *The Peter Sellers Collection*, Junkin's performance of his self-penned 'A Right Bird' is a seemingly spontaneous reflection on a special young lady who has captured the imagination of Sellers but has left no impression at all upon Junkin. It's a joyous creation, all the more so thanks to the performers' barely suppressed giggles at the end.

Like Sellers, Tony Hancock, too, valued Junkin very highly, and in the mid 1960s, when the Lad 'imself was at his fussiest about his stooges, he used Junkin in his ITV sitcom series (*Hancock*: 'The Writer', 21 March 1963) as well as in the variety spectacular *The Blackpool Show* (ABC TV, 1966–67). In a packed career as a go-to second banana, Junkin would bring his seemingly bemused comic sorrowfulness to Tommy Cooper (*Life with Cooper*: 'Getting a TV Show', ABC, 21 January 1967), Ronnie Corbett (*Sorry*: 'A Little Something Set Aside', BBC1, 26 May 1985), Kenny Everett (*The Kenny Everett Television Show*, BBC1, 1981–82), Jim Davidson (*The Jim Davidson Show*, Thames Television, 28 February 1980), Sid James (*George and the Dragon*: 'TV Conflict', ATV, 20 May 1967), Eric Sykes ('Sykes and a Uniform', BBC1, 9 November 1965), and *Terry and June* ('To Catch a Thief', BBC1, 5 September 1980). Junkin was particularly memorable as the beleaguered police officer in 'The Baddies' episode of *The Goodies* (BBC2, 14 January 1972). John Junkin did beleaguered very well.

He was a favourite, too, of Frankie Howerd, supporting him in the pilot of *Up Pompeii!* (BBC1, 17 September 1969) and his ITV success, as another Police Sergeant, in *The Howerd Confessions* (Thames, 23 September 1976). As the eighties became the nineties and Junkin's thirty-year run as a dependable comic support came to an end, he gave both Hywel Bennett and Rowan Atkinson good old-fashioned pomposity, in *The Return of Shelley* ('Wages of Virtue', Thames, 5 December 1989) and *The Return of Mr Bean* (Thames, 3 April 1991) respectively.

He was born John Francis Junkin in Ealing, on 29 January 1930. As a schoolteacher, he would supplement his income by moonlighting as a comedy scriptwriter. From the outset there was a mournful cynicism and dour charm at work; 1950's radio comedians Ted Ray and Jimmy Logan maximised it to the hilt.

The 1960s was to be Junkin's decade (and not just because he was taught how to wet-shave by George Harrison). While moronic comedy is to the fore, there's real pathos behind his deep affection for his wayward wards. Junkin's theatrical talents had flowered under the auspices of Joan Littlewood. She was a tough, challenging influence, providing Junkin with a training ground that allowed him to impress with serious performances on television: as a disgruntled army sergeant in *Redcap* (the 'Paterson's Private Army' episode, ABC, 21 May 1966), and a disgruntled farmer in *All Creatures Great and Small* ('The Playing

Field', BBC1, 24 September 1988). These weren't one-note grumps though; Junkin's characters had heart. He believed 'the secret is to survive as an actor. I'd play Hamlet, walk the high wire, try anything.'

However, it was as a comic scribe and stooge that Junkin earned his bread and butter. Working from his garden shed, he wrote material for Morecambe and Wise, Ronnie Barker and Marty Feldman. It was with the latter, in his seminal sketch show *It's Marty* (BBC2, 1968–69), that John Junkin first shone bright as a performer. The series went from the sublime to the ridiculous in a matter of seconds and Junkin was called upon to play everything from a 'chocks away!' RAF fighter pilot to a bare-kneed Eastern European folk dancer. But he was most often cast as the officious face of authority. Be it travel agent or shop assistant, Junkin's man in a suit gamely tried to appease and satisfy the relentless customers from Hell or Hull or some such place. For example, he played a bemused and slightly concerned bank manager faced with Marty in full garden-gnome garb looking to secure a mortgage on a property; and there was a string of recurring sketches in which he encountered an aged Marty with his even more aged wife. The wife in question was, of course, Tim Brooke-Taylor, who remembered that even at such heights of popularity one could be almost anonymous: 'A man was obviously waiting to get Marty's autograph after a recording. He spotted John and muttered, "Oh, there's the other one!" Then he saw me and said, "There's the *other* other one!" That put us in our place!'

It was again with Tim Brooke-Taylor, and Barry Cryer, that Junkin would form a comedy troupe that could have been called The Three Other Ones. (The Three Stooges had already been taken.) First on radio (BBC Radio 2, 1973–79) and then on television, *Hello Cheeky* (Yorkshire, 1976), as it was actually named, was a self-proclaimed ragbag of old jokes, silly voices and even sillier songs, all done with a cheerful delight not seen since the halcyon days of knockabout goons Olsen and Johnson [qv]. The trio's agenda for *Hello Cheeky* was to present a comic book of whiz-bang jokes and daftness: if you didn't laugh at one joke there would be another one you probably wouldn't laugh at coming up a few seconds behind it!

It was a laudable stance to take, although, perhaps wisely, the BBC could only perceive it as an audio cornucopia and were reluctant to take those surreal word pictures onto television. That gauntlet was picked up, instead, by Yorkshire

Television. It is a raucous joy, and that joy is all the more joyous because of the ramshackle anarchy on display – the insane costume changes, dodgy stock footage, and relentless, gut-churning, tear-inducing puns created one of the most unfettered comedy spectacles British television had ever known. Nothing has come close to it since.

Junkin's film career had scaled the heights – larking around with

With Joan Sims, promoting the ATV sitcom *Sam and Janet*, June 1967.

the Beatles under the direction of Richard Lester a peak – but any discussion of his cinematic oeuvre with him would usually revolve around Junkin's complaint that he had never done a *Carry On*. He didn't regret it, he just fumed at the fact that everybody seemed to think he had. The confusion may have arisen because he'd taken a side-step on the evolutionary scale and joined the team of the saucy seventies *Confessions* romps. In fact, the part of the bombastic boss in *Confessions from a Holiday Camp* (1977) is arguably Junkin's finest film performance. The much-maligned and unfairly dismissed sub-genre of the British sex comedy can often lack in both sex and comedy but on occasions, as with *Confessions from a Holiday Camp*, they can be genuinely funny. Amongst the forest of pubic hair and single entendres you can dig deep and find a glorious performance like Junkin's. It wasn't going to win him any awards but it proved that he could give the tits-and-bums knockabout fun some quality – quality it didn't always justify, but quality none the less. He certainly did that as the short-tempered father of *Rosie Dixon – Night Nurse* (1978). Before the expected scenario of relentless hospital bed-hopping, the scenes featuring Junkin are quite brilliant. His grumpy parental advice is played like domestic sitcom. Junkin finds dignity within the sex comedy, embodying a down-trodden world of stale toast and hard-luck stories. Even at his personal nadir, Junkin found an inner John Osborne.

Bring Me Sunshine: Barry Cryer and John Junkin celebrate being the new writers for *The Morecambe and Wise Show*, at Thames Television, in June 1978. Following the Christmas Show they took Eric 'n' Ernie out to lunch to offer up their resignation!

*EastEnders* was a lifeline; Junkin had continued to write for top comedians Joe Pasquale and Jon Culshaw but now, suddenly, he was a national figure, albeit one of hatred and distrust in the form of the mysterious and unpleasant Ernie, an abusive care-home worker from the disturbing past of Billy Mitchell (played by Perry Fenwick). Junkin was in the soap for only a matter of months, but it was a terrifying and powerful performance.

Subsequently he excelled as the embittered, wheelchair-bound Albert Moss in *The Football Factory* (2004), but it was to be his last hurrah, if also a reminder that there was a time when, throughout the 1960s and 1970s, his face was everywhere. Though he was once likened to 'a lugubrious potato', few other actors could turn misery to merriment as effortlessly as John Junkin could.

TREAT YOURSELF TO *The Least Worst of Hello Cheeky* (BBC Records: REH189, 1975), the essential compilation of the carnivalesque radio show, with musical outbursts from the Denis King Trio. It's all the funnier when it's all in the mind, y'know.

# Time for a quick drink in the Colonnade Bar...

It's the interval and this place is always packed. There's veteran West End musical star Bobby Howes, slurring his words as he re-enacts his guest appearance in Hammer's *Watch it, Sailor!*, while long-suffering, forever-bothered barmaid Olive Sloane polishes the optics and reluctantly pours him another double. Sonnie Hale is nursing half a pint as he recalls the glory days of the London Palladium before the Second World War; Lupino Lane is valiantly attempting to cheer him up with a rousing singalong of 'The Lambeth Walk'. Frank Fay is cracking wise, to himself, with his back to the room.

Freddie Frinton may be largely forgotten in his home country, despite a namecheck for his sitcom *Meet the Wife* in The Beatles' 'Good Morning Good Morning', but he's swanned in, chuffed over his eternal fame in Scandinavia, and constantly lapses into scenes from his short film *Dinner for One*. Hollywood's greatest drunks, Arthur Houseman and Jack Norton, sip orange juice as they reminisce about working with Stan and Ollie, and with W.C. Fields. Houseman has just slipped a large vodka into his own glass; rake-thin Claude Lester necks it

As long as you've acknowledged 'Willie' in the window, welcome to the Colonnade. A little slice of Georgian Brighton.

from the bottle. He's escaped from his locked dressing room, taken a stroll on the prom, and is now taking a little forbidden Dutch courage before going back on for the second house.

Mel Blanc feverishly twiddles the knobs of the bar's radio set in the vain hope of hearing himself with Jack Benny or with George and Gracie, and refuses a bowl of carrots – much to everyone's amusement. 'What's up, doc?', cracks the 'Hoo-Hoo'ing buffoon Hugh Herbert. Everyone laughs – everyone but Leslie Henson and Sid Field. These two are more than happy chatting to a mutual best friend: an invisible six-foot rabbit by the name of Harvey. Meanwhile, Sid Fields is only interested in buying a Susquehana hat. Frank Randle, gloriously well oiled, has taken half an hour to get back on his bar stool because he's supped some ale tonight, while his spiritual, comedy-world son, Ted Lune, lanky and uniformed, staggers in with the rest of *The Army Game* lads, singing rude songs and getting frosty stares from Edie Martin, Irene Handl, Molly Weir and Norman Chappell – all in the corner with a port and lemon and a superior expression each. Eddie Bracken, a nervous-looking kid in a military uniform for another country's army, anxiously slurps his lemonade, but they were allies once upon a time so the Nether Wallop chaps soon welcome him into the group. Sydney Tafler is too busy trying to sell knock-off watches to take much notice.

Joe Penner is more interested in whether anybody wants to buy a duck. Joe King and Nosmo King enjoy a regal laugh, as Nosmo claims the throne – his name is up on every 'No Smoking' sign in every theatre, after all! Billy Cotton and his band play raucous melodies, with cockney landlady Queenie Watts pounding the old Joanna and – oh, boy – Martha Raye joining in rather too loudly for comfort. Virginia O'Brien croons the chorus, monotonous, deadpan, hilarious. Not to be beaten, true Scot Sandy Rowan rallies the troupes with rousing originals like 'I Love a Lassie' and 'Just a Wee Deoch-An-Doris'. Sir

Harry Lauder and Andy Stewart, mere pretenders to his throne, are thrilled to chant along. Cyril Fletcher offers up an odd ode but—by gad! Is that the time?

Jerry Colonna wipes froth from his huge walrus moustache and accepts one more shot from ever-cheerful Charley Chase. He's a 'Son of the Desert'; he's always happy to buy a round. Bernard Manning sits by himself, gleefully counting the box office takings from his private members club. Everybody has stood on the shoulders of Dan Leno at some time, and he happily stands on the steps of the bar, a single malt to hand. Andy Cunningham clings on to his furry pal Badger, dishing out cold mashed potato and entertaining a bewitched gaggle of kids. Marty Feldman and Charles Hawtrey, both on the lash, hold each other up over by the seating area, and Sid James has a quick drag to keep them company, having left his *Bless This House* mate Anthony Jackson watching Arsenal pulverise each successive team on an eternal loop. He knows he sees dead people, but Tony ain't afraid of no ghosts. Still that's the bell, ladles and jelly-spoons. The second half is about to begin. Pied Piper-like, Tommy Handley, the leader of our pack, congas us back to our seats. T. T. F. N.

'Have you read any good books lately?' As soon as they've finished their martinis, 'Stinker' Murdoch and Big-Hearted Arthur will see you in the second half.

# Dave King

## 1929–2002

At the beginning of the sixties, when I was fifteen years old, Arbroath in Scotland, where I lived, was a popular holiday resort with a full programme of entertainment throughout the summer on the seafront, in the newly built swimming pool and in the town centre's theatre, the Webster Memorial Hall. This particular summer, the running of the theatre had been taken over by popular Scottish band leader Lindsay Ross who, along with his partner, David Puller, offered a different show each night of the week, culminating in the Saturday night spectacular *The Black and White and Tartan Show*, the first half in kilts, the second in blackface. The rest of the week was taken up by a weekly talent contest, an evening provided by the local dancing school, and performances of the hilarious farce *Wild Goose Chase* by the Arbroath Amateur Dramatic Society, of which I was a prominent member. Star Publicity Attractions, as the company was called, was a fairly ramshackle organisation, as can be gathered from the fact that at fifteen I was in charge of publicity.

I was also part of the *Lindsay Ross Country Dance Night*, which happened on a Wednesday, the content of which was really an extended version of the first half of *The Black and White and Tartan Show* with the addition of extra acts, including myself as an impersonator of stars of stage, screen and radio. My repertoire of voices included Humphrey Bogart, Chic Murray, Terry-Thomas, Peter Lorre and Al Jolson. I wrote the script myself using jokes culled from the Corgi Book editions of the American editor Bennett Cerf's collections of anecdotes and stories such as *Shake Well Before Using* and *Stop Me and Buy One*.

About three weeks into the ten-week season, I decided that I had to move away from mere impersonations and try my hand at stand-up. The comedian whom I most admired around this time was Dave King, an almost forgotten name now but huge on both sides of the Atlantic in the late fifties and early sixties. He had a really great smile, a relaxed manner, an excellent singing voice and was very, very funny. He was the comedian I most wanted to resemble, and how better to do this than to steal his material? Plagiarism is, after all, the sincerest form of flattery.

The finale of the shambles I eventually presented before that Wednesday-night audience – what there was of it – was a mime that Dave had done a year or so back and which had convulsed me at the time. Wearing a woolly bobble hat and with one arm raised above his head, he impersonated a bored child holding a parent's hand and trying to occupy himself while the unseen parent carried on a conversation with an equally unseen acquaintance.

My version of Dave's act was not subtle. I chewed gum, pulled it out, got it stuck on my jumper, picked my nose, needed to go to the lavatory, was ignored by my parent and climaxed by appearing to wet myself, exiting legs wide apart and in obvious discomfort. The mime was sufficiently well received by the audience for me to repeat it for the remaining six weeks.

As I say, the mime that I stole was part of Dave's act in his early days. He became a much subtler performer and one of the very few British comedians to find huge success in America. And then, or so it appeared to me, he vanished. I'm looking forward to reading Robert's entry on him for when I next saw him, it was onstage in 1976 and as a straight actor in David Hare's play *Teeth and Smiles*, where he played Helen Mirren's rock star's smooth agent. No bobble hat this time, but a cashmere coat, an elegant suit – but that same really great smile.

*John Kane*

If Dave King is remembered for anything today it is for a startling run of hard men and heavies in British television and film. Guest-character roles in *The Sweeney* (in the episode 'Pay Off', Euston Films, 29 November 1976), *Hazell* ('Hazell Goes to the Dogs', Thames Television, 27 February 1978) and *The Professionals* ('Hijack', London Weekend Television, 30 November 1980), and a memorable turn as the corrupt policeman in *The Long Good Friday* (1980), are testimony to the fact, if not a forgotten actor, he is undoubtedly a forgotten hero of *comedy*.

Born David Kingshott, in Twickenham, Middlesex, on 23 June 1929, King had been a boy of many parts – baker's boy, grocer's boy, butcher's boy – before becoming a semi-professional drummer boy with a dance band. His experience playing factory canteen shows led to his first professional booking, joining the knockabout troupe of Morton Fraser and his Harmonica Rascals. His career was something of a firecracker, burning at its brightest in the 1950s, when, as a young man fresh from national service with the Royal Air Force, he worked himself upwards through regional music hall, auditioned for BBC producer Richard Afton and secured a solo spot on *Television Music Hall* in 1954. BBC TV Light Entertainment chief Ronnie Walden saw his potential and, in the wake of Benny Hill's departure in 1955, offered King the resident comedian compere slot on *Show Case*. The success of these bright and breezy television assignments prompted the BBC to give King his own monthly variety television series, *The Dave King Show* (BBC Television, 1955–57), the breakthrough for writers Sid Green and Dick Hills, and produced by Ernest Maxin, all three of whom would be instrumental in the television success of Morecambe and Wise.

In March 1954 Dave King married Jean Hart, a dancer with the Jack Billings troupe, and almost immediately landed the guest-comic spot with Jimmy Edwards [qv] and Tony Hancock in *The Talk of the Town* at the Adelphi Theatre.

King subsequently proved the comedy smash of the 1955 Royal Variety Performance at the Victoria Palace Theatre, and just six months later was lined up to wow the summer-season crowds of the Winter Gardens, Blackpool with the stage version of *The Dave King Show*. Off the back of this variety smash, in February

Norman Rossington, Dave King and Daniel Massey in heist caper *Go to Blazes*, 1962.

1956 King launched a successful, albeit short-lived, recording career with Decca Records, hitting the top twenty with such perennials as 'Memories Are Made of This', 'You Can't Be True to Two', and, in January 1958, 'The Story of My Life'. The story of Dave King's life was that he was his own worst enemy. Always desperate to push for bigger budgets, bigger pay packets and bigger exposure, he turned away from the BBC and, taking his two writers with him, headed over to commercial television.

The real lure was a plum comedic acting role as Mortimer Brewster in the August 1958 *ITV Play of the Week* presentation of *Arsenic and Old Lace*, opposite murderous old biddies Peggy Mount and Dorothy Dewhurst. Even this early King was keen to embrace drama rather than stand-up, but what the bosses at ATV really wanted was the brisk variety that had been such a success on the BBC. Showcased under the network's *Saturday Spectacular* presentation, *The Dave King Show* ran for eleven programmes from April 1958.

The sheer confidence of King in these shows came to the attention of the NBC network. He was the first British vaudevillian to really make an impact on American television, and from the May to September 1959 he hosted nineteen live editions of *The Kraft Music Hall Presents: The Dave King Show*. The programmes were scripted by his familiar writing team of Sid Green and Dick Hills, with Mel Brooks adding an authentic New York zing to the jokes.

King's time in America was only moderately successful, however, and he hastily returned home to a very accommodating ATV, and two further editions

Dave was always pugnacious and diligent about the quality of the scripts he was offered.

of *The Dave King Show* in the autumn of 1959. Although, with various production crew changes, the show would linger at ATV until June 1970, King was increasingly disillusioned by his perceived limitations on British television. He had made time to re-visit America for various guest spots, as well as break into British films. His transatlantic cache secured him a cameo as a restauranteur in the Bob Hope and Bing Crosby comedy *The Road to Hong Kong* (1962). A little later that year, King starred in one of my all-time favourite comedy films, *Go to Blazes*, in which he gleefully leads a criminal gang, supplemented by Norman Rossington and Daniel Massey, in an intensive training course in firefighting – for purely unlawful reasons. Dennis Price as the corrupt fire chief and Robert Morley as the flabbergasted pyrotechnics expert provide peerless support; and you'll be humming John Addison's contagiously catchy theme for weeks after. But this big-screen romp still surprisingly failed to ignite much interest in the cinema-going public. King abandoned dreams of a star comedian film career.

King's comeback television series for ATV, *Dave's Kingdom*, cast him as a fantasist forever inventing misadventures within his flat – his Kingdom. It lasted for just one series of six editions, broadcast from 21 October 1964. King continued to perform his live comedy cabaret throughout the sixties, often taking the Talk of the Town, in London, but he eventually even tired of that. Thus started the earnest transformation into a steady and efficient character actor. Only very rarely did he return to full-blown comedy, but when he did – as in the 1971 Frankie Howerd romp *Up the Chastity Belt* – his performance was a scream. A final funny flurry came in 1980 and, rather nicely, it was a reunion with King's old writer Sid Green. 'Tell it to the Judge' was part of London Weekend Television's *Comedy Tonight* series and cast King as hard-bitten C.I.D. officer Detective-Inspector Vic Saggers. It perfectly mirrored his new tough guy persona, but no series was commissioned. Instead, Sid Green wrote *Fancy Wanders* (LWT, 1980). King starred as the eponymous character, an out-of-work day-dreamer whose innermost thoughts were shared with the audience. He would even have conversations with statues – much like Sid Green's Gurney Slade creation from twenty years earlier.

As vulgar scrap merchant Harry Brock in Garson Kanin's *Born Yesterday*, Greenwich Theatre, 1973. Lynn Redgrave was his Billie Dawn.

King would occasionally pop up in a television role up until the the mid-1990s; notably as Jack Duckworth's scallywag older brother, Cliff, in *Coronation Street* (Granada, 1994–95), and Roy Hutton in *Heartbeat*: 'Unfinished Business' (Yorkshire Television, 19 November 1995): Dave's performance of a cuckolded kleptomaniac railwayman charmingly bookended on the soundtrack by snatches of his own recording of 'Memories Are Made of This'. Occasionally he would talk of the restless ambition and petulance of youth that had rattled the cage of the BBC and thrown a thoroughly successful comedy career off course. Still, at the time of his death, in London, on 15 April 2002, at the age of seventy-two, Dave could reflect on a gloriously scattergun talent that had got him to the very top and had very nearly kept him there. Memories are made of this, indeed.

> TREAT YOURSELF TO *Memories Are Made of This* (Vocalion: B0000DB3T1, 2003), a collection from King's Decca Records output, including 'The Birds and the Bees', 'Hotta Chocolatta', 'Shake Me I Rattle' and twenty more recordings including, of course, the title track. These are, indeed, the dreams you will savour.

# Roy Kinnear

## 1934–88

I can't imagine Roy Kinnear ever auditioning for a part, though I am sure he had to every now and again. I just see a script in progress and the first thought being, 'I wonder if Roy Kinnear is available.' More than that, I imagine writers thinking, 'Shall we add a character that could be played by Roy Kinnear, just a cameo to liven things up?'

He seemed ever present in my childhood. I think of him first as someone cowardly and cunning; the nerviness of a shyster showing his hopes of hoodwinking you just a little too glaringly. The surnames of the characters he played are a delight in themselves: Wormsley, Webley, Quilby, Happychap and Skern. His turn as the put-upon, weak, cowardly but – in this case – not quite so conniving headmaster in *Hardwicke House* made him part of the most mysterious sitcom of my teenage days; a comedy about a bleak secondary school, it was pulled from the schedules with rumours of government involvement, the secretary of education seeing it as too damning a view of the system.

Every performance was memorable, whether working with Charlton Heston or Dick Emery. Perpetually employed and always pitch perfect, he brought a sweaty delight to the screen; also a fine pairing with Brian Murphy in the now rather underrated *George & Mildred*. He could play opposite anyone, including Sean Connery in my favourite Sydney Lumet movie, *The Hill*. You'll find him a useful bridge in any game of 'Six Degrees of Kevin Bacon' – see how many links it takes to get you from Brad Pitt to Henry McGee.

*Robin Ince*

To dismiss Roy Kinnear as a one-note performer is to pride yourself a fool. His stock-in-trade, a roly-poly, prematurely balding, breathlessly eager, perpetually bamboozled bumbler, was at the heart of every character and each was unquestionably cut from the same cloth but man, oh man, what quality that cloth was. The infinite inventiveness and just sheer joy that Kinnear brought to each and every one of his performances make his all-too-soon-curtailed collection of workmen, taxi drivers and lowlifes all the more treasurable. From a glorious association with Joan Littlewood to his ill-fated return to Richard Lester's *Musketeers* franchise, Kinnear could lift even the poorest of scripts with a confusedly raised eyebrow or cynical put-down.

He was born Roy Mitchell Kinnear on 8 January 1934, in Wigan. A student at the Royal Academy of Dramatic Art from the age of seventeen, his professional career began with the repertory company of the Newquay Theatre. Credits included the 1955 production of *The Dashing White Sergeant*, a play by Charles Campbell Gardner and Rosamunde Pilcher. Roy's comedy credentials were fully crystallised in 1962 when he joined David Frost and the *That Was the Week That Was* team, and, as a vital cog in the satirical machine, Kinnear not only sat on the razor's edge for a generation but also became one of the most familiar faces on British television. As a result, he was rarely out of the public consciousness for the next quarter of a century.

His performances are so brimful of laughter-fuelled joy and sun-kissed affection that to wallow in his recorded legacy is as life-affirming as walking barefoot through long grass on a summer's day. There's the dogged, uncultured

Marty Feldman with Roy, as Professor Moriarty's incompetent assistant, *The Adventure of Sherlock Holmes' Smarter Brother*, 1975.

nightclub owner Lucky Dave, desperately trying to avoid the sharp-witted, get-rich-quick – or at least get-solvent-now – patter of Anthony Newley in *The Small World of Sammy Lee* (1963). As Walter, the sweaty, desperate seller of the weird and wonderful in Hammer's *Taste the Blood of Dracula* (1969), Roy's wide-eyed comic relief naturally comes a cropper to the fangs of Christopher Lee's Count.

His work-shy interactions alongside Warren Mitchell's Alf Garnett – in which, during a complex discussion about life, the universe and everything, Kinnear can juggle props and political observations and still demolish the contents of his over-stuffed lunchbox while not missing a beat – are dexterous masterclasses; and he melts with self-pity as cuckolded airline steward Richard Burton in *The Galton and Simpson Playhouse*: 'Naught For Thy Comfort' (Yorkshire Television, 10 March 1977).

He cropped up twice as a guest of the Goodies, one of them as Nero, in 'Rome Antics', on 7 April 1975, literally rubbing a copious quantity of grapes over his body as he takes decadence to new heights. Previously, in 'The Lost Tribe of the Orinoco' (BBC2, 22 October 1971), Kinnear pounced upon an audacious script, which focused on natives who chanted 'Boom! Boom!' after every punchline, to deliver a layered and generous pastiche of Rider Haggard and Kipling.

In a television advertising campaign to promote living in Peterborough, and investing in the Peterborough Effect, Roy played an earnest Roman centurion who let the train take the strain en route to the new-town and, wandering round the city centre in search of the old slave market, he became quite the poster-boy for the place in the mid-'80s. The Peterborough Development Corporation, who had commissioned the adverts, claimed a world first in having a television commercial in Latin with English subtitles! Kinnear was the supercilious and suspicious Mr Lloyd in *The Boys in Blue* (1982), skilfully supporting Tommy Cannon and Bobby Ball in their sole film outing; and Kinnear was simply born to elevate *The Zany Adventures of Robin Hood* (1984) to the realms of genius as the slovenly Friar Tuck. Talking of outrageous adaptations of literary classics, there's also Paul Morrissey's *The Hound of the Baskervilles* (1978), which pitted

As Hoskins, caught up with Russian ballet dancer Rudi Petrovyan (Lewis Fiander), *Not Now, Comrade*, 1976.

Peter Cook and Dudley Moore against Conan Doyle's integrity and delighted in the near-incoherent ranting of Kinnear as Selden the Axe Murderer. It's truly one of the funniest, most complete film cameos you could ever hope to see, one that can leave me breathless with laughter.

Walt Disney Productions, a perennial lover of the British comic actor, cast Roy as a bumbling law-keeper in *One of Our Dinosaurs Is Missing* (1975), and a bumbling law-breaker in *Herbie Goes to Monte Carlo* (1977). On the subject of films for all the family, there's his majestic, hilarious, deadpan performance as Mr Salt in *Willy Wonka & the Chocolate Factory* (1971). That 'Nuts!' to Gene Wilder still resonates down the decades. Then there's *Just Ask for Diamond* (1988). One wishes the film had stuck to its much more satisfying, Anthony Horowitz's source material, working title of *The Falcon's Malteser* (a play on *The Maltese Falcon*, you see. Come on, keep up!) but nevertheless it boasts Kinnear as the unshaven and disinterested manager of the most run-down boarding-house hovel in cinema history.

While gloriously ripping the educational system apart in *Hardwicke House* (Central, 1987), a perennially repeated Kinnear was concurrently delighting even younger kids as the narrator of *Bertha* (BBC1, 1985–86), the animated series about

On location in Almeria, with John Lennon for Richard Lester's *How I Won the War*, 1967. Roy was back in Spain for Lester, filming *The Return of the Musketeers*, in September 1988, when he fell from his horse and was taken to hospital in Madrid; he died from a heart attack at fifty-four.

a factory machine that could manufacture anything, and as the voice of Bulk in *SuperTed* (BBC1, 1983–86), the dunderhead baddie who rejoiced in a reunion with Victor Spinetti's character, Texas Pete, for more hare-brained schemes of world domination.

And all this even before strolling into the impressive acreage farmed by director Richard Lester: that earlier evil alliance with Victor Spinetti, with Roy as the almost apologetic sidekick in The Beatles romp *Help!* (1965); the forever cuckolded chump Clapper in *How I Won the War* (1967); the plastic-mac man in the post-apocalyptic satire *The Bed Sitting Room* (1969); d'Artagnan's cynical servant, Planchet, in *The Three Musketeers* (1973) and its sequels; and, in what is arguably Kinnear's finest performance of all, the cheerfully up-beat Social Director Curtain in *Juggernaut* (1974), determinedly keeping a smile on his face and desperately trying to cheer everybody up as the North Atlantic ocean liner careers ever onwards to certain disaster. If one performance can sum up Kinnear's gift, it is this one. While all the world is going to hell in a handcart, the rainbow optimism of Roy Kinnear provides a glimmer of hope, however bloody futile that hope may be. Boy, do we need him now.

TREAT YOURSELF TO *Cowboys – The Complete First Series* (Network: B0042OFoLO, 2011), the most consistently strong sitcom for Roy Kinnear in a leading role, as the head of Joe Jones Limited, the dodgiest firm of builders in the business. If you're left with any leftover reddies at all, there's also the *Complete Second Series* (Network: B005VDLO60, 2012).

# Dennis Kirkland

## 1942–2006

Benny Hill is my favourite comedian. Dennis Kirkland was Benny's favourite director. Reason enough to reserve him a seat at comedy's top table.

*Tony Slattery*

Comedy film directors who are continually acknowledged by the majority of casual film fans as great comedy directors tend to be those who directed themselves: Charlie Chaplin, Jacques Tati, Buster Keaton... And then there was Dennis Kirkland. His mini-films with Benny Hill – for they were always something more than just television sketches – have stood the test of time just like Kirkland knew they would. Without a hint of arrogance about his own contribution, he once told me: 'You know, in the year 2086 or something, people will still be laughing at Benny Hill. What we did together will always be funny. They'll probably be playing them on children's television by that time!'

That crack about children's television belied the fact that even a decade after Hill's death Kirkland was still evangelistic about the innocent fun at the heart of his comedy. The supposed sexism that saw Hill's legacy flippantly dismissed by many commentators was irksome to him. But if you have come here for a debate then you are in the wrong place: I'm taking Benny Hill's genius as read. What we have here is a salute to his long-time director, a director who embraced a proven golden nugget of British comedy and made him international.

I got to know Dennis Kirkland while I was writing my book on Benny Hill in 1999. Over the next couple of years, we seemed to continually bump in to each other around Soho or Broadcasting House. Invariably, in fact *every time*, these impromptu meetings would end up with an hour or so in the pub. This happened so frequently that it seems to me we must have properly arranged to meet on at least one or two of these occasions, but I can't remember the phone calls that set them up. All I do remember is the sheer joy when I heard that rather fruity, nasal voice, cry: 'Robert! What the hell are you doing here? The Yorkshire Grey is calling...'

On one of these occasions I was meeting my then girlfriend, Melanie Clark, later in the day, so I had steered Dennis to the hostelry in question, possibly the Argyll Arms. Dennis and I, with pints in hand, were chatting, when at one point I could tell his attention was wavering. I looked around and there was Melanie. We hugged. Dennis was awe-struck. Melanie had an hourglass figure with a lot of sand at the top. With perfect timing Dennis said: 'Benny would have *loved* you...'

And indeed Benny would, for, like Chaplin, both he and Dennis knew that a young lady was instrumental to his comedy – particularly, in Benny's case, a well-endowed one. This attitude never contradicted his dismay at the sexist brickbats. As Dennis would winningly explain, Benny Hill often *was* sexist – against the men. They were the fools and the fall guys, Benny's repertory company of stooges, arguably forgotten in the shadow of the star of the show but allowed – and, indeed, encouraged – to steal the scene. Dennis would lovingly observe: 'My God! Look at them. The boys are back in town!' There was Little Jackie (Jackie Wright), forever being slapped on his bald head; the unflappable Henry McGee, dubbed 'Super Stooge' by a devoted cast and crew; the perpetually pickled Bob Todd (who the band Half Man Half Biscuit described as resembling 99 per cent of gargoyles), hardly able to stand up, never mind stand up for himself; the dashing Jon Jon Keefe, whose charm was always capsized by embarrassment. These were the fools in love. Against such opposition, the women always came out on top.

Like another much-missed drinking buddy of mine, Vince Powell [qv], the work of Dennis Kirkland is not so much forgotten as

Den directing his friend and comic muse Benny Hill, for Thames Television's internationally renowned sketch show.

misunderstood. Another memorable drinking tale with Dennis Kirkland involved Powell: supping one or two in the Compleat Angler, Teddington, Dennis spotted Powell across the street, rushed outside the pub and gave him an impeccable Fred Scuttle salute. Happy days.

Still, even when Benny Hill is paraded as a relic of political incorrectness, Dennis Kirkland's gleeful direction, coaxing his star through complex slapstick, is a pivotal contribution that hardly even gets a footnote. When the two met, Benny Hill had been a British television star for a long, long time. *The Benny Hill Show* had started on BBC Television in 1955 and had got considerably saucier – a Donald McGill postcard come to life – by the time Hill moved to Thames in 1969. Dennis Kirkland wouldn't enter Benny Hill's life until the third act, but when he did, he made all the difference.

Born on 2 December 1942, in South Shields, Northumberland, Kirkland had wanted to be an actor. Quick-witted and likeable, he was a natural performer; indeed, he revelled in his stand-up audience-warm-up before *The Benny Hill Show* recordings at Teddington Studios. Dennis had entered the television industry as a props man at Tyne Tees and then joined ATV as a floor manager. In 1968 he moved to Thames Television and it was here that he first encountered Benny Hill: 'I walked into the rehearsal room and there was Benny doing the old Marcel Marceau mime stuff, pretending he was trapped in a giant bubble. I just burst out laughing and he stopped, looked at me and smiled, and said: "Well, you can stay!"'

As soon as Kirkland took over as Benny Hill's director in 1979, the comedy was taken up to eleven. Not only that, but the very British Benny Hill finally broke big in the United States. His brand of robust variety conjured memories of the shows of Dean Martin and Red Skelton and Jackie Gleason. Long since diluted on American screens. For the next decade, Dennis would produce and direct Benny's best-known and most celebrated work – work celebrated around the globe. Benny would be feted in France, revered on the Rhine, and praised along the Pacific Rim. Under Kirkland's direction the whole world fell in love with Benny Hill. Just as Britain turned her back on him.

At its very best, *The Benny Hill Show* could deliver the most beautiful comedy on television. In the show broadcast on 15 September 1986, there was the clown performing a cheeky striptease that went beyond the realms of surrealism as he stripped down to his bare bones and then into nothingness. There was the homage to Charlie Chaplin with Benny as the sad-faced tramp falling in love with a mysterious girl and losing her. Perhaps most delightful of all, in the 25 April 1984 edition, there was the twist on the usual high-speed chase sequence as a persistent hair in the gate finally forces Benny to stop in his tracks, reach towards the camera lense and pluck it out before continuing.

Then, of course, there were the girls. Love them or loathe them, the Hill's Angels became a signifier for the smash-hit comedy show. As far as Dennis Kirkland was concerned, they were strong characters and a strong link to the variety halls in which Benny's career had started. Despite huge worldwide audiences, Thames Television executives were increasingly uneasy at the sexist accusations thrown at *The Benny Hill Show*, and it was Kirkland who tenderly steered Hill into safer terrain. For his shows in 1989, the sexy ladies were toned down and instead Kirkland introduced Hill's Little Angels, a gaggle of mischievous kids. These included Hill's Angel Sue Upton's five-year-old son, Richard, and three-year-old daughter, Louise, as well as Dennis Kirkland's daughter, Joanna. The only persuasion Kirkland needed was to remind Hill that it was an echo back to his silent screen hero. Nearly seven decades after *The Kid* (1921), the connection to Chaplin was complete.

Sadly the change wasn't soon enough. Less than a fortnight after the May 1989 edition of *The Benny Hill Show* was transmitted, Hill and Kirkland attended the Cannes TV Festival. As honoured guests, and representatives of Thames Television, both were dumbfounded to return to Britain, get summoned to Thames, and bluntly be told that *The Benny Hill Show* was being axed. Tabloid pressure and public opinion finally did for the world's most famous comedian. Hill masked his bitterness by going on a pampered tour around Europe and the Americas, then he was back with Dennis Kirkland for a new tailor-made programme that reflected this international standing. *Benny Hill's World Tour* was shot at Teddington Studios, their comforting home from home, though only the New York edition was completed before Benny's death, in April 1992. A Central Television contract for *The New Benny Hill Show* was among his unopened mail.

Kirkland would try to resurrect the style and spirit of his favourite muse with larger-than-life comedian Freddie Starr, an experiment that proved very successful albeit largely unheralded today. Two specials in 1993 and a series of five *Freddie Starr* sketch shows in 1994 were produced and directed by Kirkland. Brash, colourful, outrageous, and full of under-cranked mime, these Starr showcases for Central Television are clear signs that if Hill had lived Kirkland would have made sure *his* Central shows would have been business as usual. A one-off, last appearance by Bob Todd, larking about in the Freddie Starr Olympics, made the Benny Hill homage complete. And a very funny homage it was too.

Kirkland had worked with other comedians before, of course. He had started in children's television, directing *Rainbow* in the early 1970s, with that cloth-faced double act George and Zippy, both voiced by versatile actor Roy Skelton. At Thames Television on 28 August 1978, Dennis directed *The Tommy Cooper Show*, and came closer than most producers to capturing the full music hall gusto of Ken Dodd in *The Ken Dodd Laughter Show,* six half-hour sketch shows broadcast from 8 January 1979. Kirkland had directed many episodes of the Jon Pertwee-fronted crime panel show *Whodunnit?* (Thames Television, 1972–78) and was even entrusted with producing two of Eric Sykes's celebrated noisy 'silent' comedies – noisy because, despite the lack of actual dialogue, they were splattergunned with bangs, thumps, cries, and laughter. The frantic removal comedy film *It's Your Move* (Thames, 18 October 1982) and the wonderfully

Even on international promotions for *The Benny Hill Show* Den and Ben couldn't resist some risqué slapstick for the cameras.

macabre *Mr H is Late* (Thames, 15 February 1988) were jam-packed with the cream of British comedy, from Bernard Cribbins to Cannon and Ball; both films cast beloved talisman Bob Todd, as an old removal man and elderly undertaker, respectively.

But it was Benny Hill who remained the focal point of Kirkland's life, almost more so after Hill's death, for Kirkland was forever being asked to remember and, rather annoyingly, defend the comedy of Benny Hill. Until his dying day, Kirkland would remain bitter about the way Thames Television had treated Hill; mostly he felt they had continued to exploit his television legacy with lucrative repeat screenings across the world while never giving him the equivalent of a posthumous pardon. The red mist would really descend when he remembered the hastily cobbled-together clip-show obituary that Thames put out on the night of Benny's death: 'It was loads of the work we had done over the years and the final caption simply read "Thank you." Yes, I thought, you're thanking him now the poor old love is dead. The bastards!'

Early in 2006, Dennis was admitted to hospital where he contracted an infection, dying on 16 February. He was sixty-three. At his funeral Chas & Dave sang 'Ain't No Pleasing You' and the instruction to wear something pink was adhered to by all. It was a joyous celebration: very affectionate, very funny, very Dennis.

TREAT YOURSELF TO *Benny Hill – Complete & Unadulterated Set 6: The Hill's Angels Years (1986–1989)* (A & E : B000J10F8M, 2007), the complete batch of Benny's last shows from Thames Television. With the star now rather reined in, Kirkland could take him back to Chaplinesque pathos and add clever television-focused satire such as 'The Crook Report'. The perfect collaboration, tightened by the censorship of political correctness.

# Patsy Knox

## 1924–84

It seems that I've always been aware of Patsy Knox, without ever knowing it. As a child with a strong fascination for ancient Egypt, I was engaged and amused by the comical dance styling of Wilson, Keppel and Betty. Even before the advent of the internet, it wasn't too difficult to see footage of the trio: British television stations were, at that time, far more inclined to screen films and footage from bygone entertainment eras than they are today. Consequently, I well recall the unveiling of British pop artist Nicholas Munro's larger-than-life sculpture of the trio, *The Sand Dancers*, at the Sands Hotel in Edinburgh – now held by the Treadwell Gallery in Vienna – which received considerable local press coverage in newspapers and on television.

Wilson, Keppel and Betty, with minimal props and a painted backdrop of the sphinx and pyramids of Giza – peculiarly reminiscent of that used by pioneering director Georges Méliès in his 1903 short film *Le Monstre* – succeeded in capturing something of the flavour of

Egypt, during the interwar years, as it existed in the public imagination. Although comedic, the act was determinedly Orientalising, exotic, somewhat erotic and distinctly arcane, conjuring up an imaginary Egypt at the height of Western Egyptomania.

Patsy Knox, although not the original 'Betty', provided the perfect foil to her two angular, stomping colleagues, being lithe, elegant and achingly modern, with an ability to hurl herself around the stage like a veil-festooned floor gymnast.

It is impossible to fully appreciate the degree to which this act has been absorbed in the public consciousness – elements of Wilson, Keppel and Betty's Egypt of the 1920s are certainly discernible in The Three Stooges' *We Want our Mummy*, Universal's *Mummy* sequels from 1940 to 1955, *Carry On Cleo*, the sketches of Morecambe and Wise – featuring a fabulously vocal Janet Webb in the 'Betty' role – and, most recently, in 2018, in the Charles Court Opera's London staging of *King Tut: A Pyramid Panto*.

Sometimes it's easy to forget how parochial our understanding and appreciation of modern culture – particularly comedy – can be. In 2011, while delivering a lecture on cinematic representations of Cleopatra at the internationally renowned Ny Carlsberg Glyptotek, Copenhagen, I encountered some baffled looks from my learned audience in explaining the nature of the *Carry On* series. I had no such difficulties when it came to 'Cleopatra's Nightmare': one slide of Wilson, Keppel and Patsy Knox was all that was required for instant recognition. This, I think, perfectly demonstrates the act's sustained and international legacy.

*John J. Johnston, Egyptologist*

The pages of this book are littered with splendid variety turns that once thrilled packed auditoriums and now languish in the mists of time. Wilson, Keppel and Betty is not one of those acts. This spirited, hilarious and double-jointed cash-in on the 1920s Tutankhamun craze gave the eccentric dancers Jack Wilson and Joe Keppel fame, fortune and a forty-plus-year career on the music halls.

The droopy moustaches and knobbly knees remain popular culture icons that are immediately and warmly recognised. The British Film Institute reports that the scratchy clip of Wilson and Keppel performing the sand dance is the single most-requested piece of film in their archive; everybody from the Goodies to the Chuckle Brothers have paid tribute to their sand-dancing antics. The routine has been used to sell dog food and telephone services – the notorious 118 men owe much to the look of Wilson and Keppel.

The act was Steampunk Rock. Johnny Rotten was a huge fan, and a clip of the act appears in the Sex Pistols documentary *The Filth and the Fury* (2000). Jonathan Richman's 1977 hit 'Egyptian Reggae' featured them in its music video, and they even inspired the Bangles hit 'Walk Like an Egyptian'. Wilson, Keppel and Betty encouraged the entire Western world to walk like an Egyptian, and to laugh at themselves as they did it.

So, what's to forget? Betty was a glamorous counterpoint to the eccentricity. She may be lacking from the most famous surviving clip, but she's always name-checked when the act is referenced. Well, the crucial point is that there were lots of Bettys. Lots and lots of Bettys. Up to ten have been identified over the years but the one that appears in the vast majority of the all-too-few remnants of footage of the act is not actually a Betty at all. She was a young lady by the name of Patsy Knox; a forgotten hero if ever there was one. So sit back: do I have a tale to tell you.

Patsy Knox was born in Salina, Kansas, just a year after her parents had married; after just another year, they were divorced. Her mother, Betty Knox, had been born Alice Peden before marrying Donald Knox, but was known as Betty throughout her life – the original, you might say!

After her divorce, Betty Knox went on the stage as a dancer and comedy stooge, notably as a double act with Vaudevillian Jack Benny. Liverpudlian Jack Wilson and County Cork man Joe Keppel had met and teamed up during a stint with Colleano's Circus. By 1928 they were settled in America and looking for a woman to join the act. Pretty and plucky, Betty Knox fitted the bill and for fourteen years their 'Cleopatra's Nightmare' routine wowed audiences throughout America and Europe.

At this time, young Patsy was being brought up by her drifter father Donald. She would have rather been with her mother, for she too had long nursed theatrical ambitions. Her mother was by this time firmly established in Britain, and in 1938 Patsy travelled from New York to join her. Patsy was fourteen years old and determined to make it big in show business.

Patsy's fledgling education at drama school was rudely cut short when Betty decided to leave the act. The year was 1941, and with the storm clouds of the Second World War threatening to engulf her own country, rather wonderfully Betty was determined to kick the sand off of her shoes and get her hands dirty as a war correspondent.

Frank Owen, the then editor of the *Evening Standard*, called her bluff and offered her a job. The salary was a lot less than the fifty quid a week she was making with Wilson and Keppel but the challenge was too good to ignore and, it is alleged, she said: 'Give me two weeks to break my daughter into the act and I'll take it...' And that was that.

Patsy's potential career as a legitimate actor was scuppered; from now on she was a hoofer – and a hoofer in her mother's footsteps. So it was that Patsy Knox became the new Betty, debuting at the Hippodrome, Preston on 30 May 1941. While the original Betty was making a name for herself in the papers, daughter Patsy was making her name – or rather, consolidating her mother's name – in dance, on sand, in various provincial theatres around England. Patsy made her first London appearance with the act at the Streatham Hill Theatre in August 1942.

The reaction of Jack Wilson and Joe Keppel to all of this is lost, but if the records are to be believed the act simply went from strength to strength. Wilson had always been the businessman of the outfit. He would become the engine of the act, both making the bookings and choreographing the routines. He was also in charge of the all-important Egyptian props and scenery. Keppel's sole offstage duty was to make sure there was plenty of sand! He insisted on only Bedfordshire sand and would take sackfuls of the stuff as far afield as Las Vegas to preserve the precise *sound* of the act. (This is also the only way of telling Keppel apart from Wilson; if the footage you're watching features one of our moustachioed heroes dishing sand out of an Egyptian urn, it'll be Joe.) Betty Knox had been in charge of the costumes and this responsibility was bequeathed to Patsy. She would lay out the Egyptian attire, the headdresses and the exotic, skimpy dresses.

Alfie Bass as the giant in the Christmas Eve 1973 special 'The Goodies and the Beanstalk'.

Following a year in the West End at the Theatre Royal Haymarket from October 1976, Bill Fraser reprised his role of Lord Porteous for the 1978 regional tour of *The Circle*.

Eric Barker, Kenneth Connor and Leslie Phillips on the Front of House still that gives away the denouement of *Watch Your Stern* (1960).

Michael Bentine teamed up with this incontinent scavenger for unpredictable chat show appearances and this 1983 session utilised for both a BBC record compilation and a HarperCollins anthology.

During this 1983 Bournemouth summer season Billy Burden struck up a firm friendship with Wendy Richard, ten years before *Grace & Favour*.

Michael Bentine headlined an all-star cast as Horace Quilby in *The Sandwich Man*, released in cinemas in July 1966.

It was mirth and magic all the way with Marti Caine and Paul Daniels, at the North Pier Pavilion theatre, Blackpool, for the summer season of 1978.

Funny girl Marti Caine was one of British variety's brightest stars for twenty years.

Ronald Shiner took on the mantle of Will Hay in *Top of the Form*, for a spring 1953 release. Shiner's schoolmaster is more cunning than befuddled.

The Chad Valley Whack-O! board game capitalised on the huge success of Jimmy Edwards' late-fifties BBC TV series about the school 'for the sons of gentlefolk'.

A previously unpublished snapshot of Jimmy Edwards, from August 1987. Across the road is the parish church of St. Andrew and St. Mary the Virgin, Fletching, East Sussex, which is now Jim's final resting place.

The sheet music to accompany the 1899 Gus Elen recording of 'The Golden Dustman': a lament of a working man with aspirations of the high life.

Gus Elen as featured in a pack of Snap cards from the end of the Victorian era. You can never have enough Gus cards in a game of Snap!

Gus Elen as featured in Series No. 4 of 'Star Artistes', the card set issued with Cohen, Weenen & Co. cigarettes, in 1907.

The sheet music for Gus Elen's 1895 recording of 'It's a Great Big Shame!'. All together now...

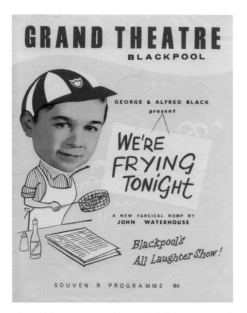

Proud Lancastrian Jimmy Clitheroe starred as naughty schoolboy Jimmy Bright in *We're Frying Tonight* for the 1963 summer season.

Charlie Drake starred in *Little Old King Cole* (man and boy), 'a new pantomimical fantasy', at the London Palladium, from 20 December 1961. The theatre was taking bookings into April 1962.

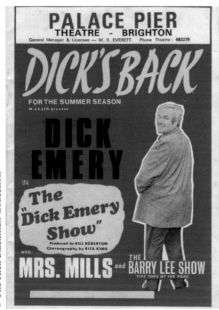

You could see Dick Emery's back – and his front! – when he took Brighton for the 1968 summer season.

A stunning Arnaldo Putzu *Look-in* cover sees Potter (Deryck Guyler) and Miss Ewell (Joan Sanderson) encounter the rather hirsute new pupils of *Please Sir!*, who had joined for the fourth TV series from 18 September 1971.

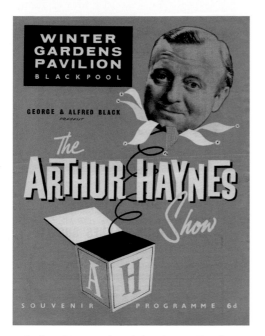

Arthur Haynes played the Winter Gardens Pavilion, Blackpool, for the 1962 summer season. Regular television stooge Nicholas Parsons was also in the cast.

Nat Jackley and Tessie O'Shea starred in *Out of This World* at the Opera House, Blackpool, for the 1950 season.

Friends and cohorts Nicholas Parsons and Arthur Haynes promoting the twelfth series of *The Arthur Haynes Show*, 1964.

Debbie Linden cheerfully covering her modesty in the mid-1980s, when she was one of the most popular Page Three girls under the sun.

Debbie brought authentic glamour to the extensive stage tour of *Page Three Girls Reveal All!* in 1988, aided and abetted by veteran comedian Ken Platt.

Star comic Ken Platt supported Hollywood singing star Alan Jones and fledgling double act Morecambe and Wise in the 1953 summer season revue at the Winter Gardens Pavilion, Blackpool.

Ken Platt was one of the most colourful and crowd-pleasing panto clowns, as often as not delighting, and signing, as the clumsy Kenny Cucumber.

Albert Modley reigned supreme with his *Modley's Merrymakers* spectacular at the Central Pier, Blackpool, for the 1953 summer season.

Having departed Broadway in 1945, Olsen and Johnson toured *Laffin Room Only* and, typically, as visiting American comedians, even stormed the notorious Glasgow Empire.

Like one of his heroes Buster Keaton, Pierre Étaix relished a twilight renaissance and remains effortlessly elegant here at his home in Paris in 2015, just a year before his death.

Ken Goodwin, game for anything to promote his 1982 album, which features songs such as 'Ukulele Man' and 'April Love' between the live comedy.

The 1962 album of Michael Bentine's surrealist sketch show boosts an amusingly apocalyptic cover taken by celebrated glamour photographer Edgar Brind.

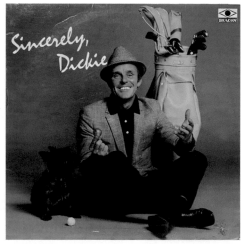

These 1969 recordings showcase Dick Emery's serious singing on such tracks as 'If You Love Her', which peaked at no. 32 in the charts.

Dickie Henderson's 1969 album unleashed the all-round entertainer on such standards as 'Everytime We Say Goodbye' and 'Fly Me to the Moon'.

The 1968 album collection of Charlie Drake's greatest hits, with statuesque glamour girl Valerie Leon very nearly in the spotlight!

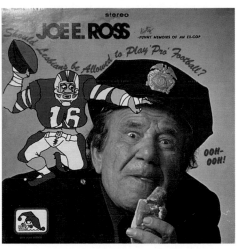

Thirty minutes of dirty jokes and still basking in the former telly cop fame that *Car 54, Where Are You?* gave him, Joe E. Ross asks a vital vaudeville question on Laff Records, from 1973.

An exhaustive 1983 compilation for the German market. Jack Davis, founding artist for *Mad* magazine, caught the zany energy of Spike Jones time and time again.

The original, rather nightmarish, cover for Mike and Bernie's gallop through the Walt Disney songbook and beyond. Released to enthral and entertain in 1967.

© Carol Royle

A gloriously battle-scarred portrait of Derek Royle as Cap'n Andy Hawks, in Wendy Toye's 1971 production of *Show Boat*, at the Adelphi Theatre.

Having wowed the West End, the 'Monsewer' was the only original star to take on the 1965 *Forum* tour. Dave King replaced Frankie Howerd as Pseudolus.

Dave King is smoking-hot as master criminal Bernard in *Go to Blazes* (1962). More's the pity then that it was his only starring comedy vehicle for the cinema.

'I Never Said That.': Tom E. Murray and Annie Purcell in *The Forty Thieves*, the Theatre Royal, Glasgow pantomime for the 1904–05 season.

Ken Goodwin stood up once more for *The Comedians Christmas Cracker*, a Granada Production for ITV broadcast on 28 December 1993.

Hugh O'Brian and Buddy Hackett subbed for a reluctant Abbott and Costello, with Spike and his Slickers elevated to top spot for *Fireman, Save My Child!*, released in May 1954.

Alan Bennett's intricately vulgar play packaged as a *Carry On*-style seaside romp for a 1983 tour with Patsy Rowlands as the battleaxe wife Muriel Wicksteed.

Released in January 1935, *Treasure Blues* cast Thelma Todd as a pancake-flipper resolute in aiding her chum on an inherited hunt for sunken wealth.

Rebranded the Valentin-Karlstadt Museum in 2001, the Munich collection of curios includes a fur-trimmed toothpick and a device for reading between the lines.

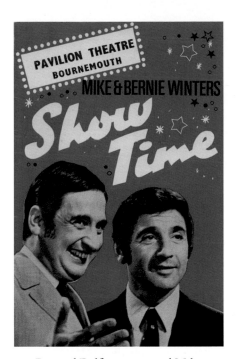

Bernard Delfont presented Mike and Bernie Winters at the Pavilion Theatre, Bournemouth, in 'A Summer Spectacular', for 1971.

It was the North Pier, Blackpool, for Mike and Bernie's variety extravaganza, for the summer season of 1968. Impressionist Mike Yarwood was in support.

In 1969 it was Harry Worth's turn to be in the pink at the North Pier, supported by 'Britain's Happiest Piano Player' Mrs Mills.

Harry gave his benevolent but bewildered King for the Wimbledon Theatre's 1986–87 pantomime season.

The stunning one-sheet cinema poster for Mario Zampi's funeral farce. Clearly Tutte Lemkow had originally been cast as Whisper ahead of Joe Melia.

The boys were ditzy ditch-diggers caught up in a pharaoh's curse in the comedy horror *Mummy's Boys*, released for Hallowe'en 1936.

Raymond Griffith as Confederate spy Jack in his 1926 masterpiece, one of the funniest film comedies of all time.

The effect of the trio was of hieroglyphics coming alive in an English variety theatre. As often as not carried onstage in a litter held aloft, Patsy would fill in the time during a particularly troublesome costume-change for the men by performing an exotic – and, yes, often erotic – with

*A Ray of Sunshine* (1950), 'an irresponsible medley of song and dance' from Adelphi Films.

Patsy adding a veil dance and even incorporating acrobatic flips – anything to keep the audience wowed enough before the trio were reunited for the grand finale, when all three would perform *that* dance.

The music was always the same: Alexandre Luigini's 1875 composition *Ballet Egyptien*. This had been given a hep makeover thanks to an arrangement by piano-caresser extraordinaire Hoagy Carmichael. It was the perfect accompaniment.

As the years rolled by, Wilson's need to concentrate on the props was gradually reduced for he jettisoned the staircase and sarcophagus. In the end, the act was frugally performed in front of a backcloth depicting a sphinx smiling benignly. Patsy would add to this cheap illusion of the mysterious Nile by adopting a Cleopatra mask. Hilariously, she would also end up in a Wilson and Keppel mask so that all three of the trio adopted lanky moustaches. The sight of that hourglass figure and shapely legs topped off by a full Dali was bizarre and funny indeed.

Patsy's forgotten status is all the more upsetting when one considers that it is her and not her mother that the casual viewer is most likely to see. It is Patsy who appears as part of the team in their rare film appearances in *Variety Jubilee* (1943) and *Starlight Serenade* (1944). It is Patsy whose high kicks and belly-dancing wriggles enthral in the National Film and Television Archive collection. And it was Patsy who boosted morale with benefit concerts during the war years, and appeared on the bill of the Royal Variety Performance in 1945 and again in 1947.

The most special of specialty acts, still topping the bill after all those years, in *Variety Cabaret*, at the Alhambra.

Perhaps her crowning glory came in July 1950, when, as a regular attraction at the London Palladium, Wilson, Keppel and Betty found themselves supporting Frank Sinatra. For Patsy that was the tops, and it was then that she decided to leave the group, while on a high.

A glut of Bettys followed. The last was ballet dancer and ex-Windmill Theatre girl Jean MacKinnon, who simplified the choreography to make the act easier for her fast-ageing cohorts, thus propelling the old boys on for another decade.

By 1963, however, the funny bones of Wilson and Keppel had become old bones and the act that had spanned the era from the Charleston to the Watusi was disbanded – but the legend, well, lingered somewhat.

But what of Patsy Knox? She married, becoming Patsy Gilchrist, and was last heard to have been caring for her ailing mother – in Dusseldorf of all places – before Betty Knox died, with impeccable timing, in 1963 – the very same year that the act she had helped to create finally came to an end. Patsy settled in Pearland, Texas, where, I'm happy to imagine, she would have danced between the raindrops for another twenty summers or so.

Keep dancing...

TREAT YOURSELF TO a jaunt to the London Palladium, 8 Argyll Street, W1. A cathedral of variety, the sandy steps of Patsy Knox are ingrained in the very timber here. Take a bushel of Bedfordshire sand, and the hand of the one you love, and dance. Dance for the joyous legacy of Patsy.

# Debbie Linden

## 1961–97

A dear girl. And so good.

*Mollie Sugden*

In the late 1970s and early 1980s British television was awash with glamour girls clad in black stockings and suspenders. From commercials for fast-food restaurants or cars to family variety spectaculars and situation comedies, and at sporting events and press junkets: anything remotely designed to entertain was decorated with a saucy blonde in a bikini. The sauciest and blondest of these was Debbie Linden, a model, actress and deliciously self-effacing sexual fantasy figure who, for a handful of years, seemed to be everywhere.

Debbie was born on 22 February 1961, in Glasgow, to Neil and Rosemary Linden. Her father was well known locally as a cabaret performer, and the young Debbie was swiftly bewitched by the glamour of show business. The vivacious young girl thoroughly enjoyed the opportunities to show off in school plays and Christmas shows, and took lessons in ballroom- and tap-dancing. Attractive, outgoing and determined, by the age of thirteen she was bikini-modelling and at just seventeen she caught the eye of Benny Hill. With its reputation for scantily clad ladies, it was almost inevitable that Debbie's very first television appearance would be on *The Benny Hill Show*. She featured in the Boxing Day 1978 edition, as well as joining Hill for publicity photographs, and she hastily followed it up with work on *The Dick Emery Comedy Hour* (Thames Television, 6 June 1979), *The Jim Davidson Show* (Thames, 15 January 1981), and as Lewis Collins's girlfriend in the 'Runner' episode of *The Professionals* (London Weekend Television, 8 December 1979).

Her most relaxed and productive partnership was with Kenny Everett. She embraced Everett's cheeky, knowing deconstruction of the glamour girl and enjoyed her gyrating along with the near-bondage-style dance routines of Hot Gossip. She even popped up in Everett's only big-screen venture, *Bloodbath at the House of Death* (1984). Admittedly, her role of 'Attractive girl' was hardly dramatically taxing but, still, she was very much part of Everett's troupe.

Debbie could also handle a decent part but, unsurprisingly, in her underwear she was rarely called upon to do very much other than look seductive. However, director Pete Walker certainly saw something more than a scantily clad winning smile when he cast her as the outrageously flirtatious teenager Carol in *Home Before Midnight* (1979). The controversial plot revolved around a twenty-eight-year-old songwriter, played by James Aubrey, being accused of having underage sex with a fourteen-year-old girl, played by Alison Elliott. By association, Linden's character is also fourteen, but she is no virginal shrinking violet. The two girlfriends, finding themselves stranded in the middle of nowhere, try to hitch-hike a lift back to the city. Linden's provocative style leaves no doubt that she's ready, willing and able to do absolutely anything to get home, as a goggle-eyed lorry driver appreciates.

The film, naturally causing a mild sensation, was followed by less challenging cinema work: Linden was a milkmaid in *The Ghost Sonata* and Mavis the wayward schoolgirl in *The Wildcats of St Trinian's* (both, 1980), in which, as early as the opening scene, she has stripped and is strolling into the ocean. She knew it was her body that got the call from the producer and she had no qualms about exploiting it.

Later television roles, as Brenda in the 1984 Christmas Day special of *Just Good Friends* and Margie in *Bergerac* (in the 26 January 1991 episode 'The Evil That Men Do'), allowed her to keep most of her clothes on. But glamour was definitely to the fore as Doreen in the first series of Roy Kinnear [qv] sitcom *Cowboys* (Thames, 1980) and for her best-loved and most high-

Debbie Linden and Lisa Vanderpump bringing sexy back to Frank Launder's *The Wildcats of St Trinian's*, 1980.

profile television role, that of Old Mr Grace's seductive secretary in *Are You Being Served?* Always dressed in short skirts and low-cut tops, with a fetching purple streak in her hair, Linden joined a revolving door of decorative *Are You Being Served?* typists (Moira Foot, Penny Irving, Candy Davis) but, although she was employed only for series eight, in 1981, and appeared only in the first five episodes, her lap-sitting confidence and self-aware innuendo alongside Kenneth Waller really made an impression. However, Linden's character wasn't even given a name. Her talents are, rather derogatorily equated to a fast car's: in her first episode, 'Is It Catching?' (9 April 1981), it is stated that she has had: 'one owner since new, very sporty, and capable of high speeds if you put your foot down!' For the remaining three episodes of the series, her character's scraps of dialogue were shared out between Louise Burton as yet another sexy secretary and Vivienne Johnson as the sexy nurse, and the only explanation for the absence of Debbie's character is talk of a course she had had to go on. Within the cast, however, Debbie's problems were a well-known secret. At that time, a diet of cocaine and Valium fuelled her life and she had become addicted to the slimming drug she had been taking since her teens. *Are You Being Served?* co-star Mollie Sugden, beloved as the unforgettable Mrs Slocombe, said: 'I remember going home one day and saying to my sons that I was so upset because I thought the pretty little girl was on drugs. She used to have a faraway look on her face some of the time

Hill's Angels Head Girl Sue Upton shows Debbie the ropes during a 1978 press push for *The Benny Hill Show*.

and we all suspected something.' Mr Humphries actor John Inman confirmed this: 'I suspected she was ill while she was in the show. She was often poorly and very peaky when we were filming.' Still, although her contribution was brief and anonymous, the nation's temperature remained high from the memory for several years to come.

Debbie also played Layla in the 1987 *The Comic Strip Presents...* film *Eat the Rich* but this intriguing association failed to ignite. Instead, by the summer of 1988, she was a glamorous hostess on Yorkshire Television's *3-2-1*, and cavorting with Ken Platt [qv], on tour with *Page Three Girls Reveal All!*. Her last television role was on 18 February 1994, when she played as woman with a buggy in 'Ducking and Diving', a one-off storyline in *The Bill*. Quite the ignoble farewell.

Work had dried to a trickle by this point, and disappointment in the business had caused Linden's reliance on alcohol and drugs to spiral out of control. Living on benefits in bed-and-breakfast accommodation in Kingston upon Thames, she turned increasingly to heroin, and was forced to sell her body to feed her addiction. With little money left, she moved in with her mother and brother, ready to start a six-week detoxification programme at Tolworth Hospital. But administrative complications meant this was downgraded to an outpatient treatment, and in her traumatic last few days she made two attempts to slash her wrists. Her distraught mother even tried to get doctors to section her under the Mental Health Act. After phoning home to her mother from a call box, Debbie admitted herself to Kingston Hospital. She was found slumped in the corridor dying of a drug overdose. She never regained consciousness.

There is a nasty underbelly of show business that is peppered with tragic tales of attractive and talented people who are picked up, chewed up and spat

out. At the age of thirty-five
Debbie valiantly told her old
bosses at the *Sun* that she was
planning a modelling comeback.
For Debbie, the pressure of
younger competition, addiction
and the shift from objectifying
glamorous females, thus severely
reducing her opportunities, was
all too much. She was just thirty-
six when she died on 5 October
1997. Still, there's a bittersweet
joy in watching her cheerfully
cavorting with the great and
good of British comedy. The
fates were not on her side, but
for a choice few years she was

Perched upon the knee of Old Mr Grace
(Kenneth Waller) to launch series eight of *Are
You Being Served?*, with Frank Thornton, Mike
Berry, Vivienne Johnson, Arthur English, Milo
Sperber, John Inman and Nicholas Smith,
spring 1981.

one of the most beautiful, busiest and best. Lest we forget.

T REAT YOURSELF TO *The Kenny Everett Naughty Joke Box* (Videospace/
Thorn EMI: B0026M2NQY, 1981). There's something extremely apt
about celebrating the comedy legacy of Debbie Linden with a lovely old
VHS tape: a design classic, a little obsolete now, but lovely to look at, and
fabulously functional if you have the right equipment. It is anarchic – a
shabbily-thrown-together, excitingly potty-mouthed excuse for Everett
to introduce such club comics as Fogwell Flax and Lennie Bennett – but
the ever-smiling Debbie gives it glamour during the era in which she
shone at her brightest and most alluring, and makes a valuable record of
this actor in her happiest of collaborations.

# Hugh Lloyd

## 1923–2008

The perfect feed.

*Ray Galton OBE*

Hugh Lloyd's ascent from jobbing character actor to star comedian was pretty meteoric. His first job was as a reporter on his local rag, the *Chester Chronicle*, but following his wartime experience with the Entertainments National Service Association and his subsequent work with various regional repertory companies, he gained variety experience in Swindon and several years at the Windmill Theatre. By the late fifties Lloyd was a reliable stooge for such top television comedians as Bob Monkhouse (*My Pal Bob*, BBC, 1957), Bill Maynard (*Mostly Maynard*, BBC, 1957), Tommy Trinder (*Trinder Box*, BBC, 1959), and Charlie Drake (*Charlie Drake in The Angry Young Plumber*, BBC, 23 December 1959).

Hugh Lloyd really lucked out when he caught the eye of BBC producer Duncan Wood. The result was a lengthy and long-lasting stint with Tony Hancock, playing everything from a man from the council ear-marking a beloved tree for felling to a competition representative delivering the star prize of a night out with Jayne Mansfield. Lloyd was notable as the beleaguered, jobsworth librarian in the classic *Hancock's Half Hour* television episode, 'The Missing Page', 11 March 1960, and successfully kept in with the lad 'imself to appear in several editions of *Hancock*, in June 1961. His most memorable appearances are as the attendant in 'The Lift' and as the deceptively cheery fellow blood donor who swipes the eponymous star's wine gums. Hancock's fleeting renewal of his faith in humanity, and its inevitable crash, is a highlight of television comedy.

Such was Lloyd's impact as a familiar character actor of authoritarian bureaucracy that he was hastily elevated to star status himself and teamed with Terry Scott for the domestic sitcom *Hugh and I* (BBC Television, 1962–67). Today Scott, though wildly under-appreciated, is still remembered, even though back in the day it was Hugh Lloyd's moniker in the show's title that carried the greater weight and panache. The two stars had been pals for many years and shared many a stage together, so the natural friendship, petty rivalry and sheer good humoured joy of *Hugh and I* was all but spontaneous and effortless.

The situations themselves were never anything more than pedestrian; they didn't need to be. Just to spend thirty minutes in the warm embrace of a couple of dear chums was enough to generate five years from the format. The two even made a gag appearance together, during the historical pageant climax of film comedy *Father Came Too!* (1964). Terry is an executioner; Hugh is Mary, Queen of Scots! However, a May 1967 edition of *Comedy Playhouse*, simply entitled 'Hughie', failed to ignite much interest. Scripted by Johnnie Mortimer and Brian Cooke, it embraced Hugh's loveable persona and cast him as a contended guest of Her Majesty's who, after a decade, is so indoctrinated in prison life that he begs to be allowed back in. Patrick Cargill [qv] was the welfare officer left a quivering wreck by Lloyd's ambitious attempts to break back in (few could do quivering wreck as well as Cargill).

The *Comedy Playhouse* debacle fell just four months after the sixth and final series of *Hugh and I* was transmitted, although a short-lived resurrection, *Hugh and I Spy*, came hot on its heels in early 1968. The characters remained the same though the concept was now far more 007, with the unwitting friends caught up in a different, cliff-hanger espionage adventure for each of the six episodes.

South Parade Pier Theatre
**Southsea**

RICHARD STONE
By arrangement with ED. W. JONES, M.B.E.
PRESENTS HIS SPECTACULAR PRODUCTION OF

**LET'S MAKE
A NIGHT OF IT**

STARRING
TERRY **SCOTT** AND **HUGH LLOYD**

PROGRAMME
A

Price Sixpence

Hugh and him played *Let's Make a Night of It* for several summer seasons, here in Southsea until 19 September 1964.

Lloyd and Scott had a complete makeover in 1969, when the sitcom *The Gnomes of Dulwich* (BBC1, 1969) was transmitted. The delightful premise saw the duo as a couple of garden gnomes, Small and Big respectively. With gently sentimental and stupidly satirical scripts from Jimmy Perry, the six episodes are among the most hotly searched-for treasures in television archives.

Lloyd and Scott remained friends and colleagues for several years after *Gnomes*, including the celebrated BBC Television pantomime of *Robin Hood*, on Christmas Day 1973, which, typically, cast Scott as the Bad Robber and Lloyd as the Good Robber. Both were also onstage in different pantomimes at the time, with Lloyd appearing in *Cinderella* at Lewisham Concert Hall.

While great swathes of Hugh's television work is still missing, believed wiped, his commercial series with Peggy Mount, *Lollipop Loves Mr Mole* (ATV, 1971–72), again written by Jimmy Perry, fares better than *The Gnomes of Dulwich* – slightly. At least some material survives from the series: two black-and-white film prints of the thirteen colour episodes. Hugh would return to the Perry universe years later when, in 1991, he was cast as the drunken butler, Selfridge, in *You Rang, M'Lord?* (BBC1, 'A Day in the Country', 22 December 1991, 'Come to the Ball', 3 April 1993, 'The Truth Revealed', 10 April 1993). Producer David Croft, who had helmed the first series of *Hugh and I* thirty years earlier, gifted Lloyd a fine character turn. From gloriously inebriated cries of 'Clear H'off!' during the picnic to unassuming sobriety as the plot thickens, here is an actor within the very skin of his role. And displaying clear gratitude for the quality of the scripts. In a throwback to the 1950s, Lloyd had once again happily resigned himself to playing support in other people's television shows; after *You Rang, M'Lord?* he was back for David Croft and director Roy Gould in *Oh Doctor Beeching!* ('Action Stations', BBC1, 14 September 1997), and he had been Mr Carey in Johnny Speight's *In Sickness and In Health* (BBC1, 1990–92). There had been the role of a petulant train ticket collector in a couple of episodes of the Southern series *Hogg's Back* (Southern 20/27 October 1975), starring Derek Royle [qv]. And it was while appearing on this show that Lloyd nurtured a fruitful association with writer

Peggy Mount as Maggie Robinson, or 'Lollipop' as Hugh's Reg Mole calls her.

Michael Pertwee. The two collaborated on *Lord Tramp* (Southern, 1977), starring Hugh as a cheerful, ever-helpful vagrant who unexpectedly inherits a fortune and title, and uses his untold riches for the good of the community. It was a heart-warming six-episode run and, if nothing else, his character's name, Hughie Wagstaff, highlighted the potency of his marquee value.

Onstage he enjoyed lead roles in regional tours of *Big Bad Mouse* and *Boeing-Boeing*, summer seasons of *Don't Tell the Wife*, and more than two years in the relentlessly popular farce *No Sex Please – We're British*, and various high-profile appearances in everything from Noël Coward (the multi-character portmanteau *Tonight at 8.30*, at the Lyric in 1981), to Anton Chekov (playing Firs in *The Cherry Orchard*) and John Webster (Grisolan in *The Duchess of Malfi*, both for the 1985–86 season at the National Theatre, with Ian McKellen).

That splendid Oscar-winning actor Anthony Hopkins is also a comedy enthusiast – he does a brilliant Tommy Cooper impression – and gleefully cast Lloyd as Thomas Prosser in the film *August* (1996), his inventive reimagining of Chekov's *Uncle Vanya* set in 1900s North Wales. Victoria Wood, another towering

A very charming man: Hugh in a favourite publicity pose.

talent who delighted in keeping the familiar faces near, cast Lloyd in her *As Seen on TV* series and in the 30 November 1989 *Victoria Wood* episode 'Over to Pam'. Lloyd's cult telly stock was high and reached the stratosphere with the role of the time-aware, rather mysterious, rather bewitching Welsh beekeeper Goronwy Jones in the 1987 *Doctor Who* story Delta and the Bannermen. This was the era of Sylvester McCoy and his question mark umbrella; the John Nathan-Turner produced years of scattergun casting of fascinatingly incongruous guest-turns at every opportunity. Lloyd's performance is arguably the most beguiling. It's certainly one of the most charming.

He continued to crop up on television, on his own terms and always with a jowly twinkle: memorably in *Foyle's War* (in the episode 'Eagle Day', ITV Studios, 17 November 2002), *Doc Martin* ('Aromatherapy', ITV Studios, 1 December 2005), and as Father Christmas in the BBC1 superhero sitcom *My Hero*, on 22 December 2000.

He was disarming company too. In the sixties, when the *Observer* asked its readers who should be made president in replacement of the queen, the majority said either Peter Ustinov or Hugh Lloyd! Hugh once said of himself: 'I'm not so much an actor, but more of a performing dog with a wagging tail and anxious to please.' It is a winning quality that enriches every project lucky enough to have included him.

TREAT YOURSELF TO *Lord Tramp – The Complete Series* (Simply Media: B002VSCAD4, 2009), a delightful rags to... well, rags – but in a stately home – story. Hugh gives an endearing performance, positively dripping with that eager-to-please quality that so endured him to audiences. A handful of lovely turns from Alfie Bass gives this some extra forgotten heroic clout too.

# Harry Locke
# and Tommy Godfrey

## 1913–87 and 1916–84

Both instantly recognisable, and both terrific actors. What I really love about Tommy and Harry was their ability to flit seamlessly from comedy to drama. You knew where you were with Tommy and Harry. Predictably fine performances with well-timed lines; stalwarts of TV and film; a casting director's dream. Why weren't they big stars? Who knows. Luck, probably. They were certainly good enough. Their fate was always to play supporting roles as character actors.

My father, Sam Kydd, who first worked with Harry in *Passport to Pimlico* in 1949, was a big fan of his. They were subsequently together in *Angels One Five*, *Treasure Island*, *Reach for the Sky*, *Devil on Horseback*, *I'm All Right, Jack*, and *Sink the Bismarck*, as well as several 'tellies'. I have a memory of Harry coming to our flat when I was little so they must have been good mates. I remember seeing Harry on TV whilst watching with my dad, who was singing his praises. My dad never minced words when a 'difficult' actor was on the box. Harry, however, was a good 'un.

Tommy and my dad were also in *Passport to Pimlico* together. They were in similar TV shows, playing cockney villains in *Softly Softly*, *Z Cars*, *The Persuaders!* and *The Avengers*. Surprisingly, Dad was never in *Love Thy Neighbour* or *Mind Your Language*, in which Tommy had big stints. I think casting directors tended not to cast them together as there was a similarity. I always thought they could have played a couple of cockney brothers in a sitcom!

Jonathan Kydd

To be frank, the pages of this book could be stuffed to the gills with loving salutes to that glorious, unsung body of character actors who peppered post-war British film and television with a seemingly never-ending run of blink-and-you'll-miss-'em supporting turns. These priceless players were as often as not eagerly shoehorned into a production to add an air of familiarity and, simply, work as brilliant shorthand for the characters. Norman Mitchell was your go-to chap for the bumbling copper, while Victor Maddern could always be relied upon to cock a snook at authority. Norman Rossington was the personification of the clumsy British squaddie, while Marianne Stone was the perennial secretary. Dora Bryan was the dial-a-barmaid and lady of easy virtue, Thorley Walters and Richard Wattis the bewildered bureaucrats, George Woodbridge the eternal pub landlord and Warren Mitchell the spiv on the corner with a ready supply of nylons and knock-off watches. Thora Hird was the sniffy, disapproving mother-in-law, Colin Gordon the officious authority figure with a perpetual frown. Sam Kydd, meanwhile, has become legendary as the backbone of the industry, the joke being that he was in *every* British film from D-Day to the death of punk. He wasn't, of course.

As a way of celebrating all those fantastic character actors, I turn to a couple of my personal, often forgotten favourites. Harry Locke was an actor of long-standing repertory experience but, like that of so many others, his fledgling career was interrupted by Second World War duties. He served with the Intelligence Corps (with distinction) and as soon as he was demobbed, in 1946, he was back in the business, as both a useful stage actor and variety comedian. He set out his stall of overly familiar cab drivers, work-shy servicemen and small-time, jobsworth authority figures and it's clear his comedy credentials are vast, including George Formby's last film, *George in Civvy Street* (1946), and a spot alongside Terry-Thomas in *Carlton-Browne of the F.O.* (1959), and Benny Hill in *Light Up the Sky!* (1960). Locke is the frantic AA man in Galton and Simpson's *Comedy Playhouse* March 1963 episode 'Impasse', desperately trying to be the referee between feuding motorists Bernard Cribbins and Leslie Phillips. He's the bemused night porter in the first *Randall and Hopkirk (Deceased)* episode, 'My Late Lamented Friend and Partner' (ITC, 21 September 1969), and was a favourite of producer Betty Box, giving support as a train ticket collector in *Upstairs and Downstairs* (1959), a hospital porter in *Doctor at Large* (1957) and as the knowing confidante Jessup in *Doctor in the House* (1954).

It was laughing gas for Betty's husband, producer Peter Rogers, too, who employed Locke as an instant signifier for all things bedpan-and-thermometer across a decade of *Carry On* films. Locke was Mick the orderly, always happy to place a bet for a patient, in *Carry On Nurse* (1959); the less-than-careful ambulance driver, fearlessly taking every bend in Maidenhead (much to the chagrin of bad patient Frankie Howerd), in *Carry On Doctor* (1968); and a rather ruddy hospital porter, once more, in *Carry On Again, Doctor* (1969).

Locke's final film appearance was as the barman in the gloriously gruesome Peter Cushing and Christopher Lee chiller *The Creeping Flesh* (1973), and his final credit of all was as the gardener in the May 1977 *Just William* London Weekend Television episode 'William and the Wonderful Present'. Reassuringly full-circle that, for one of Locke's very earliest television appearances had been with Robert Sandford in the 1951 BBC production of *Just William*. Careers never have such symmetry. Harry Locke's legacy is as the rank and file of the great British character actor. He was never called upon to carry an entire production, nor would he have wanted to; he was content just to keep working – and work he did. Locke is the cinematic equivalent of that ever-present lollipop man on the street; his was a largely thankless task, but a day in, day out vocation. I like to think that this goes a little way towards being a symbolic gong for services to nose-to-the grindstone reliability.

Now, step up to the plate: a brother-in-arms. Short, squat, stuffy, sarcastic and lots of other words beginning with S, Tommy Godfrey carved out a unique, lengthy career as the butt of the joke and the punch in the punchline. He would look almost naked without a cigarette dangling from his gawping mouth. Overalls and a bag of tools were his stock-in-trade, and a pint of beer was rarely more than an arm's stretch away – in other words, he was the working man. He was the situation comedy dogsbody who would wander into a scene, deliver a few gruff put-downs and happily wander off again. If, in the interim, a pot of paint fell over him, then all the more hilarity.

The archetypal cheeky chappie, born on 20 June 1916, in Lambeth, South London, Godfrey would only ever grow to five feet, five inches tall. One imagines he looked exactly the same as a baby – with a cigarette! His career started with an eccentric dance act with his sister on the bottom rungs of variety-theatre bills. A skilled tap dancer with the skinniest (and most hollow!) legs in the business, Tommy subsequently joined forces with Joyce Randall and Sylvia Heath to form the dance act Godfrey, Randall and Deane. He then developed a solo act for variety. It would be a long and winding road to his being cast as Teddy Knox in 1982 for *Underneath the Arches* at the Prince of Wales theatre, but it was clear that an old pro was in the house.

Still, it is as a familiar bit-part player that he is probably best remembered, having made his film debut as a bus conductor in the 1949 Ealing Studios classic *Passport to Pimlico*. The roles would rarely be any bigger and his career would never really stretch him much further than this but, oh, what a long career it was. Over thirty years later he was still giving his all when he was cast as – you guessed it – a bus conductor in *The Great Muppet Caper* (1981). I like to think it is the same bus conductor: a hard-working, grouchy, do-the-job-and-take-the-money sort of bloke, stuck in a rut for most of his working life. He'd hardly aged. He certainly hadn't developed his acting skills, and why the heck should he? He gave the public and the producer what they wanted: familiarity. By then he had become one of the most familiar and welcome faces in British comedy, notwithstanding the fact that even the most hardcore Brit-com fan would struggle to put a name to that face.

The 1970s was the kindest decade of all, for it gave him not one, not two, but three unforgettable sitcom characters. The first was as the cockney blue-collar worker Arnold Pugh in all twelve episodes of *On the House*. Broadcast by Yorkshire Television from 24 September 1970, it was written by Sid Colin and starred Kenneth Connor as Gussie Sissons,

*Light Up the Sky!* (1960): Tommy Steele, Benny Hill and Cyril Smith gather round Harry, who had already played Roland Kenyon at the Strand Theatre.

chief labourer for building firm Thomas Clackwood and Sons. John Junkin [qv] pitched in as the site foreman, Derek Griffiths was a cocky carpenter and Robin Askwith a long-haired layabout – what else?

From 1972 to 1976 Tommy Godfrey was at Thames Television playing Arthur in *Love Thy Neighbour*. As often as not, his bar-based rants with racist wag Jack Smethurst and half-pint chum Keith Marsh did very little to further the plot of the show; it was all about subtly undermining the ridiculously superior attitude of the honky. Intrinsic to the balance of the comedy, Godfrey's performance was always likeable and level-headed. True, his character would agree with some of the racist sentiments, but as often as not to pinpoint the misunderstanding of the white-supremacist audience – an audience that took *Love Thy Neighbour* to heart almost as much as Britain's black community did.

Godfrey ended the decade with another Vince Powell [qv] smash hit. Between 1977 and 1979 he played the caretaker, Sid, in *Mind Your Language*. As per usual, Godfrey's performance was as often as not away from the main action of the comedy. Instead he would have lovely little vignettes pondering the issues of his day, or fleeting exchanges with the harridan head of the school, played with piercing efficiency by Zara Nutley. More than any other role, it allowed a softer, more understanding side of Tommy's character to develop. That's 'character' used loosely, because Godfrey never really played anything other than the cockney butterball. He was a master at it.

Most of the top comedians of the day welcomed Godfrey as support. Sid James did a spot of painting and decorating with him in the film version of *Bless This House* (1972). Tommy Godfrey had a face born to play a used car salesman, and he did just that in the Benny Hill short film *Eddie in August* (1970). There was *A Little Bit of Wisdom* ('Public Enemy', Associated Television, 16 April 1974), with Norman, and *The Howerd Confessions* (Thames, 16 September 1976), with Frankie. He even played a high court judge in *The Goodies* episode 'Goodies in the Nick' (BBC2, 5 January 1974), and *Casanova '73* (BBC1, 1 October 1973), with Leslie Phillips. Tommy blended perfectly with the broadest strokes of Dick Emery (*The Dick Emery Show*, BBC1, 1972–73) and provided a rigid prop for Tommy Cooper (*The Tommy Cooper Hour*, Thames, 1974–75). At one point he was even cast as 'The Amazing Godfrey'.

There were the expected one-shot sitcom appearances: in the 'Mouse' episode of *Sykes* (BBC1, 16 November 1972); *On the Buses*' 'Mum's Last Fling' (London Weekend Television, 13 February 1970); and, best of all, as the avaricious Uncle Nobby in the *Steptoe and Son* episode 'Oh, What a Beautiful Mourning' (BBC1, 6 March 1972). He had the permanent air of the four-ale bar about him and was a huge boon to seventies situation comedy.

Godfrey was happily dragged into the salacious world of the sex comedy too, guest-starring with Robin Askwith in the 1977 UK stage tour of *The Further Confessions of a Window Cleaner*. That same year Tommy had filmed *Come Play with Me*, with Mary Millington. He even found himself posing with her for *Park Lane* and *Playbirds* magazines. His smile could have run Battersea Power Station.

Even more intriguing were the serious roles. He played Mr Lillyvick in the 1968 BBC production of *Nicholas Nickleby* and Sam Billings in the science fiction chiller *Doomwatch* (1972). His Everyman honesty made him a recurring presence in *Z Cars* and *The Wednesday Play*. For a time, he was *the* taxi driver, playing one in *The Saint* – 'The Power Artists' (ITC, 9 March 1968) and *Department S* – 'The Last Train to Redbridge' (ITC, 14 January 1970). He was a newsvendor and a school porter; a ticket tout and a drunk. And, of course, he was a pub landlord – in Amicus Productions' *The Vault of Horror* (1973). He was everywhere and everyone.

And that's the point. When you go to meet your maker, my friend, I recommend you take the bus. Because you know what? The bus conductor will be Tommy Godfrey and, oh yes, Harry Locke will be the bus driver. You know it. Have your fares ready, please.

Tommy Godfrey is the work-shy Alf Murray, more hindrance than help to Sidney James and Peter Butterworth as they do some emergency repairs on the new neighbour's home, *Bless This House*, 1972.

TREAT YOURSELF TO the sparkling restoration Blu-ray of the 1963 classic *The Small World of Sammy Lee* (Studiocanal Vintage Classics: OPTBD3066, 2016). If ever there was a film Tommy Godfrey and Harry Locke should have both been in, it is this, and it's much more than their usual cough and a spit. Godfrey is the hard-working, cheery cafe owner, desperately oiling the flagging machinery of Anthony Newley's try-anything-to-make-a-buck anti-hero. Locke, meanwhile, is given real Soho low-life clout as the stage manager of the strip club that provides the backdrop to much of the action. He's seen it all (quite literally) but exudes that never-flagging mentality of 'the show must go on, however terrible it may be'. If you want the small world of Harry Locke and Tommy Godfrey in one tasty, easily digested mouthful, this is the film for you.

# Malcolm McFee

## 1949–2001

I am proud to champion Malcolm as a forgotten hero of comedy. We played in many pantomimes as a double act and his timing was always superb. He had an instinctive and intelligent approach to comedy, getting laughs effortlessly, and unselfishly helping others to get a laugh. His Peter Craven character in *Please Sir!* was an authentic portrayal of an East London teenager which was both funny and believable. We got to know each other well on many theatre tours; he had a great sense of humour, which he demonstrated in a tour of *The Lads from Fenn Street*, especially when he parodied Christopher Timothy doing a *Sun* commercial or Noele Gordon in *Crossroads*.

He also loved Dylan Thomas's *Under Milk Wood*, in which we toured together, and I have fond memories of his brilliantly performed Nogood Boyo – a comic and well-observed characterization. I am delighted that Malcolm is remembered in this book.

*David Barry a.k.a. F.A. Frankie Abbott*

There have been a fair few instances where an actor in a sitcom has successfully created a role and subsequently been replaced. The reasons vary, from incapability to unavailability, from the box-office requirement for a bigger star name for the film version to the death of the original actor. However, for me, no one's absence was more keenly felt than that of Malcolm McFee. Having played the blond-haired, wisecracking, effortlessly cool schoolkid Peter Craven in every episode of *Please Sir!* up to that point, McFee was unceremoniously replaced by Leon Vitali for the spin-off series *The Fenn Street Gang*. This new Peter Craven was scheming rather than endearing, slow not savvy. Vitali did all right for himself – he went on to be an executive producer for Stanley Kubrick – but as an actor he was no Malcolm McFee.

Thankfully, McFee was re-recruited for the second series of *The Fenn Street Gang* and all was definitely right with the world of British comedy again. McFee fitted the easy charm and winning grin of the character he had created as though he had never been away. The problem was, he had: that first series just doesn't hang together like it should. With one vital component missing, the engine doesn't run smooth.

The reason for Malcolm's absence was down to his own popularity. Following the success of *Please Sir!*, McFee found himself in great demand. He'd been playing Ivor in Peter Nichols's *Forget-Me-Not Lane* opposite Joan Hickson and Michael Bates [qv], and when it transferred to the Apollo Theatre in April 1971 the management refused to release him from his contract. McFee was desperately disappointed, not least of all because the Thames deal was worth two hundred quid a week more to him than the stage assignment.

*The Fenn Street Gang* never seemed to fully get to grips with what it wanted. Carol Hawkins had already replaced Penny Spencer to play Sharon in the 1971 *Please, Sir!* film, and stayed for the spin-off series, *The Fenn Street Gang* (London Weekend Television, 1971–73). The theme tune changed at least once – as did, by necessity of the return of McFee, the opening credits. That montage sequence for the second series forever cemented his stance as the coolest dude in the neighbourhood. The gang, snapped in an amusement arcade, display playful and subversive antics, with McFee looking totally relaxed, getting away with murder. Aside from some instances of excellent out-of-his-depth panic acting,

McFee would remain largely relaxed and getting away with murder for the rest of the series' run. When the credits were animated for series three, Malcolm was the chilled one in a flashy sports car. Of course he was!

It would be more of the same when *The Fenn Street Gang* got its own spin-off series, in *Bowler* (LWT, 1973). The eponymous anti-hero was a rather gauche, nouveau-riche wide boy, played by George Baker, who had popped up in *The Fenn Street Gang* orchestrating a couple of dodgy deals in which Peter Craven and his naive chum Frankie Abbott got embroiled. If anyone was going to be just on the wrong side of the law, it was McFee's Craven. An Artful Dodger for the flared-jeans generation, he was a smooth-talking operator who McFee skilfully managed to make both confident and shy. It was an attractive performance and one that, for better or worse, overshadowed his entire career. Not that McFee minded too much: 'People often come up to me in the street and shout "Wotcha Peter!" he once said. 'I've got so used to it now that I don't think anything of it; I just turn round and give them a wave!' Besides, he admitted, he was very much like Peter Craven: 'I even look like him.'

Born Malcolm Raymond McFee, on 16 August 1949, in London's Forest Gate, he was educated at the Plaistow County Grammar School in the early 1960s, and despite immortalizing them on television he explained that his actual school days weren't very memorable: 'I was a little lad at the time and I was used as a sort of "front man": the others would push me forward to be cheeky to a teacher or a prefect and then the big lads would come and back me up if I needed help!'

McFee had started out in repertory theatre before making his television debut as Terry, a right likely lad, in 'Sisters & Brothers', an episode of the Associated-Rediffusion drama *Sanctuary*, broadcast 24 July 1967. 'The early days of my acting career got rid of all my illusions about "stardom" and being an "overnight success",' he later reflected. 'It involves a lot of hard work and not very much money.' The hard work paid off when first-time film director Richard Attenborough cast him as the last of three youthful brothers killed in action in *Oh! What A Lovely War* (1969). It was a small role but it got him noticed. Typically, McFee was more interested in the flocks of beautiful models that came with such film exposure. Already naturally cool and enjoying a hit at the cinema, McFee notched up his hip image quota when he was signed as the drummer with The Abstracts.

The role of Peter Craven came before he was twenty, and the kids of *Please, Sir!* became akin to rock stars; they were as much a part of that tail-end love-in vibe as Jimi Hendrix's frilly shirt collection. The show itself

Mr Hedges (John Alderton) surrounded by the pupils of 5C, promoting *Please Sir!* .

wasn't expected to last more than a month, but within weeks its popularity made it a flagship comedy for London Weekend Television. McFee was philosophical about the role: 'I enjoy playing Peter Craven but very few of the things that happen to him have ever happened to me. I love my job but as far as I'm concerned it's just a job – like anyone else's.'

This first flush of success brought other memorable television appearances, including *The Rivals of Sherlock Holmes* episode 'The Case of Laker, Absconded', on 9 December 1971, in which Malcolm played a sullen and callow youth disinterestedly working as a clerk in a travel agency. It was a role he could have phoned in before breakfast, but it was what producers wanted of him – on many, many occasions.

He cleverly tempered his indestructible situation comedy charm opposite Sid James and Sally Geeson in the 28 May 1973 *Bless This House* episode 'A Girl's Worst Friend Is Her Father', when papa Sid desperately tries to matchmake his wayward daughter with the very reluctant young chap from his office.

*The Sweeney*'s 'Messenger of the Gods' on 7 September 1978 saw McFee as another unwilling potential spouse, this time to Dawn Perllman, playing the daughter of Diana Dors. The charmingly intimidated rogue Lukey Sparrow was pure McFee and he played it with crisp confidence. He was a shoo-in, too, for the 7 January 1980 *Minder* episode 'Monday Night Fever'.

However, in later years he turned his back on television to concentrate on theatre, in particular regional theatre, becoming a highly respected actor and

Lock up your daughters... and fry up your chips! Pals Malcolm McFee, David Barry and Peter Cleall were on tour as the lads from Fenn Street, 1974.

director in the environs of his Essex home.

One of his last television appearances, in *Goodnight Sweetheart*'s 'It Ain't Necessarily So' (BBC1, New Year's Day 1996), gives him a lovely cough and a spit as a cheeky cab driver. The old charm is still there in buckets.

At the time of his death, from cancer at just fifty-two, on 18 November 2001, Malcolm was in rehearsals to play the dame in *Beauty and the Beast* at the Elgiva Theatre, Chesham. At his funeral, a poignant school reunion of David Barry and Penny Spencer rallied to say their final farewells.

It's a whimsy, but for me Malcolm McFee is forever young. For sure, he went on to other great roles, but he never again quite found that sweet spot of Peter Craven – he's out there somewhere, running down a London backstreet, a slightly iffy roll of bank notes in his back pocket, lipstick on his collar, and beaming that winning grin that can melt stone...

TREAT YOURSELF TO *Please Sir! – The Complete Series* (Network: 7952732, 2008): not only every single television episode of the happiest days of Malcolm McFee's life, but also the feature-film version too. That's an awful lot of Fenn Street fun for your buck!

# Moore Marriott
# and Graham Moffatt

## 1885–1949 and 1919–65

Every now and then, the people that support the leaders in their field – the backing singers, if you will – rise up and take on their own unique and in some ways more impressive places within that field. Moore Marriott and Graham Moffatt did just that. I am a huge fan of Will Hay and my absolute favourite films of his are the ones including Marriott and Moffatt: timeless genius-silliness, slapstick and wordplay delivered perfectly and hilariously with great chemistry and attention to detail. Moffatt holds his own as the insistent, wiser loyal friend and Marriott's utterly charming daftness and physical timing makes him comic perfection. Forgotten? Never! Unsung? Definitely! But they have etched themselves into every double act and comic ever since.

*Bob Golding*

Although never officially a comedy double act in the strict sense of the term, Moore Marriott and Graham Moffatt, like Sid James and Tony Hancock a generation later, just clicked together. It was aesthetically pleasing. Like a dovetail joint, the pairing fitted perfectly: the old, bewhiskered, toothless one and the slovenly, overweight, cheeky one; one a master craftsman of film technique and make-up, the other not so much an actor as a brilliant re-actor; one an experienced pro with a CV stretching back to the dawn of British cinema and literally hundreds of credits to his name, the other a loveable chancer who fancied the perceived easy life of a film star and, when it came, grabbed his lucky break and ran with it. Together Moore Marriott and Graham Moffatt found a mutual high level of blissful slapstick. In characterisation they were equally stupid, in plot line wheezes they were equally incompetent, and in film mayhem they were equally hilarious.

George Thomas Moore Marriott was a veritable star of silent films. Indeed, in 1928 he was dubbed the English Lon Chaney, thanks to his chameleon-like ability to disappear into a role. The previous year alone had seen him age through the decades of a military life, in *Victory*, essay a perilous young man in *Carry On!*, play the disgruntled Beppo in *Passion Island* and chill as Fleet Street's demon barber's in *Sweeney Todd*. The *Sunday Herald* declared him 'one of the greatest character actors on any screen'.

Marriott prided himself on his box of props, make-up and theatrical tricks. Already toothless himself, he had four separate pairs of dentures to aid his new characterisations, including one he used to perfect a decrepit-old-man performance he could easily deploy for either poignancy or laughter.

Although Marriott remained frantically prolific, he began to slip down the cast list as soon as sound came to prominence, supporting Arthur Wontner's Sherlock Holmes, as Mordecai Smith in *The Sign of Four* (1932) and cropping up alongside Leslie Fuller [qv] and the young John Mills in *A Political Party* (1934). By the time he was cast in the Will Hay comedy *Dandy Dick* (1935), Marriott was reduced to an uncredited role as a stable boy. Always keen to earn a few more shillings on any picture, Marriott suggested to star comic Hay that he could utilise his tried-and-tested 'old man' character to also work as stunt man and double. Hay acquiescened and the deal was struck. As a result a firm friendship developed between the two, and a comedy legend was ignited.

Graham Victor Harold Moffatt was a star-struck youth when he happily wrangled himself a job as a call boy at Shepherd's Bush Studios. As a confidante and carefree gofer between director and star, he quickly became a favourite with the studio hierarchy, in particular that

Graham Moffatt, Moore Marriott and Will Hay in *Oh, Mr Porter!*, 1937.

affable Aldwych Theatre farceur and director Tom Walls [qv], who took such a shine to the chubby cherub that he secured him a tiny part as a choirboy in his film *A Cup of Kindness* (1934). There followed a handful of other appearances (all uncredited), including a pageboy in Maurice Elvey's *The Clairvoyant* (1935), an office boy in *Stormy Weather* (1935), again directed by Tom Walls, and, fittingly enough, a call boy in the Jessie Matthews musical *It's Love Again* (1936).

Moffatt was back as yet another rotund office boy in *Where There's a Will* (1936), for director William Beaudine, crucially meeting and working with Will Hay for the first time. It was instant comedy chemistry, with the insolent back-talking of Moffatt just what Hay needed for his stock-in-trade sniffing outrage and out-of-his-depth bluster. By the time Hay, Beaudine and producer Michael Balcon reconvened for their next comic vehicle, the dream team of Moore Marriott and Graham Moffatt was in place. It was a gloriously happy accident that happened in the Indian summer of 1936. The film was *Windbag the Sailor*, and the old one and the fat one gelled from day one. With comic characters aged Jerry Harbottle and gluttonous Albert fully formed and rich with invention, the Gainsborough Pictures comedy was a hit for the Christmas season. The scenario is classic Will Hay. Playing tall-tale-telling barge captain Ben Cutlet, he regales anyone who cares to listen with his epic maritime escapades, but when his bluff is called and he is persuaded to captain the unseaworthy *Rob Roy* to the West Indies, the fun really begins. Over the following four years, the trio churned out five further comedy smashes.

Sending festive greetings in promotion of
*Where's That Fire?*, 1939.

*Oh, Mr Porter!* (1937) could well be their masterwork, with the pseudo-ghostly goings-on down at Buggleskelly train station providing a rich seam of spiralling comedy ('Next train's gone!', y'know). *Old Bones of the River* (1938), a timely parody of Zoltan Korda's 1935 film *Sanders of the River*, took the team back on the ocean waves, with Harbottle and Albert now mates on the ancient paddle steamer the S.S. *Zaire*. *Convict 99* (1938) delighted in Marriott tweaking his usual character to become Jerry the Mole, master tunneller. The plot cleverly taps into Will Hay's best-loved comic persona, as an incompetent schoolmaster, by having his character sacked from his natural habitat of the classroom before being enlisted in the prison service.

While the film was enjoyable, *Ask a Policeman* (1939) wisely returned to the close-knit, public-service shenanigans that had worked so well with *Gladstone* the steam train in *Oh, Mr Porter!*. With the team in their most purple of purple patches, for me *Ask a Policeman* is their most consistently satisfying film. Released in the summer of 1939, the frantic goings-on in Turnbotham Round police station gave the trio some particularly good cross-talking routines to work with. Besides, any film that allows Moore Marriott to play a character even older than Harbottle, and to usher in a truly delightful cameo as his own father, is already worth the ticket price. The scene concerning the disliked black fruit-pastilles is tear-inducingly funny. Some forty years later, co-writer Val Guest would resurrect the idiot-copper-versus-idiot-smugglers for the Cannon and Ball film *The Boys in Blue* – another hit in my book.

The final outing for Hay, Marriott and Moffatt came with *Where's That Fire?* A final Hay film too for Gainsborough, in association with American distribution by Twentieth Century Fox, it was shot towards the end of 1939 for an early 1940 release, by which point Britain was at war. The film gained near-mythical status. Long thought lost it re-emerged in a largely unheralded BBC television screening in 1975. The expected knockabout business is complemented by Charles Hawtrey's annoyingly inquisitive schoolboy, and the scene where our hapless heroes try to navigate a fireman's ladder through far too small an aperture is near slapstick perfection.

When Will Hay signed his contract with Ealing Studios, the winning trio was forced to disband, with Marriott and Moffatt staying with Gainsborough Pictures. Hay's triumphant run with Marriott and Moffatt is bookended by films employing a 'silly ass' comedian in support. Claude Dampier was the painfully stupid Theo P. Finch in *Boys Will Be Boys* (1935) while, once settled in at Ealing, Hay was teamed with the gloriously befuddled characterisations of Claude Hulbert in two films: *The Ghost of St Michael's* (1941), and, Hay's film swansong, *My Learned Friend* (1943).

Concurrently, over at Gainsborough, Moore Marriott and Graham Moffatt were enjoying success opposite celebrated radio comedians Arthur Askey and Richard Murdoch [qv] in three films: *Charley's (Big-Hearted) Aunt* (1940), *I Thank You* (1941), and *Back-Room Boy* (1942). The ensuing fun and frolics – and these films really are both historically fascinating as morale flag-wavers and, still, heart-warmingly funny – laudably featured the Harbottle and Albert characters gleefully stuck in aspic. Moore Marriott and Graham Moffatt were their hilarious idiot selves in these films but Artur Askey's silly little-man comic persona completely lacked the pseudo-intellectual grandeur at the heart of Will Hay's performance. The collaboration with Askey and Murdoch wallowed in a mutual idiocy: lightweight candy floss comedy films.

Even during the halcyon Hay years, Marriott and Moffatt each independently supported knockabout, six-man troupe of zanies, The Crazy Gang. The fat boy was, as you might guess, Albert the pageboy in the manic *O-Kay for Sound* (1937), while the old man was, naturally, back in grey whiskers for *The Frozen Limits* (1939) and *Gasbags* (1941). The two worked with dial-a-stooge efficiency – always. Even away from comedy, Moffatt was used to potent effect in the Michael Powell and Emeric Pressburger films *A Canterbury Tale* (1944) and *I Know Where I'm Going!* (1945). Moore Marriott, meanwhile, etched an unforgettable performance as the ill-fated, plot-driving postman in *Green for Danger* (1946). The fact that he is almost unrecognisable from his popular comedy turns is a clear testimony to his underrated acting skills. Indeed, it's a lovely throwback to his roles from silent cinema.

Both actors remained active in film until the end of the decade, when, having just brought his usual aged joy as Grandpa to the comedy film *High Jinks in Society*, Marriott died on 11 December 1949. And while it seems strange to say Marriott was only sixty-four, he was only sixty-four! Bizarrely, as if by some sort of combined fate, Marriott's death seemed to curtail Moffatt's lucrative screen career too. After a mumbling cameo as a country yokel in *Mother Riley Meets the Vampire* (1952), Moffatt gave up the acting ghost completely, having taken over as landlord of the Swan Inn at Braybrooke, near Market Harborough. Decking out the bar with photographs from his acting career, during his ten-year tenure Moffatt happily regaled customers with tales from his life in film.

Suitably enough, he can be seen as a very drunken member of a drinking team in *The Larkins* sitcom film spin-off *Inn for Trouble* (1960), while his relocation to become landlord of the Englishcombe Inn in Bath had afforded him one final film appearance. Val Guest, writing, producing and directing the thrilling smallpox-outbreak drama *80,000 Suspects* (1963) on location in Bath, stumbled into the pub, discovered Moffatt behind the bar and urged him to make an appearance for old times' sake. And there he is, in the line-up for an injection. It's the most painfully poignant but fitting of film-career farewells. Moffatt died, in Bath, on 2 July 1965, aged just forty-five.

As for those golden comedies of the late 1930s that he made alongside Will Hay and Moore Marriott, they are undoubtedly the closest anybody has ever got to preserving the carnivalesque spirit of the music hall on celluloid within a tangible narrative. Cocking a snook at authority, advocating the power of teamwork while never for one second descending to mawkishness, these films are as relentlessly funny and socially relevant now as they were when they were made eighty-odd years ago. That's quite an achievement. Long may they reign – and they will. You know they will.

TREAT YOURSELF TO *The Ealing Studios Rarities Collection, Volume 9* (Network: 7953967, 2014). Moore Marriott and Graham Moffatt star in *Cheer Boys Cheer*, the 1939 comedy directed by Walter Forde, featuring Edmund Gwenn and Nova Pilbeam as polar opposites in a battle of the breweries. Jimmy O'Dea is the lead comedian, and it's quite a performance, upstaged only by sterling support from our lads. Marriott is Geordie here, while Moffatt is, reassuringly, playing Albert. Albert Baldwin, to be precise. Just lovely. However, one treasurable moment lifts this film to a whole new level: while celebrating the very ethos of beer in the local hostelry, Moore Marriott momentarily forgets himself and calls Graham by his real name – really! It creates an instant warm glow that is way beyond price.

British cinema's funniest fat boy, Graham Moffatt. A delirious, one-note comic genius.

The real, youthful Moore Marriott – he wasn't quite fifty when he made his first film with Will Hay – happily displays portraits of his aged Harbottle creation.

# Ray Martine

## 1928–2002

If you want to see what Ray Martine was all about, try and find an episode of *Jokers Wild*. There he sits alongside the greats of his era – Les Dawson, Ted Ray, Arthur Askey and, of course, Barry Cryer – and he appears not to have a clue how to tell a joke correctly. He stumbles, meanders, gets the punchlines wrong – and yet, laugh for laugh, is a match for any of them. He was joyously gay and Jewish, instantly loveable, and authentic.

*David Benson*

Ray Martine has a claim to fame for being quite possibly the very worst comedian within these pages ever to make a living in this cockamamie business we call show, and is quite possibly the very worst comedian to appear within these pages. His stage persona was simple: he was the Jewish queen; a short-dark-haired – latterly longer-greying-haired one-liner joke machine who seemed to revel in his inability to time a joke. He would dish out a seemingly never-ending supply of single entendres, Christmas-cracker puns and thinly veiled camp insults to his audience. Personally, I adore him.

Barry Cryer, who over several relentless years happily sent up Martine on the Yorkshire Television panel show *Jokers Wild*, remembers that 'we all wanted Ray on every joke on every show, particularly Les Dawson. Les was the best player of the game and knew that Ray's delight in his own feebleness as a comic was a gift. Les's expressions of sheer disbelief at Ray's jokes were a continual source of joy for me.' *Jokers Wild*, which ran from 1969 to 1974, invited a revolving array of comics and comedy actors to spin out jokes on a given theme. Barry Cryer would, in the main, dish out the subjects (and as often as not would also strike with a killer of his own). The denouement of the show would be the sixty-second routine, in which one of the comic panellists would be selected to talk – amusingly, hopefully – for a whole minute. Ray Martine was perfect for this. His jokes may have been awful but at least they were quick; he could squeeze a torrid of whimsy into the allotted time. Whether each joke received the desired laugh from the studio audience was quite another thing. And therein lay the fun!

Although *Jokers Wild* brought Martine his biggest fame – albeit as a sort of figure of fun for the others – he had already scored huge success as a club comedian in the early 1960s. He looked like an effeminate, man-child Lenny Bruce. Indeed, his comic style was very much based on the more laid-back cool of American club comics. He always claimed that he had picked up the vibe during his national service with the Royal Air Force in the United States, and that adding his own cockney, Jewish, bitchy gayness to the mix actually attracted loyal crowds to his stand-up routines. Very much gay rather than just camp, his knowing comments on the attitude to gay men – and, indeed, gay marriage, with him often erroneously referring to his husband – made him something of a cult hero on the London circuit, a veritable bar room idol, loved by all.

The most celebrated and vibrant remnant of those halcyon days is his long-playing record *East End West End*. The East End side has him in his absolute element; it is evocative beyond words. Recorded just before Christmas 1962, in the Deuragon Arms in Hackney, it's the expected barrage of limp-wristed puns and acidic put-downs. It certainly appeals to the local beer-and-skittles gang. Martine, with a not unpleasant way with old standards, could croon up a storm like Tony Bennett with a slight head cold. And his treatment of hecklers is impeccable. He was so good that when Daniel Farson, known as an investigative journalist rather than a talent scout, spotted him, he booked Martine to perform in his own East End pub, the Watermans Arms. As Farson noted in *Never A Normal Man: An Autobiography* (HarperCollins, 1997), he was immediately struck by 'the waspish Ray Martine making mincemeat of his hecklers'. It was no idle observation. Despite the relentlessness of one particular heckler on the LP, she can't defuse him and quickly crumbles when hit by Martine's own rapier wit: 'I think I deserve a big hand and so does she – right across her mouth!'

The patter hardly changed for the West End side of the album, recording Martine's February 1963 appearance at the slick and sophisticated Establishment club on Greek Street. Here Martine injects a few slick and sophisticated jokes into the routine, before happily embracing the essence of the East End pub. He also attempts to capture the spontaneity of the Hackney heckler incident but an obvious plant amongst the revellers is unconvincing, Martine muttering: 'You sound like an actor... in British film!' It's a clever deconstruction of the nature of heckling. Martine and his accomplice try to work out a bit of business; it fails and the routine continues as if nothing has happened. In reality, this was his stage trickery at full pelt, and it's brilliant. Martine eagerly exposes the desperate third-rate comedian that lurks just beneath the surface – and I mean just beneath the surface. In that moment he actually reveals himself as really a far better comedian that he ever tried to let on. This was his cleverness. There is camp playfulness within the taunting, playground humour, with Martine – as ever – dropping in off-colour and crude humour alongside the infantile observations. Indeed, besides the obligatory Harold MacMillan joke ('Chubby from Checkers'), this could easily have been back in Hackney as opposed to among the cocktail-socialist clientele of Peter Cook and Nicholas Luard.

Throughout his career, Martine would stumble and amble through truly terrible jokes; at points he would appear to forget not only the punchline but the entire routine. This wasn't just a case of spoonerisms; it was simply comedian's block. He would say the completely wrong word and make no sense to anyone, not even himself. He would stop himself, reveal that mouth full of pearly-white teeth in a wide, winning grin, shuffle his feet rather awkwardly... and plough on with a chuckle. He had us in the palm of his hand, simply because we liked him. He was a superb comedian. Superb.

His performing residency at Daniel Farson's East End pub had brought him in close

Ray browses the *TV Times* during a *Jokers Wild* programme recording, March 1970.

professional contact with two other raucous, outrageous and uncompromising Londoners: the danger-tinged drag act of Rex Jameson [qv], Mrs Shufflewick, and the cockney sitcom star, real-life pub landlady and caterwauling singalong specialist Queenie Watts. The combination was incendiary to say the least, and Associated-Rediffusion were eager to capitalize, recording a pilot for television called *Stars and Garters* in 1963. Martine was the show's popular emcee with his comic observations on homosexuality, religion, politics and pretty much every other touchy topic in the book, until October 1965. Still, it was the working men's clubs – particularly those in the North of England – that gave him his bread and butter: a live and lively audience who wanted to laugh and to be shocked. Ray Martine was the very man.

This cool cachet made him something of a signifier for the Swinging Sixties. Indeed, he would return to the hip 'n' happening Establishment in 1965 for the film *Primitive London*. In what was little more than a staged exposure of the underbelly of the West End's pub and club scene, Martine simply had to perform his routine for the crowd. As usual it was edgy, hesitant, and very funny.

Other film and television roles came his way, though they were never more than cursory guest-appearances, such as his wordless cameo as a taxi driver in *The Avengers* episode 'The Girl from Auntie' (ABC Television, 22 January 1966). But he could always be relied upon to add some pithy comments to television panel shows such as *Juke Box Jury* or *Don't Say A Word*.

Then came *Jokers Wild*, which rode the crest of popularity for a couple of years before being demoted in the southern regions, in 1973, to a daytime slot.

Chums Dick Vosburgh and Marty Feldman pitched in some gags for Ray's *East End West End* album.

In the North of England, however, where the show was based, it remained a popular primetime hit.

Martine had by this time moved to Newcastle. Although he continued to eke out a career as a stand-up comedian and after-dinner speaker in the area, by the 1980s he had effectively retired. Martine enjoyed a quiet life away from the spotlight, establishing an antiques business and settling down domestically, as friend and colleague Barry Cryer remembers, 'not only did he get married – which was a tremendous shock to all of us who knew him – but he got married to a woman! Unbelievable.'

When the end finally came, it was some months before the public and the profession were made aware of it. His sole living relative, a nephew, finally confirmed that he had died in a Newcastle nursing home on 19 June 2002. He was seventy-three. I like to imagine that he spent his final minute cracking as many hospital jokes as possible. For Ray Martine, that would be an awful lot.

Perhaps, in the end, one should reflect on Martine's peak, in London, in the early '60s. A time when his comic talent was caught like lightning in a bottle and, as the sleeve note of the *East End West End* album asserts: 'the warmth of his personality and his love of life came across to all who stood and watched him.' Yes, even to Les Dawson.

TREAT YOURSELF TO that original *East End West End* album (Piccadilly: NPL38007, 1963). It perfectly encapsulates what made Ray Martine such a success, not to mention the contrasting, vanished worlds of London in the shallow end of permissiveness, unfiltered and before your very ears and forming a unique backdrop to Martine's relentless excuse for a comedy routine. And he really was a fantastic comedian. Just listen.

# Zeppo Marx

## 1901–79

Design is the Zeppo Marx of management disciplines – the one that everybody seems to forget.

*Tahl Raz*

Just like Ringo Starr and The Beatles, Zeppo Marx has for far too long been thought of as the weak link in a world-conquering quartet. The freeloader, if you will. This, as any true comedy connoisseur – or musicologist – will testify, is arrant nonsense. Although Metro-Goldwyn-Mayer's crowd-pleasing Marx romps without Zeppo, such as *A Night at the Opera* (1935) and *A Day at the Races* (1937), are justly regarded as classics, the big-budget, love-interest-happy powers that be at MGM had stripped the Marx Brothers of their relentless, inspired, pure anarchy – and of Zeppo. The likes of Alan Jones and Tony Martin might have been able to grin the grin and carry a light-jazz tune better than any attempt Zeppo might have made, but the truth remains that the five comedy classics the Marx Brothers had made at Paramount Pictures, each headlining

The *Four* Marx Brothers, are totally unrivalled in gag-per-blink quota. Dripping with wit, wheezes and wild, wild women, the Paramount five are the Marxes' greatest legacy. Quite frankly, without Zeppo, the Marx equation doesn't add up. The team needed four beautifully buckled wheels to merrily roll along.

The youngest of Minnie's boys, Zeppo was born Herbert Manfred Marx on 25 February 1901, in New York City. Despite his brother Groucho often maintaining that 'offstage Zep was the funniest one of us', he never intended to join the act. The young Zeppo was something of a tearaway so Minnie was keen for him to be involved and focused, but there was simply no room, for the act already had four brothers, with Gummo to the fore, accompanied by his cigar-chomping, piano-poking, harp-plucking bros.

But in 1918, with the First World War raging in Europe, Gummo joined the army, making a hole in the line-up. Zeppo eagerly stepped into the breach during the successful run of stage musical *The Cinderella Girl* and would remain a core member of the brotherhood until March 1934. Sixteen years is no brief contribution!

After years touring variety theatres, the brothers fully hit pay dirt in 1925 when musical comedy *The Cocoanuts* was staged at the Lyric Theatre on Broadway. After the Great White Way had had its way with it, the show enjoyed a further two years on the road. *The Cocoanuts* made legends of the Marxes, and while the 1929 film version is obviously and charmingly primitive and stagy, it still captures the rollicking, finger-flicking swagger of the piece. Fundamentally, sound comedy on film started here.

The brothers had already scored a second triumph on Broadway. *Animal Crackers* opened at the 44th Street Theater on 23 October 1928, and, like its predecessor, enjoyed a lengthy tour. Also like *The Cocoanuts*, *Animal Crackers* went before the cameras, for a 1930 cinema release. The Marx Brothers and Paramount were canny indeed. The stage run had honed and tuned the basic material and, with the laughter of thousands of real people still ringing in their ears, they were psyched to recreate it on film for posterity.

These first two films, more than any of their others, capture the essence of the brothers on the road. They also highlight just how quickly Hollywood was learning to speak; the filming techniques vastly improve in just ten months. The

Marxes themselves hit the floor running. They are the most deft and engaging of spoken-word clowns. All except Harpo, of course. He was just too funny for words. *honks horn*

By January 1931 The Four Marx Brothers were at the top of the comedy tree. Ahead of their time? Rubbish. They were of their time; the rest of us just haven't caught up yet.

The Perfect Four-Sided Triangle: Zeppo, Groucho, Harpo and Chico promote their greatest film, *Duck Soup*, 1933.

They had even taken London. A limited run of *Animal Crackers* at the Palace Theatre was a sell-out. Zeppo was also being funny, much to the cocked snook of history. The four brothers had been working together for so long at the time that each could happily jump in and take over the comedy duties of any of the others. Groucho, quoted in his son Arthur's book *My Life with Groucho: A Son's Eye View* (Robson Books, 1998), confirmed that Zeppo 'was so good as Captain Spaulding that I would have let him play the part indefinitely, if they had allowed me to smoke in the audience!' In actual fact, Zeppo was even better than this, and it was common knowledge that if Groucho was sick, he would make sure he was fit again pretty damn quick in order to prevent his younger brother getting too used to the enthusiastic applause.

When the four elements were working as they should, Zeppo was the young, off-kilter, good-looking romantic lead. He had a winning combination of cheeky confidence and lip-biting awkwardness, a joyful parody of the sort of boy-next-door college-student type that every Hollywood musical of the time had in spades. Zeppo wasn't so much a product of his time but a comment on it; a comedian giving a parody of this gauche, tongue-tied type with which Hollywood was awash. Basically, he was Rudy Vallée laughing at himself. It's a glorious joke that went missing in action – even Groucho failed to notice it, or maybe Groucho was just undermining his brother's position during the lucrative,

'Sweet Adeline': One of film comedy's great
entrances – but are there three voices or four?

coasting years of MGM, and game show *You Bet Your Life*, when he said: 'except for the chorus girls, being a straight man in the Marx Brothers wasn't fun for him. He wanted to be a comedian...'

At Paramount in 1931 Zeppo *was* a comedian. *Monkey Business* was a suitably nautical romp for the four brothers to make; the stowaway storyline is a delightful fantasy sideways reading of just how they managed to get home after those London dates. The opening scene, with the camera panning across four barrels and our four brothers-in-arms uniting in an unforgettable rendition of 'Sweet Adeline', remains one of the greatest opening shots of any comedy film, ever.

*Horse Feathers*, the following year, gave Zeppo the lead role – that of the short and innocent college football ace, son of Groucho and obsession of femme fatale Thelma Todd [qv]. It is quintessential Zeppo, with all the elements for a spot-on swipe at the Hollywood romantic. It is impossible not to see it as that; the sharp, savvy unit of The Marx Brothers wouldn't have had it any other way.

And then there was *Duck Soup*. Ah, wonderful, wonderful *Duck Soup*. Glorious, glorious *Duck Soup*. Always and forever up there in that fiercely argued list of top comedy films of all time. For me, its place in the top five is secure for good, and it has held pole position more than once. No harps; no pianos; no fluff and bluff. Just undiluted Marx Brothers thrown lock, stock and four smoking barrels into an explosive and contentious plot of politics, espionage and a world on the brink of war. This was no fairy-tale land. This was really happening. It *is* really happening; the fact the Marxes could squeeze laughs from this material is a miracle. The fact it still packs a punch today is the thing of comedy black magic. Zeppo, as usual, is the officious, slightly strait-laced young chap, handsome in a cock-eyed, Marx Brothers kind of way. Again, that was all part of the joke. This wasn't Ramon Novarro buckling his swash in earnest. This was Zeppo Marx doing all that being Zeppo Marx entailed – with a sense of humour. Here was a comic genius. Cary Grant agreed, and he was no slouch in that department. Not only did Grant go on record as saying Zeppo Marx was his favourite Marx Brother, but that he was also an influence on his own light-comedy playing. So there.

Premiered in November 1933, *Duck Soup*, for all intents and purposes, closed the book on Zeppo as an official Marx Brother. There could be no better epitaph. He is engaging, zestful and – yes, dammit – funny throughout. Along with Chico and Harpo, he also has cause to impersonate Groucho, and does it brilliantly. For the briefest of moments, we can see why Groucho was so nervous, even if those nerves were all very much cigar-in-cheek.

It's only a mock dismissal of Zeppo's comedic skills that can explain Groucho's quote about his youngest brother's *not* being a comedian within the team. No, the truth was that, despite MGM's willingness to throw big money at the team, the studio – which boasted more stars than there are in heaven – was clearly not willing to fork out the huge fees that the four-man team demanded. Basically, the brothers had to be more cost-effective, and to achieve that they had to downsize. It's almost ridiculous in retrospect, but Groucho's view was 'we're twice as funny without Zeppo'. Just, no.

The Zeppo gap was filled with the latest good-looking, winning band-singer, preferably under contract and, thus, cheaper; the Harpo whimsy was indulged; Chico was let off the leash; and Groucho could, at times, find himself completely smothered by overbearing production values. In the immediate wake of his retirement from the team, Zeppo joined his brother Gummo in theatrical management – including management of The Marx Brothers, no less!

But Zeppo's heart was really in mechanics. Even during the years on the road with The Marx Brothers, it was Zeppo who was the engineer when the car broke down. When America joined the war in 1941, Zeppo found his true vocation – as an inventor. While Groucho, Harpo and Chico were gloriously mugging at the big store or planning a night in Casablanca, Zeppo was doing hard graft for the

Zeppo married Barbara, his Riviera Hotel showgirl, on 18 September 1959. The couple divorced in 1973.

war effort. It might appear rather jingoistic and distasteful now, but it remains an impressive line on the Zeppo CV. Yes, through his Marman Products Company Inc., Zeppo Marx invented, patented and sold what became known as the Marman clamps. These tricky little devices helped hold the 'Fat Man' atomic bomb within the Bockscar and the Enola Gay, the B29 bombers that did their unspeakable patriotic damage on Nagasaki and Hiroshima. Quite a thing for that bloke who stood around and smiled a lot in *The Cocoanuts*, right?

There was much, much more to Zeppo's engineering genius than that. He also invented the Marman Twin, a pioneering motorcycle powered by a drone airplane engine. That didn't quite make the grade because of the expense in production. His Vapor Delivery Pad was far more successful. It replaced repeatedly applied towels soaked in hot water with a continuous distribution of moist heat over a patient's body, thus vastly reducing the problem of too much heat being lost. Even more inventive was his wristwatch specially designed for cardiac cases, which monitored the pulse of a patient and alerted medical staff if the heart rate became dangerously high or low. The latter was patented in 1969, with two of his famous brothers dead and the Marxes a lasting legacy in American vaudeville.

Despite lingering sadness at his departure from the team – nearly forty years before – and distress at his contribution being undermined, Zeppo could at least assure himself that he had become the wealthiest of all the brothers. Still, money can't buy you happiness. Zeppo's second marriage, to ex-showgirl and socialite Barbara Oliver née Blakeley, had ended in divorce when that dashing hound-dog Frank Sinatra came a-sniffing round his neighbourhood. Cuckolded, divorced and having to sit back as Barbara married Ol' Blue Eyes, Zeppo ended his days in Rancho

Mirage, California, living just off of Frank Sinatra Drive. Ooh fate, you are awful sometimes...

Zeppo died on 30 November 1979. He was seventy-eight. It was cancer of the lung that finally got dear Zeppo. Whatever it was, I was against it. Even as late as 1976 his

The four Marx Bothers at Paramount.

contribution had been mocked. 'Fours', a track on the sublime Dory Previn album *We're Children of Coincidence and Harpo Marx*, includes her lyric assuming we know that Zeppo is only so-so. However, in the January of 1977 the brothers had been inducted into the Motion Picture Hall of Fame. Gummo died that April, Groucho in the August. The last Marx standing, Zeppo had lived long enough to see the team recognised as true comedic visionaries.

But however many times I see later photographs of a sticky-up-haired, thick-bespectacled, extremely comfortably-off Zeppo with his soon-to-be-gone powder-puff blonde wife on his arm, I, for one, can't help but still see that dark-haired, eternally happy, aquiline, slightly naive, slightly embarrassed and slightly knowing young man who was a Marx Brother. At their peak, the Brothers were four – four of equal talent and importance, and Zeppo was one of them. Hooray for *that* Captain Spaulding...

TREAT YOURSELF TO *The 4 Marx Brothers at Paramount 1929–1933* (Arrow Academy: B06W5B9SZJ, 2017), a luminous Blu-ray collection featuring all five Zeppo-friendly Marx Brothers classics, from *The Cocoanuts* to *Duck Soup* (well, it makes a change from soup to nuts). Film comedy has never been this good. Seriously!

# Glenn Melvyn

## 1918–99

All through my fifty years in the business, two words have always been in my thoughts. These two words are: 'What luck!' What luck to have met, in the far off days of weekly rep., a marvellous comedian called Glenn Melvyn who gave me my first TV job and taught me how to stutter.

*Ronnie Barker OBE*

It's a safe bet that even in fifty years' time Ronnie Barker will still be heralded as the finest comedy actor we have ever had in this country. His seamless shifts of characterisation and beautifully nuanced performances will stand as a benchmark of quality – and he owed it all to Glenn Melvyn. When honoured by a BAFTA Tribute in 2004, Ronnie fully acknowledged the inspirational character comedian with the impeccable comic stutter, in his acceptance speech; when interviewed on television about his comedy roots, Barker pinpointed Melvyn as a key part in his success. Indeed, after demobilisation in 1945, Melvyn had joined Frank H. Fortescue's Famous Players, a successful repertory company based at the Tudor Theatre, Bramhall, in Cheshire; a later alumni of the group was one Ronnie Barker, a fledgling actor in small parts who, sponge-like, eagerly devoured the comedy tricks of the trade that Melvyn was already well versed in and displaying to the young actor week in, week out. Barker even made his television debut opposite Melvyn, on the 8 May 1956, episode of ATV situation comedy *I'm Not Bothered*. Melvyn was a comedy catalyst.

Born Aron Clempert, in Manchester, on 12 November 1918, Melvyn was the son of performance pros, his father John being an escapologist in the music halls,

Askey and Melvyn caricatured for
*The Love Match.*

often throwing down the gauntlet to Houdini himself, while his mother was Nellie Carson, part of song-and-dance act The Carson Sisters. Talent was clearly in the genes, for during his rep. days Melvyn's sister Zelda wrote a successful play, *Wearing the Pants*, while he wrote *The Love Match*. Impresario Jack Hylton staged it at the Palace Theatre, Shaftesbury Avenue, from November 1953 through to the June of 1954. It starred Arthur Askey and Glenn Melvyn himself as a couple of football-crazy engine drivers who move heaven and earth to get back from work in time to watch the big match. A Group 3 feature-film version, starring much of the West End cast, was released in February 1955, with Thora Hird playing Askey's wife, and Shirley Eaton and James Kenney his children. Director David Paltenghi retained the breezy joy of the stage success and the poster tag line promising it's 'Full steam ahead for riotous rollicking fun' certainly didn't fail to deliver. The play itself proved so popular it toured Scotland for several summer seasons and played to capacity crowds at Blackpool's Grand Theatre and the Futurist Theatre, Scarborough.

The rapport Melvyn had enjoyed with Arthur Askey was further utilised in the big-screen comedy *Ramsbottom Rides Again* (1956). Askey played Bill

As book-maker George Summers in *Over the Odds*. Frances Cuka proves distracting.

Ramsbottom, with Melvyn as his slow-witted sidekick Charlie Watson. In this glorious British Western, our hapless heroes begin their journey at a Yorkshire pub before stowing aboard a steamer to pick up the estate of big-hearted Arthur's rooting, tooting grandfather Wild Bill Ramsbottom. Suitably, the inheritance is a saloon, and our boys bump into dreaded outlaw Black Jake (Sidney James) and Indian chief Blue Eagle (Jerry Desmonde) [qv]. Having also featured in *The Love Match*, playing Vera, Askey's daughter Anthea crops up on this lonesome trail too, with Shani Wallis as his screen daughter, Joan. Betty Marsden is his long-suffering wife, Florrie. The whole epic, happily mocking the influx of cheap Westerns onto British television, was shot on the wide open prairies of Beaconsfield Film Studios, Buckinghamshire. It was also the last film directed by the prolific and influential John Baxter. Wagons roll!

As well as sparring with Arthur Askey on-screen, Melvyn continued to write for the stage, producing works at the Blackpool Grand Theatre and, as often as not, with even dafter Danny Ross [qv] in tow, starring in them too, including *Pillar to Post*, in 1960, and *Friends and Neighbours*, in 1958. Most successful of all had been, inevitably, a sequel to *The Love Match*. *Love and Kisses* was the 1955 summer season smash at the Grand Theatre, Blackpool, and subsequently became a television series for Jack Hylton's company at Associated-Rediffusion. Arthur Askey was back as Bill Brown; now an ex-engine-driver, he was working as a crafty pub landlord, with Anthea Askey cast as her father's on-screen daughter, alongside Glenn Melvyn, back as the befuddled, stuttering stooge, Wally Binns. From the autumn of 1966 Glenn enjoyed a year in stuttering support of Frankie Howerd in the Prince of Wales Theatre revue *Way Out in Piccadilly*. Years later Ronnie Barker would happily incorporate the unique Melvyn stutter for his penny-pinching shopkeeper Arkwright in the BBC TV series *Open All Hours*. It was a debt Barker acknowledged repeatedly, most charmingly in a tangible employment of his old cohort and comedy mentor, as co-writer and actor in *The Ronnie Barker Playhouse* (Rediffusion, 1968).

That such a pivotal mentor to Barker is largely forgotten is a crime. While Glenn Melvyn peacefully passed away, in Kingston-upon-Thames on 9 March 1999, at the age of eighty, the sheer joy he generated lives on. On a particularly quiet night, in the wee small hours of a

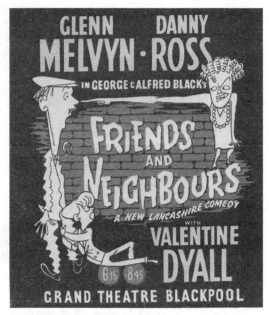

Dumb & Dumber: Glenn Melvyn and Danny Ross formed a hugely successful comedy partnership, enjoying repeat summer season success at the Grand Theatre, Blackpool, for producers George and Alfred Black. *Friends and Neighbours*, 'A New Lancashire Comedy' written by Melvyn, played to packed houses in 1958.

Blackpool-beach morning, you can just about hear the distant thunder of belly laughs reverberating sixty-odd years after the hoardings for *The Love Match* were ripped down. That's quite some legacy.

TREAT YOURSELF TO *Long Lost Comedy Classics: The Love Match* (Showbox Home Entertainment: BoooOIOPBI, 2007). It is unquestionably Glenn Melvyn's funniest, finest and most influential piece of work.

# Eric Merriman

## 1924–2003

You could always rely on Eric to deliver on the good, funny material.
Every time.

*Denis Norden CBE*

There are a few vital figures in the history of comedy who did everything right.
They contributed important, funny scripts to the golden age of radio. They were
acknowledged and respected enough to associate with the great and the good
of the industry. They may even have created not one but two programmes that
happily expanded into long-running afterlives. But still these figures have fallen
through the cracks and are forgotten. One such man is Eric Merriman. Joining the
cream of comedy writers – Ray Galton, Alan Simpson, Spike Milligan, Johnny
Speight, Eric Sykes and Terry Nation – Merriman was signed to the writers' agency
Associated London Scripts. As Merriman recalled in the outline of his unfinished
and unpublished autobiography, *Wouldn't It Be Funnier If...?*, the agency had an
office 'above a greengrocer's in Shepherds Bush, near the BBC Television Centre,

and was a unique set-up. It was terrific fun and the agency contained some of the greats of British comedy writing. We were the first generation of scriptwriters as up until this time, most comedians were writing their own material.'

Merriman had been writing gags from the age of twelve, sending his topical jokes to national newspapers. Soon his boyish enthusiasm led to him being paid to write short stories for children's annuals. When he left school at the age of sixteen he joined the staff of *The Scout* magazine as a subeditor, while moonlighting as a skit-writer for *The Gang Show*, and subsequently becoming a caption-writer for *Picture Post*.

As for many of his generation, the Second World War interrupted his blossoming career. He joined the Royal Air Force in 1943, with service life made bearable by joining a dance band as both singer and drummer. The service also indulged his passion for athletics.

Although Merriman trained as a wireless-operator and tail-gunner, the conflict came to an end before he saw active service. Upon demob he returned to the offices of *Picture Post*. Boredom soon set in, however, and he took a job selling advertising space in the *Financial Times*. This was hardly the most riveting of assignments, so, in the mid-fifties, the young Merriman began writing sketches for radio, submitting a handful to the popular variety show *Henry Hall's Guest Night*, writing material for performers such as Dickie Henderson [qv] and Kenneth Horne. A hugely impressed Horne phoned his good friend Richard Murdoch [qv], who was hosting *Variety Playhouse* at the time; Merriman was soon writing for that too. By the time Jack Buchanan took over as the suave master of ceremonies, in June 1956, Merriman was scripting the sketches for regular guest stars Jack Hulbert and Cicely Courtneidge.

By then it was clear to the industry that a brilliant new comedy writer was on the scene. While still employed by the *Financial Times*, Merriman was signed up to write for a fresh BBC Television situation comedy starring Terry Scott and Bill Maynard. *Great Scott, It's Maynard* ran for three series, from October 1955 to December 1956. For Merriman it was something of a double life: 'I used to leave the *Financial Times* – pretending I had an important advertising meeting – in pinstripe suit, with bowler hat and umbrella, and attend rehearsals at the television studios!'

But it was radio and a further association with Kenneth Horne that gave Merriman the opportunity to write arguably the most satisfying scripts of his career. Fashioning the outrageous magazine-show-style format with co-writer Barry Took, the spiralling anarchy of *Beyond Our Ken* was perfect for the urbane and unflappable Horne, the figure of avuncular respectability round which the glorious eccentrics Kenneth Williams, Betty Marsden, Hugh Paddick and Bill Pertwee foregathered. Following a pilot recorded the previous October, from July 1958 the BBC ploughed on with a series of twenty episodes, plus a Christmas special. It was an almost instant smash, with millions of British homes planning their Sunday roast around the broadcast. The gallery of grotesques within *Beyond Our Ken* became part of the nation's consciousness. There were a couple of crackers for Hugh Paddick: his very unsubtle Frankie Howerd parody, Hankie Flowerd, and the slovenly teen idol Ricky Livid. Kenneth Williams picked up a long-running catchphrase from the wily old rustic Arthur Fallowfield, whose response to almost every question he was asked was: 'The answer lies in the soil!' Together, Williams and Paddick etched the effete twosome Rodney and Charles, who would stroll around Soho making outrageously bitchy observations. The duo were very much the prototype for *Round the Horne*'s bona fide double-act of Julian and Sandy. Recalling work on the show, Merriman said, 'One of my proudest moments was when I was introduced to Prince Philip, who told me that the Royal Family had tapes of every show on the Britannia!'

From the start of the third series of *Beyond Our Ken*, broadcast on 19 April 1960, through to the final curtain at the end of series seven, on 24 November 1963, Merriman took over all of the scriptwriting. Barry Took had left the series over a disagreement and was writing television scripts with Marty Feldman. When Merriman decided to rest the radio series and make a return to television, the BBC was desperate to keep the format going. Making an outrageous tweak or two to what was otherwise the exact same show, Barry Took, with Marty Feldman in tow, returned to the fold and, from March 1965, unveiled *Round the Horne*. The rest is comedy history –and as far as the show was concerned, so was Eric Merriman.

Not that Merriman was bothered, at least not at the time, for the BBC had commissioned a television series that was not only scripted by him but presented by him too. Undoubtedly the very phrase Merriman said to producer John

Street when asked what the new show was going to be called, *Call It What You Like* was a typically vague title for a typically vague collection of sketches performed by June Whitfield, Gwendolyn Watts, Tony Tanner, Joe Melia and the occasional reliably adaptable guest star such as Frank Thornton or Ronnie Stevens. Billed as 'a sort of television show', it ran for six episodes in the spring of 1965.

*Beyond Our Ken:* Williams, Ron Moody, Bill Pertwee, Betty Marsden, Horne, Patricia Lancaster, Barry Took and Eric.

Subsequently Merriman would write special material for *The Val Doonican Show* (BBC1, 1965), *The Norman Vaughan Show* (BBC1, 1966) and *The Dave Allen Show* (BBC1, 1968). Merriman also wrote and presented *Mild and Bitter,* a spring 1966 sketch show featuring June Whitfield, with support from Peter Jones and James Beck. *Mild and Bitter* comprised experimental, pioneering comedy commissioned by channel controller David Attenborough for the fledgling BBC2, and is almost completely forgotten today. Bizarrely, in an industry that thought radio was dead, it was *Round the Horne* that would carve out characters that would live on for another fifty some years and counting.

Merriman was still hard at it into the seventies, writing for *The Stanley Baxter Picture Show* (London Weekend Television, 1972), *An Evening with Francis Howerd* (BBC2, 1973), and *Scott On...,* reuniting the stars of that show, Terry Scott and June Whitfield, for a BBC1 *Comedy Playhouse* episode on 7 May 1974. Co-written with John Chapman, *Happy Ever After* cast Scott and Whitfield as Terry and June Fletcher, middle-England suburbanites suddenly in a very empty house following the departure of their children. It was a brilliantly simple idea, and with the expert playing of Terry Scott as a petulant man-child and June Whitfield as his tolerant, focused wife-cum-mother, the BBC were quick to commission a series.

Widening the series' parameters to include the domestic housing of eccentric Aunt Lucy, played by Beryl Cooke, and the reappearance of daughters Susan and Debbie, played by Pippa Page and Caroline Whitaker, Merriman wrote all but three of the episodes. It ran over six series and culminated in a ratings-winning Christmas special in 1978.

Then came a further disagreement. Both Merriman and Chapman felt the series had run its course but, once again, the BBC was reluctant to let such a popular series go. As with *Beyond Our Ken*, the title remained with the writer, so in 1979 the BBC rechristened the show *Terry and June*, renamed the central couple Terry and June Medford, and kept the ball in the air for another eight years. In all that time, Chapman and Merriman were commissioned to write just two scripts for the series. And again, it's *Terry and June* that – for good, bad, or indifferent – is the title that's remembered.

At around this time, Merriman was also proving himself a popular and regular radio and television panellist on antique valuation show *Going for a Song* and word definition game *Call My Bluff*, as well as acting as the Programme Associate of Thames Television's celebrity quiz *Password*, and writing and producing such telly spectaculars as *Sammy and Bruce* (London Weekend Television, 1980), headlining Sammy Davis Jr and Bruce Forsyth.

Merriman wrote the extraordinary ITV Christmas film *Quincy's Quest* for Tommy Steele. A delightful, often unsettling fantasy set in a toy store, this film haunted my imagination for decades after I saw its first transmission in December 1979. Having finally tracked it down again for the first time since the age of nine, I'm happy to report it's as bonkers and as beautiful as I remember it.

In the early 1980s Merriman would write for Russ Abbot (*Russ Abbot's Madhouse*, London Weekend Television, 1980), Dick Emery (*The Dick Emery Show*, BBC1, 1981), and Mike Yarwood (*Mike Yarwood in Persons*, Thames, 1982), but his passion for television comedy, as well as his patience with television executives, was waning. Merriman's last regular television-writing credit was on *The Little and Large Show* (BBC1, 1983–84).

Still, once a writer always a writer, and, as he proudly stated, in the 1990s Eric Merriman: 'Started writing with my son, Andy, during which time we have recorded several radio series, *Mr Finchley Takes the Road* (BBC Radio 2, 1993), and *Mr Finchley Goes to Paris* (BBC Radio 2, 1994), starring Richard Griffiths, and *Minor Adjustment* (BBC Radio 4, 1996), starring Peter Davison and Samantha Bond and featuring my granddaughter, Sarah, who has Down's Syndrome.' Andy Merriman has also gone on to write several essential biographies, including ones on Hattie Jacques and Margaret Rutherford, as well as

Chalk it Up! *Beyond Our Ken* producer Jacques Brown, star Kenneth Horne, stooge Betty Marsden and scriptwriter Eric Merriman, 1960.

*A Month of June*, a radio anthology series for June Whitfield. Heart-warmingly apt, that.

Despite such a pivotal career in comedy, Eric Merriman's contribution to long-running laughter-makers is often reduced to a mere footnote, if that. Even his contribution to the *Carry On* franchise – material for the West End revue *Carry On London!* which ran at the Victoria Place from October 1973 – looked about to be forgotten when a wooden scroll, commemorating all the *Carry On* writers, was commissioned to be installed at Pinewood Studios. Thankfully, after a little bit of a fight, Eric Merriman's name was included. Merriman seems to have fought for just recognition quite a few times throughout his career. But forgotten? Not on my watch...

TREAT YOURSELF TO *Beyond Our Ken – Series 3* (BBC Worldwide Ltd.: B01N59V1X3, 2017), all fourteen episodes from the hilarious radio series that saw Eric Merriman take full control of the scripts. It's Hornerema to the maximum. With a warmth, wit and wisdom adding true comedic depth to the crazy characters and outrageous situations, it's a high point in radio humour.

# Christopher Mitchell

## 1947–2001

Christopher Mitchell is one of the unsung heroes of British comedy. Although best remembered as Gunner Nigel 'Parky' Parkin in the massively popular and critically underrated BBC sitcom *It Ain't Half Hot Mum*, Christopher also played police officer Terry Hoskins in *Only Fools and Horses* and had film roles in a string of saucy old-school sex comedies. These notably included the Derek Ford-directed *What's Up Superdoc!* (the 1978 sequel to the previous year's *What's Up Nurse!*), 1973's *The Sex Thief* and 1970's *This, That & the Other*.

Gunner 'Parky' Parkin was Mitchell's most memorable role, however. Parky was the youngest member of the Second World War Royal Artillery Concert Party created by comedy geniuses Jimmy Perry and David Croft, based on Perry's own experience of a similar troupe in India. We first see Parky in the opening episode of series one, when he signs off a letter to his mother Edith with the immortal words: 'I've now been out in India two days, and it ain't half hot, Mum.' Mitchell brings warmth and likeability to the role. Still a teenager at the start, Parkin is determined to become part of the concert party and tries his hand at everything from ventriloquism to comedy and singing, the recurring joke being that the lad is as clumsy as a bear in a Mr Blobby suit and never does anything right. Battery Sergeant Major Williams (the wonderful Windsor Davies) wrongly believes that Parkin is his illegitimate son – he'd had a fling with Edith when stationed in Colchester – and consequently treats him with far more tolerance and affection than he does everyone else. While this bellowing human bulldog brands the rest of his motley crew 'a bunch of pooftahs' and other pleasantries, he compliments 'lovely boy' Parkin frequently, telling him he has 'a fine pair of shoulders', and ignores his many blunders. When the rest of the gunners find out that the Sergeant Major believes Parky is his son, they welcome the lad into their number. They realise Williams will do everything he can to keep him from being sent into battle – and consequently keep them out of danger too. They even change Parky's blood group on his medical file so it matches Williams's, offering 'proof' of a paternal link.

On one occasion, because Parkin has no performance skills, he is appointed battery clerk. The consequences are predictably grim. Williams orders him to 'remove the mess by the officer's lines' – referring to a pile of old beds that are waiting to be thrown away. Misunderstanding the instruction, the bungling twerp promptly destroys the officer's mess. Another time, Colonel Reynolds tells him to order 200 tent pegs and instead Parky orders 200 tents. He turns twenty-one in series four (in an episode titled 'Twenty-One') and somehow he makes it through the war (and all eight series) unscathed.

Christopher's own father was the Sheffield-born actor Norman Mitchell (real name Norman Mitchell Driver), who appeared in over sixty films, had thousands of TV roles, and performed in rep. and with the Royal Shakespeare Company; during the Second World War he served with the Royal Army Medical Corps. Christopher died from cancer aged 53, just a month before his dad.

*Garry Bushell*

It's true to say that Christopher Mitchell liked a drink. This was a raging, destructive love tryst that informed the very earliest days of his acting life, when he was one of the best-looking men in the business. Like those other legendary, professional booze-hounds Robert Newton, Keith Moon and Oliver Reed, Chris ended his days as a bloated, hirsute bon viveur. Every morning was kick-started by the day's first can of lager. Every evening ended with him yelling 'Shithead!' in his garden as people passed. They would look round, outraged or shocked, only for Mitchell to grin innocently and say: 'What? It's the name of my cat!' And it was! The intoxicated imp.

He was the son of actors Pauline and Norman Mitchell, his mother retiring to raise the family while his odd-job father chalked up a list of film and television credits as long as Mr Tickle's arm. Near the end of their lives, Norman and Chris teamed up for a gloriously ramshackle semi-rap video on a lovely little ditty called 'Down the Pub'. It was that kind of relationship.

Chris had been set against a career on the stage. As a revolt against his parents, he wanted to be a farmer, but the lure of the greasepaint, the excitement, the money and, perhaps most importantly of all, the girls, finally tempted this most handsome of chaps to tread the boards. His godfather was Alan Badel, who was acting opposite Norman the very moment Chris was born on 21 May 1947. It seemed fated after all. Even while studying farming in Lingfield, Sussex, the fifteen-year-old Chris Mitchell was also writing and performing in the end-of-term play. It was a tongue-in-cheek murder mystery with each character mocking a different one of his teachers. Chris played every part, with the exception of the games master; there was another young man who could mimic him much better and Chris conceded the part to him.

By 1963 Mitchell had abandoned farming for good, attending a private drama school and quickly proving integral in productions of *Twelfth Night* and *The Taming of the Shrew* staged for local secondary schools. He honed his craft in Butlins repertory theatre and earned his money in adverts. For three years in the 1960s he was the face of Macleans toothpaste; it put him firmly on the map and led to a few small roles in television shows such as *Dixon of Dock Green* (in the episode 'The Hard Way', BBC1, 14 September 1968), *Z Cars* ('Funny Creatures, Women', BBC1, 27/28 September 1971) and playing Detective Constable

Hardiman in *Crossroads* (ATV, 1980). He had found himself in much demand as a gauche, sly or just plain sleazy man about town. He could be thuggish (as in *The Protectors* episode 'The Bridge', ITC, 4 January 1974) or priggish (as in *Doctor at Sea*'s 'But It's So Much Nicer to Come Home', London Weekend Television, 14 July 1974), but his lightness of touch steered his career towards comedy roles from the outset, as often as not as the shy-witted romantic. His first film appearance was in the stylish and extremely hip Swinging Sixties orgy *Here We Go Round the*

The *It Ain't Half Hot Mum* gang, demobbed for 'The Last Roll Call'.

*Mulberry Bush* (1968), scripted by Hunter Davies from his own novel. Barry Evans [qv] is the undoubted star but it is Mitchell, in loud sports car and confident clothes, who sums up the era in pinpoint shorthand.

As a heavily moustachioed, bushy-haired ladies' man in the 1970s, Chris was a shoo-in for the obligatory sex-comedy roles; indeed, he starred in one of the very best, the 1978 romp *What's Up Superdoc!*. Chic Murray plays a Scottish henchman, Harry H. Corbett is the prime minister. It's that kind of film! Mitchell happily spent the entire shoot walking around starkers and making love to a string of beautiful women – at least acting making love to a string of beautiful women! And he really made love to most of them too (all but one, apparently). He was naive and sweet and vulnerable, in performance as in real-life.

In the early 1980s he landed the memorable supporting-copper role opposite Jim Broadbent in the *Only Fools and Horses* series-three classic 'May the Force Be With You' (BBC1, 8 December 1983). With his trademark rather simple but endearingly sweet style, Mitchell's Police Constable Terry Hoskins is the nice and easy face of the London constabulary. He's on the side of Del Boy and Rodney, for a start. He even explains that the only people who fear Broadbent's corrupt Chief Inspector Roy Slater more than the criminals themselves are the other coppers. It's a relaxed and winning performance, and it's hardly surprising that Chris got the call back when a copper was needed for the feature-length special 'To Hull and Back'. However, even before the age of forty, Chris's drinking had started to get the better of him and he was gaining a reputation for unreliability. But *Only Fools and Horses*'s writer, John Sullivan, was adamant: he wanted the Broadbent and Mitchell team back together. It was his show, and no matter how many times he heard Mitchell dismissed as a lush, it couldn't change his mind. Sullivan won the argument, of course. In the event, it was Mitchell's last great performance. An awful lot of people saw it, too: on its first broadcast, on Christmas Day 1985, it received an audience of 20 million. When it was repeated the following New Year's Eve the figure was even higher, at 21 million!

The role that made Chris a beloved face to millions of telly-viewers was already long behind him: that of the tall, lanky and gormless Gunner Parkin in the hit BBC situation comedy *It Ain't Half Hot Mum* (BBC1, 1974–81). Mitchell told me that, for a young chap in 1973, the biggest dilemma when deciding whether to accept the role or not was that his shoulder-length hair would have to be chopped. The role was well worth it.

The latest Jimmy Perry and David Croft hit came slap-bang in the middle of their runaway success with *Dad's Army*, and like that eternal classic, the new series was to be set during the Second World War. This time it was in the jungles of Burma, however, with our British lads braving the deserts, foreign customs and just plain heat of battle. The comedy was camp, carefree and hugely engaging, of course, and the concert-party antics gave all the team the chance to drag up and mince about – even Mitchell. Although his speciality was a particularly embarrassing ventriloquist act based squarely on the incompetence of Sandy Powell [qv], Mitchell was also teamed with the no-nonsense Sergeant Major Williams, unforgettably essayed by Windsor Davies, the premise being that the bombastic Sergeant Major was convinced the dashing Parkin was his illegitimate son. One episode, 'The Pay Off', screened on 8 November 1977, guest-starred

Norman Mitchell as the pompous Captain Owen. Much tabloid fodder was found in 'Who's the Real Daddy?' publicity photographs. The series proved so popular that the *It Ain't Half Hot Mum* stage show took the Pier Theatre, Bournemouth, for the summer of 1979, before touring the country. The fun times Chris shared with pal Ken MacDonald could fill a book on their own! Through eight series of top-rated comedy, the Sergeant Major mollycoddled Parkin while running the rest of the lads ragged. It was a joyous joke and one to which the very last episode gave the perfect pay-off. Croft and Perry knew the value of a pulled heartstring as much as a tickled funny bone and that last poignant moment, with Windsor Davies and Mitchell in the railway waiting room, back in Blighty and subtly acknowledging an emotional connection, remains one of the high points of British telly. The episode was broadcast on 3 September 1981, and Chris remembered: 'They were very clever at writing sad scenes which still retained great humour. When the Sergeant-Major was left in the cafe at the railway station and Parkin goes in and says: "You can come and stay with me and Mum if you like," it was heart-breaking, with that whole idea of Windsor being my dad coming together for the close. It was David Croft who told me to play it all slightly lighter. I played it with sadness in rehearsal but David said: "No!" His experienced direction gave that scene its warmth. It was the perfect end to the series.'

Alas, British telly is unlikely to see it again. Despite the show being Jimmy Perry's personal favourite, and it having enjoyed repeats throughout the 1980s, the BBC has now seen fit to pass a remit to shelve *It Ain't Half Hot Mum* for good, whether for being racist, homophobic or just plain past its sell-by-date. I can imagine Mitchell's annoyance if he had lived to hear this. As it happens, he didn't. It was cigarettes that got him in the end, with his brief but dogged battle with cancer cutting far too short a life of happy performances, outrageously fun times and genuine kindness. I have cherished memories of countless bottles of red wine, hilarious barbecues and candid conversations shared with him into the wee, small hours. I clearly remember helping him find blank video tapes in order to record the heavily edited repeats of *It Ain't Half Hot Mum* from UK Gold in the 1990s.

I have bittersweet memories of Mitchell's funeral: a cremation. Just as the coffin slid out of sight, my dear old dad leaned over to me and whispered: 'It ain't half hot mum...' Mitchell would have loved that. Indeed, he was very

WHAT'S UP NURSE!
raised above than
a temperature
Now comes

**WHAT'S UP SUPERDOC!**

As Dr Todd, being held up by his *Ain't Half Hot* chum Melvyn Hayes. The lucky lady is Maria Harper.

proud of being the only person in the entire series ever to say the title; he says it once in the first episode and once in the last. Nobody else could ever seem to get it right on telly, he remembered; the continuity announcers always seemed to trip over their tongues with it. Even the vicar performing Chris's funeral service stumbled over his words when he mentioned the title. That would have made him laugh.

Stuart McGugan, the Scots hardman and Mitchell's good friend on the show, was the only old cast mate to make the funeral. His message of condolence read: 'Representing the boys who entertained you!' Yes, I welled up too.

TREAT YOURSELF TO *It Ain't Half Hot Mum – Complete Eighth Series* (2entertain: B002KSA3TS, 2009). It is the very last series of Christopher Mitchell's crowning comic glory, allowing the actor to fully indulge in poignancy and sentiment alongside the expected hilarity and slapstick comedy that made it a flagship comedy series for the Beeb. Mitchell once told me: 'at the end of the day, on my tombstone or something, I can actually say that I made some people laugh and I'm very proud of that. It's the biggest high ever. It's magic.' It certainly was, my friend. It certainly was.

# Albert Modley

## 1901–79

Albert Modley is the greatest comedy force to come out of my home town of Leeds. He was something of a local hero who conquered the whole country with his likability and trustworthiness. A comedian of the people, for the people.

*Barry Cryer OBE*

Few figures sum up the image of the working-class Northern comedian more than the dogged, irrepressible and just plain likeable salt-of-the-earth chap that was Albert Modley – both onstage and off it, it would seem. There was no 'side' to him at all. He wore a flat cap and by-gum trousers. He had worked with his hands – both as a boxing champion and a railwayman. He was as honest as the day was long, and he was funny for the simple reason that he was truthful. He was one of us. And one of a kind.

Modley was born in Leeds, West Yorkshire, on 3 March 1901, and died in Morecambe, Lancashire, and in the three-score-and-ten years between he entertained millions of people with his performances onstage, on the radio and even in low-budget feature films. Two of these, for director Jack Raymond, were huge hits in the North of England. *Up for the Cup* (1950) cast Modley as Albert, a Lancastrian loom-maker who journeys to London to cheer on his team in the FA Cup. *Take Me to Paris* (1951) also cast him as Albert, this time a disgruntled jockey who gets involved with a crime ring and ends up chasing the baddie up the Eiffel Tower. That familiarity, of playing Albert, was key. Through all the farcical fun, he was always Our Albert, not just loved by his audience, but adored by them.

Billed as 'Lancashire's Favourite Yorkshireman', he rose through the ranks of working men's clubs and lunchtime concerts to secure his own touring variety roadshow on the Moss Empire circuit under the esteemed auspices of theatrical impresarios Lew and Leslie Grade. Not bad for the lad who had skipped his way through school and followed his father's lead as a physical training instructor while still a teenager. As well as proving himself a dab hand with his fists – he was a Yorkshire amateur champion at the age of sixteen – Modley was a champion diver too.

Jobs as a grocer's boy, and then with his local butcher, were a means to an end. A life on the railways proved an early and lasting commitment, and he tried his hand at most of the jobs it offered, a stint looking after the parcels being particularly lucrative for later laughs. His work as a butcher's boy had involved riding horses through the streets, but the parcel office proved a veritable Noah's Ark. Pitying the cooped-up animals awaiting transit, Albert gave monkeys, pigeons and all kinds of livestock a bit of breathing space whilst in his care, resulting in animals of all sizes running amok in his workplace.

Modley always seemed to charm his way out of trouble, though, and it was not by his bosses' choice but his own choice – or rather, on the advice of his wife, Doris – that he finally left the railway after seven years' hard toil. It was also Doris – whom young Albert had known since school days – who persuaded him to try his luck on the stage.

She had long noticed her man's talent to amuse, and not just at amateur nights or after a few pints down the local. Modley had gained quite a reputation among the passengers who, either by delay or cancellation, found themselves with time on their hands at his train station of employment. His quick wit, earthy humour, and robust mockery of authority formed the perfect antidote to wasted hours on a draughty platform.

Modley's natural home was in the Northern clubs, but he secured an early break when producer Francis Laidler spotted him and offered him principal

We Three Kings of Comedy: Eric Morecambe, Albert Modley and Ernie Wise, in Morecambe.

comic, Buttons, in the production of *Cinderella* that packed them in at the Alhambra Theatre, Bradford, during the 1932–33 season. Over the years Albert would notch up a lucky-for-him thirteen pantomimes for Laidler.

Modley's summer seasons were also busy. Indeed, in 1932 he had appeared in seaside variety *The Arcadian Follies* for producer Ernest Binns, and would subsequently headline in his own comedy spectaculars, including *Modley's Merrymakers* and *On with the Modley*. There was nothing like a great pun on your name for a title to highlight just how high you had climbed the show business ladder. Modley was a sensation. With just one look to the audience, he had them in the palm of his hand. He was a comedian of the people, and his familiar exclamation of: 'Ehh! Isn't it grand when you're daft?' was soon a guarantee of gales of laughter.

And as sure as night follows day, and Cole precedes Porter, with a popular catchphrase on everybody's lips, BBC Radio was quick to sit up and take notice. Modley's style was perfect for the pioneering *Variety Bandbox* and he quickly established himself as one of a hand-selected group of resident comedians. Although he virtually personified 'visual', his skill with a lugubrious shaggy-dog story, not to mention his talent with a multiple range of musical instruments – including the xylophone, harmonica, trumpet and drums – made him worth his weight in gold on the wireless.

Onstage, he would deploy his drum kit in a sketch that cast him as a disgruntled tram-driver, continually looking back at his imagined passengers and signifying potholes and various obstacles with a dexterity of mime that transfixed crowds,

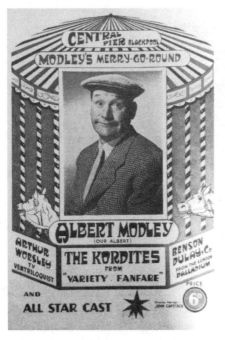

Dazzling daftness was to the fore,
Blackpool, summer 1954.

even those who had seen it year in, year out. It was a stage mainstay; a classic. At his peak Modley really was as taut and as tight as the skin on his drum, stooped in concentration and earnestness as he milked the crowd for every laugh in them.

In other sketches, he adopted the guise of a cheeky schoolboy – an incongruous sight at the best of times – skilfully goading his mildly under-the-weather mother by rushing out not for the doctor but the undertaker, and thus setting up the pay-off: 'I was cutting out the middle man!' The disruptive urchin also featured in a sketch involving a call-back to his previous life in a lost-property office and undoubtedly planted seeds in the minds of Terry Scott, Benny Hill, Marty Feldman and every other turn who has donned a sailor suit and turned back the clock to childhood for comic effect.

On 20 May 1949, *Music-Hall*, the television home of variety, eagerly showcased Modley's act, while appearances on *Stars at Blackpool* (BBC, 28 August 1953), *The Good Old Days* (BBC, 1959–71), *Saturday Bandbox* (ABC TV, 9 June 1962), and *Looks Familiar* (Thames Television, 1977) kept his comedy popular with the masses and over the decades. Tastes changed but Modley's comedy soldiered on. He even proved an unforgettable guest opposite the new crop of turns, delivering pitch-perfect routines on Max Bygraves's eponymous show, *Max* (Thames Television, 5 March 1970); and *The Leslie Crowther Show* (London Weekend Television, 1971), with Modley a regular in the six-week run, with fellow old-stagers Arthur English and Chic Murray.

But it was the variety theatre that was Modley's first and last love. With it, he had faced the worst of times – being pelted with heavy old pennies when playing Limerick during a tour of Ireland – and he had experienced the best of times

– appearing on the bill of the Royal Variety Performance at the Opera House, Blackpool, in 1955, when his natural, playful and affectionate subversion reached fever pitch. The Opera House had no royal box for the royal guests. A box was specially constructed and, for aesthetic balance, a dummy box was constructed on the opposite side of the auditorium, never intended for use and empty on the evening of the performance. Everybody dutifully bowed towards the occupied 'ashtray' – except Albert. He finished his turn with a flourish, bowed dramatically to nobody in the empty box, looked up, clocked the situation, turned to the audience and said: 'Have they gone?' A belter – and, in a business of apocryphal anecdotes, true to boot.

Modley never really retired. He just sat at home, wallowing in his glorious past with anybody who happened to be visiting, waiting for the phone to ring to call him back to action. Thankfully it did ring; quite a lot. Two of his final assignments came from the pen of Alan Bennett, a writer who has the spirit of the North running through him like a stick of Blackpool rock. Reassuringly nostalgic, the *Play for Today*, 'Sunset Across the Bay' (BBC1, 20 February 1975), produced by Innes Lloyd, cast Modley as Arthur, the cheerful friend to the retired central character. Alan Bennett's script, under the pinpoint direction of Stephen Frears, even allowed space for Modley's music hall routines and catchphrases, during comic catch-ups on the allotment. All based in Modley's beloved Morecambe too. As was *All Day on the Sands* (London Weekend Television, 24 February 1979), also written by Alan Bennett, with Stephen Frears producing. Having felt the heartbeat of the Morecambe seafront in Modley during the filming of the earlier play, Frears used him again, once more on location in his town of residency; it was certainly handy for the location shoot! He is credited as Albert. He's fundamentally playing himself. No, it's more romantic than that. He's playing the spirit of Morecambe. It's that grand, and that poignant, for the film was broadcast on 24 February 1979. Modley had died just the day before. It was his fond farewell, but not his epitaph.

His grandchildren Debbie and Leann ran Modley's restaurant, on the seafront right next to his home of forty years and by the beloved Alhambra Theatre that had been his second home for almost as long! The restaurant's

As Albert Entwhistle in the 1951 film comedy *Up for the Cup*. Fellow Forgotten Hero Harold Berens is the auctioneer.

walls were plastered with yellowing photographs and fading playbills from Modley's life in show business.

Modley's influence continues to haunt the clubs and music halls and piers of Britain. A seven-year-old wag by the name of Mike Craig had seen Modley's act at the Dewsbury Empire and never forgot it. Modley remained Craig's ultimate comedy hero, inspiring him to be a writer, performer and champion of all things variety. That's just part of Albert Modley's legacy. Practically the embodiment of the hard-working comedian, he was simultaneously of his time and for all time.

TREAT YOURSELF TO a trip to Morecambe: if you seek his monument, simply look around you!

# Robert Moreton

## 1922–57

Humorous writers tend to be sad at heart

*Josef Škvorecký*

That's an inscription that could have been writ large across Robert Moreton's *Bumper Fun Book*. He was a legitimate actor who had been the juvenile lead in a tour with the Old Vic and was subsequently cast as Coombe in the Noël Coward film *In Which We Serve* (1942) – and cast by Coward himself, no less.

Moreton showed a leaning toward comedy from early in his career, however, and, as a budding gag-writer, sold jokes to established turns Lupino Lane and Tommy Handley, neither of them slouches on the off-the-cuff one-liner themselves. It was during his service with the Royal Air Force during the Second World War that Moreton fully developed the comedic persona that would serve him for the rest of his all-too-short life. His sophisticated manner and rather superior air simply added to the incongruous appeal of his Christmas-cracker-quality wisecracks contained within that seemingly exhaustive collection of one-liners in his mythical *Bumper*

Original educator Robert Moreton, alongside fourteen-year-old Julie Andrews, Archie Andrews, Hattie Jacques, Peter Brough, Max Bygraves and Eric Speer, 1950.

*Fun Book*. The fact that he seemed not to know how precisely to tell a joke or why exactly what he was saying was funny made the routine all the funnier.

Upon demob he launched himself on to the variety circuit. By 1950 he was a veritable hardy perennial of BBC Radio platforms *Variety Bandbox*, *Workers' Playtime* and the rest of the corporation's popular entertainment packages, building up a loyal audience and impressing the bigwigs at the BBC enough to cast him as the very first tutor on *Educating Archie*. An instant success, the show was the star-making vehicle for lofty ventriloquist Peter Brough.

But while that naughty Archie Andrews was the pivotal force behind the weekly misadventures, he needed a rock-solid barrier to bash his wooden head against. Robert Moreton was custom-made for the part. Incorporating his familiar, ponderous, rather hesitant upper-class delivery, the show afforded him enough opportunity to indulge in his hilariously shaky grasp on the art of joke-telling. There were false starts, jumped sections, ridiculously elongated shaggy-dog stories and perfectly mistimed punchlines; when the whiz-bang did indeed hit home and raise an almighty guffaw from the studio audience, Moreton would pause with delight, cradle the microphone and intone his favourite catchphrase: 'Get in there, Moreton!'

The tutor on *Educating Archie* would be a revolving door of opportunity for the great and good of comedy. Upon Moreton's departure, at the end of series one, Tony Hancock stepped up to the plate with a tour-de-force performance that almost totally eclipsed what Moreton had achieved. Still, Moreton retained enough cachet to keep on working the variety halls across the country, relentlessly pedalling his *Bumper Fun Book* and finishing every solo spot with a song.

Moreton was the star comic in *Bumblethorpe*, from the combined mad genius of writers Peter Ling, Spike Milligan and Larry Stephens [qv]. This search for someone answering to the name of Bumbethorpe was broadcast from 12 November 1951. Moreton would also lend comic support to Richard Hearne [qv] in the Mr Pastry film *The Time of His Life* (1955). Still, as desperation to get a laugh set in, Moreton turned to the new craze of rock 'n' roll, performing American rhythm and blues with a perfectly clipped English accent, enunciating every word. The laboured routine went through initial hilarity, and into self-parody, before entering the realms of shocked awkwardness as he sensed himself losing his audience. When his audience did indeed turn away from this once-great comedic turn, it broke him. Ironically, scriptwriters Ray Galton and Alan Simpson sent up this wildly unsuitable variety trend in order to embrace 'the now' in the February 1957 *Hancock's Half Hour* radio episode 'Hancock in the Police', where, equally ironically, Moreton's ex-*Educating Archie* chum Hattie Jacques decries Hancock and Bill Kerr's music hall act for dropping their usual repertoire in favour of whistling the Freddie Bell and the Bellboys hit 'Giddy Up A Ding Dong'. Whether it was a deliberate poke in the ribs at Moreton or not, it sadly exposed his reduced standing in the profession.

Within just five years, Moreton had gone from radio superstar to virtually unemployable. He ended up running a flower stall on Westminster Bridge, accepting the very occasional theatrical assignment with alacrity. Tragically, in a final black-dog mood of frustration and depression at the telephone never ringing with work, on 22 July 1957, he committed suicide. He was just thirty-five.

TREAT YOURSELF TO *Four Hilarious Attempts at Educating Archie* from the BBC Radio Collection (BBC Enterprises Ltd: ZBBC1135, 1994). There's only one example from series one, and thus only one outing for Robert Moreton, in an episode first broadcast 30 October 1950, but it's a real beauty. As Moreton would have said: 'what are you waiting for, wooden-heads?!'

# Gladys Morgan

## 1898–1983

Gladys Morgan was one of my dearest friends for years and we worked together a great deal in variety around the country. She was the mother of the company. Her dressing-room door was always open, and there would always be a cup of tea for anybody who came along.

I first met her when she had just started out in the business, playing the music halls of Lancashire. In those days she was performing with a Northern accent. I was appearing in the radio series *Welsh Rarebit* as one of the four members of The Adventures of Tommy Trouble gang, a regular sketch in the show. I saw her act and went round to see her afterwards, and I remember sitting in her dressing room, chatting about her getting into radio. When I mentioned *Welsh Rarebit* she said, 'I'd love to do it!', but I had to tell her that it was a programme designed to showcase Welsh performers. She stopped me in my tracks when she said, 'Well, I *am* Welsh!' She explained that she only performed with a Northern accent because that was the way to get work in Northern theatres!

I went back to my producer, Mai Jones, and told her about Glad. She really wasn't interested. Amazingly, she said women performers were not popular! I countered that nonsense with the fact that she was using Maudie Edwards: 'Ah! But she's a singer. Comedy is very different!' I persevered with the cause and told Mai that Gladys was appearing in Pontypridd the following week and that she really should go down to the theatre and see her act.

She reluctantly went to see Gladys and offered her a two-minute spot between two musical numbers on *Welsh Rarebit*. Mai saw Gladys as filler between the songs, basically, but when Gladys came out with her cheerful humour, singing voice and *that* laugh – that hilarious shrieking laugh – well, the audience reaction was incredible. The laugh that *her* laugh got almost lasted for her full two-minute spot. The people never did stop laughing.

*Wyn Calvyn MBE*

Affectionately known as the Little Comedienne with the Big Laugh, Gladys Morgan was a towering presence in the music halls. She was not only a character comic but a business brain. At the peak of her fame she was one of the nation's favourite laughter-makers and the undisputed head of a family who delivered the ultimate package in variety.

Gladys Mabel Morgan was born in Swansea on 7 November 1898, making her professional debut at the tender age of eleven performing at the Old Panopticon in Cardiff. She was a versatile all-rounder, and it was with a light song-and-dance turn that she first came to prominence, until one particular audience began to laugh uncontrollably at her act. Morgan was mortified by their reaction, and even an offer by the management to turn her act into a speciality comedy routine for the second house performance didn't help. In fact it made things worse: the young Morgan not only dismissed the opportunity, she balked from going back onstage, and locked herself in her dressing room!

But she quickly realised that if comedy was her route to theatrical success, then comedy it would have to be, and she gradually started incorporating comic patter between her increasingly silly song-and-dance numbers. She had already met Frank Laurie – formerly of variety troupe Carrie Laurie's Juveniles – and the two married, and became a successful stage double act throughout the twenties and thirties. Morgan was the stooge to Laurie's comedian, but when agent Charlie Ellerman saw the act during a week's cine-variety in Liverpool, he cannily suggested they switch and allow Morgan to be the funny one.

Morgan's act of satirical observation and lowbrow knockabout was populated by a gallery of working-class bumblers and eccentrics. These were people her audience really knew, and she was clever enough to know that her characters had an 'everlasting quality' that all the family and each successive generation could identify with.

Her time with the Entertainments National Service Association during the Second World War opened her eyes to a more world-weary truth in her comedy that made her characters even more accessible. It was her comedic second-sight which infused the Morgan Family act, which included her husband Frank, her daughter, Joan Laurie, and Joan's husband, Bert Hollman, who also managed the team.

Morgan's personal breakthrough had come on 21 December 1950, when, after some frantic chivvying from Wyn Calvin, BBC Radio producer Mai Jones asked her to submit a script for consideration for *Welsh Rarebit*. The show wore its Welshness very much on its sleeve (the signature tune, written by Jones herself, was 'We'll Keep a Welcome in the Hillsides'), serving its original purpose – to keep Welsh servicemen in touch with home – as well as showcasing such beloved homegrown stars as Harry Secombe and Stan Stennett. By the time Morgan was accepted, the format of *Welsh Rarebit* had been extended to an hour-long variety spectacular featuring Maudie Edwards, David Lloyd, Albert and Les Ward, and The Lyrian Singers. Morgan's finely etched characterisations soon became an eagerly awaited favourite with listeners: 'I had hugged the hope of winning through in my native country', she said, 'no matter how hard or how long I had to work.' It had taken nigh on forty years of hard work but with *Welsh Rarebit* she became a national sensation. Characters such as her rowdy, loud-mouthed busybody who had just returned home from holiday, and her disgruntled failed talent contestant, tapped into the comic subconscious of her audience.

Morgan was so popular that the BBC risked uprooting her from regional security and tried her out in front of a supposedly more sophisticated London audience. As a trial run she was asked to perform before thousands of BBC employees at the National Radio Show at Earl's Court ahead of an attempt to launch her nationally in 1952 with a plum spot on the last knockings of *Variety Bandbox*.

She proved such a hit in that flagship BBC variety series that

Frank, Gladys, Bert and Joan gleefully take the London Palladium, 1961.

she landed a supporting role in heavyweight *Variety Bandbox* alumni Frankie Howerd's starring vehicle, *The Frankie Howerd Show*, first transmitted on 23 November 1953. With scripts by Frankiephiles Eric Sykes, Ray Galton and Alan Simpson, success was pretty much guaranteed, and by the second series, from 22 February 1954, Morgan's popularity was such that the very introductions could get away with affectionately mocking her: '...*The Frankie Howerd Show*, in which Frankie introduces the vitality of The Tanner Sisters, the versatility of The Hedley Ward Trio, the voice of Lee Young, the nimble fingers of Dolores Ventura, and apologises for Gladys Morgan.'

Now a Howerd satellite, Morgan's marquee value soared as she continued to play the variety halls and peddle solo broadcast spots on *Variety Fanfare*, which was 'heralding Variety in the North', and the factory employees' mainstay, *Workers' Playtime*, live from a canteen 'somewhere in Britain'.

From September 1958, Morgan found a comfortable niche on radio's *Educating Archie*, which had become a veritable playground for the comedy elite over the years. Morgan's stint came near the end of those halcyon days of Peter Brough and the loveable wooden-head Archie Andrews. She played the cheerful but clumsy cook whose culinary expertise was relentlessly the butt of the little chap's insults. Bernard Bresslaw, fresh out of uniform from his star-making role of Private 'Popeye' Popplewell in the Granada situation comedy *The*

Bernard Bresslaw and John Amery join Gladys on the bill at the Birmingham Hippodrome, 1959.

*Army Game*, was, in the wake of 'I Only Arsked!', happy to embrace another marvellously moronic catchphrase: "Ullo. It's me, Twinkletoes.'

The series left the airwaves in 1960 but Morgan wasn't downhearted. The family were relishing a lengthy run alongside Frankie Vaughan at the London Palladium at the time, followed by three tours of South Africa. They then headlined all-star cabaret on three world cruises.

Towards the end of the sixties, however, Morgan's health was failing. She made a handful of final radio and television appearances before retiring to her beloved Worthing. She died there, on 16 April 1983, at the age of eighty-four.

All but forgotten save for a distant, ever-fading yellow light radiating from a thousand and one vintage wireless sets in the collective memory of the nation, the legacy of Gladys Morgan was finally acknowledged on 11 December 2012, when her daughter, Joan Laurie, along with Roy Hudd and that Clown Prince of Wales, Wyn Calvin, unveiled a plaque on her former home, at 30 Salisbury Road. The next time you are West Sussex-bound, take a moment, ponder at her threshold, and remember that huge, infectious laugh of hers. You'll feel better for it, I assure you.

TREAT YOURSELF TO *The Wild Affair* (Network: 7954151, 2014), a rare film outing for Gladys Morgan, in which she plays the delightfully dithering Mrs Tovey. Based on the William Sansom novel *The Last Hours of Sandra Lee*, the 1965 film also stars Nancy Kwan and Terry-Thomas – without his trademark moustache!

# Lily Morris

## 1882–1952

Always top of the bill, right up to her death.

*Jimmy Perry OBE*

Her legs and arms kicked out and spun round at alarming angles and with impressive speed; she was like a marionette with extra stuffing who was as light on her feet as a vanilla soufflé – this is how I remember Lily Morris, and for me it was music hall love at first sight. Not yet into my teens, and I was hooked, watching that essential treasure trove of joy *Turns*, a weekly celebration of variety acts long gone, hosted by the infectiously enthusiastic Jimmy Perry. The Lily Morris performance was culled from the 1930 film showcase *Elstree Calling*.

It seemed to my young head only a matter of days later that the BBC were following up this revelation with a screening of the very atypical 1934 Will Hay film *Radio Parade of 1935*. It was a film that held much fascination for me; indeed, it included performances from quite a lot of people who have made the pages of this very book. Even at that relatively young age, I realised it was something important, and the *Radio Times* itself trumpeted that it was a television premiere. A television premiere for a film that was nearly fifty years old? How extraordinary – and what's more, it promised Will Hay – who I adored and still do to this day – and a Dufaycolor animation sequence. I was sold. Neither disappointed, although Hay's performance was stern and muted as the humourless Head of the National Broadcasting Group, an extremely thinly veiled satire on the BBC – for NBG also read No Bloody Good, and instead of BBC Director-General John Reith, Hay is William Garland – get it! However, what did delight, sometimes unexpectedly, was the wealth of music hall veterans who were dragged kicking and screaming into Elstree to do their stuff.

My instant favourite was this Lily Morris. Like Will Hay, she was called upon to do something very different from her usual act (not that I realised this at the time). As the Corporation's cleaner, Morris dismissed and decried the politics of the place, and sang as she swept the corridors of power. Interestingly, she was partnered by fellow eccentric variety great Nellie Wallace, making a rare foray in front of the camera and teamed for the one and only time of their careers. An uneasy double act, for sure, but one that works on so many levels but it wasn't Nellie that I warmed to but Lily. With this film and her *Turns* appearance lovingly recorded on video tape, I could watch and re-watch this plump shadow from a pre-war world of depression, poverty and always keeping cheerful.

Still, it was that vintage performance of her greatest comic song 'Why Am I Always the Bridesmaid?' that delighted me. It can still make me melt into a puddle of delight. Dressed in a billowing floral dress and donning a bedraggled, heavily adorned hat, this is Lily Morris in her comfort zone. She sings the plaintive lyrics with a distressed urgency and dances around the stage like a possessed toddler, sniffing, shaking and earnestly strangling a tightly gripped posy of flowers. The song is a classic of the music hall but it's all in the performance. You can practically feel Lily's pain. It's at turns tragic and hilarious. Even after all these years, I just want to give her a big old hug.

Born Lilles Mary Crosby, on 30 September 1882, she was a London girl and made her stage debut as a singer, later playing a fairy in the 1894 Drury Lane pantomime. By her late teens Morris was already established as a top music hall performer, carving out a very successful career as both a soubrette and as a principal boy. By the outbreak of the First World War she was making her first recordings and topping the bill in variety theatres. Sharing the same common touch and integrity of Marie Lloyd, Morris was beloved as one of the people. Indeed, she resurrected Marie Lloyd's 'My Old Man Said Follow the Van' for an earlier Will Hay film, *Those Were the Days* (1934).

Morris sang of unrequited love and over-indulgence, often at the same time. One of her best-loved numbers, 'Don't Have Any More, Mrs Moore', is a hymn to sobriety, while 'Because He Loves Me' is a delightfully childlike celebration of infatuation.

Photographed by Ian Douglas Campbell-Gray at his Hyde Park studio.

By 1925 she had cracked America. Her performance at the New York Hippodrome warranted an unprecedented number of encores. Her winning charm had captured the hearts of her audience. As one critic wrote: 'Every word and syllable she utters is a joy to the ear.' In 1927 she performed before the King and Queen in the Royal Command Performance at the Victoria Palace Theatre. The following year she made her triumphant return to New York, for a sell-out run at the Palace Theatre.

Over the next decade she would pack theatres on both sides of the Atlantic with her tried-and-tested collection of familiar ditties. They were the dying embers of the music hall, for sure, but Morris wasn't content to simply be one of the pall-bearers. Her performances were full of gusto; the audience would have felt embarrassed if they hadn't joined in at the choruses. A living, breathing, frantically moving spectre from a time of sheer fun, Lily encouraged the feel-good, lift-your-spirit-with-spirits ethos of the classic music hall era.

She retired from the stage in 1940, as she approached the age of sixty, although she subsequently had a half-hearted stab at character-acting. She played the irascible Lady Randall opposite Arthur Askey in *I Thank You* (1941), but neither she nor the film-makers could resist lightening the tone for her final scene. In an emotional and stirring climax, she breaks character to entertain Londoners sheltering from

As Principal Boy, starring in
*Jack & Jill* at the Prince's
Theatre, Bristol, for the 1907–08
pantomime season.

the bombing in an underground station. As she sings 'Waiting at the Church', the sternness and indeed the acting is completely wiped away. She is back in her prime, performing for the audience who loved her. It's pure Lily Morris, absolutely no Lady Randall.

That could have been that, if it wasn't for the death of her chief rival, Nellie Wallace, in the September of 1948. Though now sixty-six, Lily was persuaded to come out of retirement to fill Nellie's shoes in the Don Ross revival show *Thanks for the Memory*. (Even in the late 1940s, the need for pre-rationing nostalgia was insatiable; sing-songs of the old favourites did the heart good.) The lure of the theatre was too great to resist and she seemed fully set to resurrect all her old favourites for many years to come. Sadly, after a couple of years spent travelling the country with the *Thanks for the Memory* package troupe, Morris was forced to pull out due to ill health.

Morris's husband, Archibald McDougall – who she had married in the February of 1907 and who had become her manager – died in August 1952; Lily herself died less than two months later, on 3 October. She had just turned seventy. She is buried in Southgate Cemetery; the gravestone bears the name of McDougall, not Morris. It's very apt: the name Lily Morris does not belong in a graveyard. That ever-propelling, life-affirming, roly-poly bundle of London determination and happiness is a vital part of the nation's spirit. For ever.

TREAT YOURSELF TO *Don't Have Any More Missus Moore and Other Ballads* (Old Bean: DOLD504, 2002), the definitive collection of Lily's greatest hits, with not just the absolutely essential title number, as recorded on the Regal label in 1927, but an alternative version of it, released on Columbia the following year, as well as a live rendition recorded at Collins' Music Hall in 1950. Joyous.

# Richard Murdoch

## 1907–90

My first introduction to radio comedy was *Much-Binding-in-the-Marsh*, with Kenneth Horne and Richard Murdoch. What a great start. (I only recently discovered that Squadron Leader Richard Murdoch shared an office with Wing Commander Kenneth Horne. No wonder we won the war.) My heart always sank when they sang the song (with new lyrics every week); it meant the show was coming to an end and I'd have to wait another week to hear these wonderful voices tickle me pink. Not to mention Sam Costa with his 'Good morning, sir. Was there something?' Little did I realise that forty years later I'd be sharing a stage with 'Dickie' Murdoch in a summer season play, *Bedroom Farce*, at the Athenaeum Theatre, Plymouth.

Richard Murdoch is one of the reasons I entered comedy. A very good reason. Oh, I can hear the voice now...

*Tim Brooke-Taylor OBE*

For me, Richard Murdoch was always a bit of a stinker – in the nicest possible way. He was clearly of decent stock, and decent education – indeed, he was first at Charterhouse and then Pembroke College, Cambridge, performing with the Cambridge Footlights in a halcyon, P. G. Wodehouse era, light years before Peter Cook made the place his own. After leaving university, Richard Murdoch was a member of the chorus for that dapper song-and-dance man Jack Buchanan, and appeared on the West End stage with that energetic entertainer Stanley Lupino.

To my teenage self, Richard Murdoch was the delightfully dotty but impeccably mannered old barrister 'Uncle Tom' in *Rumpole of the Bailey*. He had been playing the role on an irregular basis since the first episode, 'Rumpole and the Younger Generation' on 3 April 1978, so he would have certainly popped into my consciousness while I was a kid and certainly before my twin interest in radio comedy and the Second World War saw him fire my passions in a most satisfactory way. As a comic eternity, Murdoch was charming, reassuring, and reliable. A thoroughly fine chap to have on your side.

If one can have a good war, Murdoch had a good war. Having been conscripted into the Royal Air Force and serving with Bomber Command, in 1943 he accepted a posting at the Air Ministry, and, yes, shared that office with Kenneth Horne. You couldn't make it up: the following year the two were teamed for the radio comedy *Much-Binding-in-the-Marsh*, set in a fictional RAF station. Joyous art imitating fraught life, the gentle subversion at the heart of the comedy made it a BBC staple until 1950 (with a brief sabbatical to Radio Luxembourg). Still, you can't keep a good format down; in 1970 Richard Murdoch and madcap singer and fellow *Much-Binding-in-the-Marsh* favourite Sam Costa resurrected the satirical signature tune for *Frost on Sunday*. Murdoch was still doing it for *Wogan's Radio Fun* in December 1987.

However, it was an earlier partnership, with big-hearted Arthur Askey, that ignited my interest. Back in my dim and distant youth of cutting-edge comedy from *The Young Ones* and *The Comic Strip*, the Askey and Murdoch films were regularly screened on television. Already forty years old and as alternative as tomato sauce is to ketchup, these breakneck farces made as a morale-boosting parry and thrust against a very real threat of buzz bombs were pretty much my perfect Friday night in!

Askey and Murdoch first teamed up on the radio show *Band Waggon*, for producer John Watt, and the pairing was one of glorious serendipity. Originally conceived as a showcase for popular dance bands, it was the comedy patter of Askey that linked the musical numbers and that always raised the bar of quality. Deemed a failure after just six episodes, the show was almost scrapped by the BBC but, instead, out walked writer and straight man Freddie Birtwell and in walked a personable young actor by the name

'You silly little man!': Stinker and Big-Hearted Arthur at the microphone for *Band Waggon*.

of Richard Murdoch. The chemical reaction of Askey and Murdoch made an instant improvement, and for Christmas 1938 entertainment catalyst Jack Hylton was presenting a stage version at the Prince's Theatre.

As Askey himself said, his dear chum 'Dickie' Murdoch was everything he wasn't. Classic comedy was the inevitable outcome, with the radio series introducing charwoman Mrs Bagwash and her desperate daughter Nausea. Neither of them spoke, allowing Askey and Murdoch to riff around their presence and react to the occasional grunt from the mother and the frequent thud as the offspring fainted.

The shared domicile of Askey and Murdoch eventually became something of a menagerie, with Basil and Lucy the pigeons, Hector the camel, and Lewis the goat: 'A goat in the flat? What about the smell?' pleads 'Dickie'. 'Oh, he'll get used to it!' Askey reasons. The sound man had a field day with this, eventually dressing up for the bestial parts and taking a well-deserved bow to the audience.

It's almost a cliché to say that radio greats such as the *Band Waggon* duo cracked jokes that won the war, but their cheerful, optimistic broadcasts really were crucial. The banter between Askey and Murdoch became part of the consciousness of a worried nation, while Syd Walker, as a cockney rag-and-bone man, would finish

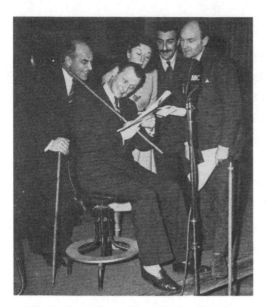

The 100th *Much-Binding*, with Ken, Dickie, Maureen Riscoe, Sam Costa and Maurice Denham, 1949.

every shaggy-dog story with 'What would you do, chums?' It was just one of a handful of catchphrases – 'Doesn't it make you want to spit?', 'Don't be filthy', 'Hello playmates' and 'Light the blue touchpaper and retire immediately' – that would resonant for decades. (I still use the latter in everyday parlance.) Such popular recurring items as 'Chestnut Corner' or 'Don't Stop Us Even If You've Heard Them Before', and the very whistleable theme tune 'Dear Old Pals', remain poignantly evocative of a community united.

However, even before the outbreak of war, it was thought that the fun had run its natural course. The intended last show, broadcast in March 1939, allowed the forever ad-libbing friends to look back on their monumental success ('We were so nervous in those days we used to write everything down!'). The nostalgia trip came ahead of a London Palladium summer season with Tommy Trinder – who had originally been earmarked as the star of *Band Waggon* – from 3 July 1939.

In August 1939 a film version was released – Askey and Murdoch's first flick together. It was a very fair recreation, with the pals separated by class but bound by poverty, struggling to make their way back into the business and being forced to live atop the roof of Broadcasting House. Every time I walked by the place I used to fantasise that they were still up there. It's a comforting thought to this day. Less comforting was the declaration of war during the shooting of the film, and by the time it was released, in the spring of 1940, the pair were entertaining the troops in France.

Two more films followed in quick succession, both outstanding revivals of hoary old potboilers, with *Charley's (Big-Hearted) Aunt*, in 1940, and *The Ghost Train* the following year. The latter was a spirited remake of the Arnold Ridley-penned ghost romp, with the original film role of Jack Hulbert cut up and split between the two of them. Askey took on the knockabout slapstick, while the love-sick romance was embodied in Murdoch. He was the Zeppo Marx [qv] of the operation.

One final film venture, *I Thank You* (1941), saw our heroes once more playing out-of-work variety comedians, desperate to stage a show against the threatened onslaught of the Blitz.

The BBC hadn't done with *Band Waggon* either, for when war was declared they begged and pleaded Askey and Murdoch to return for the good of the nation. They eventually relented, and during those dark, dark days at the end of 1939, eleven further episodes of *Band Waggon* were broadcast. It was such a relief, that a comment from one member of the house was recorded in the pages of *Hansard*: 'We are getting back to normality: *Band Waggon* will be back on the air next week.'

With Old Nasty – as Askey and Murdoch referred to Adolf Hitler – defeated, the team were back for one last, belated hurrah, on 13 November 1947: a special edition broadcast to mark the BBC's Silver Jubilee, with Askey and Murdoch resurrecting classic material with cheery apology, and Fred Yule stepping in for the late Syd Walker. It's fair to say that *Band Waggon* changed the entire feel of radio comedy in Britain.

In glorious middle age, could Askey and Murdoch do the same for British television? Well, no, but 1958's reunion for Associated-Rediffusion's *Living It Up* was a delightful attempt, with scriptwriters Sid Colin and Talbot Rothwell nostalgically carrying on as if the years had melted away, casting the boys as themselves again, now living atop – you guessed it – Associated-Rediffusion's Television House, on Kingsway.

There was one final flourish, when the BBC brought back the dynamic duo once more – this time for the corporation's Golden Jubilee in 1972. Clearly the years hadn't withered their mutual respect and comedic connection, and *Ah! Happy Days!* saw Dickie and Arthur, in the company of Arthur's celebrity daughter Anthea, revisiting their old BBC flat only to discover that in the interim the Corporation had been using their electricity supply to broadcast all their programming.

For Murdoch, after *Much-Binding-in-the-Marsh* there had been a third radio classic in the series *The Men from the Ministry*, Edward Taylor's pinpoint-accurate lampooning of the languid trials and tribulations of Whitehall civil servants.

Broadcast from 1962, it co-starred Wilfrid Hyde-White, with Deryck Guyler [qv] replacing him in 1966. Murdoch was concurrently spotting the deliberate mistakes in Ian Messiter's panel game *Many a Slip* (BBC Light Programme, then BBC Radio 2, 1964–73); while onstage, in 1968, he was Aubrey Allington in *Tons of Money*, at the Mayfair Theatre. He toured America, and played the Shaw Festival in Canada, as William the waiter in *You Never Can Tell*, in 1973. The following year he toured South Africa, as Colonel Barstow, in *Not in the Book*, and joined Bernard Bresslaw and Peter Butterworth in *Babes in the Wood*, at the Princess Theatre, Torquay. In 1977 Murdoch played Sir William Boothroyd in a UK tour of *Lloyd George Knew My Father*.

Murdoch's Indian summer included an appearance in the *Blackadder* episode 'Witchsmeller Pursuivant', on 13 July 1983. There was the gleeful BBC Radio 2 indulgence – and quite right too! – of *A Slight Case of Murdoch*, in April 1986 when, with Ronnie Bridges at the piano, Murdoch enthrals a live audience with songs and stories from a sixty-year career. In the 1986 film of *Whoops Apocalypse* he gave a kiss to his comic past as another man from the ministry, played Colonel Wainwright in *Never the Twain* ('Born to Blush Unseen', Thames Television, 24 February 1988), and enjoyed a regular role as the Worshipful Wizard opposite Stanley Baxter in *Mr Majeika* (TVS, 1988–90). Murdoch had spent 1989 touring as Lord Caversham in Oscar Wilde's *An Ideal Husband*, before settling into a West End run at the Westminster Theatre.

It was a final hurrah in *Rumpole of the Bailey*'s 'Rumpole and the Quacks', broadcast just six weeks after his death, that neatly rounded off Murdoch's long and illustrious career. An avid golfer, on 9 October 1990, Murdoch was enjoying a round on the Walton Heath course, in Surrey, when he died. He was eighty-three. An elegant final bow, indeed.

TREAT YOURSELF TO *Memories of Band Waggon, Happidrome and Other Great Wireless Comedy Shows* (EMI/World Records Limited: Retrospect SH388, 1980), an evocative collection featuring almost a full side of *Band Waggon* material from 1939, with Murdoch particularly excelling in the 'Fireworks' exchange. A glorious time capsule.

# Tom E. Murray

## 1874–1935

A forgotten hero of comedy if ever there was one. Amazing expressions –
so versatile. Just look at that face!

*J. F. Derry*

The British Film Institute have long held a two-minute film made by the
pioneering Mitchell & Kenyon company for the Imperial Bioscope of
Edinburgh. It features the antics of an unidentified comedian in an Ali Baba
turban as he animatedly reacts to an unseen associate on a wall-mounted
telephone. Thanks to painstaking research, by the University of Edinburgh's
J.F. Derry, in 2017, we now categorically know this comedian is Tom E. Murray.
Filmed on 12 December 1904, when Murray was starring in *The Forty Thieves* at
the Theatre Royal, Glasgow, it was used to promote the state-of-the-art movie
camera technology of Lizars Optometrists. Despite the film's brief running
time, we see Murray displaying a breathtaking array of comic expressions –
moments of joyous laughter, delicious face-pulling and amused reactions to

jokes – which quickly turn sour as the conversation ends with Murray losing his temper, threatening fisticuffs down the line and ultimately ripping the telephone from the wall. A winning, defiant look into camera at the very end shows a performer of style and confidence breaking the fourth wall and engaging his unseen audience with a self-aware charm. We are lucky to have him, he seems to be saying. And I think he was right.

Here is an artiste with a sense of modernity; the scene could have been filmed six weeks ago, rather than six weeks after the death of his comedic counterpart, Dan Leno. For while the legendary Leno was wowing the pantomime audiences at the Drury Lane Theatre, this mischievous, rubber-faced clown was doing something very similar four hundred miles north.

Tom E. Murray's portrayal of Mother Goose was discussed with bated breath in the four ale bars of Scotland: a cock in a frock with absolutely no pretence of feminine charm; legs astride, cheap linen skirt, a semi-bald wig giving an air of grotesque to this beguiling and endearing spectacular of a leering, cheering man happily reducing himself to affectionate ridicule simply to entertain.

Born in Boston, Massachusetts, Murray made his London debut in June 1896, sending up show business as his absent-minded stage-manager character Fitzallerton Scroggs in *On the March* at the Prince of Wales Theatre. *The Echo* described 'his quaint jests, his droll anecdotes, and his funny dances' and noted that Murray was 'the success of the evening'. He mocked himself and his public with playful arrogance, delighting in such cynical songs as 'He's All Right Now'. *The Evening News*, also celebrating Murray's debut, described him as 'a genuine humorist', while the *Pelican* enthused: 'it was quite wonderful how he held a crowded house'.

In September 1902 Murray opened at the Theatre Royal, Hull, in *An English Daisy*, a new musical comedy written by Seymour Hicks and Walter Slaughter, concerning the upper-class Daisy Maitland pretending to be a humble flower-seller. Murray was given the star comic role of Hiram Out. The *Daily Mail*'s 'Before the Footlights' column of 30 September 1902 noted: 'Mr Murray's part has clearly been written with a special view to his humouristic idiosyncrasy. That idiosyncrasy is particularly his own. We know no actor whose vein of humour is like to it. It might be hard, under analysis, to say why one laughs at Mr Murray, but the fact remains that not only one, but everyone laughs. A man must be funny who can make people do that. In the second act... Mr Murray has a talking solo. He treated the audience to a string of superb nonsense last night, and set them screaming. Even the ladies in the dress circle laughed.' The paper also observed that 'the songs given to Hiram Out are thoroughly quaint and appropriately odd'.

*An English Daisy* transferred to Broadway in 1903, then it was panto time again. Murray had already given his celebrated Mother Goose at the Shakespeare Theatre, Liverpool, with the *Pantomime Annual* describing him as 'one of the finest comedians... As a raconteur Mr Murray has few equals. He

His signature pantomime role of Mother Goose, 1907.

possesses a chuckle that is worth millions to any man who wishes to set others smiling. His admirers are legion, and in Liverpool he has long been recognised as a prime joker. Mirth and Murray are interchangeable words, and no one will know that fact better than he who goes to see Mr Murray as Mother Goose.'

Murray effortlessly consolidated his forte for pantomime with appearances in *The Babes in the Wood* and *Jack and Jill*. The 1903–04 season saw Murray starring at the Kennington Theatre, Kennington Park Road. Beatrice Willey was Morgiana, Laddie Cliff played the donkey boy and Albert Felino was Abbas his 'intelligent donkey'!

The Kentucky *Courier-Journal* on Valentine's Day 1904 celebrated the success of one of their own in the old country: 'Murray has been the bright, particular star of one of the best of the suburban pantomimes, playing Ali Baba in *The Forty Thieves*, and has increased his popularity so much that it probably will be a considerable time before he is seen in the United States again.'

Indeed, it was back to *The Forty Thieves* (and that priceless Mitchell & Kenyon film) in 1904, with Annie Purcell in support, while the 1905–06 season saw the production back at the Theatre Royal, with Ruth Lytton as Morgiana. Albert Felino was reassuringly back in the saddle, or rather with the saddle back on!

A 1902 pose for the *Sketch* magazine, promoting *An English Daisy*.

In 1908 M. Witmark & Sons, of Shaftesbury Avenue, published *Tales I Have Told!*, an autobiography ('some true, some by Tom E. Murray') and part joke compendium of extracts for one shilling. By 1911, not only was Murray starring in a new musical comedy called *The Harem Doctor* at the Queen's Park Hippodrome, Manchester, but he had also written the book of the show, and the programme proclaimed the production 'under the entire personal supervision of Tom E. Murray'. He was a true auteur at the top of the profession.

However, Murray rapidly tired of the war clouds over Europe and made for home. As an article headed 'Murray in Town', published in the *New York Clipper* in February 1916, noted: 'Tom E. Murray, the comedian ... who has been in England for many years, has just returned for a visit until the war is over. Mr and Mrs Murray have been ten months coming home, having practically made a trip around the world partly for pleasure and incidentally to dodge the submarines. Mr and Mrs Murray are on their way to Palm Beach for six weeks. Mr Murray has been entertained while here by members of the Lambs Club, Screen Club and White Rats.'

The Murrays never did return to England, and although Tom continued to perform, he never recaptured that staggering, inventive, whirligig comedic joy he had generated on the British stage. A lost clown, caught in one hundred or so seconds of celluloid aspic.

TREAT YOURSELF TO at least one pantomime each and every season. Smile at ancient, oft-repeated jokes, introduce each and every new generation to the glories of the dame and the Uglies, and spare just one thought for Thomas E. Murray. His sparkle and sheer exuberance resides deep within the art.

# David Nixon

## 1919–78

I first produced and directed *The David Nixon Show* in the late sixties and I instantly became a great admirer of his professionalism, and enjoyed every series that I was privileged enough to produce for him. At the beginning of each and every series, David would take George Martin, Ali Bongo and myself to the Terrace Bar at the Thames studio in Teddington, Middlesex, purchase four gin and tonics and, overlooking the weir at the Thames Tide End, say 'Thank you' for the opportunity of being awarded another series. David never took anything for granted, especially his own 'celebrity'. He was a wonderful human being, who died far too soon.

*Royston Mayoh*

If all the telly magicians went on a day trip to the seaside, Tommy Cooper would be the one laughing too loud and drinking you under the table and David Copperfield would make the coach disappear. David Nixon looked like he would probably rather stay at home with a nice cup of tea and a good book. He was a gentle man and a gentleman. In my dim and distant formative years, Nixon was a constant and reassuring presence, like beans on toast, and Tizer.

David Porter Nixon was born in Muswell Hill on 29 December 1919. His father, a solicitor by profession, was a keen amateur magician. He took young David to the music hall to see his favourite conjurers, including Nevil Maskelyne, David Devant and, most notably of all, Stanley Collins. With his elegant dress suit and gentlemanly manners, Collins charmed the audience, and with slick, black hair, a perfectly maintained moustache, stiff, starched shirt, a flower in his buttonhole and a seemingly endless barrage of bon mots, he certainly charmed David Nixon, who would soak up the tricks and soak up the image, even though Nixon's own hair prematurely thinned to what he claimed was: 'the best-loved bald head in show business'.

Nixon's enthused passion for magic was consolidated with a gift of an Ernest Sewell magic box from his auntie. At the age of eighteen he joined The Magic Circle. A past bout of pneumonia prevented Nixon enlisting during the Second World War but his magic skills, not to mention his proficiency on the double bass, made him an ideal candidate for the Entertainments National Service Association.

After being demobbed, in summer 1946, Nixon joined the variety Fol-de-Rols show in Scarborough and during his four-year association joined the troupe on the West End stage. Along the way Nixon had befriended another young hopeful, Norman Wisdom, the two forming a long-lasting double act that honed each man's comedic prowess. As a team, Nixon and Wisdom wowed the London Casino, while as a solo act Nixon became a favourite at the Windmill Theatre. Nixon now added a touch of song and dance to his act, and would happily work front of house too.

In 1947 Nixon married singer Margaret Burton, and made early television appearances in the variety platforms *Café Continental* and *Showcase*, in August 1951. A frequent film, television and radio turn with appearances on *Variety Half Hour* (Harold Baim Productions, 1954), *Garrison Theatre* (BBC Television, 1953–54), and *Variety Parade* (BBC Television, 28 August 1954), it wasn't until that year, when he was recognised as a 'personality' on the panel game *What's My Line?*, that Nixon became a true star – all without so much as a dove disappearing up his sleeve! Alongside other popular regulars, such as Lady Isobel Barnett and

There was always something adorable just about to come out of David's hat!

Gilbert Harding, Nixon's mild-mannered, affable and just plain sweet attempts at guessing the professions of a string of slightly awkward-looking members of the public was pretty much the benchmark for sophisticated playtime at the BBC. Everyone involved became something of a national treasure overnight.

He was also sans tricks when in 1964 he was offered the job of hosting early editions of the British version of *Candid Camera* on commercial television, displaying yet more genteel affection for Average Joes acting daft. No one but David Nixon could have done it with such understanding and kindness. He would take on non-magical jobs throughout his career, notably narrating the 1960 Mermaid Theatre production of Erich Kastner's *Emil and the Detectives*.

Still, television magic was the thing for David Nixon, and by 1955 he was hosting *It's Magic*. Such was his popularity that a subsequent success, *Comedy Bandbox*, was, from January 1966, hastily rebranded *David Nixon's Comedy Bandbox*. With his sleight of hand at its slickest and his name carrying enough clout to make the titles, his shows for ITV included *Here's David Nixon* (1963), *Tricks 'n' Nixon* (1963), *Nixon at Nine-Five* (1967) and *The Nixon Line* (1967–68). *Tonight with David Nixon* (ITV, 1969) rounded off his sixties television career in style. Having appeared on the television specials of everyone from Arthur Askey (*Before Your Very Eyes*, Associated-Rediffusion, 18 February 1955) to Harry Secombe (*Secombe at Large*, BBC, 30 May 1959), it was time to team up with that raffish fox-around-town Basil Brush, a force of nature so laid back he was practically horizontal and a comedy partner who was more than capable of matching Nixon's charming and erudite badinage. Not since the halcyon days

Promoting *Cinderella*, with wife Paula Marshall, who sadly died in a car crash soon after the season ended in 1956.

of the Western Brothers [qv] had there been a double act of such suave and crystalline delivery.

On 9 March 1970 came *David Nixon's Magic Box*, a show that two years later, on 8 May 1972, morphed into *The David Nixon Show*. This would be his major platform until 1977, with magic at the forefront of a variety bill that eagerly embraced the best in comedy and song. It was distilled joy, with the likes of Anita Harris, Lynsey de Paul, Les Dawson and Matt Monro on the guest list. Nixon was even happy to bring in other magicians, notably a young pretender to his throne by the name of Paul Daniels, who appeared in the edition broadcast on 2 June 1975. Daniels spoke with deep affection about the opportunity for the rest of his days.

Nixon was also very happy to lay his wand aside to be a charming master of ceremonies. He had presented the inaugural *Christmas Night with the Stars* in 1958, brought good grace to *Whose Baby?* from January 1973, indulged a passion for chess by presenting Thames Television's *Checkmate*, and revelled in guest – and subsequent team captain – duties on *Jokers Wild* (Yorkshire Television, 1969–71), stringing out gentle shaggy-dog stories to the delight of all.

He was a victim of Eamonn Andrews, surprised with the big red book of *This Is Your Life* at the Magic Circle's HQ in 1973. He returned the following year to guest on Arthur Askey's *This Is Your Life* profile, and it is testament to how beloved he was by the profession that when regular host Eamonn Andrews was profiled in his very own *This Is Your Life*, the special guest presenter was David Nixon.

Throughout the seventies, Nixon was a welcome cog in the variety circuit, guesting alongside everyone from Val Doonican (*The Val Doonican Show*, BBC1, 6 January 1973) to Larry Grayson (*Shut That Door!*, ATV, 4 April 1973), but it was his own show that allowed him to fully take advantage of television-studio trickery. Embracing the relatively new revelation of chromakey, he was able even to interact with himself during one particularly mind-blowing magic routine. Purists bitterly complained that this was beyond magic – it was cheating! We kids didn't care. For me, David Nixon was a cross between a beloved uncle and telly wizard Catweazle. He was adored by everyone, and it was an adoration not lost on advertisers, who eagerly signed him up to endorse the new-fangled, proto-synthesizer, the Mellotron. Nixon liked the electro-mechanical musical instrument so much he even invested in the company, and his relentless advertising campaign did much to sell thousands of units across Britain.

His appeal for the children of the nation was certainly not lost on pantomime producers, who had long seen the potential of casting Nixon as the likes of Wishee-Washee in *Aladdin* (BBC Television, 1951) or Buttons in *Cinderella* (the Palace Theatre, 1955–56, with his wife, Paula Marshall, as Dandini). There was always a moment to break that fourth wall, or to break away from the plot, simply to delight the youngsters with some magic tricks. Moreover, it was an opportunity for Nixon to quieten those who condemned his television japery. Onstage, the magic was as real as magic can be.

Besides, the criticisms were totally unfair. The use of camera trickery was pioneering rather than fraudulent. Indeed, since boyhood he had built all his own tricks. These were proper tricks; tricks you would expect to see in a proper magic show: sawing a member of the audience in half, producing a bunch of flowers out of thin air, or performing a particularly fiendish mind-reading card trick he called Nap Hand.

Nixon's skill was manifold. He made classic, unfathomable magic tricks look effortless and easy. He delivered them with a winning smile and good humour, a manner that made every single member of his audience putty in his hand, and with the ability to make the general public feel like part of the act. Nobody was ridiculed or bewildered. They were simply amazed.

Nixon's line in off-the-cuff comic observations and running commentary was natural and beguiling, and he subtly dropped flights of fancy into the act, Trojan Horse-like, bending traditional tricks to his televisual whim. It is unsurprising, then, that his appearance as a castaway on *Desert Island Discs*, in

February 1956, saw his choice of book as Lewis Carroll's *Alice in Wonderland*. He really was the Mad Hatter made flesh.

He also seemed eternally grateful for the privilege his huge talent had earned him. A tireless worker for show business charities, he was proud to be King Rat of the fraternity of the Grand Order of Water Rats for two consecutive years, in 1976 and 1977. Sadly, he failed to dodge the bullet of a fifty-a-day cigarette habit, laudably keeping the lung cancer private as he continued to honour his charity, television and pantomime commitments. He only spoke out when doctors gave him the all clear, using his experience as his platform to launch an appeal to raise £100,000 for cancer research at Bradford University.

Sadly the cancer returned, and Nixon died peacefully at home in Chipstead, Surrey, on 1 December 1978 at the ridiculously young age of 58. He worked until the very end: the Tuesday before his death, he had been reunited with his old partner in comedy Basil Brush for a seasonal special, *Basil Brush's Magical Christmas*, broadcast on 23 December. We watched in a daze; this man was like family.

There was something heart-warming about him leaving the stage in the company of that sassy fox. It was a bittersweet farewell, indeed. For my generation, enthralled by David Nixon's faultless ability to charm and bewitch, it was simply twenty or thirty years too early.

TREAT YOURSELF TO the Blu-ray of Agatha Christie's *The Spider's Web* (Stratx: B071PFLP73, 2017). A lavish Technicolor feature from Danziger Productions for Christmas 1960, Glynis Johns stars as the spirited Clarissa Hailsham-Brown. Peter Butterworth is the law, Inspector Lord, while eccentric couple Jack Hulbert and Cicely Courtneidge are two of the suspects. The film also features a rare guest-star acting turn from David Nixon as the manservant, Elgin. There's absolutely nothing up his sleeve... Or is there? As the poster screamed: 'Don't tell your friends the end... They won't believe it!!!'

# Larry Noble

## 1914–93

The company plays without pretentiousness, but with every nerve
stretched, with every talent at its full height.

*Harold Hobson*

The Whitehall Theatre farces made a legend of actor-manager Brian Rix, and
quite right too. For fifteen years, Rix's unique brand of breakneck, trouser-
dropping, frantic door-opening and frantic door-closing romps put the West
End audience in his pocket. The plays were as often as not wonderful old pot
boilers. They didn't need to be anything else, for they were populated by some
of the finest farceurs around. One of the finest, and most unheralded, was Larry
Noble, an actor who could imbue the corniest line of hackneyed dialogue or the
most laboured scene-direction with such energetic clout that you just couldn't
help but laugh, in spite of yourself. Diminutive of stature but a powerhouse of
face-pulling, scenery-chewing, little-man angst, Larry Noble was like a wind-up
toy that had been wound up just that one or two winds too many. A glorious

409

Larry, as Grandad Blunt, arrested by Leo Franklyn and Brian Rix, during rehearsals for BBC TV's 'A Policeman's Lot', February 1959.

performer, too large for anything but the Whitehall Theatre.

Laurence Keith Noble was born and bred in Huddersfield on 13 December 1914, and his life in the spotlight started early. He relished his barking, drum-beating and other tricks of the trade to attract crowds to his father's collection of collections – be it his waxwork museum, fairground exhibits or sideshow curios.

The need to make a living dragged Noble into a proper trade, however, first as a trainee dental mechanic and latterly as a door-to-door salesman, where his ability to sell absolutely everything served him well. Like most of his generation, the natural flow of his life and work was rudely interrupted by war service; in Noble's case, and already working as a bellboy for the P&O Line, with the Merchant Navy. Upon demob, he seized the opportunity to join the Barnsley-based repertory company, the Denville Players, while they were on tour in Halifax. Noble subsequently joined Frank H. Fortescue's Famous Players touring company, making his West End debut in Henry Sherek's 1944 production of Colin Morris's 'Play of Adventure' *Desert Rats*, at the Adelphi Theatre.

It was another Morris play, *Reluctant Heroes*, that gave Noble his biggest break, from 12 September 1950. It introduced him to Brian Rix's Whitehall Theatre company, and he made such a mark playing against the spirited barked orders of Wally Patch's character, Sergeant Bell, that, apart from Rix himself, Larry Noble remains the only cast member to have starred in all five first nights of the Whitehall farces between 1950 and 1965. He also played Polignac the manic French jockey in John Chapman's *Dry Rot*, which played for four years from 31 August 1954; the clumsy waiter, Smogs, in Chapman's *Simple Spymen*, from 19 March 1958; the excitable solicitor, Arnold Piper, in Ray Cooney and Tony

Hilton's *One for the Pot*, from 2 August 1961; and finally, it was more Cooney mayhem, playing the nervy Bobby Hargreaves in *Chase Me, Comrade!*, from 15 July 1964. Closing on 21 May 1966, there had barely been a week between productions in all that time.

Having proved himself indispensable onstage Noble had been at the top of Brian Rix's list when putting together a series of farces for television, and he became a mainstay in *Laughter from the Whitehall* (1957–59), and *Dial RIX* (BBC, 1962–63) as well as appearing in several of the *Brian Rix Presents*

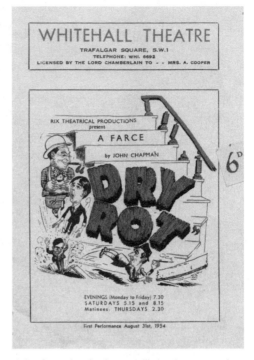

The farce that had Larry 'happily putting his foot through the stairs every night for nearly four years'!

farces, memorably essaying Albert Boyle in *Will Any Gentleman?* in 1961, the Reverend Arthur Humphrey in *See How They Run* in 1962 and, finally, in 1965, a celebratory resurrection of a tireless comedy from a different era, the Aldwych farce favourite *Rookery Nook*, in which Noble played Harold Twine. In the meantime Noble had also gone full circle and reprised his role of Trooper Morgan in the 1951 film version of *Reluctant Heroes*. Larry Noble had carved out a comic niche as the beleaguered little man with the weight of the farcical plot upon his shoulders.

After some 6,000 performances on the boards of the Whitehall Theatre, Noble decided to take his career in other directions. This included a glut of diverse and diverting television, including the 1966 *Doctor Who* story 'The Massacre' starring William Hartnell, the semi-regular role of Barney Chubb in five 1965 episodes of *Emergency Ward 10*, and as hire purchase dealer Fred Nuttall in *Coronation Street*, in 1966. As it turned out, he only made it through

WHITEHALL THEATRE
TRAFALGAR SQUARE, S.W.1
Telephone: WHI. 6692
Licensed by the Lord Chamberlain to Louis Cooper

RIX THEATRICAL PRODUCTIONS
present

RELUCTANT HEROES

A FARCE
by
COLIN MORRIS

6D.

Evenings at 7 p.m.
Matinees:
Thursday & Saturday at
2.30 p.m.

(First Performance
September 12th
1950)

PROGRAMME

Larry created the role of Trooper Morgan in *Reluctant Heroes*, in 1950.

two episodes before embarking upon a relentless run in supporting comedy roles. There was the role of a telephone engineer in *Marriage Lines* (in the 'First House' episode, BBC1, 27 May 1966), *Six Dates with Barker* as the dogged Sergeant Bowles in the celebrated 15 January 1971 episode 'The Phantom Raspberry Blower of Old London Town', Mr Godby in the John Cleese scripted *Doctor at Large* episode 'It's All in the Mind', on 13 June 1971, the 'Operation' man in the 4 May 1975 *Doctor on the Go* episode 'When A Body Meets A Body', written by George Layton and Jonathan Lynn, Mr Dingle in the 15 January 1976 *Happy Ever After* episode 'Old Folks' Party', hilarious antics on *The Dick Emery Show* (in the editions broadcast on 26 October 1976, and 24 September 1977), and a couple of *Last of the Summer Wine* episodes: as the tight-fisted Mouse in 'A Quiet Drink', on 2 April 1975, and as Gordon in the Boxing Day 1978 special 'Small Tune on a Penny Wassail'. Stage work allowed Noble to let his acting chops bristle, with notable successes including Baptista Minola in Mervyn Willis' 1975 New Shakespeare Company production of *The Taming of the Shrew*, Jacob Engstrand in Ibsen's *Ghosts* and Mr Hudson, the chilling 'Chelsea Breather' in John Bowen's *Little Boxes*, at the Duchess Theatre. He was Sam in *The Homecoming*, at the Palace Theatre, Watford, opposite and directed by Harold Pinter in February 1969, played Lickcheese in *Widowers Houses*, at the Royal Court, in 1970, and created the role of Alfredo Amoroso in the original production of Eduardo de Filippo's *Filumena*. It ran at the Lyric Theatre for eighteen months from November 1977, under the direction of Franco Zeffirelli. The previous summer, under the direction of Roger Redfarn, Larry had taken on the role of aged Mr Grainger in the stage version of *Are You Being Served?*, at the Winter Gardens Pavilion,

Blackpool. The film version would feature Andrew Sachs, as Spanish hotel manager Carlos. Sachs had played Larry's Whitehall farce characters on tour before joining the West End company with *Simple Spymen*. As Spanish waiter Manuel in *Fawlty Towers* Sachs became a slapstick legend but Larry wasn't bitter.

Having met and married Pamela Plant, the daughter of Blackpool comedian Jimmy Plant, in 1947, it took Larry thirty-eight years of relentless work to realise he was missing out on a lot of quality time between their two homes in Hampstead and France. On his 71st birthday and soon after joining a load of aged pros in Terry Gilliam's *The Crimson Permanent Assurance*

A Fabulous West End Drip! Larry's cast photograph from the programme for *One for the Pot*, which enjoyed a four-year run at the Whitehall Theatre, from the summer of 1961.

(1983), Noble did the unthinkable and formerly announced his retirement in *The Stage*. Wouldn't you know it, just as soon as he had made his decision he was offered a tasty role on telly but he stuck to his guns. After all that knockabout farce and running around in the evenings, Larry Noble had more than earned his final handful of years sedately taking it easy. Larry slipped peacefully away on 9 September 1993, two months shy of his seventy-ninth birthday, and without a broken bannister or a dropped pair of trousers in sight!

TREAT YOURSELF TO a night at Trafalgar Studios, which occupies the old Whitehall Theatre. Larry Noble was absolutely passionate about the place and his spirit of knockabout joviality is in the very brickwork.

# Ole Olsen and Chic Johnson

## 1892–1963 and 1891–1962

John Sigvard 'Ole' Olsen (born 6 November 1892) and Harold Ogden 'Chic' Johnson (born 5 March 1891), professionally known as Olsen and Johnson, are two of the most influential comedians the world has seemingly forgotten. Their greatest successes occurred onstage, in vaudeville and on Broadway, but while the venues they played launched the illustrious film careers of W. C. Fields and the Marx Brothers, Olsen and Johnson's antics never transferred to motion pictures with the same impact. Nonetheless, the rapid-fire gag format Olsen and Johnson perfected with *Hellzapoppin'* did transmogrify into the sixties TV smash *Laugh-In* as well as the eighties big-screen hit *Airplane!*, with its similar use of wild sight-gags, puns delivered in a deadpan style, and slew of 'literal jokes'. Even Mel Brooks's 1976 *Silent Movie* features an identical premise as Olsen and Johnson's *Crazy House*, the story acting as a slender clothesline to hang wild gags and celebrity cameos upon. Olsen and Johnson were sui generis.

While they're not household names today, the moulds they forged were never broken and helped shape modern comedy.

*Alan Spencer*

I love Frankenstein's monster as much as the next wolfman. I really do. I've got the Universal Monster back catalogue in every format and in every variation, from several creaky old VHS sell-throughs to the latest shiny Blu-ray, but I occasionally get a little frustrated with dear old Universal Studios. Why, oh why, does it re-package the glorious monster cycles time and time again? (This is a rhetorical question; I realise it's for the money.) I pine for Universal's sorely neglected comedy archive. It's only Abbott and Costello who seem to get a fair crack of the whip and, even then, the Bud and Lou exploits most forcefully exploited are – yep, you guessed it – those in which they meet the monsters.

While Abbott and Costello were the world's best-loved comedy double act in the early 1940s, Universal Studios was also the haven for another pair of extremely funny men. Unlike Bud and Lou, or Stan and Ollie over at Fox, Ole Olsen and Chic Johnson didn't particularly look like a double act. There was no thin–fat, smart–stupid contrast at play in their comedy. Ole and Chic were as fat and stupid as each other!

They also made the funniest film in the history of world cinema – and at a time when most of the Pythons weren't even born. The film in question is *Hellzapoppin'* (1941) and there has never been anything quite like it before or since. It simply reeks of America just before the Second World War. It is slick, sassy and silly – very, very silly. It's from an era when 'swing was king', when chaps were zoot-suited and booted, jitterbugging was the latest dance craze and nothing was really in black and white, despite the film being in black and white.

*Hellzapoppin'* begins on a high: in Universal Studios' idea of what hell really looks like – Dante's *Inferno* as told by *Capt. Billy's Whiz Bang*. Our makeshift heroes arrive via a New York taxi with Olsen's killer first line: 'That's the first cabbie who ever went straight where I told him to!' – and we're in. That one line pretty much sets out the stall for the rest of the film.

Every cinematic cliché is exposed and ridiculed. Like the wildest of Chuck Jones cartoons, Ole and Chic wander through disparate film sets, change costume with ease, break the fourth wall to hold a conversation with the cinema projectionist (played by our favourite dour underdog, Shemp Howard [qv]) and even send up Hollywood's latest and greatest hits. Stumbling over a sleigh bearing the legend 'Rosebud', Chic wryly comments: 'I thought they burnt that!' Ah, contemporary cinematic mockery at its finest.

It's dangerously satirical too: the film specifically addresses how Hollywood executives always get things so dreadfully wrong when adapting a hit show. *Hellzapoppin'* had indeed been a smash hit on Broadway. The property and pet project of Olsen and Johnson themselves, it opened at the 46th Street Theatre on 22 September 1938. It was the wackiest, messiest and maddest thing in the world – ever! Think the Crazy Gang and Mel Brooks in a blender with a side order of The Mighty Boosh. Naturally it caused a riot on the Great White Way. No one had seen anything quite like it before. Performers were planted in the audience for unexpected interruptions of the comedy; musical numbers were disrupted and would often simply grind to a halt in mid-lyric; and no pretty chorus girl was safe from a hasty disrobing. Quite simply, it was a revelation. It ran for 1,404 performances!

The genius of the film version is in the lengthy, on-screen studio discussions desperately trying to work out just how to film the unfilmable. The director, played brilliantly by Richard Lane, simply can't stand the pressure; he even wanders into the action at times. It's that kind of film. It's also the kind of film where Olsen can get away with the 'Coat of Arms' gag: his coat has several arms stitched on to it. Yes, the jokes are that obvious and that's the very point. It is a joyous, relentless, free-wheeling, convention-crushing cavalcade of laughs. The sort of comedy Hollywood just wouldn't make. But they did. And how!

Unlike pretty much everyone else who has even heard of Olsen and Johnson, my besotted-fan worship of them does not start and end with *Hellzapoppin'*. Oh, no. In the wake of the film's success and its continued dominance of Broadway, Universal starred the duo in three further comedies. Although *Crazy House* (1943) was almost completely swamped by bizarre vaudevillian turns and paper-thin plot padding, it still lifts my comedy spirits, if only for one of the greatest opening scenes: laden down with floozies, fops and all the fun of the fair, the travelling madhouse of Olsen and Johnson crashes through the gates of Universal Pictures, much to the chagrin of everyone there. 'Olsen and Johnson are coming!' screams a property man in warning. A mass exodus ensues. Even Nigel Bruce, in character as Universal's favourite sleuthing second banana Doctor John Watson, has got the wind up him. He rushes onto his own sound stage and there is Basil Rathbone with pipe in hand and tongue firmly in cheek. Naturally he knows what is going on: 'Olson and Johnson have arrived!' he mutters. As per usual,

Ole and Chic in a publicity pose for the spooktacular *Ghost Catchers*, 1944.

Watson is dumbfounded: 'How do you know?' he blusters. Rathbone deploys his perfect pause before intoning: 'I am Sherlock Holmes. I know everything!' Anything after was bound to be an anticlimax, and the rest of *Crazy House* just can't live up to that truly extraordinary opening five minutes.

Admittedly, while *Hellzapoppin'* had its icky love stories and eccentric guest-turns, these were remorseless send-ups, safe in the hands of towering maniacs like Mischa Auer and Martha Raye. The atypical Hollywood romantic interlude between Jane Frazee and Robert Paige leads to a wonderfully schmaltzy song; within moments of it starting, however, the screen displays a caption instructing the young 'Stinky' Miller to go home. These continue to disrupt the song until, both of them furious, Frazee and Paige stop the song and address the boy in the audience. A sheepish shadow on the screen shows the boy leaving and the song continues.

*Ghost Catchers* (1944) was even better – or is that worse? It's a ramshackle, feeble, cheap and cheerful haunted-house romp. It has rather too many speciality acts and musical numbers but it's still glorious, and I absolutely adore it. Any film that has that perpetual screen drunk Jack Norton as a real ghost has to be a winner. Moreover, Lon Chaney Jr., clearly chilling on the Universal backlot, is dragged in and stuck in a grizzly-bear suit. For beer and giggles, no doubt.

They ain't afraid of no ghosts. Actually, they are!
Ole and Chic promoting *Ghost Catchers*.

Bob Hope had sort of done the haunted-house comedy to death five years earlier, with box-office hits *The Cat and the Canary* (1939), and *The Ghost Breakers* (1940), over at Paramount but, for me, *Ghost Catchers* is right up there with the best comedy frighteners of them all. Rarely discussed, and even more rarely seen, it is hardly the equal to *Hellzapoppin'* in the surrealist stakes but it's rollickingly good: hair-raising and rib-tickling fun in unequal measure. A joyous slab of Hollywood moonshine.

Sadly the same cannot be said of *See My Lawyer* (1945), which poked fun at the insane American legal system but saw fit to keep Olsen and Johnson out of much of the action. The whole point of their comedy was to observe, disrupt and comment; with *See My Lawyer*, Universal finally got control back, complete with romantic storyline and structure. Ole and Chic are in there, pitching passionately, but it hardly *feels* like an Olson and Johnson film at all. Strait-jacketed and restricted, Universal didn't take them to court for crimes against comedy but the studio did quietly said bye-bye to the duo and turned its full highly amusing attention to frightening the bejesus out of Abbott and Costello.

Ole and Chic weren't downhearted. There were plenty more puns in their armoury and their long-standing partnership was rooted in loyalty. They had been the closest of friends since first meeting in 1914. Olsen was a serious violinist, Johnson a ragtime pianist, and when Ole's quartet, College Four, needed a replacement piano man, Chic got the job.

Before long they were cracking jokes and making each other laugh between musical numbers. More and more, the comedy took over. Wacky, irreverent, and eager to amuse, these guys would do anything to get a laugh. The Olsen-and-Johnson style was born. Radio was king and it loved Olson and Johnson.

They became major celebrities in the Midwest, so much so that Warner Brothers offered them a film contract, starting with *Oh Sailor Behave!* in 1930. Traces of the duo's future film madness seep through the three features they made at Warners but the straitjacket of Hollywood was still too tight. They were picked up by Poverty Row studio Republic Pictures who indulged their madcap style on the tiniest of budgets and the shortest of filming schedules. These jolly japes had absolutely no ambition to be high art and win an Oscar. Their last film there, *All Over Town* (1937), teamed them with a performing sea lion!

With the useful experience of making comedies for Republic Pictures, Olsen and Johnson were very happy to get their hands dirty while making films. No demands, no frills, just sheer, exuberant hard work and gratitude at being in the business. These gleeful pranksters were always ready to lighten the situation with a knowing chuckle or a virtual poke in the ribs. Moreover, they still held creative ownership of the *Hellzapoppin'* brand. These professional fools were no idiots, presenting a touring package-show of *Hellzapoppin'* featuring other performers in their stead, while they played the Winter Garden Theatre with more of the same with *Sons O'Fun*, from 1 December 1941, and *Laffing Room Only*, from 23 December 1944. Now they returned to their biggest triumph and continued to play to packed, enthused houses, even playing the West End of London, at the Princes Theatre, from 10 April 1948.

Not only that, but a new beast had entered the homes of America, and Olsen and Johnson were relentless in their working of it: television. It was their medium. Their material was neither rare nor well done – deliciously and deliberately so – and they happily caused mayhem as early as 1949, when they were hired by NBC to front the ambitious variety series *Fireball Fun for All*. Despite the title being a bit of a mouthful, it valiantly tried to resurrect the scattergun spirit of *Hellzapoppin'* in a pokey television studio. Still, there was a feeling of homecoming at NBC. The radio show *Fleischmann's Yeast Hour*, hosted by crooner Rudy Vallee, had fully catapulted the boys to regular and national stardom from 1932 with their section 'The Padded Cell of the Air', which allowed them to break and bend the conventions of broadcasting as only they could.

Chic and Ole, with Claudia Dell, in *50 Million Frenchmen*, released on Valentine's Day 1931.

*Fireball Fun for All* proved successful enough for a further NBC offering, *All-Star Revue*, from 1951, before Ole and Chic found a natural home, from 1957, on ABC's *Popsicle Five-Star Comedy*. This was a kids' programme but the boys took this supposed demotion on the chin. They cleverly reasoned that their sort of uncontrolled insanity was just what children wanted. Consequently they didn't change a thing. Well, perhaps there were a few less chorus girls with their skirts ripped off – still, they had an outlet for that, too, having been wowing Las Vegas for years. These weren't desolate men.

The end came only in the late 1950s, when, reluctantly, Johnson was forced to retire through ill health. The two had been firm friends for over forty years at the time and, with a typical show-must-go-on attitude, Olsen clowned on alone. He had struck up a friendship with Bud Flanagan, swapping ideas and gags for each other's respective stage antics – one can only imagine the undiluted joyful bedlam that would have resulted if The Crazy Gang had joined forces with Ole and Chic. What a partnership that would have been! Olsen may have been at half strength but the insanity kind of lingered and he was embraced as stooge and sparring partner by younger pros like Mr Television himself, Milton Berle, the vaudeville wise-cracker whose intimate and relaxed style had made him America's best-loved small screen comic.

It was during one such Berle engagement, on 5 February 1961, that presenter Ralph Edwards surprised Olsen with the *This is Your Life* book. The final guest to appear was none other than Chic Johnson, striding onto the stage with all the verve and irreverence of the glory days. When Ole and Chic got together, the years could not dim the joy of each other's company and their shared delight in the corniest of gags. It was the last time the two would perform together.

Chic died on 25 February 1962, Ole on 26 January 1963. Both were seventy and, as befits close buddies who had spent much of their lives together, they are buried in adjacent plots in Las Vegas.

So, Universal Home Video, if you're reading this, how about a four-film Blu-ray collection of the sheer genius and life-affirming lunacy of Ole Olsen and Chic Johnson? And give *Hellzapoppin'* the special-edition treatment while you're about it. Come on, Frankenstein's monster even makes an appearance!

The Broadway show made Olsen and Johnson stars, with *Funzapoppin*, a sequel of sorts, opening at Madison Square Garden, on 30 June 1949. However, it's the 1941 *Hellzapoppin'* film that is Ole and Chic's most precious cultural bequest.

TREAT YOURSELF TO a copy of *Hellzapoppin'* – if you can find one! Long restricted in America due to copyright being tied up in the stage show, there is nonetheless a long-out-of-print British VHS release (PolyGram: 634 868 3, 1991). The transfer isn't up to much but, hey, it's better than nothing. It's quite possibly the funniest film that has ever been made. You had better believe it! As Ole Olsen used to always say: 'May you live as long as you laugh, and laugh as long as you live.'

# Ken Platt

## 1921–98

In 1960, aged seven, I went with my family on our first summer holiday, to Butlins Pwllheli on the beautiful North Wales Coast. My brother, sisters and I loved the funfair, the chairlift and the swimming pool. The highlight, though, for me, was the nightly variety show. The Sunday show always had a surprise top-of-the-bill: 'Please welcome,' said the compere one night, 'from radio's *Variety Fanfare*, the one and only, Ken Platt!'

As the audience around me applauded excitedly, on to the stage strode a kindly-looking man in a sharp suit, who said in a broad Lancashire accent: 'I won't take my coat off – I'm not stoppin'.' As gales of laughter echoed around the theatre, I was hooked. There then followed a warm, funny routine about everyday working-class life. He had the audience in the palm of his hand and I knew instantly what I wanted to do for a living when I grew up. I can't remember any of the jokes but that opening line, said as if he'd just called in to our house to see my dad, has stayed with me to this day.

Catchphrases can't be manufactured. They have to touch the audience in a special way. Ken Platt certainly did that for me that night. When I eventually got into show business, I would finish my cabaret act by saying: 'Don't get up – I'll see myself out.' Not bad, but not as good as 'I won't take my coat off – I'm not stoppin'.' I never got to meet Ken, but I thank him for that first inspiration to do what I do.

*Les Dennis*

The well-worn cliché goes that, if you were around at the time, you know exactly where you were and what you were doing when you heard that President Kennedy was shot. Well, I wasn't around at the time but I can certainly tell you where I was and what I was doing when I heard that Northern comedian Ken Platt had gone to meet his maker. Suitably enough, I was on a lonely hillside somewhere just outside Holmfirth in West Yorkshire. At the time I was chatting to Robin Banks and Denis Mawn, club turns and actors employed by the BBC as stand-ins for Compo and Clegg in the long-running situation comedy *Last of the Summer Wine*. As usual when the three of us were chatting between camera set-ups, the conversation invariably lead to old comedy. Somehow our chat had turned to Ken Platt and one of my good companions sadly said that he had just passed away in a hospital in Blackpool. He had been a comedy legend, but he had died a forgotten man.

A Northern hero, born on 17 February 1921, and bred in the area, Platt had toured the music halls and working men's clubs for much of his professional career but, sadly, had been forced to retire from the business following a stroke in 1990. It was a sad and silenced last decade eased only by the constant love and attention of his partner and former manager Brian Robinson.

Ken had been bewitched by show business from a very early age and his parents maintained that he always made them laugh as a child – as parents are wont to do. The young Platt clearly had talent though. He also had a hero – a hero who would inspire and inform his entire career.

George Formby was Britain's biggest box-office draw and Ken idolised him. So much so that, at the age of fifteen, he saved up enough money to buy a banjolele of his own. Billing himself as 'George Formby the Second', Platt entertained audiences at his local music hall. It's only fair to mention that the real George Formby had much more claim over the title, for Formby's father, George Formby senior, had reigned supreme in the music halls for many years. Indeed, George Jr would go to his grave insisting that his dad was by far the better comedian – as sons are wont to do. Still, Ken Platt gleefully championed the Formby legacy.

He clearly learned his music hall history as well as his craft, for his billing eventually became 'Ken Platt "the pocket George Formby"'. It also spoke volumes that he considered himself far inferior to the performing legend he emulated. But the moniker sold tickets and that's what it was there for.

Platt had a natural, likeable style of comedy of his own though, and by the late thirties audiences and venue managers were taking notice. That was until the Second World War intervened. He joined the army in 1942 and was posted to North Africa. Platt wasted no time in joining The Forest Mummers concert party and, subsequently, was transferred to the Combined Services Entertainment, with which he toured Italy, Greece, Scandinavia and Corsica.

The immediate years following demob could make or break a successful star fresh out of battle dress, and Platt found the going extremely tough throughout the late 1940s. His parents had bought a greengrocers in his home-town of Leigh, in the Borough of Wigan, Greater Manchester. Young Ken was forced to begin working in the shop. Importantly, he kept cheerful and kept cracking jokes. In fact he just couldn't help himself. One regular customer was BBC scriptwriter and producer Ronnie Taylor, and in the summer of 1950 he offered Platt the opportunity to audition for the BBC.

The North of England, if not quite another country, was certainly treated as something of a minority audience that demanded its own tailor-made entertainment. The flagship radio show for the region was *Variety Fanfare*, a sort of *Variety Bandbox* with added whippets. Ken quickly established himself as a favourite and became the show's resident comedian. Radio was a natural medium for him. He delighted in spinning his tall tales and cheery one-liners. He also had a killer catchphrase. Every performance would start exactly the same: he would stroll out in front of the audience and mutter the immortal words: "Ello. I won't take my coat off – I'm not stoppin'.' A belter.

Something of a throwback to the halcyon days of variety and music hall, even at the peak of his success, Ken's warm-hearted delivery, easy smile and engaging personality were irrepressible and nostalgic. He starred as Idle Jack in his first pantomime, *Dick Whittington and his Cat* at the Sheffield Lyceum Theatre for the 1952–53 season, alongside Morecambe and Wise, and revelled in the cheerful audience participation and extreme silliness. By 1954 he had became such a popular variety turn that impresarios George and Alfred Black headlined him for the summer season at Blackpool. It was the pinnacle for a Northern

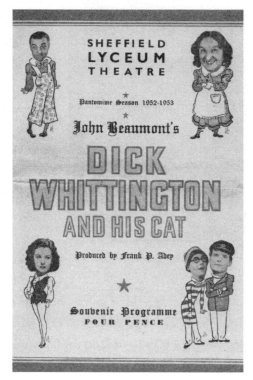

With Tony Heaton, Lynnette Rae and Eric 'n' Ernie in the 'Magnificent Yorkshire Comedy Pantomime'.

comedian; Ken Platt was at the top of the world. The following year he toured in *All-Star Variety* with that sensational singer 'with the Giggle in Her Voice' Alma Cogan, and from 26 September 1956 joined the cast of radio's *Educating Archie*, the melting pot for great swathes of the cream of British comedy. That boisterous screen Scot James Robertson Justic was the tutor, while Ken proved an ideal stooge for the wooden-head, gleefully deploying his 'I won't take my coat off – I'm not stoppin'' introductory catchphrase, week in, week out.

Like many a great comedian, Ken embraced the television game show, hosting dozens of episodes of *Spot the Tune* from 1957. The format – having started on NBC Radio in 1952 – was reworked in 1976 for the much more familiar British television series *Name That Tune* with Tom O'Connor and required contestants to guess the identity of a popular dance-hall number from the few bare notes played live in the studio by the Peter Knight

FEET UP!
By BOB MERRILL

FEATURED AND BROADCAST BY
KEN PLATT

Sheet music for 'Feet Up!', another of Ken's daft ditties.

Orchestra. Platt's winning and seasoned way with members of the general public was a godsend to the show. In 1962 he consolidated his popularity with the popular package *Saturday Bandbox*.

In 1960 Platt had broken into acting with David Kirk's play *Love Locked Out* at the Alhambra Theatre, Morecambe, and subsequently enjoyed huge success in Bernard Delfont's production of Sam Cree's *His Favourite Family* at the Pier Theatre, Blackpool, for the summer season of 1968.

The sixties were kind to him, but as the years rolled by he increasingly found himself on nostalgic package tours. His endearingly old-fashioned style had become just a bit *too* old-fashioned. By the end of the decade he was a playing an Edwardian milliner's shop managerial apprentice in the situation comedy *Wild, Wild Women*, and fully embracing old time music hall on *The Good Old Days* (both BBC1, 1969). Still only in his forties, he would send up his long career in antique gag-telling, dredging up golden oldies from his years on 'steam radio'.

This set the seal for the rest of his career. Save for the occasional spot of acting – a bit as a delivery man in the 25 February 1971 *The Liver Birds* episode 'The New Flat', for example – often as comedy character Kenny Cucumber, he worked the panto and summer seasons with unflagging energy and good humour. A 1980s holiday in, say, Great Yarmouth or Scarborough, could be enhanced and tinged with the flavour of variety's heyday with a modest but fun-packed bill featuring Ken Platt, one of the last great links from the golden age to its final, declining days. He was a towering laughter-giver.

TREAT YOURSELF TO Ken Platt's gloriously silly single 'Ting Tong Tang' (Parlophone: R4507, 1958). The flip side delights with the seasonal sentimentality of 'Snowy the Christmas Kitten'.

# Sandy Powell

## 1900–82

A charming comedian. Simply charming.

*Tim Vine*

As a kid, Sandy Powell was one of my favourite comedians, and I came to him from both ends of his career. On the one hand, he was an aged, doddery old gentleman who popped up on variety shows, as often as not struggling through his ramshackle ventriloquist act. The mounting hilarity of his ineptitude provided inspiration for Eric Morecambe's turn with a dummy. At the same time, Powell would pop up, beaming and in black and white, in clip shows and compilation films. I don't recall ever seeing one of his features in its entirety at the time, but I remember he was a boundlessly enthusiastic force of nature in round spectacles. One vignette, in which he gleefully explained the ever-escalating disasters that awaited his companion back home, had me on the floor in hysterics. Powell would relentlessly and cheerfully elaborate on the catastrophe with: 'There you are again, y'see...' The mere thought of

Sandy, at the peak of his recording and broadcasting fame, in the mid-1930s.

it is making me beam. Here was a master comedian, and he knew it. He was at the top for over fifty years.

Born Albert Arthur Powell on 30 January 1900, in Rotherham, in the West Riding of Yorkshire (where, upon his seventieth birthday, a pub was named in his honour), he took to the stage as a child, decked out in a Little Lord Fauntleroy suit by his mother. It was a salute to his extremely hard-of-hearing old ma that gave Powell his lifelong catchphrase. During one particular broadcast he dropped his pages, and filled the gap by bellowing: 'Can you hear me, Mother?' down the microphone. It instantly caught the imagination of the listeners, and the manager at his next venue, in Coventry, insisted he start the act with the line. Powell kept it in for good.

A bright and breezy teller of tall tales and silly stories, Powell was a likeable character comedian, quick of wit, and down to earth. Not only did he revel on radio, but he was also a canny pioneer of recorded comedy. Although happily at ease onstage, he really saw his live theatre assignments as an advertising platform for his 78rpm recordings. These invariably cast him as himself, Sandy Powell, in various occupations, and increasingly hilarious situations. Between 1929 and 1942 he notched up eighty-five such records, first on the Broadcast label and subsequently with Rex. Powell had turned down an offer of a £60 flat fee. Instead he negotiated in favour of a penny royalty per side. The first of these discs, *The Lost Policeman*, sold almost half a million copies. That's a million sides at one penny each in Sandy's pocket! His final recording, *The Lost Policeman in the Blitz*, issued in 1942, was a lovely comedy call-back that caught the zeitgeist of the war, and sold almost as many copies. In total over that fourteen year period Powell's comedy discs sold nearly eight million, racking up a tidy income of £60,000.

My variety-brother, Rick Blackman, is a benchmark of quality, but the fact remains that he didn't rate Sandy Powell at all. One glorious drunken weekend, he was decrying his vast collection of Powell 78s. I, also in my cups and envious of said bundle of Sandy, said I would gladly take them off his hands. The following morning, like a music hall Father Christmas, Rick had deposited a heavyweight record box, crammed with Sandy Powell, at the bottom of my bed: a treasure trove.

Throughout the 1930s, Powell also starred in a run of hugely successful films. *Home from Home*, as per usual starring Sandy as Sandy, this time struggling to cope with life after a prison sentence, was released in 1939. That year he was voted the fifth most popular star at the British box office.

A mainstay of pantomime and summer seasons, along with his Starlight variety theatre company, Powell took the Pier Theatre, Eastbourne, throughout the 1940s and 1950s, with this good Yorkshire lad earning the moniker Mr Eastbourne from a loyal local audience.

With old age came the nostalgia tours and memory-lane appearances, including four editions of *The Good Old Days* (BBC1, 1965–79), the 1980 Royal Variety Performance from the London Palladium in honour of Her Majesty Queen Elizabeth the Queen Mother's eightieth birthday (by coincidence, it was Sandy's too) and, finally, candid reflection on his place in the life and work of club comic and *Hi-de-Hi!* star 'Paul Shane's Rotherham' for the documentary *Comic Roots* (BBC1, 16 August 1982).

Right to the end, he had a cheerful, effortless comic way with him. Rather beautifully, just before his death on 26 June 1982, Sandy returned to the Coventry Theatre to unleash that heart-warming gravelly voice for one final 'Can you hear me, Mother?' It was just lovely to spend some time in his company. It still is.

AS YOU HAVEN'T got a chum as generous as my pal Rick Blackman, treat yourself to the 78rpm recording *Sandy, the Film Star* (Rex: 8041, 1933), a joyously tongue-in-cheek embrace of his very real big-screen stardom. Powell is never more winning and hilarious than on intimate audio, and this is one of his best. For the full nostalgic fix you may have to fork out for a wind-up gramophone-player as well, mind you, but it'll be worth it.

# Vince Powell

## 1928–2009

When Vince wrote *Mind Your Language* in the seventies, Britain was rapidly evolving into a multicultural society. Like other writers, Vince saw it as a ready source of new material. He was also acutely aware that the most effective way of achieving acceptance and tolerance in such a society was through humour. In *Mind Your Language* the focus of ridicule was never the foreign student. Its humour lay in the vagaries of the English language and the students' resulting frustrated attempts to master it.

I still remember with glee the bewildered Greek student trying to understand the rules of cricket. 'When you're out of the pavilion, you're in, and then when you're out, you're back in...' It was an old joke, but Vince's genius was not just in writing new material, but in sometimes cyphering the familiar through completely new and fresh situations and characters. That's why Saturday evenings saw twenty million viewers watching Vince's show and why he earns his place in this book.

I'd always wanted to tell Vince how much I owed him and how much I appreciated his work. When Robert included the cast's thoughts on commentaries for the three series DVDs of *Mind Your Language*, I finally found the opportunity to articulate that gratitude and admiration. I know Vince listened to it. I hope he listened wearing his customary, ever-present smile.

*George Camiller (Giovanni Cupello, Okie-dokie!)*

There are two very good reasons why the Lamb and Flag pub in Covent Garden is so dear to my heart. One of them is that it was the boozer of choice of Vince Powell and me after London meetings, lunches in the Concert Artistes' Association, memorial services at St Paul's – the Actors' Church; anything really.

Over the last ten or fifteen years of his life we spent many a joyous hour in that pub, happily arguing about football (Powell was a Manchester United fan; I, Arsenal) and agreeing about politics, but it was comedy – and, more to the point, the misrepresentation of his comedy – that formed much of our conversation, particularly after a glass or three of Pinot Grigio. For you see, Vince already seemed like a forgotten man, even then, and the situation hasn't improved in the years since his death.

Powell would eagerly accept invitations from television producers to be a heavily edited talking head for some rather disrespectful nostalgic clip show, hopeful that he could make the case for his back catalogue but fully aware that his work would once again be cited as the prime example of seventies sexist and racist humour.

Powell would proudly talk of the huge viewing figures that *Love Thy Neighbour* (Thames Television, 1972–76) attracted, and that black families in Britain would call it 'their show'. Rudolph Walker and Nina Baden-Semper always out-witted the white couple, Powell would say in his defence. He and the show were never racist. For that, Powell explained, you had to look to Australia. Lordy, the Australians were *really* racist. At the peak of Love *Thy Neighbour*'s popularity, Powell took a stage show version on a nationwide tour of Australia. The problem was that it was the seventies, an era when only two British actors were permitted work visas. Powell was shocked to discover that one white actor (Jack Smethurst) with two black actors was still acceptable; in other words, a black actor was considered to be worth exactly half a white actor. It was racism at work in the very fabric of a nation, and Powell wrote the show to pinpoint exactly that problem in the United Kingdom. It was an irrefutable fact that if a black family moved into your neighbourhood in the 1970s, the property price would plummet. *Love Thy Neighbour* was written to expose this disgrace not condone it.

It was the comedy of language that was the butt of the jokes in *Mind Your Language*, inspired by the faux pas of Powell's Parisian au pair girl, who would enquire each morning whether there was any post from home by asking: 'Have I had any French letters today?'

Still, by the 2000s Powell couldn't get arrested as a scriptwriter – and, boy, how he pitched and pitched and pitched ideas for new television shows. He had new sitcom idea after new sitcom idea, but no bites. And here was the man who, with his late writing partner Harry Driver, had created some of the most important, inspirational and just plain laugh-out-loud-funny comedies ever seen on commercial television.

Vince had channelled his early experiences as a tailor into *Never Mind the Quality, Feel the Width* (Thames, 1967–71), which starred Joe Lynch and John Bluthal as a pair of bickering East End tailors, one Irish Catholic, the other Jewish. There was *Nearest and Dearest* (Granada, 1968–73), which pitted Hylda Baker against Jimmy Jewel, an uneasy sister-and-brother-partnership forced to run their late father's pickle factory. *Pardon the Expression* (Granada, 1965–66) starred Arthur Lowe in a spin-off for his *Coronation Street* character Leonard Swindley, now a fully fledged comic creation, sparring with his bewildered bosses, embodied by Paul Dawkins playing Ernest Parbold in the first series, and by Robert Dorning as the rather more bombastic Wally Hunt in the second. *George and the Dragon* (ATV, 1966–68) was the first of Vince Powell's memorable association with Sid James, here cast as George the chauffeur, who was forever battling the puritanical ways of Peggy Mount as Gabrielle Dragon, the housekeeper to their mild-mannered employer, played by John Le Mesurier. *Two in Clover* (Thames, 1969–70) followed, with Sid and pal Victor Spinetti upping sticks from the City and running a farm – with hilarious consequences.

Clearly conflict was a big part of what made these comedy scripts tick, but Powell was no fool when it came to television. When the bosses at Thames

Television were searching for another Sid James vehicle, all the usual suspects were suggested: Sid the boxing promoter; Sid the pub landlord; Sid the dog-track owner. But Powell was adamant that it was time for the public to see Sid the family man. Although the bosses weren't convinced, Sid stood up and said: 'I know

Vince wrote over 500 plots for *Coronation Street*. Here, in November 1966, with Annie Walker actress Doris Speed.

Vince is right!' The result was *Bless This House*, Sid's biggest personal television success and one he worked on right up until the month of his death, in April 1976.

Powell's co-writer Harry Driver had himself died in November 1973, aged just forty-three, but Powell wrote on alone, creating *Bottle Boys* (London Weekend Television, 1984–85), which starred Robin Askwith as hapless milkman David Deacon; and *Odd Man Out* (Thames, 1977), in which Blackpool fish 'n' chip shop owner Neville Sutcliffe (played by John Inman) inherits a seaside rock factory in Littlehampton, West Sussex. This situation afforded befuddled co-star Peter Butterworth the unforgettable catchphrase: 'How's your rock, cock?' Across the eighties Powell scripted thirty-two episodes of *Never the Twain*, starring Donald Sinden and Windsor Davies, for Thames Television, as well as three series of *For Better or For Worse*, starring Gorden Kaye and Su Pollard, for BBC Radio 2, from 1993. Powell also wrote copious material for literally hundreds of episodes of Cilla Black's people shows *Blind Date* and *Surprise, Surprise*.

Many of Powell's television shows transferred to the big screen, and he gleefully wrote the scripts, most memorably *For the Love of Ada* (1972), featuring Irene Handl and Wilfred Pickles, *Never Mind the Quality Feel the Width* (1973), and *Love Thy Neighbour* (1973), for Hammer Films. Talk of a *Mind Your Language* film came to nought, although alumni from the series Dino Shafeek and Albert Moses contributed bookend cameos to, and Françoise Pascal

*Love Thy Neighbour* on the big screen, starring Nina Baden-Semper, Jack Smethurst, Rudolph Walker and Kate Williams, released shortly after the third TV series, in July 1973.

was offered the lead role in, *Carry On Emmannuelle* (1978). Powell anonymously salvaged the original, lacklustre, Lance Peters script, surreptitiously meeting the film's director, his friend Gerald Thomas, in a lay-by, and handing over the final draft just days before shooting commenced. Vince certainly had plenty of tales to tell when he sat down to write *From Rags to Gags – The Memoirs of a Comedy Writer* (Apex Publishing Limited, 2008).

Less than a year after its publication, on 13 July 2009, Vince died, in Guildford, Surrey. He would have turned eighty-one on 6 August.

Powell wrote good old-fashioned belly laughs, and millions loved it; they still do. I can still see Vince getting more and more irate at the state of modern comedy – he was something of a curmudgeon when it came to this, and although he listened as I defended the high quality of the recent past, he seethed through gritted teeth as he cited comedy writers supreme Johnny Speight, Eric Sykes, Spike Milligan and the rest, who had gone to their graves whizzing with new ideas and trying to get a commission from fresh but inexperienced heads of light entertainment. Vince Powell felt he was a living dinosaur. If nothing else, his incredible legacy of accessible television comedies deserves to be remembered and celebrated against the only criteria that really matters. Are they funny? Yes they are.

TREAT YOURSELF TO *The Complete First Series – Mind Your Language* (Madman Television: MMA5001, 2008). All thirteen episodes are included, complete and uncut, along with tasty audio commentary from Vince Powell himself as well as from cast members Françoise Pascal, George Camiller, Albert Moses and Ricardo Montez, educatedly moderated by yours truly.

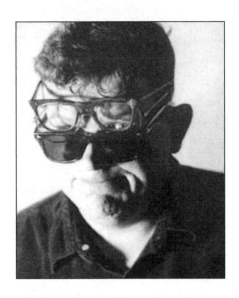

# Hovis Presley

## 1960–2005

Hovis was a legend. Full stop.

*Craig Campbell*

The least surprising thing to learn about the Bard of Bolton, Hovis Presley, is that he was not born Hovis Presley, but Richard Henry McFarlane, on 9 June 1960. He was a shambolic, rather disgruntled, ale-quaffing chap whose ear and eye for subtle detail and life's irritating little foibles made him one of the most refreshing and celebrated poets and comedians of the flash, cynical nineties. Presley was the very nemesis of Thatcherite Britain. His mentality was never 'Greed is good' but 'Life is bloody hard.' If those concerns, worries and personal doubts had to be there – and, indeed, they did have to be there – well, at least he could make them funny for people. It was something of a life-mission statement but one he never wanted to gain fame and fortune from. His only desire was to be heard. And, perhaps, to momentarily cage his moderately annoying inner demons.

His talent to amuse first emerged during his school days at Thornleigh Salesian College in Bolton. His teachers, genuinely impressed by a comedy sketch he had written, requested its inclusion in the end-of-term revue. Presley reluctantly agreed to perform it, despite his shy, introverted persona, but only if five Curly Wurly chocolate bars were provided as props. Doubtless these sweet treats were subsequently dished out to school chums as a way of countering any embarrassment from his unwanted notoriety.

He took his talents to the streets, literally, founding the busking band Dr Stroganoff Treacle Hammer and His Supporting Wall of Sound. Presley was on washboard and comedy-dancing duties. The outfit even won second place in a Bolton Council busking contest. It was the perfect accolade; first place would have been just too showy.

After graduating from Bradford University, his life took a turn for the exotic. He landed a job working on the German railway and later found himself teaching English in Cairo. Reassuringly, his writing remained rooted in normality and disillusionment. By the late 1980s he was back in his Bolton comfort zone with enough material to tackle the North East comedy circuit. He had also changed his name. An almost Orwellian conception combining the fantastic and flamboyant with the down-to-earth and working-class, Presley was in honour of Las Vegas-era Elvis while Hovis was the brown bread relentlessly marketed at the time as a lowly but delicious product of cobbled streets and flat caps. Hovis Presley was the perfect nom de plume. It also gave him an identity to hide behind. He was a slovenly, laconic and almost apologetic comedian who treated the wave of laughter for his pearls of wisdom with sheer disbelief: this wasn't an act.

Like Jake Thackray [qv] before him, Presley was at his happiest writing his poetry down rather than performing it. To that end, he published his priceless collection, *Poetic Off Licence*, in 1993.

He would have undoubtedly preferred to avoid public appearances but he realised that it was his voice, and his voice alone, that could do full justice to his mournfully funny verse. The place to be in the North East at that time was Chorlton Buzz Club, which had opened in 1989. It is no stretch of the imagination to say Hovis Presley became the club's first star attraction. Indeed, his popularity helped to build the local comedy circuit, a trend fuelled by performers such as Dave Spikey and Steve Coogan. It's clear that later talents, such as Peter Kay and Johnny Vegas, followed in the world-weary, unpretentious footsteps of Presley. Unlike those stadium-fillers of the naughties, though, Presley's success remained local, and that was exactly the way he liked it. He was a hero of his own backyard.

Presley relished a tour he did with Graham Fellows, in the guise of his keyboard-fingering alter ego John Shuttleworth. Bolton's finest Radio 1 disc jockey Mark Radcliffe, bewitched by Presley's ability to summon up the angst of his generation, invited him on to his show time and time again. But Presley, being Presley, would turn down offers of bigger comedy venues in the south, almost just because it would mean him having to spend a night away from his beloved home in Bolton. He preferred to stay in Bolton, running his 'alternative to alternative comedy clubs' at the Balmoral Hotel. He was a contented man, nursing his First World problems within this comforting venue: surrounded by the people that he trusted; the people he knew would get what he was writing and talking about.

But that looked set to change for ever in the summer of 1997. A second Edinburgh Festival Fringe show, *Wherever I Lay My Hat, That's My Hat*, was fast gaining a reputation amongst comedy admirers and theatre critics. Five-star reviews were flying around his head and his throwaway, monosyllabic and permanently disinterested comedy delivery was seen as surreal, postmodern and just sheer brilliant by sell-out audiences.

Even his poetry collection had been expanded and re-packaged as the sarcastically jolly *Poetic Off-Licence Holiday Annual*. The bigwigs were sitting up and taking notice. This was crunch time – and Presley couldn't handle it. Distressed by the acute media interest and lucrative offers being piled up on to the table, Presley disappeared mid-run and the remaining shows had to be cancelled. The situation became so serious that the police were called in to try to trace him. When he was finally found, a few days later, he was visibly shaken, unkempt and unable to return to the glare of the spotlight.

He turned, instead, to charity gigs and intimate social clubs in which it was he, and not the corporate men, who could call the shots. These working men's

THE STAND COMEDY CLUB PRESENTS:                    The sell-out success of 1997

# HOVIS PRESLEY

## MUTINY
Aug 8 - 30 (not 17, 18)
4.05pm
£5 (£4)

## ON THE
featuring
Steve Warwick
on guitar

## BONTEMPI

brilliant northern
comic - Guardian

'Above all, Hovis never stops being funny'
William Cook, The Guardian

'hilariously deadpan poetry...curmudgeonly beer-bellied
exterior conceals a superbly devious comic intelligence'
Scotsman

THE STAND COMEDY CLUB
5 York Place
☎ 558 7272
WHERE THE FRINGE COMES ALIVE

Back at the Edinburgh Fringe for a third August of
angst, in 1998 at the Stand Comedy Club.

variety shows effortlessly merged poetry, music, comedy and darts into a relaxed evening of beer and belly laughs. It was all very much Hovis Presley, and Hovis Presley only.

Presley appeared on television on very rare occasions, notably on the Carlton Television game show for kids, *Mad For It*, and the Channel 4 comedy platform *Gas*. For a short time, between 1997 and 1998, he would be accompanied on guitar by regular stage cohort Steve Warwick. It was about as commercial as Presley had ever wanted to be. Alas, half-hearted notions about actually recording his work with Warwick came to nowt, but his 18 March 1998 performance on *Gas* preserves the greatest surviving rendition of the poem that is undoubtedly his greatest hit: 'I Rely On You'. A bludgeoning, beleaguered, deathly, devoted torrent of words delivered by Presley as a monotonous dirge, it perfectly kicked sentimentality into touch in favour of a realistic truth that togetherness is simply better than being alone. 'I rely on you, like a handyman needs pliers, like an auctioneer needs buyers, like a laundromat needs driers, like *The Good Life* needed Richard Briers' is a typically joyous moment. Presley was asked countless times by engaged couples if they could use the stanzas in place of the traditional wedding vows. He would doubtless be tickled pink to know that today the poem is included in the official Salford Register Office choice of verse.

Peter Kay, something of an unofficial protégée, was so enthralled by Presley that when he was planning his new Channel 4 situation comedy *Phoenix Nights* in 2000, he offered Presley a leading role. The offer was turned down, although Presley's friend and champion Dave Spikey did appear in the show, with huge success. Presley himself didn't want to get tied down to the commercial treadmill. He was still writing poetry, though, and on very rare occasions he would return to telly to perform. He finally accepted the invitation to take part in *Whine Gums*, BBC3's celebration of comic verse. Presley only really agreed because friends and contemporaries Steve Coogan and John Cooper Clarke were also on the bill but, as usual, Presley nailed it. And he stole it with one wonderful moment. A poetic short story: 'I met a girl who changed my life, I asked her if she'd be my wife. She said: "I already am. Will you stop drinking!"'

He was still writing such cutting, hilarious verse as late as 2004, when he delivered one of his most bitingly funny couplets in 'I've Bitten Off More Than You've Had Hot Dinners'. The poem itself isn't much longer: 'I once spent an evening with Lola or Layla. She said, Make me breathless. I hid her inhaler.'

Again, as with Jake Thackray, Presley returned to teaching for the last few years of his life, particularly relishing his role teaching comedy to drama students at Salford University. He would use his tact and influence to secure stand-up spots for his most promising students, at the new breed of North East clubs like the Frog and Bucket Comedy Club, and XS Malarkey, in Manchester. Though reluctant to perform at these venues himself, he would turn up to support his students. A true man of the people, Presley's idea of happiness was a pie and mash, a pint and a football match. Among his proudest achievements was when one of his students secured the job of match announcer for his beloved Bolton Wanderers.

The glorious thing about Presley's last years was that he really was happy – at long last. In the spring of 2005 he said: 'If I'd known life at forty-four could be this much fun, I wouldn't have spent so much of my teens worrying!' In May the same year he suffered a massive heart attack, and after six weeks in a coma, on 9 June, he died at the age of forty-four. To slightly misquote his own work: as good times go, he went.

TREAT YOURSELF TO Presley's exquisite collection *Poetic Off Licence* (Flapjack Press: 978-0-9932370-0-3, 2015). Funny, heartbreaking, and about as human and unique as you can get. And proceeds of this edition go to support the Hovis Presley Memorial Fund which, since being set up by Presley's family and friends in 2005, has raised over £18,000 for his favourite charities.

# Cardew Robinson

## 1917−92

I didn't enter 'showbiz' until relatively late in life – I was in my mid thirties. In 1979 my professional theatre engagement was a pantomime at the Nell Gwynne Theatre in Hereford. I clearly remember being overjoyed to be working alongside Cardew Robinson, whose adventures I had followed weekly in the *Radio Fun* comic many years previously. Above all, he was welcoming and helpful to me as a very green newcomer to the business. I spent quite a lot of time in his company between shows and had as much pleasure listening to his reminiscences of his life in variety as he evidently had reliving them for my entertainment.

One moment which has stayed with me concerns an incident during rehearsal; the show was *Aladdin* and Cardew was playing Widow Twankey. We were in the middle of a scene during which Aladdin (the lovely Linda Lou Allen) was being arrested by the Chinese policemen (myself and David Redgrave). On the spur of the moment, I ad-libbed, 'Here we go – another Chinese takeaway!' Cardew laughed and said,

'That's a great gag – I'm having it!', which he did for subsequent performances. I wasn't miffed – I was flattered. I didn't begrudge him in the least; he was always so good to me. He even took the trouble to write to me after the panto saying that those six weeks in Hereford had been a high spot in his career, having played dame for the first time – a part which he had always been scared to take on but which he was delighted to find he could play, and play it memorably he certainly did!

During the run of the show, I caught a nasty cold and completely lost my voice. Recalling how Chico and Harpo Marx used to communicate by whistling, my fellow Chinese policeman and I devised a scheme whereby I would whistle my lines and he would translate them into words. Proud of our plan, we went to Cardew's room to explain the idea. Less than ten seconds into our demonstration, Cardew leapt to his feet and summarily ejected us into the corridor! I had committed the cardinal theatrical sin: whistling in his dressing-room!

*Terry Pearson*

The year 1992 was something of a rites-of-passage one for me. Although I had already been trying to place my very first book *The Carry On Companion* with a publisher for several years, it was the year I started to actually make some headway. In the wake of Frankie Howerd's death, that April, I made my very first broadcast on BBC Radio. Shortly afterwards the cameras began to roll on *Carry On Columbus*, the first new *Carry On* film in fourteen years, and I was invited on to the set. It was also the year I attended my first show business bash. In October 1992 I found myself walking the streets of London towards the former home of Sid James. The Dead Comics Society were unveiling a blue plaque to the memory of my greatest comedy hero and I just had to be there.

Nearing the address where I had been asked to present myself, I spied a tall, albeit slightly stooped, old gentleman in a camel coat, strolling in the same general direction. Crossing to the same side of the road, I was able to tentatively look back to see who it was: none other than Cardew 'the Cad' Robinson!

In those days I was much younger and prettier, and certainly way out of his target audience – but there were two reasons that I knew who he was nonetheless. First, he had fairly recently recreated a snatch of his old comedy routine on the December 1987 Terry Wogan special *Wogan's Radio Fun*, which I had taped off of the telly and watched and re-watched hungrily; but even more importantly, he had been in a *Carry On* film. Although the part had been written for and offered to Tommy Cooper, it was Robinson who landed the guest-role of the Fakir in *Carry On... Up the Khyber* (1968). His outrageously bad variety act is one of the outstanding performances in a film packed with outstanding performances. Bernard Bresslaw's disgruntled: 'Fakir... off!' line is all the sweeter thanks to Cardew's pathetic attempts to entertain.

All of these thoughts and feelings raced through my brain as I thought, I've got to talk to him. So I slowed my walking to a snail's pace, allowed him to get parallel to me, stuck out my hand and said, like a sap: 'Mr Robinson, I'd just like to thank you for all the laughs you have given me.' The face of this old man lit up. He flashed me that trademark toothy grin, like dawn breaking in a graveyard, clutched my hand with a vice-like grip and said the immortal words: 'Cheers, son. I'm surprised you know who the fuck I am!'

Just over two months later, on 28 December 1992, the Cad was dead, at the age of seventy-five. His later years had been fairly fallow ones, and even when he did get work it was never the most glittering of assignments. The productions themselves may have been high-prestige, but simply being billed as a 'lawyer' in Roman Polanski's *Pirates* (1986) or a 'peasant' in Mel Damski's *A Connecticut Yankee in King Arthur's Court* (1989) was hardly going to worry BAFTA. Still, film director Lewis Gilbert cast him as Mr Londoner in *Shirley Valentine* (1989), one of his most memorable twilight appearances, while producer–director Alan J. W. Bell signed him up for 'Happy Anniversary Gough and Jessie', a November 1989 episode of *Last of the Summer Wine*. Robinson's central role, as Gough, proved that, even at over seventy, his skills for physical comedy and dial-a-gurn facial reactions were as efficient as ever. He ends the episode, drunk, in a skip, with a traffic cone atop his head, and merrily singing 'The Little Yorkshire Rose'. Joyous.

He had been born Douglas Robinson, on 14 August 1917, in Goodmayes, Essex, and started performing in school concerts while a pupil at Harrow County School. Already a towering beanpole, as a comically incongruous sight he effortlessly made his classmates laugh. It never occurred to him that he could make a living out of it, so he started work at a local newspaper, which inconveniently folded within weeks. Buying a copy of *The Stage*, he spotted an advert placed by comic and theatrical impresario Joe Boganny recruiting for his Crazy College Boys troupe. Robinson remembered the gang as 'a sort of downmarket

Fakir, off! With Terry Scott and Roy Castle in *Carry On... Up the Khyber*, Pinewood Studios, 1968.

Will Hay team. It consisted of Boganny himself and his dog, whose sole purpose was to walk across the stage with a false dog's head tied to its backside!'

As well as a dog, this acrobatic slapstick troupe often included midgets and, squeezing into his predecessor's tiny costume for this music hall revue, Robinson who had just one line. In response to Boganny's exclamation 'You're late. Where do you come from?', Robinson replied 'From a little place called Cookeroff.' Boganny would then hit Robinson on the head and get the pay-off with 'Well, you Cookeroff back again!' That's showbiz. By 1934, The Crazy College Boys were playing the Lyric Hammersmith and the Balham Hippodrome at the same time and on the same night. After the first house at the Lyric they would rush to the Hippodrome for two performances, before hot-footing it back toHammersmith for the second house!

At the outbreak of the Second World War, he joined the Royal Air Force and auditioned for Squadron Leader Ralph Reader's RAF Gang Shows concert party. Robinson was promoted to flight sergeant and put in charge of RAF Gang Show Unit Five, touring Britain, Belgium, Holland and the Far East.

It was in 1942 that Robinson launched his greatest comedy creation, Cardew the Cad of the School. The character was inspired by his boyhood obsession with *The Gem*, a weekly magazine that featured Charles Hamilton's hilarious stories from St Jim's school for boys. The majority of these stories were written by Charles Hamilton, using the pen-name of Martin Clifford, although he was best known as Frank Richards, the creator of Billy Bunter, and the St. Jim's wheezes were very much cut from the same cloth. Robinson's favourite character was the

Cardew the Cad of the School at the peak of his popularity in the 1950s.

sophisticated, no-good swine Ralph Reckless Cardew. With his long, striped scarf and that often demented, wildly grinning visage topped off with a little striped school cap, Robinson created a winning stage persona for himself.

After the war, he continued his association with Ralph Reader and toured with the RAF Gang Show managed by impresario Tom Arnold. A hit on radio's *Variety Bandbox*, Robinson became the show's resident comedian, as often as not adopting the school cap for the recordings, and enthralling listeners with his weekly bulletins: 'Here is the news from St Fanny's and this is Cardew the Cad reading it'. He created an entire population for the school, including the rotund headmaster Dr Jankers, the gluttonous schoolboy Fatty Gilbert and the overly protective Matron. The Cad himself was a kind of cross between Flashman and Terry-Thomas, an image emphasised with his favourite catchphrase: 'This is Cardew the Cad saying "Car-dew do...".' The character was so popular that the Douglas was formally relinquished in 1954 and he became Cardew Robinson for ever more.

The following year he scripted and starred in a feature-film vehicle for The Cad, *Fun at St Fanny's*. Perhaps one of the most treasured of the lowbrow but historically important productions from Adelphi Films, it was directed by veteran Maurice Elvey and recruited a gallery of comic grotesques and glamour girls. It was Cardew's only starring vehicle on the big screen. He did, however, notch up a glut of memorable supporting roles: he was part of Peter Sellers's trusted troupe of comic props and was cast as the shop steward in the Sellers films *I'm All Right Jack* (1959), as Midgley, the undertaker, in *Waltz of the Toreadors* (1962), a postman in *The Wrong Arm of the Law*, and a tramp in *Heavens Above!* (both, 1963). These amusing coughs and spits afforded Robinson the opportunity to flex his comedic muscles away from The Cad character. A lanky and lugubrious loon, he could be the fall guy or the punchline. Guaranteed a laugh on his first appearance, producers were swift to appreciate that Robinson could bring scene-stealing clout to even the tiniest of bit parts.

On television, Cardew left his mark in two episodes of *The Avengers* (as the minister in 'The £50,000 Breakfast', on 28 February 1968, and Mr Puffin in 'The Interrogators', on New Year's Day 1969) and on 25 March 1960 he had made a legendary contribution to *Hancock's Half Hour* as the only old comrade who hasn't changed a bit in 'The Reunion Party' (or has he?). He was also part of Spike Milligan's television team for *Milligan In Autumn* (BBC2, 1 October 1972), and *Q6* (BBC2, 1975): a happy band of brothers, including David Lodge and Peter Jones and John Wells [qv], who would plug into Spike's insanity and try to keep up with it.

From 19 August 1964 Robinson played King Pellinore in all 650 West End performances of Frederick Loewe's musical *Camelot*, at the Theatre Royal, Drury Lane; and he recorded a very inventive comedy album, *Cream of Cardew*, released on the Columbia label in 1967. It was a burst of activity that should have kept him at the top, but it just didn't happen for him. The title of his book *How to Be a Failure* (M & J Hobbs, 1970) was tinged with heavy irony.

However, veteran variety cachet granted him access to the poorly paid but now cult world of the British sex comedy. His little railway-ticket-collector song and exclamation of 'Sod it!' as he nips his finger in *What's Up Nurse!* (1977) still makes me laugh far more than it really should. I simply can't help myself; he just was a very funny man.

A rather delightful coda: Robinson's family are now largely based in Florida. His granddaughter, JoJo Sunshine, with her brother and his boyfriend, formed Bluejay, a band voted Miami's best in 2015. Their cousin, the son of Cardew's daughter Lindy, is the successful rapper Wrekonize. Fancy that!

TREAT YOURSELF TO the recently polished-up and revived classic *The Adelphi Collection: Fun at St Fanny's* (BFI: B0058OL8FY, 2011), for it is, for better or for worse, a film that has Robinson's hands all over it. Just before his death he introduced a very rare screening of it at the Museum of London, and more recently it was screened at the National Film Theatre. He would never have believed it.

# Joe E. Ross

## 1914–82

The man's appalling eating habits were legendary. A big slob. He was eating and he looked up at me and he had stuff all over him. He said: 'I am much better with solid foods.' He was exactly what he played on television.

*Norm Crosby*

Despite being the equally billed co-star of the classic early 1960s situation comedy *Car 54, Where Are You?*, Joe E. Ross is less known and certainly less respected than his colleague. For example, take the beginning of *Twilight Zone: The Movie* (1983), one of my all-time favourite opening scenes. In it, a bored motorist, played by Albert Brooks, and his hitch-hiking passenger, played by Dan Aykroyd, endure a monotonously long car journey through a thick fog and an awkward silence. To lift their spirits, they play 'TV themes': each hums or la-las a telly tune and the other has to guess what the show is. When Dan Aykroyd does the theme to *Car 54, Where Are You?*, he adds the clue 'Fred Gwynne was in it' – not Joe E. Ross, but Fred Gwynne.

If Ross is remembered for anything at all, it's for being a complete schmuck on the set of *Car 54*. His arrogant attitude and disregard towards properly learning his great swathes of delirious dialogue drove creative genius, producer, and chief writer Nat Hiken to such distraction that he almost had a nervous breakdown. The 'Ooh! Ooh!' that Joe E. Ross became most famous for was born of his stalling for time while he desperately tried to recall his next line. The 'Ooh! Ooh!' could signify pain, or pleasure, or indeed panic, and so popular did the exclamation became that scriptwriters would add it for an assured laugh of familiarity. Still, apparently Ross was not only an unreliable performer but he was also an unpleasant man whose bad manners and messy habits repelled all of the other cast members. By the start of the second series, Ross had almost got himself sacked. Hiken, it seems, had an eye on the supporting actor Al Lewis, proving popular as Officer Leo Schnauser on the show, as the perfect candidate to take over as Gwynne's co-star. As the wide-mouthed, angst-ridden Schnauzer, Lewis had had several episodes centred around him. The contrast with the towering Gwynne was similar to that with Ross, too; for Hiken, Lewis was a godsend. An actor who knew his lines!

Ross heard rumours of his imminent dismissal and broke down in tears in front of Hiken. He wept about the lack of work he was facing and the need for money. It was probably the best acting performance he ever gave, although, truth be told, he did need the money. A heavy gambling habit, boozing sessions and a love of chorus girls and strippers – who he would nonchalantly bring on to the *Car 54, Where Are You?* set at the Biograph Studios in the Bronx, claiming them as 'advisors' – all certainly ate away at his earnings.

Hiken gave in and Ross remained for the rest of that second series – but it was the last. Despite winning an Emmy Award for Outstanding Directorial Achievement in the May of 1962, the situation with Ross was losing Hiken respect with the bosses at NBC. Moreover, the station only offered Hiken a third series as long as he agreed to them buying part ownership of the format. He refused, siding with the show's sponsors, Proctor and Gamble, in an attempt to place it with CBS. They had no suitable time slot available. Thus, coupled with the Joe E. Ross headache, Hiken shelved the show if favour of new projects. None were forthcoming and Hiken died a disillusioned and broken man, just five years later.

It had been Hiken who had catapulted Ross into the big time in the first place. Born Joseph Roszawikz, on 15 March 1914, on the Lower East Side of New York, Ross had started his career as a singing waiter in the Bronx, performing to the very lowest of common denominators, with lowbrow humour in the lowest-brow strip clubs. As a writer, Hiken had an ear for natural dialogue and as a producer he wanted that dialogue spoken by real people. That vaudevillian Catherine wheel Phil Silvers was at the very peak of his powers as Sergeant Ernie Bilko, but the supporting cast of *The Phil Silvers Show* (CBS, 1955–59) is awash with non-actors who became stars through Hiken's words. Ross was one of them. While in Miami to cast the show's second season, Hiken spotted Ross doing his stand-up routine and duly cast him as ramshackle army camp chef Mass Sergeant Rupert Ritzik. Ross stayed with the show until the bitter end, in 1959.

Just before finding this fame on television, Ross had teamed up with another comedian, Dave Starr, who was, if anything, even more lowbrow than himself. The duo's slapdash vaudevillian shtick is immortalised in the 1955 film *Teaserama*, a glorious record of Bettie Page's extraordinary burlesque routines too.

*The Phil Silvers Show* was exactly what Ross needed. He had dallied with films in Hollywood before but these had been no more than bit parts. Perhaps the best was his very first, in *The Sound of Fury* (1950), which cast him as a nightclub entertainer. It was pretty much his usual act, but cleaned up for the masses. Still, in 1956, television was king and *Bilko* was reigning supreme. It gave him regular money and plenty of female company, which amounted to the same thing for Ross. It is alleged that all eight of his wives were ex-prostitutes, simply because it was cheaper to marry them than to hire their services!

Countless stories have been told about Ross turning up on set in a dishevelled state. His clothes would be covered in food (he was the messiest eater in the business), his breath would smell of booze, his skin marinated in the cheap perfume of his latest squeeze. Worst of all, his memory for lines was atrocious. His brain was numb with excess, so how could he expect to deliver a performance as well? But deliver he did, and Hiken remained in love with that lived-in face, whisky-stained voice and the truthfulness of a slob from the slums.

This wasn't acting. It was reality. Method without thought.

The amount of dialogue he had to learn for *Bilko* was as nothing when compared with *Car 54, Where Are You?*, however. Naturally, Phil Silvers himself had taken the brunt of the workload, but when Hiken cast Ross and another *Bilko* refugee, Fred Gwynne, to take the leads in his new series, it was allegedly a recipe for disaster. However, I take exception to this commonly held opinion. Sure, Ross wasn't the best actor in the world, but you believed him; more than that – you actually loved him.

The NYPD's less than finest: Gwynne and Ross as reluctant partners Muldoon and Toody, in *Car 54*.

Officer Toody was the childish idiot struggling with a job he couldn't do, often breaking the laws he was employed to uphold, and living with an overbearing wife, Lucille (played by Beatrice Pons), who continually put him down. So he was a slob who preferred to go tenpin bowling or watch television to conversing. So what? He was a real character and, as such, a pioneering figure in American television comedy.

When *Car 54* came to an end, however, Ross went back to the nightclubs. The difference was that now he had fame. He would walk out in his stage suit carrying the police cap he had worn as Officer Gunther Toody for sixty half-hours. He would tell tall tales of his time on the show. He even recorded an album, *Love Songs From a Cop*, which was released on the Columbia label in 1965 and showcased heartfelt covers of such favourites as 'My Melancholy Baby', 'It Had To Be You', and 'Are You Lonesome Tonight?'.

Ross's return to television, in 1966, was in the lead comic role at last. It was an odd era on the box. Sitcoms could be based around aliens or talking animals. They could even be populated by Universal creature-feature wannabes – witness his *Car 54* buddies Fred Gwynne and Al Lewis in *The Munsters*. The

*It's About Time* threw astronauts into prehistoric times, with Imogene Coca and Joe E. Ross as Shag and Gronk!

weird-concept show for Ross was *It's About Time* (CBS, 1966–67), created by producer Sherwood Schwartz, already with a hit on his hands at CBS with *Gilligan's Island*. *It's About Time* cast Ross as Gronk, a bumbling caveman who encounters modern-day astronauts transported back in time. Blessed with a face fit for gurning and an aggressive sense of physical comedy, Ross shone in the show, but it was a flop and lasted just the one season of twenty-six episodes.

Ironically, for such a bum, Ross found a niche in the films of Walt Disney. He had bits as a detective in *The Love Bug* (1968), and as a nutty sailor in *The Boatniks* (1970). However, 'The Mouse Factory' soon lost Ross to the relentlessly productive sausage machine of Hanna-Barbera. It was that distinctive gravel-voice that really paid his bills. His television trademark exclamation of 'Ooh! Ooh!' was beautifully deployed for the lame-brained Botch in *Help!... It's the Hair Bear Bunch* (CBS, 1971–72), and for the knuckle-headed Sergeant Flint in *Hong Kong Phooey* (ABC, 1974). He even reprised Officer Toody himself for 'Car 54', the very last episode of *Wait Till Your Father Gets Home*, on 8 October 1974. In the animated universe Officer Toody is still a New York cop, a decade after the original, live-action series ended, and now he's looking to earn a little money on the side with a childcare business: with the expected hilarious consequences.

All this family entertainment didn't stop Ross doing his dirty stand-up material, however, and in 1973 he recorded an album on the notorious Laff Records label charmingly called *Should Lesbians Be Allowed to Play 'Pro' Football?*. As with his previous recordings, the cover featured him in his policeman's outfit, though it was ten years since his greatest success had ended. In the mid 1970s Ross eagerly took the meal ticket from coughs and spits in such exploitation epics as *Linda Lovelace for President* (1975), *The Happy Hooker Goes to Washington* (1977), and *Gas Pump Girls* (1979).

Phil Silvers visits his old *Bilko* buddies Fred Gwynne and Joe E. Ross on the set of *Car 54, Where Are You?*. Nat Hiken, creative genius of both shows, seems delighted to have him back. Between seasons, in June 1962, Ross and Gwynne had starred in the creepy comic romp 'Seven Keys to Baldpate' for the *Du Pont Show of the Week*.

Show business mythology says that Ross died on the job – in the theatre, that is. Living at the time in a housing complex in Hollywood, he was hired to play two houses of a particularly shoddy nightclub on 13 August 1982, for a fee of just $100. Straight after completing the first set, Ross clutched at his heart, sat on the edge of the stage, and died. His widow, attempting to get his fee to pay for the funeral expenses, was given just the fifty bucks Ross had earned for the first show.

His gravestone has the last laugh, though. Along with only his name and the years he lived, it simply reads: 'This man had a ball.'

TREAT YOURSELF TO *Car 54, Where Are You? – The Complete Second Season* (Shanachie: B006UI5ARY, 2012). Not only is it a happy, healthy wedge of thirty classic half-hours of comedy, but the bonus feature is a ten-minute televised recording of Ross's stand-up routine, complete with dreadful jokes, tales from Hollywood and a mightily fine impression of Wallace Beery in *The Champ*. Ooh! Ooh!

# Patsy Rowlands

## 1931–2005

I worked with Patsy Rowlands when I was recording the series *In Loving Memory* in 1982. Patsy played the part of Tiger-Lily Longstaff and the part required the two of us to share a brief embrace. As usual when recording scenes like this, we were both rather awkward and skirted around it until Patsy suddenly said to me under her breath: 'What the hell. I'm game if you are!' With that she seized me by the lapels and gave me a full-on snog. I hadn't expected that and clearly neither had the director, Ronnie Baxter, who was rendered speechless and forgot to say 'cut'. When we finally surfaced for air he said, 'That'll do.' Needless to say, we didn't need a retake.

*Christopher Beeny*

If we can stretch a point just slightly, and you count Patsy Rowlands' cut-and-paste contribution in vintage clips within the compilation film *That's Carry On* (1977), then one can conclude that she made the exact same number of *Carry On* films as Barbara Windsor. However, while Barbara is the iconic bubbly blonde forever linked to that saucy seaside-postcard world, poor old Patsy Rowlands is hardly ever mentioned. In truth, between 1969 and 1975 Rowlands chalked up nine appearances in the film series. In all that time she missed just one film, but her name made it on to only one of the posters, and disappointingly that happy, smiling face of hers was never caricatured alongside the rest of the gang for the promotional campaigns. Not once.

The one film that actually gave her a poster roll call was *Carry On Girls*, the twenty-fifth film in the series, shot at Pinewood Studios and on location in Brighton in the spring of 1973. Certainly, the role – that of the bored, slovenly wife of Mayor Kenneth Connor – was one of her very finest. Dressed in a crumpled blue dressing gown, with a cigarette almost permanently drooping from the side of her mouth and her transistor radio continually blasting out pop music, this was the frumps of Donald McGill or the matriarchs of Giles made flesh.

Rowlands was particularly effective opposite the flared nostrils of Kenneth Williams. In *Carry On Loving* (1970), for example, she transforms herself from dour, humourless housekeeper to a split-skirted, make-up-heavy vamp in order to scupper the romantic advances of Hattie Jacques towards her beloved employer.

Like that other neglected prop of the series, Peter Butterworth, Rowlands was grateful just to be in the team and would happily take on any role, however small. Even to these cough-and-spit parts she always brought sincerity and truth. Witness her role as the ill-fated Queen of Henry VIII (Sid James) in *Carry On Henry* (1971), where she is led to the guillotine by an overly jovial Terry Scott while Kenneth Williams brays and minces around on the sidelines. Only Rowlands remains calm and serene. Her performance could have come straight from a serious BBC production, and that is what was needed. The actual comedy of the scene is in safe hands. Rowlands brings acting dignity to the sequence and, as a result, defuses any hint of bad taste.

It should come as no surprise, then, that when Rowlands graduated from the Guildhall School of Speech and Drama she attained the highest marks in the country. Having made her stage debut in a touring production of the musical *Annie Get Your Gun* in 1951, her landmark role was as Thetis Tooke in *Valmouth*,

The Peter Rogers repertory company, on location at St. Peter's Church, Burnham, Buckinghamshire, for the *Bless This House* film, 1972.

a Sandy Wilson musical based on the novel by Ronald Firbank. Rowlands stopped the show with her number 'I Loved A Man' and stayed with the production when it transferred to the Saville Theatre in 1959.

The darling of the in-crowd, she was cast as Sylvia Groomkirby in N. F. Simpson's surrealist play *One Way Pendulum*, which opened at the Royal Court Theatre, on 22 December 1959 before transferring to the Criterion Theatre the following June. From 5 December 1962 Patsy again took to the stage of the Saville Theatre, as Avril Hadfield opposite Laurence Olivier in David Turner's *Semi-Detached* for director Tony Richardson.

Her early film roles included several high-prestige pictures, such as John Schlesinger's *A Kind of Loving* (1962) and Tony Richardson's *Tom Jones* (1963), with her saucy young Honor energetic, fresh and strong within that juicy and ribald framework. Much of her career would be juicy and ribald.

Patsy was well aware of her natural, girl-next-door looks. She was all too often cast in the wallflower role: the dowdy friend of the leading lady or the troublesome sister who no one wants to marry. Whether it was opposite Norman Wisdom in *A Stitch in Time* (1963) or alongside Gudrun Ure as children's telly heroine Supergran (in 'Supergran and the Course of True Love', 3 February 1985), this was Rowlands's destiny.

The 1970s was something of a boom decade. She had joined the *Carry On* team, as Kenneth Williams's long-suffering secretary in *Carry On Again, Doctor* in the Spring of '69, and eighteen months later was cast as Sid James's next-door neighbour Betty in *Bless This House* (Thames Television, 1971–76); when the *Carry On* chaps made the film version, Rowlands was a shoo-in. Sally Geeson, who played Sid's daughter, Sally, remembers, 'It was already a wonderfully happy cast, and when Patsy signed up it was clear from the start she was going to be a joy to work with. She would throw her head back and laugh her head off in the rehearsal room, and she had such an infectious laugh. The part of Betty required a dry, somewhat straight-faced delivery which Patsy was absolutely superb at. She was fun, funny; she didn't need to work at it. Sid often commented on her great talent. He wept tears when he really laughed, and he would pull his hankie from his pocket to wipe his eyes. Sid thought so highly of her, he would pop his arm around her shoulder and praise her. You would often see them both chatting away like the good friends they were.' This mutual respect is tangible on screen. Within the series it is a hate-hate

As Mildred Bumble, transformed from cynical slob to bra-burning feminist in *Carry On Girls*, 1973.

relationship, with Sid milking huge laughs from his sarcastic reactions. Whether it's Betty's continual cadging of sugar or soap powder, or her nagging of her man, Trevor (played by Anthony Jackson), Patsy brings a miserable misanthropy to the table that lifts Sid's comedy into orbit.

*The Galton and Simpson Comedy* episode 'An Extra Bunch of Daffodils' (London Weekend Television, 24 May 1969), was another plum part, with Rowlands playing the sweetly duplicitous Mrs Evans opposite Stratford Johns, while the *George & Mildred* episode 'The Twenty-Six Year Itch', for Christmas Day 1979, indulged her in typically joyous domestic situation comedy shenanigans. As well as her gallery of roles in the *Carry On* films, she also appeared in just one episode – but one of the best – of the television series *Carry On Laughing*, 'The Nine Old Cobblers' (ATV, 8 February 1975). A less-than-subtle variation on the Lord Peter Wimsey story *The Nine Tailors*, it starred series favourites Jack Douglas and Kenneth Connor as bulging detectives Lord Peter Flimsy and his man Punter. Patsy Rowlands was the endearingly naive Miss Dawkins, caught up in the murderous goings-on concerning a bell that forewarns death. And it's funny!

With Christopher Beeny in *In Loving Memory*: 'They Shoot Undertakers Don't They?', Yorkshire TV, 27 February 1982.

In 1975 alone Patsy notched up turns opposite top telly titter-providers Frankie Howerd (as Clementina in *A Touch of the Casanovas*, Thames Television, New Year's Eve 1975), Les Dawson (as a diligent Post Office clerk in the *Dawson's Weekly* episode 'All Pools Day', Yorkshire Television, 8 July 1975), Hylda Baker (as Clarissa Cholmondeley-Burnside in the *Not On Your Nellie* episode 'High Society', London Weekend Television, 31 January 1975) and even that foxy comic legend Basil Brush and Mr Roy North in *The Basil Brush Show* (BBC1, 18 October 1975).

In the 1980s Patsy supported Thora Hird in the Dick Sharples-scripted Salvation Army situation comedy *Hallelujah!* (Yorkshire, 1983–84), played the befuddled Netta Kinvig opposite Tony Haygarth in Nigel Kneale's sci-fi sitcom *Kinvig* (London Weekend Television, 1981), and enjoyed one of her favourite jobs as Thelma, the cheerful and caring confidante to Dick Emery and Barry Evans [both, qv] in *Emery Presents... Legacy of Murder* (BBC1, 1982). Later BBC television comedy roles ranged from the anarchic (*Bottom*, the 'Parade' episode, BBC2, 22 October 1992) to the traditional (Ray Galton and John Antrobus's *Get Well Soon*, BBC1, 1997), while she popped up in such popular BBC costume romps as *Vanity Fair* (1998), *The Canterbury Tales* ( 2000), and *The Cazalets* (2001).

Onstage she was the Duchess in Mike Ockrent's 1986 production of *Me and My Girl* at the Adelphi Theatre, was directed by Lindsay Anderson in *The March on Russia* at the National's Lyttelton Theatre in 1989, and played the housekeeper in Cameron Mackintosh's 1994 revival of *Oliver!* at the London Palladium, enjoying a lengthy run opposite a glut of fine Fagins from Jonathan Pryce to Jim Dale. From 1997 she played Mrs Potts the teapot in the stage version of Walt Disney's *Beauty and the Beast* at the Criterion Theatre, and was back at the National, excelling as Mrs Pearce in Cameron Mackintosh's 2002 revival of

*My Fair Lady*. Her energetic participation in the 'I Could Have Danced All Night' number regularly stopped the show. At the time of her death, from cancer, on 22 January 2005, just three days after her seventy-fourth birthday, her long-time agent Simon Beresford said: 'She never complained, particularly when she was ill. Patsy was of the old school.'

Rowlands was as endearingly sweet and as ever-so-slightly naive as many of her characters, and could often be bullied and sent up by far less talented and experienced members of a cast simply because she was sneered at as a *Carry On* person. Despite this, her dignity and good humour stood firm, and her affection and pride for the *Carry On* films stood firm too.

Happily, she lived to see her part in the *Carry On* legacy re-evaluated and celebrated during film festivals at such bastions of popular culture as the National Film Theatre and the Barbican Centre; as well as

One of the very best. Signed to the author. The accompanying letter, reflecting on the joy of filming with Dick Emery and Barry Evans, apologised for the handwriting. Patsy's son had borrowed her best pen to do his homework!

taking part in audio commentary recordings for three of her films, for DVD release. Never malicious and always the consummate professional, Patsy's place in the *Carry On* hall of fame is secure. Because of the *Carry Ons*, and not in spite of the *Carry Ons*, she must also be remembered as one of our very finest comedy actors.

TREAT YOURSELF TO *Carry On Girls* (ITVDVD: 5037115038135, 2003), undoubtedly Patsy's finest contribution to the *Carry On* series. At turns sarcastic and spirited, it's a performance of depth, adding real emotion to this tail-end *Carry On*. This special edition DVD also features Rowlands, June Whitfield and Jack Douglas on an audio commentary track, allowing you to spend a full eighty-five minutes in her company – something I was delighted to do as the moderator of the recording, and several more times within and without the *Carry On* series. Joyous, raucous times, each and every one.

# Derek Roy

## 1922–81

The great enabler. A catalyst for comedy.

*Barry Took*

It's fair to say that Derek Roy is one of the most pivotal and important heroes residing in the pages of this book. Without him the careers of arguably the most influential movers and shakers of British comedy may never have got kick-started.

Already a variety comedian of renown by his early twenties, Roy toured the music halls, performed summer seasons of variety, and became a popular mainstay of pantomime. Indeed, his celebrated run as Buttons in *Cinderella* at The Regal, Edmonton, for the season of 1947–48, which he also produced, proved so popular that BBC Television ran it as a live event over two consecutive nights, 30 December and New Year's Eve, 1947. The production was life-changing for Roy, for two reasons. Firstly, it introduced Roy to his wife Rona Ricardo, who was wowing the audience as Dandini, and secondly it led to BBC Radio signing him up for his own starring vehicle on the Light Programme. First broadcast on 5 October 1949, *Hip-Hip-Hoo-Roy!* was a wonderfully puntastic title heralding the star comedian as 'Doctor Roy – the Melody Boy' for a pioneering collection of sketches, one-liners and monologues, largely written by Bob Monkhouse and Denis Goodwin. Supported by regular guest-comics such as Alfred Marks and Robert Moreton [qv] and musical interludes from Cherry Lind, and the Stargazers, Roy was able to develop his playful use of radio, with a chatty, intimate style which fully connected with the audience tuning in at home. Roy also used the series to surreptitiously drop in often near-the-knuckle, and abstract comedy.

Most importantly of all, Roy's *Hip-Hip-Hoo-Roy!* gave a very early writing opportunity for a young ex-gunner by the name of Spike Milligan. Despite being four years Roy's senior, Milligan was very much the minion in this situation, and energetically and gratefully took the opportunity, slipping in madcap anarchy with alacrity. Milligan even enjoyed the odd appearance on the show, launching the embryonic loon that would become the slow-witted Eccles – freewheeling surrealism in a variety straitjacket. With Goon catalyst Jimmy Grafton also on *Hip-Hip-Hoo-Roy!*'s writing team, *The Goon Show* was literally round the next corner.

With *Hip-Hip-Hoo-Roy!* proving popular the BBC gave Derek Roy another show. On paper, and with hindsight, *Happy Go Lucky* was a failure. If anything, it's a footnote in history of how not to build up a comedy star. First broadcast on 2 August 1951 and vaguely structured as a 'light-hearted blend of comedy and music', the format was never fully agreed upon, the personnel came and went like shifting sands, and the star's determination to leave his mark all but scuppered his relationship with the humourless bigwigs at the Corporation. However, it was Derek Roy who, later in that 1951 run of *Happy Go Lucky*, had picked up two chums, Ray Galton and Alan Simpson (who had met in the Milford tuberculosis sanatorium). The comedy writing appeal of the two was based purely – or impurely – on Roy's love of a joke they had written about a fictional game called 'Jane Russell Pontoon' (the same as ordinary pontoon 'but you need 38 to bust!'). So impressed was he that Roy signed them up as his personal joke-writers for *Happy Go Lucky*. A recurring skit they wrote for the show, the 'Eager Beavers', cast all sorts of young men destined for comedy immortality, though none more so than Tony Hancock. The all-conquering

THE CONGRESS THEATRE, EASTBOURNE

Duncan C Weldon & Louis I. Michaels
For Triumph Theatre Production Ltd
PRESENT

ANITA HARRIS
as
Dick Whittington
WITH GUEST STAR
DORA BRYAN

DEREK     KEN
ROY       ROBERTS

ROBERT MARLOWE    NINA BROWN
AND
HARRY H. CORBETT
AS ALDERMAN FITZWARREN

Directed by Robert Marlowe
Choreography by Denise Shaune   Written by John Morley
Musical Director Trevor York   Fights arranged by Ian McKay

Derek gave his Dame in a thigh-slappingly good cast, 27 December 1976 to 29 January 1977.

triumvirate of Galton, Simpson and Hancock would, within the space of a couple of years, redefine radio comedy for a generation and set the highest of standards for situation comedy for eternity. The fact is, without Derek Roy and *Happy Go Lucky*, the three may never have met.

Roy's entire career seems defined by his talent as a conduit for other people. Although Roy was the star turn and long-term master of ceremonies on radio's *Variety Bandbox*, if that show is remembered at all today, it is, again, as an early playground for future legends such as Morecambe and Wise, or Frankie Howerd. But it was Roy's almost clinical knowledge of the mechanics of a good joke well told that acted as the cement of *Variety Bandbox*. From 1951 Roy was also a regular fixture on *Variety Ahoy!* – another showcase for singers and comics which, if remembered at all today, fits in place as an important, early cog in the comedy career of Dick Emery [qv].

These radio variety shows capture the essence of Derek Roy's comic charm. He had a winning personality that effortlessly outshone his rather nondescript appearance. In the nicest possible way, he was perfect for radio. While he looked like the branch manager of a sleepy village bank, his personality could power a small city.

That said, he did become something of a familiar face in the 1950s. He chalked up a notable appearance – as himself – in the film *Come Dance With Me* (1950), directed by Mario Zampi [qv], alongside Max Wall and a handful of other radio personalities including Anne Shelton and *The Third Man*'s zither score composer and player Anton Karas. Most intriguing of all, Roy's presence was considered enough of an attraction for him to join the rank and file for ITV's launch night on 22 September 1955. Throughout the decade Roy continued to pop up on television and stage, although those he had undoubtedly helped up the ladder had long ago usurped him in popularity. He returned to pantomime for a large-scale New Year's Eve 1960 television presentation of *Aladdin* from the Scala Theatre, this time giving his dame, Widow Twankey, opposite headlining Irving Davies and larger-than-life Alfred Marks as Abanazar.

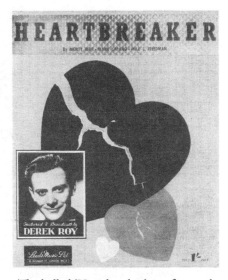

The ballad 'Heartbreaker' was featured in many of Derek's late forties radio broadcasts, sending the song up the sheet music chart.

After that and apart from the odd call for more Panto duties, Roy became something of a forgotten man. By the time cancer finally took him, some twenty years later, on 15 March 1981 – while Derek was still a relatively young man, at the age of fifty-nine – his death barely warranted a mention. Now, another forty years on, though his legacy has faded to near dust, Roy's skill, kindness and wisdom in noticing and nurturing the comic talents of others demands celebration. It's no hyperbolic boast to say that without him the landscape of British comedy today would be very different indeed.

TREAT YOURSELF TO Derek Roy's recording of 'Oh! You Beautiful Doll' (Oriole: CB1410, 1957), a lovely rendition of the standard, with the rather intense 'Liechtensteiner Polka' on the B-side. Even a scant six minutes of recorded whimsy is enough to show what the great man could do.

# Derek Royle

## 1928–90

I did the TV series of *Hogg's Back* with Derek Royle in 1975. It used to be shown at around 5 p.m. on a Monday. He played a very accident-prone character called Dr Hogg and I was his assistant, Pearl. Each week we travelled through disastrous events which involved falling into ponds, crashing into things and, once, driving into the back of a removal van and being driven away!

Derek was huge fun to work with. He was very energetic – and a trained acrobat! He taught me how to fall or faint on a particular spot for the camera. I was pregnant with my second son during the series and became rather large, so had to be filmed just looking out of windows, or round doors, so that my rather large tummy couldn't be seen!

*Jacki Piper*

There are certain supple persons of yoga or circus or dance who, even in their dotage, can perform feats of athletic, even balletic, dexterity to leave a teenager gaping. One such person was Derek Royle, a performer of true genius. He was slight of status, prematurely bald, with a near-permanently perplexed expression, but Lord, how he could fall down! As a spontaneous master of slapstick and of physical clowning, Royle was of the Keaton class. He really was that good.

His was a talent born of years of practice and pratfalls, pain and perfection. He was so good at falling down, at expertly extracting every single laugh from the most mundane, relentless physical business, that that expert farceur Brian Rix utilised his talents at every opportunity, making Royle a staple of his hugely successful, long-running farces staged at the Whitehall Theatre. Royle's characters were often absent-minded and distracted professional men, and the sheer force of his slapstick skill made every movement a thing of comic beauty. His ability to take a tumble and roll straight back into action was as second nature to him, and performing eight shows a week, year after year, only sharpened his talents.

By the time television embraced Rix's trouser-dropping roustabouts, Royle was at the peak of his game, chalking up several appearances in *Brian Rix Presents...*, as Sidney Pudney in 'Keep Your Wig On', on 19 April 1968; the accident-prone waiter in 'Clutterbuck', on 22 July 1970; and Herr Winkelkopf in 'Lord Arthur Savile's Crime', on 25 September 1970. These prestigious Rix productions showcased an untouchable force of nature, and the association led to regular work in 1972's *Six With Rix*.

By the time the sixties had started to swing to a psychedelic beat, Royle's timeless art of mime, mayhem, and self-mockery had already made him something of a legend, and he was cast in the ambitious Beatles love-in travelogue *Magical Mystery Tour* (1967). Royle's Jolly Jimmy is both cheerful and sinister, rather like one of those old-time amusement arcade dolls laughing hollowly at everything and anything. He has an air of carefree holiday fun about him but plays the role with a sense of otherness too; a sort of disconcerting pantomime Wazir.

Royle happily lent his considerable talents to the greater glory of others over the years, including Tommy Cooper (in the 'Getting a TV Show' episode of *Life with Cooper*, ABC TV, 21 January 1967), Dick Emery (*The Dick Emery Show*, BBC1, 4 October 1975), and Benny Hill (*The Benny Hill Show*, Thames Television, 2 January & 27 May 1985).

As Will Kempe in John Mortimer's *Will Shakespeare*, 1978.

In the 12 March 1979 *Fawlty Towers* episode 'The Kipper and the Corpse', Royle's humble and sweetly pathetic performance as Mr Leeman – soon to become the deceased in the title – at once gives charm and pathos to the black humour with a meek performance that expertly counterbalances the disgruntled turn of the kipper-craving doctor played by Geoffrey Palmer. It is testament both to the quality of that John Cleese–Connie Booth script and to the unselfish pratfalling of regular Andrew Sachs that the Basil/Manuel/Leeman equation adds up so perfectly.

From the start of his television career (with appearances in the ITV medical soap *Emergency – Ward 10*, in 1963, and *The Wednesday Play* 'The End of Arthur's Marriage', BBC1, 17 November 1965) to its tail end (with roles in *A Dorothy L. Sayers Mystery* 'Strong Poison', BBC2, 25 March 1987, and *The Bill* episode 'Traffic', Thames Television, 11 July 1989), Royle was given interesting, albeit small, opportunities in television drama. None suited him more so than his featured role as the workhouse registrar in *Wonderworks: Young Charlie Chaplin* (Thames, 1989). If anyone could bring the spontaneous spirit of silent comedy to this Emmy-award-nominated children's television favourite, it was Royle. The part was a straight one, of course, but the essence of the clown within was palpable.

Undoubtedly Royle's finest television role was as the unemployable doctor, Horace Hogg, mistakenly assigned for general practice and slapstick hilarity in *Hogg's Back* (Southern Television, 1975–76). Running for nineteen episodes over three series, the show was effectively Royle's own comedy lexicon – a playground for his tried-and-tested comedy moves, allowing him to fall down at every opportunity and muddle his way through hilarious misadventures in motor cars, shopping centres and camping sites. It was the perfect vehicle for him, and included Jacki Piper as support in the first seven episodes, with Wendy Richard coming in as replacement stooge Colette – although, in his muddled way, Dr. Hogg still calls her 'Pearl' – for the rest of the first series. The comedy dynamic shifted slightly in series two, with Pat Coombs drafted in as housekeeper Mrs Mac. She proved equally as skilled as Piper and Richard had been in the position of Derek Royle's slapstick companion. Frustratingly, this near-perfect knockabout collection of comic business for all the family remains almost as forgotten as

Derek met Jane Shortt during their days with the Yeovil Repertory Company, in 1953. They married three months later.

Royle himself. Written by Michael Pertwee, and with splendid comedy turns – including Robert Dorning, Michael Ripper, Sam Kydd and Reg Lye – strolling in for the occasional scene-stealing guest-spot, it deserves celebration. During the first scene of the fifth episode, Royle is hit on the head by a falling painting, flamboyantly tripped up onto a bouncy mattress, and proceeds to climb up the wrong side of a ladder. He eventually ends up in a wicker basket with a skeleton. It was that kind of show. Gloriously so.

Ironically, it was in a role forever associated with another actor that Royle ended his days. By the February of 1989, 'Allo, 'Allo had been running for five series and had made something of a star of Jack Haig. The son of music hall performers Bertha Baker and Charles Coppin, Haig had richly enjoyed an Indian summer as the outrageously amorous Monsieur Roger Leclerc, whose reveal from an easily penetrated disguise – with the line 'It is I, Leclerc' – became one of the most eagerly awaited catchphrases in a show awash with eagerly awaited catchphrases. Following Haig's death in July 1989, and with the sixth series pending, David Croft picked up the phone to Derek Royle; he was a good fifteen years younger than Haig but had long been playing characters beyond his years. Alas, Royle was not a well man. By the time his first episode, 'The Ghost of René', had been transmitted on 2 September 1989, he was already suffering from the cancer that floored him the following January. Indeed, his

Derek was one of the few select people that Ringo allowed to try out his precious drum kit, during the making of *Magical Mystery Tour*, at West Malling Airfield, 1967.

association with *'Allo, 'Allo* lasted just eight episodes, with the series returning with the third and final Leclerc, Robin Parkinson, almost exactly a year after Royle's death on 23 January 1990.

It was a rather ignoble last hurrah, for the part was forever associated with Jack Haig and each successive incumbent of the role was only ever an understudy mirroring the moves of the master.

Still, Royle's legacy is rich indeed. It's a heritage cherished and upheld by his actress daughters Carol and Amanda Royle. Undoubtedly one of the finest and funniest physical clowns you are ever likely to see, Derek's work remains a blueprint for how to be a slapstick comedian. Students of comedy, take note.

TREAT YOURSELF TO the political romp *Don't Just Lie There, Say Something!* (Strawberry Media: B01E4AMID8, 2016). Derek Royle excels as that decrepit and inept and troublesome 'Watchdog of British Politics' the Right Honourable Wilfred Potts. Not only is the film a priceless record of his physical slapstick grace opposite Brian Rix, but it's non-stop laughter: every short-sighted misunderstanding and comedy trip is sheer poetry.

# Sabrina

## 1936–2016

Askey loved her. Hancock loved her. We all loved her. She was stunning-looking, of course, but she was funny too. With a genuine instinct of what would and would not get her a laugh.

*Alan Simpson OBE*

The fifties was the golden era of the blonde bombshell. While America had Marilyn Monroe and Jayne Mansfield and Mamie Van Doren, Britain had Diana Dors and Vera Day and... Sabrina.

This vision of loveliness first came to my attention via my healthy appetite for 1980s reruns of Arthur Askey films on television. Suddenly, within the knockabout chaos of comedies like *Ramsbottom Rides Again* (1956) and *Make Mine a Million* (1959), there emerged this gorgeous goddess with a whistle-worthy figure and a twinkle in her eye.

And then the BBC screened *Blue Murder at St Trinian's* (1957), and I was well and truly smitten. There was my Sabrina, in a wordless, sexy cameo, wearing a slightly

Reunited with Arthur Askey, years after their 50s hey-day, and still displaying the charms that made the name Sabrina synonymous with glamour.

revealing negligee, tucked up in bed with a study book, as Virginia the school swot. Beautiful *and* smart. Within the film's plot, the Pride of the Force were completely distracted from their duties. I could totally relate. And it was made just twenty odd years before. Not *that* long ago.

Then my dad dropped the happy bomb. I had two degrees of separation from Sabrina. During the fifties – her decade – my dad had served in the Royal Air Force. The two large mounds on the underside of the Hawker Hunter jet fighters were called 'Sabrinas', for obvious reasons, but my dad's connection was far cooler than that. He served in the RAF with Sabrina's brother! He was a jolly cove, apparently, and very proud of his sister's pin-up status. So much so that he had asked his fabulous and famous sibling for a handful of publicity postcards to hand out to his RAF pals. My dad had kept hold of his, and would I like it? Would I! I still treasure it. Obviously.

Sabrina was born Norma Ann Sykes, in Stockport, Cheshire, on 19 May 1936. At the age of sixteen, that tremendous top-heavy hourglass figure of 42-19-36 took her to London. Producers were hungrily on the lookout for pretty girls to be decoration in British film and television, and with the fashionable peroxide-blonde locks and more front than Blackpool, Sabrina was the perfect fit.

Her most unlikely champion came in that diminutive whirligig of variety, Arthur Askey, who instinctively knew there was comedy gold in them thar hills. The contrast between his funny little man and this statuesque stooge became something of a nationwide craze.

Sabrina debuted in the third series of Askey's popular BBC Television show *Before Your Very Eyes*, in February 1955. Despite the BBC publicity machine dubbing her 'the bosomy blonde who didn't talk', a label that clearly inspired her St Trinian's casting, Sabrina did talk. Great swathes: in that distinctive and very alluring breathy voice. The slight lisp somehow made her even more attractive. *Before Your Very Eyes* scriptwriters Talbot Rothwell and Sid Colin had a field day with her, concocting

Guest-starring in *Blue Murder at St. Trinian's* (1957). Lionel Jeffries plays the distracted and dastardly Joe Mangan.

ever more saucy sketches for this sensational siren. She even heated up the radio, where she was certainly all talk, returning to the BBC to play the Good Fairy in the Christmas Day 1956 Light Programme Panto *Puss in Gumboots*, opposite Frankie Howerd, as the goodie, and Dennis Price, as the baddie. Sabrina's fame was instantaneous, and her fulsome figure became a frequent popular culture reference point in 1950s radio comedies *The Goon Show* and *Hancock's Half Hour*. In the January 1958 episode, 'The Scandal Magazine', Sid James illustrated Hancock's naivete by suggesting he'd believe him if he said Sabrina was Arthur Askey's mother: 'She's not, is she?' came the momentarily stunned reply.

Sabrina was a star. One of the most talked about and photographed celebrities of the age.

She was rather cruelly nicknamed The Hunchfront of Lime Grove, after the home of the BBC studios where she worked, but she took it with good grace. It was all grist to her publicity mill. Mind you, when *Before Your Very Eyes* was poached by the fledgling commercial channel for producer Kenneth Carter, from February 1956, Sabrina happily took Askey's advice and went over to the other side with him. The nickname immediately lost its relevance!

She would happily make gag appearances as herself – famous for being famous – in the chase through a television studios scene in the Norman

Cor, blimey! Sabby's 42.5-19-36 vital statistics launched a thousand quips and she was in on every single one of them.

Wisdom film *Just My Luck* (1957), as the special guest of *The Frankie Howerd Show* (ATV, 17 August 1958), again for producer Kenneth Carter, and wallowing in her status as an English Glamour Girl on *The Steve Allen Plymouth Show* (NBC, 9 March 1958).

Having toured the world in promotions and cabaret appearances, she once more tried her luck in America. In 1967, she married Hollywood doctor Harold Melsheimer and stayed there. She kept in touch with Arthur Askey, who, in *Before Your Very Eyes – An Autobiography* (The Woburn Press, 1975), confirmed: 'Whenever she visits this country, she usually calls on me, and she looks a million dollars, with her American grooming and her mid-Atlantic accent. Who said I wasn't a talent-spotter!'

In 1974, her marriage was on the rocks and her fame on the wane, but she settled in a gorgeous house in West Toluca Lake, Los Angeles, and was philosophical about her fabulous, fading youth. Still, her image was still potent enough for the prominent rubber bumpers on the new MG Midget sports cars to be nicknamed 'Sabrinas'. They still are!

And British viewers with long memories would have been amused to hear Simon Cadell, as entertainment manager Jeffrey Fairbrother, have a phone conversation about Sabrina's celebrity appearance at the Maplins holiday camp, in the *Hi-de-Hi!* episode 'Peggy's Pen Friend' (BBC1, 15 January 1984), set in 1959.

Sabrina died on 24 November 2016, at the age of eighty, rather lost and in pain but still beautiful. For me she is forever in a glorious time-eddy somewhere in the late 1950s. That sexiest of sex symbols: one clever enough to make money on the brand, and to be in on the joke.

Before Your Very Eyes: Arthur Askey and Sabrina remain one of the most incongruous but joyous comedy double-acts of the 1950s.

TREAT YOURSELF TO *The Sid James Collection: Make Mine a Million* (Optimum Home Entertainment: OPTD1962, 2011). Before your very eyes, this DVD, actually starring Big-Hearted Arthur Askey, is the perfect 1950s time-capsule. An early satire on television commercials and commercial television,

Sabrina's fame reached down under, with an appearance on the Australian day-bill poster for *Make Mine a Million* (1959), which hints the new man in her life could be Sid James!

it allows fifties small screen pioneers to happily send-up their own images. Sabrina has a glorious cough and spit having her lips touched up by Askey, which was more than enough to warrant guest star status. What's more, her face and her bust made it onto the film's poster! 'Juliet with the built-in balcony' indeed.

# Leslie Sarony

## 1897–1985

In the arena of comic song, the unbridled brilliant Leslie Sarony is the greatest tunesmith of them all. His long, staggeringly productive career is unequalled. 'Gorgonzola', which really is just about a piece of cheese, had originally been recorded in the 1930s, which was also when Leslie became the very first artist to have a record banned by the BBC with his immortal 'Oompah Oompah (Stick It Up Your Jumper)'. However the 1980 recording is the one, mainly because I don't think there is another record where everyone in the studio is obviously having such a tremendous time. Chief among these is organiser Roy Hudd, who can be heard singing with all his heart high above the chorus, his famous toothy smile fair beaming out of the grooves on this irresistible Pollyanna platter.

I must say until I heard this song I had no idea that the cheese had such a reputation for having a life of its own. In this song it is regarded as a living moving thing like a cat or a dog: 'It's very labour saving when a dinner party comes. You just leave it on the table and it eats up all the crumbs.'

Quite often at BBC London I would play this as my last song of the afternoon. Hearing the station then having to come straight out of this fun-soaked, upbeat mayhem of Sarony sunshine and into whatever grim, fear-inducing headlines the 5 p.m. news was hoping to panic the populace with used to make me laugh like a drain.

*Danny Baker*

Compact in frame, with a knowing glint in his eye, a loose-limbed dancing style and a pleasant, uncomplicated, pure vocal delivery, Leslie Sarony pretty much personifies the sheer fun of 1930s British variety. As a songwriter he churned out literally hundreds of classic comedy and romantic numbers over a career lasting some seventy years. Not only did he perform these witty little ditties in music halls across the country but some of his numbers were successfully covered by some of the biggest acts of the day. Moreover, 'Jollity Farm', a ribald number from 1929, was recorded forty years later by those doyens of wacky musicality the Bonzo Dog Doo-Dah Band. In 1979, The Goons, in their final three-man reunion, recorded a variation of 'Rhymes' written by Sarony. The comedy baton of Sarony's surrealistic nonsense hotly passed on to the next generation who in turn inspired the next. Ad infinitum.

Born Leslie Legge Sarony Frye in Surbiton, Surrey, on 22 January 1897, he became a professional entertainer in the early 1910s when he joined the juvenile touring troupe Doc Park's Eton Boys and Girton Girl. (Leslie was one of the boys, of course!) Reflecting during the 1979 recording session for his EMI album, he said: 'We looked as if butter wouldn't melt in our mouths. It would, you know. And it did!' He was a gloriously dirty little devil was Leslie Sarony.

While with the troupe Sarony heard about auditions for *Escalade*, a spectacular revue at the London Hippodrome. It was the first West End show to have a lavish staircase onstage. Such was the rush to be the first venue to boast one that the show opened in mid-rehearsals. The Musical Director told an unprepared Sarony that as long as he danced up and down that staircase, they would play! He must have been doing something right, for when the London Hippodrome staged the comedy revue *Hello Tango* in 1913, Sarony was back in the cast. But his fledgling success was rudely interrupted by the outbreak of the First World War. Having lied about his age ('and my height'), he served with some distinction with the London Scottish Regiment and was stationed in France and Salonika for the duration of the conflict.

The war was instrumental in the start of his hugely prolific songwriting career. For instance, at one point England was facing a shortage of cheese while Malta was drowning in the stuff. Sarony, who was entertaining in Malta at the time, explained: 'they could have built blocks of flats with it! We had it every day, for every meal, dished up in all sorts of ways. We were cheesed off with it!' It proved the inspiration for his parody of the popular song '365 Days'. His version went: 'Three hundred and sixty-five days, we've had the cheese dished up. Three hundred and sixty-five days, for breakfast, tea and sup! They tried hard to fake it, but what bloke's ever take it, and cold on the table it stays. The West Yorks have charged it, the cooks camouflaged it, three hundred and sixty-five ways...'

Immediately upon returning back to Britain, Sarony threw himself back into show business with pantomimes, summer seasons, revues and musicals: in the cast for 1924's *Whirl of the World* at the London Palladium, and in the original production of *Show Boat*, with Paul Robeson, which opened 3 May 1928, at the Drury Lane Theatre. Sarony's star was already in the ascendant but he was always adding to his considerable list of talents. Frustrated by the poor musical accompaniment he often had to endure, he taught himself to play the ukulele. This not only made him an even more self-sufficient variety turn but also inspired one of his greatest comedy songs, the Titanic-referencing number 'He Played his Ukulele as the Ship Went Down'.

He had his first song published in 1926. The song was 'Too Too', and that same year saw him recording for the first time, with gargantuan xylophonist Teddy Brown. Sarony later estimated that his complete songbook ran to nearly five hundred titles and that his recording career had covered 'every company in the country'.

By the late 1920s Sarony had become one of Britain's best-loved entertainers, both onstage and in popular guest-spots on radio, peddling his ever-growing repertoire of self-composed comic ditties. He even toured the Continent, dancing, singing and joking with Jack Hylton and his band, to great acclaim. 'I did lots of recordings with Jack,' Leslie remembered in 1979. 'He would ring me up at twelve o'clock at night and say, "I want you to do four titles tomorrow." I'd turn up to do them in one go as you couldn't edit in those days. They were all done direct onto the wax.'

In 1928 he was invited to star in the short film *'Hot Water'* and *'Vegetabuel'*, which utilised the new Phonofilm sound system. The film featured Sarony's tried-and-tested comedy patter alongside two character performances of the titular songs. He performed 'Hot Water' as a rough-and-ready cockney bloke standing outside a pub, while 'Vegetabuel' was performed, at the same locale, with Sarony in the guise of a campaigner for vegetable rights. (And this nearly sixty years before Nigel Planer's Neil took on the same cause in *The Young Ones*.) Sarony, with such winningly eccentric lyrics as 'Don't be cruel to a vegetabuel' was a firm favourite with audiences.

It's clear who was the clown in the Two Leslies. Sarony and Holmes enjoyed a sparkling partnership from 1933 until 1946.

Strange, then, that in 1935 he decided to share the wealth and form a double act with Leslie Holmes. The act, reasonably called The Two Leslies, was an immense success. Apart, the two men were each at the top of their game; together they were even more than the sum of their parts, consolidating huge popularity and, along the way, writing one or two new rules for abstract absurdist humour. Their partnership lasted until just after the Second World War and their contribution to the nation's morale is incalculable. With their greatly embellished version of 'We're Gonna Hang Out the Washing on the Siegfried Line' the home fires were not just burning, they were roaring. And it was Sarony who, during recording, ad-libbed the opening line: 'Mother dear, I'm writing you from somewhere in France'. His own personal delight with and subsequent public appreciation of the line dictated that they would keep it in for the dozens of radio and variety performances of the song to come.

From 1946 Sarony teamed up with another variety performer, Michael Cole, but the magic spark that had ignited with Holmes was lacking. By the end of the decade cracks were already showing so, as a solo act again, Sarony continued to tour the variety theatres with his collection of comic songs. Hits like 'The Old Sow' could never be left out for, although the song had been originally recorded by music hall

In old age Leslie was ever-ready to rebel rouse until he was 'stone cold, under the mould and making the daisies grow'.

singer Albert Richardson, Sarony's rendition had proven so popular that audiences would bay for his blood if he didn't find time for a snatch of 'Susannah's a funniful man', complete with pig snort effects for the old sow. There was also 'Pegatty Leg', which allowed him a moment of bearded disguise and some impressive stiff-legged dancing. He would rejoice in this wooden-legged hornpipe for decades.

As for 'I Lift Up My Finger and I Say "Tweet Tweet"', that song, written in 1929, remains a pantomime perennial to this day. In 1979 Sarony recalled: 'I wrote this while I was in *Show Boat*. Two chorus girls were having a "barney" in the wings, calling each other everything under the sun. I got between them and said, "Now, whenever anyone calls me names, I lift up my finger and I say: 'Tweet tweet, shush shush, now now, come come.'" I don't know why I said it but it shut them up and I went back to my dressing room and wrote the song.' Many people on Twitter could learn from Sarony's simple, calming lesson!

Never content to rest on ancient laurels, though, Sarony successfully carved out another career for himself as a versatile character actor. Throughout the 1960s and 1970s he would pop up in a wide variety of hit television shows. He played Arthur Giles in *Crossroads* (ATV, 1964), aged waif Bert Taylor in *Nearest and Dearest* (Granada Television, 1969), and Jack Hardcastle in *The Gaffer* (Yorkshire Television, 1981). He played loads of old-man-with-a-kick. There were episodes of *The Sweeney* ('Ringer', Euston Films, 2 January 1975), *Target* ('Fringe Banking', BBC1, 13 October 1978), *The Chinese Detective* ('Hammer and Nails', BBC1, 7 May 1981) and *Minder* ('You Need Hands', Euston Films, 20 January 1982). He racked up a *Steptoe and Son* ('And Afterwards at...', BBC1, 4 October 1965) and composed the theme song for the short-lived – pun intended – comedy series *That's Your Funeral* (BBC1, 1971).

He even played Shakespeare, cast as Gregory opposite John Cleese's Petruchio in the 23 October 1980 BBC Television presentation of *The Taming of the Shrew*.

Still, it was the comedy songs that remained deepest in his heart. It was a proud old man indeed who saw these silly compositions recognised. In 1975 Sarony was the recipient of a Gold Badge from the British Academy of Songwriters, Composers and Authors. At the end of 1979 he recorded fourteen of his old numbers for a celebratory project instigated by music hall aficionado Roy Hudd and orchestrated by musical director Don Shearman. Sarony recorded the lot in one take, over one day, before departing in a taxi for a filming job in the North of England that evening. He was still delighting in resurrecting favourite old compositions and theatrical anecdotes for *The Old Boy Network*, BBC2's love letter to variety survivors, broadcast 2 September 1981.

Eager to work 'til he dropped, Leslie played one of the ancient pirates in Terry Gilliam's support Monty Python short *The Crimson Permanent Assurance* (1983). Terry Jones remembered he 'was so excited to meet Leslie Sarony when he was on set. I was playing a window cleaner. He had written and performed so many of those old records I had collected in the 1950s. He was something of a hero of mine, and there he was right in front of me, and more energetic than the rest of us put together!'

Sarony also played the gatekeeper in the Paul McCartney film *Give My Regards to Broad Street* (1984), and was exuberant as ever even just before death finally came, on 12 February 1985. He had filmed a sketch for *Victoria Wood: As Seen On TV* which was screened three days later, and doubtless he was singing 'Ain't It Grand To Be Bloomin' Well Dead' on the way to his own funeral.

TREAT YOURSELF TO that *Roy Hudd Presents Leslie Sarony* album (EMI: RTRS101, 1980). According to Hudd's sleeve notes: 'At ten-thirty in the morning Leslie arrived at Anvil Studios and started to sing while I sat in the control box with our recording engineer, Eric Tomlinson. Eight bars in we looked at each other and Eric said, "He sounds exactly like he did in the thirties!" It was all still there, the immaculate diction, the timing and the just suppressed chuckle. A greatly overused word but the session was "Magic!"' Indeed it is; an eternal, twilight joy with one of the true greats of British comedy. Lest we forget.

# Larry Semon

## 1889–1928

Without Larry Semon we may never have had Laurel and Hardy. What a terrifying thought. Thanks, Larry!

*Jeffrey Holland*

There's a memorable sketch starring Ronnies Barker and Corbett which cast the two comedy heroes as silent slapstick clowns. Ronnie B. is big and burly, in the Eric Campbell mould, Ronnie C. the weedy and put upon, all Charlie Chaplin angst and grit. The genius of the skit is that it mocks not so much the beloved stars of 1920s Hollywood but the somewhat irksome 1960s trend of cobbling together celluloid treasures from forty years earlier and slapping on an overly cheerful narration. In this case, the narration merrily relates the sad spiral into alcoholism, self-destruction and poverty of the hapless stars on screen. It is very funny. It is also very poignant. And the sketch is practically a pathos-tinged kiss to Larry Semon.

Today, if he's known at all, Larry Semon is remembered as the star and director of *The Wizard of Oz* – no, not the one with Judy Garland, but the sadly neglected version from 1925, in which Semon played the Scarecrow. It was only his second feature film as a director, and a very assured piece of film-making it is. Alas, the production's excessive budget and relative box office failure set the seal for his rapid decline. These days it is best known for featuring a certain Oliver Hardy as the Tin Man – back in the days when Ollie was a good, jobbing heavy and Larry Semon was one of the biggest comedy stars in the business. Nearly eighty years on, the ultimate backhanded compliment saw the film released to home video as part of *The Oliver Hardy Collection* in 1999.

While Semon wasn't exactly born in a trunk, his father was the celebrated vaudevillian magician Zera the Great. In fact, during his jam-packed, all-too-brief life, Larry himself found some fame in the art of illusion when he and his sister joined his father's act (their mother was Zera's assistant). His father died in 1901 at the age of 54, when young Larry was shipped off to be educated in Savannah, Georgia.

The traces of magic didn't leave quite so easily, however, and having moved to New York to study at art school Semon quickly gleaned a reputation as a clever and talented cartoonist. By the age of eighteen he had been summoned to the White House by President Taft to immortalise the commander-in-chief in caricature.

And Semon happily basked in the reflected glory of his famous father. Moreover, he even broke the code and readily accepted a rather questionable assignment to reveal how his father's magic tricks had worked. The series of illustrated articles for the Philadelphia newspaper the *North American* went by the sensational heading of 'Mysteries of Magic, Past and Present, Exposed'. The byline was no less sensational, screaming that the contents were compiled 'by Lawrence Semon – son of the late Professor Zera Semon, one of the most noted magicians of his day'.

Larry had already supplemented his earnings as a graphic designer and cartoonist by performing comedy monologues in vaudeville, and in 1915 he was spotted by a talent scout and offered a contract to act in films for the most prolific of studios, the American Vitagraph Company. It was goodbye, drawing board, and hello, Hollywood. As a small-part actor in the short films of star comic Hughie Mack, Semon eased himself into the catbird seat as soon as Mack left the studios. In 1917 Semon starred in and wrote and directed his first comedy

As director, scriptwriter, producer and scarecrow, *The Wizard of Oz* (1925) remains Semon's most accessible work.

success, *Boasts and Boldness*. It was slapstick of the basest kind but it proved extremely popular.

Semon, a white-faced simpleton sporting a derby hat, had a keen, cartoonist's eye for visual tomfoolery. His work was a celebration of messy chaos – in a bakery; on a farm; anywhere – destruction, dirt and the disintegration of dignity were his calling cards. And it was just what America needed. In April 1917 the country had declared war on Germany. The world needed laughter, and people like Larry Semon were happy to oblige. In the film *Plagues and Puppy Love*, released in October 1917, he was playing Larry. Now so famous that he could, for all intents and purposes, play himself in the eyes of his audience, Larry Semon became a comedy personality. So much so that his films were sold all around the world. In France he was known as Zigoto; in Italy, Ridolini; in Spain, Jaimito. He was a valuable commodity. By the end of 1918 he had directed himself and Stan Laurel in *Frauds and Frenzies*. The film was well received but Semon had got himself a bad reputation with studio executives. Graduating from ten or twelve minute one-reel comedy shorts to double length two-reelers, the budget for Semon's films had not just doubled but tripled. It was Semon's perfectionism that was the cause, with his impressively fertile imagination dictating that his sight gags and special effects got more and more elaborate. This was laudable, of course, but with fame and fortune came extravagance. His marquee value was such that his films were now advertised as 'A Vitagraph-Larry Semon Comedy' and, with his name so prominent and ticket sales on the increase, Semon felt more and more justified to push the budget to breaking point and beyond. It was such behaviour that saw Vitagraph sue the star in 1920. As *Motion*

*Picture News* reported, the studio set the figure at nearly half a million dollars for the 'increased costs through delays, carelessness and waste'. As a result of this litigation, Semon was forced out of his original contract. The press began speculating that this would signal Semon's leap to a bigger, more prestigious studio like Fox. The fates and fortunes of

Semon wrote, directed and starred as Larry Cutshaw in *Bears and Bad Men* (1918). Stan Laurel works the bowler hat!

Harold Lloyd and Buster Keaton were shifting and, as *Movie Weekly* noted, with First National releasing Charlie Chaplin, 'Larry would automatically fill the comedy gap.'

It's almost impossible to grasp the fact that, at his very peak, Semon was being bracketed with the three greatest clowns of the silent era – perhaps of any era. Indeed, Semon's stardom was such that, despite having its feathers ruffled, Vitagraph was still keen to exploit his talents. Clearly aware of his box office worth, Larry Semon showed no signs of having curbed his exorbitance. Oliver Hardy, a frequent co-star, recalled years later that during production of *The Sawmill* in the winter of 1921, Semon rejected the idea of a mere painted backdrop for the briefly seen log cabin setting. Instead he insisted on building a real log cabin! As far as the studio was concerned the authenticity of the structure didn't justify the huge addition to the budget. It certainly didn't make the joke any funnier, but Semon's worldwide popularity saw the star clown get away with it. In 1922 Vitagraph made him his own producer. It was a canny move that not only boosted his ego but gave him responsibility for his own excess. Semon was now underwriting his own productions and, with renewed freedom and just a smidgen of smugness, he hungrily embraced feature films.

His first feature, *The Girl in the Limousine*, was released in July 1924. Something of a lost classic, it was popular enough at the time to allow him the indulgence of *The Wizard of Oz* (1925), a film that playfully twisted the

Bossy butler Oliver Hardy tells Larry where to go in *The Girl in the Limousine* (1924), with Charles Murray and Larry Steers. Alas, the film is missing, believed lost.

original source material into a children's fantasy very much of Larry's own imagination. The film's flight of fancy, involving farmyard antics, lovelorn slapstick and the wonderful world of Oz, all springs from the dreams of Larry Semon, in old man make-up, as a sort of toy-making wiseman cum storyteller, complete with adorable cuddly dolls of the principal characters. And Larry plays not one but three different characters in the film: this eccentric, kindly narrator; a bumbling farmhand; and the scarecrow. It's a confused, and as often as not confusing, film, but its big heart is most assuredly in the right place. The surreal and sometimes rather chilling imagery marks Semon out as a visionary director, too. The film's less than glowing box office returns must have been a blow; Larry made just two more feature films on rapidly diminishing returns – *My Best Girl* (1925) and *Stop, Look and Listen* (1926) – before crawling away to lick his wounds back in the safer and cheaper waters of short films.

This late burst of activity through 1927 and 1928 produced such focused and polished work as *The Stunt Man, Oh, What a Man!, Dummies* and *A Simple Sap*, all of which he also wrote and directed but our star had the air of a distraught man screaming at the wind. His personal life was a shambles; it always had been. At the height of his fame, in 1922, he had pursued and married his frequent leading lady Lucille Carlisle. A brilliant comic and bewitching screen presence, she only seemed to shine under Larry's guidance. Seeming to treat her career with the infectious glee with which she treated the rest of her life, Carlisle preferred to vanish off to New York for wild times, returning days, even weeks, later to a haunted husband. The marriage lasted a year.

When British comic *Film Fun* launched in January 1920, Larry was one of its funny folk headliners. Following the Arbuckle scandal, regular feature 'Fatty Arbuckle's Schooldays' became 'Larry Semon's Schooldays'.

In 1925, the year Semon made *The Wizard of Oz*, he, rather sweetly, married his Dorothy, actress Dorothy Dwan, but the match coincided with Semon's career downturn, his later shorts being distributed by the Poverty Row Educational Pictures. Full of bravado to the press, in July 1927 he told *Moving Picture World* he was planning on building his own Hollywood studio, on Ventura Boulevard, but shortly afterwards he was declared bankrupt.

A comedic tour de force, Semon was forced to tour the vaudeville halls in order to eat. Working himself into a nervous breakdown and consumption, he was back in Los Angeles by 1928, unhappily billeted in a sanatorium in Victorville, where, on 8 October 1928, he died at just thirty-nine. Pneumonia and tuberculosis were the official causes of death for this 'Clown of Tragedy', as the *Los Angeles Herald* called him. This master of slapstick's roller-coaster experiences in Hollywood couldn't have done him a lot of good either.

TREAT YOURSELF TO *Klamottenkiste: The Very Best of Larry Semon* (Zyx Records: B00026YMVU, 2004), which, despite not being the greatest of print quality, does present a rare, albeit incomplete, collection of Semon shorts. These gems include *The Star Boarder* (1919), with Larry's first wife, Lucille Carlisle, as leading lady, and *The Rent Collector* (1921), featuring supporting turns from both Stan Laurel and Oliver Hardy. It's cinematic archaeology.

# Ronald Shiner

## 1903–66

'It's me beak which made 'em larf!' he'd say. And he insured that beak for something like £20,000. Just in case it got bashed into shape, I suppose! What a performer!

*Bernard Cribbins OBE*

The steamrolling, hyperactive, fist-clenching, foot-stamping, gloriously unchanging film performances of Ronald Shiner had just one setting – and it wasn't 'subtle'! Instead, at the peak of his powers, in the early 1950s, his unique brand of loud, brash, cheerfully working-class cockney skulduggery headlined a string of not very original but always totally enjoyable big-screen vehicles. He was a Xerox Will Hay in the school-daze *Top of the Form* (1953), where his corrupt schoolteacher led, Fagin-like, a band of overage crooks including Gerald Campion and Anthony Newley. Charles Hawtrey, that sentimental Will Hay satellite, refused a role in the film, out of respect for his master.

*Innocents in Paris* (1953) followed the misadventures and misfortunes of a group of British holidaymakers in France. Typically, Shiner plays a fast-talking, sharp-shooting Royal Marine determined to make the most of a Parisian night on the tiles, funded by the pooled dosh at his unit's disposal. *Up to His Neck* (1954) was another nautical, naughty comedy, directed by John Paddy Carstairs and starring Shiner as marooned sailor Jack Carter: a life of native paradise with a grass-skirted Hattie Jacques seemingly less appealing than a commando mission to recover a purloined submarine.

By the mid-fifties Shiner had found his niche; suddenly, every single film he was associated with seemed to have a nautical flavour. Val Guest's *Carry On Admiral* (1957) offered up the supporting turn of Salty Simpson, forever pleading for the return of his borrowed oilskins; *Not Wanted On Voyage* (1957) starred him opposite farceur extraordinaire Brian Rix as a couple of likely-lad cabin stewards; *Girls at Sea* (1958) saw director Gilbert Gunn bask in a little Shiner sunlight when Ronald was cast as Marine Ogg alongside strait-laced star Guy Rolfe; while the film version of *The Navy Lark* (1959) ruffled a few feathers when Shiner, filling the shoes of Jon Pertwee, the CPO in the radio series, landed the part of Chief Petty Officer Banyard! Only Leslie Phillips survived the radio cast cull, signing up as the slow-witted Lieutenant Pouter, but Shiner connived and cavorted so expertly that few minded (Jon Pertwee notwithstanding).

Shiner's early life had been colourful, to say the least. A proper Londoner, Ronald Alfred Shiner kicked his way into the world on 8 June 1903. He went to Canada in 1920 and, having lied about his age, was just seventeen when he joined the Royal Canadian Mounted Police. Whether this Mountie got his man or not went unrecorded but, clearly disillusioned with the Canadian life, after two years Shiner moved back to Britain. Then he chalked up various short-lived bursts of employment: as a farmer, a greengrocer, a milkman, and, most suitably of all, a clerk in a betting shop. He also endured three years' army service which at least allowed him the opportunity to perform. His raw skills at comedy proved popular in military camp concert.

In the 1930s Shiner fell into life as a film extra and bit-part player, with early credits including *Wild Boy* (1934), starring Bud Flanagan, Chesney Allen and Sonnie Hale; the Leslie Fuller [qv] comedy *Doctor's Orders* (1934);

As Albert Higgins, the cabin steward tailing jewel thieves on a cruise to Tangier, in *Not Wanted on Voyage* (1957).

and the Stanley Holloway musical comedy *Squibs* (1935). Shiner worked tirelessly throughout the thirties, and by the end of the decade was getting a billing, a decent pay packet and named characters, notably supporting George Formby, Will Hay and Arthur Askey in a glut of films at both Ealing and Gainsborough Studios. Perhaps the most typical of these is his penultimate association with Formby, the 1943 Home Guard comedy *Get Cracking*. Shiner plays a right nasty piece of work, all bluster and bombast, with leading lady Dinah Sheridan seeing straight through his manipulative ways. Still, it proved to be the blueprint for his own success; add just a dash of humanity and a pinch of joy to that hard-nosed type and – bingo: instant Ronald Shiner stardom.

It was the role of crafty spiv Sam Porter in the Whitehall Theatre farce *Worm's Eye View* that really made him a star, playing for over 1,700 performances from its opening night on 18 December 1945. As the very personification of a cheerful black marketeer, Shiner's typically raucous performance was singled out for praise. Shiner stayed in the cast for the six-year run, and reprised his role for the Associated British-Pathe Technicolor film version, released in April 1951.

His film star status blossomed as a result, so much so that by 1952 he was voted Britain's most popular male cinema star. It seems almost impossible to believe now, but Shiner really had that indefinable special ingredient. He was reassuringly nonplussed about his success, seemingly as amazed at his huge popularity as everybody else was. However, behind that lackadaisical bravado there was a comedy actor of high energy and panache. He certainly held his own in the scene-stealing stakes against seasoned scene-stealers: Margaret Rutherford in *Aunt Clara* (1954), James Hayter in *Keep it Clean* (1956), and Ted Ray in *My*

*Wife's Family* (1956). He was perhaps at his happiest at the race track, alongside Brian Rix and Sid James, in the farcical romp *Dry Rot* (1956); and his khaki capers comic strip delighted readers of *Film Fun*.

By this time he had already become the landlord of the Blackboys Inn, a fourteenth-century East Sussex pub,

'Guv'nor Shiner' welcomes Diane Hart and Ted Ray behind his bar. At the time the three were shooting *My Wife's Family* (1956).

although the self-proclaimed 'Guv'nor Shiner' still took on occasional acting roles into the early 1960s. He was Widow Twankey opposite Bob Monkhouse's knowing Aladdin at the Coliseum for the 1960–61 season. It was a lavish production, and Shiner and Monkhouse thoroughly enjoyed themselves on the Cole Porter number 'No Wonder Taxes Are High'. Gilbert Gunn had pitched a khaki answer to *Girls at Sea*, provisionally entitled *Girls in Arms* but finally released as *Operation Bullshine*, in June 1959, with Shiner in support of Donald Sinden, and the girls in question being Barbara Murray and Carole Lesley. Shiner's rather ignoble cinematic end came with *The Night We Got the Bird* (1961), in which his special guest 'disappearance' saw him reincarnated as a parrot. It was that kind of film. His billing, although last, was in huge type on the poster, testimony still to his lingering place at the top table of British film comedians. He died, in Hailsham, East Sussex, on 29 June 1966, just three weeks after his sixty-third birthday. His final choice on *Desert Island Discs* had been Billy Cotton's recording of 'Maybe It's Because I'm a Londoner'. So Ronald Shiner.

TREAT YOURSELF TO *Keep it Clean* (Odeon Entertainment: ODNF125, 2008), one of a handful of great Ronald Shiner star vehicles available to watch in the comfort of your home and to treasure forever. This one cast him as Bert Kane, a wily advertising agent who is determined to put the sex back into crumpet!

# Johnnie Silver

## 1917–67

I do not see why you should not be in the game.

*Max Wall*

Social media can be a blessing or a curse, but if you use it well it can be very special indeed. During the course of writing this book, my dear and learned friend Danny Baker – who Chris Addison, quite rightly, maintains could have put this book together in his sleep – was re-reading the candid memoir of absurdist comic genius Max Wall, and happened upon a mention of Johnnie Silver. He took to Twitter to ask the nation for more, and copied me in. At the time I knew as much as the book revealed: not much. But up stepped Pete Southcombe, theatrical ephemera archivist and kindly Twitter warrior who has a fund of contemporary reviews and playbill matter at his fingertips. So here's what we have on the effervescent (and I can't remember when he effferwasn't) Johnnie Silver. The story starts with Max Wall, who looms large in Silver's legend.

In the early 1950s Wall was wont to tour the regional theatres with his act and, on occasions, spontaneously audition local turns: like a one-man *X Factor*. 'I am trying to find unknown people whose talent could be developed', he explained. 'Then I will find the right spots for them. The stage is crying out for new people but there is no organisation for finding them.' After two months of this, and having discovered a dozen or so possibilities, Wall played the Coventry Theatre and attracted thirty would-be stars.

One of these was our man Johnnie Silver. A polished amateur, he was then a travelling salesman by trade, although he had become very popular

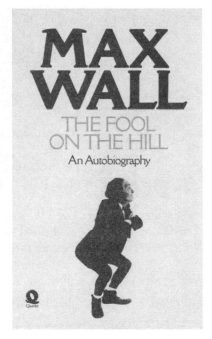

Max Wall's revelatory and unputdownable memoir, which salutes the 'ill-fated' Johnnie Silver.

performing in Coventry pubs and already made three radio broadcasts. During the late 1940s he had also played a handful of variety theatre dates with *ITMA* star Tommy Handley. Max Wall saw huge potential in Silver's barrage of one-liners and funny stories, and took him under his wing.

Wall arranged for him to perform a string of after-dinner engagements around the country but Silver told Wall: 'I am looking for a way of getting into the legitimate theatre.'

Having secured him a guest-spot on *Meet Max Wall* (BBC Television, 4 December 1955), Silver played the Windmill Theatre for two successful seasons. Fellow comic grafter Barry Cryer remembers that 'Silver never used to be in his dressing room. That was the big joke at the Windmill. He would turn up to the theatre in his stage suit and with a clean shirt on. He was ready to do the six shows a day we had to do back in those days, but he was never in his dressing room. In-between shows he was always in the pub!'

The Windmill Theatre, Great Windmill Street, London, in 1957, when Johnnie and Beryl Silver were working the legendary venue.

Silver at least spent enough time in the theatre to meet and fall in love with the principal dancer, Beryl, and the two married. Soon after turning professional in the late fifties, Silver emigrated to Australia. The club audiences there were harder than at home, and for Silver the reliance on booze before going onstage increased. As Max Wall notes in his book, Johnnie Silver was 'ill-fated', and it was a heartbroken widow who announced to the British press that he had passed away in Australia on 20 January 1967. He was only forty-nine.

One favourable review of Johnnie Silver's stage act describes 'some brilliant comedy and an unforgettable "budgie" story'. I thought there's only one man who would know the joke today – but even that filing cabinet of comedy Barry Cryer drew a blank: 'If I heard Johnnie tell it, I've forgotten it. Which is not like me at all! Have you heard this one about a parrot...?'

TREAT YOURSELF TO Max Wall's *The Fool on the Hill: An Autobiography* (Quartet Books: 0704320800, 1975), the most frank and candid of showbiz tales. Oh, and get yourself a bottle of single malt to drink as you read it too. Here's to Johnnie!

# Dennis Spicer

## 1935–64

Dennis Spicer had unique ventriloquist ideas we see nowadays all over again, such as the Human Dummy routine. He used two people for this and sung between the two, so using three voices, and he made it look easy. He was a highly skilled technician of our art who I greatly admire and it was such a loss at such a young age and at the height of what was to be only the beginning of his stardom.

I have acknowledged Dennis in many shows and seasons, performing his version of the song 'Old MacDonald Had a Farm' which he had performed at the 1964 Royal Variety Performance. My recreation was made even more special as I had members of his family in the audience. His sister Rose Dalton and niece Karen were sat in the front row. As I ended the speedy number, Rose and everyone around her rose to their feet and I was extremely proud to have paid tribute to one of the best British ventriloquists we've ever had. I have to add I still never learned the song or executed it as well as he did because Dennis was a master craftsman of his generation, and I am sad we never got to meet.

I'm so pleased he's a part of the book as I want people to remember him not for how we lost him but for what an exceptionally unique entertainer he was.

*Steve Hewlett*

From the haunted souls of Michael Redgrave, in *Dead of Night* (1945), and Anthony Hopkins in *Magic* (1978), to the 2007 James Wan film *Dead Silence*, there has long been a bewitching creepiness attached to ventriloquists and their muses. Beautifully belying this connotation is the fact that Britain's best-loved professional ventriloquists have been the most affable and thoroughly likeable bunch of entertainers. One thinks of Keith Harris (from my own childhood) and most recently the reigning patron saint of ventriloquists, Steve Hewlett. Then there was Dennis Spicer, the unfairly forgotten master of his art who reached the top but was cruelly denied the opportunity to utilise his fame.

Recordings of his act are scarce, though thankfully his highest theatrical achievement *is* preserved in the archives. On the evening of 2 November 1964 Spicer performed before the Queen and Prince Philip in the Royal Variety Performance: here was a turn at the top of his game and delighting in cheeky references to the regal occasion. As well as his usual puppet associates, including a Bengal tiger called Rikki Tikki and a one-eared monkey by the name of Maxwell – who would delight the crowd by proclaiming: 'I only have one hear-hole!' – Spicer also introduced a dummy corgi to his set. This dog of cloth and plastic revelled in biting soldiers. Allegedly, Her Majesty was charmed by the miscreant mutt, not to mention by Dennis Spicer himself. As well as his usual stock-in-trade, Spicer added an element of mystery to the act with the aid of the diminutive Kenny Baker dressed-up as a vent's dummy and perched upon Spicer's knee: the illusion's concept being that as Spicer bowed to the audience, he whistled for his dummy who jumped off the chair and ran off the stage as Spicer made his exit. Perfectly creepy, in a family-entertainer kind of way.

Born Dennis George Spicer on 13 January 1935, in Hillingdon County Hospital, the family settled in Coventry while Dennis was still a toddler. At the age of eight he borrowed a book on magic from his local library and eagerly pored over a section about ventriloquism. Before you could mumble 'a gottle of geer' he had grabbed his sister's one and only doll, cut open the jaw, attached a piece of elastic and instantly created his first dummy. Makeshift but effective.

Combing the luscious locks of both Doddy and James Green, at the Blackpool Opera House, in the summer of 1964. Ken Dodd treasured this battered snap for over fifty years.

Before long he was holding impromptu concerts in his back garden and charging the local children a halfpenny admittance. He was that delicious cliché: a natural-born entertainer. His father encouraged his passion with frequent trips to the variety theatre, and a performer at the local working-men's club sold him his first dummy proper for the princely sum of fifteen shillings. Dennis called his sidekick Enoch and the two were off on the path to fame and fortune: that very evening, his father secured him his first booking – at the tender age of ten! The gig, at the Railway Club, Coventry, proved a hit.

Father would continue to guide his talented son, sitting in patiently during every performance. There was a visual code for his onstage son to take note of. If Father gave Mother a gentle prod, he had seen Dennis's lips move. A stroking of his earlobe signified that Father had noticed his son's audibility level drop.

Before Dennis was a teenager he had secured himself a decent agent in Sid Starr, who booked him on a solid round of cabaret and club appearances. As often as not Spicer would involve his sister June in the act. Dennis would put his puppet down, leave the auditorium and then invite June onto the stage to continue the conversation with Enoch. It was a trick uniquely Spicer's at the time.

At the age of seventeen, Spicer left home, turned professional and landed a job with the Aqua Rhythm Rhapsody at the Queen's Theatre, Barnstable. The year was 1954, and that summer he joined the Resident Revue Company at the Butlin's

Holiday Camp in Filey. The following year he enlisted at the Clacton Butlin's, pitting his ventriloquial skills opposite knockabout comedians Joe Baker [qv] and Jack Douglas. It was during the 1955 season that Spicer truly became a star. There were more puppets now, including a blonde teenage girl who was hip to the latest jargon. However, his dearest stage companion was one Jimmy Green. Rebranded James Green when the act became a more sophisticated, international hit, here was an impish, cheeky, entertaining little urchin who perfectly fitted Spicer's intimate stage presence. James Green was a friendly irritation, playfully undermining Spicer onstage and making for some hilarious routines. The comic success and audience approval of the dummy fuelled Spicer's stage confidence too. Now Spicer didn't just drink a glass of water while holding a conversation with his puppets, like lesser stage ventriloquists, Spicer chatted with James Green while drinking a pint of beer! This was a class act in every way.

It was a slight lapse in concentration owing to a bit too much booze taken during the act that actually worked in Spicer's favour and took him into the big time. During one performance Spicer himself started talking in the voice of James Green, and made the puppet open its mouth only to answer in Spicer's natural voice. It was a switch-around error that delighted the audience, and from that moment on it became an integral part of the act. The lure of laughter had now superseded the simple desire to impress his audience with his skill, but for Spicer comedy was very much an enchantment of his act. This was no deliberately hopeless ventriloquism turn, like the slapdash incompetence of Sandy Powell [qv]. No, this was perfectly timed, smartly turned-out and with a certain knowing – a continuous grin and a wink shared between auditorium and audience. No-one was in any doubt just how fabulous Dennis Spicer was at his chosen craft. They even liked him in Glasgow when, for the 1958 summer season, he appeared in the spectacular variety *Five-Past Eight* shows, at the Alhambra.

He had already made his debut on BBC Television, on the 21 February 1955 edition of *Showcase*. Compère work on *The Centre Show* followed that June, and *The Stage* reviewer was impressed, reporting that: 'Dennis Spicer was a great success, changing places with his regular dummy on occasion and challenging the camera to close up on his lips, which were motionless – although you could see his tongue moving like mad!'. In July 1955 Spicer was booked for another television appearance, on *Variety Parade*, and, from October 1955, was a regular turn on *The Dave King Show*. The security of a long-term contract with the BBC made his marriage that month all the sweeter. Ever the showman, Spicer's best man was none other than his stage partner in comedy James Green. Naturally, he gave a hilarious speech!

He was now represented by the Forrester George agency, and variety assignments, summer season slots and pantomime commitments were guaranteed, as often as not with fellow Forrester George star Ken Dodd. The two became firm friends, first appearing together alongside Jimmy James, Roy Castle and Jimmy Clitheroe [qv] for producer Peter Webster in *Let's Have Fun* on Blackpool's Central Pier in 1956. A performance was filmed and, edited to a half-hour film, released in cinemas that June.

Fun was clearly what it was all about, where Spicer was concerned. Barry Cryer recalls the time that he and fellow comedian Ted Ray encountered the young ventriloquist at Tyne Tees Television in Newcastle. Cryer remembers: 'Dennis had arrived late so, apologising, he hung James Green on a hook on the wall and, leaving his case unattended and unlocked, nipped off for a desperate loo break. Now both Ted and I knew that the stage props of the ventriloquist were a closely guarded secret. It was never done to poke around in their bag. Anyway, Ted looked at me and said: "Come on, Baz. Let's have a peek!" I protested meekly: "Oh, we can't!" as we both looked into the bag! There was all kinds of weird and wonderful puppets and tricks within but, suddenly feeling guilty, Ted turned away. At that moment Dennis reappeared in the dressing room and, from his hook on the door, James Green said: "They had a look in your case, Dennis!" Oh my God. The chills that went down my spine. Dennis had a winning twinkle in his eye, though!'

From 16 October 1956, Dennis made the first of eleven appearances on the BBC Television variety series *Vera Lynn Sings*. Continually touring the country, by the early sixties his agent, Dave Forrester, had an eye on the lucrative international market.

On 7 October 1962 Spicer wowed America on CBS's *The Ed Sullivan Show*, returning for four more engagements over the following two years. Spicer toured Australia, even sparring with celebrated Down Under ventriloquist

Snuggled up with Sabrina during the televised tea party *All Star Invite*, which launched the new strand of BBC programming for women in 1955.

Ron Blaskett in Melbourne. He even broke into the Indian market, playing Calcutta to great acclaim and enjoying the management's challenge to the audience, promising 1,000 rupees to anyone who could see his lips move. Nobody claimed the prize!

There had been many years of mutual respect and friendship between Dennis Spicer and Ken Dodd – he even allowed his dummies to mingle with Doddy's Diddymen – and the two turns were back together again for the summer season of 1964. With support from jazz singer Rosemary Squires, theatrical impresarios George and Alfred Black presented *The Big Show of 1964* at the Blackpool Opera House.

Following the Royal Variety Performance in the November, Spicer was booked to be the Guest Star in *The Dora Bryan Show*, at the Manchester Opera House, for the Christmas season.

Negotiations too had already started for Spicer to play a residency at the London Palladium in early 1965, to be followed by a tour of North America. But, before all of that, first there were a couple of charity commitments to honour. Just two weeks after the Royal Variety Performance, on 16 November, Spicer travelled to Leeds to perform in two benefit concerts. The first was an afternoon show for inmates at Leeds prison, the second an evening performance for the newly established Leeds and District Jewish Convalescent Home. Driving home to Potters Bar after the show, he had a head-on collision with another vehicle on the A1 in Lincolnshire. Spicer was killed instantly. Bizarrely, police called to the scene spent precious minutes struggling to find a trapped child in the wreckage after tiny shoes were found in the footwell. They were, of course, from the feet of James Green.

Dennis Spicer was buried in North Mimms, Potters Bar. Showbiz pals Tommy Cooper, Jimmy Tarbuck and Ken Dodd were in attendance. His widow, June, was initially reluctant to mark the grave, not condoning the use of headstones, but in 2001 the family agreed that the Magic Circle could unveil a memorial plaque at the site. Spicer was already one of the finest the business had ever known, and he was not yet thirty. One can only imagine what joy he and James Green, along with

The Vent and his Muse. Dennis Spicer: one of the true greats of British variety.

Maxwell the Monkey, Puppy Doll the Poodle, Sexy Rexy the Wolf and Rikki Tikki the Tiger, not to mention his many other friends, could have given in the decades denied him.

As it is, he leaves a few brief pieces of telly footage, a suitcase of variety playbills and an undimmed warmth within anyone who had the good fortune to see him do his extraordinary thing.

TREAT YOURSELF TO an unbeatable night of variety the next time Steve Hewlett hits your town. An avid student and historian of the ventriloquial art, Steve has even played Wilton's Music Hall with Archie Andrews. His first UK tour, *Thinking Inside the Box*, was filmed at the Haymarket Theatre in our mutual home town of Basingstoke, Hampshire, and his cheeky old man character Arthur Lager is already a beloved classic. Steve has the spirit of Dennis Spicer in his very bones.

# Larry Stephens

## 1923–59

One of the joys in the fifties was the radio! We had a beaten up old radio in our house, where some of my brothers gathered around and hooted with laughter at the extraordinary antics of *The Goon Show*. What a programme that was. An amazing and exciting new brand of humour much admired and much copied in the school playground.

Whilst the programme was playing we waited for the classic moments to arrive, and how we screamed with laughter when they did: 'He's fallen in the water.' 'You dirty, rotten swine, you! You have deaded me!' 'I got a rise yesterday.' 'How much?' 'Eight inches.' Innuendo that was repeated endlessly in the playground the following day. Absolutely unmissable! Little did I know at the time that the forgotten hero behind this inspired lunacy was Larry Stephens. Sadly he died far too young, some saying the pressure overcame him.

*Bernard Holley*

Lawrence Geoffrey Stephens is one of the most shadowy of figures in British comedy. His contribution to *The Goon Show* is immense, and to call him forgotten is rather a moot point. His legacy of surreal and silly satire is timeless: sending up authority figures from a lowly us versus them position. Mocking, sometimes maliciously, but always with a smirk; a true foot solider of comedy. His work continues to make people laugh. His humour was so anarchic and so beautifully realised by The Goons themselves that the Stephens name will live on forever in the annals of comedy. Perhaps it is simply best to call Larry Stephens 'unknown' – or, as he was described by his friend and fellow Goon pioneer Spike Milligan in a 2007 radio tribute, 'the man who never was'.

Stephens was perfectly in tune with Spike Milligan. Both men were jazz fanatics; Stephens was skilled on the piano, and as often as not his playing paid for the drinks. Though he had trained as an accountant, he had already tasted a few drops of fame as a jazz pianist before the Second World War broke out. Both Milligan and Stephens had faced the terror of the war; Stephens had been a commando captain and had dealt with the traumatic aftermath by turning to alcohol – and to writing insane comedy, of course. It was during the war that his natural sense of the absurd and his love of off-colour, barrack-room humour became fully developed.

However, it wasn't Spike Milligan but that other Star in Battledress, Tony Hancock, who proved to be Stephens's earliest comic muse. Hancock had made a mark on pantomime and variety by the late 1940s but was still far from stardom when Stephens first wrote material for him. They became the very best of friends – Stephens was even best man at Hancock's first wedding – and as early as 1952 Stephens started developing a situation-comedy format for Hancock. *Vacant Lot* was very much in the mould of *Hancock's Half Hour*, which would emerge two years later, abandoning variety turn guest spots and musical interludes to present a character-driven half-hour of situation comedy. The seed of the idea – a dull life led in the fictional seaside town of Churdley Bay – was adapted by Stephens to become *Welcome to Welkham*, produced by Peter Eton, and which made it to a single broadcast episode on the Light Programme, on 19 July 1953. This failed to ignite for one simple reason: Hancock wasn't in it. Instead, *PC 49* lead Brian Reece – a likeable enough chap but no comedy genius – starred in his stead.

Stephens and Hancock remained friends, though. It certainly wasn't Stephens's fault that Hancock was replaced; writers had little to no clout in the hallowed halls of the Beeb. Still, Hancock's star was shining at its brightest after three series of *Hancock's Half Hour* on BBC Radio. Theatrical impresario Jack Hylton had been successfully showcasing him in the revue *The Talk of the Town*, at the Adelphi theatre, but sick of performing the same routines night after night, Hancock left the show. He did agree to Hylton's offer of his own television series, however, and Stephens eagerly accepted a personal invitation to write for *The Tony Hancock Show* (Associated-Rediffusion, 1956–57). Just a few weeks after the end of the first series, in June 1956, Hancock starred in the first *Hancock's Half Hour* for BBC Television, while in June 1957, Stephens was busy at Granada, as a pivotal force in the writers room of *The Army Game*. It would be the first sitcom smash for commercial television, but it was BBC Radio that saw Stephens's flights of fancy reach full potential.

He had already become Spike Milligan's filter and rock of comic stability. Stephens' absurdist humour was no less manic or unfettered but he could lasso Spike's flights of fancy and work them in to a half hour script. Stephens was great on jokes. He was also great on plots. His had a beginning a middle and an end. Not necessarily in that order, but they were there! Together, Spike's wildly dissident ramblings and Larry's moulding in to Goon logic saw *Goon Show* scripts of imperishable genius result. This was particularly true of the very early days, when Spike was as unfocused by his distrust of Michael Bentine [qv] as by his inability to get his inspired crackpot ideas down on paper. Stephens's skill at writing focused insanity is a key reason as to why the short film *The Case of the Mukkinese Battle-Horn* (1956) captures the essence of The Goons so well, despite the, initially unplanned, absence of Harry Secombe. The singing welshman had secured another gig. Besides, Peter Sellers had already pocketed a fifth of the meagre budget of £4,500. Thankfully Spike Milligan and Dick Emery worked cheap, folks, and Larry Stephens was like a kid in a sweet shop with zany visuals to bring his insanely inspired word pictures to life. The whole wonderful concoction is quite arguably the funniest film ever made in Britain.

However, as early as 1952 Stephens's appetite for rum and whisky led to disputes with Milligan, and the BBC was at a loss over the lacklustre and destructive behaviour Larry was displaying. In February 1954 it decreed that Stephens had broken his contract by failing to deliver the commissioned scripts for *The Goon Show* on time. As a result, he was out of a regular job and his work would only be considered on a freelance, script-by-script, basis. Outraged by his treatment, Stephens pledged never to have anything else to do with *The Goon Show*. To that end, in late '54 he teamed up with Jimmy Grafton to write *The Forces Show*. It wasn't that far from Goon folklore for it was Grafton who's pub, the Grafton Arms, had seen the birth of the Goons in the first place: a warm place of liquid refreshment where these fledgling fools who were to shape comedy history

An unknown lieutenant with the unknown man of British comedy. Stephens served as a captain during World War II.

could mingle, experiment, and bond with like-minded lunatics. Still, *The Forces Show* was regular work in both senses of the word: a weekly pay packet was assured, and the material comprised slightly abstract links for host Alfred Marks – another member of the Grafton Arms family – to introduce an hour of variety turns.

The pledge to permanently detach himself from the Goons was never going to stick, however, because Stephens needed the money and Milligan needed him. A wildly disorganised Spike, quietly going even more insane with the burden of solo script-writing duty through the winter of 1956, tried to tempt Stephens back to *The Goon Show* by promising to pay him a regular salary from his own pocket. An official BBC contract was never signed.

Delighting in this two-finger salute to the old Corporation, the Stephens–Milligan collaboration was resurrected at the eleventh hour for the sixth-series classic 'The Choking Horror'. The writing partnership was better than ever. This episode which, patching up a 'lover's tiff', was suitably enough transmitted on Valentine's Day 1956, is a Goon masterpiece; in an insanely funny premise, hair is infiltrating the great monumental buildings of London, *Quatermass*-style. Even fifty years on, the lengthy discussion about giving the Royal Albert Hall a haircut or providing a wig to the bald St Paul's Cathedral can leave listeners dumbstruck and joyful, gasping for breath. At the epicentre of 'The Choking Death', as with much Goon humour from these traumatised survivors of World War II, is a cynical treatment of warfare. Still raw after a decade, the futility and farce of conflict is perfectly punctured here. When it is announced that the second year of battle has been reached, Milligan unleashes his mad Eccles character, who does burst forth with a chorus of 'Happy Birthday'. Moreover, the barrack-room-style character names are as outrageous and daring as ever. Even the notorious Hugh Ampton makes an appearance, played with impeccable relish by Peter Sellers wallowing in his impersonation of Laurence Olivier. The material from Larry Stephens for this series, though limited, was of the highest standard.

It was hardly surprising, then, that, in a memo of Wednesday, 19 December 1956, producer Pat Dixon wrote: 'will you please note that Larry Stephens will be the part author of all the remaining *Goon Show* programmes. This is at the request of Spike Milligan.' Thus the set-up was etched in stone.

Not only were the best *Goon* scribes back together again, but Stephens was enjoying a burst of renewed comic creativity and working as a script doctor for the best comedians in the business. He could ascertain with lightning speed what line needed a word alteration, or whether a joke worked better before or after another joke. His increased contribution to the seventh series of *The Goon Show* – working on twenty-three episodes broadcast from October 1956 – gave it a freshness and maturity that helped reign in and enhance 'The Spectre of Tintagel' (1 November 1956), 'The Mystery of the Fake Neddie Seagoon' (29 November 1956), and 'The Missing Boa Constrictor' (21 March 1957). The established *Goon* characters would now break out into hits of the day – the David Whitfield catalogue was lovingly plundered – while both Spike and Larry displayed a delirious obsession with penguins: the flightless birds would pop up at the most unexpected moments – and, a decade or so later, inspire a similar passion in the Monty Python team, to boot. The cornucopia of Neddie's

'Needle Naddle Noos', and gushy, gaseous emission from Major Bloodnok pretty much redefined what British humour stood for.

Forever present at recordings and a continual crutch of support for a beleaguered and flagging Milligan, Stephens's absent-minded but very, very pleasing habit of doodling Goonish caricatures on scripts became legendary. His eye for what these soundscape-characters actually looked like was inspired. Indeed, when vintage scripts were reworked for *The Telegoons*, in the early 1960s, the spirit of Stephens was all over the design of the puppets, consciously or subconsciously inspired by how he saw the characters in his head.

In 1957 Milligan and Stephens had also combined their not-unimpressive musical skills to write 'Whistle Your Cares Away' as part of Spike's Decca Records contract. Goonish humour was to the fore, naturally.

However, despite enjoying the writing process, Stephens was still surviving on at least a bottle of hard liquor a day. For the first episode of the eighth series, 'Spon', in September 1957, Milligan had, once again, been forced to write alone. This time the cracks had become too severe, and this batch of *The Goon Show* would feature the last original co-writing credits for the Spike-and-Larry team; as well as a rare solo outing for Stephens, on 'The Stolen Postman' (transmitted 9 December 1957), and a new Goon writing partner in Maurice Wiltshire: the two concurrently working together on scripts for *The Army Game*. Stephens's last original script, 'The Seagoon Memoirs', was written with Wiltshire, and broadcast ten days before the Christmas of 1958, though his influence still prevailed over Milligan's unleashed genius. The two would socialise often in order to discuss the shows over and over again.

However, Stephens's already-high blood pressure was inflamed by his excessive alcohol intake, and on 26 January 1959 he suffered a massive cerebral haemorrhage and died. He was just thirty-five.

Various rumours abound as to the circumstances of his death. If not exactly suicide, his relentless reliance on booze was thought to be a very concerted effort to end his life early. Tales exist that he died literally before the very eyes of Spike Milligan as they enjoyed a late dinner and a chat about the next batch of *Goon Show* scripts, for the winter of 1959–60. However, the most likely scenario for Stephens's end seems to be that, in the company of his wife Diana,

Compendium Volume NINE · Vintage Goons

The ninth *Goon Show Compendium* from the Beeb Beeb Ceeb. Collect them all, folks!

he was driving to meet Spike for dinner in a London restaurant when the fatal haemorrhage struck.

His death is certainly the reason that *The Goon Show* broadcast on that 26 January 1959 was a hastily resurrected Stephens classic from December 1954. 'Dishonoured' was brushed down partly in tribute and partly in last-minute desperation, to be performed as 'Dishonoured – Again'. And that 1959–60 series, truncated to just six episodes, all written by Milligan alone, would form the very last series of *The Goon Show*, the final show being transmitted a year and two days since Larry's death. One hopes it gave the spirit of Larry Stephens one final chuckle at the expense of the BBC.

TREAT YOURSELF TO *The Goon Show Compendium Volume Nine – Vintage Goons* (BBC Physical Audio: 147133161X, 2014). Everyone has to start somewhere, and you may as well start here: thirteen episodes recorded for the BBC Transcription Services, and lovingly remastered. A delicious re-heat of some old fourth series classics from 1953/54, including 'The Mummified Priest', 'The Giant Bombardon', and 'The Albert Memorial', especially conjured up anew for an autumn 1958 season of 'Vintage Goons'. These benefit from both that first flush of Stephens genius, coupled with the clarity of his last months. Polished, definitive Goonery, but be warned: *The Goon Show* is infectious! To aid you through the dreaded lurgy may I humbly recommend *It's All in the Mind: The Life and Legacy of Larry Stephens* (Unbound, 2020), a sublime biography penned by Larry's second cousin, Julie Warren. The book gave me much Larry-fuelled laughter through lockdown.

# Jake Thackray

## 1938–2002

I first heard Jake singing on the Bernard Braden show and I immediately recognised a tremendous talent. He wrote a new song for the show every week, and each one was different from the last. His output was tremendous, and his gentle voice was that of a young Noël Coward. I fell in love with each and every song and swore that I would record as many as possible. Alas, only one surfaced on an LP I made way back in the early seventies called *This is Me*. This song was the lovely 'Lah-Di-Dah'. Back then, I only sang it once in public. That was in 1973 when I was hosting the live TV show *Sunday Night at the London Palladium*.

Instead of giving me a big-production number, as was their wont in those days, I told them I would just like to sit in the footlights with my legs dangling over the edge, with a handheld mic and a small spotlight on me so that people could just focus on the words of the song. It worked, and I had hundreds of letters from Jake's fans thanking me for promoting him. Seems like I'm doing it again, and I cannot sing his praises enough.

In my one-man show I delighted to introduce to American audiences such memorable songs as 'The Bantam Cock', 'Leopold Alcocks', 'Lah-Di-Dah' and 'The Castleford Ladies Magical Circle'. They love them. Any more and I shall have to call it, *The Jake Thackray Song Show Plus a Little Bit of Jim Dale*.

*Jim Dale MBE*

I arrived rather late to the Jake Thackray party but once I heard those dulcet tones for the very first time I was immediately embraced by his lilting manner and four-ale-bar charm. I had heard at least one of his songs years before actually discovering who he was. It was Jim Dale's recording of 'Lah-Di-Dah' that had bewitched me and, as Thackray himself might have said, made the Thackray bank balance look a little less sick. Still, that one song – a delicious, wary love letter of devotion to his new bride despite the eccentricities and annoyances of her family – was my full extent of Thackray knowledge. And I didn't even realise he had written it.

Then my mum, bless her, heard me listening to *This is Me* and recognised the song. 'Ooh, me and your Dad used to love him...' she said. 'Yes, it's Jim Dale!' I replied, probably a little too curtly. 'No, the man who wrote it...' she insisted. Looking at the credit, I mumbled: 'Umm... Jake Thackray?' 'Yes,' she gushed. 'He was lovely. He used to pull all those funny faces when he sang on the Esther Rantzen shows...'

And indeed he did. From the late 1960s Thackray sang a seemingly inexhaustible supply of self-penned satirical songs on *Braden's Week* (BBC1, 1968–72) – the Bernard Braden consumer show that gave Esther Rantzen her big break. Following the show's cancellation in the April of 1972, producer John Lloyd took just a year to elevate Rantzen to host, for another, much longer lived, BBC1 consumer show, *That's Life!* As with the Braden programme, Thackray was recruited for regular topical musical interludes, giving his usual world-wise and laconic commentary on human follies and international news. He was part of the show from 1974 to 1977.

Bernard Braden, not only a champion of Thackray but someone who innately understood the creative drive behind his voracious output, had penned the sleeve notes for Thackray's second EMI album, *Jake's Progress*, in 1968. Braden observed that: 'writing a new song each week isn't easy, and Jake usually selects a subject by Tuesday. Our designer, Don Giles, spends several days arranging a suitable set for a song about an old lady who lived in a room above a rural post office. On Saturday afternoon Jake wanders in with a look of abject apology. The song hadn't worked out to his satisfaction, so he's written instead a number about a trendy girl who lives in sin in Swiss Cottage. It's a mark of the quality of Jake Thackray that Don Giles happily goes to work improvising a new set which will be seen on the air in a matter of hours.'

Thackray was an observer of life, with the wit of an Oscar Wilde or a Thomas Sheridan. He also had the laid-back attitude of a strolling folk musician. There was not an ounce of arrogance in him, irony yes, but never arrogance. He saw people and events with a clear vision, and sang about what he saw. Once I'd discovered Thackray, I went round every second-hand record shop I could find in search of Thackray albums. There weren't that many. He only recorded four studio albums in his whole career, but what joy is to be found in that cough-and-spit vinyl. Songs about coquettish maidens and brigadiers, drunken village idiots and Home Counties witchcraft. It was basically a *Doctor Who and The Daemons* folk festival.

His greatest influence was the Frenchman Georges Brassens – 'the greatest of all singing dogs', as Jake often and enthusiastically referred to him during live sets – and Thackray's adaptation of Brassens's 'Le gorille' ('The Gorilla') is positive proof of the inspiration. The cunning guitar licks, the raw and bawdy lyrics, the gorilla a bon viveur living life to the full. The Brassens influence runs throughout Thackray's work, retold via a Yorkshire mentality of ramshackle country buses and whisky-sodden highwaymen. He would always cite the night of the inauguration of Cardiff's Sherman Theatre, when he opened for Brassens, as the pinnacle of his career. The date was 28 October 1973 and Thackray himself had pleaded long and hard to persuade a reluctant Brassens to appear.

As for my own rites of passage, I may have found his music, but where was Thackray himself? In those steam-driven days before the Internet, it was almost impossible to find anybody who had actually heard of him, never mind whether he was still around. I never did track him down, alas, though I got very close to it. I later found out that in May 2002, record producer David Harris had been spearheading a determined group of fellow Thackray admirers. The Jake Thackray Project had one mission: to make Thackray's fantastic back catalogue digitally available. In November 2002, a forty-two-song collection was released, initially in a limited edition run of 200 copies.

On Christmas Eve 2002 Thackray died. Out of money and in the drink, he had withdrawn from public appearances save for the occasional benefit performance or just for the sheer joy of it, at St Mary's Catholic Church, in Monmouth, South Wales. Having embraced his Roman Catholicism with even greater vigour in later life, this was his sanctuary from baying audiences and EMI executives. It was a fitting, quiet end to a life, but it's dispiriting to know it ended on the cusp of a Thackray revival. Journalist, Jake admirer and friend Victor Lewis-Smith researched and compiled a loving, telly-archive-packed salute, *Jake on the Box* (BBC2, 6 October 2006) which, in turn, in pre-production had fuelled a definitive, vault-squeezing CD retrospective, *Jake in a Box*, which EMI had released in May 2006.

Thackray himself had not been idle in those years away from the limelight. As well as the occasional special-guest appearance at folk festivals, for four years during the 1990s he wrote a weekly column of wit and wisdom for the *Yorkshire Post*. He was a natural journalist: the eye for detail and ear for gossip that had informed his lyrics was put to peerless work within the pages of the local paper. It was something of a full circle for this gentle figure who had always shunned the bright lights of show business and simply wanted to share his vision of the world.

Born John Philip Thackray on 27 February 1938, Jake was brought up in Kirkstall, a poor part of Leeds but a love for the more fanciful quirks of the Yorkshire countryside had blossomed and matured. A three-year teaching stint in Lille, France, gave his stoic toughness a sheen of sophistication. It also introduced him to the music of Brassens, an intelligent love affair that brought a magical, fairy-tale quality to Jake's storytelling. Yes, he revelled in the reality of the boozers and the blousy girls and the bilious blaggards that would populate his songs. There was a fundamental understanding of this world, and of his place within it: his songs had a playful, pleasing sense of the fun and the absurd at work. There was the frantic, higgledy-piggledy frenzy of the 'Jumble Sale' and the mild-mannered infatuation of 'The Little Black Foal'; the making-do romance of 'The Blacksmith and the Toffee-Maker' and the raucous wanderlust of 'It Was Only a Gypsy'.

Thackray's education was also clearly defined within his work. His schooling was strict Jesuit, in a Roman Catholic college in Leeds, and his degree – at the University of Durham

A candid snap of the charming chansonnier: at his home in Monmouth, 1978.

– in English. His love of words and guilt from pleasure were pretty much the foundations of his songbook.

He had some poetry published soon after he graduated, but had yet to pick up a guitar and put those words to music. Jake's French odyssey changed all that. The poetry was crucial, yet still he practised tirelessly to gain competence on the guitar, picking away at the strings night after night. A 'two-bit player' in comparison to his idol, but Thackray always was far too modest. He was now a folk singer with something to sing about. He returned to Leeds an invigorated man.

Teaching at Intake High School in Bramley, Leeds, this self-taught, embryonic Swinging-Sixties troubadour took to composing songs for his pupils, most famously warm and humorous riffs on the Christmas story. Both 'Remember Bethlehem' and 'Joseph' had an air of schooldays choir practice about them and are all the more endearing for that. An EMI recording for December 1967 was overproduced and overpopulated, with the John McCarthy Choir all but drowning out Thackray's simple re-telling of the tale. Strange really, considering that the disc's producer, Geoff Love, would do sterling work producing subsequent Thackray recording sessions. He happily came to the conclusion that all this introspective and perceptive folk singer needed was the accompaniment of his own rhythm guitar.

The Christmas single failed, but that first jaunt to Abbey Road, in the March of 1967, had given Thackray the confidence that he actually had something to

Jake, lost in his own lyrics, in concert.

say. Moreover, he had a keen ear for local gossip and booze-fuelled scandal. It was his inspiration to write. These songs were bawdy and brilliant: Hogarth cartoons set to music. Thackray himself later summed up his double-barrelled talent as 'the holy and the horrid'. These were never intended for the class-room, but instead were performed in the pubs and the clubs in the West Riding of Yorkshire; becoming even more familiar in the Northern region thanks to regular exposure on local BBC Radio and the television series *Look North*.

His music had now been heard by the masses. More importantly, it had been heard by The Beatles. The Fabs, at Abbey Road recording *Sergeant Pepper's Lonely Hearts Club Band*, were admirers of this quirky prophet. John Lennon made himself known to Thackray and told him: 'I like your gear, man' (as only one of 'the beautiful people' could get away with talking).

This humble schoolteacher faced with such unbridled praise from the biggest rock stars on planet earth did little to appease the over-awed Thackray when he nervously entered the recording studio. He was more at home with his nylon-string guitar, warbling away in his wood-alcohol baritone to the pupils he still taught or the dogs he was at turns bemused and beguiled by – or, better still, just himself. He was well and truly in the eye of the psychedelic storm in super-cool London and he didn't take to it one little bit. Nonetheless, the album he released in 1967, *The Last Will and Testament of Jake Thackray*, is sublime, with the stripped-down version – unheard until the 2006 box set – superior still. Here, that voice drives home each and every lyric with the intensity and purity of an artist at ease within his skin. 'The Statues', a song John Lennon particularly enjoyed, includes the evocative phrase of being as drunk as penguins. It is a lyric I use often myself – I hope Thackray would be pleased. Moreover, a cactus must always be referred to as a potted hedgehog or, at the very least, a son of a cucumber.

Thackray returned to Abbey Road in 1969 to record his second album, *Jake's Progress*. (Again he bumped into The Beatles – as you do – who were putting finishing touches to *Abbey Road*.) Mercifully, *Jake's Progress* was a return to basics, including beautiful, cynical love songs like 'Sophie' and knowing exposure of Satanic masses in 'The Castleford Ladies Magic Circle', which celebrates old dears each with 'a Woolworth's broomstick and a tabby cat'. There was even the uproarious 'Family Tree' – basically a three-minute version of today's TV show *Who Do You Think You Are?*.

Two more albums appeared in the 1970s: *Bantam Cock* and *On Again! On Again!*, which reiterated his passion for liquor, ladies and layabouts. He would play festivals throughout the 1970s and 1980s, and would even accept bigger gigs such as the Royal Variety Performance, but his favourite audience was the back-room bar, not the London Palladium. He would often balk at the enormity of the task at the last minute, pulling out of high-prestige assignments with next to no notice. Naturally, such behaviour did not endear him to backers and management, but he happily played the strolling player, even fronting his own perfect showcase, *Jake Thackray and Songs* (BBC2, 1981). This was Jake performing for his people, huge audiences packed in a tiny pub space, with a sincere and sweating Thackray plucking old familiar songs from the recesses of his memory. With an intimate acoustic guitar accompaniment by John Etheridge, as well as various guest-stars from folk's hall of fame, such as Ralph McTell and Alex Glasgow, this was very much Jake's happy place. A beautifully representative album of the series, also called *Jake Thackray and Songs*, was released by Dingles Records in 1983. The record was Thackray's last original release.

The years that followed would see minor interest in his old hits – EMI released a best-of package, *Lah-Di-Dah*, in 1991 – but, typically, only with death would he be fully reassessed. Now we have Jake Thackray festivals and all his albums in our CD collections; there are tribute acts and kind words – but still his place in the legacy of folk music and British comedy is far from secure. Yet through his songs you can tap into the follies and foibles of the British man. One perfectly turned phrase in that hound-dog voice of his can put a smile on the face and a pin in the heart. Who else could or indeed would rhyme 'Turkish moussaka' with 'knackered'?

An alternative pose from the *Jake's Progress* album session was utilised for this 1975 compilation release from EMI.

His rollicking, cheering and unsentimental 'Last Will and Testament' put it as clearly as anyone could. Here was a man who lived life one day at a time, and when that life was over the only thing to do was to 'get the priest and then go get the booze, boys... Let best beef be eaten, fill every empty glass... you can play on my guitar and sing my songs, wear my shirts, you can even settle my debts. You can kiss my little missus if she's willing then, but no regrets, boys...'. With a pint in your hand and one of his unforgettable songs on your lips: that's the perfect salute to Jake Thackray. Long may it continue.

TREAT YOURSELF TO *Live Performance* (EMI Records: B000F0UVBS, 2006). It's a fascinating soundscape of a genius running scared, and despite his clear and ever-lasting dislike of big, live events, this concert, recorded in 1970 at London's Queen Elizabeth Hall, sees him at the very top of his game. Polished and packed out with previously unreleased material, this two-CD release is the definitive starting point for the Thackray newcomer. It also includes the very best version of 'The Lodger', an exhaustive and exhausting tale of sex that is nothing short of distilled ribaldry.

# Thelma Todd

## 1906–35

I absolutely love Thelma Todd. My grandad used to cry with laughter when watching Laurel and Hardy; one of his favourites was *Chickens Come Home*, featuring Thelma Todd. I am so thrilled that she has been remembered in this super book.

*Fiona Everett*

There was a time in my formative years when it seemed I was forever being cast in the role of Roger Daltrey's juvenile alter-ego from the seminal Who classic 'Pictures of Lily'. But it was hardly surprising, being a young lad rather obsessed with classic films made some forty years before I was born, that the flaxen-haired leading lady I worshipped from afar, through the portal of old movies on the telly, would no longer be the twenty-something beauty in skimpy pre-Hays Code fashion. Bless my younger self.

Perhaps the most upsetting revelation was the fate of poor Thelma Todd. Dad didn't actually say, 'She's been dead since 1935,' and I'm not entirely sure I

Patsy Kelly and Thelma are daredevil air stewardesses in the comedy two-reeler *Air Fright* (1933).

cried all night, either, but the emotional stomach-punch of that horrible information remains an indelible memory. For, indeed, by the time I learned of her existence, the blonde, bubbly and eternally blooming Thelma Todd had been dead for decades, her death almost the blueprint for Jean Harlow, Marilyn Monroe and half a dozen other celluloid sex goddesses whose passport to fame and fortune came out of a bottle and a lusty studio executive.

For me, Thelma Todd – or Hot Toddy or the Ice Cream Blonde as she was affectionately known in her Hollywood heyday – was continually cropping up in the classic comedy films in the television schedules of my youth. In a way, she still is continually cropping up; a down-to-earth, earthy, and very sexy sex symbol. A knowing representative of the high society flapper girl who is still getting laughs in high-definition. Growing up, my heroes were the earliest talking comedians of Hollywood's Golden Age and Thelma Todd, funny and feisty, at turns seductive and deadpan, with a comedic scowl that could stop traffic, was a vital cog at the heart of much of their best work. No one else could unleash wanton desire so convincingly as in her screen seduction of Groucho Marx; and no one could turn Stan Laurel into an ashen-faced man-child as quickly as Todd did. She made British comedian Stanley Lupino even hotter under the collar in *You Made Me Love You* (1933). She even put the nose of the great Durante out of joint – no mean feat.

However, if Thelma is remembered today at all, it is for her death. In the week before Christmas 1935 she had attended a party held by Lupino and his soon-to-be-hot-Hollywood-property daughter Ida. The following morning Todd was found dead in her car, apparently a victim of carbon monoxide poisoning. Still, the circumstances smelled like week-old herrings: there had been a violent argument with an ex-lover at the party, and bizarrely her car and body were found in the garage of the ex-wife of her current squeeze, film director Roland West, Thelma's lip bloodied. However, the homicide bureau closed the case almost immediately, with a lukewarm statement claiming that Thelma Todd's death was 'accidental', although noting that she had had 'possible suicidal tendencies'.

Todd's last film appearance was in the 1936 Laurel and Hardy feature film *The Bohemian Girl*, although you would be hard-pressed to spot her in the final cut now. A regular with Stan and Ollie and producer Hal Roach for nearly ten years, Todd had completed her work as the leading lady of the film but her sudden death prompted Roach to reshoot most of her scenes. The only remnant is a brief gypsy musical number where she dances with all her usual mixture of allure and coquettishness.

Born on 29 July 1906, Thelma Alice Todd had wanted to be a schoolmistress before her stunning good looks tempted her into beauty pageants. In 1925 she was named Miss Massachusetts. Unsurprisingly, Hollywood came a-knocking and the following year she made an uncredited appearance as a girl at a dance hall in film-maker Herbert Brenon's weighty and worthy *God Gave Me Twenty Cents* (1926).

It was an inauspicious start but Thelma Todd was as carefree as ever. Before Brenon's film had even been released, she was cast in Sam Wood's romantic comedy *Fascinating Youth*, released by Paramount Pictures in March 1926 as a showcase for Charles 'Buddy' Rogers and, as the poster tag line had it, 'Paramount's Junior Stars'. This time, Thelma's character actually had a name: she was Lorraine Lane and positively lit up the screen.

Her first proper role and her first as leading lady to a star comedian – Ed Wynn – was just around the corner, although the film in question, *Rubber Heels* (1927), was hardly going to set the world alight. Indeed, Ed Wynn, in his film debut, was so disillusioned with the finished result that he offered Paramount a fortune to buy up every print before release; he was planning Hollywood's biggest bonfire. In the event, Wynn left America for a tour of Europe so he could escape the ordeal of promoting the film and facing the inevitable backlash. It certainly wasn't as bad as Wynn had made out, and Todd, in particular, shone as the gorgeous Princess Aline.

What Ed Wynn needed was sound cinema, for he was a man of vaudeville, of distinctive vocal delivery. Thelma Todd certainly didn't need to talk to be a star but, thankfully, her light, breezy and as often as not cynical vocal style fitted her image perfectly. She hastily became the darling of the Hal Roach short-subject comedies. The ones that seemed to showcase her talents to me, as a young lad, were those sainted classics starring Laurel and Hardy. Indeed, in May 1929, she co-starred in their very first talkie, knowingly and charmingly entitled *Unaccustomed As We Are*, playing the beautiful and beleaguered wife of frantic cop Edgar Kennedy. The balding comedy tsunami would regularly pop up in the mini masterpieces of Charley Chase, also under the Hal Roach umbrella, and Thelma was frequently his leading lady.

Importantly, by this time Todd was basically playing herself. Like Stan, Ollie and Charley, the lines had been blurred between public persona and private person. Thelma Todd was no longer just the random blonde firecracker on the dance floor or the street corner. She was Thelma Todd: a very funny lady. Her film appearances opposite Charley Chase in the likes of *Whispering Whoopee* and *Dollar Dizzy* (both 1930) convinced producer Hal Roach that he had another winner on his hands.

Thelma clearly had the potential to be a huge star. She looked fantastic and she could play comedy with her eyes closed. Moreover, she would happily muck in with the fun studio ethos. On more than one occasion she gladly cameoed in someone else's film, without credit or cash – notably as Lady Plumtree in the 1930 Laurel and Hardy short *Another Fine Mess*.

Roach's hottest property was Stan and Ollie, and his hottest leading lady was Thelma Todd. In 1931 he launched her as a new comedy star, partnered by the owl-like ZaSu Pitts. Here were the female Laurel and Hardy that Hal Roach had been desperately searching for. That first film, *Let's Do Things*, set out the stall definitively, and cast them as heightened versions of themselves: Thelma and ZaSu, a comedy duo, on a double date with a couple of blockheads. Thelma was the go-getting, confident modern girl; ZaSu was the thorn in her side. Pitts delivered much of the clumsy slapstick and social awkwardness but Todd was much more than just the decorative cement. Although the scenarios would often call on her to lose her clothing, Todd performed with a winning air of casual frustration and showed true talent for broad physical comedy. Despite Todd's flirty flights of sophistication, the pairing was very much dumb and dumber blonde.

As if to hammer home the association, and in order to drum up a bit of early interest in the Todd and Pitts shorts, 1931's *On the Loose* even roped in Stan and Ollie themselves. A riotous day on the rides at Coney Island highlighted just how good a team Pitts and Todd were, not to mention the precious, no-frills capturing of everyday Americans at leisure, caught like flies in amber.

Thelma Todd: Queen of Hal Roach Studios, Culver City, California.

The seventeen shorts that Todd and Pitts made together – utilising the comedy shorthand of playing themselves, Thelma and ZaSu – are some of the funniest and freshest you could hope to see. At the same time, Todd was also making waves in feature films – films that all too rarely get an outing on television today. For Hal Roach she was a natural shoo-in for Laurel and Hardy's ambitious restoration comedy *The Devil's Brother* (1933). Loaned out to Paramount, Todd made Groucho raise more than an eyebrow and enflamed Harpo in a couple of the earliest, wildest and very best sound comedies, *Monkey Business* (1931) and *Horse Feathers* (1932). These Marx Brothers masterpieces got in on the permissive action just in the nick of time; attitudes to sex, pool-room humour and alcohol were changing in America, and American film had to reflect that change.

Thelma, typically a vision in sheer evening gown with champagne cocktail in hand, is one of the indelible images of pre-Code Hollywood. As if to reinforce cinema's last hurrah of debauchery and free-wheelin' fun, she joined a straitjacketed Buster Keaton and an unkempt Jimmy Durante in MGM's *Speak Easily* (1932). Keaton and Durante were one of the most unlikely, and unlikable, comedy pairings of all. Individually each was a genius and a showman; together they were awkward, and not in a funny Todd-and-Pitts sort of a way. But Thelma Todd helped to massage

ZsSu Pitts and Thelma: a great double act cracking each other up with laughter, on the set of *On the Loose* (1931).

the join a little and went on to support Durante's Great Schnozzle again, in *Palooka* (1934).

Todd had also proved herself a serious actor, most notably as Miles Archer's distrustful widow in the original version of *The Maltese Falcon* (1931). One can only imagine how she would have twisted Humphrey Bogart round her little finger had she lived to reprise her role in the remake a decade later.

But it was comedy that put food on the Todd table, and when ZaSu Pitts left the Hal Roach fold to star in a string of features opposite Slim Summerville in 1933, the producer was quick to team Todd up with another loveable klutz, Patsy Kelly. The mixture was as before: smart and sexy Thelma struggling through life with her silly and slapdash friend.

By 1934 Thelma could afford to invest in a café in Pacific Palisades, Los Angeles. Thelma Todd's Sidewalk Café quickly became a Mecca for film stars and rubber-necking film fans. *After the Dance*, a rollicking Columbia Pictures crime thriller, went on general release in July 1935, just five months before Todd's death. Her performance as Mabel Kane, silly and sexy and sarcastic, also displayed a strong reading of the dramatic scenes. The short comedies with Patsy Kelly were going from strength to strength, with the latest, *An All American Toothache*, being one of the funniest and most inventive: sassy Thelma persuades her clueless chum Patsy to allow dental students to practise on her! By the time audiences got to see the film, at the end of January 1936, the sass of Thelma was no more. One would imagine contemporary viewers would have required more than laughing gas to raise a smile, but Thelma being Thelma, she left them something very, very funny.

But, Hollywood being Hollywood, there was always another blonde bombshell to fill the gap that Thelma Todd had left. Having decimated her final performance for the Valentine's Day 1936 release of *The Bohemian Girl*, producer Hal Roach ploughed on with more Patsy Kelly comedies, with two new partners in quick succession and to diminishing returns. Perhaps Thelma Todd wasn't that easy to replace after all.

Hot Toddy. One of Hollywood's finest comediennes. Period.

Today, with just a star on the Hollywood Walk of Fame and a death shrouded in mystery, it's almost understandable that Thelma's actual work gets forgotten. Understandable – but not forgivable. At her peak, she was the very best in Hollywood; a funny, sexy woman who could hold her own against comedy behemoths. Certainly more than just the average dumb blonde.

TREAT YOURSELF TO *Hal Roach: Female Comedy Teams* (Edition FilmMuseum: B004FGWFBW, 2010). A beautiful and affectionate packaging of Roach's patchily successful attempts at creating a female Laurel and Hardy, there are a tantalising ten outings for Thelma Todd here – five with ZaSu Pitts and five with Patsy Kelly. The audience-pleaser is *On the Loose* (1931), with its cameo appearance from Laurel and Hardy, but the prize is *Top Flat* (1935). Thelma, disguised as a French maid and working in a scrumptious Park Avenue apartment, contrives to convince Patsy that the place belongs to her: with hilarious consequences! This was the very last comedy short released before Todd's death and shows her in blistering form. Essential.

# Jack Train

## 1902–66

To me, Jack isn't a radio star; he isn't merely the 'Guv'nor'. He's just a real good friend and (as so many of his listeners put it in their letters) 'the sort of chap I'd like to have a drink with any time'.

*Barbara Shaw*

*It's That Man Again*, or *ITMA*, to give it its more familiar, shortened handle, was the pioneering flagship radio comedy show of the Second World War, originally conceived as a vehicle for Liverpudlian comic Tommy Handley in 1938. Scripts were worked and reworked by writer Ted Kavanagh who finally came up with the perfect sketch show structure full of indelibly memorable comic characters. Quickfire jokes and instantly memorable catchphrases were the key, and many of them passed into everyday language for years to come – you can still hear the occasional 'Can I do you now, sir?' or 'I don't mind if I do…', even if the people saying the lines have no idea from where they originated. Over sixty years since the death of Handley – and, with it, the death of *ITMA* – the show still stands as the blueprint for the comedy sketch format. Whether it's *The Two Ronnies* or *The Fast Show*, everything has directly or indirectly plundered the ethos of *ITMA*.

Arguably the forgotten genius of the show was fast-talking character comedian Jack Train. Born in Plymouth, Devon, on 28 November 1902, Train hadn't been involved with *ITMA* from the very beginning. Nor was the show – which was pretty much the foundation stone for radio comedy in Britain – an immediate success; a trial run from July 1939 lasted only four episodes before war was declared and, in any case, these shows had received only a lukewarm reception. Already prepared for the threat of bombing in London, the BBC Variety Department decamped to the safer environs of Bristol, and took with them Tommy Handley and a new cast of supporting actors, all of whom had been security cleared by the Ministry of Information. A renewed vigour spurred on a second attempt at launching *ITMA*: the overall premise was changed from a pirate radio ship – rather suitable in wartime – to a tongue-in-cheek government department. In writer Ted Kavanagh's off-kilter vision, the Ministry of Aggravation and Mysteries at the Office of Twerps may have been Handley's kingdom but the titular, totem pole of calm – like Kenneth Horne in *Round the Horne* a generation later – needed a gallery of grotesque marionettes to dance around him. For this new shine on an old idea, the fresh crop of performers to satellite Handley included Jack Train – and a myriad of eccentric and outrageous characters were created to populate the show.

Train's roles were legion. There was the eternally fussy Fusspot and the fragrantly rustic Farmer Jollop. Train was also an elderly simpleton called Mark Time who would ponder every question before replying: 'I'll have to ask me dad!' He embraced comic racial stereotypes as the Japanese mastermind Hari Kari – well, there was a war on, and to that end Train was also Funf, a thickly accented German spy with an immortal catchphrase: 'This is Funf speaking!' The echoey sound effect of this propagandist was achieved by speaking into a beer glass; indeed, Train had got the *ITMA* gig by demonstrating this wheeze to Kavanagh in the pub one evening. The phrase caught the public's imagination immediately. It is even rumoured that British intelligence would start top secret telephone conversations with this comedic gambit. The character single-handedly sent up the entire propaganda machine of the Germans, and that was the very point. At the peak of the show's popularity nearly half the population were tuning in. If Britain could laugh at *ITMA* while fighting the enemy, then the nation could take pretty much anything the enemy could throw at it.

So too, it seemed, could *ITMA*. With bombing now affecting Bristol, the department was relocated to Bangor, on the coast of North Wales. For a short time, in the summer of 1941, the show was even renamed *It's That Sand Again*.

Jack Train added to his roster of characters with Claude, who, alongside Horace Percival's Cecil, was one half of a painfully polite pair of handymen who would never walk through an open door without intoning: 'After you, Claude...'; 'No, after you Cecil...'. Train was also given the role of fidgeting gangster Lefty. Part of another double act, this time with Sydney Keith as Sam, the character proved so popular that he, along with many other favourites from the show, were plonked down lock, stock and barrel into the ramshackle but historically vital feature-film version released in 1942.

Undoubtedly Jack's greatest and most durable *ITMA* creation was Colonel Chinstrap. A permanently fermented Indian Army Officer, it was he who was responsible for the 'I don't mind if I do' catchphrase, as he continually misunderstood each and every offer made to him as an invitation to partake of a drink.

Talking in 1966, Train explained that: 'I came across the original of Chinstrap. I met him before the war with John Snagge, the BBC announcer. I was fascinated by him from the moment he said to Snagge: "I say, my boy, I've just bought a water heater on a ten-year HP agreement. The silly fools. They don't know I'm killing myself with drink!"' Delightfully, Train recounted that the old boy loved the character of Chinstrap but didn't recognise himself. 'Wonderful character,' he'd told Train. 'I knew silly buggers like that in India!' Just under a decade after first meeting him, Snagge sent Train a telegram informing him that the original Chinstrap had died. It read: 'The Colonel beat the gas company by seven months.' The *ITMA* Chinstrap enjoyed an equally charmed life himself, and was the only character to go on and flourish after the end of the series.

Jack Train played the Colonel opposite Noel Purcell in an *ITMA* spin-off radio comedy *The Great Gilhooly*, in 1950, and on New Year's Day 1954 Train starred in *At Last! The True Story of Humphrey Chinstrap (Col. Retd.)*, a BBC Home Service mockumentary about the life and times of the Colonel. Written

by Ted Kavanagh, there were
fleeting contributions from
old – in character – *ITMA*
cohorts Dino Galvani, Deryck
Guyler [qv], Horace Percival
and Clarence Wright. The next
generation of crazed comedians
gladly paid homage to the
character when Train recreated
Chinstrap for two episodes
of *The Goon Show*. In 'Who is
Pink Oboe?', broadcast on 12
January 1959, Train replaced an

Jack doing the glass trick to get the Funf voice
during an *ITMA* broadcast. Fred Yule is
amused. Tommy Handley does a fine line in
feigned shock.

indisposed Peter Sellers, with the Colonel filling the shoes of Major Bloodnok.
The sheer versatility of Sellers is proved in that episode by the fact that it took
three other actors – Kenneth Connor, Graham Stark and Valentine Dyall – to
handle the bumper bag of characters he usually embodied each and every week.
An even better *Goon* resurrection of the Colonel is 'Shifting Sands', which
gallantly killed off the character of Chinstrap but not before allowing him to
spar brilliantly with Sellers's bumptious Bloodnok. The final epitaph for his
fallen comrade sums up Chinstrap's entire comic appeal. A white stone marks
the spot and the inscription reads: 'Here lies Colonel Chinstrap. Drowned –
from the inside!'

'Without the Colonel I might never have become widely known,' reflected
Train shortly before his death. 'It's funny how luck plays such a big part in life.
Nobody has been luckier than me.' Indeed, his heritage as that greatly loved
voice from *ITMA* refused to go away. 'Now I look upon Chinstrap as another
me,' Train continued. 'I've really enjoyed that character. The funny thing is that
when I first started playing him I hardly drank at all. But people assumed I was as
big a toper as Chinstrap and they were always offering me drinks. You know, it's
amazing the number of people who still remember him – even the young ones.
I was entertaining the troops in the Far East a few years ago, and all the young
soldiers knew him, though they must have only just been born when *ITMA* was

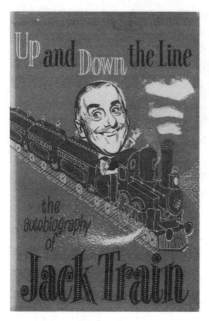

A comedian at the heart of the engine. Jack's hilarious and, at times, moving memoir, published 1956.

going. Many a time I was told: "When I was a kid we had to keep quiet in our house when *ITMA* was on." In public, people still come up to me and talk about Chinstrap. They don't recognise my face so much – it's usually when they hear me talking. I've one of the most distinctive voices in Britain. People always recognise it.'

The character had certainly boosted Train's professional life. During the reign of *ITMA*, Train had made a couple of feature films with Arthur Askey: *King Arthur Was a Gentleman* (1942) and *Miss London Ltd.* (1943). He had also found a fairly healthy living in voice-over work for animators Joy Batchelor and John Halas. In 1949 he joined a stellar cast including Joyce Grenfell, Claude Hulbert and Peter Bull to provide the voices for stop-motion animation puppets in a feature film version of *Alice in Wonderland*. Carol Marsh – in the flesh – was the eponymous hero.

By the start of the 1950s Train had become a very popular personality. He had been a regular on the radio panel game *Twenty Questions* from its start in the March of 1947. A variation on the old 'Animal, Vegetable or Mineral' parlour game, producer Cleland Finn added 'Abstract' to the mix, as well as 'The Mystery Voice' round. The show was a huge success. There was even a film, *The 20 Questions Murder Mystery* (1950), in which Train played himself, as part of the panel receiving anonymous clues to a crime! There were the occasional television appearances too. From July 1951 he appeared on the panel for *What's My Line?*, and guest-starred on *The Anne Shelton Show* (Associated-Rediffusion, 23 March 1959). He even became a radio disc jockey on *Record Express*. It was a natty pun on his surname that he never shied away from; his touching autobiography was entitled *Up and Down the Line* (Odhams Press, 1956), while autograph requests were invariably embellished with a doodle of an engine.

By the mid-1960s Jack was living in reluctant semi-retirement in leafy South Kensington with his second wife, Fay, but he appeared desperate to get back into the public eye, even if that meant agreeing to be the spokesman for an advertising campaign, as he explained. 'A new career in TV?' he pondered. 'You never know! The chocolate commercial is the only one I've appeared in, though years ago I did a few voices. I'm very good on voices and dialect, and I don't understand why I've not been offered more television work. But my only complaint is that I haven't been asked to advertise Scotch on TV.'

Clearly towards the end of his days Train wanted and needed to work, eager, as most old pros are, to dismiss any thoughts that he might not want to return, or indeed be up to returning, to the game: 'I'm still doing all right, though I would like more work. I can't afford to retire and I wouldn't if I could, but with the march of time work isn't as frequent as it was. For many years I didn't have to look for work. Now I don't know how to. I don't like to ask, but you can tell everybody I'm still at the same address – and I'm cheaper than I used to be!'

At the time, he was excited about the prospect of his first proper character-acting role for television. It was for an episode of *Turn Out the Lights*, a comedy ghost-hunting spin-off from *Pardon the Expression* starring Arthur Lowe, a series which itself had been a spin-off for Lowe's old *Coronation Street* character Leonard Swindley. Train was cast as 'Man at Meeting' in the episode 'One for Yes, Two for No'. It was an inauspicious false start: by the time the episode was screened on 6 February 1967 Train had died (on 19 December 1966), at the age of sixty-four. Alas, all episodes of *Turn Out the Lights* are missing, believed wiped, so although limited, Train's last performance has vanished like a will-o'-the-wisp: so do search your lofts. And raise a large glass to Jack Train. I don't mind if I do!

TREAT YOURSELF TO the BBC's initial *ITMA* release (BBC Enterprises Ltd.: ZBBC1011, 1988), which gathers together four historic shows on two audio cassettes: special editions dedicated to the Navy, Army and Air Force, as well as the Royal Command Performance from Broadcasting House transmitted on 4 December 1947.

# Karl Valentin and Liesl Karlstadt

## 1882–1948 and 1892–1960

Where to start on Valentin? Comedy genius, radical Dadaist, singer, breathtaking physical presence; Liesl the perfect foil. An intellectual clown who wallowed in verbal acrobatics, sometimes rendered in such a broad Bavarian dialect that even many Germans are baffled. He was a huge subversive cultural presence in the Weimar Republic, influencing the likes of Bertolt Brecht, with whom he worked. I was once assailed by a Munchener who described his own anarchic politics as Valentinian, and was surprised that I knew roughly what he meant! He is still revered by many in Germany, but beyond the silent Brecht collaboration *Mysterien eines Frisiersalons* remains largely unknown outside it. His museum in Munich is a must-visit venue and it's important that he be referenced in an English-language book!

*Richard Dacre*

It is perhaps ridiculous to include within the pages of this book a comedian who not only has a museum dedicated to him but also a statue in his honour. Karl Valentin was a colossal talent, likened to Charlie Chaplin by Bertolt Brecht, no less. Still, beyond the environs of his native Munich the dark and disturbing comic genius of Valentin is nothing more than a footnote to the work of others.

He was born Valentin Ludwig Fey on 4 June 1882. Something of a musical prodigy, he was taught to play the guitar by Heinrich Albert, the most prominent guitarist in Germany, and had studied the art of the variety clown under the distinguished Hermann Strebel. In the early 1920s Valentin found his lifelong partner in comedy in Liesl Karlstadt, herself a force of German cinema since 1913 – largely under the inspiration of Valentin. The two had first met at the Frankfurter How hotel, in 1911, when Karlstadt was still Elisabeth Wellano. Valentin suggested the stage name. Charismatic, charming and confident, Valentin was also married, with two children. Still, the nineteen-year-old Karlstadt was bewitched, and a fractious love affair began. Valentin and Karlstadt may have gone on to often play husband and wife in absurdist, abstract terms on screen over a twenty-six year association, but in reality he always refused to abandon his family for her.

Karlstadt was initially over-awed and over-shadowed by her theatrical mentor, and Valentin quickly became the most influential of figures. A white-faced absurdist. A clown in the tradition of William Shakespeare's wise observers: surreal attacks on authority via barbs of jet-black humour and energetic wordplay were the frantically beating pulse of Valentin. His influence was quick and potent, not least due to the praise lavished upon him by Bertolt Brecht, who was a journalist at the time. Having taken on a supporting role in Valentin's political cabaret in Munich, Brecht's diary recorded many subsequent encounters with this clown with a conscience. Brecht made a sincere and deliberate comparison to Charlie Chaplin thanks to the 'virtually complete rejection of mimicry and cheap psychology' within Valentin's comedy.

Later citing Valentin as one of his biggest influences, Brecht recalled: 'The clown... performed in a beer hall. He did short sketches in which he played refractory employees, orchestral musicians or photographers who hated their

Karl predicting a museum dedicated to him. Curated by his friend and colleague Hannes Konig, the collection opened in Munich, in 1959.

employer and made him look ridiculous. The employer was played by his partner [Karlstadt], a popular woman comedian who used to lad herself out and speak in a deep bass voice.' When Brecht was staging his production of *Edward II* he asked Valentin's advice on how the soldiers should look. The unforgettable reply – 'They're pale. Scared shitless' – categorically initiated the concept of Epic theatre: a sense of stark, abstract truth, experimental and bold, with Valentin himself applying chalk to the faces of Brecht's actors.

Valentin, Karlstadt and Brecht were exciting and loyal collaborators. In 1922 they posed together in a photographic parody of Munich's Oktoberfest, and the following year Valentin starred in a riotous two-reeler, *Mysterien eines Friseursalons* (*Mysteries of a Barbershop*), that Erich Engel directed from a script by Brecht. It is now universally acknowledged as one of the hundred most important German films of all time.

By the end of the 1920s Valentin and Karlstadt were one of the most popular screen pairings in Europe, and December 1929 saw the release of *Der Sonderling* (*The Eccentric*, also known as *The Odd One*), which had been shot at Munich's Emelka Studios under the direction of Walter Jerven. Never were there more apt monikers for Karl Valentin: the film is an essay in physical absurdity and political satire.

Throughout the 1930s Valentin and Karlstadt made a string of important and hilarious films, notably *Die verkaufte Braut* (*The Bartered Bride*) in 1932, *Kirschen in Nachbars Garten* (*Fruit in the Neighbour's Garden*) in 1935, and *Donner, Blitz und Sonnenschein* (*Thunder, Lightning and Sunshine*) in 1936.

Valentin and Karlstadt continued working together (as well as separately), as often as not with Valentin also producing and scripting, until Valentin's death, after which Karlstadt still proved a popular attraction, maturing into something of a Margaret Dumont for films like *Das Doppelte Lottchen* (*Two Times Lotte*) in 1950, *Feuerwerk* (*Fireworks*) in 1954 and *Schick Deine Frau nicht nach Italien* (*Do Not Send Your Wife to Italy*) in 1960.

But Karlstadt was, and forever will be, linked with the lasting legacy of Karl Valentin; today his statue in Munich is lovingly strewn with wreaths of flowers in memory of a pioneer of the absurd. Screenings of the Valentin and Karlstadt films took the absurdist genius of Samuel Beckett down hitherto unexplored tunnels and the influence continued to echo down each subsequent generation to the comedy, music, film and theatre-making of Helge Schneider. The body of comedic art that is the Valentin and Karlstadt legacy is of international relevance and importance. Each and every one of us flagrantly odd ones should tip a hat to them.

Valentin and Karlstadt, in a surprisingly staid publicity pose, 1935

In much more typically bizarre garb, promoting their 1924 Berlin cabaret *Der Wilden Buhne. The Wild Stage*, indeed.

TREAT YOURSELF TO *Karl Valentin and Liesl Karlstadt: Die Kurzfilme Neuedition* (Film101: B00166ZYVW, 2008), an essential collection of the duo's greatest short films, including *Der Firmling* (*The Firmling*), 1934, *Die Erbschaft* (*The Inheritance*), 1936, and *In der Apotheke* (*In the Pharmacy*), 1941, plus an extensive documentary, presented across three DVDs.

# Norman Vaughan

## 1923–2002

In my dim and distant past, I remember working with Norman Vaughan.
We appeared together in *Play It Again, Sam* at the Ashcroft Theatre in
Croydon. He was an excellent all-rounder with loads of energy. He had
taken on the impossible by taking over from Bruce Forsyth as compère
on *Sunday Night at the Palladium*. How could anyone forget him?

*Valerie Leon*

Like Emperor Nero wearing a red nose, Norman Vaughan could conduct his
audience with the merest up or down of a thumb – well, two thumbs, actually.
While Nero had the Coliseum, Vaughan had the Palladium. Thumbs up would
be accompanied with his catchphrase, 'Swingin'!' Thumbs down would evoke
another catchphrase: 'Dodgy!' That was all he needed. Thousands in person
and millions at home in front of the telly would be in the palms of his hands.
And there certainly were millions of them. Inheriting ITV's smash-hit variety
show *Sunday Night at the London Palladium* from boy wonder Bruce Forsyth

in the January of 1962, Vaughan had an audience of 20 million fall into his lap. He didn't muff the opportunity, and by October Vaughan had been invited to compère the Royal Variety Performance. He held court at the London Palladium for four years and the audiences didn't dip a man. No mean feat.

Comedy was in Vaughan's blood, of course, with the natural verve and wit of the confident Liverpudlian; born on 10 April 1923. He had run away from home at the tender age of thirteen to indulge, as he later explained, in 'singing, dancing and telling jokes onstage for a living'. And that's exactly what he did. The singing came first, when at the age of fourteen he joined the Eaton Boys' Choir, in Leigh, Lancashire. He may have exuded innocence but behind the warbling were the fast quips and incandescent whizz-bangs of a scallywag. These would be consolidated when he joined variety troupe Dudley Dale and His Gang. The gang were a smartly attired collection of boys who would sing and crack cheeky jokes. Vaughan would behave like a naughty schoolboy for the rest of his career, chuckling behind his hand at misfortune or innuendo, showing off in front of his adoring crowd and talking up a storm whatever the situation. He had the gift of the gab (and some) – a blessing for the stand-up, game-show host and compère.

But first came the dancing. At the age of just fifteen, he formed his own company, The Dancing Aces, and toured the country until service in the Second World War saw him posted to Italy and the Middle East. Like many of his contemporaries Sergeant Vaughan used the war to his show business advantage, staging camp concerts in which he could flex his talents for song and for dance. Not only that but his earthy humour and observational comedy patter was pushed more and more to the fore. Vaughan was very funny. And having Spike Milligan and Harry Secombe stationed alongside him didn't do him any harm either. The shows were a sensation.

But upon demob he wasn't an instant hit, and instead worked variety theatres in Australia for two years before returning home to crawl up the bills of variety theatres and seaside shows across the UK. Vaughan made his first television appearance on the variety turn *Showcase*, on 13 September 1954. He displayed a quick wit, winning smile, and a confident manner – despite later admitting that performing in-front of the camera had absolutely terrified him. ATV had heard good things and, in September 1955, Vaughan teamed up with army buddy Harry

Taking time off from the twelve-week nationwide tour of *Calamity Jane* to promote *Barbara Windsor's Book of Boobs*, 1979.

Secombe for the first of several appearances on *Saturday Showtime*, commercial television's fledgling platform for variety turns. Secombe and Vaughan were a winning combination – they had form, after all. *The Harry Secombe Show* was transmitted on 24 September 1955. The first ever sketch show on ITV, Norman Vaughan was in it too. The partnership amicably split, with Vaughan continuing to hone his skills on the variety circuit. In 1959 he became the compere for Cliff Richard's touring rock 'n' roll show. By 1962 ATV considered Vaughan more than match-fit to host their flagship variety spectacular *Sunday Night at the London Palladium* and just as the show had made Bruce Forsyth an instant television star after years of hard graft, so too did it transform the career of Norman Vaughan. He was doing very nicely on the variety theatre circuit but the level of opportunity and exposure offered by *Sunday Night at the London Palladium* was immense – it was regularly being watched by over half of the population, over twenty-eight million people. Vaughan was a bag of nerves that first night. Who wouldn't be? Pulling himself together, and pulling through, he stormed the opening comic monologue and the baying crowd took him to their hearts. It was practically a 'Bruce who?' moment, so quickly was he in charge. His knack to the introductions was to keep them bright and short; moreover, the host had to be at ease with the great British public and Vaughan was certainly that.

The game-show aspect of the programme was intrinsic to the popularity of *Sunday Night at the London Palladium* – ordinary members of the public could come along and win big prizes, as amusing interludes between the international singers, stars and speciality acts. During Vaughan's reign 'Beat the Clock' became a national obsession. Vaughan kept the contest lively, with a slightly mocking, sympathetic shake of the head when everything went belly-up. He would chuckle, point at the contestant, acknowledge the camera and play the fool like a court jester beamed into eagerly awaiting homes. It was a television revelation. Vaughan's success more than justified ATV awarding him his very own variety comedy series, *A Touch of the Norman Vaughans*. Scheduled for six editions, from 3 January 1964, the show proved so popular that the run was extended to twelve weeks.

In 1965 Vaughan handed the baton of *Sunday Night at the London Palladium* host to fellow Liverpudlian comedian Jimmy Tarbuck, ostensibly to accept an offer to star in a BBC sketch series. *The Norman Vaughan Show*, broadcast from 1 November 1966, was produced by Kenneth Carter, who had overseen Vaughan's small-screen debut in *Showcase*.

Success was sweet and money was easy when he took on a long-running advertising assignment for Cadbury's Roses chocolates throughout the tail end of the sixties. His slogan – 'Roses grow on you' – can still render people of a certain age misty-eyed with nostalgia.

Norman took to fame like the proverbial duck, headlining summer seasons and pantomimes – and, in particular, taking Blackpool by storm. The Las Vegas of the North of England was perfect for Vaughan's snappy swagger, and he enjoyed huge success there through the 1960s and 1970s. In 1972 he deployed his tried-and-tested game-show stamina and technique to take over from super-smooth host Bob Monkhouse when he left *The Golden Shot*. All the 'up a bit', 'down a bit' banter suited Vaughan down to the ground; it was the *Sunday Night at the London Palladium* game in broader strokes. Vaughan's cocky charm and easy manner was aided and abetted by glamorous hostess Anne Aston, and 'Maid of the Month', Cherri Gilham.

Leaving the show in 1973 in the more-than-capable hands of Charlie Williams, for a time Vaughan hosted *Mr and Mrs* – ordinary members of the public trying to second-guess intimate facts about each other. Not only could he host game shows with his eyes shut, Vaughan could also devise them. In 1981 he came up with the idea for *Bullseye!*, though the inspiration was hardly Archimedes-like. One day, while watching a game of darts, he thought to himself: there's a game show here if you just add general knowledge questions. Eureka!

Jimmy Tarbuck's Beatle cut is teased by Norman's old army buddy, Harry Secombe; Billy Butlin looks on, 1966.

The show made club comedian Jim Bowen a star and Norman Vaughan a very wealthy man indeed. An already comfortably well-off Vaughan didn't need to work anyway, and so he didn't, preferring to enjoy semi-retirement in his homes in Spain, Florida and Surrey. However, he happily accepted the occasional guest-spot when the smell of the greasepaint was too hard to resist, bringing his easy-going charm to *Celebrity Squares* (ATV, 1976), *Looks Familiar* (Thames Television, 1977), *Those Wonderful TV Times* (Tyne Tees Television, 1978), and *The Good Old Days*, topping the old time music hall bill, on BBC1, on 25 January 1979. Vaughan's last regular television assignment was in 1980, as a team captain deputising for Lionel Blair on the Thames charades show *Give Us A Clue*.

He had proved himself an actor, appearing with Paul Jones in *In Order of Appearance*, at the Chichester Festival, in 1977, and enjoying a nationwide tour with Barbara Windsor, in *Calamity Jane*, in 1979. Vaughan was also a very decent farceur, touring in *A Bedfull of Foreigners*, in 1980, and *No Sex Please – We're British*, in 1988.

His sporadic film roles were really breezy variations on himself: he played a television commentator in *Doctor in Clover* (1966) and a stage comedian in *Come Play With Me* (1977). And he did actually play himself in *Hear My Song* (1991), a biopic of tenor Josef Locke.

However, Norman was most at home doing what came naturally; no airs, no graces, just giggles and gaffs, all done with deep affection. One of his happiest assignments was a nine-week season at the Coventry Theatre, supporting his old chum Harry Secombe, in *The 1970 Spring Show*. Fittingly, Vaughan's last appearance was to pay tribute to his beloved fallen comrade and cohort, Harry Secombe, in *Wild About Harry: A Tribute to Sir Harry Secombe*, in May 2001. The following April, and just a week after his seventy-ninth birthday, Vaughan was knocked down by a car while crossing the road on Waterloo Bridge. He died a month later, on 17 May 2002, as a result of his injuries, in the Royal London Hospital. He was seventy-nine. A heart-breaking

With Sam Kydd, that doyen of British character actors, in 'the new lavish pantomime' *Mother Goose*, playing the Charter Theatre, Preston, for a four-week season from Boxing Day, 1974.

end to a born entertainer who had given such unmitigated joy over so many years.

TREAT YOURSELF TO Norman Vaughan's quite splendid collection of standards *Swingin' Songs for Dodgy People* (Pye Records: NPL18075, 1962) which delightfully capitalised on his *London Palladium* cachet and indulged him with such bright and breezy tunes as 'Powder Your Face With Sunshine', 'Smile Darn You Smile' and, relentlessly ramming home his 'Swinging' catchphrase, 'Things are Swinging.'

# Tom Walls and Ralph Lynn

## 1883–1949 and 1882–1962

So of their time. Those fabulous twenties. Still fabulous now.

*Peter Jones*

They weren't strictly a double act, but the joyous combination of Tom Walls and Ralph Lynn in a string of stage farces and comedy films remains one of my favourite things. They conjure a slightly naughty freedom of between-the-wars Middle England, with knowing nods to each other and to the censor, an assured faith in the mathematically perfect Ben Travers scripts and a true sense of subversion within the cosy environs of a stately home or a dusty office. The term 'Aldwych farce' may have lost its clout today, but for me it is embodied in the raffish stoicism of Walls, the monocled gusto of Lynn and a world of potent cocktails and frantic horse races.

After a stint with the Metropolitan Police, Walls became an actor in 1905, initially joining a Pierrot troupe on Brighton's pebbled beach before appearing in Robert Courtneidge's production of *Aladdin* at the Glasgow Empire

Theatre for the 1905–06 season. He made his West End debut as Ensign Ruffler in *Sir Roger de Coverley*, at the Empire Theatre, Leicester Square, before touring extensively throughout Australia in 1910 and 1911 as Peter Doody in *The Arcadians* and the Marquis de St Gautier in *The Belle of Brittany*.

By the time he returned to London in 1912, Walls's reputation for playing likeable philanderers had been sealed, and for the next decade he starred in a successful run of musical comedies, including the role of Colonel Bolinger in *Kissing Time*, at the Winter Garden Theatre, in 1919. Comedian Leslie Henson was also in the show and the two, hitting it off immediately, formed the partnership that presented the farce *Tons of Money* at the Shaftesbury Theatre in 1922. Walls gave himself a tasty supporting role, casting Henson in the lead as an impoverished inventor who masquerades as his own cousin. The show ran for two years, culminating in a film version in 1924. However, most of the plaudits were stolen by a young actor who played not one but three different characters: a crafty Mexican, an outrageous curate and a silly ass. *The Times* observed that 'he is extremely amusing. He is hardly ever off the stage, and to him in a great measure the success of the play should be due.' The actor's name was Ralph Lynn.

Lynn had made his stage debut in *The King of Terrors* in Wigan, in 1900, subsequently performing with touring productions throughout the Home Counties and America before making his London debut in the revue *By Jingo, If We Do–!* in October 1914. As the foppish and flippant Montague Mayfair, Lynn's persona appeared fully formed, and he would play variations on the theme for the rest of his days. By the time he first worked with Tom Walls he was something of a comedy certainty, and Walls, being a shrewd businessman, was not about to turn down a sure thing.

Indeed, such was the success of *Tons of Money* that Walls invested in a lease on the Aldwych Theatre. He and Henson moved their company to the premises lock, stock and two flaming Havana cigars, and presented two more long-running farces in quick succession: *It Pays to Advertise*, from 2 February 1924, and *A Cuckoo in the Nest* which opened on 22 July 1925, less than a fortnight after *It Pays to Advertise* had closed! In *A Cuckoo in the Nest*, written by Ben Travers, Walls was unwelcome guest Major George Bone while the natty playboy, Peter Wykeham, was played by Ralph Lynn. It was a triple match made

THE ONLY STORMY WEATHER YOU CAN LAUGH AT!

TOM WALLS & RALPH LYNN
STORMY WEATHER

Also JACK HOLT in "IRON FIST" with FLORENCE RICE Cert. U

BY BEN TRAVERS

WITH YVONNE ARNAUD & ROBERTSON HARE
A GAINSBOROUGH PICTURE directed by TOM WALLS Cert. A

Commencing SUNDAY

NEW GALLERY

A GAUMONT-BRITISH THEATRE

Lynn, Walls and Yvonne Arnaud, caricatured for the August 1935 newspaper campaign promoting *Stormy Weather*, from Gainsborough Pictures.

in heaven, with the original production running for 376 performances. With the befuddled, prematurely bald actor Robertson Hare also in the mix, the Aldwych Farce team was happily in situ at the theatre for over a decade.

And oh how they laughed to see such fun. The onstage combination of Walls and Lynn was unpredictable from the start. Walls, gloriously similar to his characters and reluctant to spend much time learning his lines, would float his way through the action, often openly asking for a prompt. This became so popular with the audiences that it was actively encouraged throughout the run. Lynn, on the other hand, knew his lines, as well as everybody else's too, and got so horrendously bored by about the eighth performance that he would gleefully ad-lib just to get himself through it. Again, while his fellow actors may have detested the potential minefield of such activity, full houses positively lapped it up.

A transition to cinema seemed the obvious next move, and while the West End hits kept on a-coming, Ben Travers's *Rookery Nook* was put before the film cameras in 1930. Walls and Lynn were cast as cousins Clive and Gerald Popkiss, with Walls himself in the director's chair. The stage version had run for 409 performances from 1926, and with most of the original actors back in line the film was pretty much a guaranteed winner. However, the fact that it proved to be such a huge box office success – making profits of over £100,000 – was a pleasant shock to all concerned.

It was hardly surprising, then, that throughout the 1930s Walls and Lynn would regularly feature in the Top 10 British Film Stars as based on annual ticket sales. Nor is it surprising that there was at least one Aldwych Farce at the British cinema every year for the next seven years, with Walls directing those in which he didn't appear. Indeed, he proved himself a rather brilliant comedy film director, now shamefully undervalued. Even in those primitive days he indulged in leaps of surrealism (notably the caveman dream in the 1934 film *A Cup of Kindness*) and playful convention-breaking (witness humourless law enforcer Peter Gawthorne breaking the fourth wall, just once, and no one ever acknowledging it again, in *Dirty Work*, 1934).

The repertory team that Walls secured for the Farces was impressive indeed, with future stars Cecil Parker and Mervyn Johns in officious and irritating support roles,

Tom Walls: the sartorially elegant gentleman of the turf.

Mary Brough as the alternately flighty or furious matriarch, the occasional guest-droll-role for Gordon Harker and aged eccentricity from Lynn's brother, Gordon James.

Even when the official strand of stage and film successes came to an end, Lynn and Walls were still assured headliners. In 1939 Walls took on the Alexandra Theatre in Stoke Newington, running it as a repertory theatre, and later that year returned to the Shaftesbury Theatre to produce Wilfred Eyre's farce *His Majesty's Guest*. In 1942 he produced *Why Not To-Night?* at the Ambassadors Theatre, another farce in which he took a leading role. That same year Lynn starred in a revival of *Rookey Nook*, reprising his original role of Clive Popkiss and, according to *The Times* reviewer, being 'as masterly as ever'. Fast on its heels were E. Vivian Tidmarsh's *Is Your Honeymoon Really Necessary?* and *Outrageous Fortune*, a Ben Travers play which reunited Lynn with Robertson Hare.

Tom Walls made his last stage appearance as the bombastic Edward Moulton-Barrett in the 1948 Garrick Theatre revival of *The Barretts of Wimpole Street*. For twenty years his passion had been his stable of horses near his Surrey home, including the 1932 Derby winner April the Fifth. After Walls died, on 27 November 1949, his ashes were scattered on Epsom racecourse. How very Tom Walls.

Ralph Lynn: the archetypal
monocled silly ass.

Ralph Lynn soldiered on, appearing onstage with Robertson Hare again in two more farces, back at their beloved stomping ground the Aldwych Theatre, in Ben Travers' *Wild Horses*, from November 1952 and *The Party Spirit*, at the Piccadilly Theatre, from September 1954. Peter Jones, who had co-written the play with John Jowett, told me: 'It was set in the House of Commons and ran for four or five months. Ralph Lynn was quite old at that point but he was an absolute genius – I worshipped him. It was this curious sort of nonsense but he would throw in lines: he would look at "Bunny" Hare and say, "He looks like something on a Chinese mantelpiece!" I don't know why it was funny but it always was with Ralph Lynn. He would fool around onstage without any attention to the directions he had been given, just picking up a vase of flowers, giving the vase to Hare, walking away, getting back to the script, walking back again and saying, "Quite a mistake!" and putting it back where he had found it. Lynn was quite surreal in a way but a master at what he did. Offstage Lynn took it all very seriously, interviewing actors for the other parts and saying, "You've got to try to be funny. I never try to be funny but by God I *am* funny!"' And so he was. Both of them were. Very, very funny.

TREAT YOURSELF TO *Aldwych Farces: Volume One* (Network: 7954291, 2015), a laudable gathering of the Walls and Lynn comedies inspired by and influenced by their West End success. This release features the splendid 1933 film version of *A Cuckoo in the Nest*, as well as the same year's *Turkey Time*, the perfect Christmas Day film for the classic-British-comedy-lover in your family. It's an out-of-season holiday-resort farce, and an absolute hoot. Both films are directed by Walls and showcase his and Lynn's comic prowess at the very peak of their undeniable powers.

# Elsie and Doris Waters

## 1893–1990 and 1904–78

Those charming sisters, always elegantly dressed and quite belying those favourite characters Gert and Daisy they created to huge effect on radio, were the first big-name stars to tour India and Burma.

*Bill Pertwee MBE*

Both blessed and cursed to be almost synonymous with the Second World War, the down-to-earth, gossiping characters of Gert and Daisy became as familiar a sound in London during those years as Vera Lynn and buzz bombs. Stalwarts of BBC Radio's flagship variety show *Workers' Playtime*, the characters appeared from the very beginning in May 1941, and were still working their magic and still topping the bill for the show's twenty-first anniversary edition, broadcast from a telephone-cable factory in Dagenham, on 23 October 1962. The cheery cockney songs and shaggy-dog stories of Gert and Daisy were part of that vital patchwork of beloved comedy characters that brought real comfort and reassurance to the nation. Their creators, sisters Elsie and Doris Waters, wrote all their own scripts and were proud that they never reused one of them. The characters they invented were legion – and every one of them full of heart.

Gert and Daisy's menfolk, Bert and Wally, gossipy Old Mother Butler, the neighbourhood shopkeepers: all of them were flights of fancy inspired by the glorious eccentrics the Waterses had met. Life at the East End funeral parlour where their father worked had certainly introduced some unforgettable characters. It gave truth to the Waterses' comedy, striking a natural chord with the public and creating a powerful force for good during those dark days of conflict.

It is easy to romanticise the community spirit of the Blitz and rationing and evacuation and the nice bit of haddock that Daisy forever seemed to have on offer. Through a myriad films, documentaries and misty-eyed recollections, the true sense of British strength can appear almost caricatured. But without the BBC and a clutch of working-class, ordinary performers who were eager to get their hands dirty, the morale of Great Britain would never have been so buoyant for so long. The Second World War was certainly no picnic, and anybody who lived through it remembers the true hardship. *London Can Take It!* screamed Humphrey Jennings' 1940 film poem – and she could, as long as she had characters like Gert and Daisy around. Their radio series *Ack-Ack, Beer-Beer*, which ran from 1940 until 1944, was a vital weapon – nothing less; so much so that discredited propagandist Lord Haw-Haw mocked their efforts with one snide broadcast stating that 'the good folk of Grimsby should not expect Gert and Daisy to protect them from the Luftwaffe'. But they did, in their way; Gert and Daisy were that important. Indeed, the Waters sisters were awarded the OBE for their war effort and thanked personally by Prime Minister Winston Churchill. In 1986 Elsie accepted the Burma Star – on behalf of herself and her late sister – although in actual fact the award was dedicated to Gert and Daisy!

Elsie and Doris Waters had four other siblings, including middle brother Horace, who, under the pseudonym Jack Warner, would enjoy even greater fame than theirs. In his autobiography, *Jack of All Trades* (W.H. Allen, 1975), Warner remembered that, despite their father's trade as an undertaker, 'we were certainly not a miserable family. I am quite sure that if our childhood had been shrouded in gloom, my sisters, Elsie and Doris, would have been incapable of creating two such popular vaudeville characters as Gert and Daisy.' Warner recounted that the abiding memory of their father was as a blackfaced minstrel with banjo in hand. All the children were encouraged to play a musical instrument: Elsie was a violinist, like brothers Jack and Bill; Doris played the tubular bells.

Their parents, Edward and Maud Waters, founded the E. W. Waters Bijou Orchestra, consisting of all the family, and just the family. It was *that* bijou! Before long the group was being booked for a steady flow of engagements, the largest being for a 1,400-strong audience of the inmates of Poplar Workhouse. Times were tough for East End kids but the Waterses' father kitted them out in a variety of outfits, ranging from tartan

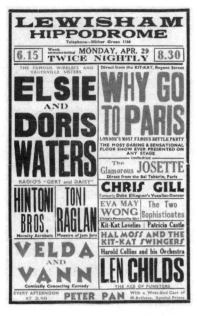

April 1940 and 'the famous wireless and vaudeville sisters' are topping the bill.

kilts to lavish white frocks. With their hair in plaits, the girls were the picture of sophistication. Their father kept the family ticking over until his death in 1926.

Having studied the piano, violin and elocution at the Guildhall School of Music, their early variety act, geared largely towards Elsie's trusty violin, was making a good living. Indeed, as early as 1927 their brother named himself Jack Warner rather than unfairly capitalise on the sisters' already-established name. They had had a burning desire to make it in show business and were unwavering in that ambition.

By 1930 they were established as a fairly upmarket music hall double act, joining the Southwold-based concert party Will C. Pepper's White Coons and subsequently broadcasting with the troupe in August 1932. The songs the sisters sang with the troupe would be upbeat and comical, often performed in upper-crust accents and with the most delicate touch on the piano. Jack Warner recalled what happened next: 'One day they were asked to record one of their musical numbers and, while waiting in the studio, they filled in their time by rehearsing part of the act they planned to do at a function that evening – an

A snapshot out of time. A signed photograph of the sisters received by the author, from Elsie, in 1987.

encounter between Gert and Daisy, two cockney women. They had just finished when the recordist entered the room and asked them what they were doing. Elsie and Doris gave him a brief rundown on their new act and he told them to go through it again. On hearing the exchanges he was so impressed that he declared, "We are going to record it now." Gert and Daisy were thus launched upon the British public. Elsie's violin went under the sofa and the sisters became Gert and Daisy upon theatre bills throughout the country.' The appeal was instant and immovable. That first recording, 'Wedding Bells', made them stars. They played the Royal Command Performance twice that decade: at the London Palladium in 1934 and at the London Coliseum in 1938.

By the outbreak of the Second World War, these unassuming cockneys were national treasures. Their Decca recording 'Gert, Daisy and the Black-Out' was a particularly timely and well-received effort from October 1939, while their 1940 recording 'Please Leave My Butter Alone' was another comic number that struck right at the heart of the British public during wartime rationing.

The pair were so popular they not only performed benefits, camp concerts and various morale-boosting broadcasts but also made their feature-film debut in an economically produced little romp entitled *Gert and Daisy's Weekend*. Released in the February of the darkest year of the war, 1942, it was a fun and cheerfully life-affirming concoction of class clashes and good-natured neighbourliness. Our heroines find themselves staying in a posh country house for the weekend, much to the initial chagrin of the landed gentry, clergy and other toffee-nosed locals, but Gert and Daisy's genuine desire to help shines through to win the day. (The scene with a frightened and tearful evacuee will melt the coldest heart.) The performances by Elsie and Doris Waters are extraordinarily good. When Gert and Daisy perform 'She's a Lily But Only By Name' – an impromptu song about a deflowered young maiden – in front of a prissy audience, the performance seems initially uneasy and under-rehearsed. Of course, they had in fact honed the song through many hundreds of renditions, so it took great confidence and pin-point practice to get the performance looking so off-the-cuff.

The film, produced by the masters of low-budget music hall comedies, Butcher's Film Service, proved to be a massive hit, particularly in the London area – so much so that Butcher's rushed *Gert and Daisy Clean Up* into production later that year for an August 1942 release. Surprisingly, the characters' names were dropped from the title for 1944's *It's in the Bag*, the third and final Gert and Daisy feature film from Butcher's, in which the ladies are all of a dither over recovering a very valuable garment that has gone missing.

The sisters were also blessed by the Ministry of Food. With slogans like 'Grow more green vegetables' and 'Eat more oatmeal' being oft-heard across the nation, a wartime cookbook became an essential household publication. Determined to stand shoulder to shoulder with the people, the sisters stuck to the rationing restrictions and fronted *Gert and Daisy's Wartime Cookery Book* (Withy Grove Press, 1941), which made sure every last morsel of food was utilised. While women were on the front line driving ambulances and, at home, working in factories and building munitions to plug the gaps left by serving men, Elsie and Doris Waters flew the female flag in light entertainment. They were worth forty Bren guns.

As with George Formby and Max Miller, the film career of Gert and Daisy stalled after the war but the act continued to play to packed variety theatres and even ventured into the more stylised and flamboyant world of pantomime. Radio was still a natural home for the pair, however. *The Floggits* was broadcast on the Light Programme, with two series and a Christmas special emerging in 1956 and 1957. A comedic soap opera with pleasingly subversive sitcom overtones, it told of the trials and tribulations of village life, centred on the village shopkeepers: Gert and Daisy. The scripts were caring and affectionate love letters to these comic characters, written by such young bucks as Dave Freeman, John Junkin [qv], and Terry Nation. The war years of these young men had been greatly cheered by Gert and Daisy. The scripts reflected this warm appreciation, and fitted Elsie and Doris Waters like an old apron. The supporting cast consisted of a load of new hopefuls, including Ronnie Barker, Anthony Newley and Joan Sims, who were as equally delighted to work alongside the two great nation treasures. Sims, in particular, was tickled pink and would incorporate traces of the personas of Gert and Daisy in her own work.

Although a success, Elsie and Doris Waters were never fully relaxed in a situation comedy format. Their ramblings had never been improvised, as such, but Gert and Daisy had been born from informal conversations, and for the stage Elsie and Doris had always moulded and shaped their own dialogue. However, with *The Floggits* the essence of Gert and Daisy was lifted lock, stock and barrel and worked into a plot. It was a loose plot though, and Elsie and Doris Waters were touched by the loving recreation of their characters. The scriptwriters were also more than happy to let them write some of their own material. In any case, the sisters had tended to do it regardless – without being told they could!

Still, when *The Floggits* had come to a natural end on radio, and a television series for the sister act was suggested, it was also down to another writer. Ironically, that writer was Ted Willis, who had created police drama *Dixon of Dock Green* for brother Jack, running to huge success on BBC Television. Willis had spotted Elsie and Doris Waters in a television advert and pitched the series to Jack Hylton Television Productions, who secured a deal with commercial network Associated-Rediffusion. *Gert and Daisy* cast the sisters as old music hall pros who had retired from the business to run a tired old theatrical boarding house. Gossip and name-dropping provided much of the laughter but, despite strong support from Hugh Paddick and Patsy Rowlands [qv], only one series of six episodes was made, and broadcast from 10 August 1959.

The BBC cast Elsie and Doris Waters in the 23 November 1963 *Comedy Playhouse* episode 'The Chars', from scriptwriters Harry Driver and Jack Rosenthal. Our heroes were cast as charwomen in the Ministry of Agriculture but not, for once, as Gert and Daisy. Elsie was cast as the rather mischievous Flo, while Doris played the bossy-boots Cissy. A third, younger char was played as a paranoid, deluded man-magnet by Ann Lancaster. Thanks to the writing talent behind the play, the script was earthy and believable.

No series resulted, however, and with changing times the writing seemed to be on the wall for Gert and Daisy. Still, there was at least one last hurrah. In 1966, the year of The Beatles' *Revolver* album and England's World Cup victory, Elsie and Doris recorded the album *Gert & Daisy Live*. It hardly rocketed up the charts, but the strength and confidence of these old-age pensioners still doing the cockney chit-chat is still something of a marvel to behold.

The duo carried on, gleefully joining nostalgia tours with the likes of Leslie Sarony and Sandy Powell [both, qv], until illness struck Doris in the 1970s. Following her sister's death, in 1978, when the headlines screamed: 'Goodbye, Daisy', Elsie continued to appear on nostalgia shows well into her dotage, always happy to talk about the good old days. Living in quiet seclusion in the spacious bungalow she had shared for many years with her sister in Steyning, near the Sussex coast, Elsie would tirelessly answer fan letters from admirers old and new, as often as not enclosing an old photograph from a stock signed by her and Doris, on which she would add a personal message in her elegantly spidery hand. I was one such new admirer to receive one: what a thrill it was, like a long-lost reply finding its way back through a time portal in the Blitz, a blast from a war-torn past popping through my letter box in the late 1980s. I could almost smell the smoked haddock.

Elsie and Doris Waters were so much more than just wartime entertainers. Nonetheless, the image that kind of lingers is of the beloved sisters singing 'Goodnight Children Everywhere' to a group of evacuated children in *Gert and Daisy's Weekend*. It takes a hard person to keep back the tears. Gawd bless ya, ladies.

TREAT YOURSELF TO Herbert Mason's once-feared-lost Gert and Daisy comedy *It's in the Bag* (Renown Pictures: 5060172961283, 2014). Barbara Mullen – best remembered as housekeeper Janet in BBC Television's *Dr. Finlay's Casebook* – stars in the 1966 support short *Miss McTaggart Won't Lie Down*. Lovely stuff.

# Rita Webb

## 1904–81

A true cinematic gem. God bless her!

*Robin Askwith*

A middle-aged woman, as wide as she is tall, is dressed in a cavernous duffel coat. Her wild, red-squirrel hair is tamped down by a green headscarf. She is a worried woman, for Fanny, her teenage daughter, has not returned home after a rock concert the night before. She spies a group of hairy, denim-clad loafers in their camper van. They are wanton, layabout musicians and, unbeknown to the woman, have her stark-naked offspring hidden under a blanket. She approaches tousle-haired cheek-monster Robin Askwith. She isn't best pleased. Her face is like thunder, lightning and every other natural disaster known to man. 'Oi!' she yells. 'Have you seen my Fanny?' 'Blimey!' chuckles Askwith. 'I saw *The Curse of Frankenstein* – that was enough!' The film is *Confessions of a Pop Performer* (1975), and the harridan of a mother is played by the unique Rita Webb.

Throughout the 1960s and 1970s, Webb worked with almost every top television comedian in Britain. A particular favourite of Benny Hill and Spike Milligan, she was also eagerly embraced by Arthur Haynes [qv], was a frequent stooge for Eric Sykes and made her finest feature-film appearances alongside Frankie Howerd. He adored her and she would reduce him to fits of giggles during a take. The 1971 film version of *Up Pompeii!* gave Webb some classy dialogue to deliver, while, later that year, *Up the Chastity Belt* incongruously cast her as Maid Marian. But she knew and loved her limitations. Speaking in 1980, she reflected: 'If they want an old hag, they send for me. After all, I'm not young and beautiful.'

Too bleedin' right, Rita. Indeed, it's almost as though she never was young or beautiful. But brilliant: yes, Rita Webb was brilliant. A born character actor, she noted that: 'at school the other youngsters were always laughing at things I said or did, but I could never understand why, but I always wanted to be an actress. I was an actress when I was three.' Olive Rita Webb was born on 25 February 1904, in Willesden. She had ambitions to be a straight actor, but variety and music hall assignments seemed to put more bread on the table. Talking to the *Sunday Post* in June 1979, she insisted that: 'I was a straight actress for seven years. I was good too. Trouble is nowadays none of the producers are old enough to remember that far back. One day I was asked to do a comedy spot, it might have been *The Army Game*. After that the comedy offers came rolling in. I had to choose between being a hungry straight actress or a fat comedy actress. Simple choice!'

Her roles were never going to be more than interesting guest-spots or supporting characters. As often as not a charlady or a landlady, with the emphasis never on the lady, her very first film, *Hindle Wakes* (1952), saw her running a Blackpool boarding house. It was shot at Merton Park Studios, a place Webb got to know very well over the years, chalking up appearances in four *Scotland Yard* shorts, including *The Tyburn Case* (1957), in which she plays a charwoman reluctantly helping the police with their enquiries. She returned to the studios for the 1969 sci-fi spectacular *Zeta One*, where she sells Charles Hawtrey a bus ticket. It was that kind of career.

Just before the Second World War, Rita met and married experienced banjo player Al Jeffery. The two remained devoted to each other for the rest of their days, and the relationship certainly eased any hurtful misgivings she may have had about the roles she was continually asked to play. Affectionately called 'Podge' by her husband, Webb could be safe in the knowledge that once she had hung up her battleaxe day clothes she could return home for dinner and an evening in front of the telly.

Nonetheless, she worked with the best directors in the business. There aren't many cockney character comedians who could claim credits under John Huston and Alfred Hitchcock, but Rita Webb could. Still, the roles were very much in her own mould. She would throw a bowl of water over the head of José Ferrer in *Moulin Rouge* (1952) and embody the down-to-earth Covent Garden market smother-mother of Barry Foster in *Frenzy* (1972). While essentially playing the same type in a different costume, her film roles were in fact fairly diverse. She was an asylum inmate in *Suddenly, Last Summer* (1959), for director Joseph L. Mankiewicz and a rustic gypsy in the Walt Disney family adventure *The Three Lives of Thomasina* (1963), for director Don Chaffey. She played a brutal masseuse in Paul Morrissey's outrageous retelling of *The Hound of the Baskervilles* (1978) and sparred with Sidney Poitier in *To Sir, With Love* (1967).

She even made a film with Gary Cooper, *The Naked Edge* (1961), an encounter she relished: 'One night he asked if I lived near the Savoy,' she later recalled. '"I live a bleedin' long way from the Savoy," I said. Anyway, he gave me a lift home in his hired limousine. That night and every night after filming. I thought to myself: "Fancy ugly old Rita getting a lift home from Gary Cooper." He was lovely.' That was the no-frills charm of the woman. Whatever the role, there was always the air of a four-ale bar about her. She was unquestionably a creation of the East End, of whelks and woodbines and wallops over the head with a frying pan, and perfectly at home opposite Sid James (in six episodes of *Citizen James* , BBC Television, November 1960 to November 1962) and Barbara Windsor (in *Sparrows Can't Sing*, 1963).

There was always serious fare amongst the comic, of course, notably in 'The Fine Art of Bubble-Blowing', the 12 May 1975 episode of *Churchill's People*, in which she was memorably teamed with Arthur Mullard, and an appearance in the *Shades of Greene* episode, 'Special Duties', on 23 September 1975 (as yet another landlady). But these were not roles to tax her, and sometimes her part would be so fleeting as if to be nothing more than glorified extra work. She was a tea lady in the Jeremy Bullock sex comedy *I'm Not Feeling Myself Tonight* (1976), and a grumpy woman at the window who shouts at Peter Sellers in *Revenge of the Pink Panther* (1978). A cough, a spit and a bleedin' rant was all she needed to do to make her mark, if that. It's why she adored *The Benny Hill Show* and returned to it time and time again from 1968 to 1980. The star clown was no mug; he would surround himself with the best and most familiar

As soothsayer Cassandra in comedic epic *Up Pompeii* (1971).

stooge stars in the business. There was no ego with Benny. The show was the thing, and when he needed a miserable old mother-in-law, an ugly blind date or a raging traffic warden there was only one person to call – Webb was on speed dial!

She brought a bit of disgusting to sci-fi telly as well. As a dishevelled charm-seller in the John Mills *Quatermass* (Euston Films, 1979), she bellows a description of her wares, accompanied by a skeleton. In *Space 1999* (in the episode 'The Taybor', ITC, 4 November 1976), the stunning Catherine Schell transforms herself into an old hag in order to escape the advances of the villainous butterball of Willoughby Goddard. Rita got the call.

She was ideal, too, for the worlds of Galton, Simpson and Speight, popping up as the conniving cockney powerhouse Ada in two episodes of *Steptoe and Son* ('And Afterwards at...', 4 October 1965, and 'Oh, What a Beautiful Mourning', 6 March 1972). In these companion pieces from the black-and-white sixties era and the colour seventies era, Webb was the personification of the grieving, thieving relation. *Till Death Us Do Part* was a natural telly home for her and, from June 1966, she appeared in five episodes across a decade, as often as not singing bawdy songs and sipping large gins in the pub with Alf Garnett and his cronies. This was Webb's world; we could merely visit it for thirty minutes.

Filming *To Sir, with Love* (1967), with Sidney Poitier, in Watney Street Market, in the East End of London.

Hers was never a flash life, but she enjoyed the luxury of a double bed adorned with the initials 'RW' in gold lettering and relished her reputation as a popular party guest. Always jolly and never pretentious, the forthright, brassy cockney with a heart of gold that she so often played was exactly what you got in real life too.

She worked until the end, and her popularity never waned. Wandering in for a quick cackle in the John Inman sitcom *Odd Man Out*, her first appearance in the 17 November 1977 episode, 'Shall We Dance?', engenders real delight and huge applause from the studio audience. You can tell they are really pleased to see her. Here Webb was cast as a female wrestler – of course.

Her last film role was as Mrs Loewenthal, the pet-shop owner in Piers Haggard's snake-in-Belgravia thriller *Venom* (1981). Sadly, she died from cancer on 30 August 1981, at the age of seventy-seven, just before the film was released. The 1980s of *Comic Strips Presents...*, Film4 and *EastEnders* would have been her very meat and drink. They were all the poorer for having missed her.

TREAT YOURSELF TO *Up Pompeii/Up the Chastity Belt* on DVD (Warner: B00009QNW7, 2003). Rita was never funnier nor more relaxed than with Frankie Howerd, and these two classics from the early 1970s see her on blistering form, soothsaying in Ancient Rome and as a plump, nagging queen's pudding of a Maid Marion in Sherwood Forest. What else do you bleeding need to know before buying?

# John Wells

## 1936–98

John was one of those more 'benign' satirists who'd come through the Oxford mill, along with others like Dudley Moore, Alan Bennett and Terry Jones (Wells was at the same college as Terry), as opposed to their more sardonic counterparts from Cambridge, like Jonathan Miller, John Cleese and Peter Cook.

His wit was just as sharp as theirs but cloaked in a deceptively gentle and ruminative style. Once he got inside the character of someone, he could produce consistently and joyfully funny material, week after week. His *Mrs Wilson's Diary* invented a whole new genre of comic writing, often imitated but never surpassed. This was followed by the *Dear Bill* letters (Wells's imaginary letters from Denis Thatcher to Bill Deedes), which once again caught the character of the author with unerring precision and skill.

He had a most-attractively dry, understated humour. His parodies were playful rather than bitter, but well informed and quite deadly. In conversation his delivery was light, almost whispery, but it paid you to listen as he could put his finger on what was funny in any situation.

He was a courteous, warm and friendly companion; a wonderful person to laugh with.

*Sir Michael Palin CBE*

Satirists are only as good as the mad reality that surrounds them; or, for the very lucky ones, their subjects are real and rather likeable madmen themselves. John Wells was blessed with playing the shadowy, bumbling and endearing figure of Denis Thatcher; the golf-club-wielding and quietly adventurous man behind the throne of Margaret Thatcher proved an irresistible target for the affectionate and knowing pokes from Wells's pen and performance. Wells's *Dear Bill* letters in *Private Eye* first appeared in the wake of Thatcher's elevation to Prime Minister, and Wells played Denis, with a rambling gait, for many years afterwards – for the duration of Thatcher's tenure at 10 Downing Street. He would even play him in a James Bond film, popping up alongside Janet Brown in the 1981 Roger Moore romp *For Your Eyes Only*.

Still, it was the West End smash *Anyone for Denis?* at the Whitehall Theatre, also in 1981, that had the real heart and soul of Wells's performance. Not only did it have a blistering pun of a title but it was the perfect showcase for Wells both as writer and performer. His onstage Mrs T, the impeccable Angela Thorne, would also co-star with him in the play's lengthy national tour, as well as in the Thames Television version of *Anyone for Denis?*, broadcast on 28 December 1982. For Christmas Day 1986 Wells would team up with Steve Nallon – Margaret Thatcher for *Spitting Image* – for a gag appearance in ITV's spectacular pantomime *Cinderella: The Shoe Must Go On*. Wells was back as Denis Thatcher for the Yorkshire Television variety show *Make a Date* on New Year's Day 1988, and in 'Send Her Victorious', the 4 December 1989 episode of *About Face*, the Central TV anthology showcase for Maureen Lipman. The script, centred on the Thatchers being kidnapped whilst on holiday, was, for all intents and purposes, a sequel to *Anyone for Denis?* and was again written by Wells. Angela Thorne and John Wells would be reunited in 1990, just after the fall of Thatcher, as a retired couple in television play *Dunrulin': An Active Citizen is a Healthy Citizen* (BBC1, 23 December 1990), another winning title, written by Alistair Beaton and John Wells, and set a little way into a future in which Mrs Thatcher has left politics and lives in retirement in Dulwich. It was the perfect sign-off for Wells's greatest comic triumph.

But there was more to him than that. Much more.

Although from fairly humble beginnings, the young John Campbell Wells, after doing his national service in Korea, headed off to St Edmund Hall, Oxford. With frightfully witty fellows such as Richard Ingrams, Paul Foot and Christopher Booker to spar with, Wells quickly established himself as arguably the funniest chap there. His comedy wasn't simply about poking fun at authority and establishment; there was too an understanding of bureaucracy there – a liking, even. Despite a love of the stage that would take wings throughout his life, it was the written word that seemed to channel the best of Wells's talents. Alongside Ingrams, Foot and Booker, Wells was recruited to write for the fledgling undergraduate newspaper *Mesopotamia*. It was certainly more fun than his language degree, although Wells passed with flying colours nonetheless.

Indeed, unlike many of his comedy contemporaries, he actually made good use of his qualification: after graduating, he taught French and German at Eton. But his mind was firmly set on performing. As the dowdy 1950s became the enlightened 1960s, Wells discovered the brave new world. In other words, he met Peter Cook.

A stint onstage at the Establishment club and an invitation to write for *Private Eye* following its inception in October 1961 gave Wells an approved passport to a life of satire. His first contribution to the magazine was a charming attack on the luvvie elan of actor Sir John Gielgud, who the magazine dubbed 'Feelgood'. But it was the regular *Private Eye* column 'Mrs Wilson's Diary' that indulged Wells to the full. A folksy, gossipy column supposedly written by Mary, the wife of Labour Prime Minister Harold Wilson, it merged the cosy middle-class opinions of a doctor's wife from pioneering radio serial drama *Mrs Dale's Diary* with the cut and thrust of savage – if shrouded – satire. The column would benefit from Wells's old and often antagonistic pal Richard Ingrams as editorial collaborator, as well as additional barbs thrown in from Peter Cook. *Mrs Wilson's Diary* would become a stage musical, with music by Jeremy Taylor and lyrics by John Wells, including numbers 'The Terrible Mr Brown' and 'Who Are the Bastards Now?'. Joan Littlewood produced at the Theatre Royal, Stratford East, from 21 September 1967, before the show transferred to the Criterion Theatre, for 175 performances from 24 October 1967. There was also a one-off London Weekend Television episode of *Mrs Wilson's Diary*, on 4 January 1969, once nervously postponed and then redressed with a re-recorded section to erase suggestions that cabinet minister George Brown, as played by Bob Grant, was in a state of intoxication! Myvanwy Jean and Bill Wallis were cast as the Wilsons. Nigel Hawthorne, a decade later the canny Sir Humphrey Appleby in *Yes Minister*, was Chancellor of the Exchequer Roy Jenkins, while David Battley [qv] was omnipresent broadcaster David Frost. And within the pages of *Private Eye*, 'Mrs Wilson's Diary' would run and run – all the way until Wilson's resignation in March of 1976. Satire needed the oxygen of reality: luckily for Wells, Margaret Thatcher was just around the corner.

If Wells had lived longer, he would undoubtedly have been labelled a 'champagne socialist' by lazy journalists. He was a man who loved to make friends, and made them easily. He delighted in the company of the rich and famous. Despite being part of the satire movement, he seemed affable to everyone, almost part of the world he was sending up. Margaret Thatcher even became a close friend, nicknaming him 'Jawn': a name that would inevitably stick. The cruel and the jealous were even heard to call him a social climber but it was a barb Wells wore well.

He married Teresa Chancellor, the daughter of Reuters guru Sir Christopher Chancellor, and spent his free time at his picturesque Sussex farmhouse not a stone's lob from Plumpton Racecourse. In his country tweeds, Wells was the image of the landed gentry toff. This is how he liked it, and he could certainly play the part. From the very start of his career he was thrown myriad roles as ineffectual officers, slack-jawed earls and fussy men from the ministry.

Not only that; John Wells was always reassuringly and doggedly at the cutting edge of the best of British comedy, from the puking and mewing days of the 1960s to the rushing-headlong late 1990s. As a writer on *That Was the*

*Week That Was* and performer on its bastard offspring *Not So Much a Programme, More a Way of Life*, he was assured a lengthy career as part of the life-support system of Britain's greatest and coolest comedy talents. He cropped up opposite Peter Sellers in *The Bobo* (1967), Dudley Moore in *30 is a Dangerous Age, Cynthia* (1968), and Marty Feldman in *Every Home Should Have One* (1970). If that wasn't enough, his place among the foothills of the beautiful people was confirmed by a role as Q's assistant in the wonderfully messy and elegantly elephantine Bond parody *Casino Royale* (1967). Rubbing egos with Orson Welles, David Niven and Woody Allen was all in a day's work, and a full fifteen years before cheekily encountering Roger Moore's official 007.

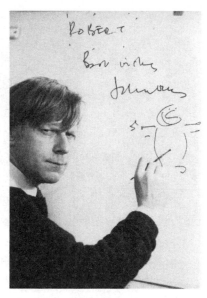

A prized postcard, dedicated to the author, complete with cheerful John Wells doodle.

Later, Wells was a shoo-in for the intricate political jousting of *Yes, Prime Minister* with his performance as Godfrey, the producer of 'The Ministerial Broadcast', on 16 January 1986, being at turns fawning, petty, and achingly undermining with continual halts and comments on the PM's television manner. From March 1982 Wells had been a loyal part of *The Kenny Everett Television Show*, on BBC1, and eagerly joined fellow architects of comic anarchy Peter Cook, Willie Rushton, and Spike Milligan, as the ghosts in *Kenny Everett's Christmas Carol*, for Christmas Eve, 1985. As a result of his comedic heritage, Wells was a darling of the younger set throughout the 1980s and 1990s. He played the judge in the terminal episode of *Filthy, Rich & Catflap*, on 11 February 1987, a doctor in 14 October 1991's *Bottom*'s ''s Up' and Uncle Humphrey in 'Morocco', a second-series episode of *Absolutely Fabulous*, broadcast 10 February 1994.

Dithering, charming and ever-so-wickedly subversive, these twilight strolls into the welcoming universe of the young pretender were meat and drink to Wells, being a gratifying acknowledgement from the likes of Rik Mayall, Adrian

Morecambe and Wise make a fuss of Angela Thorne, in Margaret Thatcher guise. The 1982 Thames Television seasonal schedule launch.

Edmondson and Jennifer Saunders that one of the titans was at play.

Wells's writings, for both publication and performance, had become even weightier and more fulfilling than the satire boom of the sixties. From *A Melon for Ecstasy* – the 1971 novel Wells co-wrote with John Fortune, which dissected the longings of a man for a tree – to a scholarly and rollicking translation of *Cyrano de Bergerac* for the Theatre Royal, Haymarket, in 1992, he continued to delight with his love of the absurd.

His final published work, *The House of Lords: From Saxon Wargods to a Modern Senate* (Hodder & Stoughton, 1997), was an eccentric history from the twilight wit of a great satirist. It is not as biting as once it might have been, perhaps, but this very English history has quite a suck. It is witty and wicked – and *very* John Wells.

Back at the acting lark, Wells had been a joy as Dr. Charles Sweet in the situation comedy *Rude Health* (C4, 1987–88). His lead role, as a rather opportunistic small town general practitioner looking to supplement his NHS income with private patients, was tailor-made for him by scriptwriters Phil Gould and Quentin Brown. The younger at heart relished his gallery of characters, including Arnold, the clumsy, perpetually sniffing, pink elephant in Ivor Wood's stop-motion animation *Charlie Chalk* (BBC1, 1987). More serious acting work for television included yet another judge, in George MacDonald Fraser's robust adaptation of *Casanova* (ABC, 1987), as well as a memorable supporting role, as an ineffectual school headmaster, in *Tinker, Tailor, Soldier, Spy* (BBC2, 1979). It was perfect casting, so much so that, from February 1997, Wells was seen as another ineffectual school headmaster, Richard Nixon, in Steven Moffat's BBC1 situation comedy *Chalk*. It was to be his final acting assignment. Too ill with the cancer that would kill him on 11 January 1998, Wells was forced to drop out of the second series.

Dying at the age of sixty-one seems all the more of a tragedy when one considers Wells's then still-glowing career as writer, satirist, actor, historian, journalist, wit, public speaker and something of a thermometer of the times. Lady Thatcher, no less, commented at the time: 'I am so sad. He brightened up our lives so much.' Amen to that. He was a national treasure of a man.

TREAT YOURSELF TO *Anyone For Denis?* (Network: 5027626492243, 2018), the 1982 Thames Television film, written by Wells, in which he also gives the definitive version of his career-defining role as Denis Thatcher.

As manipulative medic Dr Sweet picking the bones out of a second series of the Channel 4 sitcom *Rude Health*. This episode, 'A Bag of Nuts', was directed by David MacMahon, and transmitted on 18 January 1988.

# George and Kenneth Western

## 1895–1969 and 1899–1963

Oh, wonderful chaps. What joy they gave.

*Leslie Phillips OBE*

If British broadcasting during the Second World War was visualised as a scales of justice, the Nazi sympathiser Lord Haw-Haw was doubly counterbalanced by the monocled mutineers in dinner jackets and white bow ties, The Western Brothers: for every nasal 'Germany calling!', the Brits could cock a dignified snook and 'Play the game, you cads.' There really was no contest. George, the shorter of the two and the wizard of the keyboard, alongside Kenneth, who would shoot out introductory banter from a standing position, were our first and poshest line of defence.

In fact the two were not brothers at all, but second cousins. Indeed, amazingly, the two didn't even meet until they were adults. George had established himself as a composer and self-proclaimed 'entertainer at the piano' with the Roosters Concert Party. Kenneth, meanwhile, was songwriting in-between his 'proper' job at the Ministry of Transport. A canny aunt suggested the two should team up. Kenneth sent George one of his songs; George's reply from November 1924 is prophetic indeed: 'I am badly in need of a new act at the piano, but haven't up to now struck any good ideas so probably if we could have a chat sometime we might mutually assist each other... Trusting to hear from you again, and hoping to meet you in the future.' So started a career that delighted audiences for nigh on thirty-five years.

Originally billed as The Perfectly Polite Pair, their clipped delivery and frightfully English disdain was set in stone from the outset. As early as 1925 the duo were performing their satirical songs at the London Palladium. It wasn't until 1929, however, that they became The Western Brothers, with affectionately barbed songs such as 'We're Frightfully BBC' putting them firmly on the map. With wry smiles and dapper manners, the Brothers celebrated Englishness in song. Even if the Empire was crumbling or bombs were falling, the nation could still laugh at itself with such playful lines as: 'Talk about a sight, every Sunday night, in the parlour when the Company's gone; Mother on the sideboard looking very red, Father with a bonbon hanging on his head, looking for the baby underneath the bed, in the parlour when the company's gone!'

They had been releasing hugely successfully 78s of their best-loved songs for years before the company was gone, of course. A particularly popular number was 'The Old School Tie'. Indeed, their recordings for British Columbia were of such importance that they were rewarded with their own disc label emblazoned with an old school tie and the Brothers' spoof Latin motto: 'ad sum ard labor' – their version of 'I have to work hard'!

They performed relentlessly, holding great sway at the swankiest of venues such as the Cafe de Paris, and in October 1935 the Brothers were invited to perform before King George V and Queen Mary at the Royal Command Performance at the London Palladium.

They were also regular broadcasters – indeed, the 1934 film *Radio Parade of 1935* cast them as sophisticated radio announcers. The previous year had seen them script and feature in the film *Mister Cinders*, a male-centric retelling of the classic pantomime, with our cads perfectly cast as the dinner-jacketed equivalents of

The Windyridge collection utilising the illustration of Kenneth and George from the 1934 Wills cigarette card series *Radio Celebrities*.

the Ugly Sisters. By May 1938 the Brothers were pioneering radio comedy as the ne'er-do-well prefects of *Cads' College*, an outrageous, fictitious seat of learning situated in Hounds Green, Duncestern. The series gave the Western Brothers the perfect situation for their beloved comic characters: upper-crust, frightfully posh, but thoroughly decent chaps: cads with hearts of gold.

With the advent of the Second World War, their ditties of dotty Englishness turned into powerfully cheerful ear-bombs of morale-boosting propaganda. It was hardly surprising that these two experts of radio broadcasting would release a left-hook punch to the enemy in the shape of their song 'Lord Haw Haw of Zeesen', on the Columbia label in October 1939. It proved so popular that a sequel was rushed out that December. 'Lord Haw Haw the Humbug of Hamburg' proved even more popular. No wonder then that one or both of the songs would be sung as the big finish of their act. A lyric which not only mocked Haw Haw but also Russian propaganda in Uncle Boo-Hoo of Moscow, with our duo calling for three cheers for treason, was a guaranteed audience-pleaser – nothing could top Haw-Haw bashing.

The brothers seized the opportunity to entertain troops stationed overseas. During a tour of North Africa with the Entertainments National Service Association in September 1943, Kenneth wrote in his diary: 'Show in the town's Major Square. Open air with about 3,000 troops present. It was a grand sight. In the middle of the act, a note was handed to us by the Commanding Officer asking us to announce – "Unconditional Surrender of Italy". Terrific reaction, hats flung high in the air and the stage littered

– unforgettable scene!' And if that doesn't give you goosebumps, check your pulse.

Following the war, their stiff-upper-lipped polish became less and less in favour, although 'Those Radio Cads' continued performing to diminishing crowds across the country. In 1953, Kenneth told the *TV Mirror* that viewers should: 'take your feet off the table, cads. Your new 24-inch size prefects are among you.' Sadly, the small screen was not for them, and bar a couple of

The monocled mirthineers: Cousins Kenneth and George Western. Bros. for Toffs. 'Play the game, you cads!'

nostalgic recreations of classic songs they found better pickings on the road.

Naturally, as the years rolled on and tastes changed, work became more and more scarce; their final year together, 1962, saw just twenty or so appearances. Still, to be in any kind of demand in the year of The Beatles' first single was no mean feat.

On 24 January 1963, Kenneth died, at the age of sixty-three. George later reflected that 'we were more or less retired. Not from choice but because of necessity. When variety began to go there was not the work any more. TV finished us off in the end, although we kept our hand doing shows for charities and private parties. Most of our big earnings went to the income tax people.'

Following his cousin's death, George ran the sweet and tobacco kiosk at Weybridge Station. As his old catchphrase would have it, 'So what?', for he remained happy to reminiscence with older customers up until his death on 16 August 1969, at the age of seventy-four.

The Western Brothers spread jollity with laid-back ease. As George's obituary in *The Times* had it, they had an: 'entirely good-humoured, cleverly timed act ... an impudent mockery of the establishment. To them, their act was all a joke,

Old Boys: George and Kenneth Western, still raffish cads during their final days together touring the halls.

but it was a joke growing out of social realities which they shared with audiences of all classes.' Up the Cads!

TREAT YOURSELF TO *The Western Brothers – Play the Game* (Windyridge: VAR29, 2007) a lovingly compiled CD featuring twenty-two of their finest songs, including 'Bad Show Chaps', 'You Can't Take the Breed from the British', 'That's a Secret That Never Leaked Out', 'The Writings on the Wall' and, one of timeless satire, 'No One to Read Out the News (A BBC Tragedy)'.

# Gordon Wharmby

## 1933–2002

He was an asset. He went from not having a clue to giving a seasoned pro, like Dame Thora Hird, notes!

*Alan J. W. Bell*

*Last of the Summer Wine*'s epic run is peppered with forgotten fallen heroes. While the narrative of three old men refusing to go gently into that good night was the focal point, along the way the chaps were aided and abetted by a gallery of Northern ninnies. John Comer, the rotund café-owner, Sid, chalked up a decade on the Dales; after a lifetime of bit parts, Joe Gladwin became something of a star as the much put-upon bane of Nora, Wally Batty; Blake Butler, an epitome of seedy, bespectacled authority, was chief librarian Mr Wainwright in the very first episodes.

But it's a figure from the last two decades of *Last of the Summer Wine* who is the real forgotten hero of the series. Gordon Wharmby was not a professional actor when he was cast as obsessive car mechanic Wesley Pegden in 1982, and

Brian Wilde, Bill Owen, Gordon Wharmby and Peter Sallis in the *Last of the Summer Wine* episode 'The Loxley Lozenge', 1984.

throughout his twenty years with the series he was always gleefully quick to be self-deprecating and say he never became one! He simply enjoyed playing the role that made him a familiar face to millions.

A likeable, erudite man, Wharmby was being far too modest of course. Born in Salford, Lancashire, on 6 November 1933, and having served in the Royal Air Force during his national service, back on Civvy Street he worked as a painter and decorator while gaining stage experience with the Oldham Repertory Theatre. He had made the odd television appearance in the 1970s, in such fare as the *Play for Today* episode 'Spend, Spend, Spend' (BBC1, 15 March 1977), and *The One and Only Phyllis Dixey* (Thames Television, 1 November 1978), but it was director–producer Alan J. W. Bell who spotted him and would cast him as Wesley. It was late 1981 and 'In the Service of Humanity', the first episode of *Last of the Summer Wine* series six, was to be broadcast in January 1982. The plot featured Brian Wilde's bombastic Foggy removing a ladder from the side of a house, resulting in a very angry man being stranded up on a roof. Wharmby, who was far prouder of his skills as a painter and decorator than as an actor, got the part of the man on the roof. He had one line: 'Bring that ladder back!' but Bell was so impressed that he was immediately convinced he should give Wharmby the bigger part of Wesley Pegden, a regular character who made his first appearance in the following episode 'Car and Garter', on 11 January 1982. Bell recalled that, needing reassurance that Wharmby was up to the part, 'I asked him how he rated himself. "The best," he said. "Convince me," I countered. "Well, there's this big house with two floors. I can strip the wallpaper off in next to no time." I cried: "No, as an actor, I mean!" Anyway, he said, "Just give me the chance."' And so Bell did. Besides, Wesley was rarely out of his overalls. It was the dream acting job for, now ex-decorator, Gordon Wharmby!

Writer Roy Clarke was equally inspired by Wharmby. Perhaps his crowning glory was in the 1984 New Year special, 'The Loxley Lozenge'. Not an elaborate cough sweet but an exquisite engine, and a convoluted plot that stretched Wharmby as a comedy performer. He effortlessly rose to the challenge.

His success led to high-profile bit parts in other television shows: *All Creatures Great and Small* ('City Slicker', BBC1, 13 March 1988), *Agatha Christie's Poirot* ('The Adventure of the Cheap Flat', London Weekend Television, 18 February 1990), *Hetty Wainthropp Investigates* ('Lost Chords', BBC1, 5 December 1996) and, very much at home, as the ferret-fancying Horace in *Heartbeat* ('Treading Carefully', Yorkshire Television, 13 November 1994).

In 1999 I got to know Wharmby well while I was writing the BBC book *Last of the Summer Wine: The Finest Vintage*. He was a self-deprecating delight, though he relished the fame the series gave him locally: in West Yorkshire, he was a rock star. I well remember local BBC newsman Harry Gration hosting a charity fashion show. Wharmby, out of Wesley's trademark grubby overalls for once, pranced down the catwalk as if to the manor born. His grin could have melted stone. It's a memory of this lovely, minor cog in a sitcom behemoth that never fails to warm my heart.

TREAT YOURSELF TO *Roy Clarke's Last of the Summer Wine: The Complete Collection* (Universal: B075DQ4Q89, 2017) – the whole nine yards on fifty-four discs. Gordon was preparing to appear in the twenty-fourth series at the time of his death, from cancer, on 18 May 2002. The series carried on without him, until 2010, but his oil-rag dependability and droll delivery is forever part of the Holmfirth, West Yorkshire landscape. This hefty collection is his ultimate showcase. Any self-respecting comedy archivist needs this.

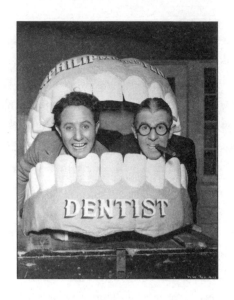

# Bert Wheeler
# and Robert Woolsey

## 1895–1968 and 1888–1938

All utter nonsense, of course, but fun for devotees of the irrational.

*Robert B. Jewell*

No other comedy team was as suited to the risqué, pre-Code Hollywood of the early 1930s as Wheeler and Woolsey. Even the Marx Brothers, who were undoubtedly sassy and saucy, covered up their most dubious smut with style and sophistication, and a sardonic raise of Groucho's painted eyebrow. There was no such subterfuge with Bert Wheeler and Robert Woolsey. Their films were a cavalcade of innuendo and bawdy humour that didn't so much tickle your ribs as give them a hefty poke. It was all done with the broadest of strokes, and with a hefty, knowing wink and a 'so sue us' grin. As with the Marx Brothers, the freewheeling world of Wheeler and Woolsey was populated with those gorgeous girls of pre-censorship Hollywood. Indeed, the two teams seemed to pass Thelma Todd [qv] between them.

Wheeler and Woolsey were also pretty much the archetypal blueprint for the screen double act. Like Stan and Ollie, Bud and Lou, and Eric and Ern, they were each distinct types: nobody was going to get these two guys mixed up. Curly-haired Wheeler was the moon-faced, doe-eyed clot who stammered and grinned; bespectacled Woolsey was the fast-talking, cigar-chomping wisecracker who would chase a piece of tail from the Bronx to California if he thought it would get him anywhere. Together they were the perfect chalk-and-cheese comedy combination, guaranteed to make their slapstick way through life. They would try everything: madcap song and dance, unrequited romance, impressions. Everything! It really was that obvious; the humour was signposted. It smacked you in the face like a wet herring, but boy did it work. For a short, glorious time, Wheeler and Woolsey were the tops. There was cynicism and cowardice in Woolsey, stupidity and naivity in Wheeler, but it was an affectionate team, both off-screen and on. In one of their earliest hits, the First World War romp *Half Shot at Sunrise* (1931), Wheeler looks for a few moments like he's about to brave no man's land alone before he typically volunteers his pal. Still, as soon as the wheels on the vehicle start exploding he's out in the wilderness himself – he wouldn't let his best friend down. This combination of risqué humour and cheerful camaraderie makes these early 1930s film a joy. The pair even made it across the pond, gaining that all-important signifier for success in Britain: a regular comic strip in *Film Fun*.

Both Wheeler and Woolsey had worked themselves out of poverty to hit the vaudeville stage during the years of the First World War. Woolsey left behind a three-year career as a jockey, scuppered due to a broken leg sustained during a fall. He had also had a stab at straight acting, and even tried a little light opera. By the mid 1920s both were big comedy stars on the New York stage, Woolsey playing Mortimer Pottle opposite W. C. Fields in the Broadway hit *Poppy*, which ran at the Apollo Theatre from 3 September 1923. Meanwhile Wheeler, who had met dancer Margaret Grae during the summer 1913 Broadway run of *When Dreams Come True*, had married his Betty three years later. The two formed a successful vaudeville comedy act. The marriage broke down, the act going with it. Bert and Betty divorced in 1926, and Wheeler went on to marry a further four times. His friend, Broadway composer and producer Gus Edwards, introduced him to the mighty impresario Florenz Ziegfeld and, under his wing, Wheeler quickly became a star comic in his own right, being employed in the *Ziegfeld Follies* from 1924.

And it was Ziegfeld that brought Wheeler together with Woolsey, albeit completely by accident. It was never planned but the two became a team from the moment they met, and their success was instant too. The year was 1927 and both comedians found themselves cast, as a pair, by that behemoth of razzle-dazzle, Florenz Ziegfeld, in the musical comedy *Rio Rita*. The show was a smash-hit Broadway success, and as soon as the run came to an end, after two years and 494 performances, Wheeler and Woolsey made the immediate and inevitable schlep to Hollywood in order to film the big-screen version. Remade a decade or so later by MGM, when the team's natural successors Abbott and Costello (who always had more Wheeler and Woolsey than Laurel and Hardy about them) took on the roles of saps abroad, the 1929 original had been a gamble on the part of RKO Radio Pictures. Talking pictures were still a relatively experimental, new-fangled gimmick and the studio was a relatively small pond in the fledgling Culver City, California – Warner Brothers it wasn't. But for this big-budget musical of fifteen reels of song, dance and knockabout comedy, the tiny studio pulled out all the stops. Not only was it all-talking, all-singing and all-dancing, it was a third colour. Just when overawed Joe Box Office thought he couldn't get any more value for his buck, the finale burst into two-tone Technicolor. The picture was a sensation, and Wheeler and Woolsey, quite naturally, found themselves in demand as movie stars for the next decade.

With the demure Dorothy Lee – a buoyant asset gratefully retained from the Broadway production – as often as not along for the ride to play Bert's coy love interest, the team churned out hit comedy after hit comedy – as often as three a year. The quality control was never a concern. As Bert Wheeler observed years later: 'they were all pretty indifferent compared to our Broadway stuff. But they all made money, so we kept on making 'em.'

Indeed, Wheeler and Woolsey were so popular a screen double act that by the 1931 short *The Stolen Jools* they were guest-starring as themselves in an all-star jamboree that also featured Stan and Ollie. They were also so popular that greedy little RKO tried to triple the takings at the box office by retaining the clout of the comedy double act *and* diluting the team into separate vehicles for Wheeler and Woolsey. Thus, audiences would be treated to the expected Wheeler and Woolsey film, plus a Bert Wheeler picture, plus a Robert Woolsey headliner. Genius. Or not. Audiences are no mugs and this less-than-cunning plan quickly saw diminished returns, leading to the team being reunited for the usual mixture of outrageous puns, childish banter and slapdash musical numbers. The fact that the musical numbers were so slapdash is a surprise, considering that future Fred 'n'

Awkwords! Woolsey, Phyllis Barry, Marjorie White and Wheeler in ditzy promotion of *Diplomaniacs* (1933).

Ginger helmsman Mark Sandrich directed the earliest efforts.

Towering directorial talent George Stevens would cut his teeth on the later films, at a time when RKO – again displaying the wisdom that kept them eternally in the shallow end – split Wheeler and Woolsey up once more, although at least this time it was within the same picture, in the convoluted murder mystery plot of *The Nitwits* (1935). Billed as 'the very first comedy musical whodunnit' (and who's to argue) the film remains probably their quintessential effort, while *Hips, Hips, Hooray!* (1934) had tried to add a touch of class. It even put the boys in top hats and tails, and Wheeler and Woolsey were categorically not top-hat-and-tail comedians; they were strictly slacks-and-sports-jackets types. Usually with patches on the elbows.

Mind you, occasionally an experiment worked surprisingly well. *Oh! Oh! Cleopatra* (1931) had transported them lock, stock and beer barrel to ancient Rome. Joyously there was absolutely no attempt to adapt their familiar screen personas to the setting of sunken baths and vestal virgins when Wheeler played Mark Antony and Woolsey was Julius Caesar. Perhaps the infant Eddie Braben

Pre-Code pandemonium: Bert and Robert publicise *Diplomaniacs*.

saw it at the New Regent Cinema in Liverpool.

Clearly the relationship with RKO was a confident one. There was no fuss and no bother, just a sense of ploughing the same field for the same assured success. Only once did things turn nasty, when a dispute over contracts saw the boys rebel and moonlight over at Columbia Pictures. This resulted in just one film, though, and *So This is Africa* (1933) was definitely a cut below what even RKO was offering. The pair's last film together, *High Flyers*, was released in November 1937. It was never conceived as their last film, of course, for there was seemingly nothing to stop the Wheeler and Woolsey juggernaut. Save the grim reaper.

Robert Woolsey was stricken with chronic kidney disease even before the production of *High Flyers*; eleven months after the film's initial release, all of which he had spent bedridden in hospital. On 31 October 1938, he died, in Malibu, at the ridiculously early age of fifty. Within months Europe was at war, America had fallen in love with Abbott and Costello, and Wheeler and Woolsey were all but forgotten.

After ten years as part of a double act, it wasn't easy for Bert Wheeler to re-establish himself but he had the talent and a bucketload of chutzpah. After a number of lean in-between years, he approached his beloved screen sweetheart Dorothy Lee for a joint tour of vaudeville theatres. She agreed and Wheeler was back, if not in the big time then at least in the hearts and minds of a nostalgic audience.

Wheeler had been an inspired choice to step in to the role of drunken dreamer Elwood P. Dowd in *Harvey*, on Broadway, in 1944. He also made two really rather excellent comedy shorts for Columbia Pictures, playing a heightened version of himself as Bert, a hapless loon with misunderstood misadventures with the boss's wife in *Innocently Guilty*, released in August 1950, and as Bert, a hapless soda jerk obsessed with detective stories, in *The Awful Sleuth*, released in April 1951. Soon after, he landed the regular role of half-breed Smokey Joe in the television series *Brave Eagle*. There was even another Broadway hit, supporting John Raitt and Anne Jeffreys in *Three Wishes for Jamie*, in 1952. Thereafter, it was bits on the small screen, second-rate nightclubs, and summer stock companies, all happy to throw Wheeler a bone or capitalise on his fondly remembered but fading marquee value. His skill for impersonations never failed him, that very last Wheeler and Woolsey comedy, *High Flyers*, utilising his talent as Charlie Chaplin.

Although enjoying solo comedy success, Wheeler had teamed up with Hank Ladd. And having been a vibrant member of The Lambs – America's First Professional Theatrical Club – since 1927, Wheeler joined forces with the much younger member, singing comedian Tom Dillon. Through the early '60s the comedy doubt act of Wheeler and Dillon played many New York night spots in Manhattan's Latin Quarter. The only shocker is that in 1963 Stanley Kramer couldn't find any place for him in the cast of *It's A Mad, Mad, Mad, Mad World* the vaudeville comedy cast to end all vaudeville comedy casts. If I had been Wheeler, I would have sacked my agent!

Wheeler carried on working – dishing out the old one-liners, and even older shtick, for anyone who would pay him to do it – until he died in New York, on 18 January 1968, a full three decades after his much-loved comedy partner. It's a shame that he didn't live long enough to see Neil Simon's *The Sunshine Boys*. Bert Wheeler was Al Lewis made flesh.

TREAT YOURSELF TO *Wheeler and Woolsey: RKO Comedy Classics Collection* (Turner Entertainment: B00BLSWWHY, 2012), which gathers nine truly hilarious feature films from their thirties golden age including *Hook, Line and Sinker* (1930), *Cracked Nuts* (1931), and *The Nitwits* (1935). They really are two of the greatest nitwits Hollywood was ever lucky enough to have.

# Albert Whelan

## 1875–1961

A master of surrealism.

*Sir Ken Dodd OBE*

Born Albert Waxman in Melbourne, Australia, on 5 May 1875, Whelan found fame and fortune as a singer and dancer in his native country before emigrating to England at the turn of the last century. Initially performing his usual eccentric dance moves for the new audience, by the time he was at his peak, in Edwardian London, he was more English than the English. Dapperly dressed and sophisticated of manner, Whelan is credited with being the originator of the signature tune, always starting his act by whistling Robert Vollstedt's 'Jolly Brothers' waltz as he removed his top hat and white gloves, then relieved himself of his cane, gleefully milking this business for all it was worth; apparently, for one memorable eight-minute spot, he only had time to shed his outer layer of clothing before he had to put it back on again and exit stage right!

When he had the opportunity to do something other than just walk onstage and walk off, Whelan proved himself an expert pianist and pitch-perfect mimic, channelling such star names of the day as American grouch Ned Sparks and cockney grumbler Gordon Harker. There's some glorious footage in existence of Whelan performing a three-way impersonation of Eddie Cantor, Donald Duck and Wallace Beery singing 'The Love Bug Will Bite You', in which he gear-shifts with flabbergasting dexterity.

Appropriately enough, it was a song called 'The Whistling Bowery

Albert put his own friendly-fire spin on the 'Chinese Laundry Blues' for a song he sang on stage and radio throughout 1942.

Boy' that, in 1905, began Whelan's fifty-five-year recording career. He made a handful of film appearances, too, almost exclusively recreations of his beloved stage routines. *Stars on Parade* (1936), shot at Cricklewood Studios, remains the most important of these; it's only a cheerful little earful of Whelan, as a tea-stall proprietor, but the film also gives the student of music hall early glimpses of Robb Wilton [qv], Arthur Lucan and Kitty McShane.

Whelan was nothing if not a canny businessman. He knew that his audience wanted the old favourites, so that's what he gave them, right up to the end, when he was still touring the surviving variety halls in nostalgia-packed bills including G. H. Elliott and Hetty King. He even teamed up with that great droll Billy Bennett (who famously sang 'Almost a Gentleman') and formed a brand-new double act: Alexander and Mose. The duo specialised in blackface banter, and gave the ever-resourceful Whelan another string to his bow: he would sign up for a bumper package of old-time variety with both Bennett and Whelan *and* Alexander and Mose. Two double acts for the price of two, performed by the same two performers. There's chutzpah!

A member of the show business fraternity the Grand Order of Water Rats, he served as its King Rat in 1948 and was a tireless campaigner for the various charities associated with this jolliest of clubs. The Whistling Wonder was still game to give a turn well into his eighties, and on 30 September 1957, was surprised, live on air, by *This Is Your Life* host Eamonn Andrews. The show described Whelan as 'a Great Entertainer and a True Gentleman of the Theatre'. Albert's wife, Rene, and their son, pianist Gordon Whelan, were in attendance. Even the ravishes of old age couldn't slow Albert down. In 1958 his left leg was amputated above the knee, at Guy's Hospital, in London. Less than three months later, and with an artificial limb attached, he was raring to get back to the theatre. Throwing down both his sticks and strolling, unsteadily, he joked: 'This is only a wooden leg. Wait till you see me on the new tin one I'm having fitted this week.' He was determined to perform again, starting with a cabaret at the Ocean Hotel, Brighton, guaranteeing: 'My act will be the same as it always was.' And it was. Albert was performing and recording until the end, finally exiting stage right on 19 February 1961. He was eighty-five and whistling, I'll be bound!

TREAT YOURSELF TO *Albert Whelan – The Whistling Boy* (Windyridge: VAR16, 2006), a definitive collection of Whelan's 78rpm recordings from the early 1930s alongside an even earlier waxing of that pioneering whistled signature tune. (There's a lot of whistling across the rest of the recordings, too.) Gems included range from the sentimental 'Sweet Carolina' to the knowing 'Oh-Oh-Oh! What a Silly Place to Kiss A Girl', plus hilarious recordings for the Imp label such as 'I'm Happy When I'm Hiking', 'My Brother Makes the Noises for the Talkies', 'I Lost My Gal Again' and 'It's An Old Spanish Custom'. But the plum in the pie is the two sides of his November 1931 release for Decca Records: the strangled lament of 'The Preacher and the Bear' and the 'short recitation written by a very tall man', 'The Three Trees'. The album is an invaluable archive of a true absurdist but the surreal, sound-effect-peppered landscape of 'The Three Trees' is on another level of abstract genius. It is a recording that never fails to delight.

# Robb Wilton

## 1881–1957

The one, for me, who stands out amongst them all as the most truly individual hero of comedy is Robb Wilton, a Lancashire comedian who specialised in a series of monologues playing establishment characters of absurd bureaucratic incompetence. Revered as an iconic master of comic timing, Wilton's influence upon generation after generation of comedians is legendary, and he is cited as having been one of the principal originators of stand-up character comedy. Both Ken Dodd and Les Dawson acknowledged him as one of their greatest comic heroes.

*Michael Armstrong*

The past is a beautiful country. They do things differently there. My own past was blessed with television schedules which filled my screen with nostalgic gems from Will Hay, George Formby and Arthur Askey, a valiant breed of entertainers who warmed the spirits of a war-torn nation – The Churchill Comedians, I call them. There was one particular favourite of mine who has, frustratingly, slipped into the mists of time. I first encountered him in the sublime comedy film compilation *To See Such Fun* (1977). In amongst the Hay, Formby and Askey – and, indeed, the Norman Wisdom, Benny Hill and Sid James – was a lengthy, very old sketch of a dithering bloke playing a fire chief. He was blissfully unconcerned about the roaring blaze burning during his watch, seemingly more uptight about the social etiquette of the situation and more interested in whether the emergency could be a good excuse to take the station dog out for a run. This gentleman was Robb Wilton, and I instantly fell in comedy love with him.

Albert Finney would recall how he first found his own talent to amuse by impersonating Wilton during his days at Salford Grammar. My dad, who had also been in short trousers when Wilton reigned, still lapsed into the stuttering gait, finger-sucking befuddlement and a nervous, 'The day war broke out...' whenever the hallowed name was mentioned. During the dark days of the Second World War this was Wilton's signature comedy opening. A monologue of contrary patriotic bewilderment would naturally ensue. My maternal grandfather was even better at it; Wilton had been his comedian. In a very positive way, Wilton was the personification of the British at war: a little bit slapdash, rather apologetic – but, by God, he would win. His sedate, very British reaction to danger and conflict has seeped into the nation's subconscious. The influence of Wilton's hesitant mannerisms and muddled determination is at play in every fibre of *Dad's Army*, where the laid-back, ineffectual but always resolute attitude to the matter in hand has secured a besotted audience for more than fifty years of repeats.

He was born Robert Wilton Smith, on 28 August 1881, in Everton, Liverpool, and blessed with the relaxed wit of the Lancastrian. His monologues were of the people, the Everyman and the everyday: of pubs and weddings, brawling and bickering. Wilton was for the working man and the working week, and he understood the distrust of authority that his class held close to its heart. Thus, in performance of his superbly silly monologues, he was the interloper: he may have worn the uniform but he did not salute the badge. He was on the side of authority, but also on the underside of it – no wielder of mighty power was he. He was almost apologetic of his position of authority; scared of it, even. Take his inept policeman who is reluctant to report a murder: he would rather do anything other than do his duty. It was almost as if he knew he couldn't handle the problem he had been given. There would be somebody else along any minute now who was actually equipped to take charge. He'd only get it wrong, and that would never do.

For all his subversion, however, his appeal crossed the class barrier. The Royals were such admirers that Wilton performed for the Command Performance at the Alhambra on 27 May 1926.

His great art was that of gentle satire and, as such, perhaps his most famous mutterings are those deeply rooted in history. And in war. There was one particularly celebrated routine in which he played a befuddled squaddie of the First World War who is convinced the war is still raging... in 1932. The humour of that situation quickly paled by the end of the decade, of course, though it was the Second World War that really gave Wilton meat for his comic potatoes. He was the zeitgeist of the conflict. With the skill of a comedic storyteller and the no-nonsense attitude of the stoic Northerner, Wilton's perfectly observed routines both tapped into and eased the public's fear. It was comedy as muffler, if you will. The dulcet tones of those reassuringly familiar opening words, 'The day war broke out...' instantly propel the listener back to the autumn of 1939, when the nation thought it would all be over by Christmas. Again.

Within Wilton's comical ramblings he is fully aware that he is a minor cog in the great scheme of things. A foot solider in the battle against the Nazis. His philosophical diatribes – often performed as one-sided telephone conversations – were given added weight by the unheard interactions from his overbearing wife. Wilton would explain, quite reasonably, that he will do his bit for the war

Robb as his celebrated comic character of the bewildered Justice of the Peace Mr Muddlecombe.

effort in his own sweet way. Ruminating on the fact that she thinks her hopeless husband will never be able to track down the dreaded Adolf Hitler once he lands in Germany, Wilton ruefully mutters: 'I've got a tongue in me head, haven't I?' If you could personify the never-weary, always-cheerful, down-to-earth spirit of the British at war, you couldn't do much better than picture Robb Wilton with an Air Raid Precautions warden's helmet atop his head.

Wilton became a highly paid draw onstage and on the radio, but film was different. In any era without Will Hay in it he undoubtedly would have become a big-screen star. Unfortunately, just as Morecambe and Wise were dominant in the days of Mike and Bernie Winters [qv], Wilton had Hay. No contest. Occasionally Wilton would appear in a slow seventh reel of a sluggish comedy, as often as not fairly irrelevant to the plot, but instantly brightening the action with a showstopping turn as one of his memorable characters.

Although never really diminishing in popularity, Wilton was certainly seen as a turn of the war years. He would tour the familiar old act and resurrect beloved routines but, like George Formby and Will Hay, he became part of that group of drolls so much identified with the war that they brought a load of unwanted baggage with them. These Churchill comedians had done their bit to keep the home fires burning but now they forever had something of the searchlight and the ration book about them. Audiences saw him as a wartime comedian, not a peacetime comedian. His Justice of the Peace, Mr Muddlecome, was different, however. Here was a timeless buffoon who was at home in almost any situation. With the expected sloppiness and almost criminally sympathetic attitude to the criminals around him, Wilton would pile on the niceness and platitudes with care and consideration, wallowing in his Lancashire roots: 'Ere, you shouldn't have done that...' his magistrate would exclaim. As disaster would mount on disaster, he would stroke his weary old chin and simply mutter: 'What a to-do!'

Towards the end of his days, Wilton was offered his last appearance, a cameo in the Arthur Askey film *The Love Match*, released in February 1955. Shirley Eaton's presence as the fresh 'n' fiery leading lady pointed to the future of British comedy at the cinema, but Robb Wilton kept one foot very much in the past. Here is a great character comedian. Steeped in variety tradition, this lampoon of the magistrate is as befuddled as ever, and very, very funny.

It remains Wilton's final comic hurrah. Wilton died, in London, on 1 May 1957. He was seventy-five. By common consent he was one of the kindest men in the business; he was certainly one of the funniest. Undoubtedly a unique comedy great. Robin Askwith, Wilton's great-nephew, certainly inherited those strong comedy genes.

That Wilton isn't remembered as one of the towering figures of the music hall generation is as much down to his lack of filmed work as anything else. It's a great pity, for he

The elder statesman of the comic monologue preparing for a radio broadcast. Almost Churchillian in repose. Quite right too...

was clearly a character comedian of true greatness. We should be grateful, then, for the handful of treasured remnants from preserved records of his greatest routines. One can never fully recapture the glory of his stage work but those precious shadowy images that capture his comic genius like lightning in a bottle are more than enough to keep him at humour's top table.

TREAT YOURSELF TO the absolutely essential CD *Robb Wilton's War* (Flapper: B00005EBUQ, 2001), which features nine Wilton sketches, including 'The Fire Station', with Florence Palmer, 'The Home Guard', recorded live in concert at Windsor Castle in 1942 and, gleefully, 'The Day Hostilities Terminated': 'My missus said to me, "What are you going to do now?" I said, "What do you mean, what am I going to do now?" "Well," she said, "there's no Home Guard, no more fire-watching, they don't want any more special constables, so what are you going to do?" I said, "I'll do something!"' All this, plus some bonus sketches from fellow character comedians Frank Randle and Billy Russell.

# Mike and Bernie Winters

## 1926–2013 and 1930–91

In 1963–64, at the Coventry Theatre, I was fortunate to appear in a superb, extravagant pantomime production of *Babes in the Wood & Bold Brave Robin Hood*. It was produced on a truly grand scale, with Arthur Askey, Anton Dolin, and Mike and Bernie Winters as the good and bad robbers, and myself as Robin Hood. A truly memorable time in my life, as I celebrated my twenty-first birthday on a two-show matinee day with a huge fan-club party between shows. After the second show, Arthur Askey gave a champagne party for me in his dressing room, at which Mike Winters made the toast and proclaimed that I would go on to become a successful actor. Prophetic, it seems!

Halcyon days that shine brightly in my box of very special memories.

*Mark Wynter*

I have a very good friend by the name of Henry Holland who has delusions that he is a man of a thousand voices. In fact, he is a man of two voices: his own and that of Bernie Winters. He is truly extraordinary at both of them. With a simple 'Eeeee... choochie face!' Bernie Winters is back in the room. It wouldn't win Henry a Perrier Award; it wouldn't even get him on *The Wheeltappers and Shunters Social Club*, but it always makes me laugh.

In fact, it's Bernie Winters who always makes me laugh. If he's remembered by anyone at all, it's usually with a shake of the head, a wan smile and 'Oh God! Him and that bloody dog!' The bloody dog in question was Schnorbitz, a behemoth of a St Bernard that in the latter stages of Bernie's career became almost as famous than he did – if not more so. Part of a legendary story that sounds apocryphal, but isn't, recalls a showbiz party where Schnorbitz fell into the swimming pool of Terry Scott and was hurriedly rescued by a quick-thinking Barbara Windsor. You really couldn't make it up. Grinning and gurning through yet another celebrity-based edition of *Whose Baby?* or some such tat, Bernie and dog were a light-entertainment staple, something akin to a novelty winner of *The X Factor*. It almost became a double act, and Bernie had known all about those.

One of my favourite jokes from the Irish master of the one-liner, Frank Carson, is: 'Do you remember those two terrible Winters we had? Mike and Bernie...' Mike, the older brother, was rather sharp and clean-cut. Fashioned like an American straight man, he was good-looking, condescending and cool with the ladies; a sort of Dean Martin without the voice. Bernie, meanwhile, was the fool: the goon with buck teeth, bulging eyes and the look of a village idiot in a suit. He was the Jerry Lewis of Islington. In terms of comedy he was a schmuck, but in terms of business he knew exactly what he was doing. Cultivating a warm, cuddly image, Bernie quickly established himself as one of the best-loved – and busiest – comedians in the business.

At least, the public liked him. But the brothers were hardly respected by their peers and, being no mugs, they were painfully aware of their limitations. Bernie once commented: 'You know, an act like Morecambe and Wise comes along just once in a lifetime. Why did they have to come along in mine?'

Good Jewish boys, born Michael and Bernie Weinstein, on 15 November 1926 and 6 September 1930 respectively, the brothers grew up quickly in a tough part of London Town. While Mike was learning to play the clarinet at the Royal

Academy of Music, Bernie had a yearning for the variety end of show business, eagerly picking up quips and routines in London's seediest dance halls. He got a job at the Regency club in Soho and worked up a comedy routine with a few stolen jokes and some shtick on the ukulele and the drums. The biggest double act in the world at the time was Abbott and Costello, and Bernie felt he needed a straight man.

During the dying days of the war, the brothers Weinstein had won a talent contest in Manchester which led to a week of touring in variety, but the act then died the death and the two split. Mike had always seen himself as a respected and wealthy economist, and he tried his luck as a street trader, while Bernie worked as a steward on a cruise liner. While Mike's entrepreneurial skills would eventually see him open a number of shops, in the early 1950s the brothers decided to have another go as a double act.

A rather ragamuffin new act developed, with the brothers initially teaming up with variety comedian Jack Parr as The Three Loose Screws before reverting to a double act once more. It was star-spotter Evelyn Taylor who really believed in them, putting them under the nose of impresario Harold Fielding. He gave them their lucky break in a summer season of variety with *The Norman Evans Show* and the brothers made their telly debut on 25 June 1955 on *Variety Parade*. An overnight success, they peddled their wares on the programme for nearly four years, by which time Lew Grade at ATV had taken notice, been impressed with what he saw, and made his pitch to lure the brothers over to commercial television.

An appearance on *Sunday Night at the London Palladium* on 22 April 1962 made them national heroes. Fresh, funny, and with a wacky, transatlantic quality to the sharp comic banter, Mike and Bernie were back on the bill on 14 October 1962. Now they were firm family favourites but it had been Harold Fielding who had again stepped in to shape their careers, and signed them up as comedy support for his rock 'n' roll variety bill with chart sensations Tommy Steele and Freddie Bell and the Bellboys. The Winters were cool. Their appearance on *Six-Five Special* in October 1957 had already made them British teenagers' favourite comedians and part of the hip generation. However, once more Bernie seemed disenchanted with the double act. He accepted some solo film work and, once again, the brothers split, only to almost immediately reunite to be a double act – this time, for good. (Again!) In 1962 they would cultivate their youth-market appeal as pretty much the star turns in Michael Winner's outrageously nonsensical pop-musical film rendition

Promoting *Blackpool Night Out* for 1 August 1965.

of Gilbert and Sullivan, *The Cool Mikado*. Their lack of acting prowess was left in no doubt, although they certainly seem more at ease in the film than Frankie Howerd does in the lead.

Later in 1962 Mike and Bernie were invited to perform before Her Majesty the Queen at the London Palladium for the Royal Variety Performance, and their continued success on television saw them host the weekly variety shows *Big Night Out* (ABC, 1961–65) and *Blackpool Night Out* (ABC, 1964–65). By spring 1966 they had been granted their own ABC series: *Mike and Bernie's Show*, a series of ten half-hours of sketches, slapstick, and special guests Lionel Blair and his dancers. Another ABC series of skits, *Mike and Bernie's Music Hall*, followed from 18 March 1967, with a further three-week run of *Mike and Bernie's Show*, from 30 December 1967. Thames Television, having launched in the summer of 1968, would be Mike and Bernie's home for the next five years, with *Mike and Bernie's Show* picked up by the network from November 1968.

A seven-week run of *Mike and Bernie's Scene*, from 27 April 1970, was the usual mix of comic bickering and quick sketches, while a one-off special, *A Tale of Two Winters*, that September, found room for some situation comedy interludes penned by Vince Powell [qv] and Harry Driver. This element paved the way for the Winters brothers to break away from the restraints of variety with a short-lived sitcom, *Mike and Bernie*, casting them as unsuccessful music hall comedians. (No real acting stretch there.) Powell and Driver were once again the writers, with the six-week series kicking off on Thames Television from

Bernie, with Leslie Crowther, in *Bud 'n' Ches*.
The ATV biopic transmitted on 16 June 1981.

14 December 1971. The final indulgence of the Thames deal, *Mike and Bernie's Show: The Redman and Ross Story*, on New Year's Day 1973, was even more telling, casting the brothers as a fictional bickering double act struggling to remain civil with each other both onstage and in shoddy variety digs. This took no acting skill whatsoever. In a combination of personal and professional wrangles, the act split once and for all in 1978.

Bernie had certainly been no stranger to working without his brother, even once the team had made it big on television. The most unlikely of showbiz friendships sprang up with multitalented entertainer Anthony Newley. (In fact, it's a fair judgment that Newley was basically Mike Winters with even more talent.) Having met on the variety circuit, the two warmed to each other immediately, and during the early 1960s Newley and Winters formed their own double act of sorts. Newley's *The Strange World of Gurney Slade* (ATV, 1960), a surrealistic deconstruction of the innards of television production, advertising and life in Britain at the time, saw Bernie pop up in the last two episodes of the six-week run. In the show transmitted on 19 November 1960, when even ITV had lost faith in the show, Bernie appears as a dazed and confused party-goer from Newley's psyche who ambles about a wood and chats to a group of schoolchildren. It was that kind of show – wonderfully so!

The unofficial team of Newley and Winters also made a break into film, and it was certainly more successful than that of the Brothers Winters. It also put Newley on the road to pop stardom, with, in 1959, an Elvis-inspired satire *Idle on Parade* (*Idol on Parade* in America) that told the tale of a rock star forced to enlist. For Newley, the film gleaned him a top-ten record in 'I've Waited So

Long' and the start of a double career as actor and all-round entertainer. Bernie pops up at the very end of the film as a gormless squaddie. It was ever thus.

Two more films followed in 1960: *In the Nick*, which saw Newley as a benign prison doctor and Bernie as one of the inmates, and, most interestingly of all, *Let's Get Married*. As well as dealing with the serious topic of abortion within the light-hearted frame of a romantic comedy, the film fully tapped in to the teamwork of Newley and Winters. There were slapstick routines, moments of buddy-to-buddy pathos and even a shared song-and-dance routine on the title number – the fact that the routine features Bernie (playing Bernie, of course) and not Newley's female lead, Anne Aubrey, makes this moment all the more fluffy and fun.

Mike, meanwhile, was doing very well for himself in America, thank you very much, running several businesses, topping up his tan and managing Muhammad Ali's agent Angelo Dundee. (Seriously!) He even wrote a book about his experiences, *The Axis of Greatness* (J.R. Books, 2008), as well as a couple of novels. *Miami, One Way* (Weidenfeld & Nicolson, 1985) was a thriller in which central character, New York talent agent Tony Florentino, agrees to travel to Miami only to get involved in a mystery set in the city's sleazy joints and exclusive clubs. *Razor Sharp* (Weidenfeld & Nicolson, 1987) was a second Tony Florentino adventure, with our hero enjoying a five-week, all expenses paid trip to London. A psychopathic killer is on the loose in the city too. This was joyous and ridiculous semi-autobiographical pulp fiction. The extraordinary aftermath of Mike's show business years was related in his twilight-years memoir, *The Sunny Side of Winters: A Variety of Memories* (J.R. Books, 2010). By that time Mike had returned from America and settled into comfortable retirement in Gloucestershire. He died there, on 24 August 2013, at the age of eighty-six. Fully reconciled with the legacy of laughter he had created with his younger brother, Mike would gleefully regale with name-dropping tales until the end. What a pro.

Bernie could hardly hope to find much professionalism in a dog, but throughout the 1980s he and Schnorbitz won the hearts of television viewers across the country. Britain loves its animals and those big, watery eyes full of love could do no wrong. Schnorbitz was pretty popular as well! Accompanied by his beloved hound, Bernie hosted *Big Top Variety Show* (Thames, 1979–82) from a three-ring circus. There were hosting duties, too, on the tiresome and tireless quiz show *Scribble* (HTV, 1987), as well as *Make Me Laugh* (Tyne Tees, 1983), a battle of stamina and joke-power between stand-up comics. Bernie guest-starred as a superiorly silly Sherlock Holmes in *3-2-1* (Yorkshire Television, 19 February 1983) and, of course, there was the hilarious nadir that is *Whose Baby?* (Thames, 1983–88), though Bernie's charm, warmth and winning grin made a nice and jolly half-hour of telly out of this most risible of formats – in which celebrities had to guess the famous parent from a fuzzy photograph of their infant offspring.

He had come late to the show, for Leslie Crowther had been the host for the first series. It was with Crowther that Bernie enjoyed the best partnership of his later years, when, in 1981, Bernie's old employer ATV cast him in *Bud 'n' Ches*, an affectionate biopic of comedians Flanagan and Allan. Bernie shared great swathes of DNA with Bud Flanagan. Both traded on their genial Jewishness and wore their patriotic charm on their sleeves. As a boy, Bernie had seen Flanagan perform, and as Bernie's stage act grew Bud became a friend and champion. Both were embraced by their audiences and not merely liked but loved. In his performance as Bud, Bernie combined his natural variety panache with accomplished acting, and some scenes are heartbreaking to watch. Remembering the film in his memoir, *One Day at a Time: The Story of My Life* (Ebury Press, 1991), Bernie wrote: 'I had sung "Any Umbrellas" on my own. The studio was blacked out and I was standing on the top of a ladder wearing a big fur coat. The camera was on a crane, high up with me, and Jack Parnell was playing the music... Up there, completely alone in the darkness, I really felt as though I was with Bud, singing beside him. The emotion of the moment got to me and I started to cry.' The reaction to the television film was so positive that the show was taken onstage. From 4 May 1982 Bernie and Leslie Crowther starred in the West End run of *Underneath the Arches,* at the Prince of Wales, with the crowning glory coming on 19 November 1984, when they performed as Bud 'n' Ches for the Royal Variety Performance. It was all the more poignant, being staged at the Victoria Palace, the former home of the Crazy Gang's comedy revues.

Bernie would be asked to sing a Flanagan and Allen number for many events after, be it charity, gala or television guest-spot. The performances are all the more remarkable considering that Bernie was dying from stomach cancer at the time. He would drown himself in vodka to kill the pain just long enough to perform. The end was certainly in sight when, from his home in Miami, Mike Winters made the pilgrimage back home to see his ailing brother. They had resolved their differences by the

Bernie with his two closest showbiz pals: brother Mike and Schnorbitz the St. Bernard. The dog was bequeathed to illusionist and actor Richard De Vere, often appearing in pantomime together at the Royal Court theatre, in Liverpool.

time Bernie died in his beloved London, on 4 May 1991, at the age of sixty. There was a genuine sense of loss across the nation. He was a goof but we loved him, and so did Mike.

TREAT YOURSELF TO *Mike and Bernie Winters in Toyland* (CBS: 63023, 1967) a long-playing record that both thrilled and rather haunted me as a child (that gloriously freakish cover of toy soldiers, two of whom are Mike and Bernie in the flesh). Listen as the brothers rattle through such nursery favourites as 'Teddy Bears' Picnic', 'Supercalifragilisticexpialidocius' and 'That Man Bat Man'. As Jimmy Tarbuck writes in his tongue-in-cheek sleeve notes: 'as singers you rate with sewing machines and Harold Wilson. As comics the Guv'nors.'

# Georgie Wood and Dolly Harmer

## 1894–1979 and 1867–1956

A perfect comic pairing.

*Mike Craig*

Born George Bamlett in Jarrow, County Durham, on 17 December 1894, the celebrated turn that would be Wee Georgie Wood was told as a youngster that he wouldn't grow any taller than four feet, nine-and-a-half inches. (That half an inch was very important to him; he never let interviewers forget it.) Straight away his mother realised she had a potential gold mine on her hands. Her mercenary response was hardly surprising when you consider she had twenty other children besides George. She put the little lad to work in the music halls from the age of five. Not that he minded. From that first time on the stage of the old Jubilee Grounds, Seaham Harbour, George seemed to revel in the attention. He made his pantomime debut in 1906 in a tour of *Sleeping Beauty*. The company also included Stan Laurel: what a pip! The two would stay in correspondence until Stan's death in 1965.

By 1908 Wood was topping the bill in variety with his impressions of Vesta Tilley, George Lashwood and other music hall greats of the day, and by 1909 he had developed his 'Nursery at Bedtime' sketch, with Dolly Harmer as his mother. The two were still together nearly twenty years later, when the 1927 Royal Command Performance presented scenes from their latest stage success, *The Black Hand Gang*, at the Victoria Palace Theatre. For Wood the sketch was a lifelong commitment. Here he was the chief of a group of mischievous, crime-busting kids. He clowned and sang and joked as a child, and, for the next fifty-odd years, he would continue to clown and sing and joke as a child.

The laughter and applause tempered his initial distress when, as a teenager, he had to face the fact that he wouldn't grow any taller. Speaking in 1975 Wood recalled his response to his diminutive size: 'I used to try to counter being small by phoney dignity.'

He was a popular star, although his forays into film were extremely scarce and, naturally, he was always cast as a character junior to his actual age. In G. B. Samuelson's production of *Convict 99* (1919), for example, he played the office boy, though he was fast approaching thirty at the time!

It was on the stage that he felt most at home. Pretty much the blueprint for every mother-and-son act that followed, from the Clitheroe Kid to The Krankies, George and Dolly were soon a guaranteed top-of-the-bill act across Britain.

Dolly Harmer was already a seasoned veteran of both variety and legitimate theatre. Born on 16 January, in Bethnal Green, London, by the age of thirteen she was a virtuoso violinist in the music halls and had chalked up a string of pantomime appearances, usually as principal boy. The first female member of the Variety Artistes' Federation, she had travelled across America, Australia and the Home Counties on various variety bills. Dolly was nearly fifty by the time she teamed up with Wood. Their meticulously rehearsed sketches of domestic life between mother and boy became music hall favourites. Performing as Georgie and Mrs Robinson, the team created such sketches as 'Thicker Than Water' and the Royal Command-approved *Black Hand Gang*. In 1930, director Monty Banks produced a four-reeler film version of *The Black Hand Gang*, from a play, *Black Hand George*, by Bert Lee and R.P. Weston.

Georgie Wood at home, larking about for publicity, with stage mother and close friend Dolly Harmer.

A headliner in pantomime throughout the 1920s and 1930s, Wood invariably played the son of the dame, typically Shaun Glenville. After such seasons, Wood would rejoin Harmer on the variety circuit, often for producer Julian Wylie. George's pantomime assignments took him everywhere, from the Theatre Royal, Glasgow, to the London Hippodrome, and just once, in 1931–32, the Wood and Harmer partnership took on the panto challenge together, in *Humpty Dumpty* at the Gaiety Theatre, Dublin. They played to packed houses.

Wood was at the peak of his fame in the early 1930s, having married vaudevillian Ewing Eaton during an American tour, the pair forming a short-lived stage act back home in Britain. The marriage was short-lived, too, but George remained a prince of variety, headlining pantomimes in Birmingham, Blackpool and Wolverhampton. He even toured South Africa, in *Cinderella*, in 1936. That same year he was given the highest accolade his peers could bestow, that of the title of 'King Rat' in the entertainment clan of the Grand Order of Water Rats.

During the Second World War, Wood and Harmer toured with theatrical impresario Basil Dean's shows for the Entertainments National Service Association, performing for troops across Europe, Africa and the Middle East. They even toured America and Australia with ENSA, with their simple, belly-laugh-inducing vignettes of misbehaviour and affection bringing great joy to overseas servicemen. It was estimated that Wood and Harmer played over five hundred shows in all.

Those ENSA shows were amongst Wood's proudest achievements. As often as not Harmer would travel right alongside Wood, and was affectionately nicknamed the 'Mother of the Forces' due to her determination to play for the troops and her personal kindness to homesick servicemen many miles from their loved ones. In his diary, Wood lovingly noted: 'Every British boy who sees her simply adores her as representing his own mother. She flies thousands of miles and at once makes friends with the crews and her fellow passengers, but there will be no medals for this wonderful old lady – and very little publicity. What does she care? Nothing! She will have a reward that transcends all such transient praise.'

Wood would often cringe when recounting his worst experiences: the recurring condescending pat on the head from a delighted adult. This was never done with malice, but the demeaning feeling it gave Wood encouraged him to

A small man with a huge personality.

use his brains to rally against the world at large. Although his mother kept a vice-like grip on his allowance from theatrical earnings, George nursed an ambition to be either a solicitor or a journalist. Distinguished barrister Norman Birkett, later the 1st Baron Birkett, was in chambers in Birmingham. The two met and became friends after Wood had performed variety in the city. Wood was an intelligent and dedicated man, and Birkett encouraged him to study law, but by then Wood was too seasoned a performer to enable such a late-flowering change of career to blossom fully. Still, George was insistent that his small stature did not denote a small intellect. He was no baby tied to his mother's apron strings, and was fully aware that his job was to make people laugh.

Although it had often been a frustration for Wood, his mother showed plenty of nous in managing Wood's affairs, and when she died, in 1946, the coffers were in good shape. That same year Wood was awarded the OBE for services to the entertainment industry, with particular reference to his work during the war years. Wood and Harmer had already dropped the mother-and-son routine, replacing it with Wood's new character of Wee MacGregor, but with Dolly Harmer now in her late eighties, both decided to retire from the stage, with dignity, in 1953.

After Harmer's death, in Hampstead, on 15 March 1956, Wood accepted the odd television assignment, notably the nautical comedy *Glencannon*, an American-

The maternal love within Dolly made her a beloved figure all over the world.

British co-production that recruited Irish Hollywood star Thomas Mitchell to play a Scottish sea captain in the backwaters of Elstree Studios! Broadcast from 14 September 1960, Wood appeared in ten of the series' thirty-nine episodes, popping up all too briefly as Cookie, the soured-faced ship's cook.

After a long and prolific career, Wood lived in relative comfort in Bloomsbury, London. Importantly, he had made and kept very influential friends during his years in the limelight. George Bernard Shaw and theatre critic Hannen Swaffer urged him to pursue a writing career, while Neville Cardus had introduced him to C. P. Scott, the then editor of the *Guardian*. 'Mr Scott liked me because I could listen and he liked to talk,' George recalled. Sticking to the topic closest to his heart, George started writing a regular column for *The Stage and Television Today*; 'Stage Man's Diary' would run for many years, keeping George Wood in the public eye until his final days.

As a man of small size, in his twenties and thirties he had revolted against his plight: 'I had a period as a crusader when I tried to right the midget's world,' he later recalled. But he soon realised that his greatest weapon was laughter. If he could make people laugh with him, rather than at him, then he had won his own personal war. He would continue to be a voice of reason until his death, at the ripe old age of eighty-four, on 19 February 1979. And funny? Big time!

TREAT YOURSELF TO *British Comedies of the 1930s: Volume 6* (Network: B017O3GAWC, 2016), which showcases *The Black Hand Gang* (1930). Love interest and gang rivalry fleshes out the running time but at its heart is the original domestic banter of Wood and Harmer. It's pure variety gold dust. The DVD also includes another Leslie Fuller [qv] feature for your collection, *Old Spanish Customers*, from 1932. Smashing!

# Harry Worth

## 1917–89

It was sometime in the mid seventies when William G. Stewart cast me as niece to Harry in 'The Family Reunion' episode of Thames Television's *My Name is Harry Worth*. I hadn't met Harry before, but Bill had formed a good friendship with him.

From the first day of rehearsals it struck me what a sweet, down-to-earth and unaffected man Harry was. Although he had a brilliant sense of humour, he definitely did not have any airs and graces. Everybody liked him on set – the other actors, the camera crew – all admired his totally brilliant comic timing.

The character he played was hilarious, always causing misunderstandings and being tremendously annoying to other characters in the plot, blissfully unaware of just how annoying he was. Harry was absolutely fabulous. He had this talent for making his performance look completely natural. He was lovely to work with. In one scene, I remember he took me to a disco for a dance. Here Harry was terribly funny: me dancing like a young girl and him bobbing around enjoying himself in his suit, large-framed glasses and smiling face. He was so funny, so talented. His familiar voice was striking; no one else sounded like Harry Worth or even vaguely resembled him. He was a unique actor.

Sometime after working together, Harry invited Bill and myself to see him in a summer season by the coast. We arrived at the bungalow he and his wife were renting; his wife answered the door and invited us in. 'Harry's just finishing his tea in the kitchen,' she said. Bill and I followed her into the kitchen and Harry was seated at a small kitchen table eating a couple of boiled eggs and toast.

A couple of hours later we took our seats in the theatre. Harry was the star of the show. To my complete surprise and delight he came on as a stand-up and a ventriloquist! This was apparently his star act before becoming famous in his television role. His ventriloquist's dummy was what looked like a wooden stick. He called it Clarence. Both Harry and Clarence had the same voice and Harry moved his lips. He was hilarious! The audience were quite literally falling into the aisles laughing, including me and Bill. He received a standing ovation. He was adored. What a remarkable man: this quiet, sweet and most natural of human beings had transformed from the husband in the bungalow eating his tea to the performer who had everyone in stitches.

*Sally Geeson*

A middle-aged man in a suit and trilby hat cautiously walks up to the corner of a shop window. Indulging his childlike whim, he cheekily obscures half of his body in the shop doorway and lifts up both his left arm and left leg. To the onlooker, the reflection looks like he is elevating himself off the ground. He chuckles with glee to himself and wanders off. The slight cock of a snook to authority could be Charlie Chaplin. The playful innocence could be Harry Langdon. But this is no silent-screen clown. This is Harry Worth and that little bit of business would launch many a half-hour of warm, good-natured comedy.

The shop window was actually the idea of writer Vince Powell [qv], who had done the same trick during his childhood days in Manchester. Worth's scene was, suitably enough, shot on the city's St Ann's Square, at the tailor's Hector Powe. It was seen in nearly one hundred half-hours of Worth comedy, and if he is remembered for anything at all, it's that iconic opening sequence. Like Maigret striking his match

Doing a 'Harry Worth' with the childlike delight that typifies his funniest comedy shows for television.

to light his pipe, or the surreal, silhouetted dancer of *Tales of the Unexpected*, that opening scene to Harry Worth's unique brand of world-weary comedy stuck in the public's imagination. Even as recently as a *Radio Times* shoot in autumn 2013, journalist Robert Peston plugged his investigation into shopping habits by, yes, posing halfway in and halfway out of a mirrored doorway. It's surprising, then, that so very little of Worth's actual work has been rescreened, and that his show and name have been unfairly neglected over the years.

He was a man of the 1960s. Not a hip, with-it sort of chap, but a typical middle-class bloke who happened to be living in an age of revolution. Like many middle-class, middle-aged blokes, the revolution passed him by and Worth's comedy was of normality, reality and everyday conflicts with life's little irritations.

This comedy of the absurd and frustration reflected an early apprenticeship alongside Laurel and Hardy, with whom Worth toured England during the 1950s, though his comedy had always had an air of apologetic embarrassment about it. His earliest days saw struggle and hardship. Born Harry Bourlon Illingsworth in Hoyland, West Yorkshire, on 20 November 1917, he was the youngest of eleven children, and just five months old when his father was killed in a colliery accident. Leaving school at the age of fourteen, the young Harry followed his father's footsteps down the mine, escaping the same fate only by taking on an even less secure life with the Royal Air Force at the height of the Second World War, in 1941.

Worth had always loved performing, finding solace from the mineshaft with the local Tankersley Amateur Dramatic Society. More significantly, he had also taught

**HARRY WORTH**

In typical gleeful pose, often used as his publicity photograph for theatre programmes.

himself ventriloquism from a borrowed book, buying his first dummy in 1936. The war years offered him ample opportunity to perform in camp variety shows in India but, nervous and dismissive of his own talents, he would always warn his audience that he was a terrible ventriloquist. This honesty won over tough crowds, and his rather slipshod work with the dummy won him laughs. He quickly realised that setting himself up as an incompetent, before anybody in the audience found out just how incompetent he really was, could be a safety net he could work to his advantage. He used it for his entire career.

Upon demob Harry started at the bottom of variety-theatre bills, including a beach concert party in Southport. His big break was kindled by pantomime principal girl Kay Flynn, who he married in 1947. She urged him to write off for an audition at the Windmill Theatre in London. As Worth's oft-used theatre programme blurb had it: 'spending practically his last penny on the rail fare, he made the trip to London, only to find that he was one of forty acts waiting to audition, impresario Vivian Van Damm never laughed once throughout his act, but, much to Harry's surprise, he booked him.' Worth started work at the theatre in 1948. It was clearly an auspicious year for he also made his television debut, appearing on the bill of the variety show *New to You*, on 2 March 1948.

Although his dummies, Fotheringay and Clarence, proved popular, he had also developed his dithering comedy patter and began with a new routine at the London Hippodrome. Top-of-the-bill singer Johnnie Ray was so impressed that he invited Worth to tour South Africa with him. Oliver Hardy, watching Worth's performance in Nottingham in 1952, advised him to abandon the dummies and cultivate his own brand of comedy. This he did, although, like

Sandy Powell [qv], Worth retained the ventriloquist routine. It got more and more unkempt, much to the delight of his audiences, and he incorporated it during much of his successful stint as Merry King Cole in pantomime, as well as in the summer season at the North Pier Pavilion in Blackpool. Worth certainly didn't need the dummies for his many broadcasts on *Variety Bandbox*, though; Peter Brough had the vent-on-radio thing all sewn up.

Through the mid-fifties Worth was still making headway on television, with stand-out stand-up spots on *Henry Hall's Guest Night*, in 1955, *Sunday Night at the London Palladium*, in 1956, and *Saturday Spectacular*, in 1957. A headlining season at the London Palladium, was followed by an appearance on the Royal Variety Performance of 1960. His adopted surname made show titles a dream. Even as late as 1988 he starred as his usual likeable bumbler self in the BBC Radio 2 domestic situation comedy *Thirty Minutes Worth*. That particular title had already served its dues, having been used for a different Harry Worth series in both 1963 and 1983! In between those two radio ventures, the title *Thirty Minutes Worth* had also been used for a Thames Television series. That was in 1972, however, by which time Harry's best work was behind him at the BBC. It's important to note that Thames had pulled off a very British coup by attracting Worth to commercial television. Up to that point, in the hearts and minds of a nation, he had been very much a BBC commodity.

Thames squeezed out three series of the show, and though it was more sketch show than sitcom, they even gave it a brief appearance in their *All-Star Comedy Carnival* on Christmas Day 1972, before returning for a second series from July 1973 and a third from the October. All that within a little over a year!

From 22 April 1974 Thames presented Worth in *My Name is Harry Worth*, his familiar catchphrase of sorts. This was a return to a more long form comedy format, pitting our befuddled hero opposite various figures of officialdom akin to *Here's Harry* (BBC, 1960–65), but it lasted just one series, under the steerage of producer–director William G. Stewart. On 12 November 1976 Worth made a surprise return to the BBC in a one-off special simply entitled *Harry*, but thereafter his television career was set in a stricter sitcom mould which moved Worth further away from playing the muddled loon in which

*Here's Harry*, the BBC TV series, was exported globally, and particularly popular in Australia.

he excelled. This had already proved something of a mistake at the BBC, however. From 8 October 1972 Worth starred as William Boot in Barry Took's brave attempt to adapt Evelyn Waugh's war journalism satire *Scoop* to the screen. Worth could certainly empathise with the central character's clumsy and foolhardy approach to life but the comedian was now past fifty, with a deeply ingrained comic persona. Audiences weren't expecting Worth to give cutting commentary on the futility of war, and the series was not re-commissioned. Worth's reign at Thames started a few days after the fourth episode of *Scoop* had been transmitted.

Worth didn't fare much better with the more cosy sofa sitcom of *How's Your Father?*, broadcast on Yorkshire Television from 27 February 1979. Playing Harry Matthews, a recently widowed father of two teenage children, Martin and Shirley, played by Giles Watling and Debby Cumming, it had the air of reheated Sid James or Patrick Cargill [qv] about it, and even the typical Harry Worth frustration with everyday life didn't quite catch alight. Great fun, all the same, and it did run to two series, coming to an end on 29 August 1980. Less than a week later, Worth was back at the old corporation, returning to the BBC for *Oh Happy Band!*, written by Jeremy Lloyd and David Croft. Here he once more played Harry Worth, but as a member of an impoverished brass band in Yorkshire. Seasoned pros including Jonathan Cecil, Tony Sympson and Billy Burden [qv] played his muddle-headed cohorts. Think *Brassed Off* meets *Last of the Summer Wine*.

Worth remained a popular performer on radio and stage almost until the end, even playing the lead in a tour of Galton and Simpson's *The Wind in the Sassafras Trees*, in the role originally played twenty years before by Frankie

Tastes in comedy may change but one should always find time to enjoy the simple, delightful antics of Harry Worth. Bye bye, now.

Howerd. Harry died, in Berkhamsted, on 20 July 1989. He was seventy-one. Kay, his loving wife of some forty summers, was still by his side.

However, Harry is forever of the 1960s. Those halcyon days of *Here's Harry* and *Harry Worth*, which simply put him in ever more ridiculous and unfathomable situations, were where his comedy thrived. There was nothing extraordinary going on in the plotting or the scripting. Everything was geared towards the bumbling, endearing genius of Harry Worth. That's all that was needed, and we loved him for it.

Regardless of the nation forgetting pretty much everything about him other than that shop window trick, Worth really is one of the most influential and skilled comedians of the television age. So when you next walk down your local high street, do me a favour. Check no one is around and do a cheeky Harry Worth. You know you want to. That way the memory will kind of live on. For ever.

TREAT YOURSELF TO *The Complete Harry Worth Collection* (Revelation Films: B004FS27JU, 2011), which includes over eleven hours of material from *My Name is Harry Worth* and *Thirty Minutes Worth* as well as a fascinating audio interview with Harry from 1987.

# Mario Zampi

## 1903–63

Mario Zampi directed me in one of my favourite films, *Too Many Crooks*. He was a very calm, kind and interested man, never one to over-direct his actors. He simply picked the people he knew could do the job – both in front of and behind the camera – and let us get on with it. When you had people like Sid James, Terry-Thomas and George Cole on set, we were all in safe hands. Mario only told you when you *hadn't* done what he expected of you. Thankfully he never told me that.

I remember meeting him for the first time and he was very concerned that my bust should be pronounced enough for one particular scene in which Terry-Thomas had to react to it. There was a suggestion that I would have to stuff socks down my blouse! Well, Mario Zampi took one look at me and decided that wasn't needed after all. That could explain why Mario's son, Giulio Zampi, who was associate producer on the film, took a shine to me and asked me out. (Unfortunately I was with someone at the time.)

The whole film was very much Mario's vision of Britain. Because he was an outsider looking in, he saw Britain in a uniquely dark, funny way. His sense of humour was very dark, but he was a very funny man and that sense of fun prevailed over the whole making of *Too Many Crooks*. It was one of the happiest of jobs. I remember him with great affection and thanks.

*Vera Day*

Born in Sora, Lazio, on 1 November 1903, as an actor in his native Italy, Mario Zampi had been something of a teen idol but an ambition to take full control of his fledgling career steered him towards film production. By 1930 he was gainfully employed as a film editor for Warner's British unit in London, and in 1937 he formed Two Cities Films with fellow Italian Filippo Del Giudice. The aim of the company was to flit between their two cities, Rome and London, but London quickly took precedence and an impressive array of prestige pictures emerged during the Second World War: *In Which We Serve* (1942), *This Happy Breed*, *The Way Ahead*, *Henry V* (all, 1944) and *The Way to the Stars* (1945).

Zampi cut his directorial teeth on thrillers but *Spy for a Day*, a 1940 romp starring Douglas Wakefield, pointed the way towards the comedy films that would make his name. A post-war merger with the Rank Organisation coincided with the production of Zampi's frantic school comedy *The Happiest Days of Your Life* at the end of 1949. Joyously pitting Alastair Sim against Margaret Rutherford, with Joyce Grenfell in tow, the fresh association with Rank was cheekily acknowledged with the last-minute addition of the gong joke: shocked at Grenfell's loud banging of the school gong, Rutherford intones:

Vera Day and Terry-Thomas in Zampi's breakneck heist comedy *Too Many Crooks* (1959).

Vernon Gray and Janette Scott, juvenile leads for the elopement drama *Now and Forever*, coaxed by Mario Zampi, Piccadilly Circus, 1955.

'A tap... I said a tap. You're not introducing a film!' *The Happiest Days of Your Life* was a box office hit, and proved Zampi could handle comic anarchy without descending into farce. At the tail end of his career Zampi returned to school to present *Bottoms Up* (1960), a rather more pedestrian effort but a thoroughly enjoyable big-screen outing for the Jimmy Edwards [qv] television series *Whack-O!*.

Zampi both produced and directed the variety-turn compendium *Come Dance With Me* (1950), showcasing Max Wall and Derek Roy [qv], and *Now and Forever* (1956), which made a grown-up film star of former child star Janette Scott. Zampi's swansong, *Five Golden Hours* (1961), starred Ernie Kovacs, Cyd Charisse and George Sanders, and remains an undervalued British–Italian film, shot through to its black heart with corruption, cynicism and greed. Very Mario Zampi, all that. Zampi's own heart failed him, in his cherished London Town, on 2 December 1963, just a month after celebrating his sixtieth birthday.

As for his cinematic legacy, it is for the five comedies he produced and directed during the 1950s for which Zampi is best remembered. Two are enjoyable minor works: the jolly, satirical espionage romp *Top Secret* (1952), starring George Cole, and *Happy Ever After* (1954), a darkly comic tale of the would-be murder of David Niven, as country squire Jasper O'Leary. Then there is Zampi's trilogy of masterworks, which kicked off with *Laughter in Paradise*. Released in June 1951, it's a jet-black farce that begins with the surreal death of practical joker Hugh Griffith and revolves around a quartet of respectable beneficiaries forced to fulfil outlandish dares in order to be allowed their inheritance. Zampi favourites Alastair Sim and George Cole give typically rich performances, with prissy Fay Compton and gung-ho Guy Middleton also playing along. Shirley Eaton, Peter Sellers and Peggy Mount were given full throttle in *The Naked*

*Truth*, released in December 1957, a deliciously cynical exposé of corrupt celebrity and the public's fascination with the real, dark meat of fame. Here Zampi winkled out arguably Terry-Thomas's finest film performance, while even this lip-smacking comedy cast are effortlessly upstaged by Dennis Price as the beastly blackmailer. Finally, *Too Many Crooks*, released in March 1959, cast Terry-Thomas once more, in an equally impressive performance as a bounder who confronts a hapless criminal gang led by George Cole. In an act of casting perfection, Zampi gathered Sid James, Bernard Bresslaw, Vera Day and debutant Joe Melia as the crooks. Too many? Perish the thought.

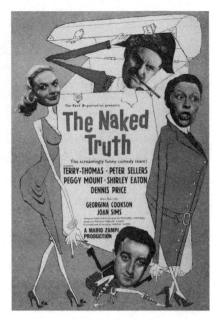

Shirley Eaton, Terry-Thomas, Peggy Mount and Peter Sellers adorn the publicity brochure for *The Naked Truth* (1957).

As the film proved, everybody in the world is bent. It was Zampi's maxim for three timelessly funny, wonderfully bleak comedy films. Anybody who can orchestrate a hearse chase through the country roads of the Home Counties has the spirit of Ambrose Bierce coursing through their veins. By all accounts a fast-talking, firm but fair kind of fellow on the studio floor, he much preferred to work in shirtsleeves and blend in with his crew. He was a jovial grafter; an enthusiastic storyteller with a cheerful streak of cynicism. That was Mario Zampi for you.

TREAT YOURSELF TO *The Naked Truth* (ITV Studios Home Entertainment: B00006423Y, 2002). Released as part of *The Terry-Thomas Collection*, this is Zampi at his darkest. One of the funniest and cruellest of British comedy films. Sheer perfection.

# Epilogue

Jimmy Wheeler plucks the string of his violin and gives a look in to the packed house of the Theatre Royal. Happy and eager to return to the Colonnade Bar, we all join in with his cheery: 'Aye, aye, that's your lot!' And it is our lot. All that remains now is for that grinning bundle of banjo-strumming energy, 'Two-Ton' Tessie O'Shea, to sing a final chorus of 'It All Belongs to Me' as we all file out. Well, the fat lady has sung. There isn't any more, Mrs Moore. As Arthur Tolcher rushes onto the stage the spotlight extinguishes just as the harmonica touches his lips: 'Not now, Arthur!', for the Ritz Brothers have donned overalls and are clearing up the aftermath – well, as always, Harry sits down on the job and barks out orders to Al and Jimmy. Frankly, this is all far from over! Henry Hall and His Orchestra play us out, and as he used to say on the wireless at the end of every episode of his *Guest Night*: 'Here's to the next time...'

The peerless Theatre Royal, Brighton. A palace of comedy and tragedy since the summer of 1807.

# Image Credits

Page 20, Eric Barker and Pearl Hackney, © Pictorial Press Ltd / Alamy Stock Photo

Page 27, Alfie Bass and Bill Fraser, © Allstar Picture Library Ltd. / Alamy Stock Photo

Page 171, Mario Fabrizi, © Trinity Mirror / Mirrorpix / Alamy Stock Photo

Page 221, Deryck Guyler, © AF archive / Alamy Stock Photo

Page 290, John Junkin, © Trinity Mirror / Mirrorpix / Alamy Stock Photo

Page 305, Dennis Kirkland, © Trinity Mirror / Mirrorpix / Alamy Stock Photo

Page 452, Patsy Rowlands, © ANL / Shutterstock

David Barry: p359, p360; Zoe S. Battley Tapley: p6, p59, p62, p63; The Rick Blackman Collection: p33, p45, p81, p158, p166, p178, p256, p296, p297, p346, p397, p423, p435, p478, p558, p562, p565, p617, p620; The Bristol Slapstick Festival: p180, p182, p239, p251, p253, p342, p500; The British Music Hall Society: p124, p167, p333, p462, p638; Carry On Films Limited: p84, p105, p109, p260, p465, p476, p477, p639; Barry Cryer: p83, p285, p308, p371; Jack Douglas: p35, p216, p432; Roy Hudd: p21, p149, p209, 291, p428; Terry Jones: p11; Andy Merriman: p384, p387, p389; Françoise Pascal: p187; Bill Roberton: p87, p89, p498; Carol Royle: p484, p486, p487, p488

All other images are from private collections, in the main the author's own personal Comedy Cottage collection.

# Acknowledgements

First and foremost, a huge thank you to everyone at Unbound, particularly Justin Pollard and Caitlin Harvey, who were there from the conception and, especially, my editor DeAndra Lupu who, with charm, dexterity and patience, effortlessly steered this epic project to completion. And to each of you who pledged your support for this book, thank you, from the bottom of all our hearts. Your name is within these pages. Put a circle round it. Thanks and sincere gratitude to the brilliant teams at the British Broadcasting Corporation Written Archives Centre, the British Film Institute Special Collections, the Colindale Library and many other invaluable bastions of research. Thanks too to Alison Young at the British Music Hall Society; Zoe Battley, Andy Merriman and Carol Royle for photos of their fabulously funny fathers; Bill Clark of Windyridge CDs for his speedy clarification, and for doing what he is doing, basically. Buy his CDs. And to my dear and valued friend of many years standing, and falling over, Rick Blackman – for shared memories and open access to his hugely impressive collection of music hall and variety ephemera. Thanks also to my mum, Eileen Ross, always the first person to read my manuscripts. Her kind and perceptive advice is always welcome. She's the top. She's Napoleon Brandy. A tip of the hat to my beloved sister, Fiona, who is an intrinsic part of the patchwork quilt of this book. We have laughed and laughed and laughed – as often as not at the same thing! And, of course, to my gorgeous and indispensable Gemma Fanning, who steered me through the lose and laughter of lockdown and the final stages of this epic labour of love. I have to thank all the friends and cohorts – dear chums, from Brian Murphy to Vera Day – who have championed the forgotten heroes within these pages, and in particular Barry Cryer, the Godfather of Comedy, who joined me in the filmed pitch for this book all those years ago, entertained subscribers with boozy memories of the great and good of giggles, as well as providing fascinating and hilarious tidbits of many turns celebrated within these pages above and beyond his official favourite. And last but by no means least, my glorious pal Terry Jones. He is the sole reason this book exists at all. This one is for you, my friend.

# A Note on the Author

Robert Ross is the leading authority on the history of British comedy. He has written a library of books, including best-selling reference works: *The Monty Python Encyclopedia* and *The Complete Terry-Thomas*; lavish celebrations: *The Carry On Story* and *The Goodies Rule OK*; and official BBC celebrations of such hit situation comedies as *Fawlty Towers*, *Last of the Summer Wine* and *Steptoe and Son*. He has also written critically acclaimed biographies of Sid James, Marty Feldman and *Carry On* producer Peter Rogers. Robert has hosted sell-out National Film Theatre events with the Goodies and the League of Gentlemen, moderated over fifty DVD commentaries and written *Doctor Who* audio plays for sixth Doctor Colin Baker. He is a frequent guest on radio and his many television credits include interviews for *What's a Carry On?*, *Top Ten: Comedy Records*, *Will the Real Basil Fawlty Please Stand Up?*, *Legends: Hattie Jacques*, *When Comedy Goes Horribly Wrong*, *What the Pythons Did Next*, *Richard & Judy* and the BBC news. Robert is a regular face on Talking Pictures TV, in conversation with such international stars as Shirley Anne Field, Vic Reeves and Rita Tushingham. He lives in Comedy Cottage, Buckinghamshire. This is his eighteenth book.

The author with Terry Jones at the Chortle Comedy Awards, Jongleurs, Camden, on 16 March 2015.

# Index

Unbound is the world's first crowdfunding publisher, established in 2011.

We believe that wonderful things can happen when you clear a path for people who share a passion. That's why we've built a platform that brings together readers and authors to crowdfund books they believe in – and give fresh ideas that don't fit the traditional mould the chance they deserve.

This book is in your hands because readers made it possible. Everyone who pledged their support is listed below. Join them by visiting unbound.com and supporting a book today.

David Absalom
Martin Adams
Chris Addison
Adelphi Films
David Adler
For Richard Adler
Keith Adsley
Antony Alldis
Jim Allen, BEM
John Allum
Jimmy Anderson
Anna Andrews
Mark Andrews
Bernard Angell
Teresa Ankin
David Archer
Simon Arthur
Stuart Ashen
James Atkinson

James Aylett
Boyce Bailey
Chris Baker
Danny Baker
Richard Baker
Neil Ballard
Elle Beer
Adrian Belcher
Neil Belton
Julian Benton
Terry Bergin
Ekaterina Berova
Tim Berry
Matt, Terri, Joseph &
    Clara Betts
Sanjay Bhandari
Dorothy Birtalan
Tim Blacklock
Rick and Christine Blackman

Holly Blades
Doug Blair
Ted Blair
Dave Blissett
Stephen Bolsover
Catherine Bolt
Nick Boorer
E. Tristan Booth
Jon Bounds
J. Patience Boyd
Chris Boyle
David Boyle
Nick Bradbury
Neil Brand
Matthew Brannigan
Robin Brecker
Morris Bright MBE
Karen & Steve Brine
Tristan Brittain-Dissont

Rachel Brock

Matthew Broughton

Aaron Brown

Antony Brown

Martin Brown

Scott, Sophie & Finlay Brown

Shirley Brown

Stephen Bruce

Phil Bruce-Moore

David Bryan

Ralph Burditt

Toni-Sue Burley

Barry Burns

Chris Burns

Anthony Butcher

Christina Caballero

James Cadman

Brian Cairns

David Callier

George Camiller

Jill Campbell

Andy Candler

Davey Candlish

Dai Cann

Barry Carpenter

Peter Carter

Linda Casey

Steven Cassidy

Dennis Cattell

Christian Cawley

Vic Chapman

Paul Charlton

Sharon Chasty

Andy Checker

Pete Chegwin

James Clarke

Jane Clinton

Geoff Coe

Elizabeth Coldwell

Paul Cole

Alan Coles

Gemma Coles

Stevyn Colgan

Charlie Connelly

Paul Constance

H E Cooper

Paul Copley

Simon Copley

Verity Coulthard

Mark Cousins

Andrew Cox

Robert Cox

Michael Cragie

Chloe Cresswell

Roi Croasdale

Andrew Croker

Sarah Cronin-Stanley

John Crowther

Gavin Culloty

Graham Cumming

Richard Dacre

Pippa Dakin

Peter Dalling

Brett Danalake

Angela Davies

E R Andrew Davis

Tony Davis

Henry Dawe

Tim Dawson

Steve Day

Verity Day

deadmanjones

JF Derry

Anne Devlin

John Dexter

Stephen Dinsdale

David Dixey

Peter Dixon

Miche Doherty

Lawrence T Doyle

Julian Dutton

Paul Duxbury

Sally Eason

Barnaby Eaton-Jones

Clare Eden

Neil Edmond

Paul Edwards

Thom Ettling

Gareth Evans

Idris Evans

Fiona Everett

Gemma Fanning

Steve & Karen Farrow

Alan Fawcus

Greg Fenby Taylor

Stuart Fewtrell

Ed and Rita Fisher

Matt Fisher

Terence Flanagan
Ian Fletcher
Sean Flynn
Alan Foster
Abbie Foxton
Mark and Jane French
Emma Fryer
Max Fulham
Mike Fury
Denise Gardner
Kevin Gascoigne
Avril Gaynor
Amro Gebreel
Rob Genders
Anthony George
Michael Gerber
Mark Gethings
Martin Gibbons
Jonathan Gibbs
Julie Giles
Chris Gill
Jessica Gioia
GMarkC
Laura Goddard
Bryan Godfree
Bob Golding
Phil Goldsbrough
Tom Goldsmith
Dave Gorman
Rod Gorman
Peter Govan
Jen Govey
Muriel Gray

Caroline Grebbell
Henry Green
John Greening
Nick Guerra
Anthony Hackett-Jones
Stuart Hadley
Tony Hannan
Terry Hardy
Simon Harper
Ken Harris
Philip Harris
Rob Harris
A.F. Harrold
Martha Harron
Joanna Haseltine
Margot Hayhoe
Jonathan Haynes
Nik Hayward
Rebecca Haywood
Paula Hazlehurst
Adrian Head
John Heffernan
Nanny Helen
John Hewer
Amanda Hickling
David Hicks
Simon Hickson
Matt Hill
David John Hill-Ilderton
Paul Hillman
Robert Hills
Paul Hitchcott
James Hogg

Mark Holgate
Henry Holland
Annie Holloway
Matt Holt
Richard Hope-Hawkins
Paul Howard
Lesley Hoyles
Gareth Hughes
Susan Hughes
Pamela Hutchinson
Romy Hutchinson
Robin Ince
Andy Jackson
Martin Jackson
Simon Jam Wall
Fiona James
Paul James
Susan James
Georgy Jamieson
Margaret JC Brown
Robert JE Simpson
Richard Jeffs
Rob Jenkins
Russell Jenkins
Titus Jennings
David John Peel
Marjorie Johns
David Johnson
Helen Johnson
Kitty Johnson
Kevin and Marion Jones
Maxine Jones
Gideon Jones-Davies

John Kane

Molly Ker Hawn

Ron Kerr

Rik Kershaw-Moore

Dan Kieran

Damon Kimpton

Darren King

Steve & Kim King

Daniel Kleinman

Doreen Knight

Matthew Knowles

Chris Ktorides

Tony Lake

Geoff Langley

Tim Langley

Andrew Langstaff

David Lars Chamberlain

Richard Latto

Daniel Lawrence

Francesca Lee

Max Lever

Allan Lewis

Monika Lewis

Will Light

Derren Litten

John & Christine Lomax

Jenny Longfellow

Stephen Longstaffe

Ed Lord

Matt Lucas

Scott MacKenzie

Siobhan Mackenzie

J.S. Majer

Kenneth Mann

Elton Maryon

Joy May

Tim May

Nicola Mayell

Angela Mayes

Gabriel McCann

Sean McCarthy

Neil McCowlen

Mo McFarland

Ronnie Mckenzie

Iain McKinlay

Mark Mclaughlan

Jonathan Meades

Steven Medcraft

Rob Medford

Jonathan Melville

Andrew Merriman

Roger Miles

Jo Miller

Margo Milne

Bryan Mitchell

Jackie Mitchell

John Mitchell

John Mitchinson

Fiona Mitford

Andrew Monk

Jim Mooney

Wendy Mooney

Delenn Moresby

Massimo Moretti

Chris Mountain

Rachel Mulberg

George Mullen

Steve Mullin

Tony Muzi

Abby Naylor

Chris Neale

Jacqui Nelson

Andrew Neve

Graham New

Mark Newman

David Newsome

Roo Newton

Al Nicholson

Margaret Nolan

Jo Norcup

Vaun earl Norman

Dr John O'Hagan

Mark O'Neill

Susan O'Neill

Dave Overall

Alan Page

Richard Parmiter

Andrea Patterson

Layne Patterson

Neil Pearson

Terry Pearson

Stephen Peberdy

Louise Penn

Christopher Pennell

Simon Pennell

Paul Perkins

Darren Perks

Claire Perry

Alexander Peterhans

| | | |
|---|---|---|
| Peter Phillips | Philippa Richards | Phil Smith |
| Craig Pickup | Claire Richardson | Tim Sommerfeld |
| Sarah Pinborough | Adam Roberts | Terry Sopp |
| Jane Pink | Alun Roderick | Sheldon Southworth |
| Peter Pinto de Sa | Steve Roffey | Karen Sparks |
| Stephen Piper | Alex Romeo | Ian Spence |
| Ford Polia | Eileen Ross | Mark Spencer |
| Justin Pollard | Carol Royle | Martin Spencer-Whitton |
| Howard Posner | Allan Russell | Richie Spillane |
| Alex Powers | Gary Russell | Darran Sproul |
| Vic Pratt | Nicola Sammons | Janice Staines |
| Barry Prescott | Mark Sampson | Jason B. Standing |
| Janet Pretty | John Sanders | Peter Stanton |
| Stewart Prodger | Nancy Sandoval | David Steel |
| Natasha Pyne | Abhilash Sarhadi | Murray Steele |
| Duncan Raggett | Dr Jean Saunders | Darren Stephens |
| Andy Randle | George Scofield | Matt Stephens |
| Gladys Rashbrook | Brian Screaton | Robert Stephenson |
| Janet Rashbrook | Paul Sharp | Hugo Stevenson |
| Marion Rashbrook | Leon Sheather | Roger Stevenson |
| Michael Rashbrook | Keith Sherratt | Robert Stewart |
| Peter Rashbrook | Mark Short | John Stine |
| Ronald Rashbrook | James Simmonds | Chris Stratton |
| Stephen Rashbrook | David Simpkin | Elstree Studios |
| Neil Rayment | Ronald Simpson | Ken Summers |
| Colette Reap | Joe Skade | James Sutherland |
| Dan Rebellato | Keith Sleight | Tristan Swales |
| Donna Rees | Jonathan Sloman | Rachel Sykes |
| John Reeve | Michael Smeeth | Steve Taylore-Knowles |
| Mike Reinstein | Adrian Smith | Anthony Teague |
| Alistair Renwick | Duncan Smith | Ben Thomas |
| Neil Rhodes | Leonie M. Smith | Rhys Thompson |
| Paul Richards | Nicky Smith | Ian Thompson-Corr |

Tracy Thomson

Karl Tiedemann

Helen Tiley

Graham Tomlinson

Anne-Marie Trace

Amanda Triccas

Chris Triccas

David G Tubby

Alwyn W Turner

Roger Utting

Jamie Vaide

Esther van Lith

Mark Vent

Royston Vince

Paul Vincent

Mark Vincent Hammett

Michael Vine

James Viner

Katey Walker

Steve Walker

Ian Walker a.k.a. Dr Soul

Alistair Wallace

Nick Walpole

David Want

Susan Warlow

Julie Warren

Paul Webb

John Welch

Annie West

Chris Weston

Katy Wheatley

Richard Wheeler

Paul Whelan

Stephen White

Barrie White-Miller

Bernard Wickham

Paul Wilkinson

John Williams

Derek Wilson

Jason Wilson

Stephen Wilson

Simon Winkler – 50 years!
    From Lisa, Jason,
        Joseph

Stephen Wise

E.L. Wisty

Ian Wolf

Kirstin Woodward

Steve Woodward

John Wright

Debbie Wythe

Owen Yapp

John Yates

Peter Young

Anna Yudaeva

Gregory Zayia